IS
AMERICA
POSSIBLE?

*You have to look at social science
results not so much as something
that will inform a decision but as
weapons in a political debate.
They are weapons that will be
used by whichever side they will
favor.*

James S. Coleman
Professor of Sociology,
University of Chicago
New York Times, January 8, 1980

IS
AMERICA
POSSIBLE?

Social Problems from
Conservative, Liberal, and
Socialist Perspectives

Second Edition

Edited by Henry Etzkowitz
State University of New York at Purchase

West Publishing Company
St. Paul • New York • Los Angeles • San Francisco

Library of Congress Cataloging in Publication Data

Etzkowitz, Henry, 1940–
     Is America possible?

     Includes bibliographical references.
     1.   United States — Social conditions — 1945-   — Addresses, essays,
lectures.   2.   Social problems — Addresses, essays, lectures.   I.   Title.
HN65.E9 1980   361.1'0973   79-27700
ISBN 0-8299-0329-1

For Nancy and Michael

CONTENTS

Page

PREFACE

Rather than viewing social reality in the light of a single framework, simultaneously using alternative theories provides a better understanding of society. Since much of social problems analysis has been developed from conservative, liberal, and socialist political theories it is appropriate to use these theories as alternative perspectives from which to view social problems. The original framework for social problems analysis in American sociology came from the liberal political tradition. Later, a conservative perspective was introduced into American sociology. Recently, socialist perspectives have been introduced into social problems analysis.

Observing society after the French Revolution, European intellectual forefathers of sociology such as Alexis de Tocqueville developed perspectives on social change that were antirevolutionary but not unsympathetic to social reform. In a later generation, Max Weber developed his ideas in opposition both to the revolutionary theories of his time as expressed by Karl Marx and to reactionary Prussian nationalists. Similarly, in their openness to social reform, the founders of sociology in America such as Albion Small, Chairman of the Sociology Department at Chicago, developed their ideas as an alternative both to conservative and radical solutions to the social issues of their time.

Sociology, which appeared in the United States as an academic discipline in the late nineteenth century, merged institutional economics with social Christianity, muckraking journalism, and an emerging social welfare profession. The first sociology department at the University of Chicago in the 1890s provided representatives of each of these groups with the opportunity to secure a place in the university. Institutional economics and social welfare provided the new discipline with its initial source of faculty while social Christianity and muckraking journalism provided an external base of support.

From the mid to the late nineteenth century economics lost interest in dealing with the major social issues created by the industrial revolution and the struggle between capital and labor. Most academic economists of that era were conservative social Darwinists who believed in the principles of *laissez faire* and non-intervention in human affairs. They held that unequal social conditions which made some people rich and left most poor, were an expression of immutable and unchangeable natural laws. Institutional economists, by contrast, were younger scholars, often trained in Germany. They conceptualized the social upheavals of the nineteenth century in institutional and social terms and believed they were amenable to planned human intervention and social reform. These scholars wanted to develop research on labor and industrial conditions but had difficulty finding academic positions in the United States. The conservative scholars who controlled American economics departments in the late nineteenth century did not want their discipline to deal with social welfare or philanthropy. When economics renounced these areas the way was opened for the birth of sociology in the United States as an independent academic discipline.

The new discipline of sociology provided arguments and data to oppose exclusionary conservative analyses of issues such as race, immigration, and minorities during the early decades of the twentieth century. Sociologists maintained that outsiders could be incorporated into American society without fundamental social change. These liberal political implications remained relatively hidden until quite recently. The overt political connections of sociology were minimized since the role of the sociologist was defined as a searcher for knowledge. Political issues such as immigration, industrialization, race relations and city life could be studied, but the use of this knowledge was to be left to others. The sociologist's job was to produce a research report. Typically, a social situation was presented in terms of what it meant for the people living in it. The Chicago school of sociology studied street gangs, hoboes, dance halls, ethnic neighborhoods, and more recently, police, drug users and unemployed black men. These sociological studies describe the difficulties their subjects encounter when their conduct differs from accepted social norms. Followers of this tradition rarely examined the top levels of major institutions such as government and big business except in subordinate appendages such as an unemployment office or factory floor. This research tradition, that brought forth a massive outpouring of monographs during the first thirty years of the twentieth century, continues into the present. The implicit political assumption of the Chicago school of sociology was that the major institutional structures and ideals of American society were valid. Reforms were necessary to give immigrants and minorities access to participate in capitalist structures and an opportunity to achieve economic success, but the capitalistic system itself was not challenged.

In the 1930s a conservative model for the interpretation of society was imported into sociology from the natural sciences. *Equilibrium theory* emphasizes the maintenance of the different parts of a society in a balanced relationship to each other. The equilibrium model was first used in the social sciences by Italian economist and social theorist Vilfredo Pareto in the late nineteenth and early twentieth century.

L. J. Henderson, a Harvard physiologist with an interest in the social sciences, offered a seminar on Pareto in the early 1930s. He introduced the equilibrium concept of society to several students who later became influential American sociological theorists, among them George Homans and Talcott Parsons. Parsons introduced this framework into sociology as an organizing principle of his paradigmatic work, *The Structure of Social Action*, wherein he reinterpreted the work of Durkheim, Pareto, and Weber to derive a model of society which embodied essential conservative principles of order and stability. Parson's student Robert Merton carried this model of society into the analysis of social problems. Merton's conception of manifest and latent functions became a means by which social behavior that appeared to be deleterious could be shown to be performing socially necessary and useful purposes. A political struggle between the adherents of the liberal and conservative approaches to sociology came to a head in the 1930s in a dispute over the control of its national association, the American Sociological Society. A conservative victory resulted in the establishment of a new journal, the *American Sociological Review*, which would present sociological theory and research from the standpoint of an independent scientific discipline, existing in isolation from direct social concerns and committed to the goal of objectivity in producing research and theory about society. The institutionalization of this approach in the American Sociological Society (later renamed the American Sociological Association to represent symbolically this shift) led to a move by committed liberals to form a separate national society to represent their approach: The Society for the Study of Social Problems (SSSP). This society provided an organizational framework for the liberal paradigm as a legitimate sociological approach, but it remained of secondary status and influence during the 1950s, when conservative sociology was dominant.

This intellectual hegemony of conservatism in sociology was broken when C. Wright Mills in the mid 1950s and others in the early 1960s charged that sociologists had not given sufficient attention to the unequal distribution of power in the United States. Mills called upon sociologists to look at this question and to focus on the relatively small group of power wielders who, he held, ran the country. Younger sociologists, especially those who had become involved in the social movements of the 1960s, heeded this call and raised further questions. The concept of "imperialism" was put forth as necessary to explain the relationship of American society to much of the Third World. This concept and other Marxist concepts, such as class, which had been earlier used by sociology in an eviscerated and weakened form, were now used by radical sociologists with its original connotations of class conflict. Radical sociologists did not always agree on either the means or ends of social change. Nevertheless, they held a common perspective on the types of questions it is important to ask about society. They wanted to investigate such topics as: the nature of the modern state, the composition of elites, the methods of attaining social change.

The breakdown of conservative theory as the dominant paradigm in sociology is related to the breakdown of the political consensus of the larger society that was based on Cold War anticommunism. Proponents of this conservative political consensus believed that America was both the wealthiest country and the most idealistic nation. The free life of the individual was the highest goal in the United States while in the Soviet Union and other communist countries the individual was forced to carry out the will of a government over which he or she had no control. America was viewed as a country in which public opinion determined public policy, if not immediately, then at least within a reasonable period of time.

For many younger Americans this belief system was shattered by the prolongation of the Vietnam War. Potential inductees into the draft were confronted with a dilemma. The code of post-World War II America did not provide an answer. The young American male's life choices were narrowed to school or a strategic occupation as an alternative to volunteering for the army or accepting the draft. Revision of the draft then narrowed the choices to the army, conscientious objection, or prison. Faced with these often unattractive alternatives, many began to question the truth of the previously taken-for-granted ideology of the freedom of the individual to determine his own life choices in American society. If a young man had to choose between going to school or going to war, was he really free?

Many sociology students entered graduate school in the sixties after participating in the civil rights and antiwar movements. They began to try out Marxist concepts on the social conflicts they had experienced. They formed radical caucuses at national and regional sociology meetings and movements within their graduate departments to give students particpation in university decision making. They organized radical student journals, such as *The Human Factor* at Columbia, *Catalyst* at SUNY Buffalo, and the *Berkeley Journal of Sociology* at the University of California, Berkeley.

The impetus that has led many younger American radical sociologists to Marxism has been the search for theoretical guidelines to understand developments in American society which the Vietnam War brought to public awareness. These issues include the concentration of economic power in relatively few hands, the use of political techniques, both covert and overt, by American corporations, the CIA, the State Department, and the military to prolong the war, and foreign aid to maintain American control over many of the underdeveloped Third World countries. Research and analyses of war-related issues published in new journals such as *WIN Magazine* or *Viet Report* and circulated in underground newspapers created in the course of antiwar movement brought basic facts about the nature of the American society to the attention of many students. The inadequacy of "modernization" as an interpretive schema to analyze developments within the Third World and relationships between advanced industrial societies and the Third World motivated a search for a new explanation. This search led to the rediscovery of imperialism as an interpretive schema and of Marxism as an overarching theoretical framework to enable sociological scholars both to understand the world and to try to change it.

The emergence of alternative sociopolitical frameworks in sociology cannot be viewed in isolation from similar developments in the other social sciences. The same process of clarification of disciplinary concepts, by making implicit political perspectives explicit, is also taking place in economics, anthropology, and political science. Often scholars from different disciplines but holding the same political paradigm have more in common than scholars from the same discipline with different politics. For example, a socialist economist and a socialist sociologist are both likely to formulate the relationships between the industrialized and nonindustrialized worlds in terms of the concept of "imperialism," whereas liberal scholars from each of those disciplines would more likely use the framework of "modernization" theory.

Sociology is emerging from its late 60s and early 70s crisis reformulated along the lines of conservative, liberal, and socialist political theories. The implicit conservative and liberal political perspectives of structural functionalism and symbolic interactionism have been revealed. Socialist perspectives, formerly viewed as non-sociological and unscientific, are emerging within the discipline. Intellectual and political disputes between adherents of differing sociopolitcal perspectives now take place within the discipline and all of these divergent intellectual traditions are increasingly viewed as legitimate sociological perspectives.

Is America Possible? makes explicit use of conservative, liberal, and socialist perspectives as a method of social problems analysis. The essential ideas of the three perspectives are presented and each social problem is discussed from all of these viewpoints. The goal is to enable students to define their own intellectual and political standpoint by applying alternative theoretical perspectives to the understanding of social problems.

I thank Susan Kirby for her excellent typing and Shelly Baker and Gary Moran for their help. I also wish to express my appreciation to West's reviewers and editors and to the students and teachers who used the first edition, for their comments and suggestions which were helpful to me in preparing this second edition.

INTRODUCTION: POLITICAL PERSPECTIVES AND SOCIAL PROBLEMS

We are all political actors. Some of us vote on election day; others do not. Some of us organize or participate in demonstrations; others do not. One person may write a letter to a newspaper to protest against the pollution of a river. Another person may express an opinion to a friend that welfare encourages poor people not to want to work. Yet another person may join in picketing the headquarters of a company that has moved its factories abroad. All of these actions, non-actions, or opinions are expressions of a political stance. Each contains within it a theory of how society should be organized and how it should be changed.

To say either that something should be different from the way it is or that the way things are is satisfactory is to make a value judgment. Value judgments say that something is "good" or "bad" or perhaps important. Everyone who enters into the discipline must face up to the question of the place of value judgments in sociology. Moreover, if there is any one area of sociology that especially demands a consideration of value judgments, it is the sociology of social problems. This is the area that defines the critical issues of where we are and where we are going as a society and that explores alternatives.

The very act of defining some part of social life as problematic necessarily involves taking a value perspective; that is, it says that something is good or bad. Making this judgment is as inevitable in everyday life as it is in the practice of sociology, if one does not totally ignore the world. To admit to such judgments is not to say that sociologists discard the scientific method in their scholarly work. Rather, each sociologist uses it in examining society, but the goals desired reflect their own perspectives.

Often students come to the study of sociology with the expectation that the discipline will provide them with a single, agreed upon set of answers to the problems of American society, that the scientific method applied to any issue will result in a specific answer indisputable by anyone who accepts the norms of science. Sometimes sociologists recognize in their writings that there is an opposing analysis to the one they have set forth. Other times, sociologists assume that because they have conducted a scientific study only one answer is possible.

I believe that, to the questions people care strongly about, different answers are likely and even inevitable, for they are usually based on different assumptions. Such differing assumptions or approaches to social problems are not random positions. Rather, they are usually consistent approaches—whether explicit or implicit—connected to longstanding political traditions. Instead of trying to submerge our political differences, let us bring them to the forefront and use them as tools of sociological analysis.

Three major frameworks—conservatism, liberalism, and socialism inform the sociology of social problems. Quite different definitions of social problems and proposals for their solution derive from these world views. Conservatives, liberals, and socialists each start from a different conception of what people are basically like. Each sets forth different goals of how society should be organized. These concepts of human nature and social institutions provide the guidelines within which social problems are analyzed.

Every political theory begins with a picture of what people are really like. This conception of human nature tells us what people have in common. It is a statement of their essential characteristics, fundamental motivations, and most desired goals. Human nature, then, is whatever seems to remain constant in human beings despite cultural, social, and psychological differences. Once the fundamentals about the nature of people are established, a political theory, on the basis of its first principles, delineates the proper relation of individuals to society. Conservatives, liberals, and socialists tell us how people live and work in groups and collectivities. Each states the principles by which social institutions operate: their purposes, reasons for existence, and sources of support.

Determining the concepts of human nature and social institutions held by an author can be helpful in defining his or her political perspective. Conservatives, liberals, and socialists hold quite different beliefs about human nature and social institutions. In the following pages we will see how ideas about what people are really like and how they act in groups are at the root of different political principles and programs.

Conservatism

Human Nature

Conservatives believe that people are essentially evil and irrational. They will do harm to each other unless they are restrained. This negative conception of human nature leads conservatives to conclude that strong social institutions are necessary for people to live together without harming each other.

Only the elite are exempted from this generally pessimistic view of human nature. These are the small numbers of persons who are fit to rule by virtue of their superior nature. Conservatives believe that some people are inherently much better than others. It is these few, identified by birth, training, or social status, who should govern the rest of us. In the United States, a conservative elite is reproduced from a combination of sources including male birth into wealthy families, individual talent, and attendance at socially prestigious preparatory schools and major universities. No single criterion is sufficient to guarantee elite membership, but the more of these statuses that an individual combines in his or her background, the likelier it is.

Social Institutions

The conservative theory of the elite exists alongside and in apparent contradiction with the view of institutions as self-regulating mechanisms. The market is the fundamental institution. In a market goods and services are exchanged, and prices are set in accordance with the laws of supply and demand. The market provides a single standard that all must adhere to. It exists independently of human volition. The operation of the market is viewed as an ideal to which all other social institutions should conform. To ignore the precepts of the market or to tamper with its operation will result in the downfall of the economy.

The essence of conservatism is institutional maintenance. Although social institutions are viewed as an expression of an autonomous moral order, they must still be vigorously defended. For if institutions break down, in the ensuing chaos each of us will lose what we have attained. This fear of the loss that may follow from social change is a powerful argument for keeping things as they are. Institutions should operate in coordination with each other, much as the wheels of a clock mesh with each other to tell time. People must adjust to the requirements of social institutions to insure that they function smoothly. Individual happiness must be subordinated to this end to insure the welfare of all.

If existing institutions are presumed to be valid, then people who disagree with them are, by definition, wrong. Individuals who do not act in accordance with institutional precepts are defined as deviant. Social deviancy is the study of people who are out of phase with what the dominant social institutions define as normal behavior. Deviants include men and women who remain single when marriage is the norm; individuals who imbibe substances that legislatures and courts have held to be illegal; people who choose not to work; individuals who have sex with members of the same sex; people who appropriate the private property of others; individuals who dress in an idiosyncratic fashion; or people who exhibit inappropriate affect (i.e., laugh at a serious occasion) when interacting with others. Although these individuals may feel that their behavior best meets their individual needs, conservatives do not accept the validity of this criterion. For conservatives, acting in accordance with accepted institutional practice is the valid norm of social conduct. People who break social rules should be negatively sanctioned so that they will get back into line or be an example to others not to follow their mode of behavior. Informal rituals of putting down inappropriate behavior, prisons, and mental hosptials are some of the means used to inhibit the spread of deviancy.

If sanctions fail to halt the spread of a deviant activity, some concessions to it may be necessary to prevent the larger institutional order from being threatened. To save society from fundamental attack, conservatives must occasionally admit some change lest what they consider to be "deviancy" get out of hand and grow into a mass social and political movement. Once generated, such a movement might escalate its goals and demand change not only with respect to particular concerns but of the entire organization of society. To prevent this occurrence, reforms that serve to preserve the existing social structure may be allowed. After change is instituted, that it has taken place is denied as much as possible. Instead, the basic continuity of the institutional structure is emphasized.

Social Problems

According to conservatives, individuals are ultimately responsible for their social condition. If you are poor, it is up to you to find a job to improve your standard of living. In the conservative view, poverty is the result of an individual's lack of success in improving his or her economic condition; it is not the responsibility of society or a result of existing social arrangements. The poor will be taken account of as a group only if they threaten to become too unruly and disrupt existing social institutions by rioting or looting. In that event, some combination of repression by the police and courts and admission into job training programs and lower level corporate employment will be undertaken by conservatives as a collective solution to a social problem.

Contemporary American conservatism views the business corporation as the model for American society. Obedience to authority must be maintained within the corporation so that goods and services will be efficiently produced and distributed. To attain social tranquility within the corporation, one problem to be solved is the discontent of the workers with mechanized labor. It must be resolved according to conservative principles, or the workers will press for socialist solutions, as in Europe, causing interminable social and political conflict. The conservative solution for labor thus alienated is to substitute artificial gratifications for the real satisfactions of meaningful, self-directed work. Some of these suggested substitutes include job security and participation in decisions about ancillary community activities conducted by the corporation (such as recreation programs and cafeterias). Successful leadership in these activities would also facilitate the access of workers to managerial positions, thus coopting leadership among the workers in order to avert potential organized opposition.

A fundamental goal of the corporation as a social institution is the expansion of the economy. The achievement of profits through corporate controlled technological development is assumed as the chief aim of each citizen as well as of the state. Adherence to this principle will give everyone an ever higher standard of living. Every individual and governmental activity may be judged by the criterion of contribution to the production of profit. If everyone shares this basic premise, the good society can be achieved.

From this perspective, the inclusion of ever greater numbers of people in the corporate system is its most certain insurance for future survival. Since social change for conservatives must be both minimal and beneficial to themselves, an expanding technology, a basic source of concern for socialist ecologists, is the sole engine they see as consistent with their view of "progress".

In examining an author's position to determine whether it is conservative, one might ask: (1) Is the author arguing in favor of continuing a social situation as it presently exists? (2) Is the author arguing in terms which call for the maintenance of social order and stability as a higher value than any other goal? (3) Does he or she consider the acquisition of private property a major social goal and interference with that goal—especially by the state—a social evil? Attainment of private property, stability, order, and maintenance of the status quo may be seen as the principle components of most conservative arguments about the nature of the good society and the means of attaining it.

Liberalism

Human Nature

Liberals believe that people are neither all good or all bad. While most people are basically good, even good people have flaws. They will act benevolently toward others much of the time but not necessarily in any and every situation. Conversely, some people who usually cannot be trusted will occasionally do good. Since people are variable in their conduct, rules and institutions should be set up to improve their behavior. But since institutions ultimately consist of people, even courts, schools, and legislatures cannot be totally relied on to insure that people will act properly.

Social Institutions

Social institutions work best when good people are in positions of power. An important liberal goal is to get the best people into positions of power. But since it cannot be counted upon that the best qualified people will always be the ones chosen to run institutions, the power of institutions should also be limited. This may be done by setting one institution to work as a check on another. Thus, even if the right people are not always in power, no single institution can do too much harm if it is properly balanced by other institutions. In the United States Constitution the President, Congress, and Supreme Court balance each other. No single branch of government can go too far in any direction without the possibility of another acting as a check and balance on its power.

This plural structure helps insure that power will be limited. With the division of governmental authority, it is unlikely that any single group could gain control of all areas of government. Different groups and interests have to compromise with each other in order to make policy. The diversity of interests and the necessity of alliances among groups insure that the desires of all groups will be represented in establishment of national policy. No single interest can push the nation too far in any direction. Various groups and interests—such as business, labor, ethnic, and racial groups—are held to be relatively equal in their access to power, and power is believed to be widely dispersed.

A basic assumption of liberalism is the taken-for-granted existence of a capitalist economic system. This economic system, as well as its allied institutions, is also seen to consist of a number of competing groups. No single economic group is belived to be able to dominate another, although governmental regulation is required to maintain this balance.

Liberals believe that all good ends are the result of "good" means—and the term "good" implies that proper procedures are not violated. A liberal holds to the principle that all ideas must be allowed to be heard. That the individual has inalienable rights, such as freedom of speech, is the heart of contemporary liberal political theory. The exercise of one's rights in the competition for power takes place in accordance with the established rules of law. In case of an unresolvable disagreement between individuals or groups, recourse may be had to the primary interpreters of these rules, the courts. All sides are expected to accept the validity of the rules as well as the decision, which is handed down from a source assumed by definition to be impartial regarding the dispute at hand.

Social Problems

Liberals view social problems as the result of flaws in institutions or in people. Institutional defects can be remedied in two ways: by replacing the people who are running the institution with persons who will do it better, or by reforming the institution. For example, if a nursing home is discovered to be offering inadequate care to its residents one solution is to replace the people in charge with individuals who will provide adequate care. Liberals do not like a person to hold a position of power for long time. Power tends to corrupt people. A good institutional structure has a procedure to replacing the people in charge on a regular basis.

If an institutional defect cannot be resolved by replacing the people in charge, the next step is to analyze the institution in question and set forth proposals to modify it so that it will be better able to achieve its goals. To continue with our previous example, if new and better qualified administrators are unable to succeed in improving conditions in the nursing home, the next step would be to undertake a study of the nursing home to see if it had adequate staff, procedures, and resources to provide proper care. If any of these areas were found to be inadequate, a recommendation for change would be in order; i.e., to increase the number of staff, enhance the quality of their training, improve the physical facilities, or provide additional activities or therapy for the residents. The proposed changes would tend to involve specific measures that fall within the framework of the existing institutional concept of a nursing home. Liberals tend not to question basic institutional principles but work within their guidelines as much as possible. The goal is to come as close as possible to the institutional ideal. Liberals realize that to achieve ideal conditions in the operation of any institution is probably beyond the grasp of human attainment. The process of social improvement is seen as a constant battle in which small gains are made on a step-by-step basis. Total transformations of social institutions are viewed as potentially dangerous even if they could succeed. It is far better to work within the existing institutions that we are familiar with than to step off into the unknown.

In liberal theory, conflict can be handled within the limits of the existing structures of society. Although these structures are not believed to be immutable to change, change—in the direction of fulfilling liberal values such as equality of opportunity—is attained at a relatively slow pace. A little at a time is gained through compromises with opponents. Liberals do not hold out for all they want. They take what they can get now—and they work for more. Contemporary liberals believe that social improvement will occur gradually through the exercise of state power on behalf of those who are poor and oppressed.

The role of social science, according to liberal practice, is to provide legitimate information for advances toward liberal political goals. This information may be used to persuade policy makers of the wisdom of implementing a social reform. It may be data which show that the public is ready to accept a social reform. It may be a theoretical framework showing that activities heretofore considered deviant are actually in accord with liberal values if viewed in the proper light.

From the liberal perspective, social problems are not necessarily related to structural conditions in society. Since the definitions of social problems are subjective, and since the subjective definitions vary according to the opinions of different groups, a social problem from this perspective is "what any group defines as problematic." As Howard Becker says:

> Consider race relations. Although clearly an area of major social concern, it is not clear what the "problem" is. For the Negro and for many white citizens as well, the problem is how to achieve as rapidly as possible the full participation of the Negro in American society. For other whites the problem is different: the possible loss of social advantages they have long enjoyed at the expense of Negroes. For many politicians and for some social scientists the problem is the tension and violence of a situation in which Negroes demand rights that whites are unwilling to grant. For professionals—social workers and educators, among others—the problem is to undo the harm done by generations of segregation and discrimination so that the Negro will be equipped to take advantage of his rights. This does not exhaust the list: parents worry about preserving the neighborhood school, realtors worry about the effect of open housing laws on their business, and diplomats worry about the effect of our racial crisis on the leaders of the new African and Asian nations.[1]

Social problems are what people think they are. Definitions of the same issue depend on the definer's place in the society. According to Becker, there is a natural history of the development of a social problem. The first step occurs when an individual or group sees some situation as problematic. Then the group convinces others so that the issue has public attention. When concern is sufficiently broad, an organization will be formed to do something about advancing a resolution of the problem.

---

1. Howard Becker, Social Problems: A Modern Approach (New York: John Wiley, 1966), p. 6.

Socialism

Human Nature

Socialists believe that people are basically good. They naturally feel concern for fellow human beings. However, the good nature of people is often subverted by existing social institutions that do not fulfill human needs. This positive view of human nature and negative view of existing institutions lead socialists to conclude that institutions must be changed so that human needs may be fulfilled.

Human needs include basic necessities and creative activity. People require food, clothing, and shelter. Human beings also share an innate desire to participate in meaningful work, leisure activities, artistic pursuits, and social interaction. While human needs are the same for all people, the potential means to satisfy them are diverse. The goal of socialism is to create social institutions that allow for the greatest satisfaction of human needs.

Social Institutions

The purpose of social institutions is to meet human needs. Our present day social institutions are the result of a historical progression that continues in motion. The general direction of historical development has been from institutions that benefit elites to institutions that meet the needs of increasing numbers of people. A great improvement in the condition of life for most people has been achieved in the transition from ancient slavery, to medieval feudalism, to modern capitalism. Nevertheless, a considerable gap remains between the level of needs that are satisfied under capitalism and what is possible under socialism.

Capitalism is based on the principle that individuals may own goods that they do not produce themselves. Property ownership allows some people to have the resources to hire other people to work for them. People who work for others in exchange for money wages give up the right to control the products of their work. Two groups of people emerge as a result of this alienation: a class that owns and controls the means of production (i.e., factories, tools, and capital) and a class that offers its labor for sale.

This two class system of owners and workers produces inequalities. Instead of food, clothing, and shelter being equally available to all as a right, access to these necessities of life depends upon one's class position. Ownership and control of the means of production enables the capitalist class to maintain their material existence at the highest level, while workers must get jobs to have adequate food, clothing, and shelter.

Socialists are opposed to a society with private property as the fundamental principle of social organization and a small elite obtaining the greatest benefits. Socialists believe that those who do the work should operate the workplaces and no special class of managers should control the work of others. Socialists hold that utility should be the criterion for production of goods, and distribution should be based on the principle of need. There should be and need be no inherited wealth, since everyone has the right to sufficient material goods and social services to ensure health and well-being. Social structures should be organized so that people may develop their individual talents while participating in a fair share of the necessary work of society—even that work which no one wishes to undertake by choice.

In general, the socialist critique of American society holds that our institutions are organized so that only a few are fully able to meet their needs. At work almost all Americans are subject to being told how to do their job. Relatively few have the opportunity to set their own goals or change the kind of work they are doing if they are dissatisfied. Still others are unemployed.

Many Americans feel that they have no real say in the decisions that affect their lives. Most Americans feel pressured by a declining personal income and rising expenses. A relatively few Americans, who have inherited wealth or hold high-paying jobs, are not subject to these constraints. These Americans have more choices than the rest of us about how they will live, where they will live, and what they will do with their free time. But even many of these more fortunate Americans are subject to the pressures of narrowly defined jobs. They must do their jobs as they are told or they will lose their prerequisites. Only the relatively few who work as artists, independent professionals, artisans, or craftspersons are able or organize their work life as they see fit. Even fewer of us work cooperatively and share equally in decision making and rewards.

Social Problems

Socialists find the cause of unequal conditions in a social structure in which a few people control most of the resources. Corporations, banks, universities, and almost all institutions in American society, with the exception of a few cooperatives, operate according to capitalist principles, which encourage the accumulation of resources and concentration of decision-making authority in the hands of a few persons.

The socialist approach to social problems reformulates the entire issue by arguing that the "problem" does not exist on the level of either differential subjective definitions of the situation or of social structures in need of modification, but that it is inherent in these structures of capitalist society. According to this formulation, specific "social problems" are surface manifestations of a form of social organization which benefits the powerful few and not the great masses of people.

Specific issues are seen as deriving from inequalities between the classes. For socialists, urban problems cannot be fundamentally resolved by reform of city government or increased federal subsidies to the cities. Inequality in housing or health care may be reduced by these measures. But since access to these resources depends upon one's position in the class structure, these problems cannot be fundamentally resolved until the domination of one class over another is ended.

What is required to solve this "problem" is a revolution by peaceful or violent means, which will replace capitalism with a qualitatively different form of human society. Until this transformation occurs, social problems will exist as inevitable features of the structural relationships of a capitalist society. Existing social arrangements are to be questioned, and if found wanting should be changed or replaced. Since social institutions were constructed by people they are always open to the possibility of being destroyed by people and reconstructed along different lines. Although people are not totally free to make and carry out whatever decision they choose, they are also not passive objects inevitably overwhelmed by external forces. No social structure can continue to exist in the face of the near total resistance of people joined together to oppose it. The very nature of the structures of control inherent in large-scale bureaucratic institutions generates opposition from those employees who are subjected to conditions in which they are kept from participating with others in controlling their work and their lives.

Martin Glaberman and George Rawick in their essay on "The Economic Institution" document how this opposition appears in the everyday life of workers in mass production industries as a necessary element in their relationships to the processes of production.

> After they enter a factory, workers find out about one another: who is glib and good at negotiating, who is strong and brave and good at blocking a plant gate or beating up a scab, who is astute as a tactician, who is a public speaker, etc. Workers also find out about the work process and the equipment: it is there to control them but it is always possible to turn the tables. In production on an individual machine, the worker finds out what makes it run. The same elementary investigation also tells him what makes it stop running. So the worker is able to have the machine running as smoothly as possible to make the work more manageable—or he can arrange for the machine to break down when he needs an extra break or is harassing a foreman.
>
> Transfer the situation to the intense cooperation of an assembly line and two changes tend to take place. It takes a little longer for workers to begin to sabotage the line for an occasional rest period because they have to be sure of those who are working around them. But the control and the struggle is moved to a wider arena than that afforded by one worker on one machine. The control can easily extend beyond the confines of one plant. In 1969 there was a wildcat strike at the Sterling Stamping Plant of the Chrysler Corporation, fifteen miles outside Detroit. The workers on the picket line were aware of the dependence of Chrysler plants around the country and abroad on their production. They knew that on the first day of their strike three main plants in Detroit would also have to shut down; on the second day, the plant in St. Louis. And so on.[2]

Socialists view the potential for fundamental social transformation as an interaction between the crises that result from the basically flawed structures of capitalist society and the social movements that result from alienation. The task of the socialist sociologist, then, is twofold: (1) to provide a clear analysis of the oppressive structures of capitalist society; and (2) to engage with others of like mind in doing both the theory and practice of constructing institutional structures based on socialist principles.

In a recent discussion of "Capitalism, Socialism and Democracy" in *Commentary Magazine* three authors, William Buckley, editor of the *National Review*, David Riesman, Henry Ford II Professor of Social Science at Harvard University, and Michael Walzer, professor of Government at Harvard stated their respective conservative, liberal, and socialist perspectives.

---

2. Martin Glaberman and George Rawick, "The Economic Institution," in American Society: A Critical Analysis, eds. Larry T. Reynolds and James T. Henslin (New York: David McKay, 1973), p. 39.

Conservative

William F. Buckley, Jr.

When I was a boy at Yale along about the time they were superannuating God, they were enshrining something called economic democracy. Many of my class-mates, by the time they had gone through the typical ration of introductory courses in economics and allied fields, were ready to live and die, if necessary, to bring economic democracy to America. In those days anything attached to democracy was osmotically desirable, democracy having been postulated as the highest civic good. We had, then, not only economic democracy as a social desiratum, but its cousin, industrial democracy. Educational democracy enjoyed morganatic privileges, and of course social democracy was tantamount to eude-monia. Henry Wallace could not give a speech without a dozen references to economic democracy, and of course it transpired that what was meant by the term was a progressive socialization of the economy. That which was capitalistic in form was disparaged quite consistently, especially by those who thought themselves progressive, as in the Progressive party which fielded Henry Wallace as its candidate during my sophomore year.

But like executive supremacy, which was good when exercised by FDR and Truman, bad when attempted by Richard Nixon, the term democracy began to suffer and, *pari passu*, economic democracy. I like to think that the bubble burst when some scholar, who flogged himself through John Dewey's *Democracy and Education*, carefully annotated twenty-two distinct uses to which Mr. Dewey had put the words democracy and democratic. There was, of course, the postwar confusion caused by the establishment of such states as the German Democractic Republic, and the endless ecomiums in the Communist and fellow-traveling press to the democratic arrangements in Stalin's Russia, which of course was what the Webbs and Harold Laski had hailed as the fountainhead of economic democracy. There were the noble dissenters—I think Sidney Hook was the most vociferous, not to say encephalophonic—who kept stressing the differences between true economic democracy and the kind of thing practiced in Russia. But doubts had begun to set in, reinforced during the 1960's by the advent of democ-racy in Africa. Democracy had been used, along with "independence," as an antonym for colonialism. And when it became clear that the expulsion of the colonizers in Africa would bring not democracy but merely an end to white rule, many Americans, rather than sort out their frustrations, simply stopped reading about Africa, even as one stops counting Bolivian coups. And I think it is correct to say that the term economic democracy tiptoed out of the workaday rhetoric of progressive politicians who, although generally the last group to recognize the uselesness of shibboleths, are sensitive to public ennui. Economic democracy was increasingly understood to be the progressive transfer of power frm the private to the public sector. There is continuing enthusiasm for this, but it tends to be inertial and dogmatic. Looking again for symbols, I think of Peter F. Drucker who in his *The Age of Discontinuity* dropped the line that modern experience has demonstrated that the only thing the state can do better than society is inflate the currency and wage war. The experience of Vietnam brings one of those two claims for the state into question.

With the demythologization of the state as the agent of universal well-being came also a revived curiosity about what it is in democracy that is desirable. Begin by admitting that the democracy that brought us Perón and Hitler is an imperfect cathedral in which to worship, and you have come a long way. If democracy can substantially diminish human freedom, it is only casually interesting that that diminution of freedom was affected by political due process. Which brought to the attention of the curious, particulary among libertarians, the startling insight that it is altogether conceivable that in a given situation one might be faced with freedom and democracy as mutually exclusive alternatives. Not entirely so, because if you surrender democracy on the grounds that democracy is heading you toward a totalitarian abyss, you have indeed given up something. But that something which you give up is not necessarily more valuable than that which by giving it up you stand to retain. Burke said it most simply when he remarked that the end of political freedom is human freedom.

It is best, I think, to ruminate on these matters by reasoning *a posteriori*. Freedom *can* be quantified. Freedom is not, in an imperfect world, indefeasible. If, let us say, a society acknowledges (1) the freedom to write, (2) the freedom to own property, and (3) the freedom to practice one's religion, it is a better state than the state that grants only two of those freedoms. But the state that grants two of those freedoms is better than the state that grants only one of them. By extension, the republic with a vigorous public sector that protects the right of property and the attendant right of economic enterprise is one which understands democracy as primarily a procedural commitment—instructing us how to make such changes in public policy as are desired by the majority, but warning us that the use of that procedural authority for the purpose of limiting substantial freedoms is intolerable. It is plain that an increasing number of intellectuals, dismayed by contemporary experience, have stopped superordinating democracy to all other specified and specifiable freedoms. Having done that, it is easier to arrive at the conclusion that a vigorous private sector is necessary for the validation of democracy. Democratic socialism, as the venerable insight tells us, is all about A meeting with B for the purpose of deciding what C will give to X. To say that democratic socialism "works" in Scandinavia is merely to say that the individual who makes that statement would rather exchange those freedoms absent in Scandinavia for those social perquisites offered in Scandinavia. If democracy is to be the servant of human freedom rather than the instrument by which to afflict the minority, then it must acknowledge the great self-denying ordinances which reasonably limit all other freedoms.

Alert intellectuals are in increasing numbers interested by what the lawyers anxious to preserve constitutional guarantees call the "slippery-slope" theory, the generic statement of which is, Give them an inch and they'll take a mile. The appetite of the socialist to govern tends to insatiability. Thus Fredom House, in the latest of its annual tables of political rights and civil rights, is instructive. The nations of the world are divided into three categories: the capitalist, the mixed, and the socialist. Only a single state is both socialist and politically free. For those interested in purple cows, that state is Guyana.

Liberal

David Riesman:

When I was a student at the Harvard Law School, I thought that there was one provision in the Bill of Rights which should be eliminated, namely, the Fifth Amendment. I knew that countries more civilized than ours allowed judges to examine parties to litigation and criminal defendants; our inhibiting of judges and lawyers because of memories of the Star Chamber appeared ridiculous to me; I did not see why people should not be called on to give an account of themselves; and enduring the Joseph McCarthy era, I felt that "taking the Fifth" made a mystery out of Communism, surrounded it with the aura of non-Communist liberals and fellow-travelers who had Communist or Communist-leaning lawyers, and supported McCarthy by this obfuscation.

And there was one provision that I thought ought to be added to the Bill of Rights, namely, the right to start a small business. Of course, in the 18th century, no one would have thought of putting this in the Bill of Rights, for it was taken for granted. When Tocqueville was here in 1831, he was impressed by the fact that priests did not have parishes given to them by the contours of the landscape; they had to be entrepreneurs to build a congregation; and he differed from most visitors from Catholic countries in regarding this as an advantage, keeping the Church and its clerics, so to speak, on their entrepreneurial toes.

Again, this judgment was confirmed by what happened to people who were blacklisted or otherwise lost their jobs during the period of McCarthyism: many of them ended up, as did Alger Hiss and other less famous people, taking jobs in small business. Had there been but a single employer in a socialist commonwealth, they would have been denied such an opportunity.

I have seen, in quite a different context, how rare is the understanding of this freedom to start a small business or nonprofit enterprise. I have sat with college and university presidents in the presence of federal officials, and watched the former ask the latter to simplify the sources of funding provided for higher education, on the ground that multiform sources of support create difficulties in fund raising and record keeping. I have heard them complain that they get money from dozens of different federal agencies, ranging from the Atomic Energy Commission to the Veterans Administration—in the latter case, via students bringing GI Bill of Rights money to help pay tuition. These academic statesmen have had wide political experience; yet I have had to point out what seems obvious: namely, that if there were a single pipeline of funding, it would be a jugular that could be cut by a single influential legislator who might be irritated by what he thought, *à la* Senator Proxmire, was a foolish bit of esoteric research, i.e., sounded foolish to a populist audience, or by some professor who was regarded as subversive to whatever was the prevailing piety of the land. If, however, sources of support are so complex that it takes the full time of academic officials and of researches even to list them all, institutions are safer, since there are decentralized sources of funding. Here I would include the "small business" of the philanthropic foundations whose fate hangs on the maintenance of the charitable deduction which certainly would not be permitted, or is most unlikely to be permitted, in a wholly socialist commonwealth which would not allow such privileges, or loopholes.

Whereas the great book of Joseph Schumpeter which has the same title as this symposium dealt with the deliquescence of esprit among the scions of affluence created by capitalism, I am here discussing something a bit tangential, namely, not so much the guilt (or decadence) of the possessors of inherited wealth in taken-for-granted entitlement as the political misjudgments among the stewards of wealth and academic institutions.

The right to start a small business sustains democracy by freeing people from the fear of offending a single regime which controls both the economy and the polity. Private wealth has been important in the independence of mind of many great thinkers, whether one has in mind Jeremy Bentham or Friedrich Engels (and, through him, Karl Marx), or artists who could afford to take risks, as Mark Twain did with some of his sardonic writings, because of money earned in the private economy.

In some respects, there is no clear-cut line here which separates a fully pluralistic capitalism from a fully totalitarian socialism. In an essay many years ago entitled "Some Observations on the Limits of Totalitarian Power," I argued that even in the most totalistic milieus, there were always apertures of freedom, if only in the form of sabotage or Good Soldier Schweik-type behavior; and the supposedly socialist state capitalism of Eastern Europe has produced its critical court jesters, its brave known martyrs, its *samizdat*, and countless nameless martyrs, as did the concentration camps. But most of us are not Sakharovs or Solzhenitsyns; we may have a modest amount of civic courage, but we are not prepared to sacrifice ourselves, and, even more poignantly, our families and friends, as martyrs to what may be a quixotic ideal—one that will rarely be heard of in a sealed or semi-sealed society. But, as Nathan Glazer makes clear, it does not follow from this that there is a continuum between a social-welfare democracy which regards itself as socialist, and an avowedly totalitarian Communism which may prefer to term itself socialist: in the latter, totalitarian control is built into the regime's organization in principle, even if it is not always successful in achieving totalistic aims in practice.

If democracy is not to become its own kind of tyranny, not of the majority, but of those who speak in its name or who can organize demonstrations or orchestrate opinion among influential groups, a certain amount of civic courage is required, in addition to private means and the right to start a private enterprise. Capitalism does not insure democracy, and public opinion manifests itself in all sorts of ways in societies that appear totalitarian, or at least succumbing to the "totalitarian temptation," when looked at from the outside. In other words, democracy is not necessarily assured by freedom of opinion, nor destroyed by its apparent absence; freedom of opinion and diversity of opinion are useful supports for democracy, helping it adapt to changing circumstance and bringing it into closer touch with world reality, but providing no guarantee.

What socialism offers to many intellectuals who would suffer from the absence of the privilege of entrepreneurship is a vision of cooperation and compassion in our oft anarchic, even solipsistically individualistic, segments of what goes by the name of capitalism. But I have also observed enclaves that might be called socialist within the United States, including small, homogeneous, often denominational colleges, and, seemingly different but also premised on cooperation and on lack of overt competition or salary differentials, experiments in communal living. People in these enclaves often make heroic efforts to minimize envy and competitiveness. But the anarchy of desire and what George Foster, the Berkeley anthropologist, years ago termed the anatomy of envy stand revealed precisely in such settings, all the more oppressive because of their somewhat claustrophobic quality. Devout socialists would say that this is because the whole society is nonsocialist or anti-socialist, hence a handicap to enclaves that would operate on different principles. I remain skeptical of such contentions.

As my collaborators and I argued in *The Lonely Crowd*, a society is safer in which some individuals pursue power and some pursue wealth. While each can be translated into the other in some degree, and some people can pursue both simultaneously, nevertheless there is some division among individuals in this respect; as I regard the pursuit of money as less dangerous, even if at times no less fanatical, than the pursuit of power, it seems to me wise to maintain a society in which such strivers for domination and preeminence can engage in competitive coexistence rather than joining in a monolithic struggle. In other words, Hobbes's war of all against all is muted when there is more than a single pinnacle for which to fight.

To return again to Schumpeter, such a society is not glamorous. Our movies praise cowboys, not chartered accountants; our mass media are obsessed, when they look at businessmen at all, with lone "jungle-fighters" (to use Michael MacCoby's term from *The Gamesman*), such as Howard Hughes, rather than with the often modest and retiring civil servants of corporate organizations whose names hardly anyone knows—they are not celebrities. The rising call for protectionism makes it evident that many large enterprises, and the labor unions with which they are linked, cannot compete on the world market in the terms of the market, but demand state aid and appeal to xenophobia to get it. Lacking real dedication, religious or otherwise, these civil servants are scarcely true believers in capitalism, but only its temporary beneficiaries. Schumpeter's question as to whether such a system can sustain itself has never been more pertinent.

Socialist

Michael Walzer:

I take the editors' statement as a call for ideological surrender from those of us who still think of ourselves as democrats and leftists. The questions are rhetorical: we are invited to acknowledge the significance of the new conservatism, to agree that we have had to rethink our positions, and to confess that socialism leads ineluctably to the totalitarian state. "Ineluctably" is a nice word. I wonder if the editors of COMMENTARY have themselves been converted to historical determinism. Political democracy, they seem to suggest, is the superstructural expression of capitalist economic relationships and totalitarianism the necessary expression of a socialist economy. I have a looser sense of historical possibility.

There has, of course, been a significant connection between capitalism and democracy. The connection is probably best described as one of mutual constraint. Democracy has functioned to set limits on the tendency of capitalism toward oligopoly in economic life and plutocracy in politics. It has prevented the direct use of economic power in the political arena, and it has made possible a certain degree of control over the indirect uses of economic power. Democratic movements have, moreover, forced the creation of social institutions that protect and care for people who would otherwise be the helpless victims of capitalist competion. I do not want to underestimate these achievements. They have made capitalist society a better place to live in than it would be given other possible political arrangements—the direct rule of the rich, for example, or the rule of military despots in the name of the rich, or the rule of fascist political parties, all of which are perfectly compatible with, though they do not follow ineluctably from, capitalist economic relationships.

At the same time, capitalism has functioned to set limits on the tendency of democracy toward egalitarianism in economic life and popular participation in politics. It has generated hierarchical structures that have proved extraordinarily resistant to political intervention. And it has produced among ordinary people a degree of passivity, a sense of their own incapacities, that makes it very difficult to mobilize large numbers of men and women for sustained and coherent politcal action. Fearful and dependent in the workplace, they are unlikely to make forthright citizens. Once again, this effect should not be underestimated. It makes democracy in a capitalist society less meaningful than it might otherwise be.

Now, these two forms of constraint give rise to a certain balance that many people find comfortable. The apathy of the masses and the partial inhibition of the high and mighty combine to produce a political regime that can be, and generally is, liberal and tolerant. Compared to the Russia of the Gulag, it is heaven on earth, and if these two were our only alternatives, political choice would be an easy matter. But it does not seem unreasonable to judge contemporary Western society by somewhat higher standards and then to call into question the current balance, even with its attendant comforts, which are, after all, enjoyed by some people far more than by others.

I do not have in mind exotic or millennial standards. The values of a liberal philosopher like John Stuart Mill will do very well. Considering the tendency of capitalism to focus men's energies on "the petty pursuit of petty advancements in fortune," Mill argued that "the spirit of a commercial people will be . . . essentially mean and slavish wherever public spirit is not cultivated by an extensive participation of the people in the business of government in detail. . . ." He would tilt the balance decisively toward democracy, for only democratic participation, he believed, could produce prideful men and women, with a sense of themselves as members of a community, committed to the general welfare, and capable of acting on that commitment. Socialism, for me, is most simply characterized as a world of such men and women. The central animus of socialist thought is directed against the slavishness that liberals also abhorred—until some of them at least came to see that it was a useful and perhaps even a necessary feature of any society founded on private property and acquiescent in the inequalities produced by the market. For it is clear that the development of participation and public spirit requires significant encroachments on the rights of private property. More precisely, it requires that the political expression of these rights, in corporate management and economic decision-making, be subjected to new sorts of popular control. Hence, democratization and socialization go together.

The state is undoubtedly the most important agent of popular control. And it is the vision of the state seized by a mass movement, but actually run by the ideological elite of that movement, that lends to the editors' questions whatever plausibility they have. Such a state is indeed frightening; its rulers might well call themselves socialists, using the rhetoric of community participation even as they further impoverished our public life and turned us all from potential citizens into actual subjects. But how is such a tyranny to be avoided? Surely the best way is to create incrementally the structured pattern of a genuine democracy. I would image that pattern as being federal in form, with a considerable degree of decentralization in both state and economy. But I do not doubt that it will be capped by a fairly powerful central government. No modern society can survive and prosper without centralized planning and coordination: capitalism too breeds its technocrats and turns them into officials.

The critical question, then, has to do with the responsibility of the people who do the planning and coordinating. Our present arrangements regularly turn these people, whatever their good intentions, into agents of the powerful few, in politics as in economics. Even more importantly, a capitalist system fails to educate large numbers of other men and women for public life, and so it is likely to generate, in its moments of crisis, movements (of the Left or Right) composed of frightened masses and authoritarian elites. The fearful prospect evoked by the editors has its source in the inadequacies and inequities of contemporary social organization. A socialist democracy, by contrast, would transform the central government into the practical expression of a carefully articulated general will—a more stable as well as a more humane political arrangement. The current balance in the West hovers between these two conditions—closer, surely, to the first. To struggle to shift the balance decisively toward the second still seems to me not a dangerous but an attractive venture.

Part 1

IS LIFE
WORTH LIVING
HERE?

Social problems originated in the analysis of
disputes arising from industrialization in the late
nineteenth and early twentieth century. Issues such
as immigration, poverty, and crime came to the
forefront as America made the transition from a
rural to an urban society. As additional areas of
society have undergone change, new social problems have been identified.

When natural resources were presumed to be
abundant and when the deleterious effects of
technology on nature went unnoticed, the environment was not a social problem. Of course, the
problem existed, but it was not yet recognized.

When a unitary world view breaks down and a
variety of positions emerge, we enter the realm of
politics. Politics involves the amassing of resources,
both material and moral, for organizing society in
one way rather than another.

Social problems are political issues. They are
disputes over how society, or some part of it,
should be organized. As soon as more than one
point of view exists about how an area of social life
should be conducted, a conflict of ideas—an

ideological dispute—takes place. When some people feel strongly enough about their ideas to try to replace one social practice with another, a political conflict—a power struggle—ensues. The struggle for power among different groups over particular issues produces social problems. The conflict of ideas over how to define, analyze, or resolve these issues produces different sociological definitions of social problems.

Each approach to social problems contains within it a different goal for what society should be. These different goals reflect the values upon which the proponents of each of the three perspectives base their analysis of what is or is not problematic in a society. For,

> ideological values are not simple statements of subjective preference. They are compound conceptions which include a recognition of all the basic human needs affirmed by other ideologies, but which advocate a particular ordering of these needs on the ground that such an order is objectively necessary for the maximum happiness of mankind.[1]

For example, conservatives, liberals and socialists each define the proper relationship of the individual to the community differently. Conservatives believe that the rights of the individual have priority over those of the community. Acquisition of private property is the prime means to individual self-realization. Freedom is defined as the ability to rise above others. Individuals oppose each other in this quest for the accumulation of resources. The state should protect the right of the individual to control his or her property.

Liberals accept the right of individuals to accumulate property but they do not believe that this right overrides all others. Different individual rights must be balanced against each other. The accumulation of property and the right to subsistence are both valid. Individual accumulation should be restricted for some if it is necessary to assure the basic necessities of life for others. The role of the state is to balance these competing claims against each other and provide an acceptable means of realizing both principles simultaneously.

Socialists do not accept the proposition that there is an inevitable conflict between the individual and society. Socialists believe that if the good of the community is secured, the life of the individual will be enhanced. Communal ownership of the means of production will insure that each individual is free from want. By eliminating the competitive struggle for property, the foundation will be laid for a society in which the creative development of all human talents will be encouraged.

Conservatives, liberals, and socialists also offer different answers to such basic questions as: Who should make decisions? How should the resources that a society has available be distributed? What are the goals that a good society should strive to achieve? Disagreements about the kind of society we want to live in are at the root of disputes over particular issues. Cities, crime, and environment are among the issues currently in dispute. These particular disputes express basic conflicts over fundamental political principles and result in quite different guides to political action.

---

1. Herbert Auerbach, *The Conservative Illusion* (New York: Columbia University Press, 1959), p. 255.

Chapter 1

CITIES

In the United States, the emergence of social problems has been associated with the growth of cities. In the early years of the Republic, when America was predominantly an agricultural nation, Thomas Jefferson predicted that the building of factories and the expansion of cities would divide Americans into rich and poor, haves and have nots, owners of industry and workers. Jefferson advised against industrialization and urbanization to avoid this division of Americans into two classes, with its attendant ills of poverty, disease, and overcrowding. He believed that almost all Americans should continue farming to avert social ills, class distinctions, and social conflict. Some farmers might be a little better off than others through harder work or the good luck of having acquired better land. Nevertheless, in a society based on agriculture, there would be an approximate equality of wealth and democratic institutions and values would be strengthened. The only exceptions to this general rule were a few wealthy merchants in seaboard cities and plantation owners (with their slaves) in the rural south. But these small groups, with their inherent seeds of inequality, would be subordinated to the vast majority of independent farmers.

Jefferson's vision of America as a nation based on small farms has been shared by many, even in the present. Although it still exists as a powerful ideology for farmers, suburban residents, and city dwellers who would like to return to the land, the theory of America as a rural nation began to break down, in the early 1800s, with the establishment of industrial cities such as Lowell, Massachusetts.

The New England merchants and manufacturers who founded Lowell built textile mills powered by the waterfalls of the Merrimack River. The mills were constructed under carefully controlled conditions to allay the fears of Americans, such as Jefferson, that democratic institutions would be subverted by the establishment of industry. The appearance of a city was avoided as much as possible. The factories were surrounded by fields, and residences were set apart from the factories to maintain a rural environment.

A unique series of policies were instituted to avoid the appearance of a permanent urban population. Young women were recruited from the surrounding farm regions. While in Lowell, they lived in boarding houses under the supervision of matrons. They worked in the Lowell mills for a few years to save money for their marriage dowries and then returned home. Through these policies the owners of Lowell hoped to avoid the creation of a permanent industrial working class and keep the members of a transient working class under close control.

For years thereafter, Lowell was seen as a model for introducing the benefits of industry into America without the evils of European industrial cities with their slums and poverty. Visiting dignitaries found Lowell to be a model for the industrialization of the United States. Even so Lowell soon had its slums, although they were kept from the sight of visitors. The elaborate plans of the factory owners made no provision for the laborers required to build canals to service the factories. A shanty town grew up adjacent to Lowell in which all the urban defects, such as overcrowding and disease, that Lowell was designed to avoid soon appeared. The factory owners decided that they could lower wages by employing Irish immigrants instead of New England farm women. The boarding houses were dispensed with, and Lowell soon resembled European industrial cities such as Manchester with their multitude of ill-paid, ill-housed, and ill-fed workers.

At the beginning of the twentieth century, Upton Sinclair, in *The Jungle,* a depiction of working conditions in Chicago slaughter houses, offered as chilling a portrait of the dehumanizing effects of factory work in America as Marx and Engels provided for Europe. Sociology was established in America during this era, partly as a response by a largely middle-class reform movement to the harsh conditions of life for workers in burgeoning industrial cities such as Chicago. Reformers included social workers such as Jane Addams, who founded the settlement house movement, journalists such as Jacob Riis, who wrote *How the Other Half Lives,* and sociologists such as Albion Small, who participated in civic associations and advised reform groups as well as business leaders on the amelioration of social problems.

The reform movement wanted to improve working conditions in factories and mitigate the ill effects of poverty without fundamentally changing the economic system or displacing its elite. Capitalism was accepted as a given, and they did not challenge the amassing of great fortunes then underway by the Rockefellers, Morgans, and Carnegies. The reformers hoped to persuade the upper class to act more responsibly to the lower classes. By encouraging industrialists to improve working conditions through legislation and moral suasion, they believed that socialist solutions could be averted. The wave of reform brought settlement houses to the slums to teach immigrants how to adjust to American life. Model tenement apartment houses were built by wealthy philanthropists to demonstrate that the poor, or at least the working poor, could be decently housed at low cost.

Socialists viewed these and other reform measures as mere palliatives that did not address the fundamental cause of urban problems. The social problems of the cities were seen as an expression of a capitalist economic system. Nothing short of a transition to socialism could make decent housing, adequate medical care, and other basic necessities of life equally available to all persons. The social conditions of working and poor people would be transformed only when they organized and demanded control of the economic wealth that they created through their labor in factories, mines, and farms.

The basic issue in dispute between conservatives, liberals, and socialists with respect to cities is the operation of the economy. Conservatives believe that the free enterprise system is the solution to urban problems. It will create sufficient jobs and opportunities to establish one's own business enabling everyone to live well. Conservatives view liberal reform measures and socialist attempts to reorganize the economy as counterproductive. The people would best be served by as little interference as possible in the affairs of the owners and managers of industry. A variety of lobbying and research organizations have been organized to protect the organization of industry on capitalist principles. The National Association of Manufacturers, the U.S. Chamber of Commerce, and the National Conference Board lobby Congress and produce studies and reports to insure that liberal and socialist proposals are beaten back.

In the conservative article "The Unheavenly City" Edward Banfield argues that the increasing criticism of urban problems does not mean that conditions are deteriorating. They are improving and the increase in criticism is an indication of this. Public standards for housing, health care, and employment have risen. Conditions in these areas are better than they used to be. We only think they are worse because our standards have changed.

Government programs to deal with problems that do exist have produced more harm than good. A natural process of improvement that is built into the normal working of our economic system will take care of these problems. For example, through a trickle-down effect good housing that is given up by the well-to-do as they move to the suburbs will become available to the poor in the cities. As immigrant groups arrived in the cities, they worked their way up the economic and social ladder. Blacks who have migrated from the south will follow essentially this same pattern of social improvement.

In the liberal article, "America's Cities are (Mostly) Better than Ever," Richard Wade discusses the historical origins of contemporary city problems and takes a guardedly optimistic view of the future. Wade agrees with Banfield that conditions of city life have improved since the late nineteenth century but disagrees with his interpretation of the black migration as simply the arrival of another immigrant group. Wade argues that the black migration from the rural south to the urban north in recent decades is distinctly different from the earlier European immigrations. The immigrant ghettos were temporary enclaves that tended to disappear as an ethnic group improved its economic condition and moved to better housing. Black ghettos continue to get larger and tend to become permanent. Economic opportunities in recent years have not been sufficient to enable blacks to achieve the upward mobility experienced by immigrant groups. Even those blacks who do not succeed in improving their economic condition are subject to racial discrimination. They are forced to remain in ghettos even when they can afford to move to the suburbs. The spread of urban problems to the suburbs offers hope for their solution. Since inner suburbs are now facing some of the same problems as cities, Wade believes that a broader coalition to obtain increased federal aid to deal with the urban crisis will be possible in the 1980s.

In the socialist article "Corporations and the City," Etzkowitz and Mack contend that deteriorating city conditions are likely to persist. Contemporary urban ills are directly connected to recent shifts in the structure of capitalism such as the decentralization of production. During the nineteenth century capitalists encouraged the growth of cities as they needed the common facilities provided by cities to conduct their business. Recent technological advances in transportation and communications enable corporations to operate successfully in remote locations. Many corporations have moved their factories and offices from central cities to suburbs and small towns. Some factories have been relocated overseas to take advantage of lower wage rates. These developments have caused major cities to lose much of their economic base. Factory jobs that were available in the cities for earlier immigrant groups are not there for blacks who have migrated to the cities. Cities have increasingly become colonial entities subject to corporate manipulation as cities fight among themselves to offer greater advantages for corporations to relocate within their boundaries. This new form of domestic imperialism increases the power of corporations vis a vis cities and creates a permanent reserve army of unemployed in our major cities.

The problem of the cities is a broad issue. It raises questions concerning the organization of the economy, racial discrimination, and the proper role of government. Although social problems were initially associated with the rise of cities, they are currently identified with their decline. Success or failure in resolving urban problems will, in the coming years, be a large part of the answer to the question: Is America Possible?

Conservative

Edward Banfield: The Unheavenly City Revisited

...the clock is ticking, time is moving..., we must ask ourselves every night when we go home, are we doing all that we should do in our nation's capital, in all the other big cities of the country.

—President Johnson, after the Watts Riot,
August 1965

A few years ago we constantly heard that urban America was on the brink of collapse. It was one minute to midnight, we were told...Today, America is no longer coming apart...The hour of crisis is passed.

—President Nixon, March 1973

The reason for juxtaposing the quotations above is not to suggest that whereas a few years ago the cities were in great peril now all is well with them. Rather it is to call attention both to the simplistic nature of all such sweeping judgments and to the fact that one's perception of urban America is a function of time and place and also, if one is a politician, of whatever winds are blowing. A few blocks' walk through the heart of any large city was enough in 1965—and is enough in 1973— to show much that was (and is) in crying need of improvement. That a society so technologically advanced and prosperous has many hundreds of blocks ranging from dreary to dismal is disturbing at least and when one takes into account that by the end of the century the urban population will be at least 20 percent larger than in 1970, with six out of every ten persons living in a metropolitan area of more than a million, the prospect may appear alarming.

There is, however, another side to the matter. The plain fact is that the over-whelming majority of city dwellers live more comfortably and conveniently than ever before. They have more and better housing, more and better schools, more and better transportation, and so on. By any conceivable measure of material welfare the present generation of urban Americans is, on the whole, better off than any other large group of people has ever been anywhere. What is more, there is every reason to expect that the general level of comfort and convenience will continue to rise at an even more rapid rate through the foreseeable future.

It is true that many people do not share, or do not share fully, this general prosperity, some because they are the victims of racial prejudice and others for other reasons that are equally beyond their control. If the chorus of complaint about the city arose mainly from these disadvantaged people or on behalf of them, it would be entirely understandable, especially if their numbers were increasing and their plight were getting worse. But the fact is that until very recently most of the talk about the urban crisis has had to do with the comfort, convenience, and business advantage of the well-off white majority and not with the more serious problems of the poor, the Negro, and others who stand outside the charmed circle. And the fact also is that the number of those standing outside the circle is decreasing, as is the relative disadvantage that they suffer. There is still much poverty and much racial discrimination. But there is less of both than ever before.

The question arises, therefore, not of whether we are faced with an urban crisis, but rather, *in what sense* we are faced with one. Whose interest and what interests are involved? How deeply? What should be done? Given the political and other realities of the situation, what *can* be done?

The first need is to clear away some semantic confusions. Consider the statement, so frequently used to alarm luncheon groups, that more than 70 percent of the population now lives in urban places and that this number may increase to nearly 90 percent in the next two decades if present trends continue. Such figures give the impression of standing room only in the city, but what exactly do they mean?

When we are told that the population of the United States is rapidly becoming overwhelmingly urban, we probably suppose this to mean that most people are coming to live in the big cities. This is true in one sense but false in another. It is true that most people live closer physically and psychologically to a big city than ever before; rural occupations and a rural style of life are no longer widespread. On the other hand, the percentage of the population living in cities of 250,000 or more (there are only fifty-six of them) is about the same now as it was in 1920. In Census terminology an "urban place" is any settlement having a population of 2,500 or more; obviously places of 2,500 are not what we have in mind when we use words like "urban" and "city."[1] It is somewhat misleading to say that the country is becoming more urban, when what is meant is that more people are living in places like White River Junction, Vermont (pop. 6,311), and fewer in places like Boston, Massachusetts (pop. 641,000). But it is not *altogether* misleading, for most of the small urban places are now close enough (in terms of time and other costs of travel) to large cities to be part of a metropolitan complex. White River Junction, for example, is now very much influenced by Boston. The average population density in all "urban areas," however, has been decreasing: from 5,408 per square mile in 1950 to 3,752 in 1960, to 3,376 in 1970.

A great many so-called urban problems are really conditions that we either cannot eliminate or do not want to incur the disadvantages of eliminating. Consider the "problem of congestion." The presence of a great many people in one place is a cause of inconvenience, to say the least. But the advantages of having so many people in one place far outweigh those inconveniences, and we cannot possibly have the advantages without the disadvantages. To "eliminate congestion" in the city must mean eliminating the city's reason for being. Congestion in the city is a "problem" only in the sense that congestion in Times Square on New Year's Eve is one; in fact, of course, people come to the city, just as they do to Times Square, precisely *because* it is congested. If it were not congested, it would not be worth coming to.

Strictly speaking, a problem exists only as we should want something different from what we do want or as by better management we could get a larger total of what we want. If we think it a good thing that many people have the satisfaction of driving their cars in and out of the city, and if we see no way of arranging the situation to get them in and out more conveniently that does not entail more than offsetting disadvantages for them or others, then we ought not to speak of a "traffic congestion problem." By the same token, urban sprawl is a "problem," as opposed to a "condition," only if (1) fewer people should have the satisfaction of living in the low-density fringe of the city, or (2) we might, by better planning, build homes in the fringe without destroying so much landscape and without incurring costs (for example, higher per-unit construction costs) or foregoing benefits (for example, a larger number of low-income families who can have the satisfaction of living in the low-density area) of greater value than the saving in landscape.

Few problems, in this strict sense, are anywhere near as big as they seem. The amount of urban sprawl that could be eliminated simply by better planning—that is, without the sacrifice of other ends that are also wanted, such as giving the satisfaction of owning a house and yard to many low-income people—is probably trivial as compared to the total urban sprawl (that is, to the "problem" defined simple-mindedly as "a condition that is unpleasant").

Many so-called urban problems (crime is a conspicuous exception) are more characteristic of rural and small-town places than of cities. Housing is generally worse in rural areas, for example, and so are schools. "Low verbal ability," Sloan R. Wayland of Columbia Teachers College has written, "is described as though it could only happen in an urban slum." Actually, he points out, all but a very small fraction of mankind has always been "culturally deprived," and the task of formal education has always been to attack such conditions."[2]

Most of the "problems" that are generally supposed to constitute "the urban crisis" could not conceivably lead to disaster. They are—some of them—important in the sense that a bad cold is important, but they are not critical in the sense that a cancer is critical. They have to do with comfort, convenience, amenity, and business advantage, all of which are important, but they do not affect either the essential welfare of individuals or what may be called the good health of the society.

Consider, for example, an item that often appears near the top of the list of complaints about the city—the journey to work. It takes the average commuter between 21 and 34 minutes to get to work (the difference in the average time depending upon the population of the metropolitan area).[3] It would, of course, be very nice if the journey to work were much shorter. No one can suppose, however, that the essential welfare of many people would be much affected even if it were fifteen minutes longer. Certainly its being longer or shorter would not make the difference between a good society and a bad.

Another matter causing widespread alarm is the decline of the central business district, by which is meant the loss of patronage to downtown department stores, theaters, restaurants, museums, and so on, which has resulted from the movement of many well-off people to suburbs. Clearly, the movement of good customers from one place to another involves inconvenience and business loss to many people, especially to the owners of real estate that is no longer in so great demand. These losses, however, are essentially no different from those that occur from other causes—say, a shift of consumers' tastes that suddenly renders a once-valuable patent valueless. Moreover, though some lose by the change, others gain by it: the overall gain of wealth by building in the suburbs may more than offset the loss of it caused by letting the downtown deteriorate.

There are those who claim that cultural and intellectual activity flourishes only in big cities and that therefore the decline of the downtown business districts and the replacement of cities by suburbs threatens the very survival of civilization. This claim is farfetched, to say the very least, if it means that we cannot have good music and good theater (not to mention philosophy, literature, and science) unless customers do their shopping in the downtown districts of Oakland, St. Louis, Nashville, Boston, and so on, rather than in the suburbs around them. Public efforts to preserve the downtown districts of these and other cities may perhaps be worth what they cost—although, so far as cultural and intellectual activities are concerned, there is no reason to assume that public efforts would not bring at least as much return if directed to metropolitan areas as wholes. The return, however, will be in the comfort, convenience, and business advantage of the relatively well-off and not in anyone's essential welfare.

The same can be said about efforts to "beautify" the cities. That for the most part the cities are dreary and depressing if not offensively ugly may be granted: the desirability of improving their appearance, even if only a little, cannot be questioned. It is very doubtful, however, that people are dehumanized (to use a favorite word of those who complain about the cities) by the ugliness of the city or that they would be in any sense humanized by its being made beautiful. (If they were humanized, they would doubtless build beautiful cities, but that is an entirely different matter. One has only to read Machiavelli's Florentine Histories to see that living in a beautiful city is not in itself enough to bring out the best in one. So far as their humanity is concerned, the people of, say, Jersey City compare very favorably to the Florentine's of the era of that city's greatest glory.) At worst, the American city's ugliness—or, more, its lack of splendor or charm—occasions loss of visual pleasure. This loss is an important one (it is surely much larger than most people realize), but it cannot lead to any kind of disaster either for the individual or for the society.

Air pollution comes closer than any of these problems to threatening essential welfare, as opposed to comfort, convenience, amenity, and business advantage. Some people die early because of it and many more suffer various degrees of bad health; there is also some possibility (no one knows how much) that a meteorlogical coincidence (an "air inversion") over a large city might suddenly kill thousands or even tens of thousands. Important as it is, however, the air pollution problem is rather minor as compared to other threats to health and welfare not generally regarded as "crises."[4] Moreover, steps are being taken to clear the air. The Clean Air Act Amendment of 1970 is expected to reduce pollution from auto emissions (by far the most serious source) to half of what they were in 1967 (the base year) by 1980 and to a quarter by 1985.[5]

Many of the "problems" that are supposed to constitute the "crisis" could be quickly and easily solved, or much alleviated, by the application of well-known measures that lie right at hand. In some instances, the money cost of these measures would be very small. For example, the rush-hour traffic problem in the central cities (which, incidentally, is almost the whole of the traffic problem in these cities) could be much reduced and in some cases eliminated entirely just by staggering working hours in the largest offices and factories. Manhattan presents the hardest case of all, but even there, an elaborate study showed, rush-hour crowding could be reduced by 25 percent, enough to make the strap-hanger reasonably comfortable.[6] Another quick and easy way of improving urban transportation in most cities would be to eliminate a mass of archaic regulations on the granting of public transit and taxi franchises. At present, the cities are in effect going out of their way to place obstacles in the paths of those who might offer the public better transportation.[7] Metropolitan transportation could also easily be

improved in those areas—there are a number of them—where extensive expressway networks link the downtown with outlying cities and towns. In these areas,
according to the Harvard economist John F. Kain, "all that is currently needed to
create extensive metropolitan rapid transit systems ... is a limited outlay for
instrumentation, some modification of ramp arrangement and design, and most
importantly *a policy decision to keep congestion at very low levels during peak hours and
to provide priority access for public transit vehicles.*"[8]

The "price" of solving, or alleviating, some much-talked-about city problems,
it would appear from this, may be largely political. Keeping congestion at low
levels at peak hours would necessitate placing high toll charges on roads at the
very times when most people want to use them; some would regard this as
grossly unfair (as indeed in a way it would be) and so the probabilities are that if
any official had the authority to make the decision (none does, which is part of
the problem) he would not raise tolls at rush hours for fear of being voted out of
office.

If the transportation problem is basically political, so is the revenue problem.
A great part of the wealth of our country is in the cities. When a mayor says that
his city is on the verge of bankruptcy, he means that when the time comes to run
for reelection he wants to be able to claim credit for straightening out a mess that
was left him by his predecessor. What he means when he says that his city *must*
have state or federal aid to finance some improvements is (1) the taxpayers of the
city (or some important group of them) would rather go without the improvement than pay for it themselves; or (2) although they would pay for it themselves
if they had to, they would much prefer to have some other taxpayers pay for it.
Rarely if ever does a mayor who makes such a statement mean (1) that for the city
to pay for the improvement would necessarily force some taxpayers into poverty;
or (2) that the city could not raise the money even if it were willing to force some
of its taxpayers into poverty. In short, the "revenue crisis" mainly reflects the fact
that people hate to pay taxes and that they think that by crying poverty they can
shift some of the bill to someone else.[9]

To some extent, also, the revenue problem of the cities arises from the way
jurisdictional boundaries are drawn or, more precisely, from what are considered
to be inequities resulting from the movement of taxable wealth from one side of a
boundary line to another. When many large taxpayers move to the suburbs, the
central city must tax those who remain at a higher rate if it is to maintain the same
level of services. The "problem" in this case is not that the taxpayers who remain
are absolutely unable to pay the increased taxes; rather, it is that they do not want
to pay them and that they consider it unfair that they should have to pay more
simply because other people have moved away. The simple and costless solution
(in all but a political sense) would be to charge nonresidents for services that they
receive from the city or, failing that, to redraw the boundary lines so that everyone in the metropolitan area would be taxed on the same basis. As the historian
Kenneth T. Jackson points out, those central cities that are declining in numbers
of residents and in wealth are doing so because their state legislatures will not
permit them to enlarge their boundaries by annexations; even before the Civil
War many large cities would have been surrounded by suburbs—and therefore
suffering from the same revenue problem—if they had not been permitted to
annex freely.[10]

That we have not yet been willing to pay the price of solving, or alleviating, such "problems" even when the price is a very small one suggests that they are not really critical. Indeed, one might say that, by definition, a critical problem is one that people *are* willing to pay a considerable price to have solved.

With regard to these problems for which solutions are at hand, we will know that a real crisis impends when we see the solutions actually being applied. The solution, that is, will be applied when—and only when—the inconvenience or other disadvantage of allowing the problem to continue unabated is judged to have become greater than that of taking the necessary measures to abate it. In other words, a bad-but-not-quite-critical problem is one that it would almost-but-not-quite pay us to do something about.

If some real disaster impends in the city, it is not because parking spaces are hard to find, because architecture is bad, because department store sales are declining, or even because taxes are rising. If there is a genuine crisis, it has to do with the essential welfare of individuals or with the good health of the society, not merely with comfort, convenience, amenity, and business advantage, important as these are. It is not necessary here to try to define "essential welfare" rigorously: it is enough to say that whatever may cause people to die before their time, to suffer serious impairment of their health or of their powers, to waste their lives, to be deeply unhappy or happy in a way that is less than human affects their essential welfare. It is harder to indicate in a sentence or two what is meant by the "good health" of the society. The ability of the society to maintain itself as a going concern is certainly a primary consideration; so is its free and democratic character. In the last analysis, however, the quality of a society must be judged by its tendency to produce desirable human types; the healthy society, then, is one that not only stays alive but also moves in the direction of giving greater scope and expression to what is distinctively human. In general, of course, what serves the essential welfare of individuals also promotes the good health of the society; there are occasions, however, then the two goals conflict. In such cases, the essential welfare of individuals must be sacrificed for the good health of the society. This happens on a very large scale when there is a war, but it may happen at other times as well. The conditions about which we should be most concerned, therefore, are those that affect, or may affect, the good health of the society. If there is an urban crisis in any ultimate sense, it must be constituted of these conditions.

It is a good deal easier to say what matters are not serious (that is, do not affect either the essential welfare of individuals or the good health of the society) than it is to say what ones are. It is clear, however, that crime, poverty, ignorance, and racial (and other) injustices are among the most important of the general conditions affecting the essential welfare of individuals. It is plausible, too, to suppose that these conditions have a very direct bearing upon the good health of the society, although in this connection other factors that are much harder to guess about—for example, the nature and strength of the consensual bonds that hold the society together—may be much more important. To begin with, anyway, it seems reasonable to look in these general directions for what may be called the serious problems of the cities.

It is clear at the outset that serious problems affect only a rather small minority of the whole urban population. In the relatively new residential suburbs and in the better residential neighborhoods in the outlying parts of the central cities and in the older, larger, suburbs, the overwhelming majority of people are safely above the poverty line, have at least a high school education, and do not suffer from racial discrimination. For something like two-thirds of all city dwellers, the urban problems that touch them directly have to do with comfort, convenience, amenity, and business advantage. In the terminology used here, such problems are "important" but not "serious." In many cases, they cannot even fairly be called important; a considerable part of the urban population—those who reside in the "nicer" suburbs—lives under material conditions that will be hard to improve upon.

The serious problems are to be found in all large cities and in most small ones. But they affect only parts of these cities—mainly the inner parts of the larger ones—and only a small proportion of the whole urban population. Crime is a partial exception, but in Chicago (so the Violence Commission was told) a person who lives in the inner city faces a yearly risk of 1 in 77 of being assaulted whereas for those who live in the better areas of the city the risk is only 1 in 2,000 and for those who live in the rich suburbs only 1 in 10,000.[11] Apart from those in the inner districts, which comprise about 10 to 20 percent of the city's total area, there are few serious urban problems. If what really matters is the essential welfare of individuals and the good health of the society, as opposed to comfort, convenience, amenity, and business advantage, then the problem is less an "urban" one than an "inner-(big)-city" one.

Although the poor and the black (and in some cities other minority groups also) are concentrated in the inner city and although the districts in which they live include many blocks of unrelieved squalor, it should not be supposed that the "poverty areas" of the inner cities are uniformly black, poor, or squalid. This can be seen from the findings of a special survey made in 1970 and 1971 by the Census of what it defined as the "low-income areas" of fifty-one of the largest cities.[12] A brief listing of some of these findings should dispel any notion that an inner-city "poverty area" is occupied only by the "disinherited."

Of the almost nine million persons aged sixteen or over who were counted, half were black and 35 percent non-Spanish white.

More than three-fourths reported incomes *above* the poverty level.

The median income of a male-headed family was $7,782 (the comparable figure for the United States population as a whole was $10,480).

Among such families, 25 percent of the white and 20 percent of the Negro reported income above $12,000.

Of the nearly two million persons below the poverty level, whites and blacks were distributed in about the same population as in the whole "poverty area" population. (Spanish families were considerably overrepresented among the poor in the nineteen cities where they were numerous enough to be surveyed separately.)

The median income of male-headed white families was $425 more than that of black and the median income of black $849 more than Spanish.

In twenty-one of the fifty-one cities, however, the blacks in poverty areas had higher median family incomes than whites and in twelve more cities the difference (in favor of the whites) was trivial—less than 5 percent.

The median years of schooling for persons twenty-five years of age or older was almost identical—10 and a small fraction—for whites and blacks, males and females; for persons twenty-five to thirty-four it was also almost identical and surprisingly high; twelve and a small fraction.

Although a large share of the income of many families went for housing, the reverse was also true: 40 percent of white and 25 percent of Negro (male-headed) families paid less than 10 percent of their income for housng. Ninety percent of the white and 80 percent of the black (male-headed) families had housing that was not overcrowded—that is, there was at least one room per person.

Of the nearly nine million persons aged sixteen or over, 478,000 (9.6 percent of those in the labor force) were unemployed. Less than half of these had been laid off; most had either quit or were just entering the labor force. Only 82,000 had been unemployed for as long as six months. Most were teenagers or unattached men and women in their early twenties, and many of these were students who wanted part-time or summer jobs.

The unemployment rate among male Negro family heads was 5.3 percent; among male white (non-Spanish) family heads it was 4.5 percent.

About 10 percent of those *not* in the labor force said that they intended looking for a job (most non-participants were housewives, of course). Asked why they did not look, "inability to find work" was given as a reason by 8,000 males and 24,000 females. Of these, 25 percent were aged 16-21. Asked what would be their minimum acceptable wage; the median figure given by black males in this age group was $83 weekly; whites expected one dollar more. Both black and white men who were heads of families expected $108.

Within or overlapping, some "poverty areas" are huge enclaves—a few have populations of several hundred thousand—that are almost entirely Negro or, in some cities, Puerto Rican or Mexican-American.[13] These enclaves—they are often called ghettoes, but this usage is extremely ambiguous—constitute a problem that is both serious and unique to the large cities. The problem arises because the enclaves are psychologically—and in some degree physically—cut off from the rest of the city. Whatever may be the effect of this on the welfare of the individual—and it may possibly be trivial—it is clear that the existence of a large enclave of persons who perceive themselves, and are perceived by others, as having a separate identity, not sharing, or not sharing fully, the attachment that others feel to the "city," constitutes a potential hazard not only to present peace and order but—what is more important—to the well-being of the society over the long run. Problems of individual welfare may be no greater by virtue of the fact that people live together in huge enclaves rather than in relative isolation on farms and in small towns, although about this one cannot be sure (such problems *appear* greater when people live in enclaves, of course, but this is because they are too conspicuous to be ignored). The problem that they may present to the good health of the society, however, is very different in kind and vastly greater in importance solely by virtue of their living in huge enclaves. Unlike those who live on farms and in small towns, disaffected people who are massed together may develop a collective consciousness and sense of identity. From some standpoints it may be highly desirable that they do so: feeling the strength of their numbers may give them confidence and encourage them to act politically and in other ways that will help them. On the other hand, the effect of numbers may be to support attitudes and institutions that will hamper progress. There is no doubt, however, that such enclaves represent a threat to peace and order, one made greater by the high proportion of young people in them. As the Commission on Population Growth and the American Future recently remarked.

> The decade 1960 to 1970 saw a doubling of the number of young black men and women aged 15 to 24 in the metropolitan areas of every part of the nation except the south. This increase, twice that for comparable white youth, was the result of higher black fertility to begin with, participation in the post-World War II baby boom, and continued migration away from southern rural poverty. The result has been more and more young black people ill-equipped to cope with the demands of urban life, more likely to wind up unemployed or in dead-end, low-paying jobs, and caught in the vicious wheel of poverty, welfare, degradation, and crime.
>
> The facts we have cited describe a crisis for our society. They add up to a demographic recipe for more turmoil in our cities, more bitterness among our "have-nots," and greater divisiveness among all of our people.[14]

The political danger in the presence of great concentrations of people who feel little attachment to the society has long been regarded by some as *the* serious problem of the cities—the one problem that might eventuate in disaster for the society. "The dark ghettoes," Dr. Clark has written, "now represent a nuclear stockpile which can annihilate the very foundations of America."[15] These words bring to mind the apprehensions that were expressed by some of the Founding Fathers and that Tocqueville set forth in a famous passage of *Democracy in America:*

> The United States has no metropolis, but it already contains several very large cities. Philadelphia reckoned 161,000 inhabitants, and New York 202,000 in the year 1830. The lower ranks which inhabit these cities constitute a rabble even more formidable than the populace of European towns. They consist of freed blacks, in the first place, who are condemned by the laws and by public opinion to a hereditary state of misery and degradation. They also contain a multitude of Europeans who have been driven to the shores of the New World by their misfortunes or their misconduct; and they bring to the United States all our greatest vices, without any of those interests which counteract their baneful influence. As inhabitants of a country where they have no civil rights, they are ready to turn all the passions which agitate the community to their own advantage; thus, within the last few months, serious riots have broken out in Philadelphia and New York. Disturbances of this kind are unknown in the rest of the country, which is not alarmed by them, because the population of the cities has hitherto exercised neither power nor influence over the rural districts.
>
> Nevertheless, I look upon the size of certain American cities, and especially on the nature of their population, as a real danger which threatens the future security of the democratic republics of the New World; and I venture to predict that they will perish from this circumstance, unless the government succeeds in creating an armed force which, while it remains under the control of the majority of the nation, will be independent of the town population and able to repress its excesses.[16]

Strange as it may seem, the mammoth government programs to aid the cities are directed mainly toward the problems of comfort, convenience, amenity, and business advantage. Insofar as they have an effect on the serious problems, it is, on the whole, to aggravate them.

Two programs account for a very large part of federal government expenditure for the improvement of the cities (as opposed to the maintenance of more or less routine functions). Neither is intended to deal with the serious problems. Both make them worse.

The improvement of urban transportation is one program. The federal contribution for urban highway construction and improvement, which as long ago as 1960 was more than $1 billion a year, has since doubled. The main effect of urban expressways, for which most of the money is spent, is to enable surburbanites to move about the metropolitan area more conveniently, to open up some areas for business and residential expansion, and to bring a few more customers from the suburbs downtown to shop. These are worthy objects when considered by themselves; in context, however, their jusitification is doubtful, for their principal effect is to encourage—in effect to subsidize—further movement of industry, commerce, and relatively well-off residents (mostly white) from the inner city. This, of course, makes matters worse for the poor by reducing the number of jobs for them and by making neighborhoods, schools, and other community facilities still more segregated. These injuries are only partially offset by enabling a certain number of the inner-city poor to commute to jobs in the suburbs.

The huge expenditure being made for improvement of mass transit—$1 billion in fiscal 1974—may be justifiable for the contribution that it will make to comfort, convenience, and business advantage. It will not, however, make any contribution to the solution of the serious problems of the city. Even if every city had a subway as fancy as Moscow's, all these problems would remain.

The second great federal urban program concerns housing and renewal. Since the creation in 1934 of the Federal Housing Authority (FHA), the government has subsidized home building on a vast scale by insuring mortgages that are written on easy terms and, in the case of the Veterans Administration (VA), by guaranteeing mortgages. Most of the mortgages have been for the purchase of *new* homes. (This was partly because FHA wanted gilt-edged collateral behind the mortgages that it insured, but it was also because it shared the American predilection for newness.) It was cheaper to build on vacant land, but there was little such land left in the central cities and in their larger, older suburbs; therefore, most of the new homes were built in new suburbs. These were almost always zoned so as to exclude the relatively few Negroes and other "undesirables" who could afford to build new houses and until the late 1962 (when a presidential order barred discrimination in federally aided housing) FHA acted on its own to encourage all-white developments by instructing its appraisers to make low ratings of properties in neighborhoods occupied by what its Underwriting Manual termed "inharmonious racial or nationality groups" and by recommending a model racial restrictive covenant.[17] In effect, then, the FHA and VA programs have subsidized the movement of the white middle class out of the central cities and older suburbs while at the same time penalizing investment in the rehabilitation of the run-down neighborhoods of these older cities. The poor—especially the Negro poor—have not received any direct benefit from these programs. (They have, however, received a very substantial unintended and indirect benefit, as will be explained later, because the departure of the white middle class has made more housing available to them.) After the appointment of Robert C. Weaver as head of the Housing and Home Finance Agency, FHA changed its regulations to encourage the rehabilitation of existing houses and neighborhoods. Very few such loans have been made, however.

Urban renewal has also turned out to be mainly for the advantage of the well-off—indeed, of the rich—and to do the poor more harm than good. The purpose of the federal housing program was declared by Congress to be "the realization as soon as feasible of the goal of a decent home and a suitable living environment for every American family." In practice, however, the principal objectives of the renewal program have been to attract the middle class back into the central city (as well as to slow its exodus out of the city) and to stabilize and restore the central business districts.[18] Unfortunately, these objectives can be served only at the expense of the poor. Hundreds of thousands of low-income people, most of them Negroes or Puerto Ricans, have been forced out of low-cost housing, by no means all of its substandard, in order to make way for luxury apartments, office buildings, hotels, civic centers, industrial parks, and the like. Insofar as renewal has involved the "conservation" or "rehabilitation" of residential areas, its effect has been to keep the poorest of the poor out of these neighborhoods—that is, to keep them in the highest-density slums. "At a cost of more than three billion dollars," sociologist Scott Greer wrote in 1965, "the Urban Renewal Agency (URA) has succeeded in materially reducing the supply of low-cost housing in American cities."[19]

The injury to the poor inflicted by renewal has not been offset by benefits to them in the form of public housing (that is, housing owned by public bodies and rented by them to families deemed eligible on income and other grounds.) With the important exception of New York and the less important ones of some Southern cities, such housing is not a significant part of the total supply. Moreover, the poorest of the poor are usually, for one reason or another, ineligible for public housing.

Another housing program that has subsidized the relatively well-off and hastened their movement out of the central city is seldom thought of as a housing program at all. It consists of benefits to homeowners under the federal income tax laws. *The President's Fourth Annual Report on National Housing Goals*, issued in 1972, estimated that by allowing homeowners to deduct mortgage interest and property taxes from their gross incomes federal revenues had been reduced by $4.7 billion the previous year.[20] The subsidies, the report said, "are worth relatively more to higher income homeowners." Renters were not benefited at all except as owners might pass some of their tax savings on to them. To dramatize the inequity of these arrangements, a tax authority testifying before a Senate subcommittee imagined what it would sound like if a housing program having the same effects were to be proposed to Congress:

> We have a program to assist people who own homes . . . . If there is a married couple with more than $200,000 of income, why for each $100 of mortgage that they have, HUD will pay that couple $70. On the other hand, if there is a married couple with an income of $10,000, then under this HUD program we will pay that married couple only $19 on their $100 mortgage interest bill. And, of course, if they are too poor to pay an income tax then we are not going to pay them anything.[21]

Obviously these various government programs work at cross-purposes, one undoing (or *trying* to undo) what another does (or *tries* to do). The expressway and (with minor exceptions) the housing programs in effect pay the middle-class person to leave the central city for the suburbs. At the same time, the urban renewal and mass-transit programs pay him to stay in the central city or to move back to it. ". . . [F]ederal housing programs over the years," the presidential report cited above acknowledges, "have contributed to rapid suburbanization and unplanned urban sprawl, to growing residential separation of the races, and to the concentration of the poor and minorities in decaying central cities."[22] In the opinion of the economist Richard Muth, expressways (" the major contributor to urban decentralization in the postwar period") and federal aids to home ownership may have caused the land area of cities to be as much as 17 percent larger than it would otherwise be and the central city's share of the urbanized area population to be 3 to 7 percent smaller.[23]

In at least one respect, however, these government programs are consistent: they aim at problems of comfort, convenience, amenity, and business advantage, not at ones involving the essential welfare of individuals or the good health of the society. Indeed, on the contrary, they all sacrifice these latter, more important interests for the sake of the former, less important ones. In this the urban programs are no different from a great many other government programs. Price production programs in agriculture, Theodore Schultz has remarked, take up almost all the time of the Department of Agriculture, the agricultural committees of Congress, and the farm organizations, and exhaust the influence of farm people. But these programs, he says, "do not improve the schooling of farm children, they do not reduce the inequalities in personal distribution of wealth and income, they do not remove the causes of poverty in agriculture, nor do they alleviate it. On the contrary, they worsen the personal distribution of income within agriculture."[25]

It is widely supposed that the serious problems of the cities are unprecedented both in kind and in magnitude. Between 1950 and 1960 there occurred the greatest population increase in the nation's history. At the same time, a considerable part of the white middle class moved to the newer suburbs, and its place in the central cities and older suburbs was taken by Negroes (and in New York by Puerto Ricans as well). These and other events—especially the civil rights revolution—are widely supposed to have changed completely the character of "the urban problem."

If the present situation is indeed radically different from previous ones, then we have nothing to go on in judging what is likely to happen next. At the very least, we face a crisis of uncertainty.

In a real sense, of course, *every* situation in unique. Even in making statistical probability judgments, one must decide on more or less subjective grounds whether it is reasonable to treat certain events as if they were the "same." The National Safety Council, for example, must decide whether cars, highways, and drivers this year are enough like those of past years to justify predicting future experience from past. From a logical standpoint, it is not more possible to decide this question in a purely objective way than it is to decide, for example, whether the composition of the urban population is now so different from what it was that nothing can be inferred from the past about the future. Karl and Alma Tacuber are both right and wrong when they write that we do not know enough about immigrant and Negro assimilation patterns to be able to compare the two and that "such evidence as we could compile indicates that it is more likely to be misleading than instructive to make such comparisons."[25] They are certainly right in saying that one can only guess whether the pattern of Negro assimilation will resemble that of the immigrant. But they are wrong to imply that we can avoid making guesses and still compare things that are not known to be alike in all respects except one. (What, after all, would be the point of comparing immigrant and Negro assimilation patterns if we knew that the only difference between the two was, say, skin color?) They are also wrong in suggesting that the evidence indicates anything about what is likely to be instructive. If there were enough evidence to indicate that, there would be enough to indicate what is likely to happen; indeed, a judgment as to what is likely to be instructive is inseparable from one as to what is likely to happen. Strictly speaking, the Tacubers' statement expresses *their* guess as to what the evidence indicates.

The facts by no means compel one to take the view that the serious problems of the cities are unprecedented either in kind or in magnitude. That the population of metropolitan areas increased during the 1960's by nearly 17 percent to a record high of 139,374,000 persons need not hold much significance from the present standpoint: American cities have frequently grown at fantastic rates (consider the growth of Chicago from a prairie village of 4,470 in 1840 to a metropolis of more than a million in fifty years). In any case, the present population increase is leaving most cities less rather than more crowded. In the 1960's, 130 of the 292 central cities lost population, and the aggregate of their loss was 2.25 million persons; this was a greater decline than in the previous decade. Density of population in the central cities fell from 7,786 per square mile in 1950 to 4,463 in 1970; the comparable figures for suburban areas are 3,167 and 2,627.[26] Looking to the future, there is every reason to expect the trend toward "decongestion" to continue. But even if it were to reverse itself, there would be no obvious cause for concern. As Irving Hoch, a researcher for Resources for the Future has remarked, there has been much sound and fury about the presumed ill effects of city size and density on health and welfare but there is little hard evidence on the subject; moreover, such evidence as points in one direction can be countered by other evidence pointing in the opposite direction.[27]

The movement of farm and rural people (mostly Negroes and Puerto Ricans) to the large Northern cities was much smaller in the 1960's than in the previous decade and the outlook is for a continued decline both because natural increase was less during the 1960's and because rural areas appear to be retaining a higher proportion of their growth.[28] But even at its height the migration of Negroes and Puerto Ricans to the big cities was no more than about equal to immigration from Italy in its peak decade. (In New York, Chicago, and many other cities in 1910, two out of every three schoolchildren were the sons and daughters of immigrants.) When one takes into account the vastly greater size and wealth of the cities now as compared to half a century or more ago, it is obvious that by the only relevant measure—namely, the number of immigrants relative to the capacity of the cities to provide for them and to absorb them—the movement from the South and from Puerto Rico has been not large but small.

In many important respects the material conditions of life in the cities have long been improving. Incomes have increased steadily. In the 1960's, for example, white income rose by 69 percent and black income by 100 percent. Despite this relative gain, the income of black families was still somewhat less than two-thirds that of whites. Housing is also better and consumption of it more than doubled in real per capita terms between 1950 and 1970. As Dean Dick Netzer has written,

> Not only has the housing improved, but also there have been huge investments in supporting public and institutional facilities—schools, roads, transit, hospitals, water supply and sewerage, airports, etc. In the twenty-year period, about $200 billion has been invested by state and local governments in new public facilities in metropolitan

areas, almost as much as the total investment in new housing in these areas during the period. This hardly supports the charge that ours is a society of "public squalor amidst private opulence."[29]

At the turn of the century only one child in fifteen went beyond elementary school; now well over half finish high school. In this period blacks have increased the amount of their schooling faster than whites; in 1900 they averaged three years less than whites, but the present generation of pupils is expected to get almost as much, or—if comparison is made among pupils with about the same test scores—slightly more.[30] (In 1972, for the first time, the percentage of black and other minority-race high school graduates enrolling in college was the same as for whites). As these figures imply, racial discrimination has declined dramatically since the Second World War. Studies made over a period of almost thirty years by the National Opinion Research Center reveal a trend "distinctly toward increasing approval of integration" with the highest pro-integration scores among the young and among residents of the largest metropolitan areas.[31]

The very movements that in some cities or parts of cities signalize, or constitute, an improvement in the situation tend, of course, to make matters worse in other places. For example, in Philadelphia the population of the districts designated "low income" by the Census dropped from more than 900,000 to nearly 800,000 in the 1960's. This happened partly because many families, black as well as white, became able to afford to move to better neighborhoods. The consequence of their moving out of the "low-income" areas, however, was to widen the income gap between those areas and the rest of the city. In other words, the poverty of the "low-income" areas has been intensified relative to other areas even though—conceivably—it may be that no one in any of them is poorer than before. (As a practical matter, there can be little doubt that the departure of the better-off families *does* entail disadvantages for those who remain.)

Surprising as it may seem, most Americans are reasonably well satisfied with their neighborhoods. A recent poll found that those who live in rural areas and in small towns are more likely to say that they are satisfied than those who live in cities, and, as one would expect, the well-off are more likely to be satisfied than the poor. But even among blacks (seven out of ten of whom are city dwellers) only 17 percent say that they are dissatisfied with their neighborhoods.[32]

If the situation is improving, why, it may be asked, is there so much talk of an urban crisis? The answer is that the improvements in performance, great as they have been, have not kept pace with rising expectations. In other words, although things have been getting better absolutely, they have been getting worse *relative to what we think they should be.* And this is because, as a people, we seem to act on the advice of the old jingle:

Good, better, best,
Never let it rest
Until your good is better
And your better best.

Consider the poverty problem, for example. Irving Kristol has pointed out that for nearly a century all studies, in all countries, have concluded that a third, a fourth, or a fifth of the nation in question is below the poverty line.[33] "Obviously," he remarks, "if one defines the proverty line as that which places one-fifth of the nation below it, then one-fifth of the nation will always be below the poverty line." The point is that even if everyone is better off there will be as much poverty as ever, provided that the line is redefined upward. Kristol notes that whereas in the depths of the Depression, F.D.R. found only one-third of the nation "ill-housed, ill-clad, ill-nourished," Leon Keyserling, a former head of the Council of Economic Advisers, in 1962 published a book called *Poverty and Deprivation in the U.S.—the Plight of Two-Fifths of a Nation.*

Much the same thing has happened with respect to most urban problems. Police brutality, for example, would be a rather minor problem if we judged it by a fixed standard; it is a growing problem because we judge it by an ever more exacting standard. A generation ago the term meant hitting someone on the head with a nightstick. Now it often means something quite different:

> What the Negro community is presently complaining about when it cries "police brutality" is the more subtle attack on personal dignity that manifests itself in unexplainable questionings and searches, in hostile and insolent attitudes toward groups of young Negroes on the street, or in cars, and in the use of disrespectful and sometimes racist language. . . .[34]

Following Kristol, one can say that if the "police brutality line" is defined as that which places one-fifth of all police behavior below it, then one-fifth of all police behavior will always be brutal.

The school dropout problem is an even more striking example. At the turn of the century, when almost everyone was a dropout, the term and the "problem" did not exist. It was not until the 1960's, when for the first time a majority of boys and girls were graduating from high school and practically all had at least some high school training, that the "dropout problem" became acute. Then, although the dropout rate was still declining, various cities developed at least fifty-five separate programs to deal with the problem. Hundreds of articles on it were published in professionals journals, the National Education Association established a special action project to deal with it, and the Commissioner of Education, the Secretary of Labor, and the President all made public statements on it.[35] Obviously, if one defines the "inadequate amount of schooling line" as that which places one-fifth of all boys and girls below it, then one-fifth of all boys and girls will always be receiving an inadequate amount of schooling.

Whatever our educational standards are today, Wayland writes, they will be higher tomorrow. He summarizes the received doctrine in these words:

> Start the child in school earlier; keep him in school more and more months of the year; retain all who start to school for twelve to fourteen years; expect him to learn more and more during this period, in wider and wider areas of human experience, under the guidance of a teacher, who has had more and more training, and who is assisted by more and more specialists, who provide an ever-expanding range of services, with access to more and more detailed personal records, based on more and more carefully validated tests.[36]

To a large extent, then, our urban problems are like the mechanical rabbit at the racetrack, which is set to keep just ahead of the dogs no matter how fast they may run. Our performance is better and better, but because we set our standards and expectations to keep ahead of performance, the problems are never any nearer to solution. Indeed, if standards and expectations rise *faster* than performance, the problems may get (relatively) worse as they get (absolutely) better.

Some may say that since almost everything about the city can stand improvement (to put it mildly), this mechanical rabbit effect is a good thing in that it spurs us on to make constant progress. No doubt this is true to some extent. On the other hand, there is danger that we may mistake failure to progress as fast as we would like for failure to progress at all and, in panic, rush into ill-considered measures that will only make matters worse. After all, an "urban crisis" that results largely from rising standards and expectations is not the sort of crisis that, unless something drastic is done, is bound to lead to disaster. To treat it as if it were might be a very serious mistake.

This danger is greatest in matters where our standards are unreasonably high. The effect of too-high standards cannot be to spur us on to reach the prescribed level of performance sooner than we otherwise would, when that level is impossible of attainment. At the same time, these standards may cause us to adopt measures that are wasteful and injurious and, in the long run, to conclude from the inevitable failure of these measures that there is something fundamentally wrong with our society.

To extent the range of present Department of Health, Education and Welfare services equitably—to all those similarly situated in need—would require an *additional* cost roughly equivalent to the *entire federal budget*, Elliot L. Richardson reported as he left the secretaryship of that department.[37] His point was that expectations, indeed claims authorized by Congress, far exceeded the capacity of the government to provide. "One can imagine," he said somberly, "a point of reckoning at which the magnitude of the ill-treated problems is fully perceived —along with a profound sense of failure. And one can only hope that the troubled reaction toward the institutions held accountable would be reasoned and responsible."

Notes

1. The 1970 Census defined as "urban" places, unincorporated as well as incorporated, with 2,500 inhabitants or more (excluding persons living in rural portions of extended cities) as well as other territory within Urbanized Areas. An "Urbanized Area" comprises at least one city of 50,000 inhabitants (the "central city") plus contiguous, closely settled areas ("urban fringe"). A "Standard Metropolitan Statistical Area (SMSA)" is a county or group of contiguous counties (except in New England) containing a city (or "twin" cities) of at least 50,000 population; contiguous counties are included in an SMSA if they are essentially metropolitan in character and are socially and economically integrated with the central city. That part of the United States lying outside of any SMSA is "nonmetropolitan." All of these definitions were somewhat different in 1960 and also in 1950.

  See Daniel J. Elazar, "Are We a Nation of Cities?," *The Public Interest*, 4 (Summer 1966), pp. 42-44.

2. Sloan R. Wayland, "Old Problems, New Faces, and New Standards," in A. Harry Passow, ed., *Education in Depressed Areas* (New York: Columbia University Teachers College, 1963), p. 66.

3. Irving Hoch, "Urban Scale and Environmental Quality," in *Population, Resources, and the Environment*, vol. III of task force reports of Commission on

Population Growth and the American Future, Ronald G. Ridker, ed. (Washington, D.C., Government Printing Office, 1972), p. 243. The figures are for 1966.

4. According to the U.S. Public Health Service, the most polluted air is nowhere near as dangerous as inhaled cigarette smoke. It is of interest also that the mortality rate from emphysema is higher in rural parts of New York than in metropolitan ones (*New York Times*, October 30, 1970) and that the state with the highest death rate from respiratory disease is Vermont (*New York Times*, December 20, 1972).

5. For data see U.S. Environmental Protection Agency, *Air Quality Data*, an annual, *Air Pollution Measurements of the National Air Sampling Network, 1957–1961*, and *The Fourth Annual Report of the Council on Environmental Quality*, U.S. Government Printing Office, September 1973, pp. 265–275.

6. This was the finding of a six-year study directed by Lawrence B. Cohen of the Department of Industrial Engineering of Columbia University and reported in the *New York Times*, December 16, 1965.

7. J. R. Meyer, J. F. Kain, and M. Wohl, *The Urban Transportation Problem* (Cambridge, Mass.: Harvard University Press, 1965), p.359.

8. John Kain, "How to Improve Urban Transportation at Practically No Cost," *Public Policy*, 20 (Summer 1972):352. Italics are in the original.

9. Arnold J. Meltsner titles his contribution to a collection of essays "Local Revenue: A Political Problem." He explains: "Officials are sometimes reluctant to raise taxes because they believe that taxes have reached a political limit. How do you know, Mr. Mayor, that the property tax has reached a political limit? Answer: I do not know; I just feel it. A political limit is a fuzzy constraint, perhaps fictitious, that local officials worry about, but have difficulty predicting. Even social scientists cannot tell when a political limit is about to be reached." In John P. Crecine, ed., *Financing the Metropolis*. Urban Affairs Annual Reviews, vol. 4 (Beverly Hills, Calif.: Sage Publications, 1970), p. 108.

In 1973 a survey of 30 cities with "serious financial problems" "failed to locate any cities in which conditions were such that timely action by local, or in a few cases, State officials could not avert or promptly relieve a financial emergency." Advisory Commission on Intergovernmental Relations, *City Financial Emergencies: The Intergovernmental Dimension*, (Washington, D.C., U.S. Government Printing Office, July 1973), p. 4.

10. Kenneth T. Jackson, "Metropolitan Government versus Suburban Autonomy," in Kenneth T. Jackson and Stanley K. Schultz, eds., *Cities in American History* (New York: Alfred A. Knopf, 1972), pp. 446 and 456.

11. *Final Report of the National Commission on the Causes and Prevention of Violence* (Washington, D.C.: U.S. Government Printing Office, 1969), footnote p. 29.

12. U.S. Bureau of the Census, *Census of Population: 1970, Employment Profiles of Selected Low-Income Areas*, Final Report PHC(3)-1, United States Summary—Urban Areas (January 1972). The low-income areas were defined by the Census Bureau in the middle 1960's for the use of OEO and Model Cities agencies. The following (equally weighted) criteria were used: family income below $3,000, children in broken homes, persons with low educational attainments, males in unskilled jobs, and substandard housing. Census tracts in the lowest quartile were defined as "low income." In 1970 the boundaries so established were

re-examined by the Census in consultation with local planning and other officials; in most instances areas were enlarged somewhat.

A Census report (distributed after the text of this book was in type) provides
data for the low-income areas of the 50 largest cities using figures from the
decennial census (a 15 percent sample) and defining a low-income area to consist
of all census tracts in which 20 percent or more of all persons were below the
poverty line in 1969. On this basis, there were 10,555,918 persons in the poverty
areas, 60 percent of whom were Negro. The median family income was $6,099; 27
percent of the families were below the poverty line and 22 percent had incomes
at least three times greater than the poverty standard. About one-third of the
families in the low-income areas paid rents of less than 20 percent of their
income; however, of the renters whose incomes were below the poverty line,
more than half paid more than half of their incomes in rent. Census tracts with a
poverty rate of 40 percent or more had 2,017,513 persons nearly three-fourths of
whom were Negro. U.S. Bureau of the Census, Census of Population: 1970 Subject Reports, Final Report PC(2)-9B, Low-Income Areas in Large Cities.

13. In *Dark Ghetto*, Kenneth B. Clark presents 1960 Census data showing that
eight cities—New York, Los Angeles, Baltimore, Washington, Cleveland, St.
Louis, New Orleans, and Chicago—contain a total of sixteen areas, all of at least
15,000 population and five of more than 100,000, that are exclusively (more than
94 percent) Negro (New York: Harper & Row, 1965), table, p. 25.

14. Commission on Population Growth and the American Future, *Population and
the American Future* (Washington, D.C.: U.S. Government Printing Office, 1972), p.
74.

15. Kenneth B. Clark, "The Wonder Is There Have Been So Few Riots," *New York
Times Magazine*, September 5, 1965, p. 10.

16. Alexis de Tocqueville, *Democracy in America*, trans. by Henry Reeve (New
York: Alred A. Knopf, 1945), I: 289-290.

17. George Grier, "Washington," *City Magazine* (February 1971), p. 47, quoted by
Bennett Harrison, *Education, Training and the Urban Ghetto* (Baltimore: The Johns
Hopkins University Press, 1972), p. 167.

18. Cf. Robert C. Weaver, "Class, Race and Urban Renewal," *Land Economics*, 36
(August 1960): 235-251. On urban renewal in general, see James Q. Wilson, ed.,
Urban Renewal: The Record and the Controversy (Cambridge, Mass.: M.I.T. Press,
1966).

19. Scott Greer, *Urban Renewal and American Cities* (Indianapolis: Bobbs-Merrill,
1965, p. 3.

As William G. Grigsby has pointed out, the "flight to the suburbs," which most
renewal projects in central cities have been intended to stop or reverse, may be a
good thing from the standpoint of the society as a whole even if undesirable from
that of the central city. "It is not understood that . . . exodus from the city has
produced a much higher standard of housing than could otherwise have been
attained, and that the market forces that produced this shift should, therefore, be
stimulated." *Housing Markets and Public Policy* (Philadelphia: University of Pennsylvania Press, 1963), p.333.

20. *The President's Fourth Annual Report on National Housing Goals*, 92d Congress,
2d Session, House Document No. 92-319, June 29, 1972. The report includes a
table (p. 48) showing the revenue cost for 1971 by gross income class.

This and another form of concealed subsidy (the noninclusion of imputed net rent in gross income reported for tax purposes) are discussed by Henry J. Aaron, *Shelter and Subsidies: Who Benefits from Federal Housing Policies?* (Washington, D.C.: The Brookings Institution, 1972), ch. 4.

21. Stanley S. Surrey, Professor of Law, Harvard University, in U.S. Congress, Senate, Subcommittee on Priorities and Economy in Government of the Joint Economic Committee, *Hearings, The Economics of Federal Subsidy Programs*, 92d Congress, 1st Session, January 13, 14, and 17, 1972, p. 45.

22. *The President's Fourth Annual Report*, p. 32. The report goes on the add: "While housing programs have contributed to these problems and in many cases intensified them, it is important to emphasize that they did not *cause* them. The causes stem from the complex interaction of population migration, comunity attitudes and prejudices, consumer preferences, local governmental fragmentation, and the impact of other federal programs such as urban renewal and the highway programs."

23. Richard Muth, "The Urban Economy and Public Problems," in John P. Crecine, ed., *Financing the Metropolis*, p. 454. See also Muth's book, *Cities and Housing, The Spatial Pattern of Urban Residential Land Use* (Chicago: University of Chicago Press, 1969). pp. 319–322.

24. Theodore W. Schultz, *Economic Crises in World Agriculture* (Ann Arbor: University of Michigan Press, 1965), p. 94.

25. Karl E. and Alma F. Taeuber, "The Negro as an Immigrant Group: Recent Trends in Racial and Ethnic Segregation in Chicago." *American Journal of Sociology*, 69 (January 1964): 382.

26. Executive Office of the President, Domestic Council, *Report on National Growth, 1972* (Washington, D.C.: U.S. Government Printing Office, 1972).

27. Irving Hoch, "Income and City Size," *Urban Studies*, 9 (1972): 320.

28. Peter A. Morrison, *The Impact and Significance of Rural-Urban Migration in the United States* (Santa Monica, Calif.: The Rand Corporation, 3P-4752, March 1972), p. 2.

29. Dick Netzer, *Economics and Urban Problems: Diagnosis and Prescriptions* (New York: Basic Books, 1970), p. 21.

30. Christopher Jencks et al., *Inequality, A Reassessment of the Effect of Family and Schooling in America* (New York: Basic Books, 1972), pp. 141–142.

31. Andrew M. Greeley and Paul B. Sheatsley, "Attitudes Toward Racial Integration," *Scientific American*, 225 (December 1971): 13 and 15.

Thomas F. Pettigrew has found that "white attitudes toward open housing have become increasingly more favorable over the past generation." See his paper on "Attitudes on Race and Housing: A Social-Psychological View," in Amos H. Hawley and Vincent P. Rock, eds., *Segregation in Residential Areas* (Washington, D.C.: National Academy of Sciences, 1973), pp. 21–84. See also Joel D. Aberbach and Jack L. Walker, *Race in the City* (Boston: Little, Brown and Company, 1973), which presents data on attitudes of blacks and whites in Detroit in surveys made in 1967 and 1971.

32. William Watts and Lloyd A. Free, eds., *State of the Nation* (New York: Universal Books, 1973), p. 80.

33. Irving Kristol, "The Lower Fifth," *The New Leader*, February 17, 1964, pp. 9–10.

34. Robert Blauner, "Whitewash Over Watts," *Trans-action 3 (March–April 1966):* 6.

35. Burton A. Weisbrod, "Preventing High-School Drop-outs," in Robert Dorfman, ed., *Measuring Benefits of Government Investments* (Washington, D.C.: The Brookings Institution, 1965), p. 118.

36. Wayland, "Old Problems," p. 67.

37. Elliot L. Richardson, *Responsibility and Responsiveness (II), A Report on the HEW Potential for the Seventies* (Washington, D.C.: U. S. Department of Health, Education, and Welfare, January 18, 1973).

Liberal

Richard Wade:
America's Cities are (Mostly) Better than Ever

More than a decade ago the phrase "urban crisis" crept into our public conversation. Since then it has become a cliché, connoting a wide range of persistent and dangerous problems confronting our cities. Moreover, the phrase, like "missile crisis" or "energy crisis," suggests both newness and immediate danger. The rioting, arson, and looting that erupted in the 1960's fortified this general impression. Presumably something unprecedented had happened. Urban life had become unmanageable; in the professional and popular view, cities were "ungovernable."

Something new, indeed, had happened. It was not that American cities had not known violence and race conflict before. They ran like thick red lines through the history of many cities. But the scale and ubiquity of the modern outbreaks had no earlier analogue. Large and small cities, both north and south, witnessed almost simultaneous explosions; the number of dead and injured and the amount of property damage easily exceeded those of anything previous. Few people predicted the rioting, hence most sought for an explanation in very recent developments—black migrations, the slow pace of desegregation, unemployment, broken families, and the Vietnam War.

Yet the fires of the 1960's were not the arson of a single decade or generation. Urban society had been accumulating combustibles for well over a century. The seventies have simply tamped down the flames while the ashes still smolder and, unless the historical sources of the present crisis are better understood and public policy changed, a recurrence, next time probably worse, is almost inevitable.

New York City's experience during the 1977 black-out to have served as the first alarm for the nation.

What baffled most commentators in the sixties was that the convulsions came at a time when urban experts confidently had asserted that the nation's cities were overcoming their afflictions. There had been, for example, a marked decline in the percentage of substandard housing; there were relatively fewer urban poor than ever before; hospital beds had caught up with need; federal programs were bringing health care to an unprecedented number of people; schools had reduced class size; new skylines attested to renewed downtown vitality; municipal government, though scarred by occasional scandals, was demonstrably more competent than it once had been.

To the historian the argument had a superficial validity. One only had to compare the city of 1970 with the city of 1900 to measure municipal progress. At the turn of the century every city had its concentrations of wretched neighborhoods where poor people huddled in run-down or jerry-built houses and in tenements lacking even toilets or running water. Primitive coal stoves provided the heat; kerosene lamps the light. Family cohesiveness, always fragile, often cracked under the weight of these oppressive circumstances. Nor were these conditions exceptional. Jacob Riis's *How the Other Half Lives* described the festering slums on New York's Lower East Side in 1890; but as the title suggests, he was also discussing the predicament of over 50 per cent of the city's population. Indeed, a congressional inquiry into urban housing at about the same time demonstrated that every metropolis matched New York's dilapidated, unsanitary, and dangerous dwellings.

Nor was there much in the neighborhood to compensate for the miseries of home life. The droppings of thousands of horses made even crossing the street hazardous. Garbage clogged thoroughfares; sanitation carts picked their way through congested avenues and alleys once a week at best. Cheap shops and uninspected markets lined the sidewalks. No traffic regulations prevented horse-drawn trucks and carts, electric trolleys, and private hacks from creating a continual cacophony, day and night. And dense smoke from coal-burning factories and office buildings rolled darkly through downtown. Worse still, crime and violence were constant companions of slum dwellers.

Three institutions attenuated the misery of the slum—the church, the school, and the saloon. And they were attractive precisely because they provided what the tenement and neighborhood lacked. The church was clean and uncongested; its friendly priest, minister, or rabbi cared about the parishioners and their families. Even the most primitive schools took the children out of the tenement and into rooms that were at least heated in the winter. The saloon was bright and congenial, and the husband could meet with friends and neighbors away from the oppressive crowding of the apartment. Yet these oases could not conceal— indeed they only magnified—the grinding deprivation of the lives of these people. Later commentators would invest the "good old neighborhood" with charm, conviviality, and livability; but to most of its residents, life was a losing struggle against filth, noise, and disorder.

The whole family was drawn into the contest. Jobs for anyone were scarce and irregular. Good, steady work that permitted the father to feed, clothe, and shelter his family on his own was very rare. The wife and children usually had to enter the already overcrowded job market. Mothers and daughters sewed, packaged nuts, made artificial flowers. Young boys sold newspapers, picked coal, collected rags, ran errands. Frequent depressions did away with even these menial tasks.

Schooling was brief. Children dropped out, not at fourteen or fifteen, but at eight or nine. Even so, education was often inadequate: classrooms were crowded, teachers poorly trained and politically selected. No audiovisual aids or paraprofessional help assisted the beleaguered instructor; the truant officer became a familiar figure in the neighborhood. Reformers sought vainly to get class sizes down to fifty and replace patronage appointments with professionals.

Conditions in the area were tolerable only because those who lived there considered them temporary. Residential turnover was high; one of every five families had a different address each year. Most, of course, moved only a short distance and often because they could not pay the rent. But a significant number found housing in more pleasant communities away from the old slum. Scholars later argued over the percentage who "made it" out; yet every resident knew someone who did; a relative, perhaps, or someone on the block or in the parish. But the possibility of escape was as much a part of the experience as confinement.

The change over the subsequent three-quarters of a century was dramatic. In 1902 Robert Hunter estimated that over half the urban population lived beneath the poverty line. By 1970 that figure had fallen to less than 20 per cent, even though the definition of poverty had been raised substantially. Density in the inner city dropped drastically; Jacob Riis found over 300,000 people per square mile living in New York's tenth ward; today, any concentration over 75,000 a square mile is considered intolerable. Public policy and private develpment removed the most visible downtown slums, though cancerous nodes remained behind. Public housing, with all its problems, replaced the most depressed and dilapidated areas. New building in the outer city and suburbs provided modern accommodations for an exploding urban population. In the sixties, experts argued over whether "substandard" housing composed 15 or 18 per cent of the total stock; judged by the same standards seventy years earlier, it would have composed more than half.

Even the crime rate was probably higher in 1900, though there is no way to prove it. Police organization was primitive, and systematic reporting of crime was still decades away. Politicians hired and fired the force; collusion between criminals and police was common. Constant gang warfare jeopardized the peace of nearly every downtown area. Political reformers always promised the "restoration of law and order."

Municipal governments were to weak to control matters. State governments granted cities only modest powers, and then only grudgingly. Corruption riddled most city halls and municipalities. Political bosses and special interests united to plunder the public till. Lincoln Steffens made a national reputation with the book entitled *The Shame of the Cities*, which chronicled the boodle, bribery, and chicanery that he contended characterized nearly every American city. Good government forces occasionally broke the unseemly ring, but usually not for long.

In short, the present city, for all its problems, is cleaner, less crowded, safer, and more livable than its turn-of-the-century counterpart. Its people are more prosperous, better educated, and healthier than they were seventy years ago.

The slow but steady improvement in municipal affairs was the result of both particular historical conditions of the twentieth century and the efforts of many generations of urban dwellers. American cities enjoyed continued growth and expansion for most of the period. They were also the vital centers of a surging national economy. As the country became increasingly urban, the best talent and greatest wealth gravitated to the metropolis, where a huge pool of skilled and unskilled labor could be easily tapped. This combination made it possible for the United States to become the most powerful industrial nation in the world.

Technological changes, themselves largely products of the urban explosion, permitted new advances in municipal management. Subways, elevateds, and automobiles facilitated the movement of people throughout the expanding metropolis, retiring horses to the country. Modern medicine increased the effectiveness of public health measures. Electricity and central heating improved the comfort of new housing, and the long-term mortgage made home ownership easier to manage. Movies, radio, and television democratized entertainment, if they did not always elevate it. New laws forced more children into schools and kept them there longer.

Though progress was often sporadic, city government widened its competence and improved its performance. Tensions between reformers and urban machines resulted in permanent gains, for after each revolt was beaten back, some improvements were always retained. Civil service slowly produced a bureacracy that, for all its clumsiness, was distinctly superior to the earlier rampant patronage system. Zoning put a measure of predictability, if not control, into land use. And nearly everywhere the quality of urban leadership was noticeably better than before. A few old-time bosses persisted, but they were viewed as quaint anachronisms rather than as the logical expressions of city politics.

This considerable achievement rested on two historical conditions: the general prosperity of the period and the ample municipal limits which permitted expanding economic activity to take place within a single political jurisidiction. Except for the Great Depression and occasional sharp dips in the business index, American cities generally witnessed sustained growth. Even wartime did not interrupt the expansion; indeed, immense military spending acted as a swift stimulus to urban economies. Municipal progress cost money—a lot of it—and American cities generally had it to spend. And when they did not, they borrowed, confident that the future would be even more prosperous.

This was, moreover, the age of the self-sufficient city. Municipal boundaries were wide and continually enlarging. In 1876 St. Louis reached out into neighboring farm land and incorporated all the area now within its city limits. In one swift move in 1889 Chicago added over 125 square miles to its territory. And in 1898 New York absorbed the four surrounding counties—including Brooklyn, the nation's fourth largest city—making it the world's Empire City.

In 1900 municipal boundaries were generous, almost always including unsettled and undeveloped land. As populations grew, there were always fresh areas to build up. This meant that all the wealth, all the commerce, all the industry, and all the talent lay within the city. When serious problems arose, all the resources of the metropolis could be brought to bear to solve them. More prosperous than either the state or federal governments, the cities needed no outside help; indeed they met any interference with the demand for home rule.

For as long as these historical conditions prevailed, American cities could make incremental progress in attacking even the most vexing problems. But after the Second World War, two divisive elements entered the metropolis, destroying its economic and governmental unity and profoundly altering its social structure. The first division was between suburb and city; the second between black and white. Actually, these fissures always had been present, but not on the same scale or with the same intensity, and certainly not with the same significance.

Suburbanization is almost as old as urbanization. American cities always have grown from the inside out; as population increased, it spilled outside municipal limits. Initially these suburbs were not the exclusive resort of the wealthy; many poor lived there to avoid city taxes and regulations. But railroad development in the mid-nineteenth century produced modern commuting suburbs: Chicago had fifty-two of them by 1874. Though suburbs grew rapidly, their numbers were always relatively small and their locations governed by rail lines. By the 1920's the automobile spawned a second generation of suburbs, filling the areas between the older ones and setting off an unprecedented building boom beyond the municipal limits.

The crash of 1929 put an end to suburban expansion for fifteen years. During the Depression, people could not afford new housing, and when war came, the military consumed all available construction material. But the pent-up demand broke loose with the coming of peace. By 1970 the census reported that more people in the metropolitan regions lived outside the municipal boundaries than within. All cities, even smaller ones, were surrounded by numerous small jurisdictions, self-governing, self-taxing—and growing.

The historical remedy to this problem—annexation of surrounding areas—was no longer available. In most states the process required a majority of the voters in both the cities and the suburbs to support consolidation and after 1920 the outlying areas were increasingly against incorporation. The cities, now with fixed boundaries, gradually lost population, while the suburbs experienced steady growth.

Moreover, this demographic change profoundly altered the social structure of the metropolis. The middle class rapidly evacuated the old city in favor of the suburbs. In turn, they were replaced by migrants from the South and from Latin America. The newcomers were mostly poor and racially distinct. With little education or skills, they were tax consumers rather than tax producers. They needed help on a large scale. Most of all they needed jobs. But industry and commerce had followed the outward movement of people. At just the time municipal government faced additional responsibilities, it saw its revenue base shrinking. Inevitably, various groups fell to quarreling over these limited resources, producing new tensions and anxieties.

The rioting of the 1960's revealed another fissure in the metropolis—the division between black and white. Some blacks always had lived in cities, even under slavery. But the "peculiar institution" had confined most to the Southern countryside. After the Civil War, former slaves without land or urban skills drifted into Southern cities, where they quickly composed a large portion of the population. The urban South accomodated the newcomers within an elaborate system of segregation. The separation of the races was accomplished both by custom and, after 1896, under Jim Crow statutes.

The massive Northern migration of rural Southern blacks in this century, however, slowly altered the racial composition of nearly every city across the country. Municipal governments adopted no new policies to deal with the influx. Indeed, they assumed that the same process that had incorporated millions of immigrants into the metropolitan mainstream would also be available to blacks. That is, the newcomers initially would congregate at the heart of town, increase their numbers, get an economic foothold, and then gradually disperse into more pleasant residential neighborhoods away from the congested center. This process, though often cruel and painful, had served the immigrants, the city, and the country well.

But the blacks' experience was fundamentally different. They did, indeed, gather at the center, and there they found what immigrants always had found: wretched housing, overcrowded neighborhoods, high unemployment, indadequate schools, littered streets, garbage-strewn alleys, rampant crime, and endemic disorder. However, the new ghetto, unlike the old, did not loosen and disperse. Rather it simply spread block by block, oozing out over adjacent communities. White residents retreated while blacks moved into new areas beyond downtown. Later a generation would grow up that knew only the ghetto and its debilitating life.

The immigrant ghetto had been tolerable because it was thought to be temporary, a rough staging ground for upward and outward mobility. Blacks increasingly perceived the ghetto to be their permanent home. And each federal census fortified this apprehension as the index of racial segregation moved steadily upward. There was, of course, some modest leakage here and there, but the barriers to escape remained formidable.

This confinement had two consequences that were different from those of the old ghetto. The first was the alienation of its black middle class. They, after all, had done what they were supposed to do: stayed in school, kept out of serious trouble, got higher education, and made good money. But they were still denied, by the color of their skin alone, that most important symbol of success in America —the right to live in a neighborhood of their own choosing with schools appropriate to their ambitions for their children.

The size of this black middle class is large; indeed, no other group has had a success story quite equal to it. In 1950 the federal census listed about 10 per cent of American blacks as "middle class"; by 1960 that figure had climed to nearly 18 per cent; by 1970 it had jumped above one-third. To be sure, it often required two breadwinners in the family to achieve this status; that, plus ambition and hard work. For these people, continued *de facto* residential segregation was especially cruel. Even in fashionable black neighborhoods, hope turned into resentful bitterness.

For the less successful, the situation was much worse. The black ghetto contained the city's worst housing, schools, and community institutions. It generated few jobs and experienced soaring unemployment. Crime rates were high, gang warfare common, and vice rampant. All this contributed to the breakdown of family life and the encouragement of dependency. Newcomers always had found it difficult to adjust to the ghetto; race compounded the problem. In the sixties, daily frustrations spilled over into violence. The young struck out against the symbols of their oppression that were closest at hand, reducing large ghetto areas to ashes.

Race, then, greatly widened the already yawning gap between city and suburb. Every important issue that arose within the metropolis reflected this division. School busing became the symbolic question: without residential segregation, no busing would be necessary. "Affirmative action" became a euphemism for introducing minorities into employment areas previously monopolized by whites. The collapse of mass transit left blacks riding in the front of the bus but with diminishing numbers of white companions. While crime rates rose in the suburbs, popular stereotypes still associated violence with inner-city minorities. In short, uniting the metropolis would have been difficult enough; the addition of race introduced an enormously complicated factor.

In the seventies the inner cities quieted down. But the new tranquillity came from black resignation rather than from a larger measure of justice. The unemployment figures contained the warning: 10 per cent in older cities; 20 per cent in the ghettos; 40 per cent among minority youth. In addition, middle-class blacks ran into all kinds of obstacles when trying to escape to the suburbs. The courts were ambivalent about legal restrictions, especially zoning, which had the effect of exclusion. And social pressures in the suburbs were often not very subtle. As a result, the ghetto still festered; indeed, its boundaries expanded each week.

Yet certain factors hold out some hope for the future. For example, suburbs are finding that they are no more self-sufficient than the cities. The same forces that led to urban decay earlier are now spreading into the surrounding communities. This is particularly true of those suburbs adjacent to the city limits. Indeed, the phrase "inner suburbs" surely will join "inner city" as shorthand for the long list of urban ills in the eighties. And for much the same reasons. They are the oldest part of suburban America. In order to keep taxes down, they allowed most of their land to be developed. Now there is no room for expansion. The new suburbanites go farther out; new industrial and commercial installations also bypass the closer-in suburbs. Large numbers of older residents, their children now gone, head for retirement areas or back to the city. Newer shopping centers in outlying suburbs skim off dollars from local merchants. Worse still, crime rates grow faster in these communities than in any other part of the metropolis.

In addition, suburban government is the weakest link in our governmental system. Until recently, residential participation in local affairs was low; most communities hired professional managers to make budgets and administer day-to-day affairs. Voting was light for local offices, and though suburbanites vote heavily Republican in national elections, suburban politics remain consciously nonpartisan. Hence, when the crisis moved in, most suburbs lacked the tradition or tools to grapple with it. By the 1970's new suburban newspapers began to reveal the often scandalous relations between some developers and many town halls. Voters increasingly turned down bond issues, even for schools. The inner suburbs' one trump card is that they still control the suburban lobby in most states. They played that card to get some relief for all local governments, hence they became the major beneficiaries. Yet neither this nor federal revenue-sharing programs could do more than postpone the inevitable fiscal impasse. When New York City slid toward bankruptcy, Yonkers, located in one of the nation's richest suburban counties, was placed in receivership.

The extension of city problems into the suburbs poked large holes in the crabgrass curtain that previously had separated the two parts of the metropolis. Now their common predicament created the possibility of a new cooperation to replace the hostility that historically had divided city and suburb. The inner suburbs were reluctant to recognize their own decline, but by the seventies they recognized that they had to trade part of their independence for outside help.

For the first time, a substantial suburban population has a stake in a united metropolis. The inner ring is no longer self-sufficient. It relies increasingly on state and federal aid rather than on its indigenous tax base. Hence, its most serious problems cannot be solved without cooperation with the city as well as with neighboring suburbs. In the 1950's the movement for metropolitan government was essentially a big-city strategy; now that concept has natural allies. To be sure, the notion of a single governmental jurisdiction is politically impossible except in a few places.

A consolidation of effort by function, however, is already imperative. In housing, education, transportation, water, pollution, and police, control depends on devising programs that employ a concentrated, cooperative regional approach. Even this requires a change in state and federal policies, which presently funnel funds into old governmental units rather than into intergovernmental ones. But the crisis of the inner suburbs has produced the necessary condition for a fundamental shift in public policy based on metropolitan realities rather than on anachronistic political jurisdictions.

New demographic changes also brought some easing of racial tensions. The massive movement of blacks from the South to Northern cities virtually has stopped; indeed, some experts detect a slight reverse of the flow. The breaking of segregation and the availability of jobs in Southern cities made them at least as attractive as Northern ones. Moreover, urban black birth rates dropped rapidly. This reduced ghetto tensions somewhat but not ghetto conditions. In addition, the election of black mayors in many parts of the country lessened the feeling of isolation and powerlessness of urban blacks. The relative quiet of ghetto in the seventies was somewhat deceptive but did provide some breathing space for the nation if the nation had the ingenuity and will to seize it.

But time is running out and we have not used it wisely to heal racial divisions or reduce urban-suburban tensions. Federal policy has neglected cities in favor of surrounding communities. Revenue-sharing formulas were based largely on population rather than on need; government installations usually were placed in outlying areas; special programs for the inner cities were either reduced or dismantled. Worse still, urban economies, historically the nation's most resilient, recovered more slowly from recurring recessions than the suburbs with their newer facilities. And the outward flow of jobs and middle-class city dwellers continued unabated. The problem is more severe in the older areas of the Northeast and Midwest. Yet the "Sunbelt" cities show the same symptoms. The acids of urban decay do not recognize the Mason-Dixon line.

The persistence of the urban crisis has led many Americans to look elsewhere for solutions. But a look outward indicates that what some thought was a peculiarly American question is, in fact, an international urban crisis. Rome's fiscal management makes New York's look frugal; the inadequacy of London's inner-city schools is more than a match for their American counterparts; Frankfurt's pollution experts travel to Pittsburgh for advice; few American housing commissioners would trade jobs with their opposite numbers in Sydney. Russian urban experts see their limited growth policies overwhelmed by illegal migration; the smog in Sarajevo would frighten even an Angelino; Rumania's ambitious satellite city plan has not inhibited the growth of Bucharest or produced any "new towns"; more than three decades after World War II, no major city in Eastern Europe has dented its housing shortage.

The record of foreign cities on race is no more instructive. British urban centers are producing their own "New Commonwealth" ghettos; not a single black sits in Parliament. Amsterdam cannot handle its old colonists of different color. Paris and Marseilles have been unable to assimilate their French Algerians. Moscow couldn't manage even a small number of African students; in Bucharest, urban renewal is gypsy removal. In Sydney and Auckland, the aborigines, though small in number, face the usual range of discrimination. Indeed, the immigration policies of Canada and Australia are designed to avoid the issue.

The fact is that no society has learned to manage a large metropolis, nor has any society succeeded in solving the question of race. If these problems are to be solved, it will be done here in the United States. Perhaps that is the way it should be. Our national history has been almost conterminous with the rise of the modern city; racial diversity always has been a part of the American experience. We have managed in the past to take millions of people with different backgrounds, languages, and religions and incorporate them into the metropolitan mainstream.

In facing the present urban crisis, we only need draw upon our best traditions. But if we do not begin to unite the metropolis and to disperse the ghetto in the next few years, the eighties will be a decade of renewed tension and turmoil and will bear out Wendell Phillip's grim prophecy of a hundred years ago: "The time will come when our cities will strain our institutions as slavery never did."

Socialist

Henry Etzkowitz and Roger Mack:
Corporations and the City: Oligopolies and Urbanization

The marxist contribution to the analyses of urban dynamics must begin to focus on the components of the capital sector as they affect the uneven development of urban regions. The effect of oligopolistic concentrations of capital is to subject cities to specific changes in housing, employment and transportation. In this paper we attempt to clarify some of the ways in which public policies—the state —facilitate corporate decentralization. Suburbanization cannot, then, be optimally explained as a flight to the closeness of community life, but must be explained in terms of corporate and state practices. Traditional questions raised by liberal theorists using a perspective focused on where things are located is not enough.

A fundamental issue confronting urban researchers and theorists, regardless of their perspective, is that of considering the city as an independent unit of analysis or that of considering the city as subsumed in theoretical perspectives other than "urban." There is serious debate as to whether or not urban has

Reprinted with permission from *Comparative Urban Research*, VI (2-3), 1978, pp. 46-53.

concrete meaning outside its census definition of a politically bounded unit of 2500 persons or more. Nevertheless, when most theorists and policy makers attempt to deal with the urban in general conceptual terms, they most often identify, either quantitatively or qualitatively, very specific areas and issues.

The new Althusserian urbanists—Castells, Lojkine, Lamarche, etc.—view the city as a mechanism to speed up the circulation of capital. They reason that the material basis of society consists primarily of industrial output in the advanced capitalist societies, and all other institutions contribute, more or less, to the accumulation of capital. Cities, seen as the concentration of people and the means of production in a tight spatial configuration, thereby contribute to this accumulation.

Castells, Lojkine, and others view the transportation, housing, and other city institutions as organized for the benefit of the capitalist class. Such institutions enable capitalists to concentrate workers near factories and enable people and goods to move swiftly from one enterprise to another. This view of the basic institutions of the city corresponds very closely to traditional urban analysis which also views the city in the same basic economic terms of infrastructure. Thus the city, in both frameworks, represents the spatial organization of the means of production of industrial society. The typical approach to studying this phenomenon has been economic base analysis, which focused upon those activities which provided the basic employment and income on which the rest of an area depended.

Traditional Views of the City

The city was depicted as the concentration of jobs, people, and retail shopping; the defining attributes of urban for an entire body of urban studies became population, density, and non-agricultural employment. The city government served to facilitate the coming together of employers and employees within the business structure in order to create the goods and services necessary for the generation of profits and wages. Urban government, through fiscal policy of taxation and spending, was to provide the infrastructural base of municipal services of streets, water, security, sewage, and often transportation and communication. These were the services that coordinated and controlled its bounded area in such ways as to allow the efficient operation of business activity. Cities were administered publicly, but for the benefit of private business activities taking place within their boundaries.

In our view of the city, capitalist institutions are also primary. We identify them as consisting of the large corporations in major industries organized as oligopolies. Rather than simply viewing the corporations in *toto* as capital, we view the effect of this type of economic organization on the rest of society. For it is the social relationships of corporations' interactions through which impacts are made, directly or indirectly, on the operation, functions, and fiscal viability of cities. The institution by oligopolies of basing point systems in which common prices are set for manufactured goods regardless of the point of origin is one example of the removal by corporations of the locational advantage that one city may have over another. The setting of prices by mutual agreement has this same effect. It is our thesis that by reducing the level of generalization from "capital," to capital as organized into oligopolies of large producers we can specifically understand how particular transportation, housing, and employment changes take place.

Corporations control the conditions within which municipal governments function through their influence on state governments, which have formal powers of control over municipalities. Increasingly, this control is expressed through quasi-public bodies dominated by corporate personnel, such as the Emergency Financial Control Board in New York City. Corporate influence on municipalities is also exercised indirectly through corporate control of state and federal regulatory agencies. On the national level the real estate industry dominates the advisory boards of the urban development agency and sets basic national policy in this area. The Snell Report to the U.S. Senate documents how General Motors and the other major automobile companies have set highway and mass transportation policy for the past several decades. In a narrow sense, this report sees GM as using agencies of government to gain and maintain control over its area of business—tranportation. From our perspective, we can see how through this control over transportation policy GM and other corporations are actually exerting control over urban development as well.

The city is a social form subsidiary to the corporate system. To the extent that it increases the circulation of capital, the urban institutional mechanism makes more capital available for the productive process. The coordination and control of resources, populations, and production facilities for business profit is, and has been, the major function of cities in America. All other functions performed in cities, and by city administrators, whether cultural, residential, governmental, or social, are secondary to its profit-enabling function. Cities were and are created and administered to coordinate, control, and provide those functions traditionally beyond the political and economic ability of individual business operations: the building and maintenance of streets, water systems, sewage, and garbage disposal systems, as well as the regulating of building and transport. Business decision makers united their influence and resources to bring together those activities needed in the allocation, production, and distribution of goods and services for the generation of profit.

Legally, an American municipality is little more than a geographically bounded tax unit established to provide services and pay for them primarily with locally collected tax revenues. The city as such is fixed in space geographically and politically, whereas employers and employees move easily across, within, and outside the boundaries of the city, taking their spending, taxes, production, and public service desires and needs with them.

While the vast majority of Americans reside in metropolitan areas, these areas, officially designated Standard Metropolitan Statistical Areas (SMSAs), are often composed of hundreds and sometimes thousands of individual (geographically based) government units, both municipalities and special service districts. Less than half of the governmentally bounded units contain as many as a thousand people. (Although more than 270 SMSAs existed in 1976, 95% of the U.S. population was within commuting distance of a metropolitan central city.) Each of these government units acts independently in both administration and service provision. Local power is ineffective and sporadic, and policy making mechanisms at the local level are weak. Functional fragmentation, even in land use policy, obscures and even usurps local government authority.

Freedom of locational choice is, in fact, freedom of employer choice and sometimes employee choices for those with economic and social mobility. Locational choice for municipalites is non-existent; they are bounded and fixed except for occasional and still rare annexations. Any locality can be conceived of as the areal expression of the interests of some land-based elite. The decisions most affecting land areas are made by corporate decision makers, a non-land-based elite.

Once a decision has been made to locate a corporate facility within an area, the corporation has a substantive stake in local policy as it affects tax structure, service levels, and regulatory action—often those very policies which brought about the original decision to locate. The corporations are organized and active in local, regional, state, and national politics to promote policies which will establish preconditions for their own growth.

The increasing dispersion of population and institutions throughout our metropolitan areas in the fifties and sixties was made possible largely by technological change and government policy. The highway and automobile, together with government housing and town policies, not only freed people to live outside the central city, but also freed factories, offices and retail stores to locate in the suburbs. While these developments made *possible* the increased outward movement of people and institutions from the central cities, they do not explain *why* people moved.

For the firm, as for the individual, the question remains: what were they trying to attain by relocation? The search for the personal ties and the security of close-knit relationships in a small communtiy has been offered as an explanation for the movement of families to suburbs. The movement to the suburbs of retail establishments is most often explained as their following the consumer to reestablish or tap the new market location. Another explantion for the suburban flight of both people and businesses is that this exodus is an escape from the high social costs of the central city: from crime, minorities, poverty, dirt, noise, and crowding.

If a city is viewed as a concentration point of relatively large numbers of people, then a city becomes its population. From the population prospective, a city moves, feeds, employs, informs, entertains, protects and houses its people. The city is also an employment center, a residential area, and the location of information gathering and disperson. The operations of a city feed, clothe, protect, inform, bathe, entertain, and house its people whether they be long time residents, daily visitors, or those just passing through.

Using a municipal framework, urban studies has typically focused on the location, structure, institutions, and social issues of politically bounded populations. This framework assumes that the political boundaries of a municipality and the activities that occur within it constitute the basic unit of analysis for understanding urban phenomena. Using this municipal framework, the Chicago School's classic monographs attempted to locate natural areas within the metropolitan complex. For instance, Ernest Burgess and his students defined 75 subareas of the city of Chicago as having a distinct identity and proceeded to compare them in terms of rates of mental illness, incidence of juvenile delinquency, and other criteria of "social disorganization" (Burgess 1930). More recently, Gans (1962), Suttles (1968), Berger (1971), and others have studied ethnic enclaves and suburbs to show the relationship between social and physical structures. The works of Dahl (1961) and Hunter (1953) on New Haven and Atlanta examine the political decision making institutions in these cities. Urban theorists such as Hawley (1971), Banfield (1970), and Berry (1973) present general urban perspectives, using population, employment, and residential data within a municipal framework.

From a municipal perspective, the central concern has been, "Where things are!" Urban studies has rarely gone beyond the original question of the location of people and institutions. The assumptions of this perspective are that a municipal area somehow controls decisions made within its own boundaries through its governmental system. A city is seen as a geographical area governed by a political mechanism which controls and coordinates activities within its boundaries. Decisions on land use and fiscal policies are viewed as the primary functions cities perform. Zoning policy enacted by the political structure of a municipal area determines the location of housing, industry, recreation, and commercial activities. Taxation and governmental expenditures determine the level as well as type of municipal infrastructure provided. The locations as well as existence of streets, schools, water systems, parks, libraries, and hospitals are decided within the municipal government's domain. This traditional perspective of urban studies is concerned with the municipal functions of land use planning and fiscal policy and how they affect and determine the social, economic, and physical structure of cities.

The Changing Need for Cities

Knowing where population, employment, or municipal institutions are located does not by itself explain the nature of urban phenomena. The municipal framework's concern with the bounded city unit fails to clearly identify the forces that create the very issues that the political city deals with. While the municipal framework does identify issues which are political responsibilities of each municipality, it does not provide us with an understanding of the very nature of the contemporary urban crisis.

Furthermore, this view of the city has clear conservative implications. For in a time of declining municipal resources, the city viewed in isolation will be seen as an institution inevitably subject to current trends and with few, if any, alternatives possible.

When the city is viewed this way, it is often assumed that various aspects (employment, housing, welfare, crime, etc.) can be dealt with as relatively separate issues. Even when it is acknowledged that one factor may impinge on another, the underlying assumption is that each may be conceptualized separately and dealt with individually with its own legislative policy and administrative structure. This constitutes the "liberal" view of the city. It is the underlying perspective from which reform legislators and bureaucrats (on whatever level of government) concerned with urban problems attend to their business. If law enforcement is a problem for local governments, then LEAA federal grants can provide hardware and software to help them cope with crime. Housing, employment, welfare, and other issues similarly defined as urban problems are each provided with legislation and a bureaucratic structure to solve them or at least to keep them under control.

Most urban scholars operate from a liberal perspective. They take separate topics as their area of expertise and focus their analyses and policy recommendations on particular issues. However, some urbanists view the city from a socialist perspective. Concepts such as use value and exchange value are employed to analyze the city in a work such as Harvey's Social Justice and the City (1973). However, the level of analysis tends to abstraction as "the city," "urbanization," and "created space" are the constructs to which Marxian theory is applied. Still, a broad overview is achieved of the relation of the city to the mode of production, as well as to other aspects of society.

Consider, for example, the effect on cities of an increasing amount of business activity being conducted within the structure of large administrative organizations rather than within and between small organizations. When industry is organized as a multitude of small producers, middlemen, suppliers, and jobbers are required to coordinate production and distribution. The garment industry located on the lower west side of Manhattan in New York City is an example of the operation of industry as a collectivity of small producers. Individual firms perform different parts of the process of making a whole garment. One business may sell cloth, another design patterns, yet another produce linings, another assemble the parts of a garment, and still another distribute the final product to wholesale and retail outlets. The location of hundreds of these small companies in a compact neighborhood makes possible easy negotiation between firms. The streets, restaurants and meeting places provide the linkages among the members of the garment industry. The city provides this industry a physical location in which the proximity of small producers to each other allows a diversity of firms to exist. And the municipal framework, while remaining largely under business control, can use public as well as private funds to provide for the infrastructural needs of workers, e.g., residences, transportation, consumption, security and entertainment. Moreover, the responsibility for the building and maintenance of streets, water works, security forces, and public transit can be shifted from business to the public sector.

By contrast, when a single firm engages in all aspects of the productive process to manufacture a final product, a city location is no longer required. Meeting places for different producers and other mediating functions that the city provided are unnecessary. These linkages between the different parts of the productive processes now take place in staff meetings in which the members of a single organization coordinate the different aspects of production. Employees of a single concern replace individual entrepreneurs. General Motors, Exxon, and United States Steel are examples of corporations that have internal coordinating mechanisms to organize production from collection of raw materials to distribution of the final product. Representatives of a few major companies meeting together in a resort or airport hotel room can replace the marketplace as a mechanism to set the price of a product.

As a result, many decision-making functions have been relocated from the central city to the suburban fringe. Many corporate decision makers no longer need to consider the infrastructure of central cities as an important factor. In fact, it is often felt that the social and economic costs of central city locations, in terms of employee attraction, transportation facilities, and security considerations, often outweigh the proclaimed benefits. (Thus changes in technology and business production functions over the past decade and the massive changes in the locations of business operations out of the central city have increased the movement of residents to the metropolitan fringe.)

The displacement of the importance of cities by corporations is, in large measure based on the existence of oligopoly—the control of an industry by a small number of corporations. By acting together, formally or informally (overtly or covertly), these corporations determine the price, profits, and costs of an industry. Additional profits (gained through control of an industry) give these corporations increased ability to act as independent entities. They may use their oligopolistic profits to fund new divisions to produce parts for their products, and so reduce dependence on subcontractors. Additionally, these corporations may achieve horizontal integration by creating divisions to provide legal and public relations services for the corporation rather than purchasing these services from outside firms. The integration process, when it is sufficiently developed, allows these corporations to choose to operate without the infrastructure of the city. And to the extent that the dense infrastructure of the city—which encourages and makes possible the creation of new enterprises—is dismantled, it will become more difficlt for new enterprises to be created.

As corporations replace central cities as the dominant mode of social and economic organization in American society, the freedom that the interstices of the central city provides is lost—not only for small business but for people. The movement of corporate offices out of established central cities to suburban areas serves to isolate employees from contacts with members of other organizations. Removed physically from alternatives of shopping or even eating somewhere else, the suburban corporate office campus becomes an eight-hour day, five-days-a-week total institution for its inhabitants. There exist few, if any, unintended or unplanned distractions from the corporate organization. Isolation gives corporate executives another lever of control over employees.

The Future of the City

The corporate decision to locate within any given area is clearly a decision to change the form of land use in the area by its presence. It is also a decision that can change the service and political relationships of the area by its demands: directly for municipal services and indirectly for operational requirements.

The conduct of urban studies must be revised because power relations in which urban decisions are made have shifted from the local and even metropolitan to the national and international levels. Decisions made by national and international corporations based on their needs and profit calculations shape metropolitan areas to a greater degree than these economic organizations are shaped by the metropolitan areas. A multi-national corporation may close an American plant and reopen it in a Third World country where labor costs are lower. This decision may have great effects on employment in a city, but there is often little a city can do to restrain or influence the departing company. A national corporation may move from a high labor cost area such as New York City to a labor cost area such as Dallas to maximize profits. Profitability is enhanced by playing one area off against the other. If the situation changes and the new area becomes more expensive, a new move may be planned.

The impact of nominally private decisions made by corporations has yet to be taken fully into account in constructing a theory of the city. We argue that the development of the modern corporation from the late nineteenth to the present is transforming the American city so that its major function is shifting from a coordinating center for the conduct of economic activity into a peripheral reservation for the containment of surplus populations. The planned operation of oligopoly within industries and negotiations between corporations from different industries increasingly supersede the market structure of the city as the locus of economic activity. An urban area is far more than just a politically bounded unit, a population grouping, or a spatial configuration of buildings and streets. To understand the nature of urban phenomena, it is important to realize how urban areas work, what the parts are, and who controls them.

Political leaders often suggest that they can persuade corporations to remain in an area that they have decided to leave. For example, in the course of the 1976 presidential campaign, Jimmy Carter promised that if he was elected President he would encourage corporations to keep their facilities in New York City. He further said that he would attempt to provide incentives to the corporations to stay in the central city. But moral suasion and even financial incentives are inadequate means to reverse or even significantly impede the trend of major corporations leaving the central city: if the structure of the modern integrated corporation no longer requires central cities as arenas in which to conduct its activities, then relocation outside of the boundaries of the central city will eventually occur in accordance with the preferences of corporate decision-makers.

If corporate planners are leaving the city for reasons other than fear of high central city taxes, then lowering taxes will not hold them. If, for reasons justified or not, corporate planners demand horizontal space, convenient parking, and easy access to residences, then the vertical buildings of central cities, the crowded and costly parking and congested access routes of many central cities, will repel them. If the relocation decisions are based on expansion needs, convenience desires, and lifestyle wants, then the central city has little chance of holding its industrial basis.

The direction and control of the economy, shifts in population, and the development and use of technology fundamentally shape urban areas. Decisions about these matters are made by the men who run major American corporations. These corporate decision-makers can move existing operations as well as establish new plants and offices. The task of urbanists is to analyze corporate location decisions in order to pierce the rhetoric of corporate responsibility and infer the urban policy that these capitalist institutions have set for American cities.

References

Banfield, Edward C. 1970. The Unheavenly City. Boston: Little Brown.

Berger, Bennett M. 1971. Working-class Suburb. Berkeley: U. of California Press.

Berry, Brian J. L. 1973. The Human Consequences of Urbanisation. New York: St. Martin's Press.

Burgess, Ernest W. 1930. Social Backgrounds of Chicago's Local Communities. (With Vivien Marie Palmer.) Chicago: U. of Chicago, Local Community Research Committee.

Dahl, Robert. 1961. Who Governs? Democracy and Power in an American City. New Haven: Yale U. P.

Gans, Herbert. 1962. The Urban Villagers. New York: Free Press of Glencoe.

Harvey, David. 1973. Social Justice and the City. London: Edward Arnold.
Hawley, Amos H. 1971. Urban Society: an Ecological Approach. New York: Ronald Press.
Hunter, Floyd. 1953. Community Power Structure; a Study of Decision Makers. Chapel Hill: U. of North Carolina Press.
Suttles, Gerald D. 1968. The Social Order of the Slum. Chicago: U. of Chicago Press.

Chapter 2

CRIME

In the colonial era criminals were subject to extreme penalties. A minor theft could result in hanging from the gallows. At times juries would not convict because of the severity of the penalties. After the revolution the criminal code was reviewed as part of a general reconsideration of practices inherited from British rule. Penalties were reduced and made proportionate to the seriousness of the offense committed. In the 1970s the problem of crime was also seen to be in the legal system, and the solution, moderate penalties that would be strictly enforced.

During the 1820s the view of crime and its causes shifted as part of the general reform spirit of the Jacksonian era. Deviant behavior came to be viewed as a product of the social environment. Individuals who committed crimes did so as a result of inadequacies in their upbringing and the collapse of family controls.

Since the problem was caused by an institutional deficit, it could be remedied by an institutional solution. Individuals who committed crimes were placed in a carefully controlled social environment. This was expected to make up for the lack of discipline in the early lives of such individuals. Prisons were established to provide an ordered routine that would remake the criminal into a law-abiding citizen. The architecture of prisons was carefully designed to remove inmates from contact with corruption. Prisoners were isolated in separate cells so that they would not be a bad influence on each other. They were provided with work to do in their cells as a means of inculcating discipline. In succeeding decades the rehabilitative intent of prisons declined with the growth of inmate populations.

The tremendous growth of urban populations in the late nineteenth century, along with mass immigration and industrialization, brought crime to the forefront of public attention again. The reform movement of the era broadened the environmental analysis of the causes of crime to include poverty, bad housing conditions, and lack of employment. While reformers tried to alleviate these social ills, the earlier solutions, reform of the legal system and penitentiary rehabilitation, were also pressed.

During the past decade crime has again become a major public issue. This time no single approach to the issue has predominated. Earlier solutions have become identified with conservative and liberal political perspectives. Conservatives would rely on heavy punishments, including the death penalty, to deter crime. Prisons are regarded as simply a means of removing dangerous persons from society. Their rehabilitative potential is minimized. Liberals look to the alleviation of poverty and other social ills as the solution to crime. Short of this they accept the necessity of removing lawbreakers from society but are concerned about the effects of prisons in training young lawbreakers to be professional criminals. Socialists agree with liberals that poverty and other social ills produce crime but believe that these social conditions can only be relieved by eliminating capitalism. Socialists argue that the issue of crime should be refocused. Corporate price fixing is also theft and should receive at least as much attention as street crime. Under capitalism, the amount stolen has little relationship to the likelihood of incurring a penalty. The underlying rule appears to be that the more you can steal, the likelier it is that you will have access to the political, social, and economic power that can keep your "theft" from being defined as crime and insure that it be considered merely as part of the normal conduct of business. Moreover, moral as well as legal criteria should be used to define criminal activity. In this view, government officials such as former Secretary of State Henry Kissinger, who initiated the secret bombing of Cambodia, should be defined as criminals for their contravention of human rights.

In the conservative article, Van den Haag argues that perpetrators of crimes, irrespective of their social postion, are solely responsible for their actions. Understanding the motivations that lead people to commit criminal acts is irrelevant. The protection of society from criminal activity is the relevant issue. The solution to crime is an effective threat that will inhibit people from engaging in criminal activity. Other proposed solutions, such as the rehabilitation of offenders or relief of poverty, do nothing to prevent crime. Inequalities will exist in any social system and individuals will always be tempted to redress inequality by breaking the law. Powerful disincentives are required to restrain people. If sufficiently strong punishments are meted out, fewer people will be impelled to act on their temptations, and crime will be reduced.

In the liberal article, Oelsner argues that poverty is the underlying cause of most crime. Persons who commit crimes are typically motivated by lack of money. The criminal justice system is overwhelmed by the huge numbers of poor persons accused of crimes. It is able to function only by reducing the level of punishments meted out. Most persons who are convicted will soon be back in court. They will continue to commit crimes since their condition of poverty persists. Nevertheless, the law, even though it is ineffective in preventing crime, most continue to be applied to poor persons. The validity of the legal system must be sustained. To reduce crime, poverty must be eliminated. Government programs should be instituted to achieve this goal. Otherwise people who need money will continue to commit crimes to get it, and the courts will continue to be filled with the poor.

In the socialist article, Platt argues that although most crime is committed by the poor against the poor, the cause of crime is not simply a matter of poverty. Significant numbers of crimes are committed by persons of middle and upper class background in the United States, and many poor countries do not have as high a crime rate as the United States. Platt identifies the high level of crime in the United States with two factors: (1) a breakdown in social and family life that is caused by the operation of the capitalist economic system, and (2) the existence of a surplus population whose labor is not required in the regular economy. It is a mistake to romanticize the contemporary perpetrators of street crime as revolutionaries. The high level of street crime divides poor people among themselves and works against the creation of group solidarity, which is necessary for effective political activity.

Conservative

Ernest van den Haag: Preventing Crime with Punishment

. . .The credible threat of punishment remains the most effective deterrent to crime.

The fundamental purpose of criminal laws is to use the threat of punishment in order to restrain persons who are tempted to do what the laws prohibit. Thus, Timothy I (1:9): "The law is not made for the righteous man, but for the lawless and disobedient."

And who is likely to be "lawless and disobedient"? Some persons are tempted to commit crimes for individual and intrapsychic reasons; others because nature or society placed them in a disadvantageous position which reduces their legitimate opportunities and, in comparative terms, increases the attractiveness of illegimate opportunities. The law is addressed to all those impelled toward crime, whatever their temptation; it would be redundant if addressed only to those not tempted to do what it prohibits. The greatest burden of the law thus is on those most tempted to violate it, usually those with the fewest legitimate opportunities and satisfactions. Rich adolescents, for example, are less tempted to steal cars, and will commit fewer car thefts than poor ones. There is no way—under capitalism, socialism, or any social system—of equalizing temptations, or individual needs, or individual responsiveness to them. Hence the law will always be more burdensome to some than to others. It is in the nature of any prohibition to affect different people differently, and to be most painful to those most tempted to do what is prohibited: they will have the greatest difficulty obeying. They will also be punished more often. To prohibit rape or theft imposes a heavier burden on one tempted to commit either offense than on a person not so tempted, whether by his circumstances or by his character.

Roughly speaking, the burden of the law will always be heaviest on those placed in the least advantageous position by nature or society—the poor or those brought up in an unfavorable family environment, e.g., by violent or cruel parents. Yet contrary to what one so often hears, it is still mainly the disadvantaged —the poor and the powerless—that the criminal law protects. In any society the rich and powerful can protect themselves. They need the law least. But the law is the only protection the poor and powerless have. They need protection against others, usually poor and powerless as well, for most crimes are committed by the poor against the poor.

The threat of punishment can deter people from prohibited acts only if credible. Else the threat becomes ineffective. And the threat remains credible only if carried out as threatened. Obviously, the threat has been ineffective with those who have already violated the law; but threats of punishment will be effective enough, if properly applied, to restrain others from crime. Threats cannot and will not restrain everybody all the time, but they are effective in all existing societies with most people most of the time—provided they are carried out when the law is violated. Else crime pays and more crime will be committed as people realize that it does.

The threat of punishment is a purely utilitarian measure. It is meant to protect society. But we also try to be just when we carry out the threat. Thus we distribute the threatened penalties only to those found guilty of crime. Further, the punishment must be as threatened, i.e., not arbitrary; and it must be proportioned to the felt gravity of the crime.

In addition to threatening punishment we can also reduce crime rates by decreasing criminal opportunities, and by increasing legitimate ones. A better social order, it is contended, may reduce the temptation to, or pressure for, committing crimes. I have no doubt that changes in social arrangements—e.g., making divorce or employment easier to get—may have some marginal effect. And I favor some such changes. But their effect has been minor, and to stress them is to misplace the emphasis.

In this country an income of $5,500 for a family of four has been decreed as the poverty line. In 1900 ninety percent of all families were below the equivalent in actual purchasing power; by 1920 the figure was 50 percent; and in 1976, 11-13 percent. If the crime rate has declined similarly, it is a well kept secret. Education, psychiatric care, etc. also have been improved, and opportunity is far more equal than it ever was. Yet these changes have not reduced the crime rate. On the contrary: the crime rate among females and blacks has increased as their opportunities have become more equal. The reason for this seeming paradox is simple enough. Social conditions were improved. But the level of effective (credible) threats against criminal behavior was independently reduced. Only if that level is maintained can social improvements reduce the crime rate. And in the present situation the most urgent task is to increase the threat level. Punishment must become more certain and less lenient if the crime rate is to be reduced. At present it is still rising.

Incapacitation for habitual offenders might reduce the crime rate by reducing the offenses of those irrationally *addicted* to crime who, when free, commit crimes regardless of legal threats. (I mean addicted to crime, not addicted to drugs. Although many offenders are drug addicts, in most cases they were offenders before becoming addicts and drug addiction contributes to rather than causes their crimes.) As long as they are incapacitated, these persons would not be able to commit the crimes from which they cannot otherwise be deterred. This would reduce the rate, say, of child molesting or of certain violent crimes committed in part for thrill and not for instrumental reasons alone. I should favor more incapacitation when possible—if and when we are able to tell the habitual law violator from others. But the practical possibilities are limited.

Unlike incapacitation, rehabilitation is not a practical possibility at all, and I doubt that it can ever be on a major scale. Let me quote a former president of the American Society of Criminology, Bruno Cormier (*The Watcher and the Watched*, p. 268): "Society must learn to accept that a delinquent treated by psychotherapeutic techniques may have benefited from such treatment even though he returns to crime." I am willing to accept that, but unlike Dr. Cormier, I do not think we should send people to prison for their health. Prisons are meant to protect society from crime—present and future—and, if convicts while benefiting from treatment still return to crime, I do not think the treatment was socially useful.

Indeed, there is no evidence that our institutions, which barely manage to teach reading and writing to children, can do any better with the behavior of adults. I need not mention all the horrors practiced in the name of rehabilitation —such as indeterminate sentences, parole, etc. But even if rehabilitation were effective, or if all non-rehabilitated convicts could be permanently incapacitated, I do not think that the rate of instrumental (rational) crimes would be reduced.

Criminals engage in instrumental crimes such as picking pockets, mugging, tax evasion, car theft, rackets, because of a combination of personality and of comparative benefits and opportunities. A different combination leads others to become dentists or criminologists. Now, if we were to incapacitate or rehabilitate all dentists, or all criminologists, presently practicing, the rate at which dentistry or criminology would be committed would remain the same (in the long run) as long as there is no change in the relative cost-benefit attractions—net gains— that determines that rate. Only if these cost-benefit factors are changed can the rate of instrumental crime be affected. They depend in part on the risk of punishment, a cost factor. Non-instrumental crimes also depend on the size of the reservoir of people attractable to, or capable of, committing the crime. But in practical terms that reservoir is unlimited, for dentists, criminologists, or criminals engaged in instrumental crimes, i.e., for all criminals except those engaged in crime irrationally.

How, then, can the crime rate be reduced? The cost of crime is the severity of punishment multiplied by the probability of its being inflicted. Thus, we will deter, *ceteris paribus*, if we punish more lawbreakers more severely.

Not everyone agrees that punishment is an effective deterrent to others. According to Boswell, Dr. Johnson attended the hanging of a pickpocket and, finding that the pickpocket's colleagues continue to work the crowd, concluded that the death penalty does not deter. The story has been repeated innumerable times. Yet the conclusion is obviously wrong. A punitive threat is deterrent when it reduces the rate at which the threatened crime is committed. The punitive threat is quite unlikely to eliminate altogether the offense being threatened. (Else, high enough penalties could eliminate all crime.) Thus, if Johnson wanted to determine the deterrent effect, he would have had to compare the amount of pickpocketing activity in the crowd attending the hanging with the amount in a similarly sized crowd without the hanging. He didn't. And even if he had not found any reduction in the rate at which the offense was committed, it would not surprise me, nor would it argue against the deterrent effect of the penalty. The pickpockets who were working the crowd were committed to their careers and had made the commitment in view of the risk of the penalty. Why then would the hanging deter them?

Deterrent effects can be expected not with respect to those already committed to their criminal careers and who made the commitment knowing the risks they took. Rather, deterrence reduces the number of new entrants so that there will be fewer than there would be if there were no penalties, or if the penalties were less severe or less certain. This is what is meant by deterrent effect. It is easy to understand why Dr. Johnson took a less than scientific approach. But those who repeat his mistake today should be blamed for their ignorance.

Liberal

Lesley Oelsner: Tens of Thousands of Indigents Jam New York Criminal Courts

Alberto Garcia stares bleakly up at Judge Milton L. Williams. Judge Williams stares back. Then the judge looks at the people who stand around Mr. Garcia: the policeman who arrested him a few hours earlier, the court-appointed defense lawyer, the prosecutor.

"How much does he have on him?" Judge Williams asks.

"Eight dollars," the policeman replies.

"He needs money to get home," the defense lawyer interjects.

"How much do you need to get home?" the judge asks the defendant.

"A dollar," Mr. Garcia says.

There is a slight pause, barely noticeable to the 50 or so men and women slumped or dozing in the spectators' section of courtroom AR-1 of Criminal Court in Manhattan, waiting for other cases to be called.

Then Judge Williams pronounces sentence:

"Seven dollars."

Mr. Garcia hands the money to a court official and walks out of court, the case closed.

Alberto Garcia is one of the ten of thousands of indigent men and women who stream through New York City's Criminal Courts. They make up the bulk of the caseload; only one out of every four or five defendants can afford his own lawyer.

Their cases reflect their poverty.

Mr. Garcia was arrested some months earlier for allegedly jumping a subway turnstile without paying his fare. A plea bargain had been arranged under which he would plead guilty to a minor charge of trespassing and, a few days later, would pay a $15 fine.

But on payment day, Mr. Garcia did not show up. A warrant was issued for his arrest; he was brought into court the day he was found. What Judge Williams did, technically, was to resentence Mr. Garcia to a lesser penalty.

There are hundreds of cases in the Criminal Courts in which defendants are supposed to pay fines but do not. Typically they don't have the money; many are afraid to come to court empty-handed, lest they be jailed.

Thousands of brutal crimes come through the city's courts: assaults, stabbings, arson. In many, perhaps most, money was the object.

Many thousands of other cases come through that are relatively minor: food taken from supermarkets, clothes stolen from department stores, subway fares unpaid by youths who leap turnstiles.

Somewhere around 200,000 defendants have cases in the city's Criminal Courts each year. The court-system officials don't know the exact number because they keep track of "docket numbers," meaning cases, rather than defendants, who may face more than one docket number each.

Defendants are entitled to free counsel if they can't afford their own. The Legal Aid Society, under contract with the city, represents the bulk of these defendants—perhaps 70 percent. Some other defendants—17,000 last year—also get free counsel, from private attorneys under programs administered by the Appellate Division of the State Supreme Court.

In Federal Court, the defendants are frequently middle class or even, as in cases of tax evasion and white-collar crimes, the prosperous. But in the local courts—the New York City Criminal Court, which is the lower-level tribunal, and the Criminal Division of State Supreme Court, the upper level—the rich are rarely seen.

The typical defendant is male, young, single, poor and, more often than not, unemployed.

A random survey of 300 defendants made for the courts in 1977 shows that only 30.1 percent were employed, 12.6 percent were students, 15.7 percent were on welfare and 41.6 percent were listed as "other unemployed."

For those defendants who were employed, more than 90 percent took home less than $200 a week and 35.2 percent took home less than $100 a week.

"It's certainly not the legal system people think of, it's not Perry Mason," said Jeremy Travis, executive director of the New York City Criminal Justice Agency, which conducted the study. "It's a net that catches people with problems."

The poverty is palpable in the courtrooms and hallways of the city's court-houses. It shows in the buses that take inmates back and forth between court and jail—the inmates who are in jail pending trial because they cannot afford bail. It shows in the shabby clothes of most of the people; it shows in the health problems of many of them.

About 40 people sit in the spectators' section of Night Court in Manhattan one weekday evening. One is a young woman with bruises on her face and a large, soiled bandage over her right eye. In the row behind her is an enormously overweight woman whose age is hard to guess. Nearby are several others with obvious weight problems, including a boy of about 10. Skin problems—rashes, acne, boils—disfigure the faces and hands of still others.

In the jails on Rikers Island, the inmates are generally "not healthy," according to Ralph Gardner, an information officer for the city's correction authorities.

The typical inmate, at least in non-drug cases, is "husky," Mr. Gardner said. But he suffers from poor nutrition, as dental checkups show. Both male and female inmates have a higher incidence of tuberculosis than normal. Some of the women are pregnant when sent to jail; typically, they have had no prenatal care.

Some of the defendants are so poor that jail can look good to them.

One day, it is cold and clammy. A man accused of disorderly conduct is brought before Judge Joan B. Carey. The prosecution case is weak. The Legal Aid Lawyer wants the case thrown out.

The defendant, however, wants to plead guilty and be sentenced to 15 days in jail. He has no money, he explains, and his welfare application has not yet gone through.

The Legal Aid attorney demurs.

The defendant says to the Legal Aid lawyer: "If you don't plead me guilty and get me some time in jail, I'm going to punch you in the mouth."

A compromise is quickly reached. The defendant pleads guilty; he is sentenced to five days in jail.

If a defendant has never been arrested before and the charge is minor—stealing meat from a supermarket or a sweater from a clothing store—the typical way of handling it is to "adjourn in contemplation of dismissal," or "A.C.D." This means that if the defendant stays out of trouble for the next six months, the charge will be automatically dismissed at the end of that time.

The A.C.D. disposition is decided on during plea bargaining between the prosecutor, the defense attorney and, often, the judge.

Judge Williams says a better approach would be to look into the defendant's life to see what is wrong that has caused the crime and try to right it.

"This is a tip-off," Judge Williams said, referring to a defendant's first arrest. "Invariably what happens is, you'll see him again, three or four times in a month. That may pass over. Then the big one comes—robbery, or assault."

"I should be able to send him somewhere and find out what's happening" at the very first incident, he says. "You could save this. Because what the hell do I accomplish, truly, with a A.C.D.—six months?"

But instead, the judge says, "My hands are tied. There's nothing I can do, except wonder."

In the Criminal Division of State Supreme Court, where felonies are handled, the typical punishment meted out is a prison term.

In Criminal Court, though, where cases are less serious, fines are frequent. In 1977, for instance, 116,711 sentences were imposed, according to the court's chief record keeper, Ida Zamist. Of these, 48,696 were fines.

The fine could be $25 or $50 or more. Defendants are allowed to pay on the installment plan and many do, often paying $10 every few weeks.

The rationale for fining defendants includes the view that a fine is less oner-ous than time in jail and that sentences must involve some hardship to be effective.

There are also arguments against fines—most obviously, that the defendants are almost all so poor that even a small fine can be a major hardship.

A few days before last Easter, Sam Jones went to Gimbels and stole two suits in the right sizes for his two young sons. He was caught almost immediately, arrested and taken to Manhattan Criminal Court.

A Legal Aid lawyer was assigned to defend him.

"Doesn't welfare pay enough?" the lawyer asked him during a quick, huddle.

"No way," he replied.

The prosecutor and the defense lawyer worked out a plea bargain. Mr. Jones—the name is a pseudonym—duly pleaded guilty. The judge duly pronounced the agreed-upon sentence: a $50 fine.

His lawyer was asked later how Mr. Jones would pay the fine if he couldn't afford clothes for his children.

The lawyer paused, then grimaced. Mr. Jones had shoplifted before, the law-yer noted.

"He's probably going to go out and shoplift again and fence it. That's how he'll pay the fine."

Judges, lawyers and others in the justice system are troubled by much of what they see in the courts. But they wonder what should—and could—be done.

The defendants who are charged with eating a meal and not paying are espe-cially distressing to many officials. Yet, says Michael Smith, director of the Vera Institute of Justice, a private organization that develops experimental justice-reform programs, "It's by no means inappropriate for an arrest to be made."

Judge Carey said, "Technically, you see, you have to arrest them. If you license the police not to make arrests for food, then you're leaving it up to them to decide in the street when to apply the larceny law. You can't do that."

There is some consensus that the justice system should increase its use of mediation as a means of resolving disputes short of prosecuting and convicting someone—especially disputes involving fights between relatives or neighbors.

Beyond that, the general view is simply that poverty in general must be alleviated.

"Jobs, economic development, education, better management of the civil ser-vice"—all are needed, Mr. Smith says.

Judge Williams, like some others, feels that the courts are burdened unfairly with problems caused by failures in other parts of society.

"It's not fair of the system to sweep everything on our doorstep, when the schools have failed, the housing authorities have failed, even the churches, and you expect us to say, in three years, we'll save him," he complained angrily.

But others seem resigned.

Robert M. Haft is a judge in Criminal Court in Manhattan who has been assigned as an acting State Supreme Court justice. He has been on the bench since 1971; before that he was a prosecutor and a defense lawyer.

One weekday night he draws Night Court duty. He sits in a small, dingy chamber behind the courtroom, waiting for the night's fare. He says there has been no real change over the years in the high proportion of defendants who are poor.

There is one obvious, basic and unchanging reason, he says: "Crime is often committed by people who need money."

Socialist

Tony Platt: "Street" Crime — A View from the Left

According to survey after survey, "street" crime ranks as one of the most serious problems in working class communities. In 1948, only 4% of the population felt that crime was their community's *worst* problem. By 1972, according to a Gallup Poll, 21% of the residents of metropolitan centers reported crime as their *major* concern.[1]

People not only *think* that they are threatened by crime; they are also taking action to defend themselves. Several years ago, Chicago citizens formed the South Shore Emergency Patrol, composed of some two hundred black and white residents, to patrol the streets at night and weekends; in Boston's Dorchester area, the community has begun crime patrols; in New York, Citizens Action for a Safer Harlem has organized blockwatcher programs, street associations and escort services for the elderly, while an armed citizens' vigilance group patrols the streets of Brooklyn on the look-out for arson and burglaries; in San Francisco, a member of the Board of Supervisors recently urged the formation of citizen anti-crime patrols to curb mugging; and in the relative peace and quiet of a college town like Berkeley, the Committee Against Rape and several neighborhood associations are meeting to plan ways of stopping violent attacks against women.[2]

The phenomenon of "street" crime has been largely ignored by the U.S. left. On the one hand, it is treated moralistically and attributed to the parasitical elements in capitalist society, mechanically following Marx and Engels's famous statement in the *Communist Manifesto* that the "lumpenproletariat may, here and there, be swept into the movement by a proletarian revolution; it conditions of life, however, prepare it far more for the part of a bribed tool of reactionary intrigue."[3] On the other hand, "street" crime is either glossed over as an invention of the FBI to divert attention away from the crimes of the ruling class or romanticized as a form of primitive political rebellion. Whether it is a form of reactionary individualism, or a fiction promoted by the bourgeoisie to cause confusion and false consciousness, or another manifestation of class strugge, is

not a matter of theoretical assertion and cannot be decided by dogmatic references to Marxist texts. What is first needed is a thorough investigation of the
scope and nature of "street" crime, concrete information about its varieties and
rates and an appreciation of its specific historical context. This essay sets out to
summarize and analyze the available information, thus providing a realistic basis
for developing political strategy.

Reporting Crime

In 1931, the International Association of Chiefs of Police developed the Uniform
Crime Reports (UCR) system and selected seven felony offenses for index purposes, on the grounds that the victims, or someone representing them, would
more likely report such crimes to the police. The seven offense groups include:
homicide, robbery, aggravated assault, forcible rape, burglary, larceny (grand
theft) and auto theft. These are the crime statistics from which trends in the
incidence of criminality are regularly reported in the media. When these
reported crimes are converted into rates per 100,000 population and comparisons
are made across time, for example 1968 to 1973, each of the index crimes, with the
exception of auto theft, increased 25% to 50%. In 1976, according to the UCR,
nearly 11.5 million serious crimes were reported to the police, a 33% increase
from 1972, and a 76% from 1967.[4]

Critics of the FBI's reporting system have pointed out that the dramatic
increase in crime rates is exaggerated and misleading since it reflects higher rates
of *reporting* crime, technological improvements in data processing, better record-
keeping systems and political manipulation by the police, rather than a real
increase in the level of crime. While there is no evidence to support sensational
media announcements about *sudden crime waves*, crime is certainly not exaggerated by the FBI. On the contrary, it is grossly underestimated.

The most accurate information about the scope of "street" crime is to be found
in the federal government's Victimization Surveys. The Surveys, part of a statistical program called the National Crime Panel created by the Law Enforcement
Assistance Administration (LEAA) in 1973, are an attempt to assess the extent
and character of criminal victimization by means of a representative probability
sampling of households, businesses and persons over the age of 12. The Surveys,
which do *not* include homicide, kidnapping, so-called "victimless" crimes (such
as prostitution, pimping, sale of drugs, etc.) and business crimes (such as fraud,
false advertising, tax evasion, etc.), are limited to personal (rape, assault and
armed robbery) and property (theft, auto theft and burglary) crimes.

Most "street" crime is not reported to the police. The Census Bureau recently
concluded that there were nearly four times as many crimes committed in 1975
and 1976 as reported to the police.[5] A 1973 victimization study found that fewer
than one in five persons report larceny to the police.[6] Some experts estimate that
only 10% of all rapes are reported; the reporting rate for wife-beating is even
lower.[7] A "self-report" study estimates that about one out of every thirty delinquent acts comes to the attention of the police.[8]

The primary reason for not reporting crimes is the belief that the police are
either incapable of solving crimes or are likely to aggravate the situation by
brutalizing or intimidating the victims. This distrust of the police is realistically

based on the extensive experiences of working class communities, especially racial and national minorities, with police brutality and ineffectiveness. According to a recent national public opinion survey, blacks think that the police are doing a poor job almost three times more than do whites.[9] (See Table 1.)

According to a recent study by Paul Takagi, black males are killed by the police at a rate 13 times higher than for white males.[10] But police killings are only a small part of the total level of state brutality directed at the civilian population. It is not an exaggeration to say that millions of Americans now alive have been beaten by the police. Data cited by James Q. Wilson, a political scientist at Harvard, show that 5% of all blacks (over one million people) and 2% of all whites (over four million people) report themselves unjustifiably beaten by the police. And sociologist Albert Reiss, in a LEAA-financed study, found that the police used unnecessary force in 3% of all police-citizen encounters, representing hundreds of thousands of cases of brutality per year. When these data are understood in the context of peer and family relationships, a very large proportion of the population on a day-to-day basis faces or fears the possibility of police violence.[11]

Additionally, the police have a very poor track record in solving and prosecuting serious "street" crime. A two-year Rand study, released in 1976, reported that substantially more than 50% of all serious crimes reported to the police receive no more than superficial investigation by detectives and investigators. Unless the patrolman on the scene makes an arrest or a patrol car accidentally stops a burglar for speeding, concludes Rand, there is little chance of a successful prosecution.[12]

The selective recruitment and militaristic training of the police, aggravated by institutionalized racism and sexism, encourage them to regard "high crime" areas as either a combat zone requiring the dispassionate objectivity of a professional soldier or a "subculture" of violence and depravity where victimization is culturally inevitable. Not surprisingly, policing the ghettos and barrios vacillates from extraordinary violence to cynical resignation.

This does not mean that all rank and file police operate in this way. There are many individual officers and a small number of progressive caucuses, such as the Afro-American Patrolmen's league in Chicago and Officers for Justice in San Francisco, who are genuinely concerned about protecting working class communities from crime. But their efforts are easily frustrated, partly because the roots of "street" crime are deeply embedded in social conditions over which they have no control, and partly because their efforts are continuously undermined and sabotaged by the political police and "red squads," who make it their business to destroy community and political organizations which are trying to combat drug pushing, pimping, rape and other forms of parasitical criminality.

Scope of Crime

According to a 1977 Gallup Poll and a survey of 70 countries, the U.S. has the highest crime rate of all capitalist and European countries. One of every five homes was victimized by crime; 15% of working class communities reported that they were afraid of being victimized by crime in their own homes, while 43% thought that crime had increased in their neighborhood.[13]

TABLE 1

Evaluation of police performance (percent responding "good")
by family income and race of respondent, eight impact cities aggregate

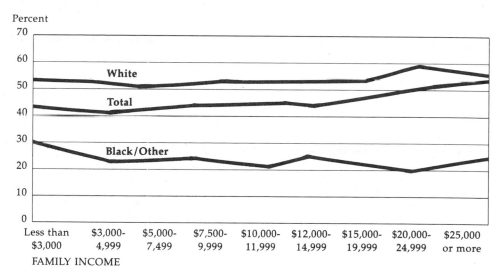

Source: James Garofolo, Public Opinion About Crime, U.S. Dept. of Justice, LEAA, 1977.

During 1974, according to the Victimization Surveys, over 39.5 million persons over the age of 12 were victimized by selected, serious crimes, an increase of 7.5% over 1973. In 1975, there was another 2% increase to nearly 40.5 million estimated incidents of victimization.[14] And the latest Census Bureau study reports over 41 million for 1976.[15] This is almost four times higher than the FBI's UCR index. Moreover, it should be remembered that these estimates do *not* include homicide, "victimless" crimes (illegal drugs and prostitution, for example) or the "hidden" figures of "white-collar" crime—price-fixing, health and safety violations, tax fraud, embezzlement, false advertising, etc.—which cause immense suffering and untold deprivation in working class communities.

The Victimization Surveys have caused considerable embarrassment to the government, which had hoped to use them to demonstrate that LEAA's "war on crime" was winning some major battles. The Surveys, however, have instead demonstrated that the rate of "street" crime has gradually increased, despite the 55% increase in criminal justice expenditures from $11 billion in 1971 to $17 billion in 1975; despite the fact that the number of police almost doubled in the decade between 1965 and 1975; despite a flourishing criminal justice-industrial complex which has upgraded the technological capacity of the police and introduced computers, weapons systems, data retrieval devices and modern communications equipment to a hither-to "backward" bureaucracy; despite the advice and thousands of research studies conducted by the "best and brightest" scholars from the most privileged universities and corporate think tanks.

Not surprisingly, the federal government recently called a halt to the Victimization Surveys, even though they were widely regarded as one of the very few worthwhile and reliable projects initiated by LEAA. The reasons for this action are quite obvious. Not only did the Surveys expose the bankruptcy and incredible waste of the government's "war on crime." They also supported the conclusion that "street" crime is not simply a *by-product* of the capitalist mode of production, a logistics problem to be solved by technocrats trained in "systems analysis." Rather, it is shown to be a phenomenon *endemic* to capitalism at its highest stage of development.

Victims of Street Crime

"Street" crime is primarily an *intra-class* and *intra-racial* phenomenon, media stereotypes to the contrary.[16] White women are most likely to be raped by white men; young black men are most likely to be robbed by other young black men; and working class families are most likely to have their homes vandalized or ripped off by strangers living only a few blocks away.

The victims of "street" crime are overwhelmingly poor people, particularly blacks and Chicanos living in metropolitan areas. LEAA's 1973 Victimization Surveys found that, with the exception of theft, families with annual incomes under $3,000 were the most likely to be victimized by serious crimes of violence and property loss.[17] Another study, using the same indices, reported that the unemployed were more likely to be victims of crime in rates two to three times higher than those employed.[18]

Racial and national minorities, especially blacks, have the highest rate of victimization. A 1975 LEAA study in the five largest cities found that:

> Blacks and Chicanos in Philadelphia and Los Angeles are most likely to be victimized by assault and robbery.
> Blacks in Philadelphia and Chicago are the most victimized by theft.
> Black family households in all five cities suffer the highest rates of burglary and auto theft.
> In Philadelphia, blacks are twice as likely as whites to be burglarized.
> In Chicago, blacks are twice as likely as whites to be victimized by auto theft.[19]

Follow-up nationwide studies, released in 1976, similarly found that the highest incidence of violent and property crime is among the poor and unemployed, specifically, the superexploited sectors of the working class, young men and single or separated women. Blacks have higher victimization rates than whites for rape, robbery and assault. Moreover, blacks over age 20 are robbed at two to three times the rate of their white counterparts.[20] (See Table 2.)

While crimes of violence account for less than 10% of "street" crimes, they are an important source of demoralization and victimization in working class communities. Rape, assault, child- and wife-beating and homicide not only cause great personal suffering to the victims and their relatives and close friends, but also undermine collective solidarity.

This is *not* a recent phenomenon. Family life under industrial capitalism, as Engels observed in *The Condition of the Working Class in England*, was "almost impossible for the worker." Impoverished living conditions, long hours of work and little time for recreation made family life a continuous round of problems and tensions. Wives and children, doubly exploited by economic dependency and male supremacist ideology, are regular targets of brutal assaults. "Yet the working man," noted Engels in 1845, "cannot escape from the family, must live in the family, and the consequence is a perpetual succession of family troubles, domestic quarrels, most demoralizing for parents and children alike."[21]

TABLE 2

	Race of victim	
Type of victimization	White	Black and other races
Base	143,217,000	19,019,000
Rape and attempted rape	90	158
Robbery	599	1,388
Robbery and attempted robbery with injury	207	473
Serious assault	108	294
Minor assault	99	179
Robbery without injury	213	589
Attempted robbery without injury	179	326
Assault	2,554	2,929
Aggravated assault	954	1,656
With injury	301	599
Attempted assault with weapon	653	1,057
Simple assault	1,600	1,272
With injury	399	289
Attempted assault without weapon	1,201	983
Personal larceny with contact	267	678
Purse snatching	57	126
Attempted purse snatching	44	47
Pocket picking	166	504
Personal larceny without contact	9,209	7,671

Source: Michael Hindelang et al., Sourcebook of Criminal Justice Statistics-1974. U.S. Dept. of Justice. LEAA.1975.

Under monopoly capitalism, social and family life is particularly difficult in the superexploited sectors of the working class, where economic hardship, a chaotic labor market, uprooted community life ("urban renewal") and deteriorating social services provide a fertile environment for individualism and demoralization. A recent study, prepared for the W.E.B. DuBois Conference on Black Health in 1976, reveals for example that about 95% of blacks victimized by homicide are killed by other blacks.

In 1974, almost 11,000 of the 237,000 deaths of nonwhites in the United States, the overwhelming majority of whom were black, were from homicide. More than six percent of the black males who died during this year were victims of homicide as were over two percent of the black females. Among blacks *homicide* was the *fourth leading cause of death*, exceeded only by major cardiovascular diseases, malignant neoplasms, and accidents. All of the infectious diseases taken together took a lesser toll than did homicide.

White men are killed by homicide at a rate of 9.3 per 100,000 compared to a rate of 77.9 per 100,000 for black men of comparable age. To put it another way, "the difference in life expectation between white and black males is seven years. Almost a fifth of that is due to homicide. . . . More than twice as many blacks died from homicide in 1974 as from automobile accidents, and homicides accounted for about 40 percent as many deaths as cancer."[22]

While the Victimization Surveys and other studies show that minorities are responsible for a higher incidence of violent "street" crimes, such as rape, robbery, assault and homicide, than whites, this does not mean that crime is simply a *racial* phenomenon.[23] Historically, "street" crime has tended to be concentrated in the marginalized sectors of the labor force and in the demoralized layers of the working class, irrespective of skin color or ethnic origin.[24] Today, it is those families with annual incomes below the poverty line which fill the police stations, jails and hospital emergency rooms. Since blacks, Chicanos, Native Americans and Puerto Ricans are disproportionately concentrated in the superexploited sectors of the working class, they are also disproportionately represented in police records and as victims of crime.

The risk of victimization is closely tied to the material conditions of life. Black women suffer a higher rate than white women because they are more exposed to the insecurities of public transportation and poorly policed streets; the elderly, living on fixed incomes in downtown rooming houses, are much more physically vulnerable than their counterparts in suburban "leisure" communities; families that cannot afford to install burglar alarms or remodel their homes into fortresses are easier prey for rip-offs and thefts; small businesses, unable to buy the protection of private security agencies, are more likely to be burglarized; apartment buildings, guarded by rent-a-cops, doormen and security fences have a lower rate of burglary than public housing projects and tenements; and working parents, hustling low-paying jobs with erratic hours in order to pay the daily bills, cannot hire tutors, counselors and psychiatrists or turn to private schools when their children become "delinquency" problems.

Crime and Class

The current high level of crime and victimization within the marginalized sectors of the working class can be partly understood in the context of the capitalist labor market. The "relative surplus population" is not an aberration or incidental by-product. Rather it is continuously reproduced as a necessary element of the capitalist mode of production and is, to quote Marx, the *"lever* of capitalist accumulation. . . . It forms a disposable industrial reserve army that belongs to capital quite as absolutely as if the latter had bred it at its own cost. Independently of the limits of the actual increase of population, it creates, for the changing needs of the self-expansion of capital, a mass of human material always ready for exploitation."[25]

For this population, the economic conditions of life are unusually desperate and degrading. The high level of property crime and petty hustles cannot be separated from the problems of survival. Commenting on the process of primitive accumulation in 15th and 16th century England, Marx observed that the rising bourgeoisie destroyed the pre-existing modes of production through the forcible expropriation of people's land and livelihood, thus creating a "free" proletariat which "could not possibly be absorbed by the nascent manufactures as fast as it was thrown upon the world." Thousands of peasants were "turned *en masse* into beggars, robbers, vagabonds . . . and 'voluntary' criminals."[26] For these victims of capitalism, crime was both a means of survival and an effort to resist the discipline and deadening routine of the workhouse and factory.[27]

But crime was not only a manifestation of early capitalism, with its unconcealed plunder, terrorism and unstable labor market. Crime was endemic to both the rural and urban poor in 18th century England.[28] And at the peak of industrial capitalism in the mid-19th century, Engels vividly described the prevalence of theft, prostitution and other types of widespread victimization in working class communities. "The British nation," he concluded, "has become the most criminal in the world."[29]

With at least 41 million persons annually victimized by serious "street" crimes in the United States, it is clear that monopoly capitalism has aggravated rather than reduced the incidence of crime. Recent studies, prepared for the United Nations report on *Economic Crises and Crime*, support the argument that the rate of criminal victimization is not only correlated with crises and "downturns" in the capitalist economy, but also with the "long-term effects of economic growth,"[30] thus giving support to Marx's "absolute law of capitalist accumulation—in proportion as capital accumulates, the lot of the laborer, be his payment high or low, must grow worse."[31] The economic underpinnings of "street" crime are underscored by the findings of the Victimization Surveys that over 90% of serious offenses are property-related (theft, burglary, robbery, etc.)[32] Not surprisingly, most "street" crime is disproportionately concentrated in the superexploited sectors of the working class where unemployment rates of 50% are not uncommon.

But "street" crime is not only related to economic conditions; nor is it solely restricted to working class neighborhoods. A series of national studies, conducted by Martin Gold and his colleagues, found little difference in rates of juvenile delinquency between blacks and whites or working class and petty bourgeois families.[33] Their latest study reports that "white girls are no more nor less frequently or seriously delinquent than black girls; and white boys, no more nor less *frequently* delinquent than black boys; but white boys are *less seriously* delinquent than black boys." (See Table 3.) Moreover, when delinquency is correlated with socioeconomic status, it is found that "higher status" boys (i.e., the sons of the petty bourgeoisie for the most part) are more likely than working class boys to commit thefts, steal cars and commit assaults.[34]

"Street" crime, like white chauvinism and male supremacy, is most brutal in (although by no means limited to) the superexploited sectors of the working class. Monopoly capitalism "emiserates" increasingly larger portions of the working class and proletarianizes the lower strata of the petty bourgeoisie, degrades workers' skills and competency in the quest for higher productivity, and organizes family and community life on the basis of its most effective exploitability. It consequently makes antagonism rather than reciprocity the norm of social relationships.[35]

Under monopoly capitalism, family and peer relationships become even more brutal and attenuated. The family as an economic unit is totally separated, except as a consumer, from the productive processes of society. Adolescents are denied access to the labor market and forced to depend on their parents, who bear the costs of their subsistence and education. As a result, millions of youth, including many of the children of the petty bourgeoisie, "become subject to an extraordinary variety of social problems that accompany the statuses of dependent able-bodied persons in our society."[36]

"It is only in its era of monopoly," writes Harry Braverman in *Labor and Monopoly Capital*, "that the capitalist mode of production takes over the totality of individual, family, and social needs and, in subordinating them to the market, also reshapes them to serve the needs of capital." While more and more of the population "is packed ever more closely together in the urban environment, the atomization of social life proceeds space. . . . The social structure, built upon the market, is such that relations between individuals and social groups do not take place directly, as cooperative human encounters, but through the market as relations of purchase and sale."

As more family members are required to work and the pressures of urban life intensify, the family is required to "strip for action in order to survive and 'succeed' in the market society." Thus, urban life, governed by capital and the profit motive, "is both chaotic and profoundly hostile to all feelings of community." The "universal market," to use Braverman's appropriate term, not only destroys the material foundations of cooperative social relations, but also permeates even the most private domain of personal life, setting husband against wife, neighbor against neighbor.[37] "In short," as Engels observed over a century ago, "everyone sees in his neighbor an enemy to be got out of the way, or, at best, a tool to be used for his own advantage."[38]

Crime As Rebellion?

There is a tendency within the New Left to glorify crime as "primitive rebellion" and interpret it as a form of spontaneous, anticapitalist revolt. There is definitely some support for this position when we examine previous historical eras.

According to Eric Hobsbawm's well-known study of criminality in precapitalist and agrarian societies, "social banditry" was a form of class struggle and often a precursor or accompaniment to peasant revolutions. "The point about social bandits," he writes, "is that they are peasant outlaws whom the lord and state regard as criminals, but who remain within peasant society, and are considered by their people as heroes, as champions, avengers, fighters for justice, perhaps even leaders of liberation, and in any case as men to be admired, helped and supported." This respect for "social bandits" was based on their defense of the oppressed and their selective theft of the oppressor's crops and property.[39]

"Social banditry" or its equivalent persisted throughout at least two hundred years of primitive accumulation, as displaced peasants asserted their traditional communal rights to subsistence through poaching, smuggling and ship-wrecking against bourgeois claims to the supremacy of capitalist private property.[40]

But not all criminality was a blow to class rule in agrarian and early capitalist societies. Peasant society was also victimized by "professional" criminals and "common robbers" who did not make any class distinctions between their victims; and the rural and urban poor in eighteenth century England were regularly demoralized by theft, robbery and other types of *intra-class* victimization.

TABLE 3

Frequency and seriousness of delinquent behavior by race and sex

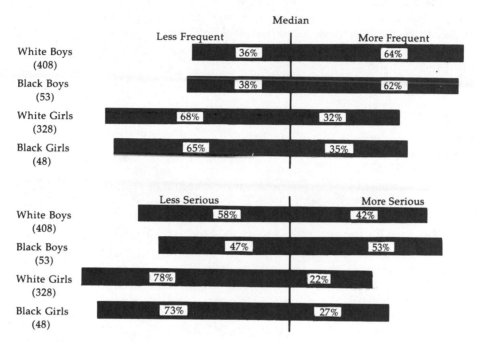

Median

	Less Frequent		More Frequent
White Boys (408)	36%		64%
Black Boys (53)	38%		62%
White Girls (328)	68%		32%
Black Girls (48)	65%		35%

	Less Serious		More Serious
White Boys (408)	58%		42%
Black Boys (53)	47%		53%
White Girls (328)	78%		22%
Black Girls (48)	73%		27%

Source: Jay Williams and Martin Gold, "From Delinquent Behavior to Official Delinquency," Social Problems 20, 2 (Fall, 1972).

Criminality as an effective, though limited, method of waging class warfare began to decline with the development of industrial capitalism. There were two important reasons for this. First, modernization reduced the means of protection and survival. The technology of communications and rapid forms of transportation, combined with economic development, public administration and the growth of the state, deprived banditry of the technical and social conditions under which it flourishes. Second, and more importantly, the organized working class developed collective, political associations which were far superior to individual criminality or even the organized self-help of banditry. As Engels observed:

> The earliest, crudest, and least fruitful form of rebellion was that of crime. . . . The workers soon realized that crime did not help matters. The criminal could protest against the existing order of society only singly, as one individual; the whole might of society was brought to bear upon each criminal, and crushed him with its immense superiority. Besides theft was the most primitive form of protest, and for this reason, if no other, it never becomes the universal expression of the public opinion of the working-man, however much they might approve of it in silence.[41]

Under monopoly capitalism, "street" crime bears little resemblance to the social banditry of Sicilian peasants, of the pastoral nomads of Central Asia or even of the rural poor in mercantile England. Contemporary "bandits" are more likely to rip off their neighbor or rob the local mom and pop store than to hold up a bank or kidnap a corporate executive. And they are more likely to be regarded as pariahs in the community than to be welcomed as heroes. Nor can theft from supermarkets and chain stores (which is widespread) be considered a modern equivalent of banditry, because bourgeois rule is not weakened by such activity, and the cost of such theft is generally passed on to the consumer in the form of higher prices or inferior commodities. It is only among ultra-leftist sects, which have no base of support within working class communities, that such banditry is still practiced and glorified.

Conclusion

The political solution to "street" crime does not lie in *mystifying* its reality by reactionary allusions to "banditry," nor in *reducing* it to a manifestation of "lumpen" viciousness. The former is utopian and dangerous because it defends practices that undermine the safety and solidarity of the working class (and glorifies spontaneity and putschism); the latter objectively legitimates the bourgeoisie's attack on superexploited workers, especially black and brown workers.

While "street" crime is associated with the most demoralized sectors of the working class, we must be careful about making mechanical and ahistorical generalizations about the "lumpen" and "dangerous class." As Paul Hirst has correctly pointed out, Marx and Engels took a very harsh and uncompromising attitude to "street" crime, not from a moralistic perspective, but out of concern for building a disciplined and principled workers' movement. "Their standpoint," notes Hirst, "was uncompromisingly political and based on the proletarian class position. Marx and Engels ask of any social class or sociopolitical activity, what is its effectivity in the struggle of the proletariat for socialism, does it contribute to the political victory of the exploited and oppressed?"[42]

Marx and Engels based their evaluation on both a class analysis of criminality and a concrete investigation of the role of the "lumpenproletariat" in specific political struggles. Thus, they argued that the "lumpen" weakens the workers' movement by living off the workers' productive labor, for example by theft, as well as by serving the bourgeoisie as informers, spies, collaborators and adventurists.[43]

The contemporary workers' movement must take an equally uncompromising stand against organized, parasitical forms of victimization and against "criminals" and prisoners who become "snitches" and agents of the political police. Pimping, gambling rackets, illegal drug operations, etc., are just as damaging to working class communities as any "legal" business which profits from people's misery and desperation.

But we must be careful to distinguish organized criminality from "street" crime and the "lumpen" from the superexploited sectors of the working class. Most "street" crime is not organized and not very profitable. Most theft, for example, is committed by individuals, and each incidence of "street" theft amounts to much less than $100.[44] Moreover, there is typically no direct economic advantage associated with crimes of personal violence—rape, homicide, assault, etc.

The condition of life in the superexploited sectors create both high levels of "street" crime *and* political militancy. The urban black community, for example, is hit the hardest by "street" crime, but it is also the locus of tremendous resistance and struggle—as witnessed by the civil rights movement, the ghetto revolts of the 1960s, and the antirepression struggles of today. Moreover, of the thousands of blacks who annually go to prison for serious crimes of victimization, many have become transformed by the collective experience of prison life and participate in numerous acts of solidarity, self-sacrifice and heroism—as witnessed by the conversion of Malcolm X, George Jackson and countless other anonymous militants in the strikes and uprisings at Soledad, San Quentin, Attica, etc.

While the link between "street" crime and economic conditions is clearly established, we must guard against economism. Crime is not simply a matter of poverty, as evidenced by the unparalleled criminality and terrorism of the ruling class. Nor is "street" crime explained by poverty, for petty bourgeois youth in the United States are probably just as delinquent as their working class counterparts, and there are many impoverished nations in the world that do not in any way approach the high level of criminality in this country. The problem of "street" crime should be approached not only as a product of the unequal distribution of wealth and chaotic labor market practices, but also as an important aspect of the demoralizing social relations and individualistic ideology that characterize the capitalist mode of production at its highest stage of development.

Notes

1. Center for Research on Criminal Justice, *The Iron Fist and the Velvet Glove*. San Francisco: Institute for the Study of Labor and Economic Crisis (1977):14.

2. *Christian Science Monitor* (November 13, 1973); *New York Times* (April 16, 1977; July 21, 1977); *San Francisco Chronicle* (January 25, 1978). According to the *Law Enforcement News* (January 3, 1978), the Law Enforcement Assistance Administration is now funding some 600 anticrime projects at a cost of $37 million.

3. Karl Marx and Frederick Engels, *The Communist Manifesto*. New York: Appleton-Century-Crofts (1955):20-21.

4. "The Politics of Street Crime," *Crime and Social Justice* 5(Spring-Summer, 1976):1-4.

5. *San Francisco Chronicle* (February 20, 1978).

6. Michael Hindelang et al., *Sourcebook of Criminal Justice Statistics: 1974*. Washington, D.C.: U.S. Government Printing Office (1975):233.

7. Center for Research on Criminal Justice:14.

8. Jay Williams and Martin Gold, "From Delinquent Behavior to Official Delinquency," *Social Problems* 20,2 (Fall, 1972):209-29.

9. James Garofolo, *Public Opinion About Crime*. Washington, D.C.: U.S. Government Printing Office (1977):28.

10. "The Management of Police Killings," *Crime and Social Justice* 8 (Fall-Winter, 1977):34-43.

11. "The Management of Police Killings":42.

12. *U.S. News and World Report* (October 10, 1977).

13. *San Francisco Chronicle* (December 22, 1977).

14. Law Enforcement Assistance Administration, *Criminal Victimization in the United States: A Comparison of 1973 and 1974 Findings.* Washington, D.C.: U.S. Government Printing Office (1976).

15. *San Francisco Chronicle* (February 20, 1978.

16. Law Enforcement Assistance Administration, *Criminal Victimization in the United States: 1973.* Washington, D.C.: U.S. Government Printing Office (1976).

17. See note 16 above.

18. John E. Conklin, *The Impact of Crime.* New York: Macmillan (1975):26.

19. Law Enforcement Assistance Administration, *Criminal Victimization Surveys in the Nation's Five Largest Cities.* Washington, D.C.: U.S. Government Printing Office (1975).

20. LEAA, *Criminal Victimization in the U.S.; 1973.*

21. Frederick Engels, *The Condition of the Working Class in England.* Moscow: Progress Publishers (1973):168.

22. Yongsock Shin, Davor Jedlicka and Everett Lee, "Homicide Among Blacks," *Phylon* 38,4 (December, 1977):398-407

23. For data on the high homicide rate among Native Americans, see Charles Reasons, "Crime and the Native American," in Reasons and Kuykendall, eds., *Race, Crime and Justice.* Pacific Palisades, Ca.: Goodyear (1972):79-95; for data on alcohol-related deaths among blacks in Georgia, see George Lowe and Eugene Hodges, "Race and the Treatment of Alcoholism in a Southern State," *Social Problems* 20,2 (Fall, 1972):240-52; for a discussion of the high rates of rape, robbery and assault among blacks, albeit from a cultural and "racial" perspective, see Michael Hindelang, "Race and Involvement in Common Law Personal Crimes," *Amercian Sociological Review* 43,1 (February, 1978):93-109.

24. See, for example, Edward Green, "Race, Social Status, and Criminal Arrest," in Reasons and Kuykendall:103-23.

25. Karl Marx, *Capital*, Vol. I. New York: International Publishers (1975):632.

26. Marx:734.

27. Dario Melossi, "The Penal Question in *Capital*," *Crime and Social Justice* 5(Spring-Summer, 1976):26-33.

28. See, for example, Douglas Hay et al., *Albion's Fatal Tree: Crime and Society in Eighteenth-Century England*, New York: Pantheon (1975).

29. Engels: 168.

30. United Nations Social Defense Research Institute, *Economic Crises and Crime*, Rome: UNSDRI (1976).

31. Marx: 645.

32. LEAA, *Criminal Victimization in the U.S.: 1973.*

33. Williams and Gold: 209-29; Martin Gold and David Reimer, "Changing Patterns of Delinquent Behavior Among Americans 13 Through 16 Years Old: 1967-1972," *Crime and Delinquency Literature* 7,4 (December, 1975):483-517.

34. Williams and Gold: 215-18. These findings have been confirmed by Paul Takagi in a current (unpublished) study of delinquency among Chinese youth in San Francisco. For a methodological critique of the Gold studies, see Hindelang, "Race and Involvement in Common Law Personal Crimes": 103-04.

35. See, for example, David Harvey, *Social Justice and the City*. London: Johns Hopkins University Press (1973).

36. Herman Schwendinger and Julia Schwendinger, "Delinquency and the Collective Varieties of Youth," *Crime and Social Justice* 5(Spring-Summer, 1976):7-25.

37. Harry Braverman, *Labor and Monopoly Capital*. New York: Monthly Review Press (1974):271-83.

38. Engels:170-71.

39. Erick Hobsbawm, *Bandits*. New York: Delacorte (1969):13-23.

40. See, for example, Douglas Hay et al.

41. Engels:250-51.

42. Paul Hirst, "Marx and Engels on Law, Crime and Morality," in Taylor, Walton and Young, eds., *Critical Criminology*. London: Routledge and Kegan Paul (1975):203-32.

43. See note 42 above.

44. LEAA, *Criminal Victimization in the U.S.: 1973*.

Chapter 3

ENVIRONMENT

From the landing of the Mayflower in 1620 to the present, Americans have had an ambivalent relationship to nature. Respect for the primeval wilderness of the American continent has conflicted with the desire to utilize its natural resources. When utilization is accepted, there is conflict over the development of natural resources for private profit or on behalf of the nation as a whole. As settlements spread across the continent and demand for natural resources increased, these questions become national political issues. Disputes over the construction of the Hetch Hetchy Dam in Yosemite National Park to provide an improved water supply for the city of San Francisco or over the lease of tideland oil fields to oil companies for development provided particular contexts for the controversies about the underlying issues.

Although much of the land area of the United States has been developed for private profit, a considerable proportion is still publicly controlled. The federal government maintains wilderness areas to protect the natural environment and holds forest, oil, and mineral reserves in trust for the nation. In recent years, the critique of the destruction of the environment for the maximization of private profit coincided with the campaign to preserve the environment for its spiritual value, to produce the contemporary environmental movement. These perspectives on the environment and their counter arguments represent the present day conservative, liberal, and socialist positions on this issue. The principle of utilization of natural resources for private gain is at odds both with the preservation of the environment in its pristine form to allow citizens the experience of direct contact with nature and with the development of natural resources on behalf of the nation as a whole.

Conservatives believe that natural resources should be developed by private enterprise. The government should be limited to preserving wilderness areas for recreational enjoyment. Government regulations to protect the environment constitute an unwarranted interference with individual freedom. Moreover, excessive government regulation of the environment will harm the economy. It results in inflation due to the increased costs of anti-pollution equipment and even in the closing of plants that become too costly to operate in accordance with environmental standards. Individuals, not government, must take the responsibility for protecting the environment. Advertising Council posters admonish drivers not to litter the roadside and request consumers to return empty bottles to recycling centers. Conservatives argue that a balance must be maintained between the protection of the environment and the growth of the economy. Industrial corporations are willing to institute reasonable voluntary safeguards to protect the environment. Protection of the environment is basically a cost-benefit problem. The costs of protecting the environment must be weighed against economic losses. Excessive concern for the environment could endanger our nation's high standard of living.

Liberals agree with conservatives that natural resources should be privately developed, but they differ in arguing that development should be strictly supervised by government. Voluntary regulation, the conservative approach, is inadequate and subject to discard, when it comes into conflict with private profit considerations. An independent body acting on behalf of the public interest is required to limit the deleterious effects of industrial development and to protect public health and safety. The Environmental Protection Administration (EPA) was established by Congress in the early 1970s. The agency sets standards to reduce pollution from industrial wastes. For example, the EPA has established rules that limit the amount of sulfur dioxide that a coal burning power plant may release into the air. An electric utility is required to install anti-pollution devices that reduce the amount of sulfur dioxide emitted into the air to levels below the federal limits, or to turn to an alternative means of generating electricity.

Liberals believe that nature is entitled to some of the same legal protections that people enjoy under our Constitution and should be treated with much the same respect that is due humans. A variety of environmental organizations have been formed to achieve this goal. Groups such as Friends of the Earth and the Natural Resources Defense Fund engage in public education campaigns, congressional lobbying, and litigation in the courts. They exert pressure on the government to maintain and expand its environmental programs. At the same time environmental groups and their congressional allies must continually defend these programs from attack. Inflation, the energy crisis, and the costs of maintaining the regulatory agencies are the arguments used by conservatives to suspend environmental protection programs. Because of their acceptance of an industrial system and economic structure that pollutes the environment through the very nature of its production processes, liberal environmentalists are fated to a perpetual struggle over particular rules and regulations. Liberals believe that this struggle, within the framework of the existing political and economic system, is the only realistic and feasible way to achieve their goals.

Socialists believe in the public ownership of natural resources. The earth's resources should not be the property of any individual or small group. Presently, many of our country's natural resources are controlled by concentrated corporate power. Oil, mining, and logging corporations develop natural resources in ways that extract the maximum profit and pay minimum attention to safeguarding the environment. As long as natural resources are allowed to be owned as private property, short-term interests in their development and transformation into capital will predominate over long-term social and environmental needs. Liberal regulatory measures, which fall short of public control, will inevitably be eroded as the result of the political influence generated by resource owners to protect and enhance their investments. Only by removing private profit as an influence can a just balance be established between utilizing the natural environment for the benefit of mankind and preserving its integrity.

In the liberal article, Barry Commoner describes the destructive effects that a variety of modern technologies have on the environment. He argues that the effects of technologies on the environment should be carefully considered before they are introduced into use. Commoner looks to a political alliance between concerned scientists and citizens to redress the imbalance between technology and the environment. This political movement would pressure Congress to institute ecologically sound standards for the introduction of new technologies and the elimination of existing technologies that have dangerous consequences.

In the conservative article, Passell and Ross agree with Commoner that many industrial technologies are harmful to the environment. They are concerned, however, that an overenthusiastic environmental movement, fearful of the ill effects of technology, will institute measures that will hurt the economy. Passell and Ross argue that a shift in economic incentives, perhaps through a change in tax policy, will be sufficient to encourage industry to give up its worst polluting technologies without a political conflict. By the profit motive, industry can be encouraged to invest in relatively non-polluting technology. Economic growth can be reconciled with environmental protection if environmentalists will modify their goals to accept a reasonable level of pollution.

In the socialist article, Molotch shows how environmental degradation is connected to the structure of the capitalist economy. When an aroused citizenry with access to political power wishes to change public policy to eliminate offshore oil drilling and its inevitable spills they are frustrated by corporate power acting to protect its interests. Environmental degradation is produced by corporations acting according to the logic of a capitalist economy. The former problem cannot be solved unless the latter is also addressed.

Conservative

Peter Passell and Leonard Ross: Effluence and Affluence; or, Growth is Not a Dirty Word

If the ecology enthusiasts have often been comically trendy, the movement is also deadly serious, and perhaps the most important and hopeful variety of reformist politics left in this country. By the late 1960's the progressive degradation of the environment had been ignored—or exacerbated—by government agencies for decades. Palliatives had often made things worse. Federal subsidies paid for hundreds of local treatment plants to cut the flow of raw sewage into our waterways; but the rivers did not become much cleaner, and the treated waste itself created a new pollution hazard by fertilizing microscopic water-plant life. Pittsburgh reduced its industrial air pollution with tough regulation of smokestack emissions, but permitted new pollution hazards to arise by virtually abandoning mass transit. Eventually, this record of social neglect and mishap drove conservationists, the young, and even the doyens of the Establishment to despair. As Aurelio Peccei, a Fiat executive, put it, "We have entirely lost the capacity for guiding the complexities of society: one can see signs everywhere."

To many liberals, this history was sobering but gave no cause for fatalism. The chances for environmental protection have always been compromised by confused planning and halfhearted financial commitments. Now that the electorate was aroused, work could begin in earnest. Surely, went the weary but plausible argument, the nation that sent a submarine under the polar icecap and a man to the moon could save Lake Erie.

A growing and well publicized group of environmentalists challenges this common-sense assertion. They predict that a modest shuffling of priorities, a few billion dollars reassigned to antipollution or mass-transit programs, will have little effect. The harsh realities of scarcity, they argue, make it imperative that we stop environmental problems at their source, that we slow the gluttonous engine of economic growth.

Technology, one hears, may work fine in outer space, but it offers scant hope of redeeming the sins we have committed against our own biosphere. Indeed, these scientists point out, technology has inadvertently magnified pollution while increasing economic output: deadly mercury-waste production has jumped dramatically since World War II, mostly as a consequence of the demand for chlorine. Synthetic pesticides, so effective in raising crop yields, threaten to reach man in toxic doses. The substitution of tough plastic packaging, impervious to chemical breakdown, for frailer cardboard means that litter remains intact where it falls.

Could we, without reliance on this defiling technology, grow nonetheless? Again, the new view is pessimistic. Growth, the environmentalists say, is drastically limited by the availability of resources. Man's appetite for depletable minerals is increasing so rapidly that most reserves could be exhausted within a few centuries. Fossil fuels—the coal, oil, and natural gas that provide virtually all of our energy—are being used up a thousand times faster than nature creates them. World supplies of crucial metals such as tungsten, zinc, nickel, aluminum, and lead are far from infinite; projected industrial demand can be accommodated from known reserves for less than one hundred years.

Even before we run out of raw materials, or poison ourselves with alien technology, casual abuse of the environment, trivial violations, may well trigger rapid natural changes that will threaten the existence of man. To assume off-handedly, then, that economic growth can go on forever is suicidal.

Behind the strong language are some reasoned, scientific arguments. Ecologists tell us that the biological accident which created and continues to sustain man is only thinly defended against diaster. Carbon, oxygen, and nitrogen, critical to life, are shuttled between earth, air, and living organisms through delicate ecological chains. Almost any economic activity disrupts these chains— the bigger its scale and the more modern the organization of work, the more disruptive it is. Coal is burned, increasing the carbon dioxide and smoke in the air. Insects are exterminated with pesticides, cutting off a food source for numerous higher life forms. Natural vegetation is cleared for farming, reducing the amount of oxygen released into the air, increasing the rate of moisture loss from the soil, and modifying the capacity of the land to resist erosion. Underground rivers are tapped for irrigation, lowering the water table. The consequences of these disruptions are rarely understood before major enviromental changes are under way. Ecological chains are complex and interwoven and we have only primitive knowledge of the effect of severing a link or two.

As a vision of future economic growth all this is grim. We seem trapped in a pattern of rapidly increasing pollution and rapidly decreasing resource reserves, with ecological disaster a constant likelihood. If history is adequate evidence on which to judge the future, the technology that has permitted us economic miracles will sabotage all efforts to break out of the circle. Anthony Lewis probably speaks for most environmentalists when he writes, "The essential is to stop economic growth." But in prescribing as the remedy an end to growth, the doomsday environmentalists have made an error not so different from those who would ignore the implications of ecology itself: the past is an uncertain measure of the future. Because growth has been associated with the rape of the biosphere for the last few centuries does not mean that we are powerless to sever the association.

Pollution is not logically inherent in economic growth, nor has the linkage always been so immediate as it has lately appeared. Consider the ambiance of the 18th or 19th-century city—blanketed by soot, layered with the excrement of horses and never far from that of men—and it becomes apparent that some kinds of pollution have *diminished* with affluence. If in many cities we have merely gotten the problem out of the chamberpots and into the waterways, that nonetheless might pass for progress.

To be sure, no such facile excuse can mitigate the pollution boom set off after World War II. Barry Commoner has argued that crucial industries—chemicals, fuels, fibers—have adopted new technologies whose effluent is more voluminous and more toxic than anything that went before. Conservationists less careful than Commoner have generalized this experience into a simple law: as Garrett Hardin puts it, Pollution = Population X Prosperity.

But the very fact that the postwar economy produced new pollutants through the application of novel technology suggests that Hardin's law is far from exact. Commoner says that most forms of pollution have increased from two to twenty times from 1946 to 1966—far exceeding the rate of economic advance. Clearly, then, economic growth does not generate a proportional increase in sludge. The increase may be far greater than proportional, as it has been, or considerably less, as it could be if we take corrective measures.

Pollution comes not simply from prosperity but also from a system of incentives which encourages dirt-producing technologies. Change the incentives, and something is accomplished against pollution. In essence, that is the economists' rebuttal to the zero growth argument. Our most grievous environmental sin is not that we consume too many things, but that we produce them in the wrong way. Air and water have been free goods for manufacturers; nobody has made industry pay for turning the biosphere into a giant garbage can.

"The Name of the Game: Profit-Ability" was the slogan in 1970 of Union Camp, a company whose paper-bag plant helps make the Savannah River one of the foulest sewers in the nation. Answering a charge by Nader's Raiders that his firm was dangerously depleting ground-water supplies, the executive vice president of the company stated: "I had my lawyers in Virginia research that, and they told us that we could suck the state of Virginia out through a hole in the ground, and there was nothing anyone could do about it." Union Camp's director of air and water protection noted for the benefit of *The New York Times* that "it probably won't hurt mankind a whole hell of a lot in the long run if the whooping crane doesn't quite make it."

Union Camp's executives may have been unusual in their public-be-fouled magniloquence, but surely not in their motive. Governor George Wallace remarked, apropos a Union Camp paper mill whose smoke reached twenty miles to Montgomery, "Yeah, that's the smell of money. She does smell sweet, don't it." Money talks, even deodorizes, and it has persuaded legislatures to slant the law in favor of polluters and against whooping cranes, asthma sufferers, and people in general. And since polluters do not have to pay for the damage they do, they go on polluting.

The profit motive for pollution, present throughout our history, seems recently to have intensified. As Commoner observes, "The new, more polluting technologies seem to yield higher profits than the older, less polluting technologies they have displaced." "The very system of enhancing profit in this industry," he concludes, "is precisely the cause of its intense, detrimental impact on the environment." The task, then, is to break the bond between profits and pollution, and strategies far short of zero growth will do the job. Strict, detailed government regulations can simply order polluters to sweep up their wastes, profits notwithstanding. New taxes on discharges can force firms to pay the social cost of the damage they do: the price of producing the Sunday *New York Times*, for example, would include a charge for cleaning up after the mill that makes its newsprint, and another fee for carting away the paper on Monday morning. Government subsidies for pollution abatement could, on the other hand, persuade firms to do research they would otherwise find unprofitable.

We do not face an either-or choice between affluence and cleanliness, but a particularized choice among less dramatic alternatives. Which method of control is most likely to survive the political hazards? Which reduces pollution at the least cost in human labor and materials? Which minimizes the dislocation that would follow if we abandon rules which favor dumping?

So far, these have not been the questions most environmentalists have asked (Commoner being a rare and outstanding exception). The environmentalists' most publicized strategy of self-denial:

> . . . if you told the suburbanite that the way his house was built, the elimination of food producing land that it caused, his long-distance drive to work, his work in the military-industrial-governmental structure, his use of power gadgets, his wife's consumption of clothing, his family's consumption of prepackaged synthetic goods, the daily pouring of thousands of food calories into the "garbage" disposal under his kitchen sink, and the birth of this third child are making the world unlivable, he wouldn't believe you. Get him to believe you.

So advises *The Environmental Handbook*, the official program guide for *Earth Day* in 1970. Dirck van Sickle's handbook on "Good Earthkeeping in America" adds some practical advice: "If you go to market by car, don't use all that polluting horsepower just to haul yourself—take a friend. Don't shop together, however; going through the aisles encourages impulse buying." "Buy 'day-old' bread at the bakery, freeze and thaw it—it will taste fresh." Abstinence, once seen as the answer to the baby glut, has now been generalized to the entire spectrum of bodily pleasures and minor self-indulgences. Instead of throwing out that Coke bottle we are urged to tote it to the community recycling center; instead of eating what we please—or what we think healthy—we are told to mind each loaf's effect on the biosphere.

Eco-scrupulosity is good propaganda. But as a strategy for directly curbing pollution, it has obvious limitations. Concerted self-inconveniencing by tens of millions of consumers would be necessary to make even a marginal impact on pollution. Air pollution in this country will be solved when the government gets the gumption to enforce some tough laws, not when every shopper makes sure to take along a friend.

In addition to encouraging consumer self-restraint, the aim of much ecological propaganda is of course to change the consciousness of businessmen. To a degree, this aim has been achieved. Not even an automobile executive would today echo the *chutzpah* of the classic letter from the Ford Motor Company in 1953 to a Los Angeles County Supervisor, quoted by Nader's air-pollution team: "The Ford engineering staff, although mindful that automobile engines produce gases, feels that these waste vapors are dissipated in the atmosphere quickly and do not present an air-pollution problem. Therefore our research department has not conducted any experimental work aimed at totally eliminating these gases." But what the auto companies have done since then (at least according to a Justice Department civil antitrust suit that the Nixon Administration conveniently settled out of court) was to agree among themselves mutually to delay the introduction of pollution-control equipment. Meanwhile, they, like the oil companies, paper manufacturers, and other new-found friends of the environment, have been furiously advertising their conversion to earth-worship.

Now that the public considers it immoral, no doubt businesses do pollute less than they did when governors rhapsodized about smoke's smell of money. But this margin of difference isn't what will save the dying ocelot or enhance the average life span. Real social progress in this country—on those occasions when it has not simply come from economic growth—has required legislation. Pollution is a federal case. Saying that, however, does not resolve the matter. There are better and worse ways to legislate the cleanup.

An appealing, simple answer is to ban pollution altogether. A Nader water-pollution report calls for "instituting a 'no dumping' policy everywhere." Recent water-pollution legislation passed by Congress (and currently hung up by the Nixon Administration's austerity drive) sets a "national goal" of zero discharge of industrial wastes by 1985. That remedy is certainly tidy. But it is also grossly and pointlessly expensive. Removing 100 percent of industrial discharges is estimated to be three times as costly as removing 97 percent and often serves no real purpose. Streams have a natural capacity to assimilate limited amounts of certain wastes; the fact that we have been scandalously abusing that capacity is no argument for ignoring it altogether. Moreover, even if industrial discharges were halted altogether, run-offs of fertilizer (both chemical and natural) and sewage spill-over from city storm drains would continue to pollute rivers. These too could be reduced, but by nothing approaching the 100 percent target for industrial wastes. As the Harvard economist Marc Roberts has argued, "The only shortcomings [of the no-dumping proposal] are that it is impossible, and if it were possible, it would be preposterously wasteful." For water pollution in general, the Council of Economic Advisers has estimated that it would cost $60 billion to remove 87 percent of the effluent; $58 billion extra for an additional 10 percent; and $200 billion on top of that for the remaining three percentage points.

Whatever we do, some waterways some of the time will not be pure enough to wash a surgeon's hands. But there is no reason why they should be. For both health and recreational reasons, we need rivers and lakes that are vastly purer than at present. But at some point, as Roberts says, "even the fish won't notice the difference." There is no reason to make cleanliness an absolute value, taking precedence over all other ways of using all that money.

A related if less extreme strategy is at the core of proposals favored by both Republicans and Democrats in Congress. This notion is to require every pollution source to make an across-the-board percentage cut in emissions. To reduce over-all pollution by 85 percent, you require each plant to cut its own contribution by 85 percent—regardless of where the plant is located or how much the abatement would cost. Again, the strategy seems straightforward; but it is administratively complicated and needlessly expensive. Plants and industries incur widely varying costs for pollution control. Some could eliminate close to 100 percent of their pollutants at minimal cost; for others, even a modest cleanup is hugely expensive. A far more efficient way to achieve the desired reduction in total pollution would be to cut back emissions at those plants where the cutting is easiest. The cost differences between the two approaches are substantial, on the order of 100 percent. A 1969 study by Robert N. Grosse estimated that a "typical city" of 2 million persons, attempting to reduce human exposure to sulfur dioxides and particulates in smog would have to spend $1.26 billion using the proportional approach, compared to $769 million using a least-cost strategy. A Delaware estuary study showed that "a dissolved oxygen level of at least three parts per million [dissolved oxygen is a commonly used index of water quality] would cost about twice as much with uniform treatment as a least-cost solution."

The lesson is not to make do with the pollution we have, but to pay some attention to costs in choosing a strategy of abatement and in deciding which pollutants must be almost completely eliminated and which allow of more modest aims. In the case of health hazards, such as sulfur oxides and particulates, something very close to 100-percent elimination in populated areas makes good sense. But other forms of pollution involve inconvenience, not death or disaster. Saying that there is no acceptable level of pollution is like saying that there is no acceptable level of auto accidents—a fine proposition but not one commensurate with a reasonable expenditure of what, even in our affluent society, are limited resources. We are more likely simply to substitute the unlimited dumping of money for the unlimited dumping of wastes.

The record of federal water-pollution programs offers blunt confirmation of this danger. In 1956, Congress authorized federal grants to states for construction of municipal waste-treatment facilities. After thirteen years and $1.272 billion of federal donations, the General Accounting Office found that the program had "no appreciable effect on reducing pollution, improving water quality, or enhancing the use of the waterways." The municipal treatment plants, where they existed, would clean up industrial wastes free. So businesses kept on polluting, since it didn't cost them anything. Their volume of *dreck* exceeded anything the municipal plants could take out.

Another form of federal subsidy, tax incentives for firms to buy pollution-control equipment with, was enthusiastically adopted by Congress in 1969. But this kind of tax "kicker" makes its own choice among methods for reducing waste. In many industries it would be cheaper to alter the basic processes or technology to produce less effluent in the first place. The tax law merely encourages firms to generate muck and then make it pure—a precise contemporary equivalent of digging holes and filling them up again.

Through wasteful subsidies for treatment plants and casual tax giveaways, the Treasury rather than the biosphere has been taken to the cleaners. All this might be forgiven if the expense fell on those who reap the largest benefits from clean water, and who can afford it best. But for the most part it is the rich who go sailing while the poor pay sales taxes. As Marc Roberts writes:

> Studies of outdoor recreation repeatedly show higher percentages of use by those in higher income groups. Indeed, the streams and rivers that flow through downtown areas, and are accessible to the urban poor by public transportation, will often be the last waterways to be cleaned up—if they are ever made usable. Such rivers are usually the most polluted by industrial output, shipping, commercial, and domestic wastes and the storm run-offs from urban streets.

In the usual conservationist argument, little is said about income distribution—it seems to be a touchy subject. Even the otherwise thorough 1971 Report of the President's Council on Environmental Quality barely grazes the question. The poor, the Council notes, have much to gain from cleaner air. Nothing is said about what the poor gain from pristine lakes which they cannot afford to visit, or how much they lose from higher regressive taxes and product prices. It is probably optimistic to expect society's decision for cleaner surroundings to be accompanied by income redistribution—or improved access—for the urban poor. But one can at least demand a decent watch on costs, since they will fall so heavily on those who least deserve them.

For many kinds of pollution, the technology of abatement is already well developed—all that's needed is a change in incentives. Jackhammer noise, for example, could be reduced 99 percent by the use of a quiet compressor, which adds only about 10 or 15 percent in cost. Builders today see no reason to shell out their own money to protect other people's ears, but a noise tax could change their minds. The price of a livable environment by this reasoning is not an end to growth, but an end to freeloading. We can, say the economists, afford to eat our cake and pick up the wrapper too.

A couple of reservations must be added to the argument for pollution taxes. Taxes on water pollution give industries the right incentive to choose less effluent-prone technologies, but they encourage efforts at water purification by each firm singly. Often, it would be far more economical to treat wastes at a common plant. For this reason, Roberts and others have proposed the creation of regional river-basin authorities. Authorities would be told to clean up their rivers and pay for it with a service charge on polluters. Since businesses would have to pay a fee for dumping, they would dump a lot less. Their fees would be used to clean up the remainder as efficiently as possible.

The electric-power crisis illustrates both the uses and the limitations of pollution taxes. Today, there is a direct conflict between clean air and electric power. Con Ed's coal-burning and oil-burning power stations generate 40 percent of the chemical pollutants and 10 percent of the smoke in New York City. The proposed expansion of the region's power capacity would be made at additional cost to the environment: more fossil-fuel facilities would increase air pollution, while nuclear plants would create thermal pollution and raise unresolved issues of safety. Recognizing the dangers, environmental groups have rallied to block further construction. The result: annual summer power shortages with no relief in sight.

Economists claim that the dilemma is artificial; the root of the problem is the gap between the price consumers pay for electricity and its actual social cost. As Redi-Kilowatt used to inform us, "Electricity is the biggest bargain in your family budget"; but the monthly power bill never included the cost to emphysema suffers in Queens.

This gap between price and cost reduces the consumers' incentives to make reasonable economies in daily use. If rates were, say, double what they are now, many of us would shut off the lights and turn down the air conditioner. Bargain rates also encourage the choice of electricity over more ecologically benign sources of power. Large users are actually charged less per kilowatt-hour. Yet the use of electric heating and cooling at least doubles the amount of sulfur-dioxide emissions.

Until recently, nobody was much intersted in designing methods to cut smokestack sulfur emissions or to remove sulfur from fuels before they were burned. Now, after much public insistence, the Nixon Administration has proposed a sulfur-dioxide emission charge and a tax on leaded gasoline. But again, taxes alone may not be sufficient to motivate business to use the cheapest antipollution technology. Research funds are needed to fuel promising new approaches to abatement in more speculative areas. For example, it may be feasible to convert fossil fuel directly into electricity without the intermediate step of generating steam to run turbines. To do so would dramatically reduce the amount of damage that each kilowatt does to the environment. One direct conversion method, the fuel cell, has already provided utility power for manned space flights. But we will not know if large direct-conversion power plants are practical until someone—probably the federal government—spends the money to find out.

Electricity could, of course, be produced in huge generating stations at isolated sites and transported thousands of miles to where it's used. (The idea is not new: the Soviets have committed vast resources to long-distance, high-tension power transmission, because they believe it is cheaper.) While this approach does not reduce pollution, it would confine its worst effects to places where few people live.

In sum, there is not a stark choice between escalating filth or a stagnating economy. Modest expenditures on pollution control can yield enormous improvements. (London, for example, has cut smoke emissions by 80 percent over the past fifteen years; since the introduction of well planned sewage treatment, fish have reappeared in the Thames. The cost of the cleanup of London air has been about 36 cents per year for each Greater London resident.) If the task of cleaning up is organized efficiently, the costs of purer air and water will be bearable—certainly less than one-tenth of the Gross National Product, the amount added by two good years of growth. Stopping growth would be a sane way to protect the environment only if society did not have the nerve to do the job directly. But people too timid to demand smokestack precipitators are unlikely to shut down factories.

Liberal

Barry Commoner: Nature Under Attack

The proliferation of human beings on the surface of this planet is proof of the remarkable suitability of the terrestrial environment as a place for human life. But the fitness of the environment is not an immutable feature of the earth, having been developed by gradual changes in the nature of the planet's skin. Living things have themselves been crucial agents of these transformations, converting the earth's early rocks into soil, releasing oxygen from its water, transforming carbon dioxide into accumulated fossil fuels, modulating temperature and tempering the rush of waters on the land. And in the course of these transformations, the living things that populated the surface of the earth have, with the beautiful precision that is a mark of life, themselves become closely adapted to the environment they have helped to create. As a result, the environment in which we live is itself part of a vast web of life, and like everything associated with life is internally complex, and stable, not in a static sense, but by virtue of the intricate play of internal interactions.

On a small scale, the dependence of environmental stability on the nice balance of multiple biological processes is self-evident. A hillside denuded of vegetation by fire and thus lacking protection against the erosion of heavy rains previously afforded by the canopy of leaves and the mat of roots can quickly shed its soil and lose its capability to support plants and harbor animals. And on this scale, the threat of thoughtless human interventions is equally self-evident; we have long since learned that brutal lumbering or greedy exploitation of the soil can permanently alter the life-supporting properties of a forest or a once-fertile plain. On this scale, too, we know, from the wastelands that surround our smelters, or from the disappearance of shellfish in a polluted estuary, that human ingenuity is rapidly creating new and more devastating hazards to the stability of the environment. We also know of numerous specific risks to particular living components of the biosphere—that DDT threatens to wipe out the birds of prey; that industrial wastes kill off a river's game fish; that sewage renders a beach unusable.

Such small-scale and specific assaults on the living environment illuminate the basic principles that govern the impact of human intrusions on the environment: (1) Because of the complex network of interactions in the environment an intrusion in one place may exert its main effect in a distant locale. Massive nuclear weapons have often been exploded on isolated Pacific Islands. But, because of the peculiarities of the lichen-caribou-man food chain on which they depend, it has been the Eskimos and Lapps living in the Artic Circle that are most seriously affected by worldwide fallout generated by these blasts. (2) Food chains and nutritive metabolism constitute a kind of biological amplifier which can enormously intensify an originally weak intrusion on the environment. Thus, DDT sprayed at a low concentration accumulates in plankton, is further concentrated in the fish that feed on plankton, ultimately reaching a peak concentration in the birds that prey on fish. In this way DDT becomes several-hundred-fold concentrated in the osprey and the eagle, which fall accidental prey to our war on insects. (3) Like any other system comprised of complex feedback cycles, an ecosystem tends to oscillate (witness the well-known interacting cycles of wolf and rabbit populations). And like other oscilating processes, an ecosystem can be driven into self-accelerating changes, and to ultimate collapse, by over-stressing at a particularly vulnerable point. Thus over-fertilization of surface waters can so accelerate the growth of algae as to deplete the oxygen content (in the dark hours)so that the algae themselves die and pollute the water. These principles tell us what is required for the stability of the environment in which we live and for its continued suitability as a place for human life. The system must accomodate itself to the stresses placed upon it in such a way as to maintain the internal processes which account for its stability.

How has the living environment been faring under these stresses? Where has the system managed to accommodate itself and achieve a new, if different, but stable balanced state? What stresses are still in the process of altering the environmental system, and what is the forecast of a new stable equilibrium? Are the changes accelerating? Is there a danger of stressing the system as a whole to the point of collapse?

The most direct human contact with the environment is mediated by the air, for a massive amount of this substance is continuously brought into intimate contact with internal metabolism through the lungs. Natural air contains only oxygen, nitrogen, water vapor, carbon dioxide, rare gases, some volatile biological products, and occasional dust. But the air that most of us breathe, especially in the cities, now contains as well: increasing amounts of oxides of nitrogen and sulfur, various kinds of dust and soot, particles of rubber and asbestos, carbon monoxide, and a wide array of poorly identified organic compounds.

Ten years ago automotive smog was a problem found almost entirely in Los Angeles, and sulfur dioxide hazards were apparent only in isolated industrial regions such as Donora, Pennsylvania. Now, New York City experiences acute episodes involving both automotive smog and sulfur dioxide. I know from personal observations that the incidence and extent of smog pollution in St. Louis has increased sharply in the last 20 years. Denver, once famed for its clear mountain air, is now subject to smog. Clearly this stress on the environment is worsening.

And while the general level of air pollution is rising there is reason to believe that the incidence of disease associated with it will rise more rapidly than the pollutant concentrations themselves. Consider, for example, the problem of lung cancer arising from chemicals such as benzopyrene which are found in the polluted city air. Air-borne organic carcinogens such as benzopyrene are capable of inducing lung cancer because of their influence on cells that line the air passages of the lungs. Laboratory studies show that the degree of the carcinogenic hazard rises with the concentration of carcinogen to which the cells are exposed and with the duration of contact between the carcinogen and the susceptible cells. There are protective mechanisms in the lung that tend to limit exposure to materials drawn in from the air, and any additional air pollutant that inhibits these mechanisms will influence the effect of a given concentration of the air-borne carcinogen. For example, sulfur dioxide tends to paralyze the ciliated cells of the lung air passages and thereby cut down the self-protective cleansing process in the lung. For this reason sulfur dioxide will extend the time of contact between a carcinogen such as benzopyrene and the lung. In this situation the risk of carcinogenesis must be measured by the *product:* benzopyrene concentration multiplied by sulfur dioxide concentration. If the concentrations of both pollutants double, we must expect that the risk of carcinogenesis may rise by as much as a factor of four.

Unfortunately, we do not yet have sufficient public health data to generalize about the quantitative relations between the level of air pollution and the medical effects associated with it. However, in the relatively sparse data available there is already some evidence that the health effects associated with pollution may be rising faster than the over-all level of pollution itself. Thus, although the concentration of organic air pollutants (a class that includes carcinogens such as benzopyrene) increases more or less proportionally with city size, the incidence of cancer in cities of different sizes seems to rise with city size not linearly but exponentially. Obviously there are other factors involved in this problem, but the present information should certainly warn us that the health effects from air pollution may worsen faster than the pollution level itself—a result expected from the multiplicative effects of air pollutants.

The dependence of human society on large supplies of fresh water is deep and pervasive. In addition to its direct biological necessity to man, water is essential in vast amount for almost every industrial process. In natural lakes and rivers, animal organic wastes are degraded by the action of bacteria of decay which convert them into inorganic substances: carbon dioxide, nitrates, and phosphates. In turn these substances nourish plants, which provide food for the animals. In sunlight, plants also add to the oxygen content of the water and so support animals and the bacteria of decay. All this makes up a tightly woven cycle of mutually dependent events, which in nature maintains the clarity and purity of the water and sustains its population of animals, plants, and micro-organisms.

We use this natural self-purifying system to control urban wastes. Sewage treatment plants add considerable amounts of organic substances to the lakes and rivers that receive their outflow, although the increment is reduced by the treat-ment. If all goes well the biological cycle assimilates the added organic materials, and, maintaining its balance, keeps the water pure. But such a complex cyclical system, with its important feedback loops, cannot indefinitely remain balanced in the face of a steadily increasing organic load. Sufficiently stressed it becomes vulnerable at certain critical points. For example, the bacteria that act on organic wastes must have oxygen, which is consumed as the waste is destroyed. If the waste load becomes too high, the oxygen content of the water falls to zero, the bacteria die, the biological cycle breaks down, the purification process collapses, and the water becomes foul.

The water pollution problem has become urgent chiefly because we are allowing the organic content of surface waters to approach the breaking point. The first large-scale warning is the death of Lake Erie, where, as a result of the rapid accumulation of waste, most of the central portion of the lake has gone to zero oxygen. The lake's life-cycle has been forced out of balance and what was, for tens of thousands of years, a beautifully clear and productive inland sea in a decade has become a rank, muddy sink.

Even universal use of present waste disposal technology will not get us out of trouble, for the treatment systems themselves elevate the nitrate and phosphate content of the receiving waters. These substances are always present in natural waters—but in amounts far less than those generated by the huge waste load imposed on them by man. And at such abnormally high levels, nitrate and phosphate become a new hazard to the biological balance. These concentrated nutrients may induce a hughe growth of algae—an algae "bloom." Such an enormously dense population tends to die off with equal suddenness, again overloading the water with organic debris, and disrupting the natural cycle. And nitrate, if sufficiently concentrated, may be toxic to man. About 8-9 parts per million of nitrate in an infant's drinking water may interfere with hemoglobin function; in a number of areas of the United States, water supplies have reached nitrate levels of 3 parts per million. In some places, physicians have been forced to replace tap water in infant diets.

In 1900 the total amount of nitrogen discharged to U.S. streams by municipal sewage was about 200 million pounds per year. Rising since then at an accelerat-ing rate, the amount reached 1200 million pounds per year in 1963 and is expected to reach about 2000 million pounds per year by 2000. From 1900 to 1940 phosphate discharged into U. S. streams by municipal sewage rose from about 10 million pounds (as phosphorus) per year to about 30 million pounds per year. But, thereafter, the rate of increase accelerated so rapidly that in 1963 the annual phosphorus burden was 250 million pounds and is expected to double again by 2000. The total oxygen demand on surface waters for degradation of organic materials in municipal sewage more than doubled between 1900 and 1960. The increase has been held in check by the production of new sewage treatment plants, but these plants do not, of course, reduce the burden of inorganic residues, such as nitrate, imposed on surface water.

Clearly our aqueous environment is being subjected to an accelerating stress, which will become so severe in the next few decades as to threaten to collapse the self-purifying biological system on which we rely for usable water.

Finally we can look at the status of the nation's soil. The soil is, of course, the basis for the initial production of nearly all of our food resources, and many industrial raw materials as well. The soil is a vastly complex ecosystem, its fundamental capabilities for supporting plant life being the resultant of an intricate balance among a wide variety of micro-organisms, animals, and plants, acting on a long-established physical substrate.

The complicated biology of the soil ties the fate of the city and industrial plant to the farm. Crop plants convert nitrates and other plant nutrients to protein. In nature, let us say a plant growing in a wood or meadow, nitrate reaches the soil chiefly as the product of bacterial decay of organic wastes—manure and the bodies of animals and plants. The natural concentration of nitrate in the soil water is very low and the roots need to work to pull it into the plant. For this work the plant must expend energy which is released by biological oxidation processes in the roots. These processes require oxygen, which can reach the roots only if the soil is sufficiently porous. Soil porosity is governed by its physical structure; in particular a high level of organic nitrogen, in the form of humus, is required to maintain a porous soil structure. Thus, soil porosity, therefore its oxygen content, and hence the efficiency of nutrient absorption, is closely related to the organic nitrogen content of the soil.

When the United States was settled, the soil system was in this natural condition, the soil cycle was in balance maintaining its nitrogen reserve in the stable organic form. Only small amounts of inorganic salts drained off into the rivers which remained clear and unburdened with pollutants. As the continent was settled, the natural soil system was taken over for agricultural purposes. Plants were grown on the soil in amounts much greater than they would sustain in nature. The organic store of nutrients was gradually depleted and crop yields declined year by year. With virgin lands always available, farmers moved westward, repeating the process of skimming from the soil the most available nutrient and leaving it when its productivity fell below a certain point, which made westward migration more attractive. This process, of course, came to an end about 1900 and from then on as crop production became intensified to meet the demands of a growing population, more and more of the original store of organic nutrients was withdrawn from the soil in the form of crops. In the Midwest the organic content of soil has declined about 50 per cent in the last 100 years. As a result, the productivity of the soil has declined.

For a time nutrients were returned to the soil by use of animal manures and imported fertilizers, especially guano. With the growth of the chemical industry it became possible to produce much cheaper inorganic nutrients as fertilizer. The heavy use of inorganic fertilizer began especially in the cotton and tobacco land of the South. Here, because of high climatic temperatures, which stimulate the breakdown of the organic stores of the soil, the soil was particularly impoverished and spectacular gains in yields could be obtained from inorganic fertilizers. In the 1940s there began a striking increase all over the nation in the use of inorganic fertilizers. The use of inorganic nitrogen fertilizer has increased about sevenfold in the last 25 years.

The result has been a massive stress of the soil ecosystem by the addition to it of huge and increasing quantities of nitrogen, phosphorus, potassium, and other plant nutrients. During heavy rains there is a natural tendency for the added inorganic fertilizer to wash out of the soil into rivers, especially in the case of nitrates. The available data show that under most field conditions an appreciable part of the added nitrogen fertilizer fails to enter the crop and instead leaves the soil in one of two forms. Part of this lost nitrogen, probably of the order of from 10 to 25 per cent of the total fertilizer placed on the soil, drains out of the soil into rivers and lakes, the amount varying greatly with local soil conditions. Another part of the added nitrogen (perhaps 5 to 10 per cent) leaves the soil because the excess nitrate and low soil oxygen content tend to stimulate bacterial formation of volatile forms of nitrogen (nitrogen oxides and ammonia). This volatilized nitrogen is caught up in rain and is washed down again to the ground, and eventually into rivers and lakes where it adds to the inorganic nitrogen already present. Investigators have been continually surprised of late to find large amounts of nitrogen in rainfall. For example, studies in Wisconsin show that rainfall now often contains as much as one part per million of nitrogen. In contrast earlier studies showed nitrogen content of rain to be of the order of .2 of one part per million.

The seriousness of the agricultural contribution to water pollution is evident from the following data: In 1964 municipal sewage in the United States contributed a total of about 1200 million pounds of nitrogen to surface waters, ultimately in the form of nitrate. In that same year agriculture added about 8000 million pounds of nitrogen to the soil in the form of inorganic fertilizers. If only 15 per cent of this fertilizer leached out of the soil into surface waters—a percentage often observed in field experiments—the amount of nitrogen imposed on surface waters would be equivalent to the amount originating in municipal sewage. And, it should be added, there is no sign that the increasing use of inorganic fertilizer will slacken in the next decade.

Thus, universal use of secondary treatment methods for urban sewage, and corresponding control of industrial organic wastes, will nevertheless burden surface waters with large amounts of the inorganic residues of treatment, especially nitrate. At the same time, nitrate leaching from fertilized farmland will probably double this burden, leading to massive overgrowths of algae which, on their death, cause a new cycle of organic pollution. By means of advanced treatment methods, it would be possible to remove inorganic nutrients from the effluent of municipal and industrial waste systems, but a corresponding control of nutrients from farmland runoff would require treatment of the total mass of surface—a forbidding task. We might undertake a huge program of controlling sewage and industrial waste only to find that rivers and lakes were dying from overfeeding by farmland fertilizer runoff.

In large part, agricultural production has increased in the United States in order to sustain the increasing population in this country and elsewhere and also to support a rising U. S. per capita consumption. In order to accomplish this increased food production we have massively stressed the nitrogen cycle in the soil by the introduction of inorganic fertilizer and this process, in turn, may stress to the breaking point the self-purifying aqueous systems upon which we depend for our urban waste disposal. This process may well turn out to be the most immediate mechanism whereby increasing population exerts a negative feedback on the quality of the environmental system sustaining it.

We have only begun to perceive the vast economic, social, and political conflicts that are being generated by the crisis in the environment. The nation is already in the throes of a tangled struggle with the problem of urban air pollution. This involves pervasive issues in transportation, power production, and basic urban design, which add enormously to the complex situation in the ecosystem itself. If coal-burning power plants contaminate the air with sulfur dioxide, shall we replace them with apparently "clean" nuclear reactors —and run the risks of radioactive contamination from waste-handling and the small but catastrophic risks of an accident in a highly populated area? If, in order to cure the smog problem we need to replace gasoline-burning vehicles with electric ones, how can the power industry and the petroleum industry accommodate this massive change?

Subtle, but vital, interactions operate in this area. For example, the New York City power industry is preparing to build a proposed water-storage generating plant on the Hudson River at Storm King Mountain in order to use excess nighttime generating capacity to store energy for daytime use. But if New York's vehicles are to be driven by electric motors, their batteries will need to be charged at night, and this will surely wipe out the nighttime excess in generating capacity that is the basis for the Storm King proposal.

Similar conflicts surround most of our environmental problems, but the ones that we have yet to confront will be vastly more serious. The economic and political impact of farm productivity on the nation is, of course, massive and pervasive. The present financial status of American agriculture is heavily based on the massive use of inorganic fertilizer. Since 1950 the cost to the American farmer of the land, machinery, and labor that he uses has increased about 80, 40, and 60 per cent respectively. In contrast, the cost of fertilizer has *dropped* about 20 per cent. The values of land, machinery, and labor inputs into farming have all declined in that period; in contrast, the input value of fertilizer has increased more than 80 per cent. Clearly any effort to limit the use of inorganic fertilizer on U. S. farms—and I can foresee no other way of ensuring the integrity of our waste disposal systems—will set off a series of explosive economic and political problems.

The crisis in the environment reveals a potentially fatal flaw in the social use of modern science and technology. We have developed an enormous competence to intervene in the natural world: We can release fearful nuclear explosions, spray insecticides over the countryside, and produce millions of automobiles. But at the same time we are unable to predict the full biological consequences of nuclear war or to avoid risks to our livelihood and health from the side effects of the insecticides or from the smog that our autos produce. In the eager search for the benefits of modern science and technology we have blundered into the accompanying hazards before we were aware of them.

In 1956 the government thought there was no harm associated with nuclear tests; but we now know from the thyroid nodules in Utah children that this was a tragic mistake. We exploded the bombs *before* we had the scientific knowledge to understand the biological and medical consequence.

We produced power plants and automobiles which envelop our cities in smog —before we understood its harmful effects on health. We learned how to synthesize and use new insecticides—before we learned that they also kill birds and might be harmful to people. We produced detergents and put billions of pounds on the market—before we realized that they would make water supplies foam and should be taken off the market. We are ready to conduct a nuclear war—even though we do not know whether the effect of the vast catastrophe on life, on soil, and the weather will destroy our civilization.

Despite their complicated scientific background, the issues generated by environmental pollution do not lie in the domain of science. No scientific evaluation can determine how to share the inevitable costs of controlling water pollution among cities, industries, and farms. Scientific methods cannot determine whether it is better to suffer the hazards of smog, or to undertake the huge economic cost of reorganizing urban transportation. No scientific principal can tell us how to make the choice between the prosperity of the farm and the welfare of the city. These are social and political issues and can only be resolved by social and political processes.

What can be done? Sometimes it is suggested that since scientists and engineers have made the bombs, insecticides, and autos, they ought to be responsible for deciding how to deal with the resultant hazards. But this would deprive everyone else of the right of conscience and the political rights of citizenship. This approach would also force us to rely on the moral and political wisdom of scientists and engineers, and there is no evidence that I know of that suggests they are better endowed in this respect than other people.

There is an alternative, which is feasible though difficult. I believe that citizens can continue to rely on their own collective judgment about the issues of environmental conservation—if they take steps to inform themselves. The nuclear test-ban treaty is a good example of how this can be done. It seems clear that one of the important reasons this treaty was approved by a vote of the Senate is that the Senators were informed by their constituents of their opposition to the radioactive poisoning of our foods by fallout. Where did the letter writers get the necessary facts? Largely from public education by many scientists who believe that these issues ought to be decided by public judgment.

Out of an original concern with fallout and nuclear war we have developed a new "information movement" among academic scientists, designed to educate the public about the scientific and technological facts relevant to the major issues of the day. This is the alliance between the scientist and the citizen, which Margaret Mead has called "a new social invention." On this alliance depends the hope that the morality of man can, at last, turn the enormous new power that science has given us from the path of catastrophe toward the goal which is common both to science and humanity—the welfare of man.

Socialist

Harvey Molotch: Oil in Santa Barbara and Power in America

More than oil leaked from Union Oil's Platform A in the Santa Barbara channel —a bit of truth about power in America spilled out along with it. It is the thesis of this paper that this technological "accident," like all accidents, provides clues to the realities of social strucutre (in this instance, power arrangements) not otherwise available to the outside observer. Further, it is argued, the response of the aggrieved population (the citizenry of Santa Barbara) provides insight into the more general process which shapes disillusionment and frustration among those who come to closely examine and be injured by existing power arrangements.

A few historical details concerning the case under examination are in order. For over fifteen years, Santa Barbara's political leaders had attempted to prevent despoilation of their coastline by oil drilling on adjacent federal waters. Although they were unsuccessful in blocking eventual oil leasing (in February, 1968) of *federal* waters beyond the three-mile limit, they were able to establish a sanctuary within *state* waters (thus foregoing the extraordinary revenues which leases in such areas bring to adjacent localities—e.g., the riches of Long Beach). It was therefore a great irony that the one city which voluntarily exchanged revenue for a pure environment should find itself faced, on January 28, 1969, with a massive eruption of crude oil—an eruption which was, in the end, to cover the entire city coastline (as well as much of Ventura and Santa Barbara County coastline as well) with a thick coat of crude oil. The air was soured for many hundreds of feet inland and the traditional economic base of the region (tourism) was under threat. After ten days of unsuccessful attempts, the runaway well was brought under control, only to be followed by a second eruption on February 12. This fissure was closed on March 3, but was followed by a sustained "seepage" of oil—a leakage which continues, at this writing, to pollute the sea, the air, and the famed local beaches. The oil companies had paid $603,000,000 for their lease rights and neither they nor the federal government bear any significant legal responsibility toward the localities which these lease rights might endanger.

If the big spill had occurred almost anywhere else (e.g., Lima, Ohio; Lompoc, California), it is likely that the current research opportunity would not have developed. But Santa Barbara is different. Of its 70,000 residents, a disproportionate number are upper class and upper middle class. They are persons who, having a wide choice of where in the world they might live, have chosen Santa Barbara for its ideal climate, gentle beauty and sophisticated "culture." Thus a large number of worldly, rich, well-educated persons—individuals with resources, spare time, and contacts with national and international elites—found themselves with a commonly shared disagreeable situation: the pollution of their otherwise near-perfect environment. Santa Barbarans thus possessed none of the "problems" which otherwise are said to inhibit effective community response to external threat: they are not urban villagers (cf. Gans, 1962); they are not internally divided and parochial like the Springdalers (cf. Vidich and Bensman, 1960); nor emaciated with self-doubt and organizational naiveté as is

Reprinted from *Sociological Inquiry*, 40 (Winter, 1970).

supposed of the ghetto dwellers. With moral indignation and high self-confidence, they set out to right the wrong so obviously done to them.

Their response was immediate. The stodgy *Santa Barbara New-Press* inaugurated a series of editorials, unique in uncompromising stridency. Under the leadership of a former State Senator and a local corporate executive, a community organization was established called "GOO" (Get Oil Out!) which took a militant stand against any and all oil activity in the Channel.

In a petition to President Nixon (eventually to gain 110,000 signatures), GOO's position was clearly stated:

> ...With the seabed filled with fissures in this area, similar disastrous oil operation accidents may be expected. And with one of the largest faults centered in the channel waters, one sizeable earthquake could mean possible disaster for the entire channel area...Therefore, we the undersigned do call upon the state of California and the Federal Government to promote conservation by:
>   1. Taking immediate action to have present offshore oil operations cease and desist at once.
>   2. Issuing no further leases in the Santa Barbara Channel.
>   3. Having all oil platforms and rigs removed from this area at the earliest possible date.

The same theme emerged in the hundreds of letters published by the *News-Press* in the weeks to follow and in the positions taken by virtually every local civic and government body. Both in terms of its volume (372 letters published in February alone) and the intensity of the revealed opinions, the flow of letters was hailed by the *News-Press* as "unprecedented." Rallies were held at the beach, GOO petitions were circulated at local shopping centers and sent to friends around the country; a fund-raising dramatic spoof of the oil industry was produced at a local high school. Local artists, playwrights, advertising men, retired executives and academic specialists from the local campus of the University of California (UCSB) executed special projects appropriate to their areas of expertise.

A GOO strategy emerged for a two-front attack. Local indignation, producing the petition to the President and thousands of letters to key members of Congress and the executive would lead to appropriate legislation. Legal action in the courts against the oil companies and the federal government would have the double effect of recouping some of the financial losses certain to be endured by the local tourist and fishing industries while at the same time serving notice that drilling would be a much less profitable operation than it was supposed to be. Legislation to ban drilling was introduced by Cranston in the U.S. Senate and Teague in the House of Representatives. Joint suits by the city and County of Santa Barbara (later joined by the State) for $1 billion in damages [were] filed against the oil companies and the federal government.

All of these activities—petitions, rallies, court action and legislative lobbying —were significant for their similarity in revealing faith in "the system." The tendency was to blame the oil companies. There was a muckraking tone to the Santa Barbara response: oil and the profit-crazy executives of Union Oil were ruining Santa Barbara—but once our national and state leaders became aware of what was going on, and were provided with the "facts" of the case, justice would be done.

Indeed, there was good reason for hope. The quick and enthusiatic responses of Teague and Cranston represented a consensus of men otherwise polar opposites in their political behavior; Democrat Cranston was a charter member of the liberal California Democratic Council: Republican Teague was a staunch fiscal and moral conservative (e.g., a strong Vietnam hawk and unrelenting harasser of the local Center for the Study of Democratic Institutions). Their bills, for which there was great optimism, would have had the consequence of effecting a "permanent" ban on drilling in the Channel.

But from other quarters there was silence. Santa Barbara's representatives in the state legislature either said nothing or (in later stages) offered minimal support. It took several months for Senator Murphy to introduce Congressional legislation (for which he admitted to having little hope) which would have the consequence of exchanging the oil companies' leases in the Channel for comparable leases in the under-exploited Elk Hills oil reserve in California's Kern County. Most disappointing of all to Santa Barbarans, Governor Reagan withheld support for proposals which would end the drilling.

As subsequent events unfolded, this seemingly inexplicable silence of the democratically elected representatives began to fall into place as part of a more general problem. American democracy came to be seen as a much more complicated affair than a system in which governmental officials actuate the desires of the "people who elected them" once those desires come to be known. Instead, increasing recognition came to be given to the "all-powerful oil lobby"; to legislators "in the pockets of Oil"; to academicians "bought" by Oil and to regulatory agencies which lobby for those they are supposed to regulate. In other words, Santa Barbara became increasingly *ideological*, increasingly *sociological*, and in the words of some observers, increasingly *"radical"*.[1] Writing from his lodgings in the area's most exclusive hotel (the Santa Barbara Biltmore), an irate citizen penned these words in this published letter to the *News-Press*:

> We the people can protest and protest and it means nothing because the industrial and military junta are the country. They tell us, the People, what is good for the oil companies is good for the People. To that I say, Like Hell!...
>
> Profit is their language and the proof of all this is their history (SBNP[2], Feb. 26, 1969, P. A-6).

As time wore on, the editorials and letters continued in their bitterness.

The Executive Branch and the Regulatory Agencies; Disillusionment

From the start, Secretary Hickel's actions were regarded with suspicion. His publicized associations with Alaskan Oil interests did his reputation no good in Santa Barbara. When, after a halt to drilling (for "review" of procedures) immediately after the initial eruption, Hickel one day later ordered a resumption of drilling and production (even as the oil continued to gush into the channel), the government's response was seen as unbelievingly consistent with conservationists' worst fears. That he backed down within 48 hours and ordered a halt to

---

1. See the report of Morton Mintz in the June 29, 1969 Washington Post, The conjunction of these three attributes is not, in my opinion, coincidental.
2. SBNP will be used to denote Santa Barbara News Press throughout this paper.

drilling and production was taken as response to the massive nationwide media play then being given to the Santa Barbara plight and to the citizens' mass outcry just then beginning to reach Washington.

Disenchantment with Hickel and the executive branch also came through less spectacular, less specific, but nevertheless genuine activity. First of all, Hickel's failure to support any of the legislation introduced to halt drilling was seen as an *action* favoring Oil. His remarks on the subject, while often expressing sympathy with Santa Barbarans[3] (and for a while placating local sentiment) were revealed as hypocritical in light of the action not taken. Of further note was the constant attempt by the Interior Department to minimize the extent of damage in Santa Barbara or to hint at possible "compromises" which were seen locally as near-total capitulation to the oil companies.

Volume of Oil Spillage. Many specific examples might be cited. An early (and continuing) issue in the oil spill was the *volume* of oil spilling into the Channel. The U.S. Geological Survey (administered by Interior), when queried by reporters, broke its silence on the subject with estimates which struck [the residents of Santa Barbara as incredible]. One of the extraordinary attributes of the Santa Barbara locale is the presence of a technology establishment among the most sophisticated in the country. Several officials of the General Research Corporation (a local R & D firm with experience in marine technology) initiated studies of the oil outflow and announced findings of pollution volume at a "minimum" of ten fold the Interior estimate. Further, General Research provided (and the *News-Press* published) a detailed account of the methods used in making the estimate (cf. Allan, 1969). Despite repeated challenges from the press, Interior both refused to alter its estimate or to reveal its method for making estimates. Throughout the crisis, the divergence of the estimates remained at about ten fold.

The "seepage" was estimated by the Geological Survey to have been reduced from 1,260 gallons per day to about 630 gallons. General Research, however, estimated the leakage at the rate of 8,400 gallons per day at the same point in time as Interior's 630 gallon estimate. The lowest estimate of all was provided by an official of the Western Oil and Gas Association, in a letter to the *Wall Street Journal*. His estimate: "Probably less than 100 gallons a day" (*SBNP*, August 5, 1969:A-1).

Damage to Beaches. Still another point of contention was the state of the beaches at varying points in time. The oil companies, through various public relations officials, constantly minimized the actual amount of damage and maximized the effect of Union Oil's cleanup activity. What surprised (and most irritated) the locals was the fact that Interior statements implied the same goal. Thus Hickel referred at a press conference to the "recent" oil spill, providing the impression that the oil spill was over, at a time when freshly erupting oil was continuing to stain local beaches. President Nixon appeared locally to "inspect" the damage to beaches, and Interior arranged for him to land his helicopter on a city beach which had been cleaned thoroughly in the days just before, but spared him a close-up of much of the rest of the County shoreline which continued to be

---

3. Hickel publicly stated and wrote (personal communication) that the original leasing was a mistake and that he was doing all within discretionary power to solve the problem.

covered with a thick coat of crude oil. (The branch visited by Nixon has been oil stained on many occasions subsequent to the President's departure.) Secret servicemen kept the placards and shouts of several hundred demonstrators safely out of Presidential viewing or hearing distance.

Continuously, the Oil and Interior combine implied the beaches to be restored when Santa Barbarans knew that even a beach which looked clean was by no means restored. The *News-Press* through a comprehensive series of interviews with local and national experts on wildlife and geology made the following points clear:

1. As long as oil remained on the water and oil continued to leak from beneath the sands, all Santa Barbara beaches were subject to continuous doses of oil—subject only to the vagaries of wind change. Indeed, all through the spill and up to the present point in time, a beach walk is likely to result in tar on the feet. On "bad days" the beaches are unapproachable.

2. The damage to the "ecological chain" (a concept which has become a household phrase in Santa Barbara) is of unknown proportions. Much study will be necessary to learn the extent of damage.

3. The continuous alternating natural erosion and building up of beach sands means that "clean" beaches contain layers of oil at various sublevels under the mounting sands; layers will once again be exposed when the cycle reverses itself and erosion begins anew. Thus, it will take many years for the beaches of Santa Barbara to be completely restored, even if the present seepage is halted and no additional pollution occurs.

Damage to Wildlife. Oil on feathers is ingested by birds, continuous preening thus leads to death. In what local and national authorities called a hopeless task, two bird-cleaning centers were established to cleanse feathers and otherwise administer to damaged wild-fowl. (Oil money helped to establish and supply these centers.) Both spokesman from Oil and the federal government then adopted these centers as sources of "data" on the extent of damage to wild-fowl. Thus, the number of dead birds due to pollution was computed on the basis of number of fatalities at the wild-fowl centers.[4] This of course is preposterous given the fact that dying birds are provided with very inefficient means of propelling themselves to such designated places. The obviousness of this dramatic understatement of fatalities was never acknowledged by either Oil or Interior— although noted in Santa Barbara.

At least those birds in the hands of local ornithologists could be confirmed as dead—and this fact could not be disputed by either Oil or Interior. Not so, however, with species whose corpses are more difficult to produce on command. Several observers at the Channel Islands (a national wildlife preserve containing one of the country's largest colonies of sea animals) reported sighting unusually large numbers of dead sea-lion pups—on the oil stained shores of one of the

---

4. In a February 7 letter of Union Oil shareholders, Fred Hartley informed them that the bird refuge centers had been "very successful in their efforts." In fact, by April 30, 1969, only 150 birds (of thousands treated) had been returned to the natural habitat as "fully recovered' and the survival rate of birds treated was estimated as a miraculously high (in light of previous experience) 20 per cent (cf. *SBNP*, April 30, 1969, F-3).

islands. Statement and counter-statement followed with Oil's defenders arguing that the animals were not dead at all—but only appeared inert because they were sleeping. Despite the testimony of staff experts of the local Museum of Natural History and the Museum Scientist of UCSB's Biologial Sciences Department that the number of "inert" sea-lion pups was far larger than normal and that field trips had confirmed the deaths, the position of Oil, as also expressed by the Department of the Navy (which administers the stricken island) remained adamant that the sea animals were only sleeping (cf. *Life*, June 13, 1969; July 4, 1969). The dramatic beaching of an unusually large number of dead whales on the beaches of Northern California—whales which had just completed their migration through the Santa Barbara Channel—was acknowledged, but held not to be caused by oil pollution. No direct linkage (or non-linkage) with oil could be demonstrated by investigating scientists (cf. *San Franciso Chronicle*, March 12, 1969:1-3).

In the end, it was not simply Interior, its U.S. Geological Survey and the President which either supported or tacitly accepted Oil's public relations tactics. The regulatory agencies at both national and state level, by action, inaction and implication had the consequence of defending Oil at virtually every turn. Thus at the outset of the first big blow, as the ocean churned with bubbling oil and gas, the U.S. Coast Guard (which patrols Channel waters regularly) failed to notify local officials of the pollution threat because, in the words of the local commander, "the seriousness of the situation was not apparent until late in the day Tuesday and it was difficult to reach officials after business hours" (*SBNP*, January 30, 1969; A-1, 4). Officials ended up hearing of the spill from the *News-Press*.

The Army Corps of Engineers must approve all structures placed on the ocean floor and thus had the discretion to hold public hearings on each application for a permit to build a drilling platform. With the exception of a single *pro forma* ceremony held on a platform erected in 1967, requests for such hearings were never granted. In its most recent handling of these matters (at a point long after the initial eruption and as oil still leaks into the ocean) the Corps changed its criteria for public hearings by restricting written objections to new drilling to "the effects of the proposed exploratory drilling on *navigation or national defense*" (*SBNP*, August 17, 1969:A-1, 4). Prior to the spill, effects on *fish and wildlife* were specified by the Army as possible grounds for objection, but at that time such objections, when raised, were dismissed as unfounded.

The Federal Water Pollution Control Administration consistently attempted to understate the amount of damage done to waterfowl by quoting the "hospital dead" as though a reasonable assessment of the net damage. State agencies followed the same pattern. The charge of "Industry domination" of state conservation boards was levelled by the State Deputy Attorney General, Charles O'Brien (*SBNP*, February 9, 1969;A-6). Thomas Gaines, a Union Oil executive, actually sits as a member on the State Agency Board most directly connected with the control of pollution in Channel waters. In correspondence with complaining citizens, N. B. Livermore, Jr., of the Resources Agency of California refers to the continuing oil spill as "minor seepage" with "no major long-term effect on the marine ecology." The letter adopts the perspective of Interior and Oil, even though the state was in no way being held culpable for the spill (letter, undated to Joseph Keefe, citizen, University of California, Santa Barbara Library, on file).

With these details under their belts, Santa Barbarans were in a position to understand the sweeping condemnation of the regulatory system as contained in a *News-Press* front page, banner-headlined interview with Rep. Richard D. Ottenger (D-NY), quoted as follows: "And so on down the line. Each agency has a tendency to become the captive of the industry that it is to regulate" (*SBNP*, March 1, 1969:A-1).

The Congress: Disillusionment

Irritations with Interior were paralleled by frustrations encountered in dealing with the Congressional establishment which had the responsibility of holding hearings on ameliorative legislation. A delegation of Santa Barbarans was scheduled to testify in Washington on the Cranston bill. From the questions which Congressmen asked of them, and the manner in which they were "handled," the delegation could only conclude that the Committee was "in the pockets of Oil." As one of the returning delegates put it, the presentation bespoke of "total futility."

At this writing, six months after their introduction, both the Cranston and Teague bills lie buried in committee with little prospect of surfacing. Cranston has softened his bill significantly—requiring only that new drilling be suspended until Congress is convinced that sufficient technological safeguards exist. But to no avail.

Science and Technology: Disillusionment

From the start, part of the shock of the oil spill was that such a thing could happen in a country with such sophisticated technology. The much overworked phrase, "If we can send a man to the moon . . ." was even more overworked in Santa Barbara. When, in years previous, Santa Barbara's elected officials had attempted to halt the original sale of leases, "assurances" were given from Interior that such an "accident" could not occur, given the highly developed state of the art. Not only did it occur, but the original gusher of oil spewed forth completely out of control for ten days and the continuing "seepage" which followed it remains uncontrolled to the present moment, seven months later. That the government would embark upon so massive a drilling program with such unsophisticated technologies, was striking indeed.

Further, not only were the technologies inadequate and the plans for stopping a leak, should it occur, nonexistent, but the area in which the drilling took place was known to be ultrahazardous from the outset. That is, drilling was occurring on an ocean bottom known for its extraordinary geological circumstances— porous sands lacking a bedrock "ceiling" capable of containing runaway oil and gas. Thus the continuing leakage through the sands at various points above the oil resevoir is unstoppable, and could have been anticipated with the data *known to all parties involved.*

Another peculiarity of the Channel is the fact that it is located in the heart of earthquake activity in that region of the country which, among all regions, is among the very most earthquake prone.[5] Santa Barbarans are now asking what might occur in an earthquake: if pipes on the ocean floor and casings through the ocean bottom should be sheared, the damage done by the Channel's *thousands* of potential producing wells would be devastating to the entire coast of Southern California.[6]

Recurrent attempts have been made to ameliorate the continuing seep by placing floating booms around an area of leakage and then having workboats skim off the leakage from within the demarcated area.[7] Chemical dispersants, of various varieties, have also been tried. But the oil bounces over the sea booms in the choppy waters; the work boats suck up only a drop in the bucket and the dispersants are effective only when used in quantities which constitute a graver pollution threat than the oil they are designed to eliminate. Cement is poured into suspected fissures in an attempt to seal them up. Oil on beaches is periodi-cally cleaned by dumping straw over the sands and then raking up the straw along with the oil it absorbs.

This striking contrast between the sophistication of the means used to locate and extract oil compared to the primitiveness of the means to control and clean it up was widely noted in Santa Barbara. It is the result of a system which promotes research and development which leads to strategic profitability rather than to social utility. The common sight of men throwing straw on miles of beaches within sight of complex drilling rigs capable of exploiting resources thousands of feet below the ocean's surface, made the point clear.

The futility of the clean-up and control efforts was widely noted in Santa Barbara. Secretary Hickel's announcement that the Interior Department was gen-erating new "tough" regulations to control off-shore drilling was thus met with great skepticism. The Santa Barbara County Board of Supervisors was invited to "review" these new regulations—and refused to do so in the belief that such participation would be used to provide the fraudulent impression of democratic responsiveness—when, in fact, the relevant decisions had been already made. In previous years when they were fighting against the leasing of the Channel, the Supervisors had been assured of technological safeguards; now, as the emer-gency continued, they could witness for themselves the dearth of any means for ending the leakage in the Channel. They had also heard the testimony of a high-ranking Interior engineer who, when asked if such safeguards could positively prevent future spills, explained that "no prudent engineer would ever make such a claim" (*SBNP*, February 19, 1969:A-1). They also had the testimony of Donald Solanas, a regional supervisor of Interior's U.S. Geological Survey, who had said about the Union Platform eruption:

---

5. Cf. "Damaging Earthquakes of the United States through 1966," Fig. 2, National Earthquake Information Center, Environmental Science Services Administration, Coast and Geodetic Survey.

6. See Interview with Donald Weaver, Professor of Geology, UCSB, SBNP, Feb. 21, 1969, p. A-1, 6. (Also, remarks by Professor Donald Runnells, UCSB geologist, SBNP, Feb. 23, 1969, p. B-2) Both stress the dangers of faults in the Channel, and potential earthquakes.

7. More recently, plastic tents have been placed on the ocean floor to trap seeping oil; it is being claimed that half the runaway oil is now being trapped in these tents.

I could have had an engineer on that platform 24 hours a day, 7 days a week and he couldn't have prevented the accident.

IIis "explanation" of the cause of the "accident": "Mother earth broke down on us" (*SBNP*, February 28, 1969:C-12).

Given these facts, as contained in the remarks of Interior's own spokesmen, combined with testimony and information received from non-Interior personnel, Interior's new regulations and the invitation to the County to participate in making them, could only be a ruse to preface a resumption of drilling. In initiating the County's policy of not responding to Interior's "invitation," a County Supervisor explained: "I think we may be falling into a trap" (*SBNP*, April 1, 1969).

The very next day, the Supervisors' suspicions were confirmed. Interior announced a selective resumption of drilling "to relieve pressures." (*News-Press* letter writers asked if the "pressure" was geological or political.") The new tough regulations were themselves seriously flawed by the fact that most of their provisions specified those measures, such as buoyant booms around platforms, availability of chemical dispersants, etc., which had proven almost totally useless in the current emergency. They fell far short of minimum safety requirements as enumerated by UC Santa Barbara geologist Robert Curry who criticized a previous version of the same regulations as "relatively trivial" and "toothless"[8] (*SBNP*, March 5, 1969:C-9).

On the other hand, the new regulations did specify that oil companies would henceforth be financially responsible for damages resulting from pollution mishaps. (This had been the *de facto* realtiy in the Union case; the company had assumed responsibility for the clean-up, and advised stockholders that such costs were covered by "more than adequate" insurance.)[9] The liability requirement

---

8. Curry's criticism is as follows:

"These new regulations make no mention at all about in-pipe safety valves to prevent blowouts, or to shut off the flow of oil deep in the well should the oil and gas escape from the drill hole region into a natural fissure at some depth below the wellhead blowout preventers. There is also no requirement for a backup valve in case the required preventer fails to work. Remember, the runaway well on Union Platform A was equipped with a wellhead blowout preventer. The blowout occurred some 200 feet below that device.

Only one of the new guidelines seems to recognize the possible calamitous results of earthquakes which are inevitable on the western offshore leases. None of the regulations require the minimization of pollution hazards during drilling that may result from a moderate-magnitude, nearby shallow-focus earthquake, seismic sea wave (tsunami) or submarine landslide which could shear off wells below the surface.

None of the regulations state anything at all about onshore oil and gas storage facilities liable to release their contents into the oceans upon rupture due to an earthquake or seismic seawave.

None of the new regulations stipulate that wells must be cased to below a level of geologic hazard, or below a depth of possible open fissures or porous sands, and, as such, none of these changes would have helped the present situation in the Santa Barbara Channel or the almost continuous blowout that has been going on since last year in the Bass Straits off Tasmania, where one also finds porous sands extending all the way up to the sea floor in a tectonically active region—exactly the situation we have here."

9. Letter from Fred Hartley, President of Union Oil, to "all shareholders," dated February 7, 1969.

has been vociferously condemned by the oil companies—particularly by those firms which have failed to make significant strikes on their Channel leases (*SBNP*, March 14, 1969). Several of these companies have now entered suit (supported by the ACLU) against the federal government charging that the arbitrary changing of lease conditions renders Channel exploitation "economically and practically impossible," thus depriving them of rights of due process (*SBNP*, April 10, 1969:A-1).

The weaknesses of the new regulations came not as a surprise to people who had already adapted to thinking of Oil and the Interior Department as the same source. There was much less preparation for the results of the Presidential Committee of "distinguished" scientists and engineers (the DuBridge Panel) which was to recommend means of eliminating the seepage under Platform A. Given the half-hearted, inexpensive and primitive attempts by Union Oil to deal with the seepage, feeling ran high that at last the technological sophistication of the nation would be harnessed to solve this particular vexing problem. Instead, the panel—after a two-day session and after hearing testimony from no one not connected with either Oil or Interior—recommended the "solution" of drilling an additional 50 wells under Platform A in order to pump the area dry as quickly as possible. The process would require ten to twenty years, one member of the panel estimated.[10]

The recommendation was severely terse, requiring no more than one and a half pages of type. Despite an immediate local clamor, Interior refused to make public the data or the reasoning behind the recommendations. The information on Channel geological conditions was provided by the oil companies; the Geological Survey routinely depends upon the oil industry for the data upon which it makes its "regulatory" decisions. The data, being proprietary, could thus not be released. Totally inexplicable, in light of this "explanation," is Interior's continuing refusal to immediately provide the information given a recent clearance by Union Oil for public release of all the data. Santa Barbara's local experts have thus been thwarted by the counterarguments of Oil-Interior that "if you had the information we have, you would agree with us."

Science was also having its non-neutral consequences on the other battlefront being waged by Santa Barbarans. The chief Deputy Attorney General of California, in his April 7 speech to the blue-ribbon Channel City Club of Santa Barbara, complained that the oil industry

> is preventing oil drilling experts from aiding the Attorney General's office in its lawsuits over the Santa Barbara oil spill (*SBNP*, Aug. 8, 1969).

Complaining that his office has been unable to get assistance from petroleum experts at California universities, the Deputy Attorney General further stated:

> The university experts all seem to be working on grants from the oil industry. There is an atmosphere of fear. The experts are afraid that if they assist us in our case on behalf of the people of California, they will lose their oil industry grants.

---

10. Robert Curry of the geography department of the University of California, Santa Barbara, warned that such a tactic might in fact accelerate leakage. If, as he thought, the oil reservoirs under the Channel are linked, accelerated development of one such reservoir would, through erosion of subterranean linkage channels, accelerate the flow of oil into the reservoir under Platform A, thus adding to the uncontrolled flow of oil through the sands and into the ocean. Curry was not asked to testify by the DuBridge Panel.

At the Santa Barbara Campus of the University, there is little Oil money in evidence and few, if any, faculty members have entered into proprietary research arrangements with Oil. Petroleum geology and engineering is simply not a local specialty. Yet it is a fact that Oil interests did contact several Santa Barbara faculty members with offers of funds for studies of the ecological effects of the oil spill, with publication rights stipulated by Oil.[11] It is also the case that the Federal Water Pollution Control Administration explicitly requested a UC Santa Barbara botanist to withhold the findings of his study, funded by that Agency, on the ecological consequences of the spill (SBNP, July 29, 1969:A-3).

Except for the Deputy Attorney General's complaint, none of these revelations received any publicity outside of Santa Barbara. But the Attorney's allegation became something of a statewide issue. A professor at the Berkeley campus, in his attempt to refute the allegation, actually confirmed it. Wilbut H. Somerton, Professor of petroleum engineering, indicated he could not testify against Oil

> because my work depends on good relations with the petroleum industry. My interest is serving the petroleum industry. I view my obligation to the community as supplying it with well-trained petroleum engineers. We train the industry's engineers and they help us. (SBNP, April 12, 1969, as quoted from a San Francisco Chronicle interview.)

Santa Barbara's leaders were incredulous about the whole affair. The question —one which is more often asked by the downtrodden sectors of the society—was asked: "Whose University is this, anyway?" A local executive and GOO leader asked, "If the truth isn't in the universities, where is it?" A conservative member of the State Legislature, in a move reminiscent of SDS demands, went so far as to ask an end to all faculty "moonlighting" for industry. In Santa Barbara, the only place where all of this publicity was occurring, there was thus an opportunity for insight into the linkages between knowledge, the University, government and Oil and the resultant non-neutrality of science. The backgrounds of many members of the DuBridge Panel were linked publicly to the oil industry. In a line of reasoning usually the handiwork of groups like SDS, News-Press letter writer labeled Dr. DuBridge as a servant of Oil interest because, as a past President of Cal Tech, he would have had to defer to Oil in generating the massive funding which that institution requires. In fact, the relationship was quite direct. Not only has Union Oil been a contributor to Cal Tech, but Fred Hartley (Union's President) is a Cal Tech trustee. The impropriety of such a man as DuBridge serving as the key "scientist" in determining the Santa Barbara outcome seemed more and more obvious.

---

11. Verbal communication from one of the faculty members involved. The kind of "studies" which oil enjoys is typified by a research conclusion by Professor Wheeler J. North of Cal Tech, who after performing a one week study of the Channel ecology under Western Oil and Gas Association sponsorship, determined that it was the California winter floods which caused most of the evident disturbance and that (as quoted from the Association Journal) "Santa Barbara beaches and marine life should be back to normal by summer with no adverse impact on tourism." Summer came with oil on the beaches, birds unreturned, and beach motels with unprecedented vacancies.

Taxation and Patriotism: Disillusionment

From Engler's detailed study of the politics of Oil, we learn that the oil companies combat local resistance with arguments that hurt: taxation and patriotism (cf. Engler, 1961). They threaten to take their operations elsewhere, thus depriving the locality of taxes and jobs. The more grandiose argument is made that oil is necessary for the national defense; hence, any weakening of "incentives" to discover and produce oil plays into the hands of the enemy.

Santa Barbara, needing money less than most locales and valuing environment more, learned enought to know better. Santa Barbara wanted oil to leave, but oil would not. Because the oil is produced in federal waters, only a tiny proportion of Santa Barbara County's budget indirectly comes from oil, and virtually none of the city of Santa Barbara's budget comes from oil. *News-Press* letters and articles disposed of the defense argument with these points: (1) oil companies deliberately limit oil production under geographical quota restrictions designed to maintain the high price of oil by regulating supply; (2) the federal oil import quota (also sponsored by the oil industry) which restricts imports from abroad, weakens the country's defense posture by forcing the nation to exhaust its own finite supply while the Soviets rely on the Middle East; (3) most oil imported into the U.S. comes from relatively dependable sources in South America which foreign wars would not endanger; (4) the next major war will be a nuclear holocaust with possible oil shortages a very low level problem.

Just as an attempt to answer the national defense argument led to conclusions the very opposite of Oil's position, so did a close examination of the tax argument. For not only did Oil not pay very much in local taxes, Oil also paid very little in *federal* taxes. In another of its front-page editorials the *News-Press* made the facts clear. The combination of the output restrictions, extraordinary tax write-off privileges for drilling expenses, the import quota, and the 27.5 per cent depletion allowance, all created an artificially high price of U.S. oil—a price almost double the world market price for the comparable product delivered to comparable U.S. destinations.[12] The combination of incentives available creates a situation where some oil companies pay no taxes whatever during extraordinarily profitable years. In the years 1962-1966, Standard of New Jersey paid less than 4 per cent of profits in taxes, Standard of California, less than 3 per cent, and 22 of the largest oil companies paid slightly more than 6 per cent (*SBNP*, February 16, 1969:A-1). It was pointed out, again and again to Santa Barbarans, that it was this system of subsidy which made the relatively high cost deep-sea exploration and drilling in the Channel profitable in the first place. Thus, the citizens of

---

12. Cf. Walter J. Mead, "The Economics of Depletion Allowance," testimony presented to Assembly Revenue and Taxation Committee, California Legislature, June 10, 1969, mimeo: "The System of Government Subsidies to the Oil Industry," testimony presented to the U.S. Senate Subcommitte on Antitrust and Monopoly, March 11, 1969. The ostensible purpose of the depletion allowance is to encourage oil companies to explore for new oil reserves. A report to the Treasury Department by Consad Research Corp. concluded that elimination of the depletion allowance would decrease oil reserves by only 3 per cent. The report advised that more efficient means could be found than a system which causes the government to pay $10 for every $1 in oil added to reserves. (Cf. Leo Rennert, "Oil Industry's Favors," SBNP, April 27, 1969, pp. A-14, 15 as reprinted from the Sacramento Bee.)

Santa Barbara, as federal taxpayers and fleeced consumers were subsidizing their own demise. The consequence of such a revelation can only be *infuriating*.

The Mobilization of Bias

The actions of Oil and Interior and the contexts in which such actions took place can be reexamined in terms of their function in diffusing local opposition, disorienting dissenters, and otherwise limiting the scope of issues which are potentially part of public controversies. E. E. Schattschneider (1960:17) has noted:

> All forms of political organization have a bias in favor of the exploitation of some kinds of conflict and the suppression of others because *organization is the mobilization of bias.* Some issues are organized into politics while others are organized out.

Expanding the notion slightly, certain techniques shaping the "mobilization of bias" can be said to have been revealed by the present case study.

1. *The pseudo-event.* Boorstin (1962) has described the use of the pseudo-event in a large variety of task accomplishment situations. A pseudo-event occurs when men arrange conditions to simulate a certain kind of event, such that certain prearranged consequences follow as though the actual event had taken place. Several pseudo-events may be cited. *Local participation in decision making.* From the outset, it was obvious that national actions vis-à-vis Oil in Santa Barbara had as their strategy the freezing out of any local participation in decisions affecting the Channel. Thus, when in 1968 the federal government first called for bids on a Channel lease, local officials were not even informed. When subsequently queried about the matter, federal officials indicated that the lease which was advertised for bid was just a corrective measure to prevent drainage of a "little old oil pool" on federal property adjacent to a state lease producing for Standard and Humble. This "little old pool" was to draw a high bonus bid of $21,189,000 from a syndicate headed by Phillips (*SBNP*, February 9, 1969:A-17). Further, local officials were not notified by any government agency in the case of the original oil spill, nor (except after the spill was already widely known) in the case of any of the previous or subsequent more "minor" spills. Perhaps the thrust of the federal government's colonialist attitude toward the local community was contained in an Interior Department engineer's memo written to J. Cordell Moore, Assistant Secretary of Interior, explaining the policy of refusing public hearings prefatory to drilling: "We preferred not to stir up the natives any more than possible."[13] (The memo was released by Senator Cranston and excerpted on page 1 of the *News-Press*.)

Given this known history, the Santa Barbara County Board of Supervisors refused the call for "participation" in drawing up new "tougher" drilling regulations, precisely because they knew the government had no intention of creating "safe" drilling regulations. They refused to take part in the pseudo-event and thus refused to let the consequences (in this case the appearance of democratic decision-making and local assent) of a pseudo-event occur.

---

13. Cranston publicly confronted the staff engineer, Eugene Standley, who stated that he could neither confirm or deny writing the memo. (Cf. SBNP, March 11, 1969, p. A-1)

Other attempts at the staging of pseudo-events may be cited. Nixon's "inspection" of the Santa Barbara beachfront was an obvious one. Another series of pseudo-events were the Congressional hearings staged by legislators who were, in the words of a local well-to-do lady leader of GOO, "kept men." The locals blew off steam—but the hearing of arguments and the proposing of appropriate legislation based on those arguments (the presumed essence of the Congressional hearing as a formal event) certainly did not come off. Many Santa Barbarans had a similar impression of the court hearings regarding the various legal maneuvers against oil drilling; legal proceedings came to be similarly seen as ceremonious arrangements for the accomplishing of tasks not revealed by their formally-stated properties.

2. *The creeping event.* A creeping event is, in a sense, the opposite of a pseudo-event. It occurs when something *is* actually taking place, but when the manifest signs of the event are arranged to occur at an inconspicuously gradual and piece-meal pace, thus eliminating some of the consequences which would otherwise follow from the event if it were to be perceived all-at-once to be occurring. Two major creeping events were arranged for the Santa Barbara Channel. Although the great bulk of the bidding for leases in the Channel occurred simultaneously, the first lease was, as was made clear earlier, advertised for bid prior to the others and prior to any public announcement of the leasing of the Channel. The federal waters' virginity was thus ended with only a whimper. A more salient example of the creeping event is the resumption of production and drilling after Hickel's second moratorium. Authorization to resume *production* on different specific groups of wells occurred on these dates in 1969: February 17; February 21; February 22; and March 3. Authorization to resume *drilling* of various groups of new wells was announced by Interior on these dates in 1969: April 1, June 12, July 2, August 2, and August 16. (This is being written on August 20 [1969].) Each time, the resumption was announced as a safety precaution to relieve pressures, until finally on the most recent resumption date, the word "deplete" was used for the first time as the reason for granting permission to drill. There is thus no *particular* point in time in which production and drilling was re-authorized for the Channel—and full resumption has still not been officially authorized.

A creeping event has the consequences of diffusing resistance to the event by holding back what journalists call a "time peg" on which to hang "the story." Even if the aggrieved party should get wind that "something is going on," strenuous reaction is inhibited. Non-routine activity has as its prerequisite the crossing of a certain threshold point of input; the dribbling out of an event has the consequence of making each of the revealed inputs fall below the threshold level necessary for non-routine activity. By the time it becomes quite clear that "something *is* going on" both the aggrieved and the sponsors of the creeping event can ask why there should be a response *"now"* when there was none previously to the very same kind of stimulus. In such manner, the aggrieved has resort only to frustration and a gnawing feeling that "events" are sweeping him by.

3. *The "neutrality" of science and the "knowledge" producers.* I have already dealt at some length with the disillusionment of Santa Barbarans with the "experts"

and the University. After learning for themselves of the collusion between government and Oil and the use of secret science as a prop to that collusion, Santa Barbarans found themselves in the unenviable position of having to demonstrate that science and knowledge were, in fact, not neutral arbiters. They had to demonstrate, by themselves, that continued drilling was not safe, that the "experts" who said it was safe were the hirelings directly or indirectly of Oil interests and that the report of the DuBridge Panel recommending massive drilling was a fraudulent document. They had to document that the University *petroleum* geologists were themselves in league with their adversaries and that knowledge unfavorable to the Oil interests was systematically withheld by virtue of the very structure of the knowledge industry. As the SDS has learned in other contexts, this is no small task. It is a long story to tell, a complicated story to tell, and one which pits lay persons (and a few academic renegades) against a profession and patrons of a profession. An illustration of the difficulties involved may be drawn from very recent history. Seventeen Santa Barbara plaintiffs, represented by the ACLU, sought a temporary injunction against additional Channel drilling at least until the information utilized by the DuBridge Panel was made public and a hearing could be held. The injunction was not granted and, in the end, the presiding federal judge ruled in favor of what he termed the "expert" opinions available to the Secretary of the Interior. It was a function of limited time for rebuttal, the disorienting confusions of courtroom procedures, and also perhaps the desire to not offend the Court, that the ACLU lawyer could not make his subtle, complex and highly controversial case that the "experts" were partisans and that their scientifc "findings" follow from that partisanship.

4. *Constraints of communication media.* Just as the courtroom setting was not amenable to a full reproduction of the details surrounding the basis for the ACLU case, so the media in general—through restrictions of time and style—prevent a full airing of the details of the case. A more cynical analysis of the media's inability to make known the Santa Barbara "problem" in its full fidelity might hinge on an allegation that the media are constrained by fear of "pressures" from Oil and its allies; Metromedia, for example, sent a team to Santa Barbara which spent several days documenting, interviewing and filming for an hour-long program—only to suddenly drop the whole matter due to what is reported by locals in touch with the network to have been "pressures" from Oil. Such blatant interventions aside, however, the problem of full reproduction of the Santa Barbara "news" would remain problematic nonetheless.

News media are notorious for the anecdotal nature of their reporting; even so-called "think pieces" rarely go beyond a stringing together of proximate "events." There are no analyses of the "mobilization of bias" or linkages of men's actions and their pecuniary interests. Science and learning are assumed to be neutral; regulatory agencies are assumed to function as "watchdogs" for the public. Information to the contrary of these assumptions is treated as exotic exception; in the manner of Drew Pearson columns, exception piles upon exception without intellectual combination, analysis or ideological synthesis. The complexity of the situation to be reported, the wealth of details needed to support such analyses require more time and effort than journalists have at their command. Their recitation would produce long stories not consistent with space requirements and make-up preferences of newspapers and analogous constraints of the other media. A full telling of the whole story would tax the reader/viewer and would risk boring him.

For these reasons, the rather extensive media coverage of the oil spill centered on a few dramatic moments in its history (e.g., the initial gusher of oil) and a few simple-to-tell "human interest" aspects such as the pathetic deaths of the sea birds struggling along the oil-covered sands. With increasing temporal and geographical distance from the initial spill, national coverage became increasingly rare and increasingly sloppy. Interior statements on the state of the "crisis" were reported without local rejoinders as the newsmen who would have gathered them began leaving the scene. It is to be kept in mind that, relative to other local events, the Santa Barbara spill received extraordinarily extensive national coverage.[14] The point is that this coverage is nevertheless inadequate in both its quality and quantity to adequately inform the American public.

5. *The routinization of evil.* An oft quoted American cliché is that the news media cover only the "bad" things; the everyday world of people going about their business in conformity with American ideals loses out to the coverage of student and ghetto "riots," wars and crime, corruption and sin. The grain of truth in this cliché should not obfuscate the fact that there are *certain kinds of evil* which, partially for reasons cited in the preceding paragraphs, also lose their place in the public media and the public mind. Pollution of the Santa Barbara Channel is now routine; the issue is not whether or not the Channel is polluted, but *how much* it is polluted. A recent oil slick discovered off a Phillips Platform in the Channel was dismissed by an oil company official as a "routine" drilling by-product which was not viewed as "obnoxious." That "about half" of the current oil seeping into the channel is allegedly being recovered is taken as an improvement sufficient to preclude the "outrage" that a big national story would require.

Similarly, the pollution of the "moral environment" becomes routine; politicians are, of course, on the take, in the pockets of Oil, etc. The depletion allowance issue becomes not whether or not such special benefits should exists at all, but rather whether it should be at the level of 20 or 27.5 per cent. "Compromises" emerge such as the 24 per cent depletion allowance and the new "tough" drilling regulations, which are already being hailed as "victories" for the reformers (cf. *Los Angeles Times*, July 14, 1969:17). Like the oil spill itself, the depletion allowance debate becomes buried in its own disorienting detail, its ceremonious pseudo-events and in the triviality of the "solutions" which ultimately come to be considered as the "real" options. Evil is both banal and complicated; both of these attributes contribute to its durability.[15]

---

14. Major magazine coverage occurred in these (and other) national publications: Time (Feb. 14, 1969); Newsweek (March 3, 1969); Life (June 13, 1969); Saturday Review (May 10, 1969); Sierra Club Bulletin; Sports Illustrated (April 10, 1969). The last three articles cited were written by Santa Barbarans.

15. The notion of the banality of evil is adapted fom the usage of Arendt, 1963.

The Struggle for the Means to Power

It should (although it does not) go without saying that the parties competing to shape decision-making on oil in Santa Barbara do not have equal access to the means of "mobilizing bias" which this paper has discussed. The same social structural characteristics which Michels has asserted make for an "iron law of oligarchy" make for, in this case, a series of extraordinary advantages for the Oil-government combine. The ability to create pseudo-events such as Nixon's Santa Barbara inspection or controls necessary to bring off well-timed creeping events are not evenly distributed throughout the social structure. Lacking such ready access to media, lacking the ability to stage events at will, lacking a well-integrated system of arrangements for goal attainment (at least in comparison to their adversaries) Santa Barbara's leaders have met with repeated frustrations.

Their response to their relative powerlessness has been analogous to other groups and individuals, who, from a similar vantage point, come to see the system up close. They become willing to expand their repertoire of means of influence as their cynicism and bitterness increase concomitantly. Letter writing gives way to demonstrations, demonstrations to civil disobedience. People refuse to participate in "democratic precedures" which are a part of the opposition's event-management strategy. Confrontation politics arise as a means of countering with "events" of one's own, thus providing the media with "stories" which can be simply and energetically told. The lesson is learned that "the power to make a reportable event is . . . the power to make experience" (Boorstin, 1962:10).

Rallies were held at local beaches: Congressmen and state and national officials were greeted by demonstrations. (Fred Hartley, of Union Oil, inadvertently landed his plane in the midst of one such demonstration, causing a rather ugly name-calling scene to ensue.) A "sail-in" was held one Sunday with a flotilla of local pleasure boats forming a circle around Platform A, each craft bearing large anti-oil banners. (Months earlier boats coming near the platforms were sprayed by oil personnel with fire hoses.) City-hall meetings were packed with citizens reciting "demands" for immediate and forceful local action.

A City Council election in the midst of the crisis resulted in the landslide election of the Council's bitterest critic and the defeat of a veteran Councilman suspected of having "oil interests." In a rare action, the *News-Press* condemned the local Chamber of Commerce for accepting oil money for a fraudulent tourist advertising campaign which touted Santa Barbara (including its beaches) as restored to its former beauty. (In the end, references to the beaches were removed from subsequent advertisements, but the oil-financed campaign continued briefly.)

In the meantime, as a *Wall Street Journal* reporter was to observe, "a current of gloom and despair" ran through the ranks of Santa Barbara's militants. The president of Sloan Instruments Corporation, an international R & D firm with headquarters in Santa Barbara, came to comment:

> We are so God-damned frustrated. The whole democratic process seems to be falling apart. Nobody responds to us, and we end up doing things progressively less reasonable. This town is going to blow up if there isn't some reasonable attitude expressed by the Federal Government—nothing seems to happen except that we lose.

Similarly, a well-to-do widow, during a legal proceeding in Federal District Court in which Santa Barbara was once again "losing," whispered in the author's ear:

Now I understand why those young people at the University go around throwing things. . . The individual has no rights at all.

One possible grand strategy for Santa Barbara was outlined by a local public relations man and GOO worker:

We've got to run the oil men out. The City owns the wharf and the harbor that the company has to use. The city has got to deny its facilities to oil traffic, service boats, cranes and the like. If the city contravenes some federal navigation laws (which such actions would unquestionably involve), to hell with it.

The only hope to save Santa Barbara is to awaken the nation to the ravishment. That will take public officials who are willing to block oil traffic with their bodies and with police hoses, if necessary. Then federal marshals or federal troops would have to come in. This would pull in the national news media (*SBNP*, July 6, 1969, p.7).

This scenario has thus far not occurred in Santa Barbara, although the use of the wharf by the oil industries has led to certain militant actions. A picket was maintained at the wharf for two weeks, protesting the conversion of the pier from a recreation and tourist facility to a heavy industrial plant for the use of the oil companies.[16] A boycott of other wharf businesses (e.g., two restaurants) was urged. The picket line was led by white, middle-class adults—one of whom had almost won the mayorality of Santa Barbara in a previous election. Hardly a "radical" or a "militant," this same man was several months later representing his neighborhood protective association in its opposition to the presence of a "Free School" described by this man (somewhat ambivalently) as a "hippie hotel."

Prior to the picketing, a dramatic Easter Sunday confontation (involving approximately 500 persons) took place between demonstrators and city police. Unexpectedly, as a wharf rally was breaking up, an oil service truck began driving up the pier to make delivery of casing supplies for oil drilling. There was a spontaneous sit-down in front of the truck. For the first time since the Ku Klux Klan folded in the 1930s, a group of Santa Barbarans (some young, some "hippie," but many hard-working middle-class adults), was publicly taking the law into its own hands. After much lengthy discussion between police, the truck driver and the demonstrators, the truck was ordered away and the demonstrators remained to rejoice in their victory. The following day's *News-Press* editorial, while not supportive of such tactics, found much to excuse—noteworthy given the paper's long standing *bitter* opposition to similar tactics when exercised by dissident Northern blacks or student radicals.

A companion demonstration on the water failed to materialize; a group of Santa Barbarans was to sail to the Union platform and "take it"; choppy seas, however, precluded a landing, causing the would-be conquerors to return to port in failure.

It would be difficult to speculate at this writing what forms Santa Barbara's resistance might take in the future. The veteran *News-Press* reporter who has

---

16. As a result of local opposition, Union Oil was to subsequently move its operations from the Santa Barbara wharf to a more distant port in Ventura County.

covered the important oil stories has publicly stated that if the government fails to eliminate both the pollution and its causes "there will, at best be civil disobedience in Santa Barbara and at worst, violence." In fact, talk of "blowing up" the ugly platforms has been recurrent—and is heard in all social circles.

But just as this kind of talk is not completely serious, it is difficult to know the degree to which the other kinds of militant statements are serious. Despite frequent observations of the "radicalization"[17] of Santa Barbara, it is difficult to determine the extent to which the authentic grievances against Oil have generalized to a radical analysis of American society. Certainly an SDS membership campaign among Santa Barbara adults would be a dismal failure. But that is too severe a test. People, especially basically contented people, change their worldview only very slowly, if at all. Most Santa Barbarans go about their comfortable lives in the ways they always did; they may even help Ronald Reagan to another term in the statehouse. But I do conclude that large numbers of persons have been moved, and that they have been moved in the direction of the radical left. They have gained insights into the structure of the power in America not possessed by similarly situated persons in other parts of the country. The claim is thus that some Santa Barbarans, expecially those with most interest and most information about the oil spill and its surrounding circumstances, have come to view power in America more intellectually, more analytically, more sociologically—more *radically*—than they did before.

I hold this to be a general sociological response to a series of concomitant circumstances, which can be simply enumerated (*again!*) as follows:

1. *Injustice.* The powerful are operating in a manner inconsistent with the normatively sanctioned expectations of an aggrieved population. The aggrieved population is deprived of certain felt needs as a result.

2. *Information.* Those who are unjustly treated are provided with rather complete information regarding this disparity between expectations and actual performances of the powerful. In the present case, that information has been provided to Santa Barbarans (and only to Santa Barbarans) by virtue of their own observations of local physical conditions and by virtue of the unrelenting coverage of the city's newspaper. Hardly a day has gone by since the initial spill that the front page has not carried an oil story; everything the paper can get its hands on it printed. It carries analyses; it makes the connections. As an appropriate result, Oil officials have condemned the paper as a "lousy" and "distorted" publication of "lies."[18]

3. *Literacy and Leisure.* In order for the information relevant to the injustice to be assimilated in all its infuriating complexity, the aggrieved parties must be, in the larger sense of the terms, literate and leisured. They must have the ability and the time to read, to ponder and to get upset.

---

17. Cf. Morton Mintz, "Oil Spill 'Radicalizes' a Conservative West Coast City," Washington Post, June 29, 1969, pp. C-1, 5.

18. Union Oil's public relations director stated: "In all my long career, I have never seen such distorted coverage of a news event as the Santa Barbara News-Press has foisted on its readers. It's a lousy newspaper." (SBNP, May 28, 1969, p. A-1.)

My perspective thus differs from those who would regard the radical response as appropriate to some form or another of social or psychological freak. Radicalism is not a subtle form of mental illness (cf. recent statements of such as Bettelheim) caused by "rapid technological change," or increasing "impersonality" in the modern world; radicals are neither "immature," "underdisciplined," nor "anti-intellectual." Quite the reverse. They are persons who most clearly live under the conditions specified above and who make the most rational (and moral) response, given those circumstances. Thus radical movements draw their membership disproportionately from the most leisured, intelligent and informed of the white youth (cf. Flacks, 1967), and from the young blacks whose situations are most analogous to these white counterparts.

The Accident As a Research Methodology

If the present research effort has had as its strategy anything pretentious enough to be termed a "methdology," it is the methodology of what could be called "accident research." I define an "accident" as an occasion in which miscalculation leads to the breakdown of customary order. It has as its central characteristic the fact that an event occurs which is, to some large degree, unanticipated by those whose actions caused it to occur. As an event, an accident is thus crucially dissimilar both from the pseudo-event and the creeping event. It differs from the pseudo-event in that it bespeaks of an authentic and an unplanned happening; it differs from the creeping event in its suddenness, its sensation, in the fact that it brings to light a series of preconditions, actions and consequences all at once. It is "news"—often sensational news. Thresholds are reached; attentions are held.

The accident thus tends to have consequences which are the very opposite of events which are pseudo or creeping. Instead of being a deliberately planned contribution to a purposely developed "social structure" (or, in the jargon of the relevant sociological literature, "decisional outcome"), it has as its consequence the revelation of features of a social system, or of individuals actions and personalities, which are otherwise deliberately obfuscated by those with the resources to create pseudo- and creeping events. A resultant convenience is that the media, at the point of accident, may come to function as able and persistent research assistants.

At the level of everyday individual behavior, the accident is an important lay methodological resource of gossipers—especially for learning about those possessing the personality and physical resources to shield their private lives from public view. It is thus that the recent Ted Kennedy accident functioned so well for the purpose (perhaps useless) of gaining access to that individual's private routines and private dispositions. An accident such as the recent unprovoked police shooting of a deaf mute on the streets of Los Angeles provides analogous insights into routine police behavior which official records could never reveal. The massive and unprecedented Santa Barbara oil spill has similarly led to important revelations about the structure of power. An accident is thus an important instrument for learning about the lives of the powerful and the features of the social system which they deliberately and quasi-deliberately create. It is available as a research focus for those seeking a comprehensive understanding of the structure of power in America.

Finale

Bachrach and Baratz (1962) have pointed to the plight of the pluralist students of community power who lack any criteria for the inevitable *selecting* of the "key political decisions" which serve as the basis for their research conclusions. I offer accident as a criterion. An accident is not a decision, but it does provide a basis for insight into whole series of decisions and non-decisions, events and pseudo-events which, taken together, might provide an explanation of the structure of power. Even though the local community is notorious for the increasing triviality of the decisions which occur within it (cf. Schulze, 1961; Vidich and Bensman, 1958; Mills, 1956), accident research at the local level might serve as "micro"-analyses capable of revealing the "second face of power" (Bachrach and Baratz), ordinarily left faceless by traditional community studies which fail to concern themselves with the processes by which bias is mobilized and thus how "issues" rise and fall.

The present effort has been the relatively more difficult one of learning not about community power, but about national power—and the relationship between national and local power. The "findings" highlight the extraordinary intransigence of national institutions in the face of local dissent, but more importantly, point to the processes and tactics which undermine that dissent and frustrate and radicalize the dissenters.

The relationship described between Oil, government, and the knowledge industry does not constitute a unique pattern of power in America. All major sectors of the industrial economy lend themselves to the same kind of analysis as Oil in Santa Barbara. Where such analyses have been carried out, the results are analogous in their content and analogous in the outrage which they cause. The nation's defeat in Vietnam, in a sense an accident, has led to analogous revelations about the arms industry and the manner in which American foreign policy is waged.[19] Comparable scrutinies of the agriculture industry, the banking industry, etc., would, in my opinion, lead to the same infuriating findings as the Vietnam defeat and the oil spill.

The national media dwell upon only a few accidents at a time. But across the country, in various localities, accidents routinely occur—accidents which can tell much not only about local power, but about national power as well. Community power studies typically have resulted in revelations of the "pluralistic" squabbles among local sub-elites which are stimulated by exogenous interventions (cf. Walton, 1968). Accident research at the local level might bring to light the larger societal arrangements which structure the parameters of such local debate. Research at the local level could thus serve as an avenue to knowledge about *national* power. Sociologists should be ready when an accident hits in their neighborhood, and then go to work.

---

19. I have in mind the exhaustively documented series of articles by I. F. Stone in the New York Review of Books over the course of 1968 and 1969, a series made possible, in part, by the outrage of Senator Fulbright and others at the mistake of Vietnam.

References

Allen, Allan A. (1969) "Santa Barbara oil spill." Statement presented to the U.S. Senate Interior Committee, Subcommittee on Minerals, Materials and Fuels, May 20, 1969.

Arendt, Hannah (1963) Eichmann in Jerusalem: A Report on the Banality of Evil. New York: The Viking Press.

Bachrach, Peter and Morton Baratz (1962) "The two faces of power." American Political Science Review 57 (December): 947-952.

Boorstin, Daniel J. (1961) The Image. New York: Atheneum Press.

Engler, Robert (1961) The Politics of Oil. New York: Macmillan.

Flacks, Richard (1967) "The liberated generation." Journal of Social Issues 22 (December): 521-543.

Gans, Herbert (1962) The Urban Villagers. New York: The Free Press of Glencoe.

Mills, C. Wright (1956) The Power Elite. New York: Oxford University Press.

Schattschneider, E. E. (1960) The Semisovereign People. New York: Holt, Rinehart & Winston.

Schulze, Robert O. (1961) "The bifurcation of power in a satellite city." Pp. 19-81 in Morris Janowitz (ed.), Community Political Systems. New York: The Free Press of Glencoe.

Vidich, Arthur and Joseph Bensman (1958) Small Town in Mass Society. Princeton: Princeton University Press.

Walton, John (1968) "The vertical axis of community organization and the structure of power." Pp. 353-367 in Willis D. Hawley and Frederick M. Wirt (eds.), The Search for Community Power. Englewood Cliffs, N.J.: Prentice-Hall.

Part 2

HOW DO WE TAKE CARE OF EACH OTHER?

How we take care of each other is at times a matter of when we take care of each other. That it is right to give aid to a person who suffers from an affliction that is beyond his or her control is a generally accepted axiom of American society. It is also generally accepted that if a person's problem is self-caused, it is the responsibility of that individual to deal with the consequences. The subject matter of this section is: How do afflictions and problems come to be viewed as either the responsibility of an individual or of society?

Whether a problem is viewed the responsibility of an individual or a society is often related to the class level of the people affected.

For example, poverty in our society is typically viewed as the fault of the poor (not being willing to work hard enough) rather than as a condition beyond their control (a structural lack of jobs for them in the economy).

William Ryan calls this psychological sleight of hand, "blaming the victim."[1] Individuals who suffer the ill-consequences of other persons' actions are made to feel that it is their own fault. Ryan offers the example of a pharmaceutical manufacturer's poster that says, "Lead Paint Kills Children," and urges parents to keep their children from eating lead paint.[2] The implied message is that if your children do eat paint and suffer brain damage it is your fault. Landlords who do not follow and city officials who do not enforce building code regulations requiring the removal of lead paint are not cited as even potentially responsible agents in these posters. Of course, there is no mention of a slum real estate industry with powerful political connections.[3]

By contrast, when a problem is viewed as the result of involuntary action and is one to which the upper class is subject, the people associated with the problem are typically viewed as in the grip of a force which is beyond their control. For example, in our society physical sickness is typically viewed as a condition which is beyond the control of the person ill rather than, as in some other societies, punishment for personal behavior or the result of an enemy's ill-will. Physical illnesses such as heart disease, ulcers, or cancer, when suffered by the upper class in our society, are not stigmatized; rather, they are dignified as unfortunate and unjustified circumstances that strike down hard-working, successful people.

On this assumption, conservatives are apt to view, as generally appropriate, the concentration of philanthropic and government funds on research and clinical care for these diseases rather than on physical ailments resulting from malnutrition or the consumption of lead paint, which affect the poor. Tuberculosis, today usually associated with the poor and undernourished, is the recipient of research and clinical funds because it is seen as a threat to those who might come into contact with its victims.

When viewed as lower class or voluntary, a problem is usually criminal-ized or at least stigmatized, and the persons associated with it are removed from the general society—imprisoned or placed in a presumably more benign total institution, such as a mental hospital. This process of problem definition by *action choice* and *class level* may be seen with special clarity when a problem which has previously been associated with the lower class becomes common to the upper class as well. The prime example of this shift and its predictable responses in terms of these factors may be seen in the response to drug use. In an earlier time, when drug use was associated primarily with the lower class, the upper levels of society viewed it with disdain as a choice of behavior undertaken by people with depraved minds and wills. As lower-class behavior, it was stigmatized and then repressed with heavy criminal penalties.

When upper-class youth began to experiment with drugs, however, the public conception of drug use underwent at least a partial shift. Drugs came to be viewed as techniques to expand consciousness and to undergo new experiences—even of a quasi-religious nature. Many upper-class parents saw drug use as a social contagion, which had swept their children into undertaking an involuntary behavior. They did not perceive it as being of their own free and rational choice. Penalties were applied with less severity as the class level of the drug user rose, and a movement to legitimate and decriminalize the use of drugs has emerged with some political strength. As drug use became associated with both the high and the low ends of our class scale, two conflicting interpretations of drug use emerged with equally contradictory effects on drug users. An upper-class youthful drug user may be admonished with a lecture from the judge and a suspended sentence, while a lower-class youth is offered a plea bargain: pleading guilty to a lesser charge and a shorter prison term. Thus, class is a prime underlying factor in the social definition of social problems.

Those social problems more frequently associated with the lower class are typically viewed as being voluntary, that is, the result of either the victim's action or inaction. Social problems associated with the upper class are typically viewed as circumstances beyond the control of the individual involved. To achieve greater specificity of analysis, however, these statements must be cross-checked with the political value positions. The view of the lower class as associated with problems of choice is a conservative position, whereas the opposite perspective on the lower class, that is, as subject to involuntary problems, is the position taken at the liberal/socialist side of the political value axis.

Notes

1. William Ryan, *Blaming the Victim* (New York: Random House, 1971).

2. William Ryan, *Blaming the Victim* (New York: Random House, 1971) pp. 22–24.

3. David Colfax "Sociology and the Politics of Poison" In Arthur Shostak ed. *Putting Sociology to Work* (New York: David McKay Company, 1974.) pp. 3–19.

Chapter 4

RAPE

In the early 1960s Betty Friedan referred to the problem that has no name:

If a woman had a problem in the 1950s and the 1960s she knew that something must be wrong with her marriage, or with herself. Other women were satisfied with their lives, she thought. What kind of woman was she if she did not feel that mysterious fulfillment waxing that kitchen floor?[1]

The problem was the mystification of sexism.

Mystification is a process by which we either fool ourselves about our oppression or are fooled by others into believing we are not oppressed when we actually are.

Subordination of females to males was accepted by both partners in the traditional marriage. In marriage the husband was the oppressor while the wife was oppressed; both accepted this as the norm. Mystification was the vehicle by which both sexes hid what was actually happening from each other. Mystification enabled men to be saved the embarrassment of the awareness that they were oppressors, while women were saved the shame of awareness of their oppression.

Family pathologies such as alcoholic husbands, psychiatric disturbances in daughters, and delinquency in sons are often attributed to either martyrdom or masochism in the wife or mother. In *Blaming the Victim*, William Ryan shows that sociologists have often been guilty of imputing the cause of a social problem to the people who suffer its effects.[2] Blaming the victim, in this case women, has also occurred in social-problems texts about such issues as abortion, rape, prostitution, homosexuality, and divorce. Typically, women's actions are seen as the cause of the problem rather than the product of the social conflicts found in a sexist society.

The sexist perspective in sociology assigns traditional roles to women, assumes that women have accepted these roles, and discusses social problems in relationship to these defined roles. A typical example of this sort of thinking is an article which proclaims: "Although most employed women have minor roles in the production process available to them, in most cases they still have an alternate choice, that of the role of housewife and mother."[3]

This statement is sexist because it assumes that women may rightfully be relegated to the home and excluded from full participation in the economy outside of the household.

The demystification of sexism by the feminist movement has made male-female relationships into a political issue, which can be argued from the perspectives of conservatism, liberalism, and socialism.

Conservatives tend to disbelieve that sexism is a real phenomenon. They argue that male and female roles are naturally different and that these differences are rooted in biological distinctions. The nuclear family is accepted as a fundamental social institution, and male authority within the family is justified. Any woman who questions male authority is viewed as a problem, not the existence of such authority. The social conflicts that have arisen from the feminist questioning of male authority are regarded as disruptive and illegitimate. Specific issues such as occupational discrimination and rape are viewed as the fault of women. Power differentials between men and women are not seen as valid criteria for analyzing these issues. Any woman who questions current social arrangements among the sexes is viewed as a problem, not sexism.

Liberals believe that sexism exists. Women have been denied rights equal to those of men in many areas of life. These differences are illegitimate and can be remedied by specific social reforms. Occupational discrimination against women can be dealt with by lawsuits and by legislation against discrimination. The relative absence of women from positions of political power can be dealt with by organizing womens' political organizations to support female candidates for public office. The struggle against each particular manifestation of sexism is viewed as the correct strategy to deal with the overall problem. The campaign for the Equal Rights Amendment to the Constitution is the broadest political effort to deal with sexism in general terms.

Socialists agree with liberals that sexism exists. However, they view inequality between the sexes as one aspect of broader social inequities. Class differences based on control of the means of production is the fundamental inequity. Inequalities based on sex, race, and age are viewed as subsidiary to this more fundamental dichotomy. Socialists view sexism, racism, and ageism as problems, primarily because they tend to divide the working class against itself. Reforms to alleviate these problems are viewed as necessary steps so that the working class may be united to engage in the larger struggle against capitalism. Only through the elimination of capitalism and a transition to a socialist society based on principles of equality can class differences and subsidiary distinctions based on sex, race, and age be done away with.

In this chapter the general problem of sexism will be examined by looking at the particular issue of rape.

In the conservative article, Edward Sagarin takes the position that the feminist effort to get the crime of rape taken more seriously by the judicial system has dangerous consequences. There is an increased likelihood that innocent persons will be convicted. Sagarin expresses great concern for the potentially wrongfully accused perpetrator, and his general attitude toward female rape victims is that many accept or even willingly participate in sexual encounters later defined as rape. The attempt to redress the imbalance of power between men and women in sexual encounters is viewed as an illegitimate attack on men. Attempts to change the way rape is defined and prosecuted will likely do more harm to men than good for women. Sagarin uses liberal arguments based on civil liberties to justify his perspective on rape. Nevertheless, his position is basically conservative because he will not admit that inequities of power exist between men and women.

In the liberal article, Pauline Bart argues that rape is an expression of sexism and symptomatic of the endemic nature of violence against women. The ability of men to rape women with little fear of punishment is a powerful form of social control over women. Narrow legal definitions of rape and sexist judicial systems allow most rapists to escape prosecution and conviction. Bart argues for a definition of rape that would include forcible sexual assaults by husbands and lovers. Pressure from the feminist movement on police, judges, doctors, and social workers can improve the treatment of women who are raped. Women and the authorities must learn to act on the premise that rape is not the victim's fault and instead to treat it as a violent assault on her person and a violation of human rights.

In the socialist article, Julia and Herman Schwendinger agree with Bart that rape and the threat of rape is a part of the reality of everyday life for women. They also support reforms to increase the protection of women. But the Schwendingers do not believe that the incidence of rape can be significantly reduced merely by attacking sexism. They view rape and sexism as connected to the inequalities built into western societies by the growth of capitalism. This socio-economic system must be changed to a socialist political economy to eliminate rape and other crimes of violence, which are produced by capitalism.

Notes

1. Betty Friedan, *The Feminine Mystique* (New York: W. W. Norton, 1963), pp. 14, 15.

2. William Ryan, *Blaming the Victim* (New York: Random House, 1971).

3. J. R. Landis, *Current Perspectives on Social Problems* (Belmont, Calif.: Wadsworth, 1970).

Conservative

Edward Sagarin: Forcible Rape and the Problem of the Rights of the Accused

Forcible rape is without question one of the most terrifying crimes in which the victim survives. The fright has an enduring quality; its consequences remain with the victim for many years or perhaps a lifetime, accounting for deep psychological problems. While the act is occurring, the fear of being seriously injured, even killed, may be similar to that felt while one is being robbed at gunpoint, with the possibility that a wrong move or an interpretation of a flicker may cause the gun to be shot. Further, in rape the stigma falls upon the most innocent victim, who is hence perceived as marred or unchaste, someone impure, as if she were more a collaborator than she claims. A relic from the era of the cult of virginity, this last absurdity may be disappearing in the Western world.

Rape is a crime for which convictions have not been easy to obtain, even when the evidence against the accused was quite strong. It is no wonder, then, that the new militant women's movement, weary of waiting for the male-dominated police, courts, and legislative bodies to put their house in order, have demanded better protection against rapists and more vigorous prosecution of the perpetrators of this heinous offense.

Successful prosecutions of rape have been difficult for several reasons:

1. A defendant will sometimes admit that there was sexual intercourse, but will claim that it was voluntary; although his claim is untrue, the woman has no evidence to establish this.

2. A woman is discouraged from prosecuting in a situation of this sort, for fear that a verdict of not guilty will stigmatize her.

3. A woman is further discouraged because, as complaining witness, she frequently has been subjected to embarrassing cross-examination about her prior sex life by counsel for the defense, particularly if the defense sought to establish that she was not an unwilling partner.

Rape, however, is unique in some other aspects that warrant careful attention. A charge of rape has sometimes been made when there has been no sexual encounter (a few examples are cited below); probably more than any other crime in which the perpetrator is actually seen at close range by the victim and even by others, the conditions make identification rather suspect; and finally, the crime of rape is probably the only illegal act that has been so inextricably interwoven with the deliberate effort to oppress the black people.

The Accusation without the Crime

The accusation of a crime where there has been none at all is not entirely unknown in other legal areas. To reverse the well-known phrase of Edwin Schur (1965), one might look into a category of victims without crimes. People have been accused of murder, when further investigation revealed that the deceased had died a natural death or had died by his own hand (that is, there was no murder) or even when the "deceased" was still alive (because of improper identification of a body or an assumption of death without the *corpus delicti*). Accusations of robbery have been made for various reasons by persons who knew that they had not been robbed (for revenge or to obtain an insurance claim); and of larceny by those who mistakenly thought that something had been taken when actually it had been misplaced.

The charge of rape may occur falsely under essentially three conditions, each of which deserves separate consideration. The first two involve instances in which there was no rape, and the third in which the crime did occur but the person accused was not the perpetrator. In sum:

1. No sexual act has taken place between the accuser and the accused, and the alleged victim has not been subjected to rape at the hands of the accused or anyone else.

2. Sexual intercourse between the complaining witness and the defendant has occured,[1] perhaps once or on several occasions, but it has been consensual; however, the woman decides to make an accusation of rape against the man.

3. The female has indeed been raped, and the perpetrator is someone previously unknown to her; in good faith, she makes an identification, but the person accused has not been the offender.

The Rape That Wasn't

It would appear that the first of the three categories can be disposed of with the least amount of difficulty. A recent newspaper story (*New York Post*, May 9, 1973) carried the headline, "Raped Girl Wasn't." A 16-year-old girl claimed that she had been raped repeatedly in New York's Central Park. When hospital tests showed that she had not been raped, the girl thereupon changed her story, saying that "she had skipped school to go to the park with a girl friend." The police and medical authorities can usually detect a lie of this sort.

There has been almost no research on this type of false claim (a sort of corollary to what is in all likelihood the much more frequent case of the girl who has been victimized in what was indisputably a forcible rape and has suppressed information about it). With little data available, it would appear that a statement that one has been raped when there has been no sexual encounter is probably rare.

However, the most blatant and frequent experience of a false accusation of rape, in the complete absence of sexual contact, forcible or consensual, involves racial matters and the entire sexual-racial mythology that has grown up in

America. It is impossible to read the history of the American South, the terrible story of lynching and of courtroom travesties, without concluding that the cry of rape was a systematic and deliberate invention of white males who made accusations against black males and who then compelled the white females to echo and support the charges. It was a cry raised for the sole and exclusive purpose of perpetrating the caste oppression of the blacks that followed the ascendancy of the Klan and the defeat of Reconstruction. Historical studies show that nothing remotely resembling forcible sexual attack had occurred in the overwhelming majority of cases for which black males were lynched, legally or extralegally.[2]

Scottsboro and After

In the 1930s, the truth about the cry of rape against pure, white womanhood was brought dramatically to the attention of the entire world in what came to be known as the *Scottsboro* case (cf. Carter, 1969; *Powell v. Alabama*, 1932). In the midst of the depression, nine black youths, the youngest only thirteen years of age and the oldest twenty, were riding the freights in Alabama, and on a train they became embroiled in a fight with two white youths. Blacks and whites, all were what was known as hobos. The whites, outnumbered, overpowered, and defeated, were thrown off the train, picked up by local authorities, and allegedly said there were two white girls on the freight who had been raped by the blacks. At the next stop, the latter were rounded up, arrested, and in a one-day trial, without representation by counsel, in an atmosphere that the Supreme Court described as "tense, hostile, and excited public sentiment," were found guilty of rape by an all-white jury. The youngest boy was sentenced to life imprisonment, the others to death.

Northern radicals entered the case, and a new defense brought forth evidence that the girls were prostitutes. One of the girls vehemently denied, through an entire series of later trials and interrogations, that she had been attacked, molested, or in any way had had sexual contact with any of the youths. A worldwide outcry, led or exploited (the words really mean the same thing, and the choice of language depends on political preferences) by the international Communist movement, joined by Negro reformist groups, liberals, and civil libertarians, stopped the hand of the legal lynchers. The result was the gradual release of the youths, the last in 1950, after nineteen years in prison and after America had entered and emerged victorious from a war to save the world from racism.

The important thing about *Scottsboro* is that it was not unique, except in that it came to the attention of the entire world. The cry that black men were raping white women was an integral and deliberate effort of the white ruling group in the South to continue to stir up fear and hatred against blacks so that the movement of the latter toward enfranchisement, legal rights, trial by juries on which their peers were sitting, and other liberties granted to white American citizens (and noncitizens too) would be effectively combatted. It was an anti-union battle cry (unionism was extremely weak in the South, and wages were far lower than elsewhere in the United States) to keep the hostility between white and black workers at a feverish height.

Of the approximately three thousand extralegal mob lynchings that took place in America from the Emancipation Proclamation to World War II, more than 90 percent of the victims were black, more than 90 percent occurred in the Deep South, approximately 20 percent of the victims were accused (if one can dignify a lynching by referring to the victims as accused) of committing rape. Investigation has led observers to state that in the great majority of instances, there was no sexual encounter (consensual or other) between the lynched individual and any white woman (Myrdal, 1944; Raper, 1933).

One might say that all that is in the past, but is it? A group calling itself the Prisoners Solidarity Committee of Norfolk, Virginia, made the following statement, published in the letters column of a radical newspaper, *The Militant*, in 1974:

> James Carrington is a young black man who has served four years of a 75-year sentence on a frameup rape charge. He is attempting to win a new trial on the basis of racist discrimination in the selection of the jury. The jury that sentenced him was composed entirely of elderly men, all white.
>
> During the trial, a doctor testified that there was no evidence of a sexual act, much less rape, and even the FBI said there was no evidence of abduction. All that the evidence showed was that Carrington had been found sitting in a car with a white woman friend on the night of April 10, 1970.
>
> The true purpose of the "trial" was revealed by the prosecutor who stated, "We're going to make an example of this boy, so that no colored man will ever lay hands on a white girl again."

The facts, as presented in this letter, have not been checked, and there may well be something that would substantiate the case of the prosecution. However, the all-white jury, the verdict of guilt in the light of the testimony of a doctor (even if there were other doctors who testified to the contrary), the barbaric sentence, and the inflammatory remarks of a local prosecutor are entirely consistent with American history. "There has been an enormous danger of injustice," wrote Judge David Bazelon in the *Wiley* case (*U.S. v. Wiley*, 1974), "when a black man accused of raping a white woman is tried before a white jury. Of the 455 men executed for rape since 1930, 405 (89 percent) were black. In the vast majority of these cases the complainant was white."

This is not to deny that interracial rape (and specifically black against white) exists, and perhaps is not as uncommon as the statistics of Menachem Amir (1971) would suggest. Eldridge Cleaver (1968) has even written of rape of a white woman has having been, at one time, a political act for him. Whether the act occurs because it was fostered by the atmosphere of racial tensions or for reasons similar to those prevailing for intraracial rape, the victim has the right to protection, and the offender should be required to face prosecution. But one must never overlook the circumstances surrounding the event in order to be certain that it is not racial persecution for a rape that never occurred.

Consensual Intercourse and the Charge of Rape

There are many instances in which an accused admits having had sexual relations with a woman, but denies that he did so without her consent. In the crime of rape there is a broad spectrum of variation from the instance where a girl or woman is grabbed from behind by someone who does not know her, brought into an alleyway entirely against her will, held down by one person while the other mounts her, or is clubbed or submits because of threat and fear. This is forcible rape, and there can be no question about the enormity of the crime, the nature of the sexual assault, and the lack of consent. On the other end of this spectrum, one finds a man and a woman (or boy and girl) having regular, consensual amorous sexual relations, she allegedly as eager as he, until some point at which she decides to say that he has raped her.

Between these polar extremes, there are infinite variations. A man may meet a woman in a bar and end up in a situation in which the girl says no when she is already half undressed, and the man either fails to control himself, decides that the girl does not have the right to deny him at that point, or believes that she merely wants more persuasion. Or it may be that a man goes out on several occasions with a woman who has already had intercourse with him, and she decides to discontinue the sexual part of their relationship; disbelieving, he uses more than persuasion—he resorts to force. Between the male's view of an act as voluntary, and the female's view as forcible, a court faces problems fraught with tragedy.

Perhaps one of the most interesting examples of injustice was the Giles-Johnson case (see MacDonald, 1971) in which three black youths were accused of rape, convicted, and sentenced to death in Maryland in 1961.[3] The men did not deny that they had had intercourse with the white complainant; they claimed that she had told them that she had had sex with sixteen or seventeen boys that week, and a few more wouldn't matter. The girl denied the statements, testifying that she had submitted out of fear. Investigation turned up a history of what a commentator called "almost incredible promiscuity." The girl had told the police that she had no idea how many men she had had sex with, including oral and group sex with six or eight men at a time (information the police did not pass on to the court). Although she was on probation at the time of the alleged rape, she denied this on the witness stand. Only after the U.S. Supreme Court granted an appeal were two men freed (in 1967, after spending six years in prison), and the third was released by gubernatorial pardon soon thereafter.

This is the sort of case that cries out for the right of a defendant to examine a complainant on her prior sexual history; on the other hand, it has been these fishing expeditions in open court of prior sexual history that have discouraged raped women from vigorous prosecution. The American Civil Liberties Union in 1976 adopted the following proposed guidelines, which appear to come as close to defending the sexual privacy of the woman *and* the rights of a defendant to a fair trial as any other legal or social document on the subject:

> There is in many rape cases a potential conflict between the right of the defendant to a fair trial and the complainant's right to have his or her claim to protection of the law vindicated without undue invasion of sexual privacy. In many cases this conflict may be irresolvable, and when that is the case the right to a fair trial should not be qualified, no matter how compelling the countervailing concerns. However, careful application by trial judges of the proper standards of relevance of testimony, control of cross-examination and argument, and elimination of prejudicial instructions unique to rape and similar cases could do much to preserve rape complainants from unnecessary imposition upon their rights to sexual privacy, without detracting from the fairness of the trial. Closed hearings should be used to ascertain the relevance of any proposed

line of testimony or cross-examination that may involve a witness' prior sexual history. The determination of relevance or irrelevance should be stated by the court on the record along with its reasons for so holding.

A determination as to the relevance of the prior sexual history of either the complainant or the defendant in rape * cases is acceptable only if it is administered fairly and free from sexist assumptions. Subject to special evidentiary rules designed to protect defendants for reasons other than relevance, the criteria for admitting evidence of prior sexual history employed in rape cases must apply equally to the prosecution and the defense. Similarly, any pre-trial screening process must apply equally to the prosecution and the defense.

Some aspects of some current rape laws clearly do not meet minimum standards of acceptability. Even where the defense is consent, the prosecution should not be permitted, as a matter of course, to introduce evidence of the complainant's prior chastity; neither should the defense, without more, be permitted to prove the complainant's prior unchastity. Unchaste witness instructions which permit an inference of lessened credibility from the fact of prior sexual activity are based on no rational inference and violate a complainant's right to sexual privacy—just as a 'chaste witness' instruction would violate a defendant's right to a fair trial if invoked by the prosecution. A statute, for example, which makes admissible evidence tending to prove that the complainant has been convicted of a prostitution offense, or even evidence concerning prior consensual sexual relations between the complainant and the defendant, without the necessity of showing a particular relevance, unconstitutionally infringes on the right to sexual privacy of such complainants.

Mistaken Identifications

In many rape cases, the victim was not previously known to the perpetrator, and she must identify him on the basis of her memory of his face, imprinted in her mind at the time of the offense. Most rape victims do see their attackers, though sometimes not very well, particularly if the entire action takes place in the dark. Sometimes there is another witness: the rape occurs in the presence of a friend or members of the family, usually bound and gagged but able to watch the scene.

For a variety of reasons, eyewitness identifications are notoriously unreliable, almost never acceptable without corroboration; a simple denial, if buttressed by a credible alibi, should be sufficient when such corroboration is lacking. The history of criminal justice is replete with honest errors, made in good faith, by people who were positive that their identification of the perpetrator could not be incorrect (MacNamara, 1969; see also Buckhout, 1974). While some persons might suggest that a rape victim usually obtains an excellent look at the face of the rapist, and from close by, this is often under conditions of extreme fright. Furthermore, in the case of interracial rape, the inability of people to distinguish

---

* While sexist assumptions and practices cause harm most often victims of rape or attempted rape, their rights can be protected if rape is treated as but one form of sexual assault by statutes and courts. We therefore urge that standards and procedures be developed to apply to all forms of sexual assault and that the phrase "sexual assault" be used instead of "rape" in policy statements, law, etc., in order to remove special legal disabilities from rape complainants.

members of other racial groups, and the tendency to confuse them with one another, is not a myth.

In New York City, during the period of late 1972 to early 1973, two men, on entirely different occasions and in unrelated matters, were arrested for rape, and each was positively identified in a police lineup. Each was accused independently by more than one victim. After several harrowing weeks, another arrest took place and it was noted that there was some similiarity in appearance of the persons being charged. In each instance, the old suspect was dismissed (*New York Times*, November 11, 1972, and May 18, 1973). Had the later arrests not taken place, and had there been no requirement for corroboration, it is unlikely that the defendants could have established their innocence in the face of more than one positive identification. Against this, they could have offered only their denials, some character witnesses, and perhaps alibis which are not usually airtight because for the ordinary person it is difficult to reconstruct his activities at a given hour some weeks or months later (perhaps he was at home watching television, or was with his family—although not unlikely, these are hardly unassailable alibis). It is entirely possible that one or both of the incorrectly accused men may have faced such a compelling array of evidence that the case would have ended with plea bargaining, resulting in a suspended sentence, a lifetime record, and a ruined career.

In a famous compilation of cases in which innocent people have been convicted, Yale law professor Edwin M. Borchard (1932:367) came to the following conclusion:

> Perhaps the major source of these tragic errors is an identification of the accused by the victim of a crime of violence. . . . Juries seem disposed more readily to credit the veracity and reliability of the victims of an outrage than any amount of contrary evidence by or on behalf of the accused, whether by way of alibi, character witnesses, or other testimony. These cases illustrate the fact that the emotional balance of the victim or eyewitness is so disturbed by his extraordinary experience that his powers of perception became distorted and his identification is frequently most untrustworthy. Into the identification enter other motives, not necessarily stimulated originally by the accused personally—the desire to requite a crime, to exact vengeance upon the person believed guilty, to find a scapegoat, to support, consciously or unconsciously, an identification made by another. . . . In eight of these cases the wrongfully accused person and the really guilty criminal bore not the slightest resemblance to each other, whereas in twelve other cases, the resemblance, while fair, was still not at all close.

An instance of false identification is recounted by a defender of the women's liberation thrust on rape. According to this writer (Lichtenstein, 1974), a woman was forcibly raped by two men who were complete strangers to her. At police headquarters, she was shown photographs of many men, and finally came to one. This was the younger of the two perpetrators, she said. The detectives had hit paydirt! Was she sure? She was 95 percent positive. All one had to do was find the culprit. Not a difficult task, for he was in prison, where he had been on the day of the offense.

Let us suppose that he was no longer in prison, but was an ex-convict, and she picked him out of a lineup. She would be told that 95 percent positive was insufficient, and having to make a decision, she might very well have decided that there was not a scintilla of doubt in her mind (it is not certain that she would have resolved the doubt against the man in the lineup, for many victims insist under such circumstances that they still retain doubt). What chance would he have against her accusation? As an ex-con, the supporters of his alibi might well have been less than model witnesses; and his lawyer could not call character witnesses without exposing his criminal record on prosecutorial cross-examination. An innocent man would be found guilty, one more case would be marked as closed, while the actual rapist would be free to continue to terrorize women.

Feminist Campaigns and Criminal Justice

The feminist campaign against rape is justified and overdue, and such a campaign cannot be conducted without insisting on vigorous prosecution. The impediments for such prosecution are formidable, and they include the harassment of the complaining witness, the delving into private and irrelevant aspects of the lives of the victim, and the stigmatization of the victim, sometimes accompanied by the exoneration of an offender. Remedies are necessary, but some of those proposed—not all, I emphasize—would challenge fundamental concepts of the administration of justice. In certain instances, writers have described situations in which no contemporary court of justice could find a defendant guilty, but the feminists nevertheless express their indignation and disgust. For example, Martha Lear (1972:55), noting that rape is seldom subject to impartial witness, states: "Thus, if two suspects were to be picked up and positively identified by the victim in a police lineup, and if they were to deny her charges, the case would be dropped for lack of evidence."

This is written as if it were a cry of anguish, clearly carrying an implication of injustice in dropping the charges. Of course, a case is never quite so simple. Suspects are asked questions concerning their whereabouts at the time of the offense. The woman's original description is compared with the men being detained, and other factors are taken into account. But if a case were as simple as Lear makes out, and consisted of nothing more than the positive identification by one victim and the denial by two accused, what is open for the prosecution but to drop the case "for lack of evidence"? Would conviction meet the standards of guilt having been established beyond reasonable doubt?

A New York detective is quoted by Lear (1972) as saying that

"when the woman never saw the guy before in her life, and she tells you he raped her in the park or in the hallways, and she identifies him . . . what more corroboration should a judge need? Why isn't this woman's word good enough?" . . .

What more corroboration should a judge need? It is a rhetorical question, and the answer is supposed to be, resoundingly, none. But such an answer makes no sense, for if he denies the charge, why isn't his word as good as hers? Because he is a man? Or because he is black? Further, if the testimony of the complainant and the defendant is equally believable, then the case must be adjudicated in favor of the accused, because of presumption of innocence and the requirement that guilt be established beyond a reasonable doubt.

However, there is always more to a case than an accusation and a denial. Was he caught on the spot? Did he have a hammer with him when apprehended that matched a weapon she had described? Did she tear part of his clothes off and did the sample match what he was wearing when caught? Did she describe a scar on his thigh which she could not have seen in the lineup, but which he actually did have? Failing all these and any other corroboration, can anyone demand a conviction on the basis of a believable accusation and identification and an equally believable and unequivocal denial?

Another story is related by Lear (1972:63) which was told to her by the girl involved. The latter claims that she invited a man to her apartment for coffee after a date, and when there, he proposed sex. She rejected the idea; he pushed, threatened, and held his fist in front of her face until she gave in. Later, she went to the police, who brought the man in for questioning, and he said, "She was perfectly willing," which ended the matter.

"Now, what do you call that?" the girl asked Lear, who replies, "I call it rape, and share her outrage that the bloody bastard got away with it."

This is an instance of a girl who had sexual intercourse in her own apartment, with a man that she was dating and who was in the apartment at her invitation. The girl comes to the police with no bruises, says it was rape, and the man says she was a willing partner. For the purposes of parlor games, you can believe whomever you wish, but the court does not have such a choice. It should not even hold a man for trial under these circumstances. Unless the country is ready to institutionalize the use of truth serums, lie detectors, and examination under hypnosis (which I am not advocating), a court must have something to balance the scale strongly against an accused in order to find him guilty.

There is another incident, narrated by Gail Sheehy (1971:66), in which a charge of force was made explicit: The young woman who was raped by a gynecologist—"my mother arranged the date"—went willingly to his room in the hospital residence. He forced her to the floor, raped her, washed his hands, and apologized. No one had responded to her screams. She gave up and let the gynecologist take her to dinner.[4]

The ancedote as told by Sheehy is quoted in full above; it is all the information available to me, and perhaps all that Sheehy had when she used the word "raped" without hedging with a description that it was a claim or an allegation. I find the story less than believable. I am intrigued by the girl who describes a meeting with a gynecologist in his office as a "date" rather than an appointment. Supposing, however, that it occurred as Sheehy relates it, passing on second-hand information as if it were gospel truth; could a court of law convict in the face of his denial? Is a jury expected to believe the woman and throw out the denial of the physician, in an instance in which she accompanied him to dinner afterward?

A militant feminist (Margolin, 1975:20) points out an "accurate figure of false accusations [of rape] is 20 percent, and most of these are detected right away." The statement is made without a citation and without a modicum of research, evidence, data, or proof. Nevertheless, if as many as one out of five accusations should prove to be false, and if "most" but not all these are easily detected, then is it not reasonable to consider that the charge leveled against the gynecologist is among the false accusations, detected or undetected?

Judge Bazelon, in the concurring opinion in the *Wiley* (1974) case, quotes the statement of Lord Chief Justice Hale (1778), that rape "is an accusation easily to be made and hard to be proved, and harder to be defended by the party accused, tho never so innocent." The U.S. Supreme Court, in discussing a case in which a man had been accused of making a solicitation to another man in a park, overheard by no one but the person to whom the invitation was made and in no way corroborated (*Kelly v. U.S.*, 1951; Sagarin and MacNamara, 1970), upheld the appeal of the defendant, on the grounds that an accusation of this sort is so easily made and so difficult to refute that it would not be accepted lightly without corroboration. Would not the same words be applicable to the gynecologist?

Guidelines

Some guidelines on rape prosecutions and defenses, particularly as they apply to previous sexual history, have been suggested by the American Civil Liberties Union, quoted earlier. It should be the aim of those who are concerned with law, order, and justice to work out mechanisms leading to greater protection of the victim, more vigorous prosecution of the guilty, with extreme probability (approaching but never attaining certainty) of exoneration of the guiltless, and at the same time to protect the constitutional guarantees of a fair trial and the protection of the rights of the accused.

Toward such ends, a sharp line of demarcation can be drawn between cases in which the accuser and the accused knew each other in the past and those in which they had hitherto been strangers. If known to each other, the nature of their previous relationship should be explored. A man may be in a woman's apartment, or she in his, with no intention or willingness on her part to participate in sexual activity. However, with lack of signs of a physical battle, and with no witness, her word cannot be taken against his.

If he claims that they had met that evening for the first time but that she had been a willing sex partner, then pretrial *in camera* testimony can determine whether examination on her past sexual history is relevant and admissable. That an investigation of her prior sexual life may indeed lead to harassment under cross-examination cannot be a reason for barring such evidence if it is deemed relevant. Ordinarily, the same could be true of the man's psychiatric and sexual history, except that an investigation of this aspect of his life cannot violate his rights as a defendant (which are greater than the rights of the complainant), and should in no way abrogate the Fifth Amendment which protects him from being compelled to testify against himself.

The complainant in a rape case might be afforded the protection of anonymity, similar to that offered to complainants in cases of blackmail. If this can be accomplished by the voluntary consent of the press and other media, it would be preferable; if it must be done by judicial decree or legislative act, it might be desirable, but that is a matter of public policy that goes beyond the question of rape; and if it involves a closed court and the denial of the right to a public trial for the defendant, it might require a constitutional amendment, and most persons concerned with justice, I would speculate, would oppose such a move as having greater potential for harm than for good.

On the question of corroboration, the testimony of a complainant, when it is denied by the accused, should always require corroboration, but this ought not to mean that each and every contention that she makes must be corroborated, nor that she should be required to bring to court a witness to the rape. Fundamentally, rape should be handled like any other crime in that the uncorroborated testimony of a complainant, in the face of a denial by a defendant, should be insufficient to convict.

A woman claiming to have been sexually assaulted should not be required to establish proof of penetration or the presence of ejaculate, but if she claims penetration, then medical evidence ought to be required. However, an assault may be indubitably sexual without resulting in either penetration or ejaculation, but to establish its sexual nature, the woman must be subject to examination and cross-examination on intimate physical details of the nature of the contact. The woman should be protected from unsympathetic police officers, and if female officers are better equipped for that purpose, then a logical argument is that they should be favored in the hiring for a rape investigation squad.

When the complainant asserts that the accused was unknown to her until the time of the attack, and he does not deny such a claim, but defends himself on the grounds of mistaken identity, then her previous sexual life is immaterial and irrelevant, and she should be protected from embarrassment of examination on that issue. However, in the absence of corroboration or confession, an identification of a stranger is suspect, and all the more so if he is not of the same race as the accuser. His alibi becomes important, although most persons cannot establish their whereabouts at a given time after a lapse of more than a few days.

What, then, can be done to reduce the incidence of rape and obtain more convictions of rapists? Greater and more vigorous work on the part of the police, careful studies of patterns of individual offenders, surveillance of their expected places of criminal offense, investigation of alibis: in other words, hard work, not the shortcuts of abrogation of civil liberties for the accused. And, above all, a massive effort to remove the sources of violence in society.

To combat the plague of rape, one manifestation of the violence so rampant in recent decades, every effort should be made to convict an offender short of denying the accused the right to a fair trial. In such a trial, he enters the courtroom an innocent man, which means clothed in the presumption of innocence, and the burden of proof is on the prosecution to establish beyond a reasonable doubt that a forcible rape was committed and that the defendant was indeed the perpetrator. The burden is never upon an accused to disprove these assertions.

It is tragic that there are so many rapes and other crimes of violence, but it is likewise tragic that the elementary principles of criminal justice governing all criminal trials should need restating.

Notes

1. In this article, I refer to the victim as the complaining witness or complainant, not the prosecutrix. It appears to me that a clear delineation should be made between the officers of the state, including the prosecutor (if female, a prosecutrix), and witnesses for the state.

2. There is a very rich fiction that offers remarkable insights into this phenomenon. Particularly pertinent is a short story by William Faulkner, "Dry September."

3. This case was reported in a tone of moral indignation about the fate of the alleged offender by Susan Brownmiller (1968). Ms. Brownmiller (1975:7-8), however, had later second thoughts about her position.

4. What apparently is the same episode, though the source is not identified, appears in Brownmiller (1975:355-60). In this version, the woman is reported as saying "we went out to have dinner. We proceeded along with the dinner as if nothing had happened. I was in such a state of shock I just went along with the rest of the date."

References

American Civil Liberties Union. "Policy on Prior Sexual History," No. 311, April 1976.

Amir, Menachem. 1971. *Patterns in Forcible Rape.* Chicago: University of Chicago Press.

Borchard, Edwin M. 1932. *Convicting the Innocent.* Garden City, N.Y.: Garden City Publishing Co.

Brownmiller, Susan. 1968. "Rashomon in Maryland," *Esquire 69* (May): 130-32, 145-47.

—. 1975. *Against Our Will.* New York: Simon & Schuster.

Buckout, Robert. 1974. "Eyewitness Testimony," *Scientific American* 231 (December): 23-31.

Carter, Dan T. 1969. *Scottsboro: A Tragedy of the American South.* Baton Rouge: Louisiana State University Press.

Cleaver, Eldridge. 1969. *Soul on Ice.* New York: McGraw-Hill.

Hale, Matthew. 1778. *Pleas of the Crown.* London: Richard Tonson.

Kelly v. U.S. 1951. 194 F.2d 150 (District of Columbia Circuit).

Lear, Martha. 1972. "Q. If You Rape a Woman and Steal Her TV, What Can They Get You For in New York? A. Stealing Her TV." *New York Times Magazine,* January 30, pp.10-11.

Lichtenstein, Grace. 1974. "Rape Squad," *New York Times Magazine,* March 3, pp. 10.

MacDonald, John M. 1971. *Rape Offenders and Their Victims.* Springfield, Ill.: Charles C. Thomas.

MacNamara, Donal E. J. 1969. "Convicting the Innocent," *Crime and Delinquency* 15:57-61.

Margolin, Debbi. 1975. "Rape: The Facts," *Women: A Journal of Liberation* 3:20-21.

Myrdal, Gunnar. 1944. *An American Dilemma.* New York: Harper & Row.

New York Post. 1973. "Raped Girl Wasn't," *New York Post,* May 9.

Powell v. Alabama. 1932. 287 U.S. 45.

Raper, Arthur F. 1933. *The Tragedy of Lynching.* Chapel Hill: University of North Carolina Press.

Sagarin, Edward and Donal E. J. MacNamara. 1970. "The Problem of Entrapment," *Crime and Delinquency* 16:363-78.

Schur, Edwin M. 1965. *Crimes without Victims.* Englewood Cliffs, N.J.: Prentice-Hall.

Sheehy, Gail. 1971. "Nice Girls Don't Get Into Trouble," *New York Magazine* 4 (15 February):26.

U.S. v. Wiley. 1974. 492 F2d 257.

Liberal

Pauline B. Bart: Rape as a Paradigm of Sexism in Society — Victimization and Its Discontents

It's cleavage to go with carnage at pro football games these days as skimpily clad cheerleaders cavort and prance to keep the fans' spirits up. As CBS sports producer Chuck Milton sees it, "The audience deserves a little sex with its violence!" (*Newsweek*, Nov. 7, 1977)

Introduction

For the past year Marlyn Grossman and I have been listening to over 100 women tell us about the violence in their lives. Originally I wanted to learn how women could avoid being raped when attacked. To find women who were nearly raped and a comparative group of rape victims, I advertized, put up flyers, and spoke anyplace people would let me, from tiny colleges to TV shows. I also tried to get publicity in local newspapers, having met with no success from the major news-papers since the study was not "news." I asked women who had been raped or nearly raped in the past two years to talk to me confidentially (they were given expenses and $25 since the study was funded by the Center for the Prevention and Control of Rape of the National Institute of Mental Health).

The women were asked about the situation surrounding the assault, about how they usually dealt with stress, about what skills they had (e.g., self defense) and about how they were brought up, the latter to test the feminist hypothesis that being brought up to be a girl and then a lady, or what sociologists call female socialization, sets you up to be a rape victim rather than a woman who avoids the rape (all other things being equal). I chose this topic because women would always ask me what to do if attacked and I had no answer since at that time the data were contradictory. I am trying to find the answer by learning what factors, especially what strategies under what circumstances, are associated with avoid-ing rape when attacked.

While listening to these stories I was overwhelmed by the amount of violence in women's lives—incest, child abuse, woman abuse, molestation, and with the intertwining of the prior violence with their response to the recent assault. Originally I thought there were two categories—(1) women who had been raped and (2) women who were attacked and avoided being raped. That analysis under-estimated the variety and pervasiveness of violence. There were some women who had been both rape victims and rape avoiders within a two year period, and more if I extended the time, women who had been raped several times in their lives (one twice on the same day by two different men in different places), and women who had avoided being raped several times. Some women recalled or

This study has appeared in *Women's Studies International Quarterly*, Vol. 2, no. 5 (1979), pp. 1-11. Reprinted by permission of Pergamon Press, Ltd. and the author. This investigation was supported in part by a National Institute of Mental Health Center for the Prevention and Control of Rape fellowship #1 R01 MH29311-01.

redefined prior incidents as rape in the course of recounting their current experiences. Some women who had been raped and had learned from their prior experience not only the damage it had done to their lives but what not to do managed to avoid being raped the next time someone tried to assault them. On the other hand at least two women who avoided being raped were shortly thereafter raped, one by her boyfriend who was "turned on" by the avoidance and the other by her husband (a wife-beater) who demanded his "marital rights" when she, like most women who have had an assault experience, was not able to have sex.

While I have not yet systematically analyzed the interviews, I have been thinking and speaking and writing about rape (Bart, 1975A, 1975B, 1975C, 1976A, 1976B) and more recently woman abuse (Bart, 1978) as well as speaking about violence against women in general and the change in ideology from one blaming the victim to one stating "women do it too" (Bart, 1978)—(e.g., Steinmetz's (1978) alleged data on battered husbands—for the past four years and would like to set out some of my thoughts.

Differences and Similarities Among Forms of Violence Against Women

In this analysis I differentiate between rape by someone you know and rape by a stranger. The reason will be apparent below.

1. Rape by someone you know, woman abuse and incest are violations of trust. Rape by a stranger is not. That is why I found (1975A) that the more intimately you know your attacker, the more likely you are to have psychological problems after the rape. However, the treatment women receive from society's institutions after being raped generally has a radicalizing effect on women who believed in the system and for them rape by a stranger can also cause a loss of trust, but in the society, not in men. One woman was raped while serving with one of the branches of the armed forces. When it became clear they had protected the rapist, she said, "I didn't believe the _____ (branch of service) would do such a thing." Another upwardly mobile young black woman and her family lost their faith in the system generally, and Mayor Daley, whom they admired, in particular, when rape charges against the two rapists were dismissed and she had no recourse. (While we may see these cases as progress, in fact, the loss of trust in the system caused severe existential depression.)

2. Victims of woman abuse and incest are ecologically locked in their situation, at least temporarily, since they share the same residence. (Even if the relative does not live in the house he has easy access to it.) There is an ongoing relationship. This is not true for rape (except for systematic husband rape).

3. Victims of all of these forms of violence have been blamed, but this is somewhat less likely for victims of stranger rape and most true for women who have been date raped and for battered women who remain in their marriage.[1]

4. In all of these situations the man has no respect for the needs of the other person and in some cases he assumes an identity of interest, e.g., the woman enjoys being raped, the father is giving the daughter necessary sex education.

5. In both kinds of rape, in woman abuse and in incest, mental health professionals traditionally have been part of the problem, not the solution.[2] Their intrapsychic approach, or what I call "It's what's inside that counts" (1972), leads to blaming the victim, and in the case of woman abuse and incest, their commitment to the importance of the nuclear two parent family emphasizes working things out rather than getting him out.

6. Woman battering is a recurrent event. Incest is sometimes recurrent. Rape (by the same person) is not recurrent (Husband rape may be an exception, but we have little information on this).

7. "Depersonalization" or splitting yourself off so that you think it is happening to someone else, not you, is a common response to these events. One rape victim told me she felt as if she were on the ceiling of the car watching the rape taking place on the car seat.

8. While stranger rape functions as a form of social control over women not attached to men (whose presence, presumably, though not always in fact, would deter the rapist), "date rape," women abuse and incest are forms of social control over women attached to men.

9. All of these events are underreported to the authorities. Stranger rape is the most likely to be reported of all of these crimes. Thus, while all forms of violence against women (including those we have not discussed, such as hassling on the street) have many elements in common and stem from our situation living under patriarchy, there are differences among them which it is useful to recognize and understand so that we may fight them more effectively.

Sexism, Social Class and Rape

We know that working class women suffer because of their class and gender, but we also know that almost all women are underpaid, relegated to the female occupational ghetto where, unless they have someone with whom they can combine their incomes, they frequently fall below the poverty level, particularly if they head families. The relevance for rape is as follows. While all women are vulnerable to rape by known assailants, one can buy a certain amount of protection from street or apartment rape by strangers. Many of the women I interviewed were raped waiting for public transportation or walking from public transportation. Sometimes they had typical female jobs, such as nurse or waitress, which meant that they usually had to leave work at late hours. One of the women deliberately chose the night shift so that she, a divorced mother (her husband had systematically beaten her) could spend time with her children during the day. If they could have afforded cars or cabs and had inside or secure parking, which is of course expensive, those particular rapes would have not occurred. Similarly if one can afford to live in an apartment with a doorman and/or an expensive security system that works, it is more difficult for rapists to enter. (When one of the women I spoke with told me she had been raped at gunpoint two houses down from where I live I truly understood what it meant to me to be able to afford locked parking and not have to search on the street for a space, having to walk by the very place she had been assaulted). Similarly many women hitchhike because it is the only means of transportation they have. One victim had no money and didn't want to spend Christmas alone. She was hitchhiking to another city to be with some friends, assumed men driving vans were gentle hippies, was picked up, assaulted, her virginity destroyed and she was dumped back on the road. Again, had she travel funds she could have avoided the rape. However, these kinds of rapes are not the majority of rapes and while some can buy some safety, as long as we live in a society where women are brutalized, women themselves constitute a class.

Sexism and Definition of Rape

Definitions, notably legal definitions, reflect the belief system of the dominant groups in society. It is therefore not accidental that the *de facto* and *de jure* definitions of rape embody sexist beliefs, and that these definitions are changing because, in part, of the impact of the women's movement. The following are two examples of sexism in the definition of rape:

1. Forcible intercourse between a husband and wife is not included in definitions of rape, a carryover of the concept of the wife as the husband's property. This law is being modified in some states so that a man can be charged with raping a wife from whom he is legally separated. It is interesting to note that, in an unpublished paper I read, the largest number of gender differences in defining what was rape was in the case of a man separated from his wife. It should also be noted that in fact, though not in law, it is extremely difficult for women who are prostitutes, cabdrivers and exotic dancers to have their charges of rape taken seriously. One male cabdriver, when hearing that I was a rape researcher told me a "funny" story about a prostitute who had intercourse with several men, none of whom paid her, and then claimed to have been raped. I asked him how he would feel if I didn't pay for the cab ride, which he would not have given me were it not a commercial transaction. He thought a bit and then said, "If that's rape then there's certainly a lot of rape around." He's right.

2. Rape is defined as penile vaginal penetration (although this definition is being changed in some states). Men think of rape as a sexual act and that is how they conceptualize sex. Moreover, this definition excludes the serious problem of males raping males, a dramatic example of rape as an expression of dominance.

Sexism and Individual Responses to Rape

1. The Double Standard

The double standard is applied to rape in two senses. In the first sense the double standard refers to conventional sexual morality where men have sexual freedom while women who stray from the path of virginity prior to marriage and monogamy after marriage are "bad." It is difficult for such "bad" women to receive just treatment from the police and courts, and people are more likely to believe she "got what she deserved" or "was asking for it." Thus, a study of college students showed that they responded more negatively to a vignette describing an assail-ant raping a virgin than to vignettes describing the rape of a divorcee or cocktail waitress (Hoffman and Dodd, 1975). This finding is similar to Elizabeth Pleck's (1978) research on court records where she discovered that in nineteenth century wife beating cases only husbands who beat "virtuous" wives were found guilty. In the archtypical situation, the situation that everyone would agree was rape, the victim would be a 16 year old virgin, raped by a black felon, while she was sitting in her parents' house, baby-sitting for her siblings, with all the windows closed and the door locked, [3] crocheting the flag while watching The Waltons on television.

A second manifestation of the double standard in the case of rape is that more stringent requirements are applied to proving guilt in rape cases than in other felonies. Thus, for example, corroboration was required in cases to prove the rape took place, a requirement not necessary for other crimes. Judge Morris Ploscowe opposed changing this requirement in New York State "because ladies lie." But a reading of history does not lead one to the conclusion that truth telling is a sex-linked male gene. Rape victims alone among all victims of crime are required to fight back to prove that it was indeed a crime, furnishing another example of the double standard in the case of rape. Such a demand requires that a woman transcend her traditional socialization which is to be "nice," trusting and compli-ant and not be a tomboy after twelve, so that she usually does not have fighting skills, or even skills in physical contact sports, such as football. Non-traditional females who are more likely to have the skill to fight back are less likely to be treated justly by the societal institutions, while traditional females are, in this situation, supposed to behave non-traditionally, without the skills to do so.

2. The Ideology of the Rapist As Mentally Ill

One of the most common ideologies about rapists, and one that invalidates the feminist analysis of rape, is that men rape because they are mentally ill. Some of the women with whom I spoke gave that reason for the rape, although their major evidence for mental illness was "Why else would he rape?" This circular reasoning psychologically protected the women because were they to believe men raped because they wanted to dominate women, that the dehumanization of women and misogyny inherent in rape are endemic in the society, that there are no data indicating that rapists are more crazy than anyone else, then women would have to confront the fact that they were always at risk of being raped as long as they lived in a sexist society.

In fact we know nothing about rapists. We know something about imprisoned rapists, but since so few rapists are convicted, fewer still convicted on charges of rape (i.e., they have not been plea-bargained) and fewer still in prison rather than on probation, by examining rapists in prison, as some researchers do, we can make inferences not to men who are rapists but to men who are losers. Even in the case of incest there is little data that the men are mentally ill. Herman and Hershman (1977) note that incestuous fathers are neither psychotic nor intellec-tually defective. "They are especially hostile toward women" and "see the sex act as an act of aggression." Clearly such beliefs characterize a large proportion of the male population. To call people holding such beliefs mentally ill makes the term meaningless since mental illness is a deviant status. If everyone is sick the term loses its analytic utility.

Psychiatric explanations of behavior have replaced religious explanations in our society. Psycho has replaced sin to account for behavior. But a feminist analysis must use a structural or institutional analysis of behavior rather than an individual one. If we are not suffering from private problems but from public issues, as we learned in our consciousness raising groups, then we have to discuss what the public issues are and why they lead to violence against women. To call rapists mentally ill is an individualistic explanation; to say that rape is the logical culmination of male sexual socialization and thus neither abnormal nor unexpected behavior is a feminist alternative interpretation.

The Ideology of the Imperative Nature of Male Sexuality

Another ideology justifying incest and rape is the mistaken view that the demands of male sexuality are so imperative that if a man becomes aroused he has no choice but to assault the woman who has stimulated him or a substitute. Masturbation is not considered a more ethical or viable alternative. This belief can account for one incest researcher explaining incest by noting that the girls are unusually charming and attractive in their outward personalities (Herman and Hirschman, 1977). What's a poor man to do? Similarly the view that the rape victims bring it on themselves by being sexily dressed, and thus break through the thin veneer of control men have over their sexual drives leaving them with no choice but rape, assumes this view of male sexuality. But no man ever died of an erection—though many women have.

In other areas of our life we are not allowed to take what we want, even if provoked, e.g., store windows are deliberately designed to make people want the products. Yet that does not legally justify breaking the glass and taking them. Only in the case of violence against women is doing what one wants in response to "provocation" a justification. Without giving any credence to the provocative dress theory of rape by answering it I want to note that of all the women interviewed only one was "scantily clad" since she was walking home from the beach in shorts. Most were wearing pants, and many were assaulted in the dead of Chicago winter dressed as if they were about to climb Mt. Everest.

It is easy to understand why men hold these views of rape which narrow the definition so most rapes are not defined as such, particularly if the man is "provoked." Since male sexual aggression is endemic, if any sex act against a person's will is considered rape, the majority of men would be rapists. They could not only be accused of rape but found guilty. But if rapists are mentally ill, since most men consider themselves sane, they are not rapists. Viewing rape as normal in our society is threatening to men. I account for Judge Simonson's defeat in Madison by realizing that men voted against him because they were threatened by his definition of rape as normal male behavior. One male newscaster told me he felt insulted by Simonson's remarks about rape being a normal response. Contrast the outrage against Simonson with the low level of response to the judge in California who freed a rapist who had assaulted a hitchhiker. The latter judge kept the definition of rape narrow and thus was acting in the interest of men. The former broadened the definition of rape and so threatened men.

In addition, just as some women have rape fantasies (never to be confused with the actual desire to be raped, since one has power over a fantasy and the essence of rape is a feeling of powerlessness), men, I have been told by male clinicians, have fantasies of being rapists. This fact, combined with general male sexual aggressiveness, particularly in dating (Kanin, 1957, 1971) can explain why women who went to court told me that the States' attorneys and judges identified with the rapist rather than with them. This identification crossed both class and race lines.[4] While racism and class bias certainly are present in the judicial system, they operate more clearly when men of different classes and/or races are involved. When, however, the case is male vs. female, particularly in instances of violence, identification along gender lines rather than along race or class lines seems to predominate, at least at this particular historical time.

It is more puzzling to understand why many women hold conventional ideologies about rape. Women jurors were never considered especially sympathetic to rape victims. One reason is as follows. To live with the knowledge that not only are all women vulnerable to rape, but that frequently they are raped by men they know (Bart, 1975A) is difficult. If, however, women believe in fact that only bad women can be raped and only crazy men who are strangers are rapists, then they can feel safe.

Sexism and the Institutional Response to Rape

In this section I will briefly discuss the response to rape by the police, the hospitals and the courts and somewhat more extensively the "helping" professions and criminology, the "scientific study of crime."

1. Police. Probably because most of the attention of feminists and then the media has been focused on the sexist treatment of rape victims by the police they have improved. Both the data I collected in 1975 and the women I have been speaking with throughout the year have relatively few horror stories about the police, some good stories, and have been delighted with the police women if they have been lucky enough to have one on duty when they called. There is no room in this paper for discussion about why and how this change came about.

2. Hospitals. Since sexist treatment of women by physicians has been a recurrent theme in the women's movement (e.g., Scully and Bart, 1973; Howell, 1974), and a radical analysis of the health care system points to the inordinate power that physicians have, it is to be expected that the hospital experience can feel like another rape. One physician told a 17 year old woman I spoke with who had been beaten and raped by two men "were you really raped or you just trying to make trouble for someone?" Increasingly hospitals have lay rape victims advocates to help demystify the process for the woman, and women who had such advocates reported good experiences to me. But the following facts must be overcome so that women, victimized by patriarchy in their rapes, are not further victims if they seek or are brought to hospitals for medical attention.

Women are examined by physicians who, be they male or female, have internalized a male perspective in medical school (except for a small group of socially concerned feminist and pro feminist students). Furthermore the women see

gynecology residents. We know (Scully and Bart, 1973, Scully 1977) that gyneco-
logical training is pervaded by paternalism at best and misognyny at worst; their
ignorance of female personality and sexuality boggle the mind. Moreover they
define the residency as a place to learn and define rape victims as people they can
learn nothing from. Thus they do not enjoy having their time "wasted" (Scully,
1977).

3. The courts. The courts are a disaster area for rape victims, as they are for
battered women (in the latter case when there are advocates, as in Chicago,
battered women fare better). Women tell me they want to prosecute their rap-
ist(s), or the man (men) who tried to rape them, out of concern for other women
not out of vindictiveness, and so that their suffering will not be meaningless.
Their pain will have some use if, through their efforts, other women are not
raped at least by this rapist. Third world women whom I have interviewed were
incredulous when I presented to them the radical argument that third world men
should not be prosecuted because the system was racist. Not only did they not
care what happened to the rapist, they did care for their female kin whom they
wanted to protect by having rapists locked up.

Not all women who want to prosecute are able to get through the various gate-
keepers prior to the court appearance (e.g., States' attorneys must believe they
have a chance of winning so as not to spoil their records). Moreover rape cases,
like most cases, are frequently plea bargained, but this plea bargain makes the
victim feel invalidated. She thinks it means people don't think she was raped.
But unless the rapist had a prior history of conviction for felony, particularly if
he was out on parole, the chances of his being convicted and sent to prison are
minuscule. Having a prior history of felony means that men and male dominated
institutions judged him and found him guilty frequently of crimes against men.
That now he raped or attempted to rape is consistent with his prior criminal
behavior. But simply raping or attempting to rape a woman is not enough.

For example, in one case the woman interviewed was a Jewish legal secretary
working for her father. She was raped in her home by two young black adolescents. Yet the white (by definition upper middle class) judge stated the infamous
Hale's dictum, "Rape is an accusation easily to be made and hard to be proved
and harder to be defended by the party accused, tho never so innocent." He
found the defendents innocent. Hale was a famous British jurist and that dictum
is quoted by every legal writer on rape. Only recently, through the efforts of the
women's movement, and probably the "law and order" people who also want
rapists convicted but for different reasons than we do, have California judges
stopped routinely reading these instructions to their juries before the juries have
to decide on the guilt of the accused.

4. Mental Health Professions. Traditionally schooled mental health professionals have a "trained incapacity," to use Veblen's term, to deal with female
victims of male violence since their analysis is intrapsychic rather than institutional. As mentioned previously in this paper such an approach is conducive to
blaming the victim. Not only does their intellectual armamentarium include
female masochism and the intrapsychic approach but, in the case of family therapists, this armamentarium is augmented by family systems theory where it is
assumed that each participant gets "something" out of what is going on. They do
not mean broken bones in the case of battered women, or sexual trauma in the

case of incest victims. In the traditional analysis of father-daughter incest the mother is complicitous and the child is seductive. Only the father is assumed to have no free will.

Marolla and Scully (1978) have reviewed the psychodynamic literature on rapists and found four types of motive statements presented, sometimes combined. They are:

a. uncontrollable impulse

b. mental illness or disease

c. momentary loss of control precipitated by unusual circumstances

d. victim precipitation

e. no societal or institutional analysis of critique of rape found

Just as the psychiatric literature suggests that women and girls are responsible for incest, it suggests that rape too is caused by women—the rapist's mother, his "frigid" wife, and the provocative victim (Albin, 1977).

5. Criminology.

Criminologists, like mental health professionals, are supposed to be experts on rape, because rape is a crime. Moreover their textbooks are used to train law enforcement personnel. Therefore Wisan's findings (1978) that current American criminology textbooks embody cultural myths and stereotypes, particularly "she was asking for it" or "victim precipiation," is both relevant and distressing. Other myths found in criminology textbooks are "women want to be raped," "you cannot rape a women," and "rape is simply explained by sexual frustration."

Victim precipitation, as used by Amir (1971) did not really mean "she was asking for it." It refers to a breakdown in communication where the man assumes the woman is interested in sex, because, for example, she had a drink with him in a bar, while she believes she is simply engaging in friendly behavior. Men and women do live in different worlds and there are different meanings attributed to events, but to call such instances where rape results *victim* precipitation exemplifies a male perspective.

Sexism and Its Implications for One Way of Avoiding Rape

In order for patriarchy to survive girls need to be brought up to believe that men, specifically men in their family and later their husbands, can be trusted and will take care of them. Conversely we are told women are not to be trusted. In order to win a caretaker of one's own, girls are told to be "nice"—it is our stock in trade. Niceness not only refers to sexual behavior but to a whole way of dealing with men in a pleasant, unassertive supportive manner. Girls who were not nice in this way came to a bad end.

But the Queen's Bench Foundation Study, *Rape, Prevention and Resistance* (1976) found that "attempted rape victims were more than twice as likely to respond in a rude or unfriendly manner", when they were approached by men who planning to assault them. Moreover "attempted rape victims were more likely than rape victims to be suspicious of their future assailants" and to trust these feelings even though they didn't know why they felt uneasy. These feelings may have arisen in the course of an apparently friendly conversation, since in over half the cases they report the attack was preceded by casual conversation. They trusted their feelings even though we have been taught that we as women are illogical, and our sense of how things are has been systematically devalued.

There are a number of examples of suspiciousness leading to rape avoidance in my own study. For example when a would-be rapist told one woman that he had a gun in his pocket and another was told he had a knife under the car seat both women said, "Show me." In both cases the men were bluffing and because the women knew there was no weapon they were able to use strategies to avoid the rape.

I therefore suggest that notable psychologist Erik Erikson's famous developmental stages be changed for women. He states that the successful outcome of the first stage is basic trust. I say that for women living in our society as it exists, the successful resolution is basic *mistrust*, at least if you don't want to be a rape victim. This perspective makes life difficult and unpleasant, but that is what we mean when we say women are oppressed.

The Role of the Woman's Movement in Fighting Rape: A Selective Chronology

Since we must have hope in order to continue our struggle, and this paper has been a woeful litany let me end with some landmarks in the role of the fight against rape by the Women's Movement.

1971 Radical Feminist Speakout on rape
Susan Griffin's "Rape-The All American Crime" published

1972 Feminist Rape Crisis centers started

1973 NOW National Task Force on Rape started

1974 Process of revising rape laws having some success. Michigan law passed at the behest of and with the support of feminists. (It went into effect in 1975)

1975 Brownmiller's *Against our Will* published

1976 Favorable outcomes of the Inez Garcia and Joann Little trials, Legitimization of rape a social problem. Mathias bill set up Center for the Prevention and Control of Rape as part of the National Institute of Mental Health to fund research. Struggle against the cooptation of the anti-rape movement and loss of the feminist analysis, e.g., the FAAR newsletter

There is no *conclusion* to this paper because we must *continue* our struggle against violence against women.

Notes

1. There are no data supporting the pervasive myth that battered wives don't leave. It takes some women longer than others for reasons which we are well aware of. Since "experts" primarily see battered women in the marriage where they are being abused, they make this assumption which leads to the conclusion that either nothing can be done for them or they must "need" the battering. It is as if one visited a pneumonia ward every day, every day saw people with pneumonia, and said, "People never get over pneumonia." Both battered women in my study had left and all my friends who were battered left.

2. This tradition is changing, notably in the work of psychiatrist Elaine Hilberman on rape (1976) and battered women, and of Judith Herman, whose article with Lisa Hirschman on father-daughter incest (1977) is a feminist classic.

3. I mention this point because I have heard people say of a rape victim, "Why did she have to have windows open?"

4. See Marilyn French's *The Women's Room* (1978) for a fictionalized depiction of this phenomenon. See also *Chicago Sun Times*, Wednesday, May 3, 1978 for additional evidence (pp. 4, 16).

Bibliography

Albin, R. S. "Psychological Studies of Rape." *Signs*, 3, 2, Winter (1977), 423-436.

Amir, M. *Patterns in Forcible Rape*. Chicago: The University of Chicago Press, 1971.

Bart, P. "The Myth of a Value-Free Psychotherapy." In W. Bell and J. A. Mau (eds.) *The Sociology of the Future*. New York: Russell Sage Foundation, 1972, 113-159.

Bart, P. (A) "Rape Doesn't End With a Kiss." *Viva*, 2, 9, June (1975).

Bart, P. (B) Rape and the Criminal Justice System. Paper presented at The Society for the Study of Social Problems, San Francisco, 1975.

Bart, P. (C) Unalienating Abortion, Demystifying Depression and Restoring Rape Victims. Paper presented at the meetings of the American Psychiatric Association, Anaheim, California, May, 1975.

Bart, P. (A) Book review of E. Hilberman, *The Rape Victim*, American Psychiatric Association, Washington, D.C., 1976, in *Women and Health*, 1, (1976).

Bart, P. (B) Book review of L. Brodyaga et al, *Rape and Its Victims*. A report for Citizens, Health Facilities and Criminal Justice Agencies. National Institute of Law Enforcement and Criminal Justice, 1975. *Women and Health*, 1, 5, September-October, (1976).

Bart, P. Victimization and Its Discontents or Psychiatric Ideologies of Violence Against Women as a Form of Violence Against Women. Paper presented at the meetings of The American Psychiatric Association, Atlanta, 1978.

Brownmiller, S. *Against Our Will: Men, Women and Rape*. New York: Simon and Schuster, 1975.

French, M. *The Women's Room*. New York: Jove (HBJ) Book, 1977.

Griffin, S. "Rape, the All-American Crime." *Ramparts*, 10, September (1971), 26-35.

Herman, J. and L. Hirschman. "Father-Daughter Incest." *Signs*, 2, 4, Summer (1977), 735-757.

Hilberman, E. *The Rape Victim*. Washington, D.C.: American Psychiatric Association, 1976.

Hoffman, S. and Dodd, T. Effects of Various Victim Characteristics on Attribution of Responsibility to an Accused Rapist. Paper presented at the twenty-first annual meeting of the Southeastern Psychological Association, 1975.

Howell, M. "What Medical Schools Teach About Women." *New England Journal of Medicine,* August 8, (1974), 304-307.

Kanin, E. "Male Aggression in Dating-Courtship Relations." *American Journal of Sociology,* 64, (1957), 197-204.

Kanin, E. "Sexually Aggressive College Males." *Journal of College Student Personnel,* 12, (1971), 107-110.

Marolla, J. and D. Scully. Rape and Psychiatric Vocabularies of Motive. Paper presented at the meetings of the American Sociological Association, September, 1978.

Newsweek, 90, 19. (1977), 5.

Pleck, E. Wife Beating in America. Paper presented at the meetings of the American Studies Association, Boston, 1978.

Pleck, E., J. Pleck, M. Grossman and P. Bart. "The Battered Data Syndrome." *Victimology,* 2, 3-4, (1977-78), 680-683.

Queen's Bench Foundation. *Rape Prevention and Resistance.* San Francisco, 1976.

Scully, D. and P. Bart. "A Funny Thing Happened on the Way to the Orifice: Women in Gynecology Textbooks." *American Journal of Sociology,* 78, 4, January (1973), 1045-1050.

Scully, D. Skill Acquisition in Obstetrical Gynecology: Social Processes and Implications for Patient Care. Ph.D. Dissertation. University of Illinois, 1977.

Steinmetz, S. "The Battered Husband Syndrome." *Victimology,* 2, 3-4, (1977-78), 499-502.

Wisan, G. The Treatment of Rape in Criminology Textbooks. Paper presented at the meetings of the American Sociological Association, September, 1978.

Socialist

Julia R. Schwendinger and Herman Schwendinger:
Rape Myths: In Legal, Theoretical, and Everyday Life

I. Introduction

Second only to the political scandals, the daily headlines in the United States newspapers decry the increase in all crimes of violence. The subject of this paper, forcible rape, is an act of violence having one of the highest rates of increase. But this amazing detail of the American crime tableau has only recently been correctly interpreted. Because of the protests raised by the members of women's groups, we are now aware of the significance of the "dark figures" obscured by official crime reports.

The dark figures are represented by the number of unreported rape cases. One factor accounting for these figures is that victims are fearful of the stigma of being a known rape victim. They are also wary of the consequences of further sexist treatment by kinfolk, friends, journalists, police, or lawyers. Indeed, some rapes go unreported because victims have been unjustifiably convinced that they are guilty of precipitating the crime. Finally, many politically conscious women do not report because they know that imprisonment will not help the rapist and that American prisons are racist, sexist, politically repressive schools of violence.

In the United States, "rape and fear of rape," according to Susan Griffin, "are a daily part of every woman's consciousness" (Griffin, 1971:27). And although it is not a subject of this article, we should add that rape is also a fear and a reality for certain men. One investigation, for instance, found sexual assaults in a Philadelphia prison to be epidemic: within the prison, "Only the tougher and more hardened young men, and those few so obviously frail that they are immediately locked up for their own protection, escape homosexual rape." Estimates indicated that an astounding number, about 1880 forcible rapes, had taken place in the prison during a 20 month period."[1]

Thus, the dark figures of rape statistics indicate that official rapes are only the tip of a statistical iceberg; but an equally dark side of this criminal phenomenon involves the sexist myths that influence the treatment of women victims. The previously mentioned reasons for not reporting rapes, for instance, are often encouraged by the common belief that it is impossible to rape a woman without her willing consent. The unjustifiable condemnation of the victims of forcible rape is also encouraged by additional myths which have no relation to the typical dynamics of this violent crime.

Because of the adverse affects of the myths, women and men who defend women's rights are repeatedly forced to seek valid information in order to contradict these sexist fallacies. Information about five of these myths is presented in this article.[2] Some of this information is derived from interviews held with victims as well as the study of the literature from the women's movement, sociologists and legal scholars. Other parts of this information are derived from direct struggles to defend the rights of the victims.[3] These struggles have stimulated theoretical insights that clarify the politics of those attempting to inform the victims, their families, friends, and outsiders with whom they must deal in the city and its institutions. They have also heightened an appreciation of the pernicious influence of common sense as well as scientific theories of rape. Consequently, the information below will be placed in a realistic and argumentative framework that can help the reader persuade others to reject these popular fallacies about women victims.

II. The Myth of the Impossibility of Rape: Resistance is the Issue

One of the insights derived from the struggle to defend the rights of the victim, is that academic discussions have notably avoided any analysis of most common sense theories about rape. But ignorance has often remained the benchmark of both scientific and common sense theories; in fact, few scientific theories about rape are commonly known and, where they exist, are often no less commonsensical and have been generally disproven. On the other hand, the most prevalent and the most significant theories about rape, the popular theories, influence the behavior of practitioners in the scientific, legal, and health professions as well as the woman and the man in the street.

It is not difficult to discern popular theories because they are implicit in questions that are repeatedly asked about rape. In fact, in some cases these questions make no sense at all unless some theoretical ideas are taken for granted in conversation. Not long ago, for instance, questions of this kind were expressed in an American "talk show" that was broadcast over the radio in the San Francisco Bay Area in California. In the broadcast, listeners were encouraged to telephone their own questions about the subjec tof rape to a moderator and three members of a women's advocate and defense group, the Bay Area Women Against Rape. These women functioned as a resource panel on the talk show.

The first person who telephoned was a man who didn't believe that a woman could actually be raped if she was unwilling to engage in sexual intercourse. He addressed the participants in a fatherly and consdescending tone:

Hello. You have someone on the program who has been talking to you whose name is Maria, don't you? I want to talk to Maria. How are you tonight, Maria? Do you *actually* believe there is such a thing as rape?

Maria answered:

Yes, there is such a thing; and the idea that rape is impossible is one of the myths we always have to deal with.

The man replied:

> I feel that there's no such thing as rape. In fact, I have taught my three daughters self-protection. Anyone can learn to use the knee and how to use the side of their hand to chop at the Adam's apple.

To this man, rape is impossible because it is easily avoided by the woman's resistance.

Before discussing the validity of this caller's opinions, it should be noted that he is not alone in his belief. A wide variety of persons share his opinion in this regard. Under different circumstances, however, this man's assertion is frequently dressed up in facetious remarks such as "a woman with her skirt up can run faster than a man with his pants down." The same idea is clearly expressed in "frankly I can't see how any woman who doesn't *want* it can be raped."

Moreoever, in the struggle to defend the rights of raped women, we have heard this belief expressed by doctors, defense lawyers, district attorneys and police officers. Usually when pressed in a discussion, a professional who makes this contention modifies the claim to "rape is impossible when all other things are equal." This modification implies that in most cases, these are typical circumstances surrounding the rape event, that the victim has an element of choice, and therefore, that the victim is morally responsible for submitting to the rapist. Consequently, the phrase "when all things are equal" connotes, in this context, certain allegedly normal conditions which govern the dynamics of rape (the attack and the defense) and justify the condemnation of the victim.

By what semantic alchemy can such a normal rape situation exist? Some persons concoct this situation by mixing such ingredients as the vigor and health of the victim or the number of her attackers. One of these ingredients is suggested by the anthropologist Margaret Mead when she says, "By and large, within the same homogeneous social setting an *ordinarily* strong man cannot rape an *ordinarily* strong healthy woman" (Mead, 1969:207, our emphasis). Both of them are involved when the legalist, Morris Ploskowe, quotes from medico-legal experts that "rape cannot be perpetrated by *one man* alone on an *adult woman of good health and vigor*" (Plowskowe, 1962:160, our emphasis).

One can readily understand why common sense would indicate that rape is impossible without willing consent, because sexual experiences are commonly based on voluntary rather than forcible participation. But the simple comparison between a typical act of sexual intercourse and a typical act of rape is highly misleading for several reasons. First of all, the "other things" indicated above by Mead and Ploskowe are ordinarily not "equal." For example, the single largest group of rape victims are female young adults; and these women are indeed representatives of the prime age group from the standpoint of health and vigor. But, in spite of this, many women in this age group are actually raped even when their resistance endangers their very lives.*Another case in point is the woman

---

* A case in point is a recent rape victim in San Francisco: a nineteen year old Japanese woman who came from Tokyo as an exchange student was attacked by a rapist with a knife. When he tried to kiss her, she bit him severely on the tongue. This bit provoked the attacker into a furious assault, and he stabbed the woman fifteen times. Veteran sex-crime inspectors said they had never known a victim to survive "such a brutal and vicious knifing."

who is suddenly raped because she is forcibly overcome by an unexpected and violent attacker.** Also, there are victims who give unwilling consent because they are fully aware of the futility and dangers of active resistance.***

It should be kept in mind that the rapist's motives involve feelings of domination, regardless of whether the victim is a man or woman. Rape is a power trip—an act of aggression and an act of contempt and in most cases is only secondarily sexual. As a result, the differences in options actually available to the victims of rape illustrate how sharply rape and making sexual love are opposite situations.

Presumably, in an *ideal* love-making situation the woman has the real choice of not engaging in a sexual act. In reality, of course, the choice involves constraint in the situations of many women, because refusal may involve social or economic risks that they are not ready to take. However, instead of being faced with any choice in rape, physical force is *always* present or implied. The woman is converted into an *object* who is issued a command: "Take off your clothes!" "Lie down and don't make a sound!" "Be quiet and you won't get hurt!" Usually the urgency of this command is accented with a knife, gun, another weapon, or a threat. Such threats may be directed to her life, her children or companion. Sometimes the woman is unexpectedly grabbed by the throat from behind and brutally flung to the ground. Mutual love-making is not on the rapist's schedule! The perceived authority, shock and surprise in the command, the weapon, and the force, ordinarily reduces the balance of power to very unequal proportions. In short, Mead, Ploskowe and the man who telephone the radio program are simply wrong on factual grounds. We have repeatedly found too many circumstances in which force or the threat of force has been sufficient to secure *willing consent* from a woman.

III. Consequences of the Myth

Belief in the myth that under ordinary circumstances rape is impossible has many consequences. Among these is that women can be "twice victimized," first by the rapist and then by other persons who humiliate and mistreat the victim,

---

** An illustration of this type of rape event is contained in Julia Schwendinger's research with rape victims. One of these victims is a nineteen year old woman who was baby sitting for a family in their house. The rapist had broken and climbed in through a window. "He came out from behind the bedroom door wearing a black mask and grabbed me from behind." Although he had a knife, she screamed and struggled with him. He threatened her, bound and gagged her, beat her up and raped her. Then he finally left by the window after she promised not to call the police. She was asked what was the first thing she did afterward and her answer was, "I went to look in the mirror to see if I was really alive."

*** This is illustrated in the rape of a woman, let her be called Ann. Friday afternoon Ann stopped in at the bar a block from her house to have a drink. Two young men whom she recognized from her neighborhood asked her to join them. They talked for a couple of hours and seemed "friendly and nice." When they invited her to have another drink in their house, she accepted. After another 45 minutes of talk, "as if by a signal" one grabbed her and the other started to tear her clothes off. They threatened to take her to San Francisco and the man who owned the house told the other to "get the gun" from his bedroom drawer. She was so frightened that she said she would give them anything if they wouldn't hurt her—that she wouldn't report them—that they could still be friends.

because they feel that she willingly consented to the rape. An example of this latter type of victimization involves the experience of one victim with her doctor:

> My experience with the doctor was much worse than with the police. The doctor said he didn't believe in a rape if a girl really wanted to resist it. He performed a little trick with me holding a cup and showing that if I moved it around he couldn't put a stick in it. He scoffed at me. Gave me no medication of any type.

The following story provides evidence of the use of this illustration among police. This story, however, also indicates the fatal flaw that underlies the illustration.

> A young man and his woman companion were having a drink in a tavern. The man recognized a police officer who came in and invited him to sit down at their table. During the conversation the officer stated that if a woman struggled hard enough it would be impossible for her to be raped. He handed her a large glass and suggested that she move it rapidly about while he would attempt to insert his billie club into it. After demonstrating how hard this [his task] could be, he suggested that she try it and gave her the club. She picked the club, and hit him across the arm with it; he released the glass and drew back in surprise.

The reversal which now made the glass accessible, more nearly approximated the power relations involved in the enactment of a true rape situation.

The doctor and the police officer are not the only persons who have used a stick and a moving cup to illustrate the impossibility of rape without willing consent. The rape victim who courageously presses legal charges against her attacker may also encounter similar illustrations in the courtroom. Defense attorneys have employed this demonstration to indicate that a healthy woman not wishing sex will resist to the utmost or to an undefined lesser degree, with the result that intercourse will not occur. But exceptions are also to be expected, and in these cases her resistance would be overcome; there would naturally be sufficient evidence of blood or bruises to demonstrate her lack of consent. To win this kind of courtroom contest, the rape victim must act like a contender for a boxing title who does not let her fans down: it must be clearly demonstrated that she didn't throw the fight. Obviously, under these legal conditions, the absence of cuts and bruises is tellingly noted by the defense attorneys. This lack of physical evidence is used to "prove" the innocence of the rapist, and moreover, the "proof" is persuasively "demonstrated" by maximizing the allegedly moral responsibility of the woman to resist the rapist to the utmost. In many cases where the accused admits the act, the woman's unbruised body is utilized as a sign of her consent thus negating the act as a rape.

Defense attorneys therefore still attempt to uphold the myth about the impossibility of rape, even though changes in rape laws have qualified any absolute standard of physical resistance. Some laws have reflected the expectation that a woman should resist as long as she has the power to do so. In a Wisconsin decision, it was stated that the woman must:

> ... exert the utmost power in the protection of herself. .... There must be the utmost vehement exercise of every physical means and faculty within the woman's power to

resist the penetration of her person and this must be shown to persist until the offense is consummated (1938, 288 Wisc. 235, 280 N.W. 357).

The Wisconsin law has remained essentially unchanged. However, most of the forcible rape laws in this country are not so rigid. In a California case, for instance, it was decided that:

> ... the female need not resist as long as either strength endures or consciousness continues. Rather, the resistance must be proportional to the outrage, and the amount of resistance necessarily depends upon the circumstances such as the relative strength of the parties, age, condition of the female, uselessness of resistance, and the degree of force manifested, which rule in some jurisdiction is expressly adopted by statute (1935, 10 Cal. App. 2d 511,52P.2d 538).

Nevertheless, the stipulation that "the resistance must be proportional to the outrage" retains the sexist imprint of the mythical impossibility of rape. In addition, it implicitly assumes that rape situations permit deliberative responses on the part of the victim. This assumption flies in the face of the elemental features of most rape situations. To say the least, little opportunity for deliberation is afforded by most rape situations, and furthermore, an overwhelming sense of fear may inhibit any impulse to show physical resistance regardless of emotional revulsion to the rapist's demands.

This inhibiting effect is understandable, considering that the *modus operandi* of rape includes at least mild violence or threats of violence. In the most highly publicized cases, rape has been accompanied by extreme brutality. Women, furthermore, have learned to fear rapists from childhood warnings by their parents and this has been reinforced by lurid tales in the mass media. Even the police themselves have often counseled women, "Don't fight back. Stay alive!" The woman's fear, in combination with the rapist's threats, undoubtedly makes rape increasingly possible in a violence scarred country like the United States. And the fear is not wholly unrealistic, because often, rapes have been converted into assaults with intent to injure or kill.

Consequently, if the *threat* of force or violence by a physically stronger man is sufficient to secure unwilling consent from many women, then any legal requirement for a show of physical resistance must go against the woman's legitimate rights in this matter.[4]

Businessmen may forcibly resist theft of their property. But no law *demands* this kind of personal resistance as a condition for the lawful protection of his property rights. Women's rights, on the other hand, seem to be another matter.

IV. The "Asking for it" and the "Uncontrollable Passions" Myths: Both Assume Consent

Various assumptions are brought into play in the evaluation of the victim's behavior *prior* to an act of forcible rape. The most common of these assumptions is that the victim "was asking for it." Another implies that an imbalance in the size of the two sexual populations increases the incidence of rape. This is thought to be true if either sex outnumbers the other. If men outpopulate women, then allegedly rape will increase because sexual frustrations among men are intensified by a scarcity of women. Conversely, if women outpopulate men, then allegedly women are forced to act more provocative sexually in order to effectively compete for sexual partners. The increased provocation, it is claimed, will increase the likelihood of rape.

These common assumptions are often symbolized by a question or a statement. For instance, in the radio "talk show" mentioned previously, one caller, a young woman this time, combined two of the above assumptions in a question and a seemingly disconnected assertion. She said:

> I want to know, what "turns a man on"; you know, [what turns on] the majority [of men]? I'm sure you've heard that the women outpopulate the men.

It should be emphasized that her query dealt with the causes of rape; therefore, whatever "turns a man on," in this context, precipitates forcible rape. The question further assumes that some aspects of the woman's behavior cause the rapist to select *her* as his victim. Finally, the statement implies that an imbalance in sexual populations is related to rape.

Let us look at each one of these likely assumptions and examine how they are often combined with moral judgments when people claim that the victim should be denied her rights, because she is seen as responsible for provoking the rapist.

The first assumption implicitly involves the victim's role in bringing on the attack. Translated into criminological jargon, rape is seen as a "victim precipitated crime." From this standpoint, it is assumed that there is something in the psychological makeup of rape victims that differentiates them from non-victims. Under ordinary conditions, therefore, women as catalytic agents may typically be seen as wearing something rapists consider provocative; their willingness to make a friendly response to a strange man's conversation is interpreted as an invitation of sorts; and the acceptance of automobile rides, invitations to dinner, or entering apartments alone with a male may be misunderstood or intentionally rationalized as a sign of their consent.

This way of thinking rarely questions the oppressive sexist norms that regulate the everyday activities of women. In this context, furthermore, the burden of responsibility for maintaining these norms continues to be placed on the woman, because an abrogation of these norms is defined as a sexually exploitable occasion. Consequently women have also been led to believe that the victim ordinarily shares responsibility for precipitating the rapist's attack. Where the believer in the shared responsibility notion is the victim herself who hitches a ride to school every day because she has no car, she will often internalize the implied guilt and ask herself, "Why didn't I know better?" There are others who accept these sexist norms: where the believer is the police officer on the case, he may actually flirt with the victim or call her on the telephone for a date. Where the believer is a well-meaning parent whose sexist attitudes have racial dimensions, he or she may be reprimand the daughter, saying "I've always told you not to hang around with black men." Where the believer is a media talk show consumer, she may worry that her actions will "turn on" a rapist to her.[5]

Also implicit in this way of thinking is once again the normalization of rape as consensual heterosexual sex: the telephone caller, for instance, identified rape with "turning on" the majority of men. Therefore at times, an important corollary of the common belief in victim precipitation assumes that rape involves a degree of overwhelming passion on the part of men. How many women have heard, "You led him on and he couldn't help it [poor fellow]." Like a source of energy, all that is needed is a flame to ignite it and the uncontrollable act is initiated!

This "overwhelming passion" idea frequently locates the rapist on a continuum in which all men are so possessed, only differing in degree. To be sure, using such logic, a woman can be seen as inviting attack by her very presence or by indicating any positive social response. The phraseology of this imputation takes the form that she "led him on" and therefore got what she deserved. A perfectly consistent extension of this kind of thinking is that the typical rapist is a maniac: in this case, virtually everyday social response whatsoever can be interpreted as a provocation.

V. Sex Role Myth: Based on False Naturalistic Premise

As indicated, the "overwhelming passion" idea often assumes that men are basically animals who are to some degree driven by innate passions. Additional notions about the innate nature of both men and women may be used in interpretations of forcible rape: for instance, the woman telephone caller above indicated that "women outpopulate men" and implied that a population imbalance had something to do with forcible rape. In this context, the presence of a greater proportion of women may signify that they will naturally compete all the harder for sexual mates; thus ensnaring men with highly provocative sexual behavior. The existence of a greater proportion of men, on the other hand, will result in an increased number of frustrated males who express their natural compulsions to become predators. As such, they forcibly seize the mates of others or attack single women who appear to be available. In either case, given the scarcity of one sex, these fallacious naturalistic premises assume that the members of the other sex will act as immoral beasts.

In scientific circles, a theory of this kind, the "sex-ratio" theory, was developed by Hans von Hentig (1951). Not surprisingly, this *male* scholar viewed the problem solely from the standpoint of *male*-sex starvation; that is, he proposed that a greater imbalance of men over women would yield a greater incidence of rape. Several studies have tested this theory and all have failed to find systematic evidence of its explanatory value. In Denmark, Svalastoga (1962) found evidence for this theory when rural and urban areas were compared, but it was insufficient as an explanation of rape when cities were compared with each other. In addition, he found a great difference in rates of rape in cities with the *same* sex ratio. On the other hand, Menachem Amir (1971) tested von Hentig's hypothesis using his own Philadelphia data and found no statistically significant patterns which confirmed it. In fact, some of his data contradicted this theory entirely. Thus, no clearly discernible patterns have been systematically found to confirm the sex-ratio theory of rape.

VI. Legalization of Prostitution Myth: Force is Unnecessary When Sex Can be Bought

Finally, the struggle to defend the rights of women often encounters myths about the relations between prostitution and rape. In a letter to the women's advocacy and defense group mentioned previously, one person wrote, "We lived in the Reno, Nevada area before moving to Los Angeles [California]. In Nevada there is legal prostitution, and I cannot remember reading about any rapes. Do you believe that legal prostitution will reduce rape attacks in California?

Popular myths suggest that the number of rapes would decrease if prostitution was legal and controlled. However, the evidence shows that this is false: three cities that had allowed open prostitution actually experienced a decline in rape and other sexual assaults after prostitution was prohibited.

In the case of Gary, Indiana, there were 95 complaints of sex crimes in 1947, 81 in 1948, and only 69 in 1949 when the houses of prostitution were closed. In Terre Haute, Indiana the closing of the vice district in 1943 was measured against reports of aggravated assaults which included sex crimes. A three year record showed: 36 aggravated assaults in 1942; 14 in 1943; and a drop to 4 in 1944. The third case involved Honolulu, Hawaii where prostitution was really big business. For the eleven months prior to September 1944, the month in which all houses of prostitution were closed, there had been 29 rapes and 559 other sex crimes. The record for the following 11 months showed a decline to 22 rapes and 404 other sex crimes (Kinsie, 1950:250-252).[6]

Behind this myth is the false notion that rape is essentially a crime of sexual passion which can easily be prevented by commercial forms of sexual relationships.[7] Rapists, however, include men who do not patronize prostitutes.[8] Furthermore, the need for sexual release is not the *primary* motive for their sexual assaults. [9] We are also convinced that both rape and prostitution degrade women and flourish primarily in an atmosphere of sexism and exploitation for individual gain. Consequently, it is important to view rape and rape justice in an historical context, rather than as an isolated phenomenon.

VII. Class Relations and Everyday Sexist Norms

Sexism and exploitation have existed for a long time; both of these relationships, for instance, were features of slave societies. Regarding Western European societies, scholars have indicated that private property and the state provided the material conditions for the subjugation of women in antiquity. The material conditions in the later historical period in Greece, for example, generated a general decline from women's prior status to one that was marked by a sharp double standard (Lecky, 1902:287-289).

Monogamous marriage among wealthy Athenian families demonstrates the economic functions of this double standard. The purpose of marriage was to "make the man supreme in the family and to propagate, as the future heirs to his wealth, children indisputably his own" (Engels, 1942:57-58). Historically the double standard and the reasons for its existence have involved these and other economic functions; and the degree of repression has fluctuated by class and by era through the centuries.

The fluctuations in the degree of repression in England during the 16th and 17th centuries have been described by Margaret George (1973). In the 16th century the status of women had improved because of economic changes brought about by the rise of early capitalist relations. Seventeenth century women, however, suffered an absolute setback from the rough-and-ready equality of performance in business and productive enterprises that had previously existed in Tudor England. At that time, middle-class women experienced a drastic diminution in status and a sharp reduction in opportunities to participate in and contribute to production and social life. Coterminous with this change, the "good woman" was increasingly becoming once again defined as "chaste," "faire," and "pious." "Woman's ambitions were encouraged to be wholly centered on the family" and in addition, the married woman was exhorted by clerics to carry herself as an inferior, who, in good conscience, voluntarily subjected herself to the husband's will (George, 1973:156-164).

It should be emphasized that this idealized version of the chaste woman was always classbound: during *antiquity*, for instance, one finds that the wealthier the Grecian family the more secluded and protected the woman's life. In 17th century England, many middle-class wives refused to be seen in their husbands' business establishments. Furthermore, the wealthier middle-class tradesmen feared that their shops would be thought "less masculine or less considerable than others" if their wives were seen working there (ibid.:158). On the other hand, the women who were poor could afford no such idle existence. In Greece, many lived as prostitutes in order to survive; a few became "successful" and notable as haetera or "companions" to wealthy men. In later centuries many working-class women still earned their living in this manner. In the Victorian period, for instance, "Virtue was a middle- and upper-class luxury which [poor women] quite simply could not afford ... Thus the working class provided a kind of sexual sewer for the wealthy. It is important to remember just how classbound the sentimental, idealized image of womanhood actually was" (Figes, 1971:82).

It should also be emphasized that in every class society the values and attitudes engendered by ruling class standards and institutions have penetrated the thinking of men and women in all classes. Thus many working-class men and women voluntarily maintain these standards and institutions even though they are inimical to their own class interests.

In light of the great significance of social class relations, it is not surprising to find that 17th century Anglo-Saxon laws about women were influenced by the general changes in the forms of class justice. These changes were affected by the state's priorities given to extending and consolidating all the institutions of civil society including the bourgeois family. Class justice was also affected by such bourgeois standards as the double standard in sexual relationships. These standards have endured and to the present day they provide the widest latitude to defense attorneys in their attempts to impeach the rape victim's tesimony in court. The rules allow the defense to introduce all the woman's past sexual relationships as evidence of her unchaste or "bad" character; yet, in the testimony of the accused man, this type of evidence is in admissible.[10]

A further example of the double standard lies in the often repeated words of Sir Matthew Hale, a 17th century jurist, who wrote that "rape is a destable crime . . . but it must be remembered, that it is an accusation easily to be made and hard to be proved, and harder to be defended by the party accused, tho never so innocent" (Hale, 1800:635, orig. 1630). In California today judges paraphrase these words in the cautionary note usually given to juries in forcible rape cases. This note follows the completion of testimony and states:

> A charge such as that made against the defendant in this case is one which is easily made and, once made, difficult to defend against, even if the person accused is innocent.

> Therefore, the law requires that you examine the testimony of the female person named in the information with caution.

As far as we know, this cautionary instruction is not expressed in other types of criminal cases. Furthermore, it is patently false: as a rule, the charge of rape is not easily made by women and it is not difficult to defend against by the defense attorneys. There can be no doubt of this because prosecutors do not usually win in forcible rape cases!

Twentieth century social movements may lead to some changes in rape laws, but the rape laws represent only one aspect of the conditions that influence rape victims. Other aspects include the centuries-old racist and classist discriminatory standards. These are combined with oppressive sexual standards imposed on such everyday activities of men and women as making themselves sexually attractive or acceptable in the clothing they wear, in the language they use, in the mannerisms they effect, and in the activities they pursue. Members of both sexes uphold these standards and employ a whole array of sanctions to enforce sexual, racial, and class inequality. Because of these normative standards, women often find that their "moral character" is regarded with deep suspicion if they travel or live alone, or conduct themselves in many ways that would rarely be questioned if they were men. Furthermore, when they adamantly refuse to restrict their lives by conforming to these norms, women face the possibility of being defined as sexual objects that can be justifiably exploited by any man.

Thus, the impact of sexual bias, for example, is certainly felt by the rape victim. She may find that by non-conformity she has forfeited her right to obtain legal protection. If by her life style she looks like a "hippie" or if she "comes out" as a righteous lesbian, she has little recourse to the law as it is practiced in our society. As with other "suspect" women, such as those who are poor and "third world," her lack of conformity becomes especially salient as police, lawyers, doctors, or even women themselves exercise their option of evaluating a victim's behavior *prior* to the act of forcible rape.

Women's movements in the United States have found that they can provide effective support for the female victims of forcible rape. And until basic political and economic changes can be made, women must continue to strive for reforms in the way their sisters are treated when they have the misfortune of being raped. Although examples mentioned earlier indicate the callous attitudes of police and doctors, the full scope of the outrageous police and hospital procedures cannot be detailed at this time. However, reforms are necessary along the following lines: police questioning should be sympathetically and courteously carried out by specially selected personnel, and the victim should have the option of choosing a woman interviewer. Since the victim knows first-hand what happened, her report should be taped or written in her own words unless she prefers another form of report-taking. In addition to being allowed to phone a parent or friend, the presence of a volunteer advocate should be made available to all victims.

A *free* medical examination at a nearby hospital is important in all cases whenever a woman reports a rape regardless of whether police "found" or "unfound" the rape (i.e., decide that the crime has or has not been committed) or consider medical attention too costly for department budgets. At the hospital, prompt, sympathetic, and discreet care must be offered by all levels of emergency room personnel from the admitting clerks to the examining doctors. In addition to specimen samples for proof of semen, the woman's entire body should be checked for injuries and medical treatment given whenever necessary. The woman needs full information verbally and in writing regarding gonorrhea, syphilis, and crabs plus prophylaxis or testing for veneral disease. Pregnancy information and safe termination periods and procedures for abortion should be stated. Follow-up arrangements should be established at this time since most victims require varying types of medical attention and emotional support during different post-rape phases. Medical treatment should include an offer of a shower, tranquilizer, and supportive conversation with an informed person who has had an experience with rape victims. From the outset, the well-founded fears and the unfounded guilt experienced by the victim should be clearly understood by all who come into contact with her so these symptoms can be alleviated rather than compounded.

Women's movements may also achieve some gains in the struggle against the double standards employed by the police and legal professionals. Because of these struggles, legislation is pending which prohibits the court from admitting any "evidence of specific instances of sexual acts of the victim involving any person other than the defendant." But it should be remembered that sexual double standards exist because they have been influential in securing the bourgeois domination of everyday life. These standards furthermore, will never be eliminated as long as this form of domination endures. Consequently women's movements can prevent rape and rape justice only by joining a political struggle with other class conscious movements. Reforming the legal structure may improve the plight of the rape victim, but it will not affect the socio-economic and ideological system that spawns these sexist crimes. Crimes of violence as we know them today have been produced by capitalism; and the contradictions of capitalism will continue to feed the hatred and contempt of certain men toward women. To resolve the contradictions, and the expression in rape of the social psychological effects of these contradictions, is to change a class system of oppression in America today to a socialist political economy and a relatively crime-free tomorrow.[11]

Notes

1. In the study of these assaults, it was deemed ironic that some of the men who were raped had been sent to prison to await their trials. And although eventually

found innocent of criminal charges, these men were even being raped in the sheriff's vans transporting them to court (Davis, 1968:8-16).

2. The five myths are: (1) rape is impossible; (2) a woman who gets raped "was asking for it"; (3) men rape because of uncontrollable passions; (4) an imbalance in the sex ratio causes rape; (5) legalizing prostitution will reduce rape.

3. Julia R. Schwendinger has worked with a woman's advocate and defense group called Bay Area Women Against Rape (BAWAR), in Berkeley, California, helping to develop many of its activities since its inception three years ago.

4. This generalization refers to rapists who are strangers as well as those who are known by the victim. We are aware of the legal complications regarding the "known" rapist, but will discuss them elsewhere. However, with regard to distinguishing between rape and "normal" male sex-initiating behavior, it should be noted that the magnitude of this problem is usually exaggerated and overgeneralized. It is *not* a fact that there is a high incidence of reporting rapes between intimates. Although reported cases may underestimate the actual number of rapes between intimates, Amir, in the only sizable American research based on police reports, found an insignificant 14% of 646 cases to be so involved. For our purpose, the actual percentage is even smaller because Amir's "intimate relation" category includes, besides a close friend or boyfriend, such people as relatives and friends of the family. The latter persons are ordinarily excluded from typical "amorous" relationships. Therefore, in the light of this research, the ambiguities between culturally approved and culturally disapproved male sexual aggression have been inordinately overemphasized and mystified in legal contexts.

5. All of these examples reflect actual incidents which have been verified by research.

6. The notion that prostitution reduces the incidence of rape is strongly contradicted by the declining trends of rape in each city closing down its houses of prostitution. On the other hand, the data underlying these trends, however consistent, should be regarded with caution, because they are based on officially adjudicated cases. Adequate data can only be obtained on the basis of the actual number of rapes. This number exceeds the reported rape cases, which in turn exceed the number of adjudicated cases.

7. If rape were really an act of passion the trends in the three examples cited in the text would have been in the opposite direction.

8. Kinsie (1950:250) overgeneralizes psychiatric relations, but the following statement is otherwise worthy of note: "The sexual psychopaths who are responsible for most sex crimes do not as a rule patronize prostitutes, nor are they apt to be concerned in any way with prostitution activities."

9. We have previously mentioned the power and dominance factors in the rape of women; these also appear in the homosexual rape of men in prisons. According to Davis (1968:15): "It appears that need for sexual release is not the primary motive of a sexual aggressor. . . A primary goal of the sexual aggressor, it is clear, is the conquest and degradation of his victim."

10. This article concentrates on the situation in the U.S.A.; hence, no space is available for an adequate discussion of modern developments in England. However, if Radzinowicz's description of English rape laws in 1957 still holds true, then the basic elements of these laws have remained essentially unchanged.

Several laws have been consolidated into one and outdated terms such as "carnal knowledge" have been modernized. There are some other changes in the defini-tion. For rape to occur, penetration rather than the older requirement of emission is sufficient. In addition to force and violence, fraud or lack of "real consent" can now qualify intercourse as rape. Consent is still an important issue. Where in doubt about lack of consent, juries at times acquit the rapist and find a verdict for a lesser offense. The archaic punishment schedule for rapists (e.g., life imprison-ment) lends itself admirably to lesser verdicts or complete acquittals. A jury can rest more easily by handing down a two year sentence for procurement of a woman by threats rather than a life sentence which applies only to rape and intercourse with a girl under 13 years of age. Also the English law, in its "majestic equality" allows a prostitute, a mistress or an "unchaste" woman to charge rape; but her sexual life is "most material in determining whether in fact she con-sented or not" (Radzinowicz, 1957:326). Thus, in spite of some changes, certain crucial double standards have continued in effect. Sex offenses are the only crimes where a very strong juridical emphasis is placed on the desirability of corroboration by a third party; and most sexual offenses against men are liable to greater punishment than corresponding crimes against women.

11. This conclusion is not utopian: regarding nations that are now socialist, comparisons between pre- and post-revolutionary periods show enormous dif-ferences in the incidence of "organized crime" and "crime in the streets" which include sexual crimes. Information from travellers, journalists, and non-nation-als who have worked for extended periods in Cuba, for instance, indicates that organized crime has virtually disappeared from Havana, which in the pre-revo-lutionary period, was the major center of organized crime in the Caribbean. Similar sources of information have also indicated changes in China in relation to prostitution and opiate use as well as other types of organized crime and crime in the streets. Finally, comparisons between the (East) German Democratic Republic and the (West) Federal Republic of Germany indicate a lower incidence and a long term decreasing trend in ordinary crime within the German Demo-cratic Republic. See, for example, "Kriminalitat and Gesellschaft," Drucksache VI/3080 Deutscher Bundestag-6. Wahlperiode, Kapital V:205-223.

References

Amir, Menachem, 1971 *Patterns in Forcible Rape*. Chicago: University of Chicago Press.

Davis, Alan J., 1968 "Sexual Assaults in the Philadelphia Prison System and Sheriff's Vans." Trans-action (December): 8-16.

Deutscher Bundestag-6. Wahlperiode, 1973 "Kriminalitat and Gesellschaft." Drucksache VI/3080. Kapitel V:205-223.

Engels, Frederick, 1942 *The Origin of the Family, Private Property and the State*. New York: International Publishers.

Figes, Eva, 1971 *The Case for Women in Revolt, Patriarchal Attitudes*. Connecticut: Fawcett Publications.

George, Margaret, 1973 "From 'Goodwife' to 'Mistress,' the Transformation of the Woman in Bourgeois Culture." Science and Society XXXVII:152-177.

Griffin, Susan, 1973 "From 'Goodwife' to 'Mistress,' the Transformation of the Woman in Bourgeois Culture." Science and Society XXXVII:152-177.

Griffin, Susan, 1971 "Rape: The All-American Crime." Ramparts (September):26-35.

Hale, Sir Matthew, 1800 *The History of the Pleas of the Crown*, I. London: E. Rider, Little-Britain.

Kinsie, Paul M., 1950 "Sex Crimes and the Prostitution Racket." Journal of Social Hygiene 36:250-252.

Lecky, William E. H., 1902 *History of European Morals, from Augustus to Charlemagne, II.* London: Longmans, Green and Company.

Mead, Margaret, 1963 *Sex and Temperament in Three Primitive Societies.* New York: Dell Publishing Company.

Ploskowe, Morris, 1962 *Sex and the Law.* New York: Ace Books.

Radzinowicz, Leon, 1957 *Sexual Offenses, IX* London: Macmillan & Co. Ltd.

Svalastoga, Kaare, 1962 "Rape and Social Structure." Pacific Sociological Review 5:48-53.

von Hentig, Hans, 1951 "The Sex Ratio." Social Forces 30:443-449.

Chapter 5

DRUGS

Drug addiction is used here to refer to the
dependence of an individual on the regular consumption of either "street drugs" or prescribed
uppers and downers[1] to make it through everyday
life. Traditionally, drug addiction has been defined
solely as the use of "street drugs" by individuals
who are labeled as deviant for breaking laws that
prohibit their use. On the other hand, when
individuals in the mainstream of society use large
amounts of tranquillizers or other mood altering
drugs on prescription, they escape the labeling of
their behavior as deviant because (1) they are using
drugs with official sanction and (2) their use of
drugs is encouraged by family, friends, or a
physician to help them conform to social norms.

Conservatives view drug use as a personal
problem. Individuals who use drugs are often
blamed for their inability to face reality or cope
with everyday life. Nevertheless, this may not be
their fault since drug use is a mental illness.
Viewing drug use from the perspective of a medical
model focuses on flaws within individuals who are
drug users. Defining drug use as a mental illness
provides a framework congruent with the desire
not to identify drug use with social conflicts. It
deflects attention from family problems, workplace
alienation, and other contexts and situations typically associated with drugs.

Some liberals view drug use as an indicator of
social disorganization. Other liberals view drugs as
a means of personal liberation. Still others agree

---

1. A partial list includes cocaine, hashish, marijuana, heroin, amphetamines, barbitu-
ates, LSD, and peyote.

with both views and argue that the meaning of drug use depends on the circumstances in which drugs are taken. When drugs are taken by individuals to avoid dealing with personal problems, this is seen as drug abuse. When many persons engage in drug abuse that is related to the same situation, a condition of social disorganization, such as the generation gap, may be identified. However, when drug use is engaged in as a technique of consciousness exploration or merely as a recreational activity, it is viewed benignly or even positively. Drug use and abuse is situationally defined for liberals, positively or negatively, depending upon the motive imputed to the act of drug ingestion.

Socialists view drugs as an instrument of social control. Addiction is seen as a way of draining the revolutionary spirit of the underclass despite apparent attempts by the state to suppress the use of drugs. Whereas some government agencies impede the importation and distribution of illegal drugs such as heroin, other agencies promote the use of legal drugs such as methadone. Both drugs control people who might otherwise become rebellious. Another instance of the social control potential of drugs is the widespread use of tranquillizers in mental hospitals to enervate and restrain disruptive patients. If people who take drugs would give up their use and react against oppressive social conditions to demand what they really want of society, a revolution might result.

In the conservative article, Kiev argues that drug abuse is a medical problem. Excessive drug use is a mental illness. Adolescents and youth are especially susceptible to this disease. An interaction of social, psychological, and biological factors causes the drug disease. The prime social cause is probably a loss of a sense of integration into a common culture. Individuals do not have control over their drug use. Drugs are disease-causing agents that produce psychiatric illness, especially in predisposed individuals.

In the liberal article, Rockwell argues that drug use is a social problem. As with other social problems, drugs follow a typical course of development. Initially, group awareness of the existence of a problem appears. This is followed by the formation of a social movement to resolve the problem. The drug problem can best be understood by comparing it to the earlier problem of alcohol. The struggle between the "wets," who advocated allowing consumption of alcohol, and the "drys," who advocated prohibition has its parallel in the contemporary drug era. The first step toward a solution is for each of the opposing sides to gain a better understanding of the other's point-of-view. When society has more tolerance for drug use, abuse will likely decrease. Users will then be less likely to be involved in a deviant subculture, which encourages the increased use and hence the abuse of drugs.

In the socialist article, Karmen argues that drugs are a political and economic problem. Historically, drugs have been used as a means of controlling subordinate populations. Drug use drains the ability of oppressed people to resist their oppressors. In the United States, the contemporary drug problem gives the state an excuse to suspend constitutional protections. Tactics used to suppress the drug trade receive a legitimacy that allows them to be used for political repression. Drug use occurs because many persons can not lead meaningful lives in the context of the present social structure. Drug use will persist until an alternative social system that allows everyone to live meaningful lives is created.

Conservative

Ari Kiev: The Epidemiology of Drug Abuse

The Need for a New Strategy

Drug abuse refers to a type of maladaptive effort to relieve psychological distress by means of a variety of naturally occurring and manufactured pharmacologically active substances or drugs which alter mood, thought, and behavior. While a propensity to use drugs to alleviate distress is a universal characteristic of human beings, the unmonitored and excessive use of such substances is symptomatic of the combined effects of psychological vulnerability and environmental pressures.

While most people acknowledge the legitimacy of the impulse to alleviate distress through the use of pain killers, sedatives, hypnotics and tranquilizers, there is a tendency to invoke moralistic notions of will power and self-control when individuals progress to the point of abuse or addiction. Abuse is here considered as the excessive and unmonitored use of drugs; addiction as a more extreme form of drug abuse where physical and psychological dependence on the drugs has developed. Popular misconceptions about the feasibility of controlling drug abuse and drug addiction through will power and self-control have unfortunately fostered various attitudes and programs which until recently have been ineffective in preventing or eliminating the problems of drug abuse and addiction.

The failure to recognize that drug abuse and addiction are symptomatic of an underlying psychiatric disorder or psychological conflict and the inclination instead to view such symptomatic behavior as deviant unfortunately has had the effect of a self-fulfilling prophecy. Treating individuals as deviants, rather than as disturbed or troubled individuals in need of medical care, leads them to behave in a deviant way. They develop a negativistic view of themselves and fail to recognize their need for medical help.

Recognizing that the individual often cannot control this distress, rational programs must be developed to deal with the motivational patterns and underlying psychological distress which lead to drug abuse. Appeals to conscience will rarely have any significant impact on the individual's ability to cope with the psychological and environmental pressures that lead to drug abuse.

The deviancy model incorrectly focuses on the symptomatic aspects of a psychological problem rather than the problem itself leading, of course, to considerable confusion about will power, responsibility, and the development of more rational alternatives for the alleviation of distress. It assumes free will on the part of the drug abuser; responsibility may be assigned to the abuser when others should assume it. Parents, for example, should take firm stands and insist on medical treatment when they discover drug abuse behavior in their children. The fact that emotional turmoil pervades adolescence should not prevent responsible adults from recognizing treatable problems. Fear of generating rebelliousness in teenagers leads many parents to deny evidence of drug abuse such as altered states of consciousness or withdrawal symptoms such as restlessness, nervousness, anxiety, tension, twitching, cramps, vomiting, diarrhea, and dilated pupils. Similarly, symptoms of depression that may result from drug abuse, such as moodiness, seclusiveness, loss of appetite, and insomnia, are sometimes rationalized as the turbulent reactions of adolescents so as to avoid much feared confrontations.

Young people themselves subscribe to the deviancy model of drug abuse. Rationalizations for drug usage—boredom, frustration, alienation, a critical attitude toward the "hypocrisy of their parents and the larger society"—may be accepted at face value and not recognized in themselves as manifestations of psychiatric disturbance.

On the campus, police raids and other official efforts to curb drug abuse have only confused the problem of drug abuse with the issues of political activism and the generation gap, thus further contributing to nonrecognition of the fundamental causes and dangers of drug abuse. Legislative and police efforts to control drug abuse often lead to an intensification of the problem rather than to its reduction.

To establish the basic premises of the remedial measures so urgently needed, one must clarify the multiple causes and the natural evolution of the phenomenon of drug abuse. As long as doctrinaire and dogmatic assertions are made about specific problems, the approach to remedies will continue to be less than adequate.

Historical Trends

The incidence of drug abuse has progressively increased since World War II. Numerous surveys have documented widespread experimentation with drugs, rising morbidity rates from drug-related illnesses such as abscesses and serum hepatitis and rising mortality rates from heroin and methadone overdoses among young people.

The broad range of usage patterns, differences in the drugs being used, and the complications involved in relying on evidence of social maladaptation such as school absenteeism and unemployment have made it difficult to obtain accurate incidence and prevalence figures relating to drug abuse.

The actual number of new cases cannot be determined accurately. Different agencies often report on the same individuals who use a range of services, a problem compounded by administrative needs to inflate figures for funding purposes.

The Narcotics Register in New York City showed an unduplicated list of 94,699 known addicts at the end of 1969. By the end of 1971 the total number of addicts in New City was estimated to be 160,000. In 1973 the Register listed 73,000 known addicts and estimated that there were 125,000 addicts in the city, a reduction attributed to treatment programs, the reclassification of many heroin addicts as polydrug abusers, and the reduced availability of heroin on the streets because of the limited importation of heroin from Turkey.

Between 1960 and 1969, 4,254 people died in New York from narcotics abuse. In 1971 there were 916 such deaths; in 1972, 924 and in 1973, 745. By contrast, in 1966 there were 388 narcotics deaths.

Deaths attributed to narcotics use include deaths due to acute heroin overdose in addition to deaths from hepatitis and other infections. If deaths from related other causes, such as homicides, suicides, and fatal accidents among heroin addicts, are included, the figures are even higher. The number of such deaths rose from 1,174 in 1970 to 1,268 in 1971 and 1,409 in 1972. The increase in such deaths was largely a result of the increase in homicidal deaths, which rose from 208 in 1971 to 324 in 1972.

In 1971 some 30,000 addicts were in treatment. The number in treatment increased to 52,782 in 1972 and to 56,522 by the end of May, 1973, which constituted 45.2% of the estimated 125,000 addicts in New York City according to 1973 estimates.

Increases in the number of cases reported reflect growing interest in the drug problem. Cases which in the past may not have been reported because they were secondary to physical illnesses are now being reported even as secondary diagnoses. Improved law enforcement reporting and the greater availability of health services also account for an increase in reported cases. The converse of this is that the drug epidemic may be far more serious than is usually considered, in that only serious cases come to our attention. There may be many more subclinical, minor forms of drug abuse in the community which are not now picked up.

If subclinical cases were to be counted, drug abuse rates would be considerably higher than what is now reported. Many drug users play a significant role in spreading the epidemic of drug abuse, very much like those people who act as carriers of infectious diseases but do not themselves manifest the disease. These subclinical users are not necessarily addicted, but they "pass on" addiction to those whose personality makes them vulnerable to heavy drug use.

The more users there are, then, the greater the increase in the number of other users. And the use of drugs creates the need for more drugs, and is thus a self-reinforcing behavior pattern. As with infectious disease, the availability of the noxious agent, be it bacteria or an addicting drug, increases the risk of developing the condition for predisposed individuals.

Tackling the Epidemic

The historical trend points to an epidemic of major proportions, calling for the institution of new corrective and preventive measures. Existing programs must be reassessed, since they have not successfully applied the most modern measures of public health and epidemiology to contain this problem. To a large extent, the problem was ignored as long as it was confined to the ghetto. Operating programs rarely attacked the earliest stages of drug abuse, concentrating attention instead on confirmed addicts in the advanced stages of deterioration, when they were least amenable to treatment. Efforts to eliminate the availability of drugs have also proven inadequate and ineffective.

Obviously, the nature and size of the drug problem must be determined. This can be done by an examination of historical trends, by means of surveys and improved reporting schemes, by the use of suitable diagnostic criteria and a uniform nomenclature, and by means of reliable instruments for differentiating among patterns of drug abuse.

The first step in studying the drug problem would be to establish correlations between drug abuse and physical and mental illness, being careful to correlate rates by age and sex. Drug abuse is a major manifestation of psychiatric disorder in teenagers and young adults. Outcome studies should reveal much about the natural history of drug abuse, the usual age of onset, background factors, and the rate of spontaneous remission.

The drugs used, their sources, the manner of use (alone, with strangers, with friends), family usage patterns, and the use of other drugs should also be studied. Measures of social performance and social deterioration may also correlate with drug use. These measures would help to assess individual social functioning and psychopathological states. A chronic schizophrenic individual may avoid social attachments and have less access to drugs. He may be less able to tolerate drugs and may be more disturbed by minimal involvement in drug usage than a relatively healthy heavy user. "High risk," therefore, has different meanings. A simple head count of drug abusers does not yield an accurate picture of the severity of the disturbances or suggest the kinds of services that are needed to really get at the problem.

The drug problem cannot be handled in isolation from other problems. The ghetto problems of poverty and poor education require different measures than the suburban problems of alienation, boredom, and affluence.

The effects of migration and adaptation to the urban industrial environment and the breakdown of the nuclear family must be assessed. Military service, frequent moving, the increased employment of mothers, affluence, TV, inadequate police forces, overcrowding, the decay of the cities, suburbanization, and increased leisure time contribute in various ways to creating a highly anomic and unstable environment and undermine the important psychological processes of identification and socialization, thus increasing vulnerability to drugs; these variables must be considered in any assessment of community problems pertaining to drugs. Drug abuse may increase as cultural integration weakens. The inadequacy of social services and resources further complicates the picture by failing to divert participants in the drug culture into much-needed rehabilitation programs and non-drug-using peer groups which might counteract the peer pressures to take drugs.

The importance of formal and informal systems for supporting adolescents through critical life stresses needs to be stressed. The absence of such support systems leaves a vacuum that is frequently filled by quasi-therapeutic peer groups which encourage self-medication and quasi-naturalistic group therapy experiences that, unmonitored, can have deleterious effects. To the extent that drugs reduce anxiety, they are often mistakenly associated with masculine virtues rather than with gratification of narcissistic dependent and regressive traits.

We must begin to look at drugs as etiological agents producing in predisposed individuals such effects as depression, personality deterioration, and progressive addiction. According to this model, social and psychological factors interact with biological factors to produce the various observed clinical pictures. The multiplicity of contributing factors accounts for the difficulty experienced in generating a simple model of this psychosocial disorder.

Studying the Problem

The popular misconceptions about drugs and drug abuse derive from various factors. The mass media seek to dramatize the problem and so contribute to much of the prevailing hysteria; the extant punitive legislation contributes to the view of the drug abuser as deviant. Those who use drugs contribute their own biases. Intellectuals who have used drugs experimentally with no serious aftereffects tend to minimize the seriousness of the drug problem and to vigorously support a civil libertarian concept of individual free choice.

One must separate the different personality syndromes, behavior patterns, and life-styles associated with drug usage, differentiating mild from serious disturbances. To the extent that the individual, the drug, and the environment are dependent variables, one can measure the decline in individual functioning in relation to the drugs used, the exposure to other users, treatment measures undertaken, and efforts made to control the availability of the drug. Only studies under controlled circumstances, using measured dosages and responses, can accurately delineate the drug effect.

Careful studies of the differential responses of different people to drugs should clarify the respective contributions of drugs, environment, and personality to the clinical picture. Some individuals become philosophical while under the influence of drugs. Others become emotional and flamboyant. Still others withdraw. Unpredictable personality disturbances, psychotic episodes, transient states of delirium, and other dissociative processes may be triggered off by certain drugs in certain negative settings. The effect of the drugs and the effect of the group atmosphere on the individual in producing these clinical states should be differentiated.

Even less is known about the synergistic effects of multidrug use. Most clinicians have limited experience with the entire spectrum of drug abuse and often have difficulty in assessing the problem. One must consider personality, the social and family environment, and past patterns of behavior and not simply label an individual who has experimented casually with drugs as a drug abuser.

A complete picture of drug abuse also requires the assessment of "burned-out" cases and hospitalized cases with major psychiatric disorders. One must differentiate those in the early phases of drug abuse from nonabusers, and from those with the personality potential to become drug abusers. One must also examine the normal range of medication abuse among nonusers. To what extent does the drug user reflect the peer group to which he belongs? To what extent does drug abuse start with the excessive use of prescription drugs, mild tranquilizers, laxatives, or other forms of medication? To what extent does marijuana usage occur in the individual's peer group? These are important considerations for assessing the extent to which the individual's behavior is governed by the shared norms of his age group or ethnic subculture.

It is also important to differentiate the different syndromes of drug abuse as they occur in different milieus and among different personality types. Just as the life-styles in Haight-Ashbury, in the theatrical world, on college campuses, and in the nation's ghettos differ, so too does the utilization of drugs in these groups vary in terms of frequency of use, types of drugs used, associated patterns of criminality, and associated ideology. Each of these correlated behavior patterns must be examined more closely, and differences and similarities among various drug abusers must be separated out from the social class and ethnic group differences. Further studies may suggest the existence of a number of syndromes characterized by differences in the psychological predisposition toward the use of popular substances, in the way in which drugs are taken, in the meaning attributed to the art of taking drugs, and in the meaning assigned to particular drugs.

Liberal

Don Rockwell: Social Problems — Alcohol and Marijuana

The current controversy over the dangerousness of marijuana will prove irrelevant in the long run. The issue is simply not medical-scientific but rather more social-political as Leifer,[1] Kaplan,[2] and Grinspoon[3] have indicated. The proof for this contention can be clearly seen through examination of a less controversial but strikingly parallel social problem—that of alcohol.

Social Problem Perspective

I intend to demonstrate that the social problems of alcohol and marijuana are isomorphic historically and that we can learn from history to intervene more intelligibly in the marijuana controversy. The social problems perspective gives great insight into the impact and unintended consequences of social control. The sociologic perspective has been largely unexamined by physicians in spite of its potential for predicting long term consequences of course of action.

Neither psychiatrists in particular nor physicians in general are aware of salient information that sociologists have accumulated which could contribute to our understanding of drug abuse problems. From the study of other less controversial social problems and social movements sociologists have been able to describe certain regular features of these phenomena. By examining these regular features vis-à-vis a more traditional American drug problem—that of alcohol —we can construct a picture of what may happen in a contemporary drug problem—that of marijuana.

There can be no doubt that much of contemporary American society considers marijuana and alcohol use a social problem. Both alcohol and marijuana abuse meet the sociologic criteria for a social problem; "a social problem arises when there is an awareness among a given people that a particular social situation is a threat to certain group values which they cherish and that this situation can be removed or corrected only by collective action."[4] Social problems beget social movements some of which solve the original problem and others of which perpetuate the problem they were designed to solve or generate new problems. These secondary or iatrogenic problems are a regular feature of social movements and the outcome of understandable forces. The social movement defines a territory for action and thus breeds countermovements. Attempts to secure or protect values meet with counterforces securing or protecting counter values. A frequent side effect of good intentions is the creation of social situations which some other people regard as troublesome; this is particularly true when the movement advocates change to solve the problem. As a movement grows it tends to become an institution, and as the organization solidifies it necessarily becomes more interested in its own life and growth than in the initial problem. Self-preservative, conservative, and appropriate functions replace the initial forces. We shall see how the original operation (social movement) is a success, but in the process the patient (the social problem) does not recover. In order to explore the relationship between social problems and social movements I have chosen to use the temperance and alcoholism movements' attack on the social problem of alcoholism as a model. I contend that this model may be equally applicable to not only alcohol, but also other drugs, marijuana in particular.

We are only now seeing the beginnings of social movements to deal with "the marijuana problem." They consist of three major forces: first, a heterogeneous group of law officers, judiciary, most physicians, educators, and much of the silent majority who view the issue as clear cut. Marijuana is to be prohibited rather vigorously—one might call this group "the drys." One explanation for the vigor of their stance comes from the recognition that this social movement serves to protect values perceived as being threatened by marijuana use. A second group opposes the first group at least partially because they perceive the "drys" as "moral entrepreneurs" who are extending the legal definitions of criminal behavior—behavior whose relativity is quite diffuse.[5] This group also hopes to avoid a polarization of attitudes, a malignant phenomenon we will return to later. This group talks pro-marijuana yet behaves anti-marijuana and represents a "middle road" view, comparable to the "mixers" of prohibition days. The third force operates considerably more visibly and vociferously while urging legalization of marijuana. This group includes many young people, users and non-users, and a scattering of adult radicals from both the far left and the far right who oppose "governmental oppression" for quite opposite reasons. These we might designate as "the wets."

A final and more nefarious force also operates but primarily on the basis of economic rather than social contingencies. As is the case with other "criminal" activities, those with financial interests in drug abuse including "dealers," perhaps organized crime, and including inevitably some members of law enforcement, stand aligned with the "drys" but for very different reasons. The liquor lobby may also be included paradoxically among the drys in this issue since legalization of marijuana would probably infringe on their sales.

I have purposely chosen the typology of wets, drys, and mixers because it both reflects the current scene and can be transferred directly back into the history of movements dealing with the social problem of alcohol.

History of Alcohol As a Social Problem

The history of alcohol problems can tell us much about the future of problems with marijuana. Consider for a moment the close parallels between alcohol and marijuana as drugs. They are in some ways pharmacologically comparable. Their initial use takes place in social settings and the purpose for their use may be similar. The major difference might be the use of alcohol as problem escape, a negative indication, while use of marijuana is the pursuit of "high", a postive indication. At any rate the "scientific" evidence about both drugs has followed parallel courses with alcohol's "scientific" course anteceding that of marijuana. It consists essentially of three phases: (a) "research" to prove its dangers—Rush in alcohol and Anslinger in marijuana; (b) a long period of little research in alcohol in 1850-1940, in marijuana 1930-1965; and, (c) a period of increasingly "hard nosed" research 1940 + for alcohol, 1970 + for marijuana. The outcome of the scientific research, however, has little relevance on attitudes and behavior. Further research and "science" can be used by either side to prove their point. Interest in the "drug" then has accomplished little. Interest in the social history of alcohol has proven much more rewarding in terms of understanding the current situation vis-à-vis alcohol.

Straus[6] and Rubington[7] among others have summarized the relevant history of alcohol in detail elsewhere. We need only sketch the salient features needed for our later discussion of the isomorphism with marijuana.

Prior to 1700 the use of alcohol in Colonial America took the form of family-centered and family-controlled imbibing of beer and wine. For economic reasons distilled spirits became increasingly prevalent during the 18th century until by the end of that century 90% of the alcohol consumed in this country was "hard liquor." Coincidentally, there was an immigration of large numbers of unattached males whose drinking was both unrelated to family sanctions and may have compensated for "the absence of the gratification, responsibilities, and the stability of family living."[6] The drinking excesses of these unattached frontiersmen—often accompanied by destructive behavior—was seen as a threat to the personal property and well-being of other citizens, and "the loss of productive manpower through drunkenness was seen as a threat to the national economy and vitality."[7] Similarily much concern is currently voiced about heavy marijuana use leading to an "amotivational syndrome"[8] and "dropping out"[9] while the image of the "psychotic"[10] marijuana user is very likely seen as a threat by much of our contemporary citizenry. Our national integrity and vitality is sapped by the "flagrant lawbreaking of the marijuana user,"[11] if we can accept the hard line view of some. So far the parallel alcohol/marijuana is quite close.

The Temperance Movement

The temperance movement for alcohol began in the latter half of the 18th century and has exerted a major continuing influence on American beliefs about alcohol and attitudes toward it. Initially, "temperance" implied the moderate use of alcohol and was espoused primarily by religious leaders who tried to use moral suasion to encourage "temperance." The negative sanctions grew, however, first against "hard liquor" and then shifted from a temperance to abstinence position. Benjamin Rush's treaties on the effects of alcohol on mind and body led the clergy to the abstinence position. The initial focus was on "drunkenness" which was condemned on moral, medical, economic, and nationalistic grounds. By the 1830's the temperance movement pervaded almost every facet of social life. In the late 1830's several changes took place in the temperance movement's concepts and goals. The emphasis moved from drunkenness to drinking and moral suasion gave way to legal sanctions against the drug "alcohol." The drunkard now served the temperance movement only as the example of the effect of "drink." National concern shifted in the direction of eliminating alcohol rather than understanding the alcoholic. Waves of legislated prohibition swept the country in the 1850's, again in the 1880's and finally in the 1910's, culminating in the "great experiment" with national prohibition in 1919. Where moral suasion had failed, legal coercion began and also failed. Prohibition legislation sought to preserve rural middle class values of sobriety, thrift, industry, self-control, and respectability. Similarly, current prohibition of marijuana serves to preserve suburban middle class values of industry, respectability, conformity, "team" mindedness against encroachment by the "dropping out," nonconformist, individualistic "marijuaniac." While legal prohibition of alcohol was defeated in 1932, it must be viewed merely as a battle lost by the temperance movement while the ultimate victory was theirs. The temperance movement, much less an open force currently, nevertheless left an indelible stamp on American attitudes toward alcohol, has defined alcohol per se as the problem and sees the solution of the problem as the elimination of alcohol.

Socialization into Alcohol Use

The pervasiveness of the prohibition mentality must be reckoned with since it has a continuing impact on problems with alcohol. The prohibition mentality pervades the current process of socialization into alcohol and other "drug" use. It is well worth recalling that the patterns of socialization in alcohol use have a rather direct effect on the extent of alcohol problems within a subculture. Snyder[12] Lolli[13] and Cahalan *et al.*[14] have outlined the social climate least likely to lead to problems with alcohol. Their findings indicate that how the person is socialized into drug use has a tremendous impact on his later potential for drug abuse. The socialization process includes a variety of factors. First, the social function of alcohol has importance. Alcohol can serve to solidify the family, as in Jewish ritual or can serve a dietary purpose, as with some Italian-American families. Alcohol use may be ritualized, tabooed, or ambivalently viewed, the latter state being typical of many Americans. Drinking in some settings is mandatory as at cocktail parties and adolescent "busts" and prohibited in other settings such as in church groups. The sanctions surrounding the use of abuse of alcohol are best learned from parents and before the child is exposed to adolescent peer use which tends to be rebellious and counter-productive vis-à-vis appropriate use. Learning from one's parents in a setting that is rather neutral or positive in terms of emotional feeling is associated with low rates of alcoholism while situations which are highly charged and ambivalent are associated with high rates of alcoholism.[15]

The temperance movement, however, does not encourage a felicitous socialization process. Its impact is at many levels and pervades the socialization process. The struggle between the wets and drys which culminated in national prohibition polarized the nation's view of alcohol and led to alcohol being symbolically a highly charged and ambivalently valued object. The ambivalence toward alcohol pervades much legislation and is best seen in legislated education about alcohol. Nearly every state under pressure from temperance groups has legislated a requirement that education about alcohol be included in the school curriculum—that education, however, takes a form acceptable to the temperance viewpoint. Thus the adolescent whose earlier socialization has not included socialization into alcohol use is exposed to prohibition-biased education—one side of the picture—while at the same time is exposed to the majority custom of adolescent drinking—the reverse side of the coin. The adolescent quickly recognizes that education and practice do not agree and that the law and the custom are quite at odds. By the late teens the prevalence of drinking equals and in quantity and frequency may exceed that of the general population.[16] The adolescent is exposed then to the worst possible socializing environment for learning appropriate use of alcohol. Drinking drops off slightly after age 21. Interestingly enough, the evidence indicates that "restricted prohibitive" schools have more drinking-related problems than more "liberal" schools.[17]

At another level the prohibition mentality strikes closer to home in the attitudes of various helping professions. A variety of recent studies (Knox,[18] Mogar *et al.*,[19] Bailey,[20] Freed[21] and Mendelson & Hyde[22]) have documented that contemporary helping professions continue to view alcoholism and the alcoholic in "prohibition" terms. Physicians in particular have negative attitudes toward alcoholics and this often contributes to the lack of adequate treatment programs. But even ostensibly more socially and behaviorally enlightened caretakers such as psychiatrists, psychiatric residents, psychoanalytically oriented social workers and workers in alcohol treatment centers continue to view the problem as a "lack of will," the treatment goals as abstinence, and the prognosis "guarded."

The Alcoholism Movement

A second alcohol movement developed both in response to the primary problem and in reaction to the temperance movement. The "alcoholism" movement began in the early 1940's with the formation of the National Council on Alcoholism and promoted the view that alcoholism is an illness rather than moral degeneracy. The idea was an old one, but until the repeal of prohibition it was culturally unacceptable. In the 1930's the scientific community became interested in alcohol and particulary in the alcoholic. The view of alcoholism as an illness is now widely shared, at least at the lip service level, by groups such as the AMA, HEW, and Alcoholics Anonymous. As a movement we see it gaining ascendence in the area of alcohol problems, but the temperance background noise is still impressive. The "sick role" for the alcoholic is not widely accepted by either the alcoholic or his helpmates. These two movements—"temperance" and "alcoholism"—have an ongoing legacy. The temperance movement polarized attitudes that have not been significantly altered by the alcoholism movement. The problem is still defined in terms of drink rather than drinkers. The drinker is important to the extent he evidences lack of "will and nerve." The alcoholism movement while counterbalancing temperance in some areas has led to increased conflict in others. The issue of sickness versus nonsickness has been heatedly argued by medicine and law alike. The sickness model alienates many lay workers in alcoholism and if adhered to would overwhelm treatment resources. Thus, both movements contribute to polarization of attitudes and to socialization practices characterized by ambivalence, preeminent peer influence, and hypocrisy, setting the stage for later problem drinking.

Other Sociologic Insights

The idea that social control—as in attempts to prohibit alcohol or to suppress marijuana—begets the very behavior it is intended to prevent has a long and distinguished history that is not well known to most physicians. The father of modern sociology, Emile Durkheim, spoke of the tendency of a society to generate and depend on deviance for its very organization. Contemporary sociologists such as Becker, Erickson,[23] and Lemert[24] have clearly established that social control often leads to increased deviance. The control process begins with designating which behaviors and actors, in the sociologic sense, are deviant. That this is a fluid and not a fixed process has been most clearly demonstrated in Becker's exposition.[5] As alcohol moved from "prohibition" gradually into the medical model, agencies of social control have shifted their interest to drugs not yet included in the "illness" model. The control process itself may provide for the learning of that behavior which is ostensibly to be eliminated. Once begun, the control process is very unlikely to be dismantled. Just as social movements grow and become self-serving, so do governmental bureaucracies. The control agencies evoke a counteraction from antiestablishment groups—primarily youths. In situations of high tension and low reciprocity—typical of the generation gap—social control is likely to be repressive and hence reduces reciprocity further and adds to tension.[25] Polarization of attitudes toward marijuana is following this pattern.

General Patterns of Illegal Consumption Offenses

Glaser[26] notes that offenses of "illegal consumption" follow certain regular patterns. The pattern applies to not only consumption of drugs or alcohol but also "consumption " of other illegal products or services such as gambling, abortion, and so forth. Initially, a type of consumption disturbs a sufficiently influential public to result in the use of criminal law to prohibit it. When consumption is not suppressed by such an effort prohibition is replaced by regulation. Regulation is resorted to often as the result of the great social costs of the attempted suppression. These costs include direct costs of supporting the control agency and indirect costs such as corruption of police and criminalization of the illegal consumer. This sequence has already occurred with alcohol and appears to be in progress with gambling, abortion, and perhaps opiate addiction.

Glaser has developed six general principles applicable to all efforts to suppress addiction:

(1) Any effort to prohibit by law the sale of goods or services in wide demand creates a highly attractive business opportunity for persons without scruples about violating the law. There is considerble evidence that there is a wide demand for marijuana. Manheimer's studies[27] indicate that 13 percent of adults have used marijuana.

(2) Police and other public officials, as representatives of the general public, are frequently reluctant to enforce rigorously any laws directed against practices that much of the public condones at least behaviorally. This leads often to selective enforcement of the law with the hapless, dependent, and incompetent being apprehended while the skillful, artful dodger escapes. Thus, although the number of arrests increase the number of convictions decrease.

(3) Competition among illegal businessmen is not regulated by legitimate agencies, but by acts of violence, so such businesses usually employ or are controlled by predatory criminals. For example, violence in the Haight Ashbury and in Detroit has been attributed by police officials to criminals in the drug scene.

(4) Offenders whose crime is the provision of service to private users can seldom be apprehended.

(5) Techniques successful in illegal selling and capital procured from it are used by the illegal sellers to acquire businesses previously operated legitimately.

(6) Any law widely violated seriously impedes other law enforcement by overloading law enforcement agencies and promotes disrespect for them. A prime example of this exists in the enforcement of laws regarding abuse of alcohol. With over 50 percent of arrests in this country for alcohol-related offenses the National Commission on Law Enforcement commented that "these arrests place an extremely heavy load on the operation of the criminal justice system."[28]

Glaser notes that in situations where an extensive supply of illegitimate consumable exists, two developments regularly occur. Consumption is increasingly regarded by the public as a health rather than a crime problem or, if impairment of health is doubted, as a matter of personal taste. Secondly, law enforcement agencies protect themselves from the impact of principle six above by shifting from prosecution of these offenses as consumption to prosecuting of them as performance, arresting only when the acts are pursued in public or involve minors. Changes in statute lag behind changes in supply and demand, but the inevitable movement is in the direction of regulation rather than prohibition. The shift from prohibition to regulation reflects the general sociological theorem of Durkheim[29] that as division of labor in society increases, i.e., increasing technocracy, tolerance for behavioral diversity also increases. Inevitably, then, the control process moves from public alarm to prohibition to regulation. Intense suppression of illegal consumption only reinforces a crime-consumable linkage.

Alcohol — Marijuana Isomorphism

We have presented the alcohol paradigm and some general theoretic concepts about drug use and can proceed now to further elucidate the isomorphism of alcohol with marijuana. Until the 1930's marijuana use was primarily medical and abuse was of little concern. The campaign against marijuana began in earnest near the end of prohibition, supported at least in part by liquor interests who foresaw potential inroads into their market. Under the aegis of Commissioner Anslinger the Federal Bureau of Narcotics began an 'educational" campaign. This campaign provided an image of the marijuana user that although notoriously inaccurate left a sterotypic picture in many peoples' minds. The image, that of the depraved sexual pervert, has persisted in the minds of the "older" generation—most certainly in the minds of people born before 1930 who currently populate the legislative bodies of the United States.

The nonuser and most of the "silent majority" have developed an image of the marijuana user which incorporates many symbolic sources of general societal tension. Marijuana is seen as a drug of the poor, the black, and the deviant, and is associated with sexual excess, insanity, laziness, and disrespect for authority. A rapidly growing majority has discovered that the marijuana prohibitionistic mythology is untrue and has proceeded to proselytize a new mythology of marijuana as a benign non-caloric euphoriant. Neither position is accurate. The prohibition movement in marijuana started where it had left off with alcohol. Legal sanctions have been operative in the area of marijuana use since 1937. The continued need for this stance is justified on the basis of the evidence that marijuana is associated with a variety of ill effects. Marijuana causes an "amotivational syndrome"[8] characterized by a "loss of virtually all activities other than drug use"—a newly described syndrome that characterizes a great many alcoholics. The stepping stone theory of heroin use has been touted as a reason for repression of marijuana—ignorning that repression per se may be the cause of the association. Oddly enough, people seem little concerned about beer being a stepping stone to hard liquor. Recent studies (*Kolansky & Moore*[10] *and Keeler et al.*[30]) demonstrating the adverse psychological impact of marijuana fail to recognize that alcohol may be similarly detrimental and its use is poorly controlled. Studies of the therapeutic effects of marijuana have not been done.

We are beginning to see the development of social movements in marijuana which parallel both the "drys" and "alcoholic" movements in alcohol. The "wets" in marijuana are only recently on the scene. Prior to the founding of N.O.R.M.L. (National Organization to Revise Marijuana Laws) it was a loosely organized coalition of marijuana advocates—most clearly seen in Amorphia, the Cannabis Cooperative, of Mill Valley, California. Likewise, as scientific research on marijuana increases we see—in perfect parallel to the situation in alcohol research in the 40's—the beginnings of the enlightened "marijuana" movement which emphasizes the personal/societal sources of marijuana abuse rather than the "evils" of the drug itself. This movement has thus far not become influential and perhaps, like the alcoholic movement, can only hope to modify attitudes slowly. While the marijuana "wets" and "drys" push their respective positions they serve to further polarize attitudes toward the drug. I have indicated earlier how such polarization can operate through the process of socialization to promote drug abuse behaviors. In addition, as Howard Becker[31] has pointed out, untoward drug reactions—particularly panic reactions and paranoid states—are promoted by the heightened discussion of marijuana combined with its illegal status. Crucial socializing agencies have rather uncritically accepted the prohibition viewpoint without recognizing its potential consequences. The alliance of legal authorities, medicine, and educators with the forces of marijuana prohibition has widened a generation gap with already alienated and "normally" antiestablishment youth. As was the case of youthful drinking in the past all current young people's "bad" behavior is attributed to the use of marijuana. Straus has called attention to the fact that adult attitudes toward youthful drinking (or marijuana smoking) often confuse drinking (or drug) behaviors with pathology. There is little evidence to show that teenage drinking patterns are linked with alcoholism, an earlier "stepping stone theory" that did not prove out. Similarly what little evidence we do have seems to indicate that most youthful drug users do drop out—drop out of drug use, that is.

Just as teenage drinking elicited a variety of social reactions from exaggeration of its extent to denial of its existence just so with marijuana. Blame assignment is common in both problems with school, law enforcement, parents, and churches all blaming each other. Both drinking and other drug behaviors may mean breaking with family or religious convictions and the mere act may evoke feelings of personal conflict or guilt, especially when drinking or smoking marijuana is associated with sexual behavior. The prevailing confusion is then compounded by the gross inconsistency between custom and the law which defines drinking as legal adult behavior and smoking marijuana as illegal adult behavior. In both the case of alcohol and marijuana prohibition the tactics have been the same. The social problem is defined as "the drug." The drug user, if considered at all, serves only as the example to be pointed out with derision. The solution in both cases is the same, eliminate the drug, a patent impossibility. The impact of the controversy is the same in both cases—polarization of attitudes thus setting up the very situation most likely to produce drug problem behavior, the very behavior that

prohibition intended to eliminate. Attitudes about the drug, alcohol or marijuana, are thus deeply ingrained and will be vociferously held regardless of the
relative paucity or abundance of scientific evidence to support either view. The
issue at stake is more clearly seen by understanding that social movements
develop to cope with social problems only when cultural values are at stake.
Concern over the imputed effects of marijuana abuse can be taken as indicators of
the values being questioned.

More recently, however, the importance of taking a global look at social issues
has achieved some semblance of scientific respectability with the recent publication of Forrester's[32] seminal work on systems analysis. Forrester demonstrates
that the short range view and local scale may often prove disastrous when considering altering social systems.[33] The evidence that the most "reasonable"
approach is not always most productive in the long run is now coming from
many fronts. For example, a recent study[34] demonstrates that allowing a tolerable level of employee theft may maximize morale and profit in certain kinds of
jobs. This is clearly an immoral and, in the face of it, an unreasonable approach. A
model similar to the one Forrester developed for population control would be of
inestimable assistance in developing national policy about marijuana in particular and drugs in general.

The sociologic and systems perspective can thus be seen to be crucial to understanding the marijuana muddle. The unintended consequences of social control
are numerous and counterproductive as presently constituted. One might speculate on ways to reverse these trends. Clearly the first order of business is to
depolarize attitudes as quickly as possible. Given the impossibility of adequate
repression of marijuana, then regulation is not only inevitable but wise. The
inevitability of regulation stems from several operative forces. First, as we have
seen, regulation results when suppression of illegitimate consumption is more
costly to a society than is its regulation. Secondly, as the values of the society
slowly shift we might expect a new recreational drug of choice to appear.
Thirdly, as cultures become increasingly diversified, tolerance for deviance
increases. Finally, the current marijuana-using youth ultimately will become
members of the establishment and thus will increasingly have an impact on
legislative bodies with progressive erosion of the sanctions against marijuana.
The more rapidly we move in this direction the less likely we are to provide a
socialization milieu conducive to drug problems. Parallel to this we must recognize that education is a crucial element in facilitating appropriate respect for all
drugs. If we continue to assume that young people, given adequate information,
will get into trouble with drugs, we have established an unhealthy self-fulfilling
prophecy. On the other hand, if we appeal to the healthy part of the ego we may
find that youths respond responsibly. This is not to say that drug problems will
disappear. It is inevitable that some section of our culture will be alienated from
the mainstream and may choose a drug dependency solution to this alienation.

The medical profession thus has a three-part obligation. First, we must recognize the social-political aspects of the "drug abuse" problem and recognize the
implications of this. Secondly, we have an obligation to aid in depolarization of
views, starting with our own. Finally, we have an obligation to improve the
socialization milieu and education in all drug use.

Notes

1. Leifer, R. "Cannabis Politica." *Psychiat. Soc. Sci. Rev.* Vol. 6: 2.(1971).

2. Kaplan, J. *Marijuana—The New Prohibition.* (Cleveland: World Publishing, 1970).

3. Grinspoon, L. *Marijuana Reconsidered.* (Cambridge: Harvard University Press, 1971).

4. Fuller, R. C. "Social Problems." In Park, R.E.(Ed). *An Outline of the Principles of Sociology.* (New York: Barnes and Noble, 1943).

5. Becker, H. *Outsiders.* (New York: Free Press, 1963).

6. Straus, R. "Alcohol." In Merton, R. (Ed.). *Contemporary Social Problems.* (New York: Harcourt, 1966).

7. Rubington, E. "The Nature of Social Problems." *Brit. J. Addict.* Vol. 64: 31-46. (1969).

8. McGlothlin, W. H. & West, L. J. "The Marijuana Problem: An Overview." *Amer. J. Psychiat. Vol. 125: 370-378. (1968).*

9. Blum, R. & associates. *Utopiates: A Study of the Use and Users of LSD-25.* (New York: Atherton, 1964).

10. Kolansky, H. & Moore, W. T. "Effects of Marijuana on Adolescents and Young Adults." *J.A.M.A.* Vol. 216: 486-492. (1971).

11. Bloomquist, E. "Social Benefit or Social Detriment." *Calif. Med.* Vol. 106: 346-353. (1967).

12. Snyder, C. R. *Alcohol and the Jews.* (New York: Free Press, 1958).

13. Lolli, G. *Alcohol and Italian Culture.* (Glencoe: Free Press, 1958).

14. Cahalan, D., Cisin, I. A. & Crossley, H. M. *American Drinking Practices: A National Study of Drinking Behavior and Attitudes.* (New Brunswich, Rutgers Center for Alcohol Studies, 1969).

15. Snyder, C. R. "Inebriety, Alcoholism and Anomie." In Clinard, M. B. (Ed). *Anomie and Drinking Behavior.* (New York: Free Press, 1964).

16. Straus, R. & Bacon, S. D. *Drinking in College.* (New Haven: Yale, 1953).

17. Sterne, M. W., Pittman, D. J. & Coe, T. "Teenagers, Drinking and the Law." *Crime and Delinquency.* Vol. 11: 78-85. (1965).

18. Knox, W. "Attitudes of Psychiatrists and Psychologists Toward Alcoholism." *Amer. J. Psychiat.* Vol. 127: 1675-1679. (1971).

19. Mogar, R. E. *et al.* "Staff Attitudes Toward the Alcoholic Patient." *Arch. Gen. Psychiat.* Vol. 21: 449-454. (1969).

20. Bailey, M. B. "Attitudes Toward Alcoholism in Social Caseworkers." *Quart. J. Stud. Alcohol.* Vol. 31: 669-683. (1970).

21. Freed, F. X. "Opinions of Psychiatric Hospital Personnel and College Students Toward Alcoholism." *Psychol. Rep.* Vol. 15: 615-616.

22. Mendelson, J. & Hyde, A. "Alcoholism Training in Medical Schools: Some Pedagogical and Attitudinal Issues." *Ann. N. Y. Acad. Sci.* Vol. 178: 66-69. (1971).

23. Erikson, K. *Wayward Puritans.* (New York: Wiley, 1966).

24. Lemert, E. *Social Pathology.* New York: McGraw, 1951).

25. Palmer, S. "On the Unintended Consequences of Social Control." Paper read at Annual Meeting Amer. Soc. Assn. September, 1969.

26. Glaser, D. "Criminology and Social Policy." *Amer. Sociologist. Vol. 6: 30-37. (1971).*

27. Manheimer, D., Mellinger, G. & Balter, M. "Marijuana Use Among Urban Adults." *Sci.* Vol. 166: 1544-1545. (1969).

28. President's Commission on Law Enforcement and Administration of Justice. "Task Force Report: Drunkenness." (Washington: U.S. Govt. Printing Office, 1967).

29. Durkheim, E. *The Division of Labor in Society.* (Glencoe: Free Press, 1933).

30. Keeler, M., Ewing, J. & Rouse, B. "Hallucinogenic Effects of Marijuana as Currently Used." *Amer. J. Psychiat.* Vol. 128(2): 213-226. (1971).

31. Becker, H. "History, Culture and Subjective Experience: An Elaboration of the Social Bases of Drug-Induced Experiences." *J. Health Soc. Beh.* Vol. 8: 172. (1967).

32. Forrester, J. W. *Urban Dynamics.* (Cambridge: MIT Press, 1969).

33. Forrester, J. W. *World Dynamics.* (Cambridge: Wright-Allen Press, 1971).

34. Zeitlin, L. "A Little Larceny Can Do a Lot." *Psych. Today.* Vol. 5: 22-28. (1971).

Socialist

Andrew Karmen: The Narcotics Problem: Views From the Left

Leftists believe that contemporary social problems are reflections of deep-seated insoluble contradictions inherent in the profit system. Because the interests of the wealthy and powerful are opposed to those of the vast majority, the solutions the ruling class chooses cause the problems working people face.

Both liberal and conservative defenders of the social order fear that an unchecked narcotics plague could lead to a state of "anomie"—the deterioration, degeneration, and demoralization of society. Conservatives seek solutions that restore and revive crumbling authority structures and traditional values. Liberals try reforms and adjustments that accommodate new realities to save the social system from its self-destructive tendencies. The radical left builds democractic mass movements against exploitation, alienation, and oppression that struggle for fundamental social changes. To leftists, heroin addiction and the street crime it generates constitute a special problem because its net effect is to hold back the growth and development of broad-based progressive forces.

This paper reviews and synthesizes the keenest insights, soundest arguments, sharpest criticisms, and most constructive proposals from leftist sources about the narcotics problems in the U.S. today.

The Problem

To understand the narcotics problem, the normative paradigm of morality and law, which limits most social science research, must be transcended in favor of an analysis that uncovers the historical links between opiates and the political economy (Chambliss, 1977: 54). Current public policies towards narcotics are not based on irrationality, ignorance, or confusion inherited from a prescientific past (Helmer, 1975:7). Criminal law is designed, enforced, and administered by self-interest groups, classes, and movements, which seek to impose their definitions of right and wrong on all of society through government. Dramatic changes in the status of narcotic users and abusers throughout history and from place-to-place demonstrate that there is nothing about this particular behavior that makes it unavoidably illegal (Reasons, 1974:102). Liberal muckraking exposes and the labeling theory about drugs divert attention from crucial political conflicts and the underlying economic forces that provoke them to an overemphasis on prominent individuals and official reactions (Galliher and Walker, 1978:31).

American society has become consumption oriented, and many habits are promoted and indulged in with abandon. Businesses, both legitimate and illegitimate, push products that meet the demand they help to create (Kenny, 1970:105). But drug addiction is more than pleasurable self-gratification and escapism. It is a predictable market response to economic and social dislocations (Yurick, 1970:23).

Heroin addiction has been and continues to be a "vice" of the lower strata of the working class. Concentration and containment of this contagion is not an unintended consequence of anti-narcotics legislation and enforcement patterns but is precisely the cause of prohibitionist laws. Rational, working-class adolescents are drawn to the illegitimate opportunity structure and illegal labor market, including the narcotics trade, during periods when jobs are scarce in the secondary pool of low-paid, unskilled work. Whether the flow is a trickle or stampede depends upon the number of entry level positions at lower echelons, the chances for upward mobility, the requirements for capital or credit, and law enforcement pressures (Helmer, 1975:3-15). Heroin addicts and salesmen are defined as "deviants" and controlled because they are unable or unwilling to perform legitimate wage labor, they use drugs to escape or transcend rather than for sociability and adjustment, and they criminally interfere with approved patterns of income and goods distribution (Spitzer, 1975:646). But to leftists, such social activities are evaluated by their contributions towards the struggle for social justice (Platt, 1978:33). Heroin addicts are classic examples of people alienated from themselves, their community, and the productive labor force. Through their efforts to ease their own suffering, they fuel racism, spread defeatism, victimize fellow workers, and legitimate repression.

Fueling Racism

The historic reluctance of white workers to support the just demands of super-exploited minorities has fueled racial tensions at the expense of a common struggle to improve the quality of life. The stereotypical identification of drug abuse as a trait of an entire racial or ethnic group has divided people who ought to be united. These splits resolve the business community's "labor solidarity" problem.

In the Old West, poorly paid Chinese immigrants who toiled in mines and on railroad construction gangs were placated with opium imported from their homeland by their employers. But when the demand for cheap labor waned, an "Oriental exclusion" campaign developed. Discriminatory laws that scapegoated the Chinese for economic hardships were passed, including the first anti-narcotics statutes, which banned opium dens. These laws were intended to harass and control the Chinese rather than to discourage the use of the drug (Helmer, 1975:31; Takagi and Platt, 1978:11).

During the years of the Great Depression, the drug of choice of Mexican farmworkers and laborers—marijuana—was misclassified as a dangerous narcotic, and outlawed. The new laws were used against the entire ethnic community to drive unneeded Mexicans back over the border (Helmer, 1975:74).

Today, grossly exaggerated claims about the involvement of undocumented workers—denounced as "illegal aliens"—from Latin America in the marijuana, cocaine, and heroin trade contributes to the hostile reception these newcomers encounter. There are disproportionate numbers of known addicts who are black or hispanic wherever minority group youths live in ghettos, hard hit by poverty, inferior education, and unemployment. But white reluctance to desegregation in schooling, hiring, and housing is stiffened by distorted accounts of heroin "epidemics" in inner city neighborhoods.

Whenever a particular drug is linked to a specific group during a period of intense competition for scarce resources and limited opportunities, the efforts to ban the drug reflect the concerns of the majority about economic security more than their fears about its harmful effects (Quinney, 1979:156).

Pacifying the Rebellious

Patient, reasoned, responsive, and sustained organizing efforts nurture the evolution of a principled and disciplined mass movement for social justice. Narcotized individuals lack the inclination, time, and ability to commit themselves to such a process. Heroin addiction is part of the solution to the establishment's "radical activism" problem.

Throughout history and around the globe, drugs have been used as a tool by those who seek to manage, manipulate, contain, and control others. The conquistadores doled out cocaine to subjugated Incas to make them dig more energetically for gold. Human lives were bartered by slave traders for rum and tobacco (nicotine). The resistance of native American Indian tribes to the settlers' encroachments was weakened by the "firewater" (whiskey) pushed on them. The

Chinese masses were dominated with the help of the "foreign mud" (opium) imported by the British East India Company.

Combat troops are given stimulants and sedatives before and after going into battle. School authorities slow down hyperactive children with Ritalin. Restless prisoners and unruly mental patients are given powerful tranquilizers, which serve as chemical straitjackets.

Right-wing conspiracy theories contend that drug dependence is cultivated by external enemies, to demoralize the entire population and sap its strength to resist subversion or even invasion. During the height of anti-Chinese sentiment in the late 1800's, opium dens were pictured as outposts of seduction and corruption. During World War I, heroin allegedly seeped in from German pharmaceutical companies and from anarchist circles. During World War II, Japan was fingered as the supplier of American habits. When the Cold War set in, the Soviet secret police were said to be behind the narcotics trade. After the outbreak of the Korean War, Communist China was charged with masterminding the traffic. At the height of the War in Indochina, North Vietnam and the National Liberation Front were suspected.

The reality is quite different. Rather than being a "communist plot," the flow of narcotics has emanated from some of the world's staunchest anti-communists —Chinese Nationalist Army units in Southeast Asia's Golden Triangle, CIA backed mercenaries and political cliques, paramilitary anti-Castro Cuban groups, and ultra conservative crime families (CCAS, 1972:56-65).

Left-wing conspiracy theories charge officials with "benign neglect" at best, or even tacit approval of heroin-taking by certain targeted populations. These accusations are based on Karl Marx's "opiate of the masses" theme—that the ruling class encourages working class escapism. Narcotics use tends to depoliticize rebellious people, dissolve their collective networks into squabbling bands, and channel or deflect their energies into self-destructive urges.

Narcotics use has been a definite alternative to radical activism for two groups in recent years—Vietnam G.I.'s and ghetto youths.

During the war in Indochina, soldiers who supported military policy gravitated toward the tradition of heavy drinking, while those who opposed intervention in Vietnam tended to identify with a marijuana sub-culture. But a concerted crackdown against pot smoking drove many disgruntled G.I.'s to take up heroin smoking, which they discovered made time pass quicker, and helped them to get through their tour of duty faster. Overseas and back home as veterans, the opiate users held the same anti-war views as servicemen in the G.I. movement but just didn't have the time or will to act on them (Helmer, 1974:76-81, 241).

Ghetto youths emerging from a consciousness-contracting euphoria became preoccupied with how to raise enough money for another fix before withdrawal sets in. They are too passive when nodding and too self-absorbed when they aren't high to fight for community control over the schools, to organize tenants for a rent strike, or to march on City Hall to demand decent jobs for all who want to work. Since narcotics pacify those who suffer most from mental and physical degradation, it's likely that some astute members of the ruling circles have decided its benefits outweigh its costs (Tabor, 1971:3; Carroll, 1974:41; Silber, 1977:52).

Legitimizing Repression

Government policy is shaped by the top executives of giant corporations and the super rich. Because of the street crime problem, attributable in part to the predatory acts of addicts, working people are driven to support the criminal justice apparatus. They come to view the police, courts, and prisons as the protectors of their possessions and even their lives, rather than as the guarantors of the property and privileges of the upper class and businesses. In the name of cracking down on the narcotics trade, dangerous precedents have been set and questionable practices routinized. Personal freedoms, civil liberties, and constitutional rights are threatened as much by official reactions as by the "evils" they are intended to snuff out. The legitimation of state repression is a particular problem for leftist critics of official policies. It is part of the solution to the dilemma of "too much freedom for dissidents," which constantly confronts those who rule.

Most street crimes are not acts of primitive political rebelliousness of the "steal-from-the-rich, give-to-the-poor" Robin Hood type, nor are they rational attempts to survive under harsh conditions; they are essentially expressions of reactionary individualism, callous, ruthless, oppressive attacks by the impoverished and alienated on fellow working people (Dod *et al*, 1976:2). Heroin addicts intensify existing intra-class and intra-racial patterns of criminal victimization (Humphries, 1979:235). The narcotics trade bleeds poor communities of funds and is as destructive of the quality of life as any legal business thriving on misery, desperation, and illusions (Platt, 1978:33).

The typical addict/dealer lifestyle is the antithesis of a "serve the people" commitment to radical change. The elite and role models in the subculture of the marginalized and excluded are professional con-artists and swashbuckling profiteers. They are armed with a polished array of "games" or "hustles," which revolve around conniving, duping, cheating, and adulterating, and are numbed by a rip-off mentality which objectifies people as "marks." Their status hierarchy is based on money-making ability, conspicuous consumption, and the enjoyment of leisure derived from living off the labor of others—capitalist values at their crudest. Immersion in the narcotics subculture is a brutalizing and conservatizing experience, which destroys egalitarian and humanitarian impulses.

But prevailing upon the authorities to "clean up" the narcotics scene doesn't enhance the possibilities of liberation either. Vice squads, the vanguard of the anti-narcotics forces, rely on undercover agents to infiltrate drug-taking circles and ferret out pushers. Small-time dealers and ordinary addicts are offered leniency or even immunity if they serve as informers and witnesses. Users and sellers are targeted for arrest, events are engineered, and cases are built against them. Dramatic raids and show trials are staged for media exposure to cultivate public support and insure funding. These tactics bear a striking resemblance to the infiltration, provocation, disruption, and discreditation of "counterintelligence" programs directed by "red squads" and the FBI against the anti-war, black liberation, and radical movement in recent years (Karmen, 1974a:210). Since the same questionable, controversial, even unconstitutional methods are rarely if ever employed against high level corporate executives or top government officials who plot crime in the suites, the lesson is clear: tactics the public tolerates in the suppression of the drug trade receive a legitimacy that facilitates political repression.

The war against narcotics has spawned other ominous practices. The no-knock law that permits authorities to break into homes without warrants or warnings to prevent the destruction of drugs as evidence jeopardizes the right to privacy (Gerth, 1972:62). The fundamental principle of "innocent until proven guilty" is undermined by the procedure of coercing suspected addicts to sign themselves into rehabilitation programs as alternatives to prosecution and incarceration. Civil commitment with compulsory treatment for indefinite periods of time has permitted the state to intervene against individuals in ways that vastly exceed the usual statutory limits on isolation, confinement, and punishment (Quinney, 1979:385). Extensive files kept on drug violation suspects can be traded back and forth between computerized systems, or amalgamated with other records, increasing the potential for abuse, harassment, and intimidation by centralized agencies with concentrated powers (Chambliss, 1975:347).

Unprecedented demands for abstinence and accountability have been imposed on captured narcotics users. Probationers, parolees, or patients in programs are routinely subjected to urine surveillence to expose and discipline any "cheaters" who ingest forbidden substances. Monitoring their drug intake through these chemical lie detector tests goes well beyond the primitive method of visually inspecting their arms for "tracks" (needle marks). These stringent constraints on the personal behavior of medicalized wards of the state raise serious questions about the limits of policing.

And Its Solutions

The emergence, growth, and development of a drug abuse control establishment makes the eradication of heroin addiction unlikely. Individual careerists, profit-oriented businesses, and empire-building bureaucracies that depend on addicts and the trouble they cause seek to manage the problem—keep it within limits—rather than eliminate it.

Disinterested parties are hard to find even to investigate a basic question like the approximate number of addicts in a community. Researchers who are sensitive to what funding sources are looking for adjust their approaches and methodologies accordingly. Computer data processing and statistical analysis encourage the adoption of broad definitions of abusers to get large sample sizes. Almost invariably, the conclusions are that the problem is serious, rates are on the increase, and action must be taken. Policing innovations, experimental treatments, and further social research are not stimulated by assessments that drug abuse and its fallout have been overestimated (Sternberg, 1977:192-195).

Different factions within the drug abuse control establishment compete for funds and contend for hegemony within the parameters of a policing/punishment vs. treatment/rehabilitation debate. Given the sustained propaganda against "dope fiends" and "junkies," it's not surprising that punishment and banishment are the prevailing gut reactions and that even those who support treatment and correction vehemently resist new facilities in their own neighborhoods (Regush, 1971:56).

Most solutions seek to reintegrate the ex-addict back into the social order, and often this simply means putting them to work. The underlying premises are that involvement in legitimate activities is a pull away from drugs and crime and that interaction with generally law-abiding citizens provides a push towards conformity. Efforts to prod addicts to take jobs ignore the likelihood that the tasks open to those short on marketable skills, and who have long criminal records, will be dreary lifelong obligations. Alienating labor is damaging to dignity and not genuinely rehabilitative (Morash and Anderson, 1978:563).

All the "realistic" solutions that have been proposed or tried are actually manipulative attempts to force addicts into compromising collaboration and rigged participation with the very same systems—family, education, occupation, criminal justice—that drove them to drugs originally (Karmen, 1974b:310). The contribution that concerned leftists can make is to help rescue the humanitarian kernels in these solutions from their reactionary shells.

Prohibition, Policing, Punishment

Voluntary (not compulsory) treatment is preferable to the quasi-military alternative of policing, but there is a role for prohibition and punishment in the overall drive against narcotics abuse.

The appropriate targets for disruption, arrest, and incapacitation are the mobsters of traditionally conservative crime syndicates and their cohorts in business and government who direct, finance, and protect the lucrative trade, but who do not use narcotics themselves. The web of corruption from patrolman to prosecutor to policymaker has actually helped major traffickers to charge addicts monopoly prices for highly adulterated junk by sparing their operations while eliminating their competitors (Tabor, 1971:4; Silber, 1977:73).

The Central Intelligence Agency has not used its global capabilities to destabilize international smuggling networks; instead, it has initiated occasional joint projects with them. The Federal Bureau of Investigation has directed much more of its counterintelligence efforts to splinter progressive movements than to break up the real enemy within. The Bureau of Narcotics and its successors have squandered their resources persecuting devotees of marijuana, psychedelic drugs, and cocaine. Police narcotics squads have concentrated on putting expendable, easily replaced street level pushers, who are addicts themselves, out-of-business (CCAS, 1972:9).

Given these realities and the miniscule odds of intercepting couriers and shipments before they reach wholesalers and retailers, the best chance to stem the narcotics tide is to dry up its sources. Poor peasants in remote mountainous areas of "free world" allies must be offered incentives to grow crops other than opium poppies. Failing this, pre-emptive buys (purchasing the opium and then burning it) should replace ineffective, dangerous, and military-oriented chemical crop destruction programs.

Legalized Heroin

Because the war against narcotics is being lost, the British system of dispensing heroin as a medicine to certified addicts has received sporadic attention in liberal and conservative circles. It would probably be welcomed by many addicts, but this is not what "liberation" and "self-determination" is really all about. Heroin maintenance means indeterminate dependence with government doctors or private practitioners and drug companies as respectable pushers.

If heroin was distributed legally and at low cost, it's likely that demogogic politicians would picture patients as "parasites getting high at the taxpayer's expense," and use addicts as a football to kick around at election time. The reality would be that a new mechanism of pacification and control was being established.

Heroin transition programs might be a more politically acceptable alternative. Specially licensed non-profit patient-worker-community-controlled clinics could provide slowly declining doses of heroin along with a full range of social services until addicts were drug-free and self-sufficient, or at least enrolled in other treatment modalities (Kunnes, 1972:178; Dubro, 1977:15).

Methadone Maintenance

At the turn of the century, heroin was touted by socially irresponsible pharmaceutical firms as the cure for morphine addiction. Methadone, a more powerful synthetic narcotic discovered by Nazi scientists, nurtured by Rockefeller money, and promoted by the Nixon Administration might merely increase the range of addictive substances available on the legal and illegal market. For those who enter maintenance programs involuntarily as a condition of probation or parole, methadone becomes a not-too-subtle mechanism for controlling immobilized, neurologically dependent, psychologicaly compelled consumers (MCHR, 1972:8; CCAS, 1972:68; Ahern, 1977:2). Ironically, they couldn't get adequate health care before they violated the narcotics laws; afterwards, they can't fend off intense medical attention (Speigelman, 1977:31).

Methadone maintenance has redeeming humanitarian features as a stabilizer for hard core addicts only when counterposed to harsher alternatives—a predatory existence on the streets, or imprisonment and punishment (Regush, 1971:124; Dubro, 1977:12).

Therapeutic Communities

Psychological profiles of the average addict tend to be under-specific because they fit the personality traits and background characteristics typical of poor young men (Helmer, 1975:148). If most addicts are not mentally disturbed, they don't need longterm psychotherapy.

Counseling services run by ex-addicts rather than professionals can serve as consciousness-raising groups where the connections between personal troubles and social problems can be explored (CCAS, 1972:76). But recruiting ex-deviants to directly preside over custodial setting smacks of "conversion"—a management strategy to coopt former troublemakers as the first line of defense and support for the existing social arrangements that generate deviance (Spitzer, 1975:649). Especially objectionable are programs employing massive group pressure to inculcate a victim-blaming ideology that holds addicts completely at fault for their own plight. In a process analogous to religious redemption, addicts are berated by each other and the staff to personalize, individualize, and internalize all responsibility and guilt for their "fall." Through public confession, self-sacrifice, penance, and self-abasement they renounce their weakness in the face of temptation. Only after a trip through hell comes the blinding insight that leads to salvation—they should adopt the work ethic and other conformist values (Yurick, 1970:72). The punitiveness, authoritarianism, and "brainwashing" in "attack-therapy" heaps further abuse on those who have suffered plenty, until their will to resist is ground down and they become faithful followers and even messianic zealots of the program's philosophy (Dubro, 1977:13).

The Real Cures

After more than a century of widespead opium-smoking, China solved its narcotics problem within two years of the victory of the revolution. A two-pronged attack was successful. Highly selective, strictly enforced, severely punitive measures were directed at major traffickers. Amnesty, massive public support, and a promise of a place in the new society were offered to small-scale dealers and to addicts (Rubenstein, 1973:61; Silber, 1977:70).

In New York's blighted South Bronx, black and Puerto Rican radicals took over and transformed the ineffective Lincoln Hospital drug program as an act of community self-defense. Political education classes and patient advocacy services were set up to de-medicalize and de-professionalize rehabilitative efforts (Kunnes, 1972:193).

To those who rule, narcotics addiction has served as a safety valve easing the labor solidarity, radical activism, and too-much-freedom problem. But addiction and criminal behavior also poses a threat by underscoring the irrationalities of the existing system—its driving need for expansion and empire; its imposition of alienating conditions; its preservation of deprivation in the midst of affluence; its waste of human resources; and its provocation of needless insecurity, fear and hatred.

The best solution to the narcotics problem is to prevent the onset of addiction in future generations. The real cure is a social system that permits meaningful lives for all.

References

Ahern, D. (1977) "Letter to the editor." *Liberation*, 20, 4, June, 2.
Carroll, D. (1974) "Dialogue with David DuBois." *Issues in Criminology*, 9, 2, Fall, 21-42.
Chambliss, W. (1977) "Markets, profits, labor and smack." *Contemporary Crisis*, 1, 53-76.
Chambliss, W. and Rhyther, D. (1975) *Sociology: The Discipline and Its Direction*. New York: McGraw-Hill.
Committee of Concerned Asian Scholars (CCAS) (1972) *The Opium Trail: Heroin and Imperialism*. Boston: New England Free Press.
Dod, S., Platt, T., Schwendinger, H., Shank, G., and Takagi, P. (1976) "The politics of street crime." *Crime and Social Justice*, 5, Spring-Summer: 1-4.
Dubro, A. (1977) "Methadone is not a government plot." *Liberation*, 20, 2, Jan/Feb: 11-15.
Galliher, J. and Walker, A. (1978) "The politics of systematic research error: The case of the Federal Bureau of Narcotics as a moral entrepreneur" *Crime and Social Justice*, 10, Fall-Winter: 29-33.
Gerth, J. (1972) "The Americanization of 1974" *Sundance*, April-May.

Helmer, J. (1974) *Bringing the War Home: The American Soldier in Vietnam and After.* New York: Free Press.

Helmer, J. (1975) Drugs and Minority Oppression. New York: Seabury Press.

Humphries, D. (1979) "Crime and the state" in Syzamanski, A. and Goertzel, T., *Sociology: Class, Consciousness and Contradictions.* New York: Van Nostrand.

Karmen, A. (1974a) "Agent provocateurs in the contemporary left movement." in C. Reasons, *The Criminologist, Crime and the Criminal.* Santa Monica: Goodyear.

Kenny, M. (1970) "Drug history: Politics and prohibition." *Health/Pac Bulletin,* June.

Kunnes, R. (1972) *The American Heroin Empire.* New York: Dodd, Mead and Co.

Medical Committee for Human Rights, Greater Boston Chapter (MCHR) (1972) "Methadone: Federal drug addiction." *MCHR News,* Summer: 1-8.

Morash, M. and Anderson, E. (1978) "Liberal thinking on rehabilitation: A work-able solution to crime." *Social Problems,* 25, 5, June: 556-564.

Platt, T. (1978) "Street crime — A view from the left." *Crime and Social Justice,* No. 9, Spring-Summer.

Quinney, R. (1979) *Criminology,* 2nd Edition. Boston: Little, Brown.

Reasons, C. (1974) "The dope on the Bureau of Narcotics in maintaining the criminal approach to the drug problem." in *The Criminologist, Crime and the Criminal.* Santa Monica: Goodyear.

Regush, N. (1971) *The Drug Addiction Business.* New York: Dial Press.

Rossman, M. (1971) "Politics of the white drug plague." *Liberation News Service,* August 7.

Rubenstein, A. (1973) "How China got rid of opium." *Monthly Review,* 25, 5, October:58-63.

Silber, I. (1977) "No drugs in the new society." *Skeptic,* No. 17, Jan-Feb:70-73.

Speigiman, R. (1977) "Prison psychiatrists and drugs: A case study." *Crime and Social Justice,* 7, Spring-Summer: 23-39.

Spitzer, S. (1975) "Toward a marxian theory of deviance." *Social Problems,* 22, 5, June:638-651.

Sternberg, D. (1977) *Radical Sociology.* Hicksville, New York: Exposition.

Takagi, P. and Platt, T. (1978) "Behind the gilded ghetto: An analysis of race, class and crime in Chinatown." Crime and Social Justice, 9, Spring-Summer:2-25.

Tabor, M. (1971) "The plague: Capitalism plus dope equals genocide." New York: Committee to Defend the Panther 21.

Yurick, S. (1970) "The Political economy of junk." *Monthly Review,* 22, 7, December:22-37.

Chapter 6

MENTAL HEALTH

Mental illness, defined as a social problem, has traditionally focused on conditions in mental hospitals. Generations of sociologists have committed themselves as patients or taken social service jobs in mental hospitals to conduct studies by participant observation. These sociological studies encouraged the development of public awareness about mental hospital conditions, which led to a movement to close the hospitals. In recent years, most mental patients have been returned to the community to have their needs provided for in non-institutional settings.

More recently sociologists have focused their attention on social conditions that may be associated with the causation of mental illness. Studies of families, sex roles, and ethnic and racial groups have been conducted to determine the relationship of those factors to the incidence of mental illness.

Finally, mental illness itself has become the subject of sociological inquiry. In these studies mental illness is viewed as an alternate system of meaning with its own validity. A mental patient liberation movement has been organized on the basis of this critique. Groups of former patients and radical mental health professionals challenge psychiatric definitions of abnormal behavior and question inhuman treatment methods.

All of these approaches to mental illness have contributed to politicizing an area of life once presumed to be apolitical and personal. Mental illness and mental health is now inextricably involved in issues of power. Psychotherapeutic power may be seen as exercised along the following dimensions:

1. Determining the boundaries of normal behavior.

2. Determining who is defined as mentally ill.

3. Determining the nature of the psychotherapist-client relationship.

4. Determining the responsibility of social structures for psychiatric disorder.

These issues are treated quite differently depending upon the political perspective taken.

Conservatives interpret mental illness as a refusal to adjust to society as it exists. They try to find ways to encourage people to make the necessary adjustments and give up their mental illness. Liberals find the cause of mental illness in specific social inequities and attempt to redress these specific ills so that the incidence of mental illness will be reduced. Socialists interpret mental illness as an individualistic depoliticized rejection of the capitalist system. They try to find ways to encourage the politicization of these skewed, but essentially valid, responses to society as it exists.

Conservatives believe that individuals are ultimately responsible for their actions. They are suspicious of the concept of mental illness since it provides a framework for people to withdraw from individual responsibility. Families also refuse to accept their responsibility to care for individual members who exhibit odd behabior. They often have them declared mentally ill and arrange for their commitment to mental hospitals. It is the responsibility of therapists to get individuals to adjust to society and to get families to accept the difficulties of dealing with recalcitrant members.

Liberals believe that mental illness is produced by a complex of biological and social causes. It results in a personal condition in which individuals cannot be held responsible for their actions. Society is responsible for caring for the victims of mental illness. Research into the causes of mental illness should be increased. The conditions under which mental patients are cared for should be improved. Increased funding should be provided for new methods of community care and treatment. Some mental illness is caused by role strain or poor social conditions. Reorganization of sex roles and alleviation of poverty would do much to reduce the incidence of psychiatric disorder.

Socialists believe that the cause of mental illness can be traced to the inequities that are inherent in a capitalist society. Individuals who feel powerless and refuse to confront oppressive conditions distort the unpleasant reality and project their avoidance into seemingly bizarre attitudes and behavior. Mental illness must be cured by transforming the social system that produces it. Mental patients and mental health professionals should first organize against the coercive use of so-called therapeutic techniques such as drugs and psychosurgery as instruments of social control and join in larger political struggles.

In the conservative article, Ludwig and Farrelly reject social causes as an explanation for mental illness. Families, poor mental hospital conditions, and society do not produce insanity. People choose to become mentally ill as a strategy to increase their power vis-á-vis their family and the larger society and to improve their living conditions. The authors view mental hospitals as quasi-socialist utopias, in which all needs are met without the patients having to exert any effort. Society needs to be protected against these freeloaders who accept the label of "crazy" to get access to the good things of life without having to work for them. Mental hospitals should be reorganized so that mental patients will be less comfortable and therefore less likely to want to settle permanently. To encourage mental patients to return to the outside world and accept their individual responsibility to support themselves, strong incentives, including punishments, should be employed. If patients will not accept the responsibility to take care of themselves, they must be forced to do so. The goal of therapy is to insure that craziness does not produce rewards for the mentally ill.

In the liberal article, Richman and Ross argue that flawed social conditions produce mental illness. Stressful conditions of everyday life, overlayed on biochemical and genetic predispositions, result in psychiatric disorder. Lack of social supports and limitations on social roles are identified as the causal agents. Women and the poor are especially subject to these constraints and are therefore more likely to become mentally ill.

Treatment of mental illness could be improved by providing additional social supports to persons when they leave mental hospitals. At present programs to encourage mental patients to leave hospitals and live in the community are not adequately supported. Most former patients end up living in isolated circumstances and in slum living conditions. Even if these programs were to be improved, they are inadequate as an approach to mental health because they only deal with the results of mental illness, not its prevention. Social reforms are required to deal with the social causes of mental illness. Social support systems, such as day care centers for mothers and better living and working conditions for the poor, would do much to alleviate psychological problems among these groups.

In the socialist article, Kupers argues that mental illness is a legitimate form of defense against assault on an individual's mind by capitalist institutions. Kupers describes the process of reification in which people come to be treated as objects in the course of producing and consuming goods. As wage earners they have lost control over determining the conditions of their lives. Rather than accept the mental numbness that results from this way of life, an individual can build up mental defenses against the loss of control over their life. Schizophrenia is a special form of awareness of the dehumanizing effects of life under capitalism, not a loss of contact with reality. It is an individual rejection of capitalism. It is not an effective protest since the special awareness of reification that comes with schizophrenia is not translated into effective political activity. Nor is it transmuted into artistic creativity. Schizophrenia is an individual protest by powerless persons against domination. Their illness is produced by reification and can be cured by revolt against the capitalist system.

Conservative

Arnold M. Ludwig and Frank Farrelly: The Weapons of Insanity

It is becoming fashionable to view mental patients, especially chronic schizophrenics, as poor, helpless, unfortunate creatures made sick by family and society and kept sick by prolonged hospitalization. These patients are depicted as hapless victims impotent against the powerful influences which determine their lives and shape their psychopathology. Such a view dictates a treatment philosophy aimed at reducing all the social and institutional iniquities responsible for the patient's plight. However, in the process of levelling the finger of etiological blame for the production and maintenance of chronic schizophrenia, theoreticians and clinicians have neglected another culprit—the patient himself. Professionals seem to have overlooked the rather naive possibility that schizophrenic patients become "chronic" simply because they choose to do so.

Undoubtedly, a myriad of authoritative articles could be quoted to refute such an oversimplified approach to this problem. We do not deny the complexity of the problem or the multitude of theoretical factors which should be taken into account for the understanding and treatment of these patients. Since we cannot at this point in time unravel twisted genes, undo the past, reform society, or eliminate mental hospitals, we are left with a more modest, but still formidable task—the treatment of the patient himself. The major problem is in dealing with what *is* and not with what should be or might have been. In our own experience, the problem is not so much modifying factors outside the patient, but rather in changing certain patient attitudes and consequent behaviors, as well as complementary, newly traditional attitudes on the part of society and professional staff, which aggravate the basic problem and prevent effective therapeutic intervention.

We have had the opportunity to observe closely and work with a group of thirty male and female chronic schizophrenics, handled with a minimum of medication and housed together on an experimental treatment unit. In a previous article, we outlined a number of characteristic attitudes and behaviors, both on the part of patients and staff, which tended to perpetuate chronicity. These characteristics comprise what we have called "the code of chronicity." Implicit in our discussion of the "code" are five important clinical "facts" which, we believe, underlie the behaviors of chronic schizophrenics. First, these patients can use their insanity to control people and situations. Second, they have an indomitable will of their own and are hell bent on getting their way. Third, one of the basic difficulties in rehabilitating these patients is not so much their "lack of motivation" but their intense, negative motivation to remain hospitalized. Fourth, insanity and hospitalization effectively pay off for these patients in a variety of ways. Fifth, these patients are capable of demonstrating an animal cunning in provoking certain reactions on the part of staff, family and society at large which guarantee their continued hospitalization and its consequent rewards.

"The Weapons of Insanity" by Arnold M. Ludwig and Frank Farrelly from the *American Journal of Psychotherapy*, Vol. 21, No. 4 (1967): 737–749. Reprinted by permission.

Related to these characteristics are a number of other important ones, which are typical of these patients and which we want to elaborate on since they are relevant to our basic thesis concerning patient behavior. These additional features have gradually come into focus for us during the various phases of our research treatment program; in this article we shall term them the "weapons of insanity." It has become increasingly clear to us that patients both have at their disposal and employ effectively an array of counter-therapeutic weapons against staff efforts to rehabilitate them. These weapons not only reach their targets but have the additional bonus of a "fallout" effect in the form of a series of predictable staff reactions. Since one of the most effective ways to cope with these weapons is first to recognize them, we have felt the need to describe them and their effects. Moreover, since we have become convinced that for rehabilitative purposes these weapons of insanity must be jammed, then there is a necessity to consider carefully the therapeutic implications and ethical issues involved. It is our purpose to do precisely this.

The Arsenal of Weapons

Squatter's Rights

The prevalent conception of mental hospitals as snake pits or horrible asylums from which all patients eagerly long to depart has little truth when applied to the chronic schizophrenic. In fact, one of the major problems in rehabilitating these patients is their adamant refusal to be dispossessed from their adopted hospital homeland. For many patients, especially those who feel emotionally and financially deprived, the mental hospital represents a "promised land" where the whole range of their needs is met.

The hospital comes to be a model of the idealized childhood home—a cruise on the "good ship Lollipop." Every effort is made to help the patient "feel at home": not only are the basics of food, clothing, and shelter provided, but also, as in the good childhood home, his psycho-social needs are met. He is protected from harm and pain, is relieved of any major responsibilities and demands, and has a wide variety of entertainment and recreation provided for him. His home gives him a ready made group of companions who, because they share similar experiences, give him understanding and a sense of belonging. The good parental surrogates never punish him, attempt to protect him from failure and frustration, try concientiously to meet his immediate needs at all levels, and do not expect him, as a child, to make decisions for which he is not ready or mature enough.

The hospital thus comes to represent an emotional gold mine where patients stake their claim. They seem to grasp intuitively the legal dictum that "possession is nine-tenths of the law". If some claim jumpers, in the guise of therapeutic staff, threaten to dispossess them, especially after their years of homesteading, chronic patiens will fight back with animal ferocity to defend their territory. This general attitude seems best epitomized by the remark of one patient who told the staff "You'll never railroad me out of here!"

All or Nothing

Ask any patient whether he wants to be rehabilitated and the invariable answer will be "yes." Try to do anything to effectively bring this about and the invariable behavioral response will indicate "no." One reason for this discrepancy between verbalization and behavior is that it requires minimal effort to utter the socially appropriate "yes" and maximal effort to do something about it.

There appear to be four basic components to the patient's view concerning rehabilitation. First, they sincerely *want* all the good things, such as status, power, love, material possessions, which can come with discharge. Second, they want an iron-clad guarantee that they will *get* these good things. If they are to prepare themselves for leaving the hospital, they want firm assurance that people will accept them, not derogate them for being a mental patient, not hold their behavior against them, not reject them, and treat them with dignity and respect. Third, they expect the good things to be *given* to them free. And fourth, they are unwilling to expend any persistent effort or expose themselves to undue frustration to acquire the good things.

Almost any therapeutic staff working with these patients will recognize the "all or nothing" principle in most of their behavior. Patients want the whole pie and are often dissatisfied with only one piece of it at a time. If they have to experience any emotional pain or stress in achieving socially appropriate goals, their most common response is to give up or say "to hell with it." This attitude and behavior is reflected in their whimsical work week or their attendance at and participation in any constructive rehabilitation program where they readily throw away all their gains at the slightest frustration or rejection—knowing full well that they can afford to do so since they can always fall back on the good will and beneficence of the hospital.

Most rehabilitation programs for chronic schizophrenics are bound to founder simply because staff have not come to grips with these patient attitudes and behaviors. The patients' problems may be explained by invoking such scientific terms as low frustration tolerance, infantile omnipotence of the wish, and poor impulse control, but these terms are only substitutional euphemisms for saying that patients want what they want, the way they want it, when they want it, and effortlessly.

Social Push-buttons

It is an interesting phenomenon that "helpless" and "confused" schizophrenics are often much more expert at producing certain reactions on the part of staff, family, and society at large than are the latter at evoking desired patient responses. Because patients have a far better understanding of our social value system with its inherent limitations than we have of theirs, they can employ a repertoire of behaviors which function as push-buttons to elicit the desired staff or social response, thereby insuring the attainment of their goal. These patient behaviors and the reactions they trigger off have an "if-then" quality to them. For example, if the patient presents any one of the following behavioral stimuli, then it will elicit a specifiable, related staff response with a high degree of probability.

a. nuisance behavior evokes irration and anger;

b. overt sexual behavior evokes outrage;

c. aggressive-combative behavior evokes fear;

d. self-destructive behavior evokes pity;

e. stubborn withdrawal evokes frustration; and

f. crazy-bizarre evokes confusion and helplessness.

When staff, family, or society become irritated and angry, outraged, fearful, pitying, frustrated, or confused and helpless, then they are automatically forced to take action in a variety of forms, the end result of which is continued hospitalization or rehospitalization.

In addition these push-buttons there is another more general one which we have termed the "tyranny of the weak." It seems to involve a somewhat different kind of process and appears to lead to a "hands off" effect or therapeutic inaction. When we begin confronting patients and "picking on them" for therapeutic purposes, they portray themselves as helpless, weak, and vulnerable while simultaneously casting staff in the role of inhumane bullies. Because they effect this type-casting so convincingly, and because we accept these complementary good-bad roles, the consequent shame and guilt aroused in us cause us to withdraw as effectively as does a wolf in response to the exposed jugular vein of another wolf in a fight. By employing this tactic, patients frequently exploit their "weakness" tyrannically over others by forcing them to make amends for "mistreating" them.

When patients are confronted with or held accountable for these triggering behaviors, they almost always invoke the following ritualistic formulae: (a) I didn't do it—you did; (b) if I did do it, you make me do it; (c) even if I did do it, I'm not to blame—I'm emotionally and mentally disturbed.

Aside from the apparent reason of assuring continued hospitalization, it appears that there are three other factors which keep patients pushing these buttons. First, they attain power and recognition. By pushing any of these buttons, patients can mobilize social agencies, communities, families and hospital staff to cope with their behavior ("I'll *make* you pay attention to me."). Second, this affords them a sense of control which reduces their feelings of helplessness and impotence. Third, they continue to push these buttons simply because they are so effective. People invariabley respond to these patient behaviors and unwittingly continue to reinforce them.

The Divine Right of Kings

One of the central problems in treating the chronic schizophrenic centers around the issue of the patient's responsibility for his actions. At the present time, the label of insanity confers diplomatic immunity or sanctuary for all patients' deviant behaviors. Patients can gratify every impulse or whim without fear of serious retaliation. They have the sanction to indulge any of their feelings because, by definition, they are presumed not to know any better or are unable to control their impulses, and therefore, cannot be held accountable for what they do.

Not only is the patient immune from retaliation by society, but he can also buy protection from his own conscience for repugnant actions by employing the ultimate excuse of craziness. Under the sacrosanct banner of insanity, he can avoid guilt and shame for normally shocking or sickening behavior. If he so desires, he can defecate when or where he chooses, masturbate publicly, lash out aggressively, expose himself, remain inert and unproductive, or violate any social taboo with the assurance that staff are forced to "understand" rather than punish his behavior.

In many ways, the modern day patient has prerogatives similar to the medieval absolute monarch with the power and sanction to gratify his every whim. Just as the divine right of kings insured that "the king can do no wrong," so, too, the mentally ill can do no "wrong": they can only engage in "sick" behavior.

The "divine right" of the mentally ill confers other advantages. Like any monarch with his retinue of servants, chronic patients also have a number of helpers or "servants" to wait on them. In any well-staffed mental hospital, professional dieticians prepare their meals, and psychiatric aides serve them; should they need some assistance in dressing, shaving, or showering, some staff person is always available. Recreational and occupational therapists make detailed plans to amuse and keep them from becoming bored. Should they get upset, some doctor or nurse is always nearby to quell their anxiety or relieve their hurts. Social workers are ready to act as emissaries with their families and diplomatically explain the patients' "illness" to elicit understanding and acceptance. It is not surprising that several patients "delusionally" have referred to us as their servants—that the hospital exists, as in fact is does, to take care them and minister to their needs.

Let the Healer Beware

The chronic schizophrenic has at his disposal a variety of techniques exquisitely designed to dampen or quash the therapeutic enthusiasm of almost any staff within a short period of time. By employing these techniques, the patient can preserve his prerogatives, continue to go his own way, and avoid being pestered about getting well and preparing for discharge.

It is very difficult to maintain or sustain any therapeutic zeal for these patients when almost every helpful or kind gesture is either repulsed, ignored, or unappreciated. Patients seem masters of counter-conditioning and extinction techniques; when staff try to rouse them from their apathy, correct their deviant behavior, or interest them in some constructive task, patients respond by stubbornly ignoring, cursing, spitting, hitting, threatening, or assaulting staff. Not only do patients seem ungrateful or even resentful of staff efforts, but some may even attempt to drive staff away further with Mafia-like threats of maiming or destroying their families.

In a situation where staff receive so little positive feedback or gratitude from patients, the usual response is for therapeutic interest to wane or become extinguished. When patients drop all the social amenities, courtesies and decencies, the predicted staff response is gradually to move from a position of helpfulness and concern for them to one of frustration and apathy.

In interpreting these behaviors, we are becoming increasing convinced that the patients' primary purpose is to discourage therapeutic efforts: they are fully aware that leaving the hospital means leaving many prerogatives behind. They seem to be constantly transmitting the message "go away and leave me be" or "if you must relate to me, do so on my terms."

Acts of Contrition

Even when patients do occasionally apologize or seem remorseful for their actions, they often employ ritualistic confession with no sustained, firm purpose of making amends. Their usual behavior is to do something bad, contritely confess their wrongdoing, ask for forgiveness, and shortly afterward repeat the same process, sometimes in a different forms, which calls into question the credibility of their acts of contrition. Their behavior can be summarized in the formula "slap —'I'm sorry'...slap—'I'm sorry'...slap..." When staff find these repetitive acts of contrition unbelievable and convey their disbelief to patients, the typical patient response is to become hurt or furious at staff for not being gullible and naive enough to accept the magic words "I'm sorry."

The purpose of the repetitive utilization of these magic words seems three-fold: first, to be granted a suspended sentence from any guilt or shame they themselves might feel at their behavior; second, to placate staff's animosity through this show of penance; and third, to secure the restoration of full privileges.

The Syndrome of "Chronic Staffrenia"

Part of the real difficulty in establishing an effective treatment and rehabilitation program for chronic schizophrenics resides in the reaction of hospital staff toward working with these patients. Caught between what they have been taught represents "good" professional treatment and their own personal (often equated with "bad") reactions provoked by the tactics and behaviors of patients, staff eventually become incapacitated in their treatment efforts. The conflict is between how staff *should* treat patients and how they spontaneously *want* to respond.

It is easy to understand the genesis of this bind. If staff accept the view that the mentally ill patient is not responsible for his actions, then it follows that the essentials of any humanitarian treatment approach must always be comprised of love, kindness, acceptance, and understanding; above all, it is professionally inappropriate to criticize strongly, to react angrily, or punish patients for their behavior since such behavior has been caused by factors beyond their control. On the other hand, day to day experience with these patients invariably arouses in staff reactions which are diametrically opposed to those which they are expected to feel.

If staff attitudes *must* under all circumstances be those of patience, helpfulness, love and acceptance, what options do staff have when they frequently find themselves impatient, helpless, angry and revolted by patients' behaviors? Not only is it difficult for staff to act persistently one way when they feel another, but this same hypocritical facade weakens the therapeutic effectiveness of their efforts. Despite the loud and clear messages from their adrenals and viscera, staff are permitted only a very limited response repertoire to the behavioral weapons employed by patients.

Staff tend to resolve the conflicts of this bind by assuming an observable set of attitudes and behaviors which oftentimes complement those of patients. We have labelled this characteristic staff reaction the syndrome of "chronic staffrenia." The components of this syndrome include apathy, weariness, minimal personal involvement, decreased enthusiasm, lack of emotional investment, and markedly decreased expectations for patient rehabilitation. Staff attitudes are depicted by such statements as "let well enough alone," or "to hell with it—it just isn't worth it." Staff increasingly withdraw and engage in perfunctory therapeutic activities which, regardless of their name, at best resemble good custodial care, and they become all too happy to settle for patient cooperation in lieu of patient rehabilitation. Any program that aims at rehabilitating chronic schizophrenics (in contrast to one that merely provides good custodial care) must anticipate this syndrome and take measures to prevent or cope with its development.

Implications for Treatment

Any therapeutic program primarily employing psychosocial techniques for the modification of chronic schizophrenic behavior must make certain operational assumptions as a basis for effective therapeutic action. The primary and most important assumption is that the patient is responsible for his actions and can muster up the necessary will power to act sanely and decently if he should choose, or be made to choose, to do so. Given this assumption, certain treatment implications follow.

First, staff must hold patients accountable for their actions, rewarding appropriate behavior and punishing inappropriate or deviant behavior. One of the problems in such a seemingly simple philosophy is that it runs counter to much current clinical thought. It is our feeling that today's dynamically oriented theoreticians have placed the onus of responsibility for the patient's behavior on such scapegoat devils as mother, society, or mythical biochemical abnormalities, rather than on the individual patient himself. With such convenient whipping boys, where everyone is to blame, nobody is to blame. If the patient cannot be blamed, then, it follows, he cannot take credit for healthy, sane behavior. We contend that holding patients responsible for both their good and bad behavior invests them with human dignity and hope; not holding them responsible is tantamount to pronouncing them hopeless.

Our own simplified view of psychotherapy dictates that the assumption of responsibility by the patient represents a prerequisite for any further constructive behavioral change. If patients are to be receptive to treatment, their attitude must include four successive components or stages which are as follows: (a) I am responsible for my behavior; (b) I want to change my behavior since it dissatisfies me; (c) I need help; and (d) I will cooperate with the help you give me. These stages not only hold for the rehabilitation of the alcoholic, juvenile delinquent, criminal, character disorder, and psychoneurotic, but for the chronic schizophrenic as well. The major problem with the chronic patient is to get him to move from a position where he denies all responsibility for his behavior or excuses it under the banner of insanity to the first of these stages. Once this is done, a major barrier is crossed.

Since staff have been commissioned to intervene therapeutically with these patients, the second treatment implication is that staff must have certain rights consonant with their obligations. In our current and legitimate concern for the rights of patients, we have overlooked or ignored the rights of those working with them. What currently obtains in most treatment programs is that staff have the "the right" to being cursed, threatened, or assaulted by ungrateful patients without being able to punish them for their actions or to vent openly their genuine feelings. However, we insist that staff should and do have certain rights: the right to expect gratitude from patients and safety from physical harm, to interact honestly with patients, to be creative, and to derive a sense of accomplishment from their work. These are not idealized luxuries but absolute necessities for treatment staff. Unless their necessary rights are encouraged, implemented and insured, we are convinced that no intensive, persistent, and concerted staff treatment effort can occur. Unless staff can demand responsible behavior and respect for their rights from patients, the counter-therapeutic tactics of patients will surely and inevitably extinguish any remnants of staff rehabilitative efforts in their regard.

A third treatment implication is that staff be genuine with patients. We propose that staff not be pressured to hide behind pseudo-humanitarian treatment slogans which decree that love and understanding are the *only* appropriate responses to all patient behaviors and that anger and even occasional hatred are antitherapeutic. There is nothing inherently wrong in admiring and liking the good qualities of patients while, at the same time, disliking and rejecting their undesirable qualities. If staff are forced to conform to hackneyed platitudes, their response, at best, will consist of perfunctory love, phony acceptance, misguided kindness or biased understanding. We believe it most appropriate that staff be allowed to give patients *accurate* and *honest* human feedback concerning the impact and social consequences of their behaviors. For example, it is unreasonable to insist that staff adopt inappropriate smiles or act kindly toward patients while brimming with anger. Our contention is that "love and understanding" are not simply insufficient, but at times are actually incongruous and damaging in response to certain patient behaviors. Staff should be allowed and encouraged to use a *whole* relationship: both to be positive, warm, and loving when patients behave sanely and well, and also to be angry, rebuking, rejecting, and punishing when patients are obnoxious or bad. The combination of Pollyanna plus Scrooge represents a more whole, integrated, human response; either alone is a travesty.

A fourth implication pertains to the so-called rights and prerogatives of the chronic patient. From our assumptions it follows that patients not be allowed to become too comfortable or settled in the hospital. It is imperative that staff feel free to usurp and confiscate the patient's "squatter's rights" and convey insistently and persistently to patients that they not only do not have the right to remain in the hospital, but that the only virgin land available for homesteading lies outside the hospital.

Other treatment implications pertain directly to jamming the various weapons which patients employ. It makes little sense to continue to treat these patients as perpetual convalescents and invalids by waiting on them and thereby encouraging and reinforcing dependency. As long as patients can continue to gain all the prerogatives and privileges without effort, there is little incentive for them to change. As long as their craziness continues to pay off without uncomfortable repercussions or sanctions, we encourage the development and perpetuation of chronicity.

Ethical Issues

In evolving a treatment philosophy for chronic schizophrenics, we have had to grapple with a number of ethical issues, posed by ourselves and respected colleagues, concerning staff attitudes and treatment approaches toward these patients. Since the direction and development of any treatment program is contingent upon how these issues are resolved, their importance cannot be stressed enough.

One of the immediate ethical issues involves the use of punishment for patients. Without delving into all the aspects of this problem, which would require a separate paper to do full justice to it, we will simply say that this issue is largely artificial or moot, for there are no psychosocial techniques for instituting human behavioral change which do not employ the very potent tools of both reward and punishment. Even those programs which espouse only benevolent approaches make liberal use of such negative reinforcements as withholding privileges, withdrawing love or approval, restraints and seclusion, ECT and drugs for the avowed purpose of "controlling" patient behavior, but the rationales offered are often only euphemistic or socially condoned excuses for subtle or blatant punishments. The issue is not whether punishments should be used; they are and will be — this is simply a fact of all clinical and social life. The real issue is whether punishments will be administered openly, non-apologetically, and in a consistent, systematic, goal-oriented manner rather than on a disguised, apologetic, whimsical and haphazard basis.

There are those who fear that once the use of punishment is openly acknowledged and condoned, it might well serve as a vehicle for sadism. We sympathize with and share this concern; however, the essence of the problem is whether the therapist uses punishment solely for his own gratification or the patient's welfare. Our position is simply that if a therapist is sadistic, he will be ingenious enough to find a vehicle for his saidsm in any type of therapeutic approach, even in benign non-directive therapies. Or, to put it differently, the beatific smile of the therapist does not guarantee that there are not fangs hidden behind it.

A critical ethical question is to what lengths will we go to implement our treatment goals? Should the goal be to maintain a chronic schizophrenic comfortably in the hospital or to undertake the more ambitious task of helping him become a relatively whole, occasionally uncomfortable person functioning outside the hospital? If we choose the latter goal (a formidable task), then it follows, that certain procedures, which might be considered drastic or extreme, will have to be employed.

It cannot be overemphasized how serious and malignant a problem chronic schizophrenia is. As the situation now stands, these patients represent serious economic, social, political, and psychological debits not only to society but themselves as well. Many represent the psychological equivalents of terminal cancer patients, devoid of any prospects of a productive existence. Therefore, we have to make the operational value choice of either preparing them for a comfortable psychological demise or using, if necessary, radical procedures which measurably increase their chance for responsible meaningful living.

In any radical procedure there must be a willingness to balance the potential risks against the possible gains. It is our impression that most professionals working in this area have been reluctant to confront the issue of risk and have chosen instead to play it safe. One way of playing it safe has been to settle for more modest treatment goals for these patients. Another way (but a valuable one at that) is to concentrate exclusively on the etiolgoical and preventative aspects of the problem. It is riskier, but at least equally important, to engage the problem here and now—that is, if we are not going to let patients psychologically rot in the mental hospitals until we engineer social change or determine the presumed biochemical abnormality underlying this disorder.

The bind we are in, whether we like it or not, is that we must deal with these patients. In doing so, we have to choose between two options. We can employ palliative procedures with the risk of keeping patients psychologically moribund or of leading to their psychological death; or we can try radical psychosocial procedures with the possibility of curing the patient, but with the risk of his getting worse. Should this latter possibility occur, the therapist lays himself open to being labelled antitherapeutic or destructive; we suspect that one reason many therapists have chosen palliative procedures is not to risk censure from colleagues and to avoid receiving such labels. Unfortunately for patients, we have been too bound to the principle of *primum non nocere* ("first, do no harm), and, as a result, have been employing a variety of gumdrop therapies for a very malignant problem.

Long ago Archimedes stated that if he had a lever long enough and a fulcrum on which to rest it, he could move the earth. It is our contention that we already have at our disposal some therapeutic levers or techniques for dealing with chronic schizophrenics. If our goal is the ultimate rehabilitation of these patients, we must begin to search for even more potent and effective levers, which may involve to some degree the use of pain, deprivation, and punishment —all socially sensitive areas in the treatment of patients. It is not enough simply to theorize about these techniques; we must demonstrate a willingness to use and evaluate them.

A final ethical issue concerns the question of whether patients should have the right to opt out of living in normal society. For those who find life and responsibility too stressful, should we provide some haven or retreat in the form of mental hospitals, where they can spend the remainder of their days in relative peace and quiet? Perhaps the ramifications of this issue could be debated endlessly; we have resolved this issue for ourselves by arbitrarily claiming that just as a person does not have the social or legal right to commit suicide, so, too, the chronic shizophrenic does *not* have the right to commit psychological suicide by giving up or opting out through prolonged hospitalization. Again, just as when a person attempts suicide, every possible technique or treatment, no matter how drastic, is employed by the physician to aid him, so, too, we contend that every possible therapeutic technique, even those seemingly drastic, should be brought to bear to psycho-socially revive the chronic schizophrenic.

Liberal

Judith Richman and Catherine E. Ross: Shifting Mental Health Policies: Psychiatry in a Social and Political Context

The current recognition of mental illness as a major social problem and the corresponding quest for improved mental health in American society can be characterized by two separate but related themes. On the one hand, the middle and upper classes frantically search for personal fulfillment through self-actualizing therapies such as yoga, transcendental meditation, marathon encounter groups, and psychic healing. At the same time, lower class schizophrenics, who previously filled the wards of mental hospitals, now populate the slums of major American cities. While the severity of distress and the life situations of these two social groups are vastly different, the link between their experiences lies in the questioning of traditional psychiatric approaches to mental illness, and the search for alternative solutions to psychological problems.

This paper describes recent challenges to mainstream American psychiatry and suggests alternative approaches to mental health care. We argue that shifts in the treatment of mental illness occur as a result of both scientific-technological developments within psychiatry and social forces outside of psychiatry. Most important is the political process in the larger society through which various social groups articulate their conceptualizations of mental illness and legislate corresponding social policies.

Challenges to American Psychiatry: The 1960s and 1970s

The Treatment of Psychosis: From the Hospital to the Community

In 1769 the first mental institution in the United States was built in Williamsburg, Virginia. Yet the severely mentally ill were rarely institutionalized: most remained in the community under the care of their families (Rothman, 1971). Persons who were considered insane and had no one to care for them in the community were institutionalized in mental hospitals whose therapeutic programs were based on humane treatment. This humane treatment, ecompassing a supportive environment and belief in the curability of mental illness, lasted a short time. By the early nineteenth century, humane treatment had given way to custodial care. With urbanization, industrialization, and immigration came a decreased tolerance for deviant behavior. The mentally ill were removed from the community to asylums in rural areas in an effort to increase order in the growing cities. Mental hospitals were overcrowded since they rarely released anyone. This overcrowding in conjunction with lack of personnel reinforced the custodial nature of the institutions. That is, many patients were kept in locked wards and given neither treatment nor support.

From the early nineteenth century, when institutionalizing the severely mentally ill became the accepted policy, to the 1960s, severe mental disorder has been treated in large institutions. While the major treatments included psychoanalytically-oriented therapy and organic treatments, such as electro-convulsive therapy, a large portion of chronic patients received custodial care, or essentially no treatment. This was particularly true of the lower-class patients in state mental hospitals (Hollingshead and Redlich, 1958). Gradually, the mental hospital was subject to a sweeping critique.

Social scientists, as well as critics within psychiatry, suggested that institutional treatment was worse than the "disease." In particular, mental hospitals were depicted as alienating social institutions, which robbed their inhabitants of a sense of autonomy and personal identity (Goffman, 1961). Moreover, the custodial nature of mental hospitals was seen as iatrogenic; it reinforced and even magnified the psychological problems of patients. Limited treatment, lack of stimulation, and low expectations for patient functioning made hospitalized patients even less capable of functioning in the larger society after treatment than they had been before treatment (Gruenberg, 1967; Wing and Brown, 1970). In addition, patients whose psychological state did improve were thrust back into a society that rejected them. The stigmatizing label "ex-mental patient" followed these individuals and made resumption of "normal" roles difficult (Scheff, 1966; Phillips, 1963). A final, though less frequently articulated critique of the mental hospital involved the notion that treatment of the individual could have limited success if the person was then returned to the same environment which caused the problem in the first place (Cowen, 1973). This critique was clearly the most radical since it challenged the notion that the locus of treatment should be the patient, per se, and alternatively or additionally defined the environment (from the primary group level to the societal) as needing "treatment."

Given the assessment that the mental hospital failed to fulfill its therapeutic function, a major shift in the treatment of severe mental disorder was initiated in the mid 1960s. Society's new mental health policy became de-institutionalization. The goal was to gradually empty the state mental hospitals and shift patient care to the community. While this change in mental health policy was clearly influenced by the academic critique of the mental hospital, two other factors contributed to the shift. On a scientific-technological level, the discovery of the phenothiazines—the major tranquillizers—made it possible to control the most serious symptoms of schizophrenia: hallucinations and delusions. From a social control perspective, the threatening behavior of schizophrenia could now be controlled by internal, biochemical restraints in place of the external restraints of the locked wards of mental institutions. From a therapeutic perspective, antipsychotic drugs alleviated the more extreme symptoms of schizophrenia (a point emphasized by drug supporters), though they also created new symptoms in the form of drug side-effects (a point emphasized by critics). Second, on a political level, the social climate in the 1960s was one of liberal optimism encompassing a commitment to social reform. Thus, the "Great Society" programs of the Johnson Administration channeled large sums of money into community mental health centers, which were to be the focus of the community support system for the newly released patients.

The initial evaluation of the community treatment of schizophrenia was positive, given the goals (modest from a radical view-point, radical from a traditional medical view-point) of maintaining patients in the community with their symptoms under control (Pasamanick *et al.*, 1967). The most optimistic accounts described ambitious programs, which intervened in all aspects of the individual's life, including the search for adequate housing and employment (Test and Stein, 1977).

In 1961 Pasamanick and his associates began an experiment aimed at assessing the feasibility of maintaining schizophrenics in the community. Two groups of schizophrenics lived at home with their families and were periodically visited by a public health nurse, psychologist, social worker, and psychiatrist from whom they received treatment, advice and social support. One of the two groups received drug treatment; the other received placebos. The home group on drug treatment did the best; 77% of them were not re-hospitalized, while only 34% of the placebo group avoided re-hospitalization. A control group, who had been in the hospital and was later returned to the community, did not fare as well as the home care drug group. Thus, Pasamanick concluded that it was feasible to maintain schizophrenics in the community if they received social support, antipsychotic drugs, and necessities such as food and housing.

By the 1970s the state of initial optimism concerning community treatment had been transformed into a clear statement of failure, revealed by newspaper headlines such as "The Problem That Can't be Tranquillized: 40,000 Mental Patients Dumped into City Neighborhoods" (New York Times, 1978). Between 1955 and 1978 the number of patients in mental institutions decreased from 550,000 to 190,000. What has happened to these ex-mental patients? Many of the elderly patients were simply transferred from one institution to another and now reside in nursing homes. Most ex-patients are unemployed: Davis and her associates, in a follow-up of Pasamanick's study, found approximately 77% of the schizophrenics in the community unemployed (1974). Many have been deserted by their families. Most are poor and supported by the state: in New York City there are thousands of ex-mental patients living in deteriorated welfare hotels. In addition, many ex-patients cannot cope in the community at all and have been rehospitalized. Sixty percent of the ex-patients in Pasamanick's study were rehospitalized during the time of the follow-up study. After these patients spend a short time in the hospital, they are released again into an unsupportive community and re-admitted at a later date. This has been labeled the "revolving door" syndrome.

A policy of de-institutionalization will only work if there is community care available for the discharged patients. But adequate community care never really developed for a number of reasons. Both the liberalism and the economic abundance of the 1960s declined. Beginning in the early 1970s, many community mental health programs had their budgets cut in a general dismantling of the social welfare programs initiated in the sixties. Halfway houses and sheltered workshops in which the mentally ill could live and work in protected environments were ideas which never materialized in adequate numbers. As Pasamanick found, schizophrenics need fairly intensive supervision and support if they are to live a decent life in the community. Although schizophrenics in Pasamanick's experiment got sufficient home care, when the experiment ended and these ex-patients received only routine state care, most deteriorated. Declining community mental health budgets combined with prevalent values to produce this inadequate care. The values of outpatient community clinics were such that they set up shop and waited for people to come to them (Cowen, 1973). Outpatient clincs made few outreach efforts or efforts to help patients in their homes. This failure in part stems from the fact that outpatient clinics are not geared to help the poor, severely mentally ill patients. Traditionally they have treated middle-to-upper-income patients with mild problems. These people are healthy enough to come to the clinic, and the possibility of curing them, in combination with their higher levels of education, make them more attractive patients. Outpatient clinics have neither the money to hire enough personnel, nor the value orienta-tion necessary to meet the needs of poor, severely disturbed ex-mental patients. In spite of the fact that the prevalence of severe mental illness is greater for the poor than for the well-to-do, the poor are less likely to see a psychiatrist on an outpatient basis (Kulka *et al.*, 1979). Thus, in many cases, the transition from hospital to community care ended as a transition from custodial care to no care.

Outpatient Treatment of Milder Disorders: From Psychoanalysis to Therapeutic Eclecticism

In the late 1950s psychoanalysis was clearly considered the elite treatment for neuroses. The Hollingshead and Redlich study of mental illness in New Haven showed that the lower classes were much less likely to receive psychoanalyti-cally-oriented treatment than higher status groups (1958). As a result, a major expansion in, and public support for, psychoanalytic training was recommended in order to make it accessible to a wider segment of the population. Since the 1950s there has been a proliferation in both the quantity and variety of psycho-therapies available and a corresponding questioning of the superiority of psy-choanalytic approaches for the treatment of psychological disorder. The major changes in psychotherapeutic orientations for the treatment of neuroses, just as the changes in the treatment of schizophrenia, resulted from socio-cultural chal-lenges to psychiatry from outside the profession, as well as scientific develop-ments within the profession.

In the 1960s psychotherapy met challenges from political activists and adher-ents of the counter-culture, who articulated a set of values clearly different from those underlying psychoanalysis. As Bart demonstrated, the values of Freudian psychoanalysis supported the Protestant work ethic (1971). They legitimized the individual pursuit of the fruits of capitalism, upward mobility, and adaptation to existing social institutions. In contrast, counter-culture members embraced the values of spontaneity, creativity, and self-transcendence in place of rationality, competition, and achievement. At the same time there was a growing awareness of the problems resulting from poverty, racism, and sexism: radicals and femi-nists challenged existing political arrangements and viewed mental illness as a product of these arrangements. And last, anti-authoritarian ideologies chal-lenged the hierarchical arrangement of the psychoanalyst-patient relationship. These alternative images of psychological health and treatment were embodied in new psychotherapies such as peer self-help therapy (Hurvitz, 1974), existen-tial and transpersonal therapy (Coan, 1977; Bart, 1971), and feminist therapy and consciousness-raising groups (Kirsh, 1974; Williams, 1976).

Economic developments, in part, influenced the changing values, which chal-lenged Freudian psychoanalysis. Whereas psychoanalytic theory reflected an economics of scarcity with an emphasis on production, the new therapies were congruent with an economics of abundance (Bart, 1971). The emphasis changed from production to consumption. The middle classes had more leisure time, and with their basic needs met, sought to improve the quality of life and to realize full potential. The emphasis changed from a concentration on problems to a concentration on health.

Through the growing middle class demand for therapy, the monopoly of psychoanalytically-oriented psychiatry was erroded. Because the demand could not be met by traditional psychiatrists, other mental health persons became involved in therapy. Psychologists, social workers and alternative therapists challenged psychoanalytic ideas.

To sum up, according to Freudian psychoanalytic theory, mental disorders had individual-level causes and individual-level solutions. Economic and value changes in the 1960s, however, produced new therapeutic ideologies. Some of these located the cause of psychiatric disorders in society but still sought to change the individual, while others set forth societal-level solutions as the only answer. Many, including feminist consciousness-raising groups, had both long-term goals of changing the place of women in society, and short-term goals of distress-reducing therapy for individuals (Kirsch, 1974).

In addition to the challenges leveled at psychoanalysis from the larger society, psychoanalysis was challenged within psychiatry as the result of the discovery of drugs to treat various disorders, such as depression, and by the development of brief psychotherapies. For example, well-designed, controlled studies of the efficacy of tricyclate drugs and brief interpersonal therapy, separate or in combination, showed that the drugs appeared to alleviate the symptoms of depression and the therapy resulted in improved social functioning (Klerman, 1976; Weissman et al., 1979.) Most important, these studies symbolized the movement toward making psychiatry more scientific by empirically demonstrating the efficacy of particular treatments (Gross, 1978). (This is in contrast to the resistance of psychoanalysis to empirical demonstrations of its utility). Perhaps the strongest empirical challenge to psychoanalysis was formulated by Jerome Frank (1974). Frank examined the evidence for the efficacy of a variety of psychological and nonpsychological interventions, such as psychoanalysis, behavior therapy, and shamanism in primitive societies, and concluded that there was little evidence for the greater effectiveness of any particular intervention. Moreover, all of the therapies were effective at least in the short run, for they provided the client with social support and a sense of hope and optimism in place of feelings of demoralization. According to Frank, successful therapies have a number of characteristics in common. They provide a supportive, caring, confidential relationship through which the client's hope is mobilized. The cure works through the suggestion of the therapist. This implies, not only that all interventions may be equally successful, but that any therapist who gives attention and the promise of cure to a distressed patient will be successful. Most important, the ideology of the therapy must be congruent with the belief system of the client. This implies that indigenous mental health workers, who share the patient's values, may be especially successful. Thus, ex-alcoholics may provide the best therapy for alcoholics, and persons living in the inner cities may provide the best therapy for the poor (Hurvitz, 1974; Albrecht, 1974). A variety of therapeutic interventions (from psychoanalysis to psychic healing) might be equally effective in the short term alleviation of psychological distress, depending on the belief system of the patients.

Society As Patient: The Alteration of the Social Structure

The preceding approaches to treatment, which have dominated mental health care in the United States, have been essentially curative rather than preventive in focus. Though the interventions are based on different conceptions of mental health and vary in the techniques they use to bring it about, most of the interventions focus on treating the individual once the distress or disorder has occurred. In part, this lack of emphasis on prevention stems from the fact that most therapists in the United States are in private practice, and in fact, they can do little to change the patient's environment.

A mental health care system oriented toward the prevention of psychiatric disorders would involve interventions to lessen or eliminate the occurence of disorder in the first place. The model for this level of intervention comes from public health, where the conquest of infectious disease resulted as much or more from environmental changes such as improved diets, drinking water, and sanitation as from the discovery of specific causal agents within the body (Dubos, 1959; Illich, 1976).

Psychiatric epidemiology suggests a multi-causal view of the genesis of mental disorders. Both genetic/biochemical factors and environmental stresses appear to play a causal role in the onset of psychiatric disorder (Dohrenwend, 1976; Weissman and Klerman, 1978). However, given a genetic predisposition, environmental factors are necessary to bring out the disorder. Epidemiologic research offers some clues to particular psycho-social factors which could be manipulated in order to prevent the onset of psychiatric disorders.

In the search for social causes of mental illness, researchers have delimited a number of characteristics which might be associated with psychiatric problems. These characteristics, such as age, sex, race, and social class, indicate ones place in the social structure and the social roles associated with the position. Of the characteristics examined, two have consistent associations with mental illness: sex and social class.

Women

Research on sex differences in psychiatric disorder shows that women have higher rates of bipolar and unipolar depression, whereas men have higher rates of personality disorders (sociopathy, drug abuse, and alcoholism) Dohrenwend and Dohrenwend, 1976; Weissman and Myers, 1978; Weissman and Klerman, 1978). Moreover, women score higher on general impairment scales taping subjective distress, including anxiety, depression, and psychophysiological symptomatology (Gove and Tudor, 1973). Social explanations of these differences have focused on the problematic aspects of the traditional female role.

According to structural arguments, married women occupy stressful roles in the family and in society, which tend to cause psychological problems (Gove and Tudor, 1973; Gove and Geerken, 1977; Richman, 1979). First, whereas most men occupy two roles—worker and head of the household—most women are restricted to a single role, that of housewife. Therefore, whereas men can focus on an alternate role if one is unsatisfactory, women have no alternative source of gratification. Second, the role of housewife is intrinsically ungratifying. That is, housewives view much of their work as boring, undemanding, and lacking meaning. Third, the role of housewife has low prestige. Achievement in American society means individual achievement in the occupational structure rather than housework in the home. This lack of achievement may be especially frustrating to women with high educational attainment. Fourth, the position of housewife wields little power, since decision-making power in the family is a function of individual economic resources (Blood and Wolfe, 1960). Housewives do not contribute financial resources to the family, and employed women usually earn less than their husbands. Fifth, the role of housewife tends to be unstructured, invisible, and ambiguous. Role amiguity—not knowing what is expected of one—is psychologically distressing. So is doing work which is invisible, since no one sees or rewards work well done. Sixth, housewives are relatively isolated. Men interact with colleagues at work. Women, especially those with young children, may be tied to the home and therefore receive less psychological gratification from interacting with others. Although the role of housewife is especially distressing, even women who work occupy disadvantaged positions compared to men. Women tend to have low status, poorly paid jobs compared to men, and often their positions are not commensurate with their education (Epstein, 1970).

One logical implication of this structural argument is that women who work will have lower rates of psychological distress than housewives. Working women occupy two roles, they have more power and prestige, they may be involved in more interesting work, and they are less isolated than housewives. This hypothesis is supported by the data. A number of studies find that working women are somewhat less distressed than housewives (Richman, 1979; Gove and Geerken, 1977; Gove and Hughes, 1979; Rosenfield, 1978). Moreover, Gove and Geerken isolate a number of stressful components of the housewife role. They find that housewives with children at home (the most distressed group) felt that others were always making demands on them, that they had no time to themselves, and that they were isolated from other adults and felt lonely.

The prevention implications of these findings include two policies. (1) Women should receive the same pay as men for the same jobs. This would equalize power and prestige. (2) Day care centers should be made available, both so that any woman who wants to work can, and so that housewives with young children can have time away from the children to interact with other adults. Both increasing the number of women in the work force and reducing the isolation of housewives with young children should decrease the prevalence of psychological distress among women.

In addition to not working and having children at home, marriage itself appears to be more stressful for women than for men. Married men are in better psychological health than married women. Yet single women are in better psychological health than single men. While marriage provides men with psychological gratification, many women find marriage stressful (Bernard, 1972; Gurin et al., 1960).

In addition to the stresses associated with adult roles in the social structure, socialization experiences as children may affect psychological well-being. Young girls are taught that being feminine consists of being dependent, helpless, and passive (Weissman and Klerman, 1977). This "learned helplessness" translates into an inability to cope successfully with stress as adults (Seligman, 1974). In addition, daughters may identify with their mothers who occupy socially devalued roles and thus develop low self-esteem. These socialization experiences may produce depressed women. Men, on the other hand, are taught to be active, aggressive, tough, and independent. While these characteristics are conducive to success in the work world, in extreme they may lead to antisocial behavior, the characteristic male disorder. Whereas women's socialization experiences and disadvantaged statuses in society may lead to feelings of depression, anxiety, and helplessness, men's experiences may produce aggressive antisocial behaviors. Less work has been done on the mental health of men, yet in terms of prevention, the stresses associated with the social positions of both men and women must be defined. Understanding these social stressors is the first step in changing the social structure to reduce them, thereby decreasing the frequency of psychological problems.

The Poor

Women occupy one type of disadvantaged position in society. Being in a low social class, as measured by having a low income, little education, and a low prestige job, is another disadvantaged status.

Persons in the lower social classes have higher rates of both psychoses and mild psychological symptoms (Dohrenwend and Dohrenwend, 1969). Bipolar depression is the only diagnosis which is not associated with low social class (Weissman and Myers, 1978). The psychological problems associated with lower class positions may result from a number of social stressors. These include lack of power, prestige, intrinsic gratification from the job, poor working conditions, unemployment, poor housing, disrupted family life, discrepancies between aspirations and achievement, and lack of resources that help one cope, such as income, education, or powerful friends.

Kohn presents a model in which stress, rigid cognitive orientations and genetics interact to produce high rates of schizophrenia in the lower social classes (1972). Not only are persons in the lower social classes exposed to more chronic social stressors (such as poverty), but they are harder hit by acute social stressors (such as having one's spouse die) because they have fewer internal and external resources available to soften the blow (Dohrenwend and Dohrenwend, 1969; Myers et al., 1971). The causes of this lack of internal coping resources are two-fold: work experiences and socialization. Persons in the lower social classes tend to have jobs consisting of routine, non-creative work over which they have no control. Rarely do they make autonomous decisions at work: they simply take orders. These objective job conditions, in conjunction with low educational attainment, lead to a limited and rigid conception of the external world, including fatalism and conformity to authority. Although this personality type stems from an accurate assessment of job conditions, it leads to inflexibility and inability to cope with unknown situations, causal factors in schizophrenia. In addition to holding this world-view themselves, lower class parents tend to socialize their children to have the same rigid cognitive orientations. These rigid cognitive orientations do not by themselves cause schizophrenia. Schizophrenia will only develop in a person who, in addition to being cognitively rigid, is genetically predisposed and under stress.

Other researchers emphasize additional aspects of lower and working class jobs which may produce psychological distress. First, jobs with low prestige are associated with job dissatisfaction and poor mental health (Gurin et al., 1960; Kahn, 1972; Quinn et al., 1971). Since a sense of self-worth stems in part from evaluations from others, holding a job which is not valued by others may lead to feelings of low self-esteem and psychological distress. In addition to low prestige, Kasl enumerates a number of specific job conditions that tend to characterize low level jobs, which are weakly associated with psychological distress (1978). They include unpleasant work conditions, including health and safety hazards, fast-paced work, excessive supervision, and long or inconvenient hours. Jobs which are perceived as uninteresting, repetitious, and not using the worker's skills are also associated with poor mental health, as are jobs with low pay. Persons at the bottom of the social hierarchy are also most likely to be unemployed, and unemployment is related to psychological distress for two reasons (Liem and Liem, 1978; Kasl, 1978). First, men are expected to be employed, so that they are evaluated negatively when unemployed. This may lead to low self-esteem. Second, unemployment means lack of income which also causes distress. Brenner found that in times of economic recession when many people lost their jobs, admissions to mental hospitals increased (1973). Both temporary job loss and chronic unemployment are associated with psychological problems.

In addition to working life, family life in the lower social classes may be stressful. First, persons in the lower social classes are more likely to live under crowded housing conditions. When persons living in crowded homes feel that they lack privacy and that others are constantly around and placing demands on them, they are likely to feel psychological distress (Gove et al., 1979). Second, family disruptions are more prevalent in the lower social classes. Divorce and separation are more frequent in the lower social class (Goode, 1956). Being divorced is associated with poor mental health, in part, because it indicates that one has lost primary group ties and social support, which are essential to psychological well-being (Myers et al., 1975; Dean and Lin, 1977). Persons who live alone under conditions of social isolation are especially prone to psychological problems. As Farris and Dunham first noted in 1939, those areas of the city characterized by the social isolation of transient men living alone in rooming houses had the highest rates of schizophrenia. Another source of family disruption is death. At every age (including infancy) a person who is poor has a greater probability of dying than a person in the upper social classes (Lerner, 1975; Antonovsky, 1972). Having a death in the family may be a stressful event with which the poor have few resources to cope. In addition to increased mortality rates, the poor tend to be in worse physical health than persons in the upper social classes, and poor physical health is associated with psychological distress (Gove and Hughes, 1979; Eastwood and Trevelyan, 1972).

Disadvantaged statuses, including those of the poor and women, carry with them stressors which increase the probability of psychological problems. A societal level prevention program based on the public health model, aimed at increasing equality and attempting to eliminate disadvantaged statuses, including the social roles and living and working conditions associated with them, may decrease the prevalence of psychological problems in these groups.

Conclusion: The Political Context of Mental Health Policy

According to Klerman, "all judgements about psychiatric illness—diagnosis, treatment, prevention, and management—are based upon social consensus within the health professions and between the professions and the society at large; (1977:221). Through a process of negotiation between various social groups, conceptualizations of mental illness and treatment are developed. Thus, mental health policies are based, in part, on nonscientific value judgements. In Klerman's view all social groups have an equal voice in the negotiation process, and no challenging groups are excluded. The outcome is that ideas about mental illness are "legitimized by consensual validation" (1977:231). We agree with Klerman's analysis in large part. Yet he ignores one important component in the negotiation process—power. Although mental health policies do develop through a process of negotiation among various professional groups and community interest-groups within a larger social context, not everyone involved in the process has equal power. We question Klerman's assumption that there will be an ultimate value consensus. Rather, groups with the most power will have the greatest influence on mental health practices. Chances are that some interest groups will not agree that the best policies are being enacted and will continue to challenge the newly accepted notions of treatment, making the process of entrenchment and challenge an ongoing one.

While Klerman ignores the power of psychiatry to command resources and influence decisions (compared with community interest-groups such as women or the poor), radical critics such as Lasch (1977) overestimate the power of psychiatrists as social control agents and conservatizing influences. They argue that people who feel unhappy, dissatisfied with their lives, and generally distressed have a revolutionary potential. That is, they will want to change the present social structure since their position in it is causing them anguish. The helping professions, including psychiatry, quell the desire for revolution by reducing individual distress. Lasch feels that the helping professions have a large amount of autonomous influence in maintaining the status quo. We question this argument on two points. First, two assumptions are made for which there is little evidence: (1) individuals will recognize that their psychological distress stems from the social structure, and (2) given this recognition, distress will translate into political action. Lasch assumes that if the helping professions had not treated psychological distress on an individual level, these people would have had revolutionary potential. But, in fact, it is unlikely that persons in poor mental health will be political activists. Persons who are psychologically distressed have low self-esteem, feel helpless to change things, feel life is hopeless, and feel that they have little control over the environment. These are not characteristics of political activists. On the other hand, successful therapy may reduce these feelings and lead to a more active, less fatalistic approach to life (Frank, 1974). The second point on which we question Lasch concerns the power of the helping professions. According to Lasch, the helping professions have an autonomous conservatizing influence: they independently dampen revolutionary fervor. We feel that the power of psychiatry must be placed in the context of the relative power of other interest groups and the general political context of society. The helping professions do not have the sole power to either suppress or induce revolution. Whereas Klerman ignores the power of psychiatry, Lasch overestimates it.

Psychiatry plays a part in the social construction of the concepts of mental illness and treatment. Its input consists of three components: values, interests, and scientific evidence on the efficacy of various treatments. Other social groups also have an input. These groups include other mental health personnel, such as psychologists or social workers, and members of the community at large, such as minorities, women, or the poor. In addition, the negotiation process among these groups occurs within a broad social and political context. In the negotiation process each group's input is weighted by its power. The more power the group has, the more it can influence policy.

To sum up, mental health practices do not develop in a vacuum. Rather, they are a function of (1) scientific advances both within psychiatry and in related fields such as psychopharmacology, (2) interaction and conflict among members of the mental health community, including psychiatrists, social workers, and psychologists, and (3) influences in the larger society, including economic developments, value changes, and political interest-group challenges.

References

Albrecht, G. 1974 "The indigenous mental health worker: the cure-all for what ailment?" Pp. 235-250 in Paul Roman and Harrison Trice (eds.) The Sociology of Psychotherapy. N. Y.: Jason Aronson.

Antonovsky, A. 1972 "Social Class, life expectancy, and overall mortality" Pp. 5-30 in E. Gartly Jaco (ed.) Patients, Physicians and Illness. N.Y.: Free Press.

Bart, P. 1971 "The myth of value-free psychotherapy" Pp. 113-159 in Wendell Bell and James Mau (eds.) The Sociology of the Future. N.Y.: Russell Sage.

Bernard, Jessie 1972 The Future of Marriage. N.Y.: Bantam.

Blood, Robert and Donald Wolfe 1960 Husbands and Wives: The Dynamics of Married Living. N.Y.: Free Press.

Brenner, Harvey 1973 Mental Illness and the Economy. Cambridge: Harvard University Press.

Coan, Richard 1977 Hero, Artist, Sage or Saint? N.Y.: Columbia University Press.

Cowen, E. 1973 "Social and Community Interventions" Annual Review of Psychology 24:423-472.

Davis, Ann, Simon Dinitz, and Benjamin Pasamanick 1974 Schizophrenics in the New Custodial Community. Ohio: Ohio State University Press.

Dean, A. and N. Lin 1977 "The stress buffering role of social support" The Journal of Nervous and Mental Disease 165:403-417

Dohrenwend, B. P. 1975 "Sociocultural and Social-psychological factors in the genesis of mental disorders" Journal of Health and Social Behavior 16: 365-392.

Dohrenwend, Bruce and Barbara Dohrenwend 1969 Social Status and Psychological Disorder: A Causal Inquiry. N.Y.: John Wiley. 1976 "Sex differences and psychiatric disorders" American Journal of Sociology 81:1447-1454.

Dubos, Rene 1959 Mirage of Health. N.Y.: Anchor Books.

Eastwood, M. R. and M. H. Trevelyan 1972 "Relationship between physical and psychiatric disorder" Psychological Medicine 2: 363-372.

Epstein, Cynthia 1970 Woman's Place. Berkeley: University of California Press.

Farris, R. E. and H. Warren Dunham 1939 Mental Disorders in Urban Areas. Chicago: University of Chicago Press.

Frank, Jerome 1974 Persuasion and Healing (revised edition). N.Y.: Schocken Books.

Goffman, Erving 1961 Asylums. N.Y.: Anchor Books.

Goode, William 1956 Women in Divorce. N.Y.: Free Press.

Gove, W. R. and M. R. Geerken 1977 "The effect of children and employment on the mental health of married men and women" Social Forces 56: 67-76.

Gove, W. R. and M. Hughes 1979 "Possible causes of the apparent sex differences in physical health: an empirical investigation", American Sociological Review 44: 126-146.

Gove, W. R., M. Hughes and O. R. Galle 1979 "Overcrowding in the home: an empirical investigation of its possible consequences" American Sociological Review 44: 59-80.

Gove, W. R. and J. F. Tudor 1973 "Adult sex roles and mental illness" American Journal of Sociology 78: 812-835.

Gross, Martin 1978 *The Psychological Society*. N.Y.: Random House.

Gruenberg, E. M. 1967 "The social breakdown syndrome—some origins" American Journal of Psychiatry 123: 1481-1488.

Gurin, G., J. Veroff, and S. Feld 1960 *Americans View Their Mental Health*. N.Y.: Basic Books.

Hollingshead, August and Fredrick Redlich 1958 *Social Class and Mental Illness*. N.Y.:Wiley.

Hurvitz, N. 1974 "Peer self-help psychotherapy groups: psychotherapy without psychotherapists" pp. 84-132 in Paul Roman and Harrison Trice (eds.) The Sociology of Psychotherapy, N.Y.: Jason Aronson.

Illich, Ivan 1976 *Medical Nemesis*. N.Y.: Random House.

Kahn, R. L. 1972 "The meaning of work: interpretation and proposals for measurement" Pp. 159-203 in A. Campbell and D. E. Converse (eds.) The Human Meaning of Social Change. N.Y.: Russell Sage.

Kasl, S. 1978 "Epidemiological contributions to the study of work stress" Pp. 3-48 in C.L. Cooper and R. Payne (eds.) Stress at Work. Sussex: Wiley.

Kirsh, B. 1974 "Consciousness-raising groups as therapy for women" Pp. 326-354 in Violet Franks and Vasanti Burtle (eds.) Women in Therapy. N.Y.: Brunner Mazel.

Klerman, G. L. 1976 "Psychoneurosis: integrating pharmacotherapy and psychotherapy" Pp. 69-91 in James Claghorn (ed.) Successful Psychotherapy. N.Y.: Brunner Mazel. 1977 "Mental illness, the medical model, and psychiatry", The Journal of Medicine and Philosophy 2: 220-243.

Kohn, M. L. 1972 "Class, family, and schizophrenia: a reformulation" Social Forces 50: 295-304.

Kulka, R., J. Veroff, and E. Douvan 1979 "Social class and the use of professional help for personal problems: 1957 and 1976" Journal of Health and Social Behavior 20: 2-17.

Lasch, Christopher 1977 *Haven in a Heartless World*. N.Y.: Basic Books.

Lerner, M. 1975 "Social differences in physical health", Pp. 80-134 in John Kosa and Irving Zola (eds.) Poverty and Health. Cambridge: Harvard University Press.

Liem, R. and J. Liem 1978 "Social class and mental illness reconsidered: the role of economic stress and social support" Journal of Health and Social Behavior 19: 139-156.

Myers, J. K., J. J. Lindenthal and M. P. Pepper, 1971, "Life events and psychiatric impairment" Journal of Nervous and Mental Disease 152: 149-157. 1975 "Life events, social integration, and psychiatric symptomatology" Journal of Health and Social Behavior 16: 412-427.

New York Times 1978 "The problem that can't be tranquillized: 40,000 mental patients dumped in city neighborhoods."

Pasamanick, Benjamin, Frank Scarpitti and Simon Dinitz 1967 *Schizophrenics in the Community. An Experimental Study in the Prevention of Hospitalization*. N.Y.: Appleton Century Crofts.

Phillips, D. 1963 "Rejection: a possible consequence of seeking help for mental disorders" American Sociological Review 28: 963-972.

Quinn, R. P., S. Seashore, R. Kahn, T. Mangione, D. Campbell, G. Staines and M. McCullough 1971 *Survey of Working Conditions*. Washington, D. C.: U.S. Government Printing Office.

Radloff, L. 1975 "Sex differences in depression" Sex Roles 1: 249-265.

Richman, J. 1979 "Women's changing work roles and psychological -psychophysiological distress" Paper presented at the American Sociological Association Annual meeting. Boston.

Rosenfield, S. 1978 "Sex differences in depression: do woman always have higher rates?" Paper presented at the American Sociological Association Annual meeting. San Francisco.

Rothman, David 1971 *The Discovery of the Asylum*. Boston: Little, Brown.

Scheff, Thomas 1966 *Being Mentally Ill*. Chicago: Aldine.

Seligman, M. E. 1974 "Depression and learned helplessness" in R. J. Friedman and M. M. Katz (eds.) The Psychology of Depression: Contemporary Theory and Research. Washington, D. C.: V. H. Winston and Sons.

Test, M. and L. Stein 1977 "A community approach to the chronically disabled patient" Social Policy: 8-16.

Weissman, M. and G. Klerman 1977 "Sex differences and the epidemiology of depression" Archives of General Psychiatry 34: 98-111. 1978 "Epidemiology of mental disorders. Emerging trends in the United States" Archives of General Psychiatry 35: 705-712.

Weissman, M. and J. K. Meyers 1978 "Affective disorders in a U.S. urban community", Archives of General Psychiatry 35: 1304-1311.

Weissman, M., B. Prusoff, A. DiMascio, C. Neu, M. Goklaney, and G. Klerman 1979 "The efficacy of drugs and psychotherapy in the treatment of acute depressive episodes. American Journal of Psychiatry 136.

Williams, Elizabeth 1976 *Notes of a Feminist Therapist*. N.Y.: Praeger.

Wing, J. K. and G. W. Brown 1970 *Institutionalism and Schizophrenia*. London: Cambridge University Press.

Socialist

Terry A. Kupers: Schizophrenia and Reification

I struggled in my attempt to exist, in my attempt to consent to the forms (all the forms) with which the delirious illusion of being in the world has clothed reality.

—Antonin Artaud[1]

It is quite impressive how fiercely many of the people who are called "schizophrenic" battle against being cast as objects for others. Being controlled or manipulated from without, being dead or a mere thing, being talked about or being schemed on are all aspects of their hyperawareness. Their only escape consequently appears in becoming the total subject of a private fantasy world. In a society where people are quite regularly treated as objects, it seems appropriate to consider how a diagnosis like "schizophrenia" comes to be attributed to certain individuals who cannot or will not tolerate this plight.

Consider an example. John D., a young man so diagnosed, is sitting quietly in a family therapy session. The awkward opening moments of this session are filled with seemingly disconnected speculations about a rash of murders in the Los Angeles area attributed to a knife-wielding "Slasher." John D. breaks in to say, "Cutthroat is the name of the game they teach us." As he withdraws again into silence, his relatives are all too quick to point out the bizarreness of his statement.

Reprinted by permission of the *Socialist Review*.

John D.'s social metaphor was taken for madness. It soon became clear that he often clothed his perceptions in irony as a way of both expressing and concealing resentment he harbored towards a family that seemed to him to be forcing him into a mold he rejected—that of an aspiring and successful breadwinner and family man. Perhaps his family's failure to understand or appreciate the metaphor was partly determined by their reciprocal resentment of his "aimlessness."

John D. refused to dull his sensitivity to the words he played on. He cleverly linked an implicit critique of competitive social relationships to a filial protest against his family's unquestioning and active complicity in this evil. The rest of the family was receptive neither to his choice of words nor to his social interpretation. They attributed this failed communication to his madness. Does his lucidity arise in the midst of personal chaos, or is chaos created out of his lucidity?

Lucid moments for John D. are often disconnected and thus seem bizarre. This in part is why he is diagnosed as schizophrenic. But a partial lucidity or consciousness and a fragmentation of everyday experience are themselves programmed by the very structure of modern capitalism.

Without supporting the idea that there *is* a "disease" called "schizophrenia"—debate currently rages on this issue—we will attempt to make the experience of at least some people so labeled intelligible within the context of social relations, rather than merely diagnostic.*Crucial to such understanding is the concept of reification—the metamorphosis of people into things in our society. Perhaps we can discover in the very conflicts that drive society the key to the conflicts within the person set so apart in society.

Psychiatry has traditionally approached schizophrenia as a disease that afflicts certain people. Like other diseases, its species can allegedly be classified. The typical signs and symptoms demonstrated by afflicted persons can be catalogued. Emil Kraepelin revolutionized the classification of these diseases in the last century by lumping catatonia, hebephrenia, and paranoia into one entity, which he entitled "dementia praecox." He differentiated this entity from the other major form of madness—manic-depressive psychosis—by certain describable characteristics. For instance, dementia praecox was thought to follow an inexorable course of deterioration of the personality while manic-depressive psychosis was characterized by cycles, not only of mood, but also of exacerbations and improvements.

Bleuler substituted the term "schizophrenia" ("split-mindedness") for dementia praecox when it was noticed that progressive deterioration did not characterize all cases. Confinement in barbaric asylums probably caused more of the deterioration than any disease process. Bleuler wanted to focus on a splitting of psychological life, rather than on a deteriorating course.

The Kraepelinian approach, or the "medical model" of "mental illness" still dominates psychiatry today. The illness is presumed to be located within the

---

* The term "schizophrenia" is a broad and ill-defined diagnostic label which is often assigned arbitrarily. The wide spectrum of people so diagnosed includes young adults who "hear voices" once but never again, individuals whose behavior is judged bizarre by strangers who spend little time getting to know them, and people who have spent a large portion of their lives vegetating in mental hospitals with little room for personal expression or growth. We cannot seriously generalize about such a diverse group of people so loosely diagnosed. We will be concerned here with a subgroup of individuals who are so diagnosed at some point and who present a somewhat consistent report of their experience.

individual. Refinements in diagnosis have occurred over the years. Disease classification systems have been altered. Research has uncovered various "causes" in chromosomes, child-rearing practices, biochemicals, or brain structure. Treatment has moved from strait-jackets and lobotomies to electroconvulsive (shock) therapy and psychoactive drugs. Prognoses have improved. But the concept of schizophrenia as an illness located within individuals has changed little. Until recently, information about family and social milieu was an afterthought, perhaps admitted to discussions of cases as a "contributing factor" to the disease process.

Challenges to the validity and utility of this medical model have been made from many perspectives. Freud insisted that there was meaning in even the craziest behavior, though the meaning was often unconscious. He sought a dynamic rather than a merely descriptive understanding of schizophrenia. (Bleuler, too, was headed in this direction.) His search was important, but short-lived because of his edict that psychoanalysis could not treat the narcissism that he held underlay schizophrenia. A dynamic psychotherapy for schizophrenia had to await the next generation of psychoanalysts, such as Frieda Fromm-Reichman, Paul Federn, and Margaret Sechahaye, as well as the "interpersonal" approach of Harry Stack Sullivan. These dynamic approaches countered the strictly descriptive medical model. But they still limited the object of their investigations to the interaction of individuals in the consulting room.

More recently, attention to "family dynamics" has resulted in an important discovery. Behavior that seems bizarre or "schizophrenic" on the part of one individual, considered in isolation, is actually quite meaningful when viewed in the context of that individual's family life.[2] The centrality of the family to any real understanding of the phenomenon called schizophrenia is firmly established. Improving family interactions can, then, be more helpful than the treatment of the isolated person. This family-centered approach is a great advance over the individual-centered medical model. But the family does not exist in isolation either.

Sociologists have gone on to show how the larger social picture can further inform the investigation of schizophrenia.[3] Certain people in society are labeled "mentally ill," and that labeling initiates a social process of behavior shaping that consolidates their role as deviants. The social equilibrium is maintained as these deviants mark by their excesses the boundaries of normal behavior. This approach has opened doors to a new understanding, but it has also tended to lose sight of the real experience of the individuals assigned to the roles. Also, these sociologists here seem to take as background an undifferentiated society rather than one in which social class is of decisive import. They treat society as a norm-abiding mass with a minority of deviants. They certainly fail to see that the conflict between classes or within the very structure of a class society effects changes in the personal lives of those cast as deviants.

The "radical therapy" movement has linked its critique of traditional approaches to schizophrenia with a critique of capitalist society itself.[4] This generally profound critique has mostly neglected what is specific to the "schizophrenic" experience. Sometimes this has led to the romanticizing of the schizophrenic experience as a heroic protest against an irrational society. Like the work of R. D. Laing, from which it borrows, this radical critique loses sight of the cold logic of a society based on profit-seeking, and misses the terror and complexity of the experience of those labeled schizophrenic.[5] A meaningful interpretation of schizophrenia cannot precede an understanding of the core structure of society.

Georg Lukacs demonstrated the centrality of the concept of reification in the work of Karl Marx.[6] This concept is critical to discussions like the present one, because, while it is defined in terms of the structure of capitalist society, its ramifications are evident in everyday experience, even the most mundane.

According to Marx, Lukacs argues, reification is a "specific problem of our age, the age of modern capitalism." Marx begins his critique of the mode of capitalist production with an analysis of the commodity form. Before the advent of modern capitalism, production was aimed at satisfying the needs of a particular family or other living-unit of producers. Because of greater efficiency of production, the point arrived where these "use-values" exceeded the demand of the individual living unit and became the objects of exchange. Products then became *commodities,* valued for their "exchange-value" more than for their "use-value." Barter then became a major form of social exchange, and accumulation of great "free" or disposable wealth became possible. Thus, with the advent of modern capitalism, the commodity became "the dominant form in society."

One class that had been initially favorably situated then progressively used its accumulations to "purchase" the means of production, including especially the labor-power of the non-propertied class. In closely following developments, the efficiency of production was further upgraded through such successive forms as home manufacture, to elementary factory organization, to mass line production. The worker, unable to own the ever more elaborate and expensive means of production, was soon left without even the means necessary to produce the use value needed by his or her own family or living unit. The worker then possessed only one last marketable "commodity" —his or her labor-power—which he or she was forced to sell, literally in order to live at all.

At this point, the worker's labor (or labor-power) becomes itself purely a commodity, something "objective" and independent of the worker, something which must be sold, and something over which the worker loses all control.

Marx describes reification in these terms:

> A commodity is therefore a mysterious thing, simply because in it the social character of men's labor appears to them as an objective character stamped upon the product of that labor; because the relation of the producers to the sum total of their own labor is presented to them as a social relation, existing not between themselves, but between the products of their labor. This is the reason why the products of labor become commodities, social things whose qualities are at the same time perceptible and imperceptible by the senses. . . . It is only a definite social relation between men that assumes in their eyes, the fantastic form of a relation between things.[7]

Lukács demonstrates how specialization and fragmentation characterize the rationalization of production necessary for the constant acceleration of efficiency and profit. Over the past century, the production process has been repeatedly analyzed into its component parts for the purpose of quantification and streamlining. Fragmented time and motion studies ("Taylorism") were carried out to insure that the waste of each worker's time and energy was minimized while output was maximized. Rationalization of the work process then proceeded to the point where "the human qualities and idiosyncracies of the worker appear increasingly as mere sources of error."[8]

The production process became fragmented for the sake of "economy." But the worker's productive life was thereby itself fragmented experientially, as each worker was assigned a specialized and monotonous task, and blocked from any sight of the whole scheme. Thus modern workers have become alienated from the product of their labor, from their fellow workers, and from themselves. A steelworker complains:

> You're mass-producing things and you never see the end result of it. . . . How are you gonna get excited when you're tired and want to sit down? It's not just the work. . . . I would like to see a building, say, the Empire State, I would like to see on one side of it a foot-wife strip from top to bottom with the name of every bricklayer, the name of every electrician, with all the names. So when a guy walked by, he could take his son and say, "See, that's me over there on the forty-fifth floor. I put the steel beam in."[9]

This fragmentation spreads beyond the factory gates, so that consciousness and everyday experience are fragmented throughout society. The false consciousness of masses is connected in important ways to this fragmentation that limits awareness of the totalities of social reality.[10]

Because of the domination of the commodity form over all relationships in capitalist society, human relationships take on the form of relationships between things (people as objects or appendages to the machine) while things themselves —the commodities—appear to have the human qualities and agency denied to people—i.e., they seem to produce their own value (commodity fetishism) and to interact independent of and external to relationships between people. People thus come to experience their powerlessness in specific ways. This is the experience of the proletariat first, but increasingly characterizes the experience of the large unbounded mass of people loosely called the "middle class" today. They feel like things, more the object than the subject of their lives. They experience the world as fragmented. They are able to determine neither the human agency behind the overall scheme nor their own abilities to make change. "Reification" describes this state of affairs.

According to Lukács, "reification requires that a society should learn to satisfy all its needs in terms of commodity exchange."[11] Reification is the outcome of this commodity exchange.

The commodity is ever more the dominant category, and reification increasingly characterizes capitalism today—this, despite runaway technology, everexpanding bureaucracy, the blurring of class lines, and a relative shift of focus from production to consumption, all of which embellish the contemporary picture. Consumerism is precisely the modern version of a society "learning to satisfy all its needs in terms of commodity exchange." Bourgeois social scientists since Weber have tended to concentrate on the embellishments while ignoring the core matter. Some of them even borrow the term reification, but apply it to subjective experience instead of to the basic structural characteristics of modern capitalist society. Contrariwise, Marxists have not adequately analyzed and explained the embellishments, so that their contention that reification is at the core of social relations often seems like mere proclamation. Increase in and deepening of current Marxist work on culture and consciousness will hopefully help narrow this gap. In any case, the status of people in capitalist society has changed little, from the time Marx described man as an appendage to the machine.

The test of reification as a useful theoretical construct lies in a rigorous examination of political economy. The evidence that reification permeates everyday life is seen more in frantic popular attempts to deny or escape its reality, than in any explicit awareness of its extent or its roots in the structure of capitalist relations. Escape takes such forms as quests for euphoria (drugs, alcohol), flights back to nature (health foods, camping), seeking after secondary intimacy or personal salvation (encounter-type therapies), thrill seeking (high-speed driving or shock movies) or just plain hedonism (credit-buying or *Playboy*-style sexuality). The very form of exclusive romantic love or the illusion of family bliss well insulated from the traumas of work serves the same purpose.[12] Any escape is sought from the deadness, emptiness, unreality, fragmentation, isolation and powerlessness of everyday reified experience. As reification is tuned out of awareness, a certain numbness sets in. The attempt not to feel reified is paralleled by a diminishing ability to feel at all, except in a few circumscribed or sensationalized situations. Of course, this denial or mass unconsciousness is not total. It is not even so much a matter of people not knowing—for instance about class inequities—but more of their not dwelling upon what can so easily be known.

The social roots of reification are particularly subject to this process. Phillip Slater speaks of a "toilet assumption"—the notion that unwanted matter, unwanted difficulties, unwanted complexities and obstacles will disappear if they are removed from our field of vision. "We do not connect the trash we throw from the car window with the trash in our streets.... Our approach to social problems is to decrease their visibility: out of sight, out of mind."[13]

It is not entirely accurate to state that numbness is the popular state of mind in capitalist society today. The modern mystification of reification is more or less transparent to large numbers of discerning people who actively attempt to transcend their reified situation. But a tension develops between this attempt to transcend and the wish to ignore discomforting revelations. The connections between personally experienced problems and their roots in the social structure are often particularly discomforting forms of knowledge, as is the frustration of beginning alone to attempt change. Here is where a convenient numbness can set in that gradually spreads to other aspects of experience. Popular attempts at personal salvation such as encounter groups, or paths to "expanded consciousness," serve to counter the ensuing sense of numbness, while steering clear of discomforting social realities. Even awareness of the need for radical social change creates discomfort, when such change would result in even short-range personal sacrifice.

This tension is highlighted by the popularity of artists and writers who refuse to be numbed. The "unmentionable" can be discussed, as long as it is "only art." Safely sealed off from the general flow of social intercourse, at least some readers can identify privately with accounts of reification, such as the following by William Burroughs:

American Housewife (opening a box of Lux): "Why don't it have an electric eye the box flip open when it see me and hand itself to the Automat Handy Man he should put it inna water already.... The Handy Man is outa control since Thursday, he been getting physical with me and I didn't put it in his combination at all.... And the Garbage Disposal Unit snapping me, and the nasty old Mix master keep trying to get up under

my dress.... I got the most awful cold, and my intestines is all constipated.... I'm
gonna put it in the Handy Man's combination he should administer me a high colonic
awready."[14]

The artist is applauded for seeing beyond restrictions of consciousness.
Appreciative audiences share this perception. But the audience is generally not
yet ready to transcend these restrictions outside the circumscribed realm of art.

The revolutionary, too, refuses to be numb—and struggles to end the basis for
reification in social relations. A well worked out alternative world view and a
feeling of solidarity with masses in active struggle support the revolutionary's
firm stand against pressures to accept the status quo and the more popular
numbness.

Others who refuse and refute areas of socially prescribed numbed consciousness are more alone in their awareness. They do not share public approval with
the artist or collective awareness with the revolutionary. John Berger has said,
"No revolution is simply the result of personal originality. The maximum that
such originality can achieve is madness; madness is revolutionary freedom confined to the self."[15]

Of course, the categories of artist, revolutionary, and madman are neither
precise nor exclusive. Overlaps occur, even as individuals cross the boundaries
from one to another. We are thus discussing conceptual trends rather than concrete insight into the special character of "schizophrenia."

Ms. Natalija A. was a thirty-one-year-old ex-philosophy student when she
went to see pioneer psychoanalyst Victor Tausk, complaining that she was being
controlled by an "influencing machine."[16] She was deaf because of an ulcer of
the ear. Tausk listened carefully to her detailed descriptions of a complicated
machine, which was manipulated by someone else, and which caused changes in
her. He then put together his own formulation about the origins of this "influencing machine." He hypothesized that inner or outer changes occurred early
over which his analysand had no control (e.g., her ulcers). Estranged from this
change, but searching for its cause, she assumed an external originator. The
image of this external originator was built up and filled in through projections,
delusions, and even hallucinations, until the detailed picture of a machine
emerged. The delusion was then consolidated, replacing the original estrange-
ment and mystery with a certainty that was both reassuring and frightening.

Ms. Natalija A. was out of touch with reality when she went to see Tausk. But to
what extent is unclear. Certainly the feeling of powerlessness and of being controlled is a real insight into reified existence. But this insight was disconnected,
so that she was unable to evaluate which aspects of her life might be under more
or less direct control; and she was unable to identify the agent and locus of that
control. In her encounter with Tausk, however, the entirety of her thought-
process was judged delusional. Her kernal of lucid comprehesion went unnoticed as she was "helped" to regain her "mental health."

Psychoanalyst Jacques Lacan writes:

> What in fact is the phenomenon of delusional belief? It is, I insist, failure to recognize,
> with all that this term contains of an essential paradox. For to fail to recognize presup-
> poses a recognition, as is manifested in systematic failure to recognize, where it must
> obviously be admitted that what is denied is in some fashion recognized.
>   ...It seems clear to me that in his feelings of influence and automatism, the subject
> does not recognize his productions as his own. It is in this respect that we all agree that

a madman is a madman. But isn't the remarkable part rather that he should have to take cognizance of them? And isn't the question rather to discover what he knows about himself in these productions without recognizing himself in them?[17]

Lacan describes paranoia. But capitalist relations of production insure that "the subject [worker] does not recognize his productions as his own." The essential paradox of recognition is located in the social relations of alienation and mystification. When it surfaces in the fragmented and personalized consciousness of certain individuals, it only perpetuates and deepens the original mystification to attribute the individual's lucid but fragmented productions to personal madness. But, of course, any other interpretation would upset the conventional numbness to reification.

This is not to say that there is no disorder in the mental life of many who are diagnosed as schizophrenic. But the labeling itself tends to accentuate the process by which people are treated as objects. The term is tied to the "medical model" and functions as a vague and loose diagnostic category to which individuals with very different kinds of problems are consigned. Domination figures centrally here. The dominated, whether they be exploited workers, oppressed minorities, or women, are most likely to receive this diagnosis as well as the harshest treatment.

Still, leaving aside the question of etiology for a moment, and leaving open the possibility of eventually discarding the entire concept of a "mental illness" called schizophrenia, it is useful to summarize some typical experiences reported by some people who have been diagnosed as schizophrenic.*

1. Fragmentation of experience with bizarreness. Human objects as well as relationships and even space and time are fragmented. Bizarreness results. Feeling is split off from idea, act from thought, one thought from another (ambivalence in thought and feeling).

2. Fusion or confusion of the imaginary with the real. Reality and fantasy merge. Word becomes thing. Reality testing is hampered. A private personal world is created.

3. Loss of boundary around ego or self. The subject is alienated from his or her productions in action, thought, and feeling. Thoughts may seem to be stolen from or inserted into one's own head by others. An illusory fusion or merging of self with other may occur.

4. Perception of self as object or thing. The sense of being the subject of one's experience is lost except for regressions to infantlike states of total subjectness. Complaints of feeling "dead" or "empty" or of being controlled by others for their purposes often predominate. Dread of an encroaching numbness develops.

5. Terror, fragility, and isolation. Impermanence and insecurity threaten, while trusting relationships with others are precluded.

This is a schematic and partial summary of experiences reported in the course of treatment by some people diagnosed as schizophrenic, or reported in the literature. Various parts of that literature accentuate one or another aspect of such

---

* A general or comprehensive description of schizophrenia would be problematic (see footnote above, p.000). Lumping people together and calling the process diagnosis can too easily confirm the worst fears of those so lumped—denying them their individuality. The following is merely my own compilation of common experiences reported by a certain number of people who have some time in their lives been diagnosed as schizophrenic.

reports. But the above categories encompass those generally held to be important by the therapists who do the reporting.

Still, it could just as well be a general description of the subjective experiences of reified social relationships throughout society. The fragmentation of a specialized and compartmentalized workplace has spread to all aspects of life. Desires and their satisfactions shaped by the mass media truly confound the imaginary with the real. Exploitation rips the product from the hands of its producer. People become things to be controlled. (Here is the key to understanding "mental illness" among workers, women, and minorities.) Isolation and insecurity are built into the ideology (e.g., the image of the "self-made man") essential to the maintenance of the machinery of competition and profit.

The very structure of capitalist society is "schizophrenogenic." [18] But common as it is, outright schizophrenia is not the plight of the entire population. Most people find a different way to live with reification.

We have discussed the reification that characterizes modern capitalism, and its denial, which results in a certain numbing of consciousness. It is often held that chaos is characteristic of the schizophrenic experience, and that lucid insight occurs only at moments of contact with the real world. Yet the hyperawareness and sensitivity of the schizophrenic experience seem to produce a more accurate picture of reified relationships than does the more "normal" numbed consciousness. We must ask at this point what goes wrong to turn potential insight into personal terror and fragmentation.

Being human is never easy. Maintaining relationships where one does not become a mere object for the other requires intense struggle, no matter what the structure of society. Discussion here should not be construed as a model of pure and unilinear causality whereby capitalism "causes schizophrenia." Real life is not so simple.* But when a society is constructed so that the relationship between people assumes "the fantastic form of a relation between things," the maintenance of human relationships becomes systematically that much more difficult. This is, for us, the problem of schizophrenia.

In the course of "normal" socialization, moments arise where the developing child is encouraged to ignore or be numb to certain events and experiences. As he or she learns which events and experiences are not to be noticed, the child is shaped into conventional consciousness. For instance, the child might be made more comfortable when he or she is numb to parental deceptions. To the extent that we can investigate or interpret pre-verbal communication and experience,

---

*   Epidemiological studies generally conclude that the incidence of schizophrenia is fairly consistent throughout the different forms of culture and society. Such a conclusion is the result of abstracting behaviors considered symptomatic of the "disease," and comparing the incidence of a certain configuration of these behaviors in different societies. This simplistic approach equates behaviors that, in the context of the different cultures and societies, have very different meanings. "Schizophrenia" becomes a common label with little substance. We will not be ready to understand what happens to the phenomenon we currently label schizophrenia in post-capitalist forms of society until we improve on this approach. However, the interpretation of schizophrenia and its relation to reification given here does assume there will be different potentialities in a society where reification should not exist, in the sense given it by Marx. Theory tells us that reification, like alienation and false consciousness can be transcended only after a revolution that ends capitalist relationships. This has not been demonstrated in practice. New potentials exist in socialist society for an end to such concomitants of capitalist relationships; so we

we should be able to demonstrate that age-specific equivalents to this process extend back even to infant-parent relations. The mixed or contradictory nature of messages is made to seem to the child a result of his or her own personal confusion.[19] Consider how the child is encouraged to rationalize that even blatantly arbitary punishment is "for his own good." Later, the child is taught not to question at what expense in human lives "the West was won." These "little deceptions" are not unrelated. If we were to explore further the intervening events, the earlier, seemingly idiosyncratic distortions of consciouness in the child's development would appear as part of a progression towards a later more systematic configuration of false consciouness in the adult world.[20] Many investigations of how the cultural norms of a capitalist society are passed along to the young uncover just such a tendency.[21] Later denials of reification are related to such childhood experiences.

Some individuals more than others, for some reason, refuse to be thus numbed. But when they proclaim their beliefs, at whatever level of development, they are denied validation in the areas where their beliefs contradict the conventional consciousness. Repeated enough in the right combination, this devalidation can create areas where these people are unable to evaluate the truth or merit of their own perceptions and beliefs. They cannot test social reality because they have no way at that moment to challenge the united presentation of the conventional view by significant others in their lives. If they refuse to surrender or alter their course, seemingly sporadic events may add up to a consistent pattern whereby they may become unable to differ with the increasingly consolidated attribution by others that they are first different, then strange, and finally mad.

Psychoanalysts sometimes speak of very complex developmental issues in terms of prototypic moments or events. For instance, Lacan describes the "mirror phase" in infant development, where the subject views itself as object, or the "I" discovers itself as "me" in the image appearing on the other side of the mirror.[22] In fact, the discovery does not occur at any one given moment. The prototypic moment of the mirror phase is really just shorthand for a series of complex events. These events include the infant's finding its thumb, recognizing a flailing hand as its own, distinguishing in other ways the "me" from the "not me," as well as the actual moment when it can recognize the mirror image of its own productions and movements.

We can speak of such a prototypic moment in the life of an individual who early in life refuses to be numb, and then later in life as a "schizophrenic" episode. As a child, he or she notices a discrepancy between his or her own perceptions and the way the world is interpreted by parents or significant others. The individual who refuses to give up his or her own perceptions in order to agree with those of the other, is left alone to deal with whatever small bit of reality it is that the others deny. If that bit of reality is strange or frightening, as would be any personalized glimpse of reified social relations, the individual left alone to confront it can be overwhelmed. Feelings of isolation, confusion, and terror can follow.

----

can hope that the potential for an end to particular personal and interpersonal experiences and problems now discussed under the rubric of "mental illness," also exists there. The discussions and investigations necessary for a real understanding of this entire topic cannot occur independent of important and continuing social struggles.

If certain of the collusive distortions of consciousness that occur between infant and parent really are microscopic subevents in the overall socialization of the child towards a "numbed consciousness," then a firm early refusal to be numb might lay some of the foundation for a later "break with reality." This kind of link would help us to understand why reports of experiences during "schizophrenic episodes" so resemble naked reification. Thus, society's attempt to deny reification may be played out in the bizarre world created for some who protest the denial.

The question remains whether or not this kind of developmental event really plays much of a part in the enactment of the social drama called schizophrenia. We are not hypothesizing that all people whose early development can be described in terms of such a prototypic moment later become schizophrenic. (Certainly the artist and the revolutionary might share such experiences.) Neither are we hypothesizing that in the lives of all people diagnosed as schizophrenic, this kind of moment stands out. We are merely hypothesizing that for some smaller but significant subgroup of people who are diagnosed as schizophrenic, this type of prototypic moment is important.

To test this hypothesis, we need merely to listen closely. We need to avoid the distortions introduced with the "medical model" or any perspective that ignores the impingement of social relations. Then, we can expect to hear reports from some schizophrenics that closely fit what we collapse here into a "prototypic moment." Since they would necessarily be recollected in age-appropriate terms, they might not be very cohesive or self-conscious. They would, in effect, be fragmented reports. But this is just how reality is presented in reified society— especially for the child.

Some of the individuals who early internalize acute but fragmented images of reified society in this way, are later considered hyperaware by others who choose to be more numb. For instance, they might be called "paranoid" when they proclaim that they are "being controlled" or that their productions "are being stolen." There are many possible routes from this experience to a full-blown "schizophrenic breakdown."

This formulation does not "explain" schizophrenia. Important questions remain. Why do only certain individuals have this kind of experience? How are these social and psychological events realted to biological ones? (Current debates about the social vs. the biological "causes" of schizophrenia cannot be very scientific from the start, since they fail to grapple with the complex interconnections that must come into play.) What are the mediations, intervening variables, and events that link social relations, childhood experience, and schizophrenia?

There is a real need for scientific investigations of these phenomena. The social perspective outlined here can frame and inform such investigations, but cannot serve as a substitute for them. But much data relevant to the development of the approach suggested here is already available, for instance in the psychoanalytic literature. It lies relatively dormant because of biased or one-sided interpretations that do not accord such data much importance.

For instance, Freud analyzed Judge Daniel Paul Shreber from a reading of Shreber's autobiography.[23] He attributed the judge's paranoia to his projected homosexual impulses. Morton Schatzman has found a different reality in certain material, available at the time of Freud's study, but ignored.[24] A very popular child-rearing manual of that period in Germany was written by Shreber's father.

The manual prescribed very rigid discipline aimed at breaking the child's will. Shreber's father had devised various machines or devices that were to be attached to children, and were presumably used by him in raising his own children, which would painfully enforce correct posture and manners. Schatzman demonstrates how accurately Judge Shreber's detailed "delusional" descriptions of the external forces controlling and torturing him match his father's actual torture-chamber methods of child rearing. Freud's interpretation seems remarkably narrow in the light of the broader perspective Schatzman brings to the case. The crucial point here is that the father epitomizes the very form of domination we have described as reification, in his practice and in his manual.[25] And this is precisely how the father contributes to the production of "schizophrenia."

The reification that permeates social relations is not always transparent to social consciousness. Still, it provides a key to understanding the complacent consciousness that characterizes capitalist ideology today.[26] Given this state of affairs, those individuals who are conscious of reified relationships but have no effective control of this mass "unconsciousness" (as the artist or revolutionary might) may end up confused and terrified. Unable to talk with others about the real world, and thus unable to struggle collectively, they suffer that world alone. Meanwhile, it is assumed that these individuals are totally out of touch with that other real world of social consciousness.

This formulation stresses the lucidity of persons eventually diagnosed as schizophrenic. Unfortunately, recognition of this lucidity has often led to the romantic notions of schizophrenia mentioned above. But individuals trapped in the social role and the private world of schizophrenia represent an important failure from a social perspective. Because of the fragmentation, terror, and isolation of their experience, they are generally able to do little to change their own plight or the social world that they experience as so uncomfortable. People who live largely within a privatized world cannot very effectively struggle against the institutions that insure their domination. Artaud observed, "So a sick society invented psychiatry to defend itself against the investigations of certain visionaries whose faculties of divination disturbed it."[27] But he still had to spend more than fifteen years of his life in asylums.

There is an encouraging alliance developing between a small but growing number of mental patients and ex-mental patients, mental health workers, and progressives in and out of the mental health field, against some oppressive and exploitative mental health practices. [28] Such a collective struggle hopefully will offer an important alternative to some who had become lost in their private worlds.

Thus, there are some striking similarities in form between the personal world perceived by some people diagnosed as schizophrenic, and the world of capitalist reification. The "schizophrenic" experience seems very related to the panic that ensues for some who refuse to be numb, but are then left all alone to deal with their experiences, realizations, and the frightening reified social world that includes the very role created for them. Schizophrenia may, like the portrait of Dorian Gray, be kept in society's attic so that no one need view the image it holds of an ugly reified world.

This essay poses more questions than it answers. Perhaps it will serve to reframe some specific investigations that might lead to a more scientific approach to the disorder in social relations some now call schizophrenia.

References

1. Antonin Artaud, *Artaud Anthology*, ed. J. Hirschman (San Francisco: City Lights, 1965), p 85.
2. See Gregory Bateson, "Toward a Theory of Schizophrenia," in *Steps to an Ecology of Mind* (New York: Ballantine, 1972); and R. D. Laing and A. Esterson, *Sanity, Madness, and the Family* (Middlesex: Penguin, 1970). See also the rapidly expanding literature on family therapy—the work of Nathan Ackerman, Jay Haley and the Palo Alto Group, Salvador Minuchin, Murray Bowen, and others.
3. See Erving Goffman, *Asylums* (Chicago: Aldine, 1961); and Thomas Scheff, *Being Mentally Ill* (Chicago: Aldine, 1966).
4. See Phil Brown, ed., *Radical Psychology* New York: Harper, 1973); Michael Glenn, ed., *Voices from the Asylum* (New York: Harper, 1974); and Radical Therapy Collective, *Radical Therapist* (New York: Ballantine, 1971).
5. R. D. Laing, *The Politics of Experience* (New York: Ballantine, 1967); and his earlier work, *The Divided Self.*
6. Georg Lukács, *History and Class Consciousness* London: Merlin Press, 1971).
7. Karl Marx, *Capital*, vol. 1 (New York: International Publishers, 1967), p. 72.
8. Lukács, p. 91
9. Studs Terkel, *Working* (New York: Avon, 1972), p. 2.
10. See Richard Lichtman, "Marx's Theory of Ideology," *Socialist Revolution* 23 (April 1975).
11. Lukacs, p. 91.
12. See Eli Zaretsky, "Capitalism, the Family, and Personal Life," *Socialist Revolution* 13/14 and 15 (1973).
13. Phillip Slater, *The Pursuit of Loneliness* (Boston: Beacon, 1970), p. 15.
14. William Burroughs, *Naked Lunch* (New York: Ballantine, 1973), p. 124.
15. John Berger, *The Look of Things* (New York: Viking, 1974), p. 135.
16. Victory Tausk, "On the Origin of the 'Influencing Machine' in Schizophrenia" (1919), *Psychoanalytic Quarterly*, vol. 2 (1933), pp. 519-.
17. Jacques Lacan, *The Language of the Self*, ed. A. Wilden (Baltimore: Johns Hopkins, 1968), pp. 96-97.
18. See Anthony Wilden, *System and Structure* (London: Tavistock, 1971), p. 108. Gilles Deleuze and Felix Guattari, in their book *Capitalisme et schizophrénie*, vol. 1 (Paris: Editions de Minuit, 1972), discuss the machine-like nature of people in reified society and propose a more socially conscious "schiz-analysis" to replace psychoanalysis in understanding and treating such a situation.
19. See Gregory Bateson on the "double bind."
20. See Lichtman.
21. See the work by Wilhelm Reich and others on the transmission of authoritarian culture to the young during the Nazi regime (*The Mass Psychology of Facism* ([New York: Orgone Institute, 1946]), and the work by Jules Henry on the transmission of competitive ways of relating to the young in contemporary capitalist society. (*Culture against Man* [New York: Viking, 1963]).
22. Jacques Lacan, "Le Stade du miroir comme formateur de la fonction du "Je," Eng. trans. *New Left Review* 51 (September-October 1968)
23. Sigmund Freud, "Psychoanalytic Notes upon an Autobiographical Account of a Case of Paranoia" (1911), in *Three Case Histories* (New York: Collier, 1970).
24. Morton Schatzman, *Soul Murder* (New York: Signet, 1974).
25. Refinements of this idea and others throughout this essay developed from conversations with Professor John Seeley.
26. See Herbert Marcuse, *One-Dimensional Man* (Boston: Beacon, 1964), and Henri Lefebvre, *Everyday Life in the Modern World* (New York: Harper, 1971).
27. Artaud, p. 135.
28. See the journals of the radical therapy movement (*Rough Times and Issues in Radical Therapy*). See also the growing literature from patients and ex-patients, presented in the works mentioned in reference 4; and in *Madness Network News*, published by the Network against Psychiatric Assault (NAPA) in San Francisco.

Part 3

WHO
GETS WHAT?

The question "Who gets what?" arises with special force under conditions of scarcity. When there is not enough of a desired good or service available to satisfy all who want it, a principle of allocation must be determined. Conservatives, liberals, and socialists disagree about what constitutes a just system of distribution.

Conservatives believe that personal economic achievement is the best criteria for deciding who gets what. Access to the basic necessities of life is not a right. Everyone must pay for what they want. Conservatives say that, "There is no free lunch." Competition among individuals is the way to organize the distribution of scarce resources. Those who want scarce goods will be encouraged to work harder to earn more money to attain their desires. Scarcity is an incentive to economic achievement that calls forth greater human effort and ingenuity. Increased economic growth results and scarcity is reduced accordingly.

Liberals agree with conservatives that people must work to get what they want. Personal economic achievement is a valid criteria for organizing the distribution of scarce resources. But it should not be the sole principle for regulating distribution.

Economic competition should be structured so that everyone has a fair chance to succeed. If a pure competitive system is not modified, some people will have an unfair advantage. Birth into a high income family assures access to better education, health care, and social connections. Individuals who have greater initial access to resources will be better prepared to succeed later in life. If personal achievement is to be a fair criteria for organizing distribution, those individuals who start from a poor or disadvantaged background must be given access to a good education and improved health care to make it possible for them to enter the competition for scarce resources at the same level as individuals from an advantaged background. Liberals justify government programs to improve conditions of life for the disadvantaged on the grounds that they are entitled to an equal opportunity. Individuals who are unable to compete for scarce resources due to mental or physical disabilities are entitled to the basic necessities of life as a matter of right.

Socialists start from the principle that everyone is entitled to the basic necessities of life as a fundamental right. The distribution of scarce resources should be conducted apart from the evaluation of personal achievement. Class difference must be eliminated so that they do not become bases of distribution. Nevertheless, as long as scarcity exists the desire to satisfy individual wants will tend to interfere with the practice of the basic socialist principle, "From each according to his/her ability; to each according to his/her needs." The elimination of scarcity is the fundamental means to achieve a socialist society. Until abundance is achieved, basic necessities such as food and health care must be allocated equally, without favoritism or special privilege.

Chapter 7

====================

HEALTH

====================

Two apparently contradictory trends are at work. The cost of health care is increasing while standards of health are declining in comparison to other western industrialized countries. In the United States, infant mortality is higher than in thirteen other countries. The life expectancy for males is lower than in seventeen other countries. Yet the number of medical personnel is increasing steadily and the amount of money spent on health care grows faster than the economy. Conservatives, liberals, and socialists view these trends quite differently.

Conservatives believe that health care should be a matter of individual choice and responsibility. Everyone should have the right to choose one's own doctor. Everyone has the responsibility to decide the amount of health care one wants. This decision is based on the choice among competing goals of how to use one's economic resources. Government should not interfere with individual choice and responsibility. If any government measure is at all justified, it should be one that provides funds to pay for treatment of catastrophic illness. Health care is best left to the management of doctors since it is their area of professional expertise. Interference with our health care system, based on principles of private enterprise and competition among hospitals and doctors, will only result in higher costs for health care without significant improvements.

Liberals believe that health care is a basic human right. Disease is something that strikes an individual and over which he or she has little control. It is not a matter of individual responsibility but one of social responsibility to care for the sick. Good health care should be made available to all persons and the United States has the resources to accomplish this goal. Such a goal can be realized without fundamentally changing the existing organization of health care. Our existing health care resources need to be better coordinated and financed. We can accomplish this by including health care in the social security system. Individual choice of doctors that conservatives desire can be retained in such a national health care system. We can achieve good health care for all Americans with only limited intervention from government. Health care should remain under the control of professionals although some input from consumers should be added as a counterbalance to doctors.

Socialists believe, with liberals, that health care is a basic human right. But they do not think that making minor adjustments in the existing system of health care will be sufficient to realize that right. A thoroughgoing reorganization of health care, in which paraprofessionals and consumers would play as important a role as doctors, is required. Along with democratization and deprofessionalization of health care, changes in the structure of wealth and power will be required to make the necessary resources available to institute a full national health care system.

Most countries have instituted some form of national health care system. Medical services are made available without regard to the individual's ability to pay for them. Britain's national health scheme established immediately after World War II is perhaps the most familiar to Americans. It is paid for out of general tax revenues with modest user fees for a few services primarily to discourage unnecessary use. Individuals may choose their own physicians, but medical care such as hospital operations are provided according to need rather than ability to pay. The increasing cost of health care in the United States has placed the proposal for some form of public health care system on the political agenda in the United States. Various schemes have been introduced as bills in Congress since 1948, but none have passed. Senator Edward Kennedy's proposals for national health insurance offered in the early seventies have received the most attention of any plan to reorganize the American health care system. The articles in this chapter focus on the question of health insurance in relation to a public health care system.

In the conservative article, Fuchs argues that the United States really does not need a new national health care plan. Existing medical resources are sufficient to meet health needs. We already have a national health care system, even if we do not call it by that name. Municipal hospitals are available to the poor, and the middle class can write off medical bills that they are unable to pay as bad debts. There is a limited amount of resources, and if funds are shifted to health care, they must be taken from other uses. The desire for a national health care system is understandable since it is a relatively non-controversial way of fulfilling the goal of equality. Nevertheless, national health care is "irrational" as it would not materially improve health care but only make it cost more. The problem is not the lack of health care; it is the movement for a national health care system.

In the liberal article, Senator Kennedy argues that good health care is a right that should be available to all. Our present system of health care is not organized to meet that goal. It is fragmented into individual practitioners, group practices, and hospitals. The quality of health care that an individual receives is greatly dependent upon how much money one has. Although existing federal programs have gone part of the way to improving access to good health care for the poor and elderly, most Americans simply cannot afford adequate health care.

Senator Kennedy proposes to establish a national health care system through an act of Congress. Individuals would pay for part of it through an increase in social security taxes; employers would contribute a share; and the federal government would pay for the rest from general revenues. The plan would also improve the way in which health care is made available, emphasizing preventive medicine, provided by local health service organizations. The Senator's proposal includes measures to limit costs and encourage efficiency so that making good health care more equally available to all citizens would only cost a small percentage more than current outlays. A national health security program should be established so that all Americans will have good health care at a cost they can afford.

In the socialist article, Ferguson agrees that national health care is a valid goal but argues that the Senator's proposal is inadequate. A national health care system should not only provide good health care to all Americans. Such a plan should also provide for restructuring the health care system so that the people, as consumers of health care, have a major say in how it is conducted. The Kennedy plan includes consumers only as appointees to health care boards. Ferguson argues that real consumer control can only come through elections. Health care must be democratized and deprofessionalized. Community health organizations should be run by consumer/health worker boards. In addition, the Kennedy proposal would tax working people more heavily than higher income persons. Insufficient income would be generated to carry out its goals. Ferguson argues that a national health care plan should be financed more heavily by taxing corporations and the rich. Only by attacking inequalities of wealth will it be possible to institute a health care system based on principles of equality.

Conservative

Victor R. Fuchs: From Bismarck to Woodcock: The "Irrational" Pursuit of National Health Insurance

Uniformity of practice seldom continues long without good reason.

—Samuel Johnson, 1775

If an economic policy has been adopted by many communities, or if it is persistently pursued by a society over a long span of time, it is fruitful to assume that the real effects were known and desired.

—George Stigler, 1975

Almost a century ago Prince Otto Eduard Leopold von Bismarck, the principal creator and first chancellor of the new German nation-state, introduced compulsory national health insurance to the Western world. Since then, nation after nation followed his lead until today almost every developed country has a full-blown national health insurance plan. Some significant benchmarks along the way are the Russian system (introduced by Lenin after the Bolshevik Revolution), the British National Health Service (Beveridge and Bevan, 1945), and the Canadian federal-provincial plans (hospital care in the late 1950s, physicians' services in the late 1960s). In nearly all cases these plans built on previous systems of medical organization and finance that reflected particular national traditions, values, and circumstances.[1]

In some health plans, such as those in the communist countries, the government has direct responsibility for providing services. In others, the production of medical care is still at least partially in the private sector, but the payment for care is through taxes or compulsory insurance premiums which are really ear-marked taxes. Even in the United States, the last major holdout against the world-wide trend, government funds pay directly for almost half of all health care expenditures and pay indirectly for an appreciable additional share through tax exemptions and allowances.[2] Moreover, most observers believe it only a question of *when* Congress will enact national health insurance, not *if* it will.

Almost as obvious (to many economists) as the rise of public subsidy of health insurance is the "irrational" aspect of such programs. Health insurance, in effect, reduces the price the consumer faces at the time of purchase of medical care and therefore induces excessive demand. Because the direct cost to the consumer is less than the true cost to society providing that care, he tends to over-consume medical care relative to other goods and services. This misallocation of resources

Reprinted with permission from the *Journal of Law and Economics*, Vol. 19, pp. 347–359. Copyright 1976 by the University of Chicago Law School.

1. Brian Abel-Smith, Major Patterns of Financing and Organization of Medical Care in Countries Other than the United States, 40 Bull. N.Y. Acad. Med. 540 (2 ser. 1964).

2. For a discussion of why the United States is the last to adopt national health insurance, see p. 358 *infra*.

results in a significant "welfare loss," which Martin Feldstein has estimated at a minimum of $5 billion per annum in the United States.[3]

Not only does society seem to be irrationally bent on encouraging people to overuse medical care, but in the free market for health insurance people also tend to buy the "wrong" kind. Most economists agree that to the extent that health insurance serves a useful purpose it is to protect consumers against large, unexpected bills for medical care. All insurance policies are actuarily "unfair," that is, they carry a load factor for administrative costs, but, if consumers are risk averse, it is worthwhile for them to pay these costs in order to protect themselves against unpredictable (for the individual) large losses. It follows, therefore, that consumers should prefer major medical (catastrophe) insurance, that is, plans with substantial deductibles or copayment provisions for moderate expenses but ample coverage for very large expenses. Instead, we observe a strong preference for "first dollar" or shallow coverage. Of the privately held hospital insurance policies in the United States, the number covering the first day of hospitalization are several times greater than the number covering long-term stays.

Another apparent irrationality with respect to health insurance was alleged by Milton Friedman in a *Newsweek* column in April, 1975. He noted that Leonard Woodcock, President of the United Automobile Workers (UAW), is leading the drive for universal comprehensive national health insurance despite the fact that such a measure is

> . . .against the interest of. . .members of his own union, and even of the officials of that union. . . .The UAW is a strong union and its members are among the highest paid industrial workers. If they wish to receive part of their pay in the form of medical care, they can afford, and hence can get, a larger amount than the average citizen. But in a governmental program, they are simply average citizens. In addition, a union or company plan would be far more responsive to their demands and needs than a universal national plan, so that they would get more per dollar spent.[4]

Friedman says that Woodcock is an "intelligent man," and therefore finds his behavior a "major puzzle."

From Bismarck to Woodcock, it seems that economists are drowning in a sea of irrationality. But other economists warn us against jumping to the "irrationality" conclusion. In particular, George Stigler has taught us to look beyond the surface appearance of political actions in search of their actual consequences and of the interests that they serve. He writes,

> It seems unfruitful. . . .to conclude from the studies of the effects of various policies that those policies which did not achieve their announced goals, or had perverse effects . . . are simply mistakes of the society.[5]

In short, when confronted with some consistent and widespread behavior which we cannot explain, we should not blithely assume that it is attributable to lack of information or bad judgment. We should be wary of what might be called the "fallacy of misplaced ignorance." It may be that the behavior we observe is more

---

3. Martin S. Feldstein, The Welfare Loss of Excess Health Insurance, 81 J. Pol. Econ. 251 (1973)

4. Milton Friedman, Leonard Woodcock's Free Lunch, Newsweek, Apr. 21, 1975, at 84.

5. George J. Stigler, The Citizen and the State: Essays on Regulation, at x (1975).

consistent with the self-interest of particular individuals or groups than it first appears.

It is to George Stigler that we are also indebteded for the "survivor principle," one of his many contributions to the study of industrial organization.[6] The basic notion is simple: if we want to learn something about the relative efficiency of differently sized firms in an industry, Stigler tells us to look at that industry over time and notice which size classes seem to flourish and which do not. Can the "survivor principle" be applied to institutions as well? If so, national health insurance seems to pass with flying colors. No country that has tried it has abandoned it, and those that have tried it partially usually expand it. It may not be unreasonable to infer, therefore, that national health insurance does serve some *general* interests. That is, there may be some *welfare gains* lying below the surface that more than offset the losses so apparent to many economists. An exploration of some of the special or general benefits that might explain the widespread pursuit of national health insurance follows.

The U.S. Already Has Implicit National Health Insurance

Some of the observed behavior would seem less irrational if we assume that the U.S. already has *implicit* national health insurance, especially for catastrophic illness. If it is true that most uninsured people who need care can get it one way or another—through government hospitals, philanthropy, or bad debts—then it may be rational for people to buy only shallow coverage, or indeed, not to buy any insurance at all. To suggest that there is implicit insurance in the United States covering nearly everyone is not at all to suggest that there is equal access to equal quality care. We know that so-called free care may often have some stigma attached to it, may be less pleasant and less prompt, and may fail in other ways as well. But it cannot be denied that a good deal of medical care is delivered every year in the United States to persons who do not have explicit insurance or the money to pay for it.

Those persons without explicit insurance are essentially free riders. Those who do carry extensive insurance, such as the automobile workers, in effect pay twice—once through the premiums for their own insurance and again through taxes or inflated costs to cover care for those without explicit insurance. If this is a significant factor, it could be perfectly rational for the automobile workers to support *universal compulsory* insurance. Why society provides implicit or (in most countries) explicit coverage for all remains to be explained.

An Attempt to Control Providers

Another reason why the UAW leaders and others may favor a single national health plan is the hope of gaining some control over the providers of medical care—the hospitals and the physicians. In recent years one of the major frustrations faced by the auto workers and other groups with extensive insurance coverage is the rapid escalation in the price of medical care. They may believe that only

---

6. George J. Stigler, The Economics of Scale, 1 J. Law & Econ. 54 (1958).

a single source national health insurance plan will be in a position to control provider behavior and stop the escalation in costs. Moreover, there is strong evidence that they are not alone in this view. One of the puzzles for economists has been to explain the traditional opposition of the medical profession to legislation which, at least in the short run, increases the demand for their services. This opposition probably stems in part from the belief that national health insurance would ultimately result in an increase in government control over providers.

Tax Advantages

Why do people buy shallow coverage—where the administrative load is high and the risk element relatively small? One reason is that when the premium is paid by the empoyer the implicit income is free of tax. Even health insurance premiums paid by the individual are partially deductible from taxable income. If the tax laws allowed employers to provide x-free "food insurance," we would undoubtedly see a sharp increase in that type of fringe benfit. But again the explanation is not very satisfactory. Why do the tax laws encourage the purchase of medical care but not in food, clothing, or other necessities? In an attempt to answer this question, we should consider some of the characteristics of medical care and health insurance that are different from conventional commodities.

Externalities

One explanation for the popularity of national health insurance that has great appeal for economists at the theoretical level is that there are substantial external benefits associated with the consumption of medical care. If this were true, then governmental subsidy of care need not be irrational; indeed it might be irrational not to provide that subsidy. The best example of potential externalities is the prevention or treatment of communicable diseases such as tuberculosis. In earlier times these diseases constituted a very significant portion of overall health problems, but are much less important today. Furthermore, if a concern with externalities were the chief motivation, it would be logical and feasible to subsidize those services (for example, veneral disease clinics) which are clearly addressed to the communicable diseases. However, even economists who are strong advocates of national health insurance, such as Lester Thurow, do not rely on the externality argument. Thurow writes, "Once a society gets beyond public health measures and communicable diseases, medical care does not generate externalities.[7]

Mark Pauly has called attention to one special kind of externality which probably is operative. It involves the satisfaction people get from knowing that someone else who is sick is getting medical attention.[8] This satisfaction could be

7. Lester C. Thurow, Cash Versus In-Kind Transfer, 64 Am. Econ. Rev., pt. 2, at 190-95 (Papers & Proceedings, May 1974).

8. Mark V. Pauly, Medical Care at Public Expense: A Study in Applied Welfare Economics (1971).

purchased by voluntary philanthropy, but the total amount so purchased is likely to be less than socially optimal since each individual's giving tends to be based on his or her private satisfaction, ignoring the effects on others. The solution may be compulsory philanthropy, that is, tax-supported programs.

A Matter of "Life or Death"

Another explanation for national health insurance that has great appeal at the theoretical level but carries less conviction empirically is that "the market should not determine life or death." This theme is advanced by Arthur Okun in his new book, *Equality and Efficiency, the Big Tradeoff,* and is a basic tenet of those who argue that "health care is a right." [9] There is considerable logic in the argument that society may be unwilling to accept the consequences of an unequal distribution of income for certain kinds of allocation decisions, such as who serves in the army during wartime, who gets police protection, and who faces other life-threatening situations. It may be easier and more efficient to control such allocations directly than to try to redistribute money income (possibly only temporarily) to achieve the desired allocation.

Although this explanation has a certain theoretical appeal, one problem with it is that the vast majority of health services do not remotely approach a "life or death" situation. Moreover, the ability of medical care to make any significant contribution to life expectancy came long after Bismarck and Lenin advocated the national health insurance. Even today, when some medical care is very effective, it is possible that housing, nutrition, and occupation have more influence on life expectancy than does medical care, yet we allow inequality in the distribution of income to determine allocation decisions in those areas. According to Peter Townsend, there is no evidence that the British National Health Service has reduced class differences in infant mortality, maternal mortality, or overall life expectancy.[10] If equalizing life expectancy were society's goal, it is not at all clear that heavy emphasis on national health insurance is an optimal strategy.

The emphasis on medical care rather than other programs that might affect life expectancy is sometimes defended by the statement that it is more feasible. Although diet or exercise or occupation may have more effect on life expectancy than does medical care, it may be technically simpler to alter people's consumption of medical care rather than to alter their diet, etc. It has also been argued that it is politically more feasible to push medical care rather than alternative strategies. The distinction between technical and political feasibility is not, of course, clear-cut because the former depends in part on what we are willing to do in the way of permitting government to intrude on personal decisions—a political question. However, to the extent that the popularity of national health insurance is said to be attributable to its political feasibility, we have really not explained much. Its political popularity is precisely the question we started with.

9. Arthur M. Okun, Equality and Efficiency: the Big Tradeoff (1975).
10. Peter Townsend, Inequality and the Health Service, [1974] 1 Lancet 1179-90.

The Growth of Egalitarianism

Life expectancy aside, one way of interpreting the growth of national health insurance is an expression of the desire for greater equality in society. British economists John and Sylvia Jewkes have written,

> The driving force behind the creation of the National Health Service was not the search for efficiency or for profitable social investment. It was something quite different: it was a surging national desire to share something equally.[11]

An American economist, C. M. Lindsay, has developed a theoretical model which analyzes alternative methods for satisfying the demand for equality of access to medical care. Among other things, he shows that if this demand for equality is widespread, there are externalities similar to those discussed by Pauly in connection with philanthropy. Thus a free market approach will result in less equality than people really demand. He also shows that the British National Health Service can perhaps be understood as an attempt to satisfy this demand for equality. He concludes, ". . . the politician's sensitive ear may read the preferences of his constituents better than the econometrician with his computer."[12]

Why the demand for equality has grown over time and why it should find expression in medical care more than in other goods and services are not easy questions to answer. Is there really more altruism in society now than before? Were Bismarck and Lenin the most altruistic political leaders of their time? Is it simply the case that equality is a normal "good," that is, we buy more of it when our income rises? If this is the explanation, what are the implications for equality in a no-growth economy?

Perhaps there has been no real increase in altruism at all. Perhaps what we observe is a response to an increase in the ability of the less well-off to make life miserable for the well-off through strikes, violence, and other social disruptions. In this view health insurance is part of an effort to buy domestic stability. It may be that industrialization and urbanization make us all more interdependent, thus increasing the power of the "have-nots" to force redistributions of one kind or another. Or perhaps there has been a decline in the willingness of the "haves" to use force to preserve the status quo.

Such speculations, if they contain some validity, would explain a general increase in egalitarian legislation, but they would not help much in explaining why this legislation has focused heavily on medical care. Indeed, is it not curious that society should choose to emphasize equality in access to a service that makes little difference at the margin in life expectancy or to economic or political position and power? A cynic might argue that it is not curious at all since it is precisely because medical care does not make much difference that those with power are willing to share it more equally with those with less. Indeed, one might argue that the more a society has significant, enduring class distinctions, the more it needs the symbolic equality of national health insurance to blunt pressures for changes that alter fundamental class or power relationships.

One egalitarian goal that has always had considerable acceptance in the United States is equality of opportunity. Thus, a popular argument in favor of

---

11. John & Sylvia Jewkes, Value for Money in Medicine 60 (1963).
12. Cotton M. Lindsay, Medical Care and the Economics of Sharing, 36 Economica 351, 362 (n.s. 1969).

national health insurance is that it would help to equalize access to medical care for children. Some recent theoretical work on the economics of the family, however, calls into question the effectiveness of such programs. Gary Becker has argued that the thrust of programs aimed at increasing investment in disadvantaged children can be blunted by parents who can decrease their own allocation of time and money to their children as investment by the state increases.[13] The increase in the welfare of the children, therefore, may be no greater than if a cash subsidy equal to the cost of the program were given directly to the parents. The ability of the "head" to reallocate family resources may not, however, be as unconstrained as Becker's model assumes. There may be legal or social constraints, or there may be a desire on the part of the head to maintain the child's obedience, respect, or affection. Thus the importance of the reallocation effect is an empirical question, about which at present we know virtually nothing.

Paternalism[14]

An argument advanced by Thurow in favor of transfers in kind—such as national health insurance—is that some individuals are not competent to make their own decisions. He writes,

> Increasingly we are coming to recognize that the world is not neatly divided into the competent and the incompetent. There is a continuum of individuals ranging from those who are competent to make any and all decisions to those who are incompetent to make any and all decisions.[15]

Thurow argues that if society desires to raise each family up to some minimum level of *real* welfare, it may be more efficient to do it through in-kind transfers than through cash grants. Even if we agree with this general argument, it does not follow as a matter of logic that subsidizing medical care brings us closer to a social optimum. It may be the case, for instance, that the "less able" managers tend to *overvalue* medical care relative to other goods and services, in which case Thurow ought to want to constrain their utilization rather than encourage it.

More generally, there is the question whether government will, on average, make "better" decisions than individuals. As Arrow has stated in a slightly different context, "If many individuals, given proper information, refuse to fasten their seat felts or insist on smoking themselves into lung cancer or drinking themselves to incompetence, there is no reason to suppose they will be any more sensible in their capacity as democratic voters."[16] Two arguments have been suggested to blunt Arrow's critique. The first is that the "less able" are less likely to vote; therefore the electoral process produces decisions that reflect the judgment of the more able members of society. Second, it has been suggested that there is considerable scope for discretionary behavior by elected representatives;

13. Gary S. Becker & Nigel Tomes, Child Endowments, and the Quantity and Quality of Children, 84 J. Pol. Econ. S143 (1976).

14. I am grateful to Sherman Maisel for suggestions concerning this section.

15. Lester C. Thurow, *supra* note 7, at 193.

16. Kenneth J. Arrow, Government Decision Making and the Preciousness of Life, in Ethics of Health Care 33, 45 (Papers of the Conference on Health Care and Changing Values, Institute of Medicine, Laurence R. Tancredi ed. 1973).

they do not simply follow the dictates of their constituents.[17] It may be that their judgment is generally better than that of the average citizen.

An Offset to an "Unjust Tax"[18]

Suppose the U.S. were defeated by an enemy in war and had to pay an annual tribute to the enemy of $100 billion. Suppose further that the enemy collected this tribute by a tax of a variable amount on American citizens chosen at random. The U.S. government might decide that this tribute tax was unjust and that it would be more equitable for the federal government to pay the tribute from revenues raised by normal methods of taxation. If the enemy insisted on collecting the tribute from individual citizens on a random basis, the government could choose to reimburse those paying the tribute.

Some observers believe there is a close parallel between the tribute example and expenditures for medical care. They see ill health and the consumption of medical care as largely beyond the control of the individual citizen—the cost is like an unjust tax—and the purpose of national health insurance is to prevent medical expenditures from unjustly changing the distribution of income. There is, of course, the question whether, or how much, individuals can influence and control the amount of their medical expenditures. Putting that to one side, however, and assuming that the analogy is a good one, there are still some questions that arise.

One might ask why the government has to intervene to protect people against the tribute tax. Why couldn't citizens in their private lives buy insurance against being taxed for tribute? The total cost and the probabilities are known; therefore private insurance companies could easily set appropriate premiums. One answer might be that this is also inequitable to the extent that some people can afford the insurance more easily than others. The government could easily remedy this, however, by some modest changes in the distribution of income.

Another problem, of course, is that some people might not buy the insurance. They would be "free riders" because if they were hit with a big tribute tax they would be unable to pay and others would have to pay in their place. Furthermore, they would be wiped out financially, so that society would have to support their families.

To be sure, the government could both redistribute income to take care of the premium and make insurance compulsory, but that becomes almost indistinguishable from a national insurance plan. The only difference then would be whether there is a single organization, the government, underwriting the insurance, or whether there are several private insurance companies.

In the tribute tax example we have assumed that the probability of loss would be identical across the population, but this is clearly not true for health insurance. One argument advanced in support of national health insurance is that it does not require higher-risk individuals to pay higher premiums. A counter argument is that individuals do have some discretion concerning behavior that affects health and concerning the utilization of medical care for given health conditions. National health insurance, it is alleged, distorts that behavior. A

17. Albert Breton, The Economic Theory of Representative Government (1974).
18. I am grateful to Seth Kreimer for suggestions concerning this section.

related argument is that medical care will always have to be rationed in some way and that national health insurance requires the introduction of rationing devices other than price and income. These devices carry their own potential for inequity and inefficiency.

The Decline of the Family

Illness is as old as mankind, and, while frequently in the past and not infrequently today, there is little that can be done to change the course of disease, there is much that can be done to provide care, sympathy, and support. Traditionally most of these functions were provided within the family. The family was both the mechanism for *insuring* against the consequences of disease and disability and the locus of the *production* of care. The only rival to the family in this respect until modern times was the church, a subject to be considered below.

With industrialization and urbanization, the provision of insurance and of care tended to move out of the family and into the market. Thus, much of the observed increase in medical care's share of total economic activity is an accounting illusion. It is the result of a shift in the production of care from the home, where it is not considered part of national output, to hospitals, nursing homes and the like, where it is counted as part of the GNP. Unlike the production of bread, however, which also moved from the family to the market (and stayed there), medical care, or at least medical insurance, increasingly became a function of the state.

One possible explanation is that the state is more efficient because there are significant *economies of scale*. With respect to the production of medical care, the economies of scale argument can fairly safely be rejected. Except for some exotic tertiary procedures, the economies of scale in the production of physicians' services and hospital services are exhausted at the local or small region level. For the insurance function itself, there may be significant economies of scale. Definitive studies are not available, but the proposition that a single national health insurance plan would be cheaper to administer than multiple plans cannot be rejected out of hand.[19] To be sure, a single plan would presumably reduce consumer satisfaction to the extent that the coverage of the plan would represent a compromise among the variety of plans different individuals and groups might prefer.

The relationship between the declining importance of the family and the growing importance of the state is complex. Not only can the latter be viewed as a consequence of the former, but the causality can also run the other way. Every time the state assumes an additional function such as health insurance, child care, or benefits for the aged, the need for close family ties becomes weaker. Geographic mobility probably plays a significant role in this two-way relationship. One of the reasons why people rely more on the state and less on their family is that frequently the family is geographically dispersed. The other side of the coin is that once the state assumes responsibilities that formerly resided with

---

19. See Maurice LeClair, the Canadian Health Care System, in National Health Insurance: Can We Learn from Canada? 11, 16 (Proc. of Sun Valley Forum on Nat'l Health 1974 Symposium, Spyros Andreopoulos ed. 1975). LeClair writes that the experience in Saskatchewan clearly indicated economies of scale in the administration of a virtually universal plan. See also further comment on this point by LeClair, *id.* at 24.

the family, individuals feel freer to move away from the family, both literally and figuratively.

It has often been alleged that these intra-family dependency relationships are inhibiting and destructive to individual fulfillment. Whether a dependency relationship with the state will prove less burdensome remains to be seen. There is also the question whether the efficient provision of *impersonal* "caring" is feasible.

The Decline of Religion

In traditional societies when the family was unable to meet the needs of the sick, organized religion frequently took over. Indeed, practically all of the early hospitals in Europe were built and staffed by the church and served primarily the poor. The development of strong religious ties, with tithes or contributions frequently indistinguishable from modern taxes, can be viewed as an alternative mechanism for dealing with the philanthropic externalities discussed previously. Moreover, at a time when technical medical care was so ineffective, religion offered a particular kind of symbolic equality—in the next world if not in this one. Thus, the decline of organized religion, along with the weakening of the family, may have created a vacuum which the state is called upon to fill.

The "Political" Role

When refugees from the Soviet Union were interviewed in Western Europe after World War II, they invariably praised the West and disparaged life in Russia—with one notable exception. They said they sorely missed the comprehensive health insurance provided by the Soviet state.[20] It may be that one of the most effective ways of increasing allegiance to the state is through national health insurance. This was undoubtedly a prime motive for Bismarck as he tried to weld the diverse German principalities into a nation. It is also alleged that he saw national health insurance as an instrument to reduce or blur the tension and conflicts between social classes.

We live at a time when many of the traditional symbols and institutions that held a nation together have been weakened and have fallen into disrepute. A more sophisticated public requires more sophisticated symbols, and national health insurance may fit the role particularly well.

Why Is the U.S. Last?

One rough test of the various explanations that have been proposed is to see if they help us understand why the U.S. is the last major developed country without national health insurance. Several reasons for the lag can be suggested. First, there is a long tradition in the U.S. of distrust of government. This country was largely settled by immigrants who had had unfavorable experiences with governments in Europe and who had learned to fear government rather than look to it for support and protection. Second, it is important to note the heterogeneity of

20. Mark G. Field, Soviet Socialized Medicine 14 (1967).

our population compared to some of the more homogeneous populations of Europe. We are certainly not a single "people" the way, say, the Japanese are. Brian Abel-Smith has noted, for instance, that the U.S. poor were often Negroes or new immigrants with whose needs the older white settlers did not readily identify.[21]

The distrust of government and the heterogeneity of the population probably account for the much better developed non-governmental voluntary institutions in the U.S. Close observers of the American scene ever since de Toqueville have commented on the profusion of private non-profit organizations to deal with problems which in other countries might be considered the province of government. These organizations can be viewed as devices for internalizing the philanthropic externalities discussed earlier in this paper, but the organizations are frequently limited to individuals of similar ethnic background, religion, region, occupation, or other shared characteristic.

Another possible reason for the difference in attitudes between the U.S. and Europe is the greater equality of opportunity in this counry. In the beginning this was based mostly on free or cheap land, and later on widespread public education. Moreover, the historic class barriers have been weaker here than in countries with a strong fueudal heritage. To cite one obvious example, consider the family backgrounds of university faculties in Sweden and the U.S. Sweden is often hailed as the outstanding example of a democratic welfare state, but the faculty members at the leading universities generally come from upper-class backgrounds. By contrast, the faculties at Harvard, Chicago, Stanford, and other leading American universities include many men and women who were born in modest circumstances. With greater equality of opportunity goes a stronger conviction that the distribution of income is related to effort and ability. Those who succeed in the system have much less sense of noblesse oblige than do the upper classes in Europe, many of whom owe their position to the accident of birth. In the U.S., even those who have not succeeded or only partially succeeded seem more willing to acquiesce in the results.

Summing Up

The primary purpose of this inquiry has been to attempt to explain the popularity of national health insurance around the world. My answer at this point is that probably no single explanation will suffice. National health insurance means different things to different people. It always has. Daniel Hirschfield, commenting on the campaign for national health insurance in the United States at the time of World War I, wrote:

> Some saw health insurance primarily as an educational and public health measure, while others argued that it was an economic device to precipitate a needed reorganization of medical practice. . . . Some saw it as a device to save money for all concerned, while others felt sure that it would increase expenditures significantly.[22]

---

21 Brian Abel-Smith, *supra* note 1.

22. Daniel S. Hirschfield, The Lost Reform: The Campaign for Compulsory Health Insurance in the United States 16 (1970).

Externalities, egalitarianism, the decline of the family and traditional religion, the need for national symbols—these all may play a part. In democratic countries with homogeneous populations, people seem to want to take care of one another through programs such as national health insurance, as members of the same family do, although not to the same degree. In autocratic countries with heterogeneous populations, national health insurance is often imposed from above, partly as a device for strengthening national unity. The relative importance of different factors undoubtedly varies from country to country and time to time, but the fact that national health insurance can be viewed as serving so many diverse interests and needs is probably the best answer to why Bismarck and Woodcock are not such strange bedfellows after all.

Liberal

Edward M. Kennedy: Good Health Care: A Right for All Americans

Each of us risks our family's health and future in a gamble that serious illness or injury will not strike us; or that if it does, the health insurance we have will cover the costs; or that if our insurance doesn't cover it all, we will be able to pay the difference without hurting our finances too seriously. As we have seen, millions of Americans lose this gamble tragically. Americans are bankrupted and forced to sacrifice their savings and family dreams on top of suffering through tragic illness and injury. For many the cost is worse than the illness. Moreover, all Americans are finding the gamble more and more risky and expensive to make. It costs more to buy good health insurance than we can afford, but it costs even more to be ill or injured without insurance. Even when we buy insurance, it is seldom good enough. The gaps, exclusions and limitations in coverage leave us financially vulnerable in ways we don't even realize until they happen.

We risk more than disastrous costs, however. We risk our family's health itself. We bet that the physician or clinic we choose has kept current with the latest in his field, reviews his work with other specialists, and generally practices good medicine. We bet that we cn get to our family doctor when we need him, and from there to the specialist, to the laboratory, to the hospital, to the nursing home, to the drugstore, and so on as necessary. We bet that there will be a place for us or someone to help us at each place, and someone who pulls together the work of all these people and institutions to diagnose and treat our illness or injury.

As we have seen, millions of Americans lose on these gambles also. Americans are given widely varying quality of care. Many of us are subjected to unnecessary surgery or treatment, while some suffer long and needlessly because the physician is simply wrong. Many others of us spend anguished hours waiting for care, trying to get help after hours or out of town, or fighting our way from one specialist to another and from doctor to laboratory to hospital, repeating tests, hearing conflicting opinions, and losing hours of work.

Americans have relied on health insurance companies and on the doctors, dentists, hospitals and other providers to assure us good care at an affordable cost. The fact is that the health insurance industry assures us only that it will raise premiums enough to cover skyrocketing hospital and doctor charges and still assure its own high salaries, profits, and sales commissions. It has failed to adequately protect Americans from disastrous health care costs by spreading the cost and risk among all Americans. It has also failed to use the enormous amount of money it pays hospitals and doctors (over $15 billion in 1969) to press those providers to offer health care more economically and in ways, at times, and in places suited to the need of the millions of Americans who pay billions of dollars in health insurance premiums. The insurance industry pays for the health care, however poorly the care is organized and offered.

Nor have the hospitals, the doctors and other providers assured us good care at affordable costs. Care is offered by most providers in ways, at times, and in places most convenient to them, and most likely to assure them a good life at a high income. That is why you can't get a doctor in the middle of the night. That is one of the reasons costs are so high. Nor do providers do enough to guarantee quality. Most medical and other professional societies do little to insure that their members keep current in their field, subject their work to the review of their peers, or otherwise assure the quality of the health care they offer. Even when these societies (or insurance companies) know who the bad hospitals, doctors, or dentists are, they won't tell the people, and they rarely take effective action of their own. Unlike other American businesses, health care providers do not feel the competition and pressures from the people who buy services that assure that the services are offered in a way and at a price most attractive to the people.

It does not make sense that something Americans value as deeply as good health care at an affordable cost should hinge on our gambles on the insurance industry, whose interest is profit and not good protection for our people. Nor can we gamble completely on providers, whose own income and life style are at stake. It is tragic that Americans continue to make such gambles with health care when we are capable of doing more.

It is perhaps even more tragic that some Americans don't even have a chance to make this gamble. They are all but shut out from good care because their incomes are too low to buy insurance or to pay for care, because their age or disability makes them unable to get through the fragmented system, or because they live in an area where there is little or no care available. These Americans must drive long distances, or wait six to eight hours in the waiting rooms of public hospitals, or face possible insult from physicians and hospitals that refuse them treatment. It is callous beyond belief that we have created a health care system so unwilling and unable to respond to people with special needs that it almost shuts out Americans who are disadvantaged by age, disability, low income, or even by the fact that they live in rural areas.

No child should grow up in America with limbs still twisted because of the lack of health care.

No American should be forced by unnecessary bad health to live in poverty and watch his family grow up without the good health care that might improve their chance for a better life.

No elderly or disabled American should be forced to suffer alone because he is no longer strong enough or wealthy enough to fight his way through the system.

No American should be deprived of good care because he must travel so far or wait so long to get it that it is practical only in emergencies or when an illness has become serious.

Indeed, the way health care is offered and paid for in America today, none of us has any real assurance that he or his family can get good health care at a price he can afford. All of us risk, to some extent, our family's health and future in a gamble we need not make. We have the knowledge and the wealth in our nation to assure ourselves and every American that good health care is available to him and his family at a price he can afford. Other nations have succeeded in assuring good health care to their people and have proven that it can be done at reasonable costs. Why not assure such care to every American? I believe we should assure good health care to ourselves, to our families, and to everyone living in this country.

Good sense and responsibility to our own deepest values demand that we make this assurance. The opportunity for health is too important to our opportunity for a full life to run the risks of our present system of paying for health care through insurance companies and leaving the providers free to offer health care as they choose. I believe the federal government should take actions on our behalf to assure that every American has good health insurance coverage, and to assure that the wants and needs of the people are a more compelling influence in offering health care than is the convenience and profit of the providers. The federal government should simultaneously take actions to improve the efficiency, the organization, the quality, and the capacity of our health care system, in order to make sure the health care system is equipped to offer every American the good comprehensive health care that his new comprehensive health insurance coverage would enable him to afford.

There are a variety of proposals before Congress addressing one or more of the problems of assuring good health care to all Americans. I believe that only one of these proposals, however, will make the fundamental improvements required in both insurance and the organization and delivery of health care. That is the Health Security Act. I believe this bill will make these changes and at the same time protect the rights of the providers and open to them new opportunities for professsional growth.

The Health Security Program

Under the Health Security Program, the federal government would become the health insurance carrier for the entire nation. Rather than relying on the insurance industry to provide good health insurance coverage, Americans, by passing this bill, would ask their federal government to provide this insurance. The bill also would call on the federal government, as insurance agent for the nation, to set up controls and incentives for dentists, hospitals and other providers to assure that the health care offered to all Americans is of high quality, of reasonable cost, and offered in ways, at times, and in places responsive to the needs of the people. In addition, the program would set aside a portion of all the funds the government would spend on health care in a Health Resources Development Fund to educate the people, build the facilities, and organize the new types of services needed to offer good care to all Americans. In short, the program calls on the federal government to make sure that every American can pay for health care, that every American has good health care offered to him in ways suited to his needs, and that enough providers, facilities, and equipment are available to do the job.

The Program Would Give the Best Health Insurance in the World to All Americans

The government would provide identical insurance coverage to all Americans for all essential health care. It would be as if the federal government issued a group insurance plan where every resident of the United States was a member. Unlike the present system, you would get the same health care coverage regardless of where you work, what insurance company your policy is with, what previous illnesses you have had, how old you are, or how much you earn in income. No one would be excluded. Every American would have a comprehensive policy with the federal government from the moment he is born until the day he dies.

There would be no deductibles, no coinsurance, and no copayment of any kind—that is, you would not have to pay the first fifty or a hundred dollars each year, nor would you have to pay part of anything more than that. Nor could you use up your insurance. There would be no upper limits on how much the insurance would pay. The insurance would pay for as much care as needed to get you well. The program would pay for eyeglasses, hearing aids, and artificial limbs, even for crutches and wheelchairs.

Moreover, the insurance would pay for the health care you receive whether it is in the hospital, in the doctor's office, at home, or in a nursing home. It would cover:

> All hospital care.
> All physician's care.
> All dental care (starting with children through age fifteen).
> Home health care.
> Psychiatric care—unlimited when given in a "comprehensive health service organization," otherwise limited to forty-five days a year in hospital and twenty psychiatric consultations.
> Laboratory tests.
> Prescription drugs for the chronically ill, and for everyone treated in a comprehensive health service organization.
> Medical care in skilled nursing homes—limited to 120 days a year.

The intent is to cover all basic medical services. In order to get time to train and equip more dentists to meet the increased demand expected for dental services, dental coverage is phased in, starting with children who are age fifteen or less when the law takes effect. Once covered, however, a person remains covered throughout his life, so that eventually everyone will be covered.

The limitations on psychiatric care is intended to move psychiatrists and other professionals to treat patients on an outpatient basis in the framework of a comprehensive health or mental-health center. In such a setting, the benefits are unlimited.

The bill proposes to pay for *medical* care in nursing homes, but not custodial care. The limit of 120 days is viewed as a limit beyond which a person seldom needs to be kept in a nursing home for medical reasons.

With these exceptions aimed at phasing in the program or changing the way health care is offered, the program covers all medical care to all Americans without limit.

The Program Would Offer
Americans More Care at Less Cost

In the early years of the program the average American family would end up paying the same amount for comprehensive health care under the Health Security Program as they would pay for less comprehensive care without the program.

The incredible fact is that even estimates of the cost of the Health Security Act by its opponents acknowledge that the amount our nation would spend on health care under this act would be only eight percent over the amount we would spend on health care just as it is today. In fact, distinguished supporters of the act insist that the same amount would be spent with the act as without it in its initial years.

Moreover, the real payoff in costs under the act would be in the future. Only the Health Security Act incorporates strong costs controls and incentives for efficiency aimed at slowing skyrocketing health care costs. Without this act, costs will continue to rise as at present. Indeed, other national health insurance proposals may well speed these cost increases by feeding more money into the existing system while taking little or no action to correct its glaring inefficiencies.

The Health Security Act would bring rising costs under control. Consequently, in later years the act would provide Americans more health care at far lower costs than they would pay without the act.

Budgeting to Control Costs The Health Security Act would place the providers of health care on a strict budget. Hospitals and other institutions would prepare budgets to cover their operation in the coming year. After local health planners reviewed the budget to eliminate unnecessary costs, such as duplicate services among hospitals in the same community, the local Health Security office would negotiate a final budget which would determine the federal government's payment to the hospital. These budgets would be designed to promote expansion in needed services, such as outpatient clinics, but curtailment or conversion of excess facilities which add to overhead costs. Once the budget is set, the hospital's costs must be kept within it.

Likewise, the federal government would establish a budget for payment of physicians, dentists, and other providers. The budget would be large enough to cover all payments to these physicians for services to their patients, would allow a controlled increase in physicians' incomes to match increased costs of living, and would be adjusted to reflect increased services.

Incentives for Efficiency and Lower Costs In addition to this tightly controlled budget process, the Health Security Program offers powerful incentives for more efficient health care.

Since the plan covers all forms of care, whether given in the hospital or in the doctor's office, there would no longer be an incentive to hospitalize patients in order to get insurance coverage. Moreover, since the hospital is paid on the basis of an annual budget and not on the basis of how many beds are filled, the hospital would feel less pressure to fill its beds in order to meet its expenses. Pressures such as these are widely acknowledged to result in many people being unnecessarily hospitalized or kept in the hospital longer than necessary. Organizations such as the Kaiser-Permanente Group Health Plan find that when these pressures are removed the number of hospitalizations is cut over fifty percent. Since hospital care is by far the most expensive form of health care, less hospitalization results in dollars saved for use in providing more health care in the doctor's office or the clinic.

In addition, the program offers financial incentives to physicians and hospitals to form comprehensive health service organizations. These are prepaid group practice organizations which offer all essential health care services for a fixed amount per person per year. Such organizations not only reduce the amount of hospitalization for their patients, but also manage to care for many more people than the same physicians can treat practicing on their own. They do this by organizing physicians of various specialties under one roof with a common supporting staff, laboratory, and other services, and by emphasizing preventive care which aims at keeping patients healthy and at diagnosing illness early, when it can be treated at the least possible cost and the least possible suffering. Can you believe that some such organizations send reminders to their patients that it is time for a checkup? Even though they are paid no more for such services, they offer them in the belief that they will pay off in the long run in less illness and lower cost of treatment. While other national health insurance bills encourage formation of comprehensive health service organizations (the President's bill calls them "health maintenance organizations"), only the Health Security Program provides the framework of comprehensive national health insurance and provides generous start-up support necessary for these organizations to be offered as a choice for all Americans of all incomes.

The program also contains a variety of other provisions aimed at increasing efficiency. It pays for home health care so that, wherever possible, people may be treated by a visiting nurse in their homes rather than being admitted to the more costly nursing home or hospital. It offers incentives for nursing homes and hospitals to form affiliations which encourage transfer of patients from the hospital to the less expensive nursing home at the point in their recovery where intensive medical surveillance or treatment is no longer necessary. Controls are established also to assure that excessively costly drugs and medical devices are not used when less expensive ones are equally good.

All of these and other provisions of the bill aim at encouraging more health care at less cost, and would result in the American taxpayer's getting more care for his dollar than in the present system. No other national health insurance program in Congress contains the wide range of carefully thought-out incentives for efficiency found in the Health Security Program.

The Program Would Ask Every American to Pay Based on What He Could Afford

Instead of paying private insurance companies, doctors, dentists, hospitals, laboratories, and others for health care, Americans would pay the federal government. They would pay for their insurance through a one percent payroll tax (2.5 percent for self-employed) and through their income taxes. The man who earns more would pay more, and the man who earns less would pay less. But all would get the same benefits. Employers would pay a tax of 3.5 percent on their payrolls, but they would be relieved of private health insurance premiums.

From these funds the government would pay directly the doctors, the hospitals, and other providers. Since both the patient and the doctor know the bill will be paid, money will no longer be a consideration for a patient seeking any health service. Americans will no longer be discouraged from seeking needed care because they can't afford it, nor will pressured doctors and hospitals have to worry about whether a patient can pay or whether his insurance will cover the care. No hospital will any longer have "charity" patients, because every American will be eligible for care at any hospital or from any doctor he chooses, and the same fee will be paid regardless of the patient's income. In this situation, both patient and physician can afford to be health-conscious rather than cost-conscious.

The Program Assures Quality of Care

As a condition for receiving payments for services from the federal government, hospitals, physicians, and other providers would have to meet national standards which would assure that institutions maintain the best possible facilities and have available adequate trained staff; that physicians, dentists, and others are current with the latest in their specialty or field; that physicians do not perform surgery for which they are not qualified; and that major surgery or specialized services are performed only after review of the need for the services by a physician in general or family practice, and in some cases by another specialist as well. The program also requires that drugs and medical devices be prescribed from lists established by specialists to indicate what drugs are safest and most effective for various purposes.

Providers who do not meet these standards will be excluded from the plan. Patients who feel they have been mistreated by the provider will be able to lodge complaints with the administrators of the Health Security Program.

Perhaps most important of all, the program offers strong incentives to physicians to organize prepaid group practices and other forms of practice in which they have a continuing need and opportunity to review the records of their fellow physicians' work and consult with them about it.

The Program Enables the Health Care System to Seek Out Those Who Need Care

The program will extend special services to Americans who are disabled or elderly, who are unable or too poor to get transportation, or who live in the country or the inner city where doctors will not presently go.

For the elderly, the disabled, and others with similar problems, the program offers home health care and emergency transportation to the doctor or the hospital. It will even pay for nonemergency transportation when getting to the doctor or the hospital is a problem. In addition, the program's Health Resources Development Fund will support projects designed to reach out to meet the special needs of these and other Americans.

Physicians, dentists, hospitals, and other providers would be attracted into shortage areas by the opportunity for practicing modern health care in these areas at an income comparable to other parts of the country—and by economic pressures. By making every American equally eligible for health care paid for by the federal government, the Health Security Program would make it possible for a physician, a dentist, or any other provider to make a good income even if he practices among the poor. This fact in itself would enable hospitals and individual doctors to open their doors to people and reach out into communities that they presently cannot afford to serve. In addition, in the process of setting up budgets over the years for regions and service areas across the country, the health service planners would move toward equal sharing of funds, and facilities among all areas of the country. This would mean that some areas of the country that currently spend unusually large amounts on health care, that have the most extensive facilities, and that receive the largest number of services would be held even, while funds to purchase care and new facilities will be diverted into areas that are currently short of services. In the future there would be more and more money to be made in shortage areas by providers while the competition for income in highly served areas would be increasingly stiff.

At the same time that financial resources to buy care are being diverted into shortage areas, the program will make funds available to health profession schools to turn out more physicians, dentists, and other professionals. Funds will also be available to institutions to develop and implement satellite clinics, computer-supported communication systems, and other mechanisms designed to enable physicians to offer the latest in health care in these shortage areas and to make practice in these areas more attractive professionally.

The Program Organizes Our Health Care

The comprehensive health service would offer all essential health services to its enrollees, frequently in the same building or complex. In all cases the patients' treatment would be coordinated by the organization, and referrals would be simplified to the greatest extent possible. The aim of the program is to establish enough such organizations to make this form of health care available to all Americans who want it.

For those who want and need assistance in finding their way through the current maze of health services, the comprehensive health service organization would be a valuable opportunity.

Moreover, by encouraging affiliations between health care insitutions, and by requiring coordinated planning of what facilities are built and where, all Americans will benefit from better balanced services.

As for fragmentation of insurance plans, it will cease. Medicare, Medicaid and other programs will be absorbed in this more comprehensive plan, and thousands of private insurance plans will cease to exist.

The Program Frees the Hospital and the Physician to Be Healers But Preserves Their Independence and Freedom of Choice

Providers would be freed of the burden of collecting from patients and from hundreds of insurance companies, freed of concern over whether special services to people with special needs can be afforded, and offered the resources to start new forms of practice or the opportunity to maintain their practice as in the past.

Physicians, dentists, and other providers can select payment on a fee-for-service basis or on the basis of a fixed amount per enrolled patient per year. They can choose solo practice, they can join a group, or they can work under salary, whichever they prefer. Clearly, different patterns of payment and practice are appropriate to different situations, different parts of the country, and different individuals.

Moreover, the people will have freedom of choice over the physician and the type of practice they prefer. Indeed, it is the essence of the plan that a choice of physicians and various forms of practice be available to the people in order that their preferences can be expressed.

There will, of course, be pressures on providers to control costs, to offer needed services, to insure quality of care, and otherwise meet the health needs of the people. While the program anticipates no decrease in providers' income, it will place financial pressures on providers to keep costs down and to improve efficiency.

These pressures, however, will be no greater than those felt by any business in America attempting to offer attractive services at competitive rates. These pressures have been constructive generally in America and they can be constructive for health care.

Indeed, on the other side of these pressures is the opportunity for providers as entrepreneurs to choose from a wider set of options for practice than has been available to them in the past—and the opportunity for those with the imagination and the will to obtain the financial resources needed to offer new forms of services and new types of practice that extend their skills and capacity as healers.

The Program Will Plan and Create the Capacity to Offer Good Health Services to All Americans

A unique feature of the Health Security Program is its planning for all areas and regions of the country and its establishment of a special fund to build the facilities and educate the personnel needed to provide good health care.

The Health Resources Development Fund, consisting of several billion dollars a year, will be used for these purposes, as well as to start up comprehensive health service organizations; set up programs of continuing education for providers; establish new forms of health services appropriate to rural and inner-city areas and to special groups such as the elderly and the disabled; and to support any new, innovative or special services by which providers can better meet the health needs of the people.

In order to allow time to create capacity to offer more health care, the program puts this Health Resources Development Fund into operation two years before the rest of the health insurance plan takes effect. Between improvements in the efficiency of existing resources and creation of new resources, the nation will be able to offer more services to more people under the Health Security Program than it could ever offer otherwise.

The Health Security Program Would Belong to the People

The program would not be run by the federal government for itself or by the providers for themselves. It would be run by the federal government for the people, and the people would be given every opportunity to shape the program to meet their needs.

At national, regional, and local levels, consumers would be in a majority on councils that would advise the government on how the health plans should be run. State and local planning agencies would advise on the needs for various services in their areas. Consumer-based community agencies would be encouraged to set up and manage their own comprehensive health service organizations, and all such organizations would be obliged to give consumers a strong say in how they offer services.

Ultimately, the people could influence their Senators, Congressmen, and President by their votes and could hold them accountable for how the program is run.

The biggest single reason, perhaps, for the problems in our health care system is that the people have had no way to influence when, where and how health care is offered and what it will cost. The Health Security Program aims at giving the people this influence.

Conclusion

We have a choice of conscience to make in America. It is a choice of whether we will assure each other and all Americans good health care at a cost they can afford. The pages of this book are filled with the tragic stories of people who have been hurt because we do not make this assurance. We can put an end to such stories, and I believe we should. I urge Americans to search their hearts to choose and to make their choice known. To take so major a step the government needs your support.

Socialist

Allen Ferguson: A Pie in Every Sky: Kennedy's Health Plan

The Kennedy-labor bill for national health insurance appears to offer free, comprehensive health care to all under one nationally coordinated system, without discriminating against the poor. It holds out the promise of complete, accessible care without making the patient pay either out-of-pocket expenses or insurance premiums. It promises to restructure the health care system to provide more personnel and facilities, organize them rationally and distribute them equitably. And it appears to give the consumer both a choice of providers and a voice in decision-making.

Is is hard to criticize the Kennedy bill for what it *promises*. The problem is that the bill promises what it cannot possibly deliver. If it passes, the Kennedy bill may provide somewhat more accessible health care for more people, and this is important. But it will *not* be able to provide comprehensive care for all; it will *not* free low and middle income people from the burden of financing a very expensive health care system; it will *not* involve the consumer or the health care worker in meaningful decision-making; it will *not* provide sufficient health care personnel and facilities; it will *not* decrease the alienation, depersonalization and impotence that people often feel while receiving health care. In this chapter, we will look at what the bill promises; we will also examine what it can and cannot achieve and why.

Reprinted from *Billions for Band-Aids: An Analysis of the U.S. Health Care System and of Proposals for Its Reform*. Edited by Elizabeth Harding, Tom Bodenheimer, and Steve Cummings. San Franciso: Bay Area Chapter of the Medical Committee for Human Rights, 1972, pp. 107–116.

The Promise – Critical Description of the Bill

The Health Security Act of 1971 (S.3 and H.R. 22) was introduced into Congress in January, 1971, backed by the AFL-CIO, the UAW, and the labor-dominated Committee on National Health Insurance. Its chief sponsors are Senator Edward Kennedy, Congresswoman Martha Griffiths and Congressman James Corman. The Health Security Act (called in this paper by its popular name, the Kennedy bill) would insure all residents of the United States for personal health care through a federally administered system. Money would come from social security and federal taxes. The money would be paid to private doctors, hospitals, group practices, and other health care providers. Three would be financial incentives for developing group practices, called comprehensive health service organizations, referred to here as HMOs because of their similarity to Nixon's HMOs. In March, 1972, Senator Kennedy introduced a related health bill, S.3327, that specifically addresses the creation of HMOs. Except where S. 3327 is cited, this chapter pertains to the Health Security Act.

Who would be served? All residents of the United States would be insured for health services covered by the bill. Non-residents and visitors would be covered only if arrangements were made with their governments. Some countries, such as England and the Soviet Union, give free health care to all non-residents and visitors without making special arrangements. The Kennedy bill can be criticized for not doing the same.

What Services Would be Provided? Covered services would include unlimited hospital, physician, optometrist and podiatrist care; home health care; X-rays and laboratory tests; emergency services; limited nursing home and psychiatric care; dental care for people up to the age of 15 (in future years up to 25); specially needed transportation; limited drugs and appliances; and supportive services such as health education, physical therapy and social work when provided by an HMO or hospital.

An estimated 30% of personal health services would not be covered under the Kennedy bill.[1] This 30% (for certain drugs, dental care for adults, and some psychiatric and nursing home care, etc.) would place a heavier—sometimes prohibitive—burden of payment on low income people and, in that way, would tend to perpetuate a two class system of care.

Who would pay and how? There would be no out-of-pocket or insurance premium payments for covered services. Instead, the system would be financed nationally, through a new Health Security Trust Fund, one half of the money coming from federal general revenues (derived from taxes) and the other half from social security payments. Employers would pay a 3.5% social security payroll tax on wages and salaries of their employees up to $15,000 per year, and employees would pay 1% of income up to $15,000. The self-employed would pay 2.5% up to $15,000.

The regressive nature of social security taxes and loopholes in the income tax structure would force working people to pay for most of the enormously expensive health care system, even though out-of-pocket and premium expenses would be eliminated. A person making $15,000 per year would pay the same number of dollars in new social security taxes as a person making $150,000; and a person making $7,000 per year would pay a greater percentage of her income than someone earning $17,000. A millionaire who avoids paying income taxes wouuld actually be subsidized for her health care by others. The 3.5% social security tax paid by employers would be passed on to workers and consumers in the form of lower wages and higher prices.

Who would be paid, how, and how much would it cost to pay them? Any qualified provider (a physician, hospital, HMO or other provider) would be paid from the Health Security Trust Fund. In order to qualify, an HMO would have to be nonprofit, but it could contract with profit-making organizations or individuals to provide some of its services. Thus, laboratories, individual practitioners, groups of practitioners, some hospitals, drug manufacturers, medical suppliers, and others would be permitted to make profits from health security payments.

Doctors could choose to remain independent and be paid directly, or they could choose to join HMOs. Funds would be limited, however, and priority in payment would be given first to physicians practicing in HMOs, then physicians in medical foundations, and last to physicians choosing fee-for-service payment.

Payment to HMOs and medical foundations would be made by capitation and these organizations would be permitted to reimburse their physicians on any basis they wish (salary, fee-for-service or other). Medical foundations and private practitioners would be permitted to use private fiscal intermediaries (such as Blue Cross) to handle payments. Although supporters of the Kennedy bill launch strong attacks against the private health insurance industry, this provision in their bill would allow private insurance to play a part. The presence of the unnecessary intermediary would increase administrative waste and profit making and decrease public accountability.

The government would reward an HMO or foundation for keeping its patients' hospitalization and other expensive care below average by paying it 75% of the money that the government saves as a result. This is a potentially extremely profitable boondoggle for the HMO, that would undoubtedly encourage the development of HMOs and at the same time intensify profit incentives in the health care industry to the disadvantage of the patient. The capitation payment system, combined with this special low utilization incentive, would encourage providers to give as little patient care as possible in order to make more money.

The Kennedy bill would also allow fee-for-service payment to continue, with its well known incentives to give expensive care and to overcharge the patient. Physicians, whether paid by fee-for-service or salary, are promised by Kennedy bill supporters that they would receive incomes "equivalent to what they now receive."[2] Thus, the Kennedy bill has a firm base in the profit motive. Whether a provider receives capitation or fee-for-service, there would be an incentive to distort health care.

One additional criticism of the Kennedy bill's financing mechanism is that the entire budget could be spent before the end of the fiscal year. This would undoubtedly lead to cutbacks in services or the introduction of out-of-pocket fees or both. The result would be a much more limited and inaccessible delivery system than that contemplated in the bill.

Who would control the health care system and how would they do it? The program would be administered by a new five-member Health Security Board in the Department of Health, Education and Welfare. The members of the board would be appointed by the President, with Senate approval. The Health Security Board would be responsible for administering the program, including making payments to providers. Administration would be carried out by the 10 existing HEW regions and 100 new health services areas within the regions.

This extremely centralized system of control would concentrate tremendous power in the hands of a few Presidential appointees. Local and regional bodies would have power only to the extent allowed by the Health Security Board.

A 21 member National Health Security Advisory Council, with a majority of consumer representatives, would advise the Health Security Board. The chairwoman of the Health Security Board would also chair the Advisory Council. The other 20 Advisory council members would be appointed by the Secretary of HEW. The Health Security Board would appoint local and regional advisory boards with a majority of consumer representatives.

Flash! Kennedy Softens

As a result of stiff resistance from insurance interests and "discussions" with Congressman Wilbur Mills (the key chairman of the House Ways and Means Committee), Senator Kennedy is abandoning even his rhetorical opposition to private insurance companies playing a large part in the health system. It appears that Mills and Kennedy will offer a legislative proposal in 1973 that will allow private companies to maintain an important share of their profitable hold on health care financing.

To quote a recent interview with Senator Kennedy in *Business Week* (June 24, 1972): "Q. Do you see any place for private insurance companies? A. Under S 3, the function of the insurance companies will be actuarial. There may very well be a role for liability insurance — for the patient in the hospital — which is one of the most lucrative parts of the business. . . I'd be reluctant to accept a tightly regulated private system, but it's at least a realistic alternative."

It is clear that the power of the insurance industry will make it politically expedient for even the most liberal legislative reformers to give private companies a "lucrative" place in their future health care plans.

No policy making role is given to consumers or health workers in the Kennedy bill. Consumers would play an advisory role only, and even then would be appointed from above rather than democratically chosen by other consumers. There is no guarantee that either policy makers or consumer advisors would represent the ethnic, economic, age, sex or geographic distribution of the populations served. To make matters worse, the chairwoman of the national advisory council would be the top appointee on the Health Security Board.

Decision-making by health workers, who are most intimately involved in the daily workings of the health care delivery system, is not even mentioned in the bill. "Providers" are mentioned, but it can be safely assumed that providers who sit on the Health Security Board and advisory councils will be doctors and administrators and will not be representative of health care workers as a whole. Health workers must be included on the councils controlling health institutions. If health workers are given the responsibility of sharing in decision making, they will care more about the institution in which they work and will be likely to do a better job for the patient. No longer will they be working for a boss; instead, they will be working for the patients, the community and themselves. The complete neglect of health workers in the decision making apparatus of the Health Security system constitutes a major weakness of the Kennedy bill.

As a result of criticism that the Kennedy bill received for its failure to give real power to consumers, Senator Kennedy introduced his HMO bill (S.3327), giving preference in federal financing to HMOs with a majority of consumers on the governing board. However, there is still no provision for democratic selection or representativeness of consumers. Even if both bills passed, consumers would be excluded from real power in the system as a whole.

An analogy can be made between an institution's response to innovation and an organism's response to a foreign body: the intruder either (1) is kept out altogether, or (2) if it enters, is isolated from the rest of the system. Consumer and worker control is such a foreign body to the health care system, and is treated as such, even in the liberal Kennedy bill.[3]

What Provisions are made for improving Quality of Care? The Health Security Board would set national standards that providers would have to meet before they could receive payment under the plan. It would also set national licensing standards for health workers. Continuing education would be required for physicians. Hospitals, nursing homes, home care agencies and HMOs would have to meet national standards in order to participate. The board would have power to terminate participation of providers who fail to meet the standards or requirements.

It has been the experience of people working in free clinics that open discussion and criticism among doctors, other health care workers and patients is the best way to assure high quality care. This process requires extensive sharing of medical knowledge among health workers and patients. Prerequisite to this kind of quality control process is control of health institutions by consumers and health workers (including professionals). The Kennedy bill sets national standards (which is a good start), but institutes no strong local quality controls. S. 3327 would make stronger provisions for quality control, but still does not assure good mechanisms for monitoring quality during the process of delivering care.

How would the delivery system be changed? The creation and initial operation of HMOs would be encouraged. This effort would tend to restructure the delivery system away from isolated solo practitioners, toward large prepaid health care organizations similar to Kaiser or the Health Insurance Plan (HIP) of Greater New York. There would be no limit on the size of HMOs and no requirement that they be located within easy traveling distance of their enrollees. HMOs under the Kennedy plan, as under the Nixon plan, could be large, impersonal organizations so efficiency-conscious that they neglect or rush the patient to the greatest extent possible.

A portion of the Health Security Trust Fund (The Resource Development Fund) would be used to restructure the health care system through nationwide health planning; alleviating shortages of personnel and facilities; developing HMOs; establishing links between hospitals, doctors and other providers; and recruiting poor and minority people for training in health care occupations.

$600 million would be allocated for this purpose during two years before Health Security benefits go into effect, and up to 5% of the fund would be allocated for resource development thereafter.

These funds are inadequate for making the needed changes in the health care system. The Public Health Service has estimated that the health worker shortage approximates half a million, including 50,000 doctors. National health insurance will increase demand for services, thus worsening the shortage. The training of these additional health workers might cost $15 billion above present health training expenditures (assuming $100,000 to produce a doctor and $20,000 on the average to train each non-physician). Kennedy's Resource Development Fund, which has many functions in addition to health worker training, is far too small.

The bill fails to state how certain desired changes in the health care system could be accomplished. How would the Health Security Board succeed in getting providers of all kinds to make linkages with each other in order to provide continuous care? What kinds of linkages would they make? Even if they did make numerous linkages, what reason is there to believe that the sum total would be a coordinated, accessible system of health care? There is no definite plan for an integrated, regionalized network of health centers and hospitals across the country. The Health Security Board would no doubt make changes here and there, but the system as a whole would remain a disorganized array of individuals and institutions, concentrated heavily in some areas and greatly lacking in others.

Why the Promise Cannot Be Kept — A Discussion

We have described the Kennedy-labor bill for national health insurance and have made criticisms along the way. How important are the criticisms, and what do they add up to?

The Kennedy bill promises comprehensive health care to everyone, free of direct charges, and it promises to be responsive to those who are served by the system. These things cannot be achieved under the Kennedy bill as it now stands for three main reasons: (1) the program would become too expensive for the sources of money available; (2) health care institutions would be controlled by providers who tend to act out of financial and political self-interest, rather than by consumers and health workers acting in their collective interest; and (3) the system as a whole is structured in such a way as to be controlled by those who already have money and power. A discussion of these points follows.

It would become too expensive for those who would have to support it. Why would the system become too expensive? First, the causes of many of the exorbitant expenses presently existing in the health care system would remain. These include profits for drug and supply companies, high incomes for doctors, extremely steep rates for hospital beds, and unnecessary administrative costs of private health insurers used as fiscal intermediaries by some physicians. With profit incentives, monopolies and shortages of services remaining in health care, the inflationary cycle would continue and health care would become more and more expensive.

The second reason why too little money would be available is that major sources of money in the country would not be tapped. Working people would pay for the health care system and the rich would be spared. Were the rich adequately taxed, an initial $50 billion per year in additional funds could be devoted to health care.

If the Kennedy bill passes without simultaneous, basic changes in the profit system and the tax structure, it will probably follow a course similar to that of Medicare. Medicare poured money into the existing health power structure. The immediate result was a considerable lessening of the financial burden for the elderly and enormous profit-making by doctors, nursing homes and others. The resultant severe inflation made care less accessible for everyone else in society. As the years go by, Medicare premiums and deductibles increase, ambulatory care is still fragmented and hard to find, chronic disease care is a national scandal, and the elderly pay more and more each year for their care.

Many will argue that the Kennedy bill is fundamentally different from Medicare and therefore cannot precipitate the same kind of crisis. They will note, for example, that Medicare was prohibited from interfering with the delivery of health care while the Kennedy bill *intends* to interfere by regulating certain costs and restructuring the system. Although this is true, there are even more fundamental similarities between Medicare and the Kennedy bill that justify a comparison.

What are the inherent contradictions in Medicare that have led to its unhappy state? First, Medicare money is extracted from the working classes in social security payments and income taxes. This is also true of the Kennedy bill. Because it does not tap the wealth of the rich, Medicare is limited in its revenues and cannot meet the costs of inflation without increasing out-of-pocket expenses. Second, Medicare pumped money through the profit-oriented system. The result was high profits and prices with little improvement in care. As we have shown, the Kennedy bill would also pump money through the profit-oriented system, though in a somewhat different manner. Even HMOs could turn out to be just as inflationary as fee-for-service medicine. Chances are that the results under Health Security would parallel those under Medicare and Medicaid—patients would begin to pay deductibles that increase each year, services would be cut, and people would generally pay more money for the same or fewer services.

Two changes are needed in the financing mechanism of the Kennedy bill in order for the plan to work. First, profit making must be excluded from the health care system. Second, the wealth of the rich must be taxed. If these two changes were made, the program would be unlikely to run out of money before the end of the year; services would not be cut and enough money would be available to train needed health workers and to build needed facilities.

It can be argued that there is one way in which the Kennedy bill could work without changing the profit and taxation systems: a reordering of national priorities away from war and toward health. Vast sums are now being poured into the defense industry which could conceivably be poured into the health care industry, thus making unnecessary basic changes in the profit system or the tax structure.

However, widespread conversion to peacetime industry is probably not possible in the present American economy.[4] The inherent structure of monopoly capitalism produces higher profits in the production of heavy machinery for waste (planes and tanks destroyed in war are the best example) than in the production of services such as health care. If more profits are made from war than from health, then the economy might decline upon conversion from defense to health spending. Without a change in the entire economy, unemployment could increase and an economic depression could ensue. The conclusion is that until monopoly capitalism is changed to another economic system, defense spending will probably not decrease markedly.

Control of health institutions would be in the wrong hands. Even if the Health Security system could somehow be adequately financed, it could not achieve what the bill promises because providers remain in control. Proponents of the bill speak of consumer participation and responsiveness to the health needs of the people, yet the bill places control solidly in the hands of providers and appointed officials. Health Security proponents also speak of the need for technical expertise and health care experience in policy making, yet many categories of highly skilled health care workers are completely excluded from decision making in the Health Security system. The question of control is closely related to the previous question of financing, for the chief providers, who would remain in control, also benefit from the profit structure. This cannot help but have a strong influence on the delivery of health care.

Here it may be objected that many HMOs will actually be consumer controlled, removing power from the hands of doctors, businessmen and managers and putting it in the hands of the people. While this is an admirable ideal (and one that should be fought for) there are several reasons to believe that such a substantial power shift would not occur under the Health Security system.

First, consumers and workers are at a disadvantage in applying for HMO grants because they are less organized than provider groups such as medical societies and hospitals, and they have fewer grantsmanship skills. As a result, HMO grants will continue to go mainly to provider groups even if the government had a general policy of consumer preference.

Second, even in a consumer-controlled HMO, the consumers who constitute a majority of the board may not be representative of the community or enrollee group. They could be all rich white males, even if the HMO is serving mostly poor people, minority people or women. In such a case, the domination of the society by a wealthy elite would continue to be reflected in the health system, though now under the banner of consumer control.

Third, even assuming a majority of consumers who reflect the enrollee composition, providers may still hold the reins. This will be true especially if the consumers are chosen by the providers rather than democratically selected by other consumers. Also, if health workers are not included in policy-making, top providers may be able to play consumers and workers off against each other, thereby defeating the purpose and potential impact of consumer control. This is particularly easy to do in health care because of the mystical powers that are falsely ascribed to doctors, and the resulting feelings of ignorance and inadequacy on the part of many consumers. This mystification could be decreased by participation of health workers (including doctors) along with consumers in the governance structure of community health institutions.

Local consumer-health worker control would be severely limited unless control of the system as a whole changes. An HMO governed by an active, representative consumer-health worker board may still fail in the goal of providing good, responsive health care in a comprehensive way if it is an isolated case trying to survive in a sea of competitive, provider-dominated, money-oriented health care institutions and funding agencies.

A community board, for example, might wish to hire four doctors at $10,000 salary rather than one doctor at $40,000, thereby offering more health care for the same budget. However, this would be almost impossible as long as other institutions continued to pay high physician salaries.

If the board of a community HMO wanted to offer chiropractic, Yoga, or even food as part of its health maintenance program, its hands might be tied as long as the funding or lending agency holding the purse strings remained dominated by providers. In a world of large, provider organizations and a centralized, undemocratic national administration—the kind of world toward which the health care system would move under the Kennedy bill — a few people-oriented, people-controlled institutions would have extremely limited power and autonomy.* The entire health care system must be made non-profit and consumer-health worker controlled in order to assure responsiveness to community needs and complete health care for everyone.

Conclusion

The Kennedy bill makes many promises to the American health consumer. And if it passes, the Kennedy bill will provide somewhat more accessible health care for more people.

But the bill will be incapable of keeping its promise of delivering free, complete health care in a responsive way to all. Its financing mechanism, which taxes working people heavily without taxing the rich adequately, would generate grossly insufficient funds. And its system of control would solidify the practice of unaccountable providers and bureaucrats calling the shots while the consumers and workers face the consequences.

The Kennedy bill promises to everyone a pie in every sky. The bill demonstrates a fundamental fallacy of liberalism: that social problems can be solved without hurting those in control. This belief is untrue. In order to achieve good health care for everyone, the rich and the corporations must begin to pay for and must cease to control health care. Only a health care plan that attacks the fundamental issues of financing and control will be credible to masses of consumers and health workers.

References

1. Battistella, R. "National Health Insurance: An Examination of Leading Proposals in the Light of Contemporary Policy Issues" *Inquiry* June 1971.

---

* This does not mean that communities should not try to establish such institutions. Repeated attempts to do so are a first step in changing the health care system as a whole.

2. "The Physician and Health Security" printed by the Committee for National Health Insurance.
3. Kaufman, J. unpublished paper.
4. Christoffel, T. *et al. Up Against the American Myth* (Holt, Rinehart and Winston), p. 73.

Chapter 8

TAXATION

Implicit in the issue of taxation is the larger issue of the role of government. For taxes are essentially the means to provide government with the resources to carry out its policies and programs. Most debates about taxation are really arguments about the scope and direction of government activities.

Conservatives are of two minds about government. On the one hand they desire a strong government and military to protect the security of the United States. On the other hand, they are opposed to the growth of government interference in domestic affairs. They fear that the growth of the state will reduce individual initiative and restrict individual freedom of action especially in the economic sphere. Conservative tax policy proceeds from these two premises. Conservatives favor increased military spending and support larger budgets for police forces. At the same time they wish to reduce taxes on the well-to-do so that their incentive to achieve economically will be increased. Conservatives generally favor sales taxes, which, they hold, will affect the entire population equally, and are opposed to progressive income taxes, which tax the well-to-do at a high rate.

Liberals also share two perspectives on government. On the one hand they favor an increase in government activity to provide solutions to social problems. Government is expected to provide such social services as job training for the unemployed, day care centers for children, and programs for the elderly. Government agencies are also required to monitor the conduct of industry. Regulatory agencies such as the Food and Drug Administration check products for health and safety hazards. When a public good must be achieved or when a countervailing power is required to balance the growing exercise of private power, a new government agency is called for. Yet liberals are also fearful that government agencies may interfere with the exercise of basic rights. Liberals oppose the extension of the power of agencies such as the FBI and the CIA. They oppose government interference with the right to privacy through bugging telephone conversations or opening the mails.

Some liberals agree with conservatives that a large military establishment is required to protect the United States from imminent foreign dangers. They believe that increased military expenditures can be combined with large domestic expenditures and that a growing economy can afford both. Other liberals believe that the military has grown beyond our actual requirements for protection. They are concerned that military expenditures will reduce funds required for pressing domestic needs. These liberals would reorder national priorities to de-emphasize the military.

Liberals believe that taxation should be fairly shared. They favor tax reform measures that would eliminate loopholes used by the rich and corporations to avoid their fair share of taxation. Liberals oppose emphasis on regressive taxes such as sales taxes whose burdens, they argue, fall more heavily on the poor than the well-to-do. In general liberals recognize the need for relatively high taxes to provide the resources for a wide array of governmental activities. Although liberals often favor small tax cuts as an incentive to economic growth, they oppose large tax cuts, which would interfere with government carrying out a broad social program.

Socialists are opposed to state power in capitalist societies. They believe that the state is under the control of the upper class and acts in its interest to the detriment of the interest of the working class. However, in socialist societies many socialists would favor a strong state. Since the state under socialism is presumed to be under the control of the working class, it is expected to act on behalf of its interest. A strong state is therefore justified both to protect the working class against the return of capitalism and to carry out programs of economic development and social services in the interest of the entire society. Other socialists, often of anarchist persuasion, are concerned about the existence of a strong state in any society, capitalist or socialist. They argue that even under socialism the state tends to develop its own interests independent of the interests of the people. Government bureaucrats tend to become a privileged class that acts in its own interests. In their opposition to the strong state (though they differ in their view of what constitutes a good society), there is an area of agreement among segments of the left and of the right that any large centers of power are potentially dangerous.

Socialists view taxation under capitalism as a form of domination. The upper class uses tax policy to collect monies from the less well-to-do to fund government programs in its class interest. They also use their political power to see that tax codes are written to allow them to pass their wealth on to their children, insuring the continuity of their class. Nevertheless, tax policy represents a potential weapon against the upper class. High inheritance taxes and heavily progressive income taxes redistribute wealth. Under socialism, taxes can be used to insure that class divisions do not reappear. Socialists who believe in a strong state favor the necessary tax policies to support it. Other socialists, opposed to a strong state, are wary of heavy taxes even under a socialist government. They are fearful that government bureaucrats who control the expenditure of these taxes may constitute themselves as a new exploiting class.

In the conservative article, Orr evaluates the effects of Proposition 13, the tax cut amendment to the California constitution, from the perspective that the scope of government should be limited. Government should only provide essential services such as fire and police protection. It should eliminate non-essential services such as job training or environmental protection studies and charge more for others such as higher education or recreation facilities. The intent of Proposition 13 may be deflected. Instead of reducing non-essential services, government bureaucrats might cut essential services to blunt the movement for reduced taxes. Moreover, if local taxes and local level government are pared, the functions that are eliminated may be pushed upward to the state and federal governments. This would have the undesirable effect of increasing big government. Proposition 13 is an important symbolic victory. It represents the taxpayers' desire to limit government, but it may be an ineffective tool to accomplish that purpose. Orr suggests a constitutional limit on the size of government and level of governmental expenditures. Such measures to halt the growth of government bureaucracy could not be coopted.

In the liberal article, Lipset and Raab argue that the success of Proposition 13 does not mean that the public no longer believes that government should provide social welfare services. Proposition 13 was a reaction to inflated property values, the existence of a tax surplus, and a belief that revenue could be cut without any decline in services. Although there is an irreversible public commitment to government programs to help the poor, there is substantial disagreement about the form which they should take. Many Americans would like to see welfare programs replaced by programs that provide jobs for the poor. While most Americans desire a socially protective government, they do not desire a large government. Lipset and Raab pose the question of whether these two apparently opposed goals are evidence of an emerging contradiction between liberal ideology and conservative practice or the basis of a future synthesis between the two.

In the socialist article, O'Connor agrees with Lipset and Raab that a tax revolt does not necessarily represent a swing to the right. Taxes are a class issue. Most taxes are inequitable levies by the ruling class on the working class. Tax exploitation is justified by arguments that if the rich pay less, everyone will ultimately benefit. Income and corporate taxes are systematically skewed to advantage the rich. More government expenditures are provided on their behalf than for the working class or the poor. There is a growing, yet inchoate revolt against taxation inequalities. If taxes were limited, the gap between revenues and expenditures would result in a fiscal crisis that could threaten the structure of monopoly capitalism. It is the task of the left to expose unfair taxes and demand that the tax burden be shifted to business. The struggle against regressive taxation must be linked to opposition to the issues of military spending and imperialism. Opposition to big government is an important issue for the left since most government programs support the expansion of corporate capitalism. A class conscious tax revolt could be an effective weapon for radical social change.

Conservative

Daniel Orr: Proposition 13: Tax Reform's Lexington Bridge?

The overwhelming acclaim given to the Jarvis-Gann initiative, which permanently cuts real estate taxes through an amendment to the California constitution, has excited much comment and speculation among quick-answer analysts. In the left-vs-right scheme of things, there is despair that Proposition Thirteen is a massive repudiation of responsibility toward society's downtrodden (especially the young and the black) on the part of the selfish propertied, or there is ecstasy that at last the voracious termites who devour the American edifice are getting a first whiff of chlordane. Those with a cost-benefit orientation have asked whether Thirteen is a good way to achieve low taxes: the possibility exists that essential public services will be interrupted, and the hardship, confusion and turmoil will be great. The Machiavellians have suggested that the government establishment, in hope of securing an early repeal, will punish the voters and subvert the intent of Thirteen by deliberately focusing most of the spending reductions in areas where the harm therefrom is greatest. There is also speculation as to why Thirteen succeeded so overwhelmingly: is it a harbinger of strong public disaffection toward big government and a first step away from continued government growth, or it is simply a peculiar and isolated response to a too-rapid increase in one particular tax?

Most of these questions can in some degree be illuminated by an analysis of the effects of tax reform on the interests of private individuals, politicians and bureaucrats. Such an analysis predicts not only the ways that Thirteen will be digested within California during the coming months, it also suggests where and how further efforts to cut the size and importance of government will occur and the kinds of responses that those who oppose such cuts will offer. Where it all ends up—perhaps as a first step in a major move to limit the scope of government—will depend almost entirely on the effectiveness that tax reformers have in selling further necessary changes to the voting public, compared to the job of undermining, neutralizing or co-opting those changes that is done by those who oppose a diminished role for government.

If we examine what Proposition Thirteen does, we quickly see that it will not be easy to extend it outside of California. California has a peculiar institution, the

Policy Review (Fall 1978), a quarterly journal of the Heritage Foundation, 513 C. Street, N.E., Washington, D. C. 20002. Reprinted by permission.

constitutional initiative, whereby voters can directly amend the state constitution through a simple majority vote, once an amendment has been placed on the election ballot by a petition with a required number of signatures. Proposition Thirteen is such an amendment. It stipulates four important things about real estate tax assessments and real estate rates. Real estate in California is assessed by elected assessors who, prior to Thirteen, regularly updated these recorded values on the basis of prices paid for comparable properties. Thirteen provides, first, that a real estate parcel shall be currently reassessed at its fiscal 1975 level unless it has changed ownership since January 1, 1976, in which case the most recent price paid is the basis of assessment. Second, the assessed value of a parcel can rise no more than two percent per year, unless the parcel changes ownership. Third, the maximum real estate tax that can be collected is one percent of the assessed value; and fourth, a two-thirds majority of both houses of the legislature is necessary in order to change these rules of taxation.

Again, features peculiar to California enter into those provisions. Assessors are elected. They operate openly, according to specific rules and are remarkably free from corruption. There is a high degree of uniformity in the assessment of different parcels. All of this has contributed to a focus of anger against the tax laws rather than against the assessors. And California real estate, above almost everywhere else in the nation, has been the object of vast appreciation in market value. During 1974-78, it was not unusual for a residential property to triple in market value in many of the larger cities of the state. This appreciation is a response to general inflation: construction labor and material costs have increased, and speculators seeking to protect the purchasing power of their wealth have looked upon California real estate as a good inflation hedge.

In California it is common that certain locally-based and locally-funded welfare programs are paid out of property tax revenues. In addition, there is widespread public concern in some urban school districts (including Los Angeles and San Diego, the two largest in the state) about the use of school revenues to pay for extensive programs of pupil transportation to achieve racial balance in individual schools. Thus, the rapid escalation in property taxes was not accompanied by any increase in the quantity or quality of property-related services, and in fact the taxes were seen by some voters as being used for purposes which are socially non-productive or even harmful.

Finally, there had been a good amount of publicity given to the fact that the State of California was enjoying a very significant budgetary surplus. Due in part to the effects of inflation on personal incomes and the sharply progressive structure of the California state income tax, revenue collections by the state were outrunning expenditures to such a degree that Governor Brown was contemplating buying the state its very own communications satellite (a program that would have been budgeted at a level near $5 billion).

The interaction of all of these factors in one time and one state assured the success of Thirteen. There was a mechanism to change the law which bypassed the potentially subversive processes of representative democracy. There was a tax on which to focus, which imposed a large, rapidly growing and highly visible burden on numerous voters,[1] and which conveyed benefits about which many

---

1. The importance of the *visibility* of the property tax to successful revolt is pointed out in James Buchanan's "The Simple Analytics of Proposition 13" (Center for Study of Public Choice, VPI, Blacksburg, Va., unpublished).

voters felt doubtful or toward which they felt hostile. There was a general perception of glut in the government sector. In short, the ingredients are a mirror image of what is usually found when a program involving new or higher taxes is successfully *imposed* (voter isolation from the decision process, highly concentrated benefits to a group of active supporters, diffusion of costs over a broad base of taxpayers).

The Effects of Proposition Thirteen

The immediate consequences of Thirteen in California will be relatively trivial. Property taxes will be lower for everyone and much lower for property owners whose holdings antedate January 1, 1976. There will be a temporary disruption of some public services (a subject we will examine in more detail shortly). The real estate game will be changed in important ways: the widespread and popular practice of "trading up"—using the price appreciation in this house to make a down payment on that larger house—will in some degree be defeated due to the assessment increases which follow on trade. These consequences all are distributive. Windfall gains are scattered among all property owners and in part are offset by higher income taxes due to lower income tax deductions. To the extent that the "business climate" is improved and incomes increase, the level of public services can be maintained without the imposition of any additional taxes, if some mechanism is found for using those higher state income taxes to pay for services previously provided out of the property tax.

In fact, the transfer of tax revenues from the local level to the state and federal levels is the most ominous and potentially the most significant effect of Thirteen. There may be an accompanying change in the balance of power and responsibility among different levels of government, which can have extremely important consequences.

The foregoing analysis identifies several features which contributed to the success of Thirteen. That analysis illuminates the issue of whether Thirteen is an excessively cumbersome tool with which to trim government fat (as was eloquently contended by Walter Heller in the *Wall Street Journal* on June 2). We have a number of examples in recent years (dating back to the Hoover Commissions and the efforts of Senator Paul Douglas in the late 1940s and 1950s) to eliminate specific ineffective government programs by selective withdrawal of their funding. That approach has seldom been successful: scalpels cannot seem to penetrate the blubber. On the other hand, we have seen that bureaucracies can continue to function while accommodating themselves to draconian across-the-board slashes in their funding (many public universities in the late 1960s offer instructive examples). Thus, the claim that Proposition Thirteen was a heedless, hasty and heavy-handed substitute for careful and judicious trimming is almost totally without merit: that latter choice simply does not exist, and the true alternative to Thirteen was business as usual.

What of the concern that bureaucrats and politicians will violate the intent of Thirteen or destroy its spirit by cutting back on services that the community deems essential, while preserving functions, offices or agencies that are peripheral or unnecessary? Will there be a confrontation in which public officials (elected or civil service) seek to demonstrate that the costs of Thirteen are very high, in an effort to start a popular movement for reversal or repeal?

Such concerns are not entirely without foundation. One problem with a sweeping and broad-based mandate like Thirteen is that the chief source of information on the costs and benefits of various government functions must be the bureaucracy itself. The bureaucracy has a strong interest in existing programs, and that interest may not coincide with taxpayer interest. For example, certain programs such as job training or environmental impact studies carry significant matching funds from the federal government. Every dollar budgeted at the local level carries an expenditure multiplier, and most of that expenditure is of benefit to the bureaucracy. It follows that the local-level bureaucrats, whose recommendations of areas for expenditure cutting will in the short run probably be highly influential, will have a strong incentive to favor such programs at the expense of activities more widely regarded as essential, such as fire and police protection. That fact, however, is not decisive. Politicians at the local level have a strong incentive to impose cutbacks in a way that will meet voter approval. There are many local governments affected by Thirteen and because interest will be high, press coverage of performance will enable comparisons to be drawn by voters between "our" politicians and "their" politicians. Whether or not elected officials directly control the budgets of their jurisdictions, they will be aware that if "essential services" are cut by more in their jurisdictions than elsewhere, vigorous political competition is likely to ensue. Those bureaucrats whose funding recommendations coincide most closely with voter preferences among governmental activities will be chosen to guide the allocation process and will benefit in personal power, status and income thereby. Because of the existence of many similar local jurisdictions and the opportunities for comparison among them, the danger is minimized that a serious effort will be made to subvert Thirteen by the imposition of excessive service reductions. Thus, it appears that everyone, including politicians and other beneficiaries of large government, will stand to gain by appearing to seek "reform" in the spirit of Proposition Thirteen.

Will Proposition Thirteen Result in Lower Taxes?

But, while it may not be possible or feasible to overthrow Thirteen by keeping bad programs and reducing good ones, there is a danger that wolves will dress as sheep, and those who hope that Thirteen augurs smaller government and lower taxes will be defeated by a more subtle and devious approach.

When it became clear that Thirteen was a resounding success, Governor Brown immediately jumped on the bandwagon. His first public act was to state that he took the mandate seriously and would work toward reform. Governor Brown is a clever man and a Democrat, and the likelihood that he will lead a serious movement to diminish the scope of government is nil. What, then, can he be up to? There are several ways that Thirteen's success can be turned to his advantage and can be made to work toward greater power for the Governor's office and for him personally. As we noted, the immediate consequence of Thirteen is to diminish the revenue-collecting potential of counties and municipalities. The revenue-generating potential of the state is, by contrast, enhanced, due to the greater taxable income and purchasing power that Thirteen leaves in private hands. This change can be used to induce greater state control of programs which previously had been controlled at the local level. It is possible to imagine a simple transfer of revenues, no strings attached, from the state treasury to the local authorities, as a means of offsetting the fiscal impact of Thirteen. But that will not happen. It will be proclaimed necessary to husband state financial resources and to exercise control over the way they are used. It will be pointed out that the size of the total tax take has shrunk, and therefore tax dollars must be stretched farther to do more. These points all will be true, at least temporarily, and their consequences will be that state bureaucracy will expand, but by less than all local bureaucracies combined contract; and substantial new powers will be vested in state government. Such a move is, of course, inimical to the frequently-voiced goal of increasing the importance of political decision-making at the local level. Competition and diversity among counties and municipalities will decline.

But what happens if taxes which are levied at the state level also come under tax-revolt scrutiny? The only state tax in California which has the attributes of burdensomeness and visibility, and hence the most logical candidate for drastic cutting, is the state personal income tax (which is one of the nation's highest, operating at a rate of eleven percent on incomes above $31,000 for married couples). California has other sources of revenue, however. The state sales tax, currently six percent on all items except food purchased for home consumption, labor services and prescription medicines, can no doubt be extended to those uncovered items and raised a notch or two. An increase in state taxes on all types of fuels could probably find support on environmental grounds. In addition, there might be considerable popular support for pricing some of the more selectively used state services, such as the state park system and the extensive state-supported system of higher education, at rates much closer to the marginal cost of use, thereby cutting down on the state's tax subsidy of these activities.

Could a constitutional amendment directed at the state income tax be successful? Almost certainly it could, under the California initiative system. The consequences, paradoxically, might be greater investment, more employment, higher *per capita* disposable income and reduced *per capita* consumption of state-provided services in California. Should that eventuate, recourse to increases in other taxes would be less necessary. But even if the tax revolt carries forward to a point that revenue-generating capabililty at the state level of government is seriously impaired, and even if the revolt spreads among all fifty states, the task confronting the advocates of small government has only begun to surface. For the federal government has shown itself to be favorably disposed toward the idea of revenue sharing with the states, and the taxing power of the federal government at present completely defies revolt.

At the federal level, tax reduction measures directed at specific individual taxes can readily be accommodated, as the record of the past fifteen years suggests. Beginning in 1963, with the Kennedy tax cut, income tax rates have fluctuated considerably, but overall the rates are considerably lower than they were in 1962. Accompanying these rate reductions have been offsetting movements which have tended to increase individual tax payments and government control of spendable revenue. First, and most important, inflation has increased taxable incomes and moved individuals up into higher income tax brackets. (The processes which cause inflation also have served directly to increase the federal government's purchasing power.) Second, certain federal taxes, conspicuously including the capital gains tax, have increased dramatically. The general tax cuts have been motivated by the Keynesian theory of effective demand and the importance of expenditure, and the capital gains tax increases have been motivated by soak-the-rich egalitarian sentiments. Both changes illustrate a rather ominous proposition: federal tax policy can blow with any political wind. The federal government is in no formal way constrained in terms of the amounts that it collects, spends, or redistributes. Only political assessment of the voter tolerance of deficits constrains the government in power, and the experience of recent years suggests that the "myth" of budget balance is increasingly less persuasive to voters.

The federal government's first mighty weapon with which to defeat tax reform, then, is inflation. Possession of that weapon stems from its monopoly over the printing of money.

Promiscuous reliance on inflation to fund government programs, however, carries its own dangers. Voters may never truly learn that *only* the monetary authority has the ultimate power to affect price levels, but high and persistent rates of inflation may nonetheless elicit meat-ax voter responses against the political establishment. The federal government possesses a second and almost equally potent weapon with which to generate the revenues which will sustain government growth, namely, the value-added tax. This is a type of tax which heretofore has never been important in the United States. It is collected from businesses and its basis is the total sales of the business, less purchases from other businesses. The total taxes paid at different levels of manufacture are hidden in the prices of goods brought by consumers, even much more so than a sales tax would be were it quoted directly as a part of the price of a purchased article, because many different manufacturers may be involved. European countries which have relied heavily on the VAT have been able to keep income taxes at fairly modest levels compared to the U.S.—France, Switzerland[2] and Germany, for example, all have lower income tax rates than does the U.S., but bar higher goods prices due to VAT. But in the U.S. the VAT appears to be strictly a federal-level tool. Use of the VAT at the state level would be extremely difficult due to the competition among states to attract new industry. An attempt on the part of California to institute a VAT would no doubt lead such "anti-progressive" states as Texas or Tennessee to advertise a more favorable tax climate, thereby stultifying California's growth—and tax base.

The Bureaucrats' Counter-Revolution

Apparently, then, it is child's play to parry or co-opt the Jarvis-Gann spirit of tax revolt. The strategy comprises two parts: (1) transferring the responsibility of funding "essential" government expenditures to more central, more powerful, and more distant levels of government; and (2) instituting less visible forms of taxes from which to make those expenditures. The whole operation must of course be accompanied by a heavy barrage of rhetoric on the efficiency gains that will be realized by a more centralized provision of services: predictably, many rhapsodies are soon to be written on how wonderful it is to eliminate costly duplication.

This all means that proponents of smaller government will have to work very hard to sell their ideas. The nation's electorate has recently not been receptive to abstract arguments based on the general principle that government is too large. Rather, government has grown because the electorate has always seemed to be

---

2. Switzerland uses a turnover tax, a sales tax charged at every stage of manufacture. The VAT is ubiquitous in the Common Market.

responsive to a "problems and solutions" approach: a problem is pointed out, and some solution or other, usually governmentally implemented, is proposed.

The appeal and success of the "problems and solutions" approach hangs on the creation of two strongly interested groups of sufficient size to assure adequate political support: a beneficiary group which stands to gain from a solution of the problem, and a group of bureaucrats and entrepreneurs who will be actively involved in implementation of the proposed solution, and whose wealth and power will thereby be enhanced. Success also depends on devising the proposed solution in such a way that no group of significant size is sufficiently harmed by it to offer serious opposition. It appears difficult, in prospect, to use this approach to reduce the size and scope of government. Can the idea be sold that the size of government is in itself a problem? Many self-interested groups, small and large, will converge in opposition to that idea, and those who still view government as the protector of the poor and oppressed will see it as an attempt to reinstitute slavery and illiteracy. Can individual programs be eliminated one by one on cost-benefit grounds? As we noted earlier, that approach has never succeeded, because of the diffusion of support and concentration of opposition.

A likely and unfortunate consequence of Proposition Thirteen-style tax reform, then, is a greater concentration of taxing and spending authority in the federal government, and a proliferation of new federal bureaus, scattered per-haps among the Departments of Treasury, HUD, HEW and Agriculture which are charged with allocating and monitoring the use of revenues which have been provided to the municipalities and countries. Certainly, Thirteen is not an agenda for full-scale reform. The net long-run impact on the individual taxpayer of all the adjustments and changes that Thirteen will induce will be higher taxes, less visible and hence less painful taxes, and a much larger federal interest in patterns of local expenditure.

As a specific agenda for tax reform, then, Proposition Thirteen is perverse. If a major objective of tax reform is to increase the efficiency of government spending (that is, to make it conform more closely to the preferences of taxpayers) then increased federal control is a big move in the wrong direction. If the objective is to make spending authorities more compliant in limiting the menu or portfolio of goods and services provided by government, the move again is in the wrong direction. People who are concerned about the growth of government (as Jarvis and Gann purport to be, and as many who voted for Proposition Thirteen proba-bly are) would do well to consider the possibility that their June 6 triumph may have set back the date when serious, meaningful fiscal reform of the federal government can take place.

It is my own reformer's perspective that in order to protect against the twin ravages of inflation and unlimited growth of government, we need a constitu-tional amendment which drastically reduces the scope of federal spending and regulating activity, accompanied by a constitutionally imposed formula requir-ing a federal budget which would, under conditions of full employment, yield a modest surplus in every year. (In a given year defined to be less than full employ-ment, a deficit is permissible; but the formula must show that if employment in that year were increased to the defined full employment level, the deficit would become a surplus.) If federal activities are to be constrained, it will be necessary to refer many necessary or desirable governmental functions back to the state and local levels. To the extent that Proposition Thirteen weakens the mecha-nisms of local government, that task is made more difficult.

The one enormously hopeful augury offered by Proposition Thirteen is that two-thirds of the voters in the nation's most populous state seized the chance to roll back taxes. This they did in the face of hysterical forecasts and threats of school and library closings, police and firefighter layoffs, garbage in the streets and on the beaches. The main task confronting tax reformers remains, however. It still must be shown that the reason those property taxes were too high and were growing too fast is to be found on Capitol Hill and that something can and must be done.

Liberal

Seymour Martin Lipset and Earl Raab: The Message of Proposition 13

The Jarvis-Gann Constitutional Amendment, limiting property taxes in California, has touched off speculation about a conservative backlash and the ascendance of a New Right in America. But analysis suggests that the trend exemplified by the "taxpayers' revolt" confounds the traditional political designations.

In 1946, according to Gallup, Americans who wanted taxes cut outnumbered those who did not by only four percentage points (48-44). By 1963, the gap was 44 percentage points (63-19). In 1969, 54 per cent of Americans told the Harris survey that they had "reached the breaking point" with respect to the amount of taxes they paid; that figure was up to 66 per cent by 1978.

Those who are unhappy use a simple consumer's measure: in so many words, only 23 per cent of the people queried by the Harris poll in 1971 thought they were getting their "money's worth from tax dollars." In this sentiment no more than two or three percentage points separated whites from blacks, Democrats from Republicans, or one income group from another. All felt put upon. In that same year, about 7 out of 10 told Harris that the time was coming when they "would sympathize with a taxpayers' revolt," involving a refusal to pay taxes— again with little difference in view related to whether they were white or black, and whether their income was around $5,000 or over $15,000.

The pressure has increased along with inflation. About one out of three Americans ranked inflation as their chief worry in 1977; in 1978, two out of three Americans did so. The "money's worth" was diminishing rapidly. In response, public officials uniformly promised tax reduction, but they did not deliver. Then the California property tax provided the dramatic breakthrough. California real-estate inflation had been brutal, often triple-digit over a few years' span. It was common for people who had bought a modest home for $20,000 to find themselves paying taxes ten years later on a home assessed at $90,000. No one was surprised to learn that the home of a Los Angeles man had been reappraised to $60,000 in 1977, and reappraised again in 1978 to $104,000, with a jump in taxes from a little over $2,000 to a little over $3,500. It became a hardship for many people to live in their own homes, and obviously there was no point in selling for the profit to buy other inflated houses at proportionally higher interest rates.

While these and other taxes were rising so much faster than income, the number of state and city employees was also increasing faster than the population. In the period 1970-75, the number of state and local employees rose by 21 per cent, while the state's population grew by only 6 per cent.

But the tipping point in the California situation was a sizable tax-generated surplus that public officials in Sacramento continued to sit on despite the growing tax lament from the public. Inflation pushes many taxpayers into higher brackets in all graduated-income-tax systems as their dollar earnings (although not their real earnings) go up. Under the Reagan administration, the California income tax had been made even more progressive than before, producing a visible and well-publicized $5.7 billion surplus by 1978. This was available for distribution, or to serve as the basis of a tax cut. But instead of proposing such remedies, Reagan's successor, Governor Jerry Brown, apparently preferred to hoard the surplus in order, according to some, to use it to advantage in his reelection year. As State Treasurer Jesse Unruh has pointed out, this enormous surplus constituted a standing public invitation to Proposition 13, the Jarvis-Gann Amendment. For this reason, Unruh has called Brown "the father of Proposition 13," although the Governor opposed the measure—with somewhat waning vigor as the polls showed increasing support for it. The polls were accurate: Proposition 13—which rolled back property taxes to 1 per cent of market value as of 1975, prohibited local taxes from rising more than 2 per cent a year, and put other checks on tax-raising—passed by nearly a two-to-one margin.

But while the surplus may have been idiosyncratic to California, it was, even for Californians, only the final straw. They were obviously using the occasion to express themselves on the matter of tax burdens in general. And indeed, this is how their vote was taken, by politicians in California and everywhere else, as well as by the American public. After the California vote, a New York *Times*/CBS News poll found that the whole country was jubilant. Again by a two-to-one margin (51-24), Americans said that they supported a similar measure for their own jurisdictions.

But if California's Proposition 13 was the messenger, what really was the message? To what extent do the taxpayers just want to keep their money, as against seeking their money's worth? What services are they willing to give up? What do they expect from government?

One stream of opinion on the subject was articulated by Senator George McGovern when he said that Californians had acted on a "degrading hedonism that tells them to ask what they can take from the needy." He also saw "undertones of racism" in Proposition 13. According to others who share this view, Proposition 13 is an expression of "mean-spiritedness" and the harbinger of the conservative and/or racist backlash which has allegedly been around the corner for the past dozen years.

There is no doubt that self-interest (which, however, is not necessarily the same thing as mean-spiritedness) was a factor in the Proposition 13 vote. A Los Angeles *Times*/CBS News election-day poll of those who voted revealed that 72 per cent of homeowners (who stood to gain) had opted for the measure as against

47 per cent of the renters (who had nothing to gain), while only 44 per cent of those with public employees in their family said they had backed the measure, as compared to 65 per cent of the total population.

What is noteworthy, however, is how many voters with an apparent interest in the defeat of Proposition 13 nevertheless went for it: 44 per cent of families of public employees, 47 per cent of renters, and 42 per cent of blacks. In these categories, the majority who voted opposed Proposition 13; but in every *economic* category, it was the other way around. Thus the measure was supported by 55 per cent of those with incomes under $8,000; 66 per cent of those in the $8-15,000 bracket; 67 per cent of those in the $15-25,000 class; and 61 per cent of those with incomes above $25,000.

A similarly mixed picture appears when we look at the vote in terms of ideological categories. As might have been expected, 82 per cent of self-designated "conservatives" voted for the measure. Yet here too what is noteworthy is the large number of self-described "moderates" (63 per cent) and "liberals" (45 per cent) who voted for it.

Clearly, then, the victory of Proposition 13 represents something more complex than a triumph of selfishness and/or old-line conservatism. In trying to understand what that something is, we might begin by noting that the evidence from a variety of opinion surveys reveals that a growing number of Americans, when asked to describe themselves politically, say that they are conservatives. In 1964, according to the New York *Times*/CBS poll, the ratio of self-described conservatives to self-described liberals was fairly even (32-27); today, the gap has widened considerably (42-23).

But what do people mean when they call themselves conservatives? Evidently it has to do with distaste for a growing, interfering, and cumbersome government. Thus in 1964, according to the Gallup poll, Americans were almost evenly split (42-39) on the issue of whether "the government has gone too far in regulating business and interfering with the free-enterprise system." By 1978, when the New York *Times*/CBS poll repeated the question, Americans had come to agree with the statement by a margin of 58-31 per cent. Not surprisingly, self-described conservatives now endorse this statement overwhelmingly (67-26); what is surprising is the fact that even "liberals" divide in favor of it by 45-35 per cent.

The percentage of people who think that "government is spending too much" has also risen steadily since 1973. But "too much" is a famous term of relativity. It may be considered too much with respect to the income of the citizenry; but it may also be considered too much with respect to the quality of the product. This is the "money's-worth" question. And the overwhelming tide of opinion, especially "conservative" opinion, identifies this government deficiency as "waste." In 1958, only 42 per cent of those polled told Gallup interviewers that "the government wastes a lot of the tax money"; by 1978, 78 per cent of Americans thought so (New York *Times*/CBS News). A vast majority of blacks also agrees with this view.

"Waste in government" was the key phrase in the Proposition 13 campaign. Mervin Field of the California poll reports that the main comment made by proponents of Proposition 13, other than "Taxes are too high," was "The time has come to cut government costs, waste, and inefficiency." Field noted that prior to election day, the California public believed that a cut of 10 per cent in tax revenues could be accomplished without any decline in state and local government services. And three-quarters of Californians in favor of the Proposition, in the

Los Angles *Times*/CBS News election-day poll, said that they did not think public services would be reduced by Proposition 13. After the California vote, a vast majority of Americans nationally (89-5 per cent) interpreted it as "a strong protest that people running government will have to respond by trimming a lot of waste from government spending" (Harris/ABC).

Does there begin to appear an anomaly in the position of those who supported Proposition 13? After all, it was reliably estimated that $7 billion in revenue would be lost to the state as a result of the measure. Surely two out of three Californians did not believe that paper clips and bureaucratic perquisites could account for that much fat. And indeed, three weeks after the election, a majority of the supporters of Proposition 13 told Los Angeles *Times* interviewers that they still favored the amendment, even though they now recognized that there would have to be some cuts in services. Was, then, the cry against "waste in government" merely a cover-up for "hedonistic" and "mean-spirited" impulses to cut services for the needy? The evidence indicates that the answer to this question is no, and that the cry against government is genuine.

In all surveys, the percentage of people who say that they trust or have confidence in the government has dropped steadily. In one recurrent poll (the University of Michigan's Survey Research Center) the percentage trusting the government dropped from 78 in 1964 to 33 in 1976. More and more Americans think that the people running the government "don't know what they're doing."

But more significant in refuting the interpretation of Proposition 13 as pure "hedonism" is the fact that the desire for government to intervene in beneficent ways has not diminished. The New York *Times*/CBS poll reports that in 1960 63 per cent of Americans agreed that "the government in Washington ought to see to it that everybody who wants to work has a job." This year, 74 per cent of the people in general—and 70 per cent of those who describe themselves as "conservative"—approved that mandate for government. In 1960, about 64 per cent of the people endorsed the proposal that "the government ought to help people to get doctors and hospital care at low cost." This year, 81 per cent of those interviewed by the New York *Times*/CBS poll agreed. In the fall of 1976, the University of Michigan's Survey Research Center asked a national sample whether they thought "government should spend less even if it means cutting back on health and education." Only 21 per cent favored spending less under such circumstances while 75 per cent opposed the cut. In the same year, 67 per cent of those polled by Gallup thought that government help for the elderly should be increased, while only 3 per cent said it should be reduced; 51 per cent thought that there should be more government support for health care and only 13 per cent said there should be less; 44 per cent felt there should be more government intervention on behalf of the unemployed, as compared to 19 per cent who believed there should be less. There was no significant difference between the attitudes of professional and business people and manual laborers, or among the various income classifications.

This common support of beneficent government intervention, substantiated by survey after survey, cannot be written off by saying that people are only interested in maintaining social programs of direct benefit to them. No doubt a certain amount of "there-but-for-the-grace-of-God-go-I" sentiment has always sustained liberal social programs; but the figures do not confirm the charge that it

is *narrow* self-interest which motivates the well-to-do and the ideologically conservative to favor government help for the aged and the needy. Rather, Americans seem to have developed an irreversible commitment to basic government
welfare programs, as they did, finally, to social security. It is now as natural to
them as getting up in the morning.

There seems to be one nagging exception to this generalization which itself
throws light on the attitudinal sets in the country. The word "welfare" constantly draws antipathy from the American public. When asked by the Los Angeles *Times*/CBS poll which services they would least like to see reduced, if services
had to be reduced, 75 per cent of Californians who voted on June 6 named police
protection, while only 11 per cent said welfare programs. (Actually, if this was an
index of "mean-spiritedness," it did not differentiate sharply between those who
had supported Proposition 13 and those who had opposed it: about 9 per cent of
the former and 14 per cent of the latter listed welfare as the leading candidate for
a cut.) The California (Field) poll also found 62 per cent choosing "welfare and
public-assistance programs" as the prime target for a cutback, as compared to the
6-8 per cent who favored cuts in fire and police departments.

This attitude toward "welfare" is by no means new. In 1935, in one of the first
surveys Gallup ever took, 60 per cent of the respondents said that the government was expending too much money for "relief" (the contemporary term for
what later came to be called welfare) while only 9 per cent replied that the
government was spending too little. The majority of Americans continued to
show disdain for "relief" all during the Depression. But the same polls which
produced these results revealed a considerable majority in favor the government's providing jobs for the unemployed, and for requiring those on relief to
accept such jobs.

This general response pattern has remained substantially unchanged over the
years. In a 1970 Harris poll, Americans approved (46-34) the proposition that
welfare should be abolished, and that welfare recipients be made to go to work.
But the same respondents overwhemingly supported (56-28) the idea that government should be increased to help the poor. Again, in a 1976 survey, Harris
found that 62 per cent favored (and only 23 per cent opposed) "a major cutback in
federal spending." However, confronted wih a list of specifics, substantial major-
ities of the same respondents *rejected* cutbacks in spending for education, health,
help for the unemployed, equal opportunity for minorities, environmental protection, and product safety. It was only on welfare that a majority (56-35) favored
a cutback.

The juxtaposition of these two answers—cut welfare, increase help for the
poor) poses a puzzle which turns up again and again. Thus in 1977, the white
population was evenly split (39-39) on whether welfare programs should be
greatly decreased, but three-quarters of them said that the government should
spend money to provide job incentives for the poor (Roper). In 1977, the American public approved by 80-13 per cent the idea that all able-bodied people should
be removed from the welfare rolls, but also stated by a similar majority that the
government should provide public-service jobs, with tax money, for those who
could not find jobs in private industry. And by about the same margin (78-15), the
American public agreed that its tax money should continue to be expended on
the aged, blind, disabled, and one-parent families with children under the age of
seven (Roper). There was no significant difference in the answers to these questions by self-styled conservatives and self-styled liberals.

The numbers may be subject to various degrees of distortion, but the answer to the puzzle is clear. Americans—especially that growing contingent of self-identified "conservative" Americans—are willing to pay taxes to assist the needy, but they are not satisfied with the way that portion of their tax money is being spent.

There are three strikes against "welfare." It still durably connotes "relief," "dole," something for nothing, economic waste. It is connected to the sometimes exaggerated, sometimes prejudiced sense of how many able-bodied people are on the rolls, or how many prefer not to work. As a program it seems to epitomize bureaucratic government at the worst; inefficient, ornately overlaid, corrupt, unfathomable, feckless.

But helping the poor by providing jobs is another matter entirely. Thus in 1972 Gallup asked: Suppose it would cost the government less money to give poor people cash payments than to have government train them, find jobs for them, and, if necessary, provide care for their children while they work? About 81 per cent responded that they would prefer the more costly program; only 9 per cent said they would favor the less expensive one.

The message, then, is: help the poor but get rid of "welfare." That "liberal" message is consistent with the nature of our new self-styled "conservative."

This hybrid political animal has, of course, been spotted before. In 1967, for example, Hadley Cantril and Lloyd Free found that many Americans were "ideological conservatives"—that is, anti-statist in their political beliefs—and "operational liberals," in the sense that they supported government action to create jobs. The number of such people is growing. More precisely, ideological conservatism has been growing as a partner to a continuingly dominant operational liberalism. This orientation is often described as neoconservatism, but it might just as accurately be called neoliberalism. The former designation emphasizes the belief that expansion of government services at the current welfare state level should, in lawyer's language, be suspect—subject to proof that a real problem cannot be dealt with in another fashion. The latter term emphasizes the continuing acceptance of collective responsibility to provide for the impoverished and the disadvantaged.

But if this hybrid phenomenon is the most dynamic force in the American political culture today, it also poses a dilemma—perhaps the new American dilemma, which, like Gunnar Myrdal's old one, also encompasses a contradiction between practice and ideology, this time in the arena of government intervention. Is it finally possible to hold down the monster state while dealing with the sheer bulk of services of every kind our society seems increasingly to need?

The "tax revolt" is perched at the edge of this huge question, whose answer will probably evolve rather than be calculated. But the tax revolt raises a more practical and immediate question as well: will the politicians quickly enough recognize and accommodate to the growing neoliberal (or, if one prefers, neoconservative) mood, or will they misread it, one way or another, according to their predilections?

If characterizing the tax revolt epitomized the Proposition 13 as "means-spiritedness," or "hedonism," or "racism" is to misread it on the one side, to interpet it as the sign of a swing to old-line conservative or right-wing Republicanism is to misread it equally on the other. For not only did California Democrats give Proposition 13 a landslide vote of support, 57 per cent to 43, but California Republicans chose the moderate Evelle Younger as their gubernatorial candidate over the more conservative Ed Davis.

Nationally, too, the same pattern is evident. The growth of tax-revolt sentiment has been accompanied by a parallel growth of identification not with the
Republicans but with the Democratic party (Democrats now outnumber Republicans by 45 per cent to about 20 per cent in the polls). In practical terms, both
Gallup and the New York *Times*/CBS polls estimate that the overwhelming Democratic majority in Congress will be renewed this November, even though the
out-party usually makes a comeback in congressional contests held in non-presi-
dential election years. In addition, the Democratic party—the party which has
stood for expanding social services—has gained overwhelming control of government from the county courthouses to the state and national legislatures, and
from governorships to the Presidency, during a period when the proportion of
self-identified conservatives and anti-tax sentiment have been increasing
steadily.

Nor are the elements of a classic right-wing extremist movement present in
Proposition 13. Howard Jarvis, who has been plumping for this kind of tax
measure for over ten years, suddenly found himself at the head of a parade he did
not assemble. He may be a culture hero at this point, but he is not a political
leader. Extra-partisan movements, whether rightist or leftist, usually make head-
way when they espouse a cause which is not embraced by one of the major
coalition parties. Such movements has always been done in by the fact that one of
the major parties, following the logic of its coalitional nature, took over their
cause in a more moderate form. That seems to have happened already in California. It remains to be seen, however, if the politicians understand exactly what it is
they have embraced.

The stong support of Proposition 13 by Democrats, in California and around
the nation, provides the clue. As the survey data show, these Democrats have not
abandoned their desire for a socially protective government. (On the contrary,
most Republicans have tended to join them in that desire.) But the Democrats
increasingly consider themselves "conservative" in their queasiness about the
way government is growing and acting.

If, then, the public mood today is against enlarging the power, scope, and size
of government in order to solve social problems, as advocated by George McGovern, Edward Kennedy, or the Americans for Democratic Action, it is also against
returning to the laissez-faire small-government philosophy proposed by Ronald
Reagan, Milton Friedman, or the American Conservative Union. Reagan, however, appears to be shifting: in a post-Proposition 13 speech he challenged his
image as a "right-wing person" by pointing out that as governor he had made the
California income tax more "progressive" and had increased welfare grants "by
43 per cent for the truly needy." Evidently he at least understands what analysis
of the tax revolt tells us—that the predominant public mood is not "right-wing"
but the neoliberal (or neoconservative) impulse to combine support of collective
social responsibility with a suspicion of growing government power.

Socialist

James O'Connor: The Fiscal Crisis of the State

The issue of taxes has always been a class issue; it is still true that "external protection and power, and the enrichment of some classes at the expense of others [are] the purpose of the tax system."[1] Every important change in the balance of class forces has always been registered in the tax structure.

In advanced capitalist states tax exploitation cannot be openly applied or instituted without some kind of ideological justification. Taxes can be either concealed, which is difficult to accomplish in the modern era, or justified on some basis of "tax fairness or equity." Failing this, there is the danger of a tax revolt, in the form of tax evasion or organized political opposition.

Even in the feudal era, the ruling class was compelled either to conceal or to justify tax exploitation. Taxes contained an "equity" criteria when they first appeared in the budgets of the feudal nobility. But they were based on the principle that different persons and classes had different rights and duties. "The nobility of eighteenth century France were serenely certain," Louis Eisenstein has written, "that they contributed special benefits to society that called for a special immunity from taxes. They . . . had incentives that had to be preserved for the welfare of others."[2]

In nineteenth-century America, the ruling class concealed tax exploitation. The working class was small and a personal income tax was not feasible; the only wealth tax was the property tax. The tariff became the most important source of revenue, one that was hidden from view because it took the form of higher commodity prices. (Because they are easy to conceal, import and export taxes today are held up as models of taxation in underdeveloped countries. Economists have written of the political "advantage" of export taxes because they hide the burden that falls on peasants engaged in export production.[3]

Today the false reasons given to justify tax exploitation revolve around two ideas—the old concept of "incentives" and the new idea of "ability to pay." Put briefly, the "incentive" rationale asserts that if profits are taxed too heavily, the accumulation of capital, and thus the growth of employment, will diminish. Similarly, the "incentives" of investors, wealthy families, and others who monopolize the supply of capital must not be "impaired." Such statements are in fact true within the framework of capitalism because those who make them threaten to sabotage production if they do not realize acceptable profits. Again in brief, the doctrine of "ability-to-pay" assumes that the benefits of state expenditures accrue to everyone more or less equally, and therefore that everyone should

James O'Connor, *The Corporation and the State: Essays in the Theory of Capitalism and Imperialism* (New York: Harper & Row, 1974), pp. 136–145. Copyright © 1974 by James O'Connor. Reprinted by permission of Harper & Row, Publishers, Inc.

1. Rudolf Goldscheid, "A Sociological Approach to the Problem of Public Finance," in Richard A. Musgrave and Alan T. Peacock, eds., *Classics in the Theory of Public Finance* (New York, 1958), p. 203.

2. Louis Eisenstein, *The Ideologies of Taxation* (New York, 1961), pp. 222-223.

3. R. Jackson, "Political Aspects of Export Taxation," *Public Finance* 12, no. 4. (1957): 291.

pay taxes according to ability, normally measured by the level of personal income. This doctrine obviously has no basis in reality, and is false, not because of its logic, but because of its premise.

Tax exploitation is still concealed—there are roughly 150 taxes hidden in the price of a loaf of bread, and about 600 taxes concealed in the purchase of a house.[4] Excise and sales taxes still remain important sources of revenue at state and local government levels. But, of more importance, tax exploitation is accepted because the ideology of corporate capital is still accepted. Only recently has this ideology been subject to challenge. Thus, both workers and the individual capitalists identify their interest closely with those of the state; and workers therefore identify their interests with those of capital.[5]

Concealing and justifying taxes are of crucial importance in the contemporary era because the fiscal burden that the owners of corporate capital place on the state is not accompanied by any willingness to shoulder the burden themselves. Superficially, it appears that the ruling class taxes itself in a number of ways—there are corporation income taxes, property taxes, and inheritance taxes, besides the individual income tax, which place extremely high marginal tax rates on high incomes. In fact, corporate capital, for the most part, escapes taxation altogether except during periods of national crisis (for example, in 1936-1939, when Congress legislated an undistributed profits tax, and during World War II, when corporate capital had to pay an excess profits tax).

First, the corporate managers completely shift the corporate income tax to consumers—mainly wage and salary earners—in the form of higher prices. Although corporate gross rates of return doubled between the 1920s and 1950s, net rates of return remained the same, even though the corporation income tax rate rose from 5 percent to 52 percent during the same period. In effect, the corporation income tax is similar to a general sales tax, levied at rate in proportion to the profit margin of the corporation.[6]

Second, the property tax falls mainly on the working class, not on the business class. One reason is that within the core cities residential properties assume the larger share, and commercial land and buildngs the small share of the total property tax burden. Property values in the central city show a relative decline owing to the "suburbanization of industry" and to the spread of freeways and the expansion of public parking facilities, office buildings, and other structures that have taken lands off the tax rolls. The flight of well-to-do workers and the middle classes to the suburbs has reduced local revenues from residential property taxes, as well.[7]

Moreover, available studies indicate that owners of tenant-occupied residential buildings usually shift the property tax to their tenants—the vast majority of whom are working people. And about 75 percent of property taxes on local

4. These were the conclusions of a study by the Tax Foundation, cited by Sylvia Porter, *San Francisco Chronicle,* 29 November 1966.
5. The situation is different in Europe and the underdeveloped countries where bourgeois ideological hegemony is relatively weak.
6. The corporation income tax in the competitive sector is also borne by the consumer because profits are too meager to absorb the tax.
7. Mordecai S. Feinberg, "The Implications of the Core-City Decline for the Fiscal Structure of the Core-City," *National Tax Journal* 17, no. 3 (September 1964): 217. From 1950 to 1960, in the ten largest U.S. cities, revenues from property taxes actually rose. If assessed rates and prices had not changed, revenues would have *fallen* by 7 percent. If prices alone had not changed, revenues would have fallen in four of the ten cities.

industry and retail establishment is shifted to consumers.[8] Thus, it is not surprising that there is general agreement among economists that the property tax as a whole is regressive.[9]

All in all, however, property taxes are becoming a relatively insignificant source of revenue. In 1902 they raised over 80 percent of all state and local government revenues; today property taxes finance about one-half of the budgets of local governments, and only 5 percent of state government budgets (the largest cities are becoming increasingly dependent on intergovernment transfers, which are financed chiefly by income, sales, and excise taxes). In the past few years, taxpayer groups and politicians in dozens of states have been actively seeking to lower property taxes. And some kinds of property taxation (for example, taxes on personal property) are being eliminated altogether in many localities.

The only other wealth tax in the United States is the inheritance tax. Nominal rates of the federal tax range from 3 percent on $5,000-$10,000 to 77 percent on $10,000,000 or more, but the actual average rate is little more than 10 percent. The difference between the high nominal rates and the low actual rates is explained by exemptions for life estates and for gifts made more than three years before death.[10]

This brief survey warrants the conclusion that the owners of monopoly capital pay few taxes on their wealth,[11] and none on their corporate income. There is no general business tax in the United States, and unrealized capital gains go tax-free. To be sure, wealthy individuals who receive dividends and interest income are taxed at high marginal rates under the individual income tax, but top corporate controllers and managers receive most of their income in the form of tax-free interest from municipal bonds and realized capital gains, which are taxed at low rates. Capital thus protects not only its profits from taxation, but also personal wealth and income. This should not come as a surprise; profits are the key to the economic survival, and personal income and wealth are the key to the social and political survival of the ruling class.

In addition to that portion of property and corporation income taxes that falls on the working class, tax exploitation takes the form of social security taxes, sales and excise taxes, and the individual income tax. The most important social security tax is the payroll tax used to finance old-age insurance. This is a regressive tax because a flat rate is applied to taxable earnings without regard to income levels; it is especially regressive for those who do not stay in the labor force long enough

---

8. Richard Musgrave's study of Michigan property taxes, cited in California Assembly, Interim Committee on Revenue and Taxation, *Taxation of Property in California*, December 1964, p. 30. Little or no shifting occurs if there exist rent controls, long-term leases or competition between landlords.

9. Dick Netzer, Economics of the Property Tax (Washington, D.C., 1966), pp. 40-62. One economist has written: "The unevenness of its base, the wide variations in rates, and the imperfections in its administration probably make [the property tax's] impact such as to move the tax system as a whole away from, not toward, ability to pay" (Jesse Burkhead, *Public School Finance* [Syracuse, N.Y., 1964], p. 185).

10. Tax Foundation, *State Inheritance Tax Rates and Exemptions* (New York, 1966), p. 165.

11. The only period in which a capital levy was remotely possible was directly after World War I in Europe, when there was considerable popular discontent with war profiteering and the conscription of manpower. The best analysis of the political economy of wealth taxation is Manual Gottlieb, "The Capital Levy after World War I," *Public Finance* 7, no. 4 (1952): 356-385.

to accumulate sufficient credited employment to qualify for primary benefits.[12] Excise taxes are applied by both state and federal governments, and most state and many local governments have general sales taxes. These taxes are altogether regressive, and fall particularly hard on low-income workers.[13] Indicative of their importance is the fact that state governments raised nearly two-thirds of their tax revenues from sales and gross receipt taxes in 1967, while state individual income taxes accounted for only 16 percent of the tax revenues.[14]

The most oppressive instrument of tax exploitation is the federal individual income tax. First passed by Congress in 1894, on the heels of more than a decade of farmer and working-class agitation against big business, the income tax was originally conceived as a class tax. The tax rate was a flat 2 percent and provision was made for a $4,000 personal exemption, and thus the tax would have fallen on only a handful of wealthy individuals. The tax was declared unconstitutional.

The modern individual income tax did not win acceptance until 1913. The historical reasons for this delay were simple: First, the development of the income tax, and, in particular, the general application of the tax by the expedient of regularly lowering exemptions, was not possible until there existed a massive propertyless working class. Second, by the turn of the century, the United States economy was producing a wide range of substitutes for imported commodities and, as a result, workers were able to avoid tariff excises by reducing their consumption of imports.

Not only was an individual income tax historically possible, it was also ideally suited to the needs of corporate capital. On the one hand, the income tax cannot be shifted to profits; on the other hand, the tax is regressive or proportional in content, although progressive in form. The myth of "tax equity" is preserved, and the reality of tax exploitation is concealed behind an elaborate progressive tax schedule, which in turn contains hundreds of loopholes deemed necessary for "economic growth," "economic stability," and "fiscal justice."

The income tax has increasingly encroached on wage and salary income since it was first introduced. The state has systematically reduced personal exemptions and credits for dependents from $4,000 (for a family of four) in 1913-1916 to $2,400 today. In 1913-1916 a single person was granted a $3,000 exemption; today, only $700. In terms of actual purchasing power, real exemptions have fallen even more. Further, popular consciousness of the tax burden has been reduced by the introduction of tax withholding—the highest form of tax exploitation. At present, 85 percent of income taxes are collected at the basic 20 percent rate, which applies to two-thirds of all returns.[15]

---

12. Ernest C. Harvey, "Social Security Taxes—Regressive or Progressive?" *National Tax Journal* 18, no. 4 (December 1965): 408.

13. Tax Foundation, *Retail Sales and Individual Income Taxes in State Tax Structures* (New York, 19620, pp. 29-30. Evidence of the class nature of these taxes is the federal excise tax reduction of 1965, which was expected to reduce excise tax revenues by almost $5 billion over a four-year period. But the tax law retained taxes on tobacco, gasoline, alchohol, and other wage goods, cutting taxes on a wide range of luxury and semiluxy commodities.

14. Bureau of the Census, *State Government Finances* in 1967 (Washington, D.C., 1968), p. 7, table 1.

15. In 1916 only 400,000 tax returns were actually taxable; taxable returns jumped to 2.5 million in 1925, 4 million by 1939, over 32 million in 1950, and more than 55 million today. In 1913 the initial rate of tax was 1 percent on the first $20,000 taxable income (after deducting personal exemptions). Today the figure is 20 percent on the first $20,000. In 1913 individual and corporation income taxes together yielded a little more than $35

According to available studies, the average rate of taxation on the highest incomes is roughly 30 percent, chiefly because of the special treatment granted to capital gains income, deductions (mainly applicable to those who receive relatively high incomes), and income splitting and exemptions (which benefit high income families relatively more than low income groups).[16] In fact, no one apart from independent professionals and small and middle businessmen pays more than a 25 percent rate because of the ease of short-circuiting income into nontaxable forms (for example, expense accounts) and to tax evasion, which is most widespread among farmers and those who receive interest income and annuities. In recent years the state has failed even to pretend that the flat tax surcharge of 10 percent is progressive, and passed a tax cut in 1965 that benefited the rich far more than the poor—for the former the decrease is permanent, but for the latter (whose money income is rising) only temporary.[17]

The Tax Revolt

In the preceding sections, we have seen that the economic surplus is mobilized for the political-economic programs of corporate capital through the budget. Monopoly capital dominates the state budget and socializes various production costs and expenses, but resists the socialization of profits. Taxation is the only source of state revenue fully consistent with capitalist property relations: the burden of taxation necessarily falls on the working class.

The fiscal crisis consists of the gap between expenditures and revenues, which is one form of the general contradiction between social production and private ownership. The severity of the fiscal crisis depends upon the production and social relations between corporate capital, local and regional capital, state employees and dependents, and the taxpaying working class at large. In the absence of a serious challenge to the ideological hegemony of corporate capital, in particular in the absence of a unified movement organized around opposition to corporate liberal and imperalist budgetary priorities—a movement that seeks

---

million; today the individual income tax alone yields about $85 billion. Most advanced capitalist countries have experienced the same trends. In Japan, for example, the number of income taxpayers rose from 1 million to 19 million from 1935 to 1949; meanwhile the ratio of personal income tax revenues to national income jumped from less than 1 percent to 10.2 percent (Sei Fujita, "Political Ceiling on Income Taxation," *Public Finance* 16, no. 2 [1961]: 183-189).

16.   Available studies also indicate that taxation *as a whole* is at best proportional and at worst regressive with respect to income, although some studies indicate a degree of progressivity in the higher income brackets. See, for example, Gerhard Colm and Helen Tarasov, *Who Pays the Taxes?* Temporary National Economic Commission Monograph no. 3 (Washington, D.C., 1941); Richard Musgrave et al., "Distribution of Tax Payments by Income Groups: A Case Study for 1948," *National Tax Journal* 4, no. 1 (March 1951); Richard Musgrave, "Incidence of the Tax Structure and Its Effects on Consumption," *Federal Tax Policy for Economic Growth and Stability*, papers submitted by panelists before the Joint Committee on the Economic Report, U.S. Congress, 1955; Richard Goode, *The Individual Income Tax* (Washington, D.C., 1964), p. 263; "Who Really Gets Hurt By Taxes?" *U.S. News and World Report*, 9 December 1968. Ross Abinati of San Jose State College has estimated that the average effective tax rate on the incomes of all strata of the working class and managers, officials, proprietors, and farmers is roughly 30-32.5 percent.

17.   S. D. Hermamsen, "An Analysis of the Recent Tax Cut," *National Tax Journal* 18, no. 4 (December 1965): 425.

to unify the working class as a whole—the fiscal crisis will continue to divide state workers from state dependents (e.g., teachers from parents, social workers from welfare recipients) and state employees and dependents from workers in the private sector (e.g., teachers and students from taxpayers as a whole).

At present, growing taxpayer resistance to heavy, rising taxes both reflects and deepens the fiscal crisis. Although "taxpayers" as group comprise the small business, professional, and working classes as a whole, tax resistance is not presently organized along class lines. In practice, tax issues are rarely seen as class issues, partly because of the general absence of working-class unity in the United States, and partly because the fiscal system itself obscures the class character of the budget. As we have seen, although monopoly capital dominates the budget, the state mediates between labor and capital, and the working class benefits materially from state expenditures. In addition, monopoly capital has developed an elaborate ideological rationalization of the budget that is integral to capital's general view that material abundance, capital accumulation, and economic growth define social well-being. Finally, as we have seen, the aggregate, effective tax rate on the incomes of both lower- and higher-income families is roughly the same, indicating that tax exploitation is not confined to poor people, who have least to lose and most to gain from radical social change.

For these reasons, tax issues ordinarily are seen as interest group or community issues, and far from helping to unite the working class, the issues act to divide it. In particular, the growth of thousands of autonomous taxpaying units —the "1400 Governments" of the New York metropolitan area and the nearly five hundred separate tax-levying bodies in Illinois's Cook County, to cite two examples—and the proliferation elsewhere of autonomous trusteeships, municipalities, and school, water, sewer, and other special districts tend to set community against community, tax district against tax district, suburb against city. The fundamental class issues of state finance—the distribution of taxation and the division of expenditures between different social classes—emerge in a new form. The core cities are attempting to force the suburbs to pay their "fair share" of city expenditures, while the relatively well-to-do suburban populations not only are defending themselves against the programs of the core cities—tax redistribution, central city income taxes, commuter taxes, consolidation or merger of tax districts and entire metropolitan areas—but also are taking the offensive by offering inducements to private capital in order to establish an autonomous industrial and commercial base.

Apart from the cold war between city and suburb, the most militant form of tax resistance is that against the property tax. Decades ago, the function of the property tax was to finance public improvements for the benefit of property owners. Today there is little or no visible connection between property taxation and expenditures financed by it; rather, there is a tendency to use property tax revenues to finance social programs that many property owners oppose. In many cities, small homeowners are mounting tax referendum campaigns aimed at downtown business interests whose properties are undervalued for tax purposes. In the suburbs, there is widespread sentiment that the property tax should be replaced in whole or in part by other sources of revenue—sentiment that right-wing and local politicians are successfully exploiting for their own purposes.

Suburban resistance to increased taxation, agitation against the property tax, and the urban-suburban cold war, not to speak of tax avoidance and evasion and the general sentiment against "spendthrift" government, arise not only because of the rising level of taxation, but also because of government expenditure priorities.

The *priorities* of corporate liberalism are under attack, not only by the black movement and the organized left, but also by a significant part of the population at large. A study conducted in the early 1960s concluded that popular sentiment ran against space spending and support for agriculture, and in favor of domestic welfare and education programs. According to this study, no single government program inspired the majority of the population sampled to agree to expand the program through higher taxation.[18] A recent Harris poll stated that "the central motive for paying taxes has begun to disintegrate." Those polled opposed foreign aid, Vietnam War spending, space and defense, and federal welfare outlays (no doubt because of racism and the prevailing ideology that stresses the importance of "individual self-sufficiency"). Favored were aid to education, pollution control, help for the cities, and other domestic programs.

What is the significance of popular attitudes on taxation and spending for the left? The tax issue is complex, and cannot be separated from the questions of the level of state expenditures and spending priorities. In the past, the left has not been able to exploit the tax issue because it has been wedded to the modern liberal tradition that has sought an enlarged government role in the economy with little or no attention paid to the structure and burden of taxation. Chiefly for this reason, the right wing has enjoyed a near monopoly on the issue of taxation.

There are some signs that the left is breaking its self-imposed silence on taxation, and beginning to link up taxes and expenditures. Some unions—in particular, state employee unions such as the Transport Workers Union in New York and sections of the American Federation of Teachers—are incorporating demands that the tax burden be shifted to business into their programs for higher wages and better working conditions. This enlarged perspective on the state finances represents an advance, but it is clear that even a general critique of the relationship between expenditures and taxation is insufficient in and of itself. Of equal importance is a theoretical and practical demonstration of the relation between state expenditure priorities and the pattern and rhythm of *private* accumulation and spending. For example, tax referendum campaigns organized around the issue of the relative burden of property taxation on residential versus commercial property should include a critique of the class character of education and urban renewal expenditures. Clearly, struggles against tax exploitation alone can have only a limited impact on either popular consciousness or the actual tax structure. Past struggles by populist, progressive, liberal, and left movements dramatically show that under conditions of monopolistic industry and administered prices it is impossible to influence greatly the distribution of the tax burden (and thus the distribution of wealth and income) without a simultaneous challenge to *both* state and private capital spending priorities.

Further, the left must begin to demonstrate the relationship between foreign and domestic spending, which, we have seen, public opinion radically separates. Struggles around regressive property and sales taxes, increases in fares for public services, and so on, should be informed by an understanding that domestic and international spending are integrally related; that is, that the maintenance of corporate liberalism at home depends upon the expansion and consolidation of

---

18. George Katona, *The Mass Consumption Society* (New York, 1964), pp. 145-146.

imperialism abroad, and vice versa. Even on the left, it is sometimes not appreciated that foreign economic expansion and imperialism are required to maintain corporate liberalism by *expanding* national income and material wealth, thus muting domestic capital-labor struggles over the *distribution* of income and wealth. And the growth of social and welfare expenditures (and the establishment of class harmony) at home are preconditions for popular acquiesence in militarism and imperialism abroad. The "welfare-warfare state" is *one* phenomenon, and military and civilian expenditures cannot be reduced significantly at the expense of one another. An understanding of the relation between foreign and domestic programs requires comprehension of the *totality* of world capitalism—a difficult but necessary undertaking, precisely because there is presently a large constituency ready to support a massive expansion of corporate liberal domestic programs (except welfare) at the expense of military, space, and foreign aid expenditures.[19]

---

19. Nixon's new-federalism program makes it especially important to link up the issues of the tax burden, domestic and overseas expenditure, and private corporate priorities; that is, to develop a perspective of capitalism as a total system. Nixon's program envisages the redistribution of billions of dollars of federal tax monies to the states and cities in an attempt to alleviate the fiscal crisis at the local level. Redistribution will benefit local politicians—now caught between their need for the support of organized labor (and thus the need to keep taxes on residential properties low) and their dependence on downtown business (and thus the need to keep taxes on commercial property low). But the funds for redistribution will not be available in the absence of economic growth, which in turn is partly dependent on more foreign expansion.

Chapter 9

INEQUALITY

Many social problems can be defined as issues of who shall have the right to valued roles, goods, and services. We are all aware that some people in our society have considerable access to "the good things in life," while others have little. Insights into whether this unequal distribution can be justified may be found by examining conservative, liberal, and socialist perspectives on inequality.

The conservative position holds that inequality is necessary for the proper organization and successful functioning of society. In the Davis-Moore theory of stratification,[1] it is argued that some people must be given more of what society has to offer in order to encourage them to fill the difficult and demanding roles of leadership in a complex society. Davis and Moore state that the executive positions which involve running large organizations are the most difficult, demanding, and least rewarding intrinsically so that great extrinsic rewards must be offered to get people to agree to be president of General Motors Corporation or President of the United States of America.

Against this conservative position, socialists argue that jobs which involve hard, dirty physical labor such as coal mining and housework merit society's rewards in the form of good pay and high status. At the same time both socialists and conservatives agree that the work which no one voluntarily wishes to do but which is necessary for society to function must be the most highly rewarded. Socialists and conservatives differ on what constitutes unpleasant labor: managerial responsibility and its ulcers or physically backbreaking tasks with their job-related injuries.

The liberal position holds that inequality is acceptable only if every member of the society is given the chance to overcome inequality. Liberals emphasize providing the means, such as education and health care, to enable those who start with a disadvantage to compete with those who have privileged backgrounds. Liberals state that access to higher positions in society should be based on merit. Liberals believe that when previous historical circumstances have disadvantaged people, government aid programs are justified to raise their health, education, and aspiration levels. Then they will have both the desire and capability of achieving success in American society.

People who want to rise from a lower to a higher status position should, the conservative formula holds, be able through education and personal achievement to equalize any status inequalities of birth. However, this prescription only holds in a society where what you know is indeed really more important than who you know. Mobility, viewed in these terms, is the upward or downward movement of the individual.

For socialists, most mobility in American society has been the result of concerted action by classes rather than an individual now and then pulling themselves up by their intellectual bootstraps. Socialists also assert that there has not been enough successful concerted action and that many groups have attained little if any improvement in their circumstances.

The socialist position is that inequality is fundamentally unacceptable and that society should be reorganized to eliminate distinctions based on inherited property. The basic form of inequality derives from the fact that members of one class control the means of production in a society, thereby making all others subservient to them. To eliminate inequality, the means of production of a society must be socialized and controlled, directed and coordinated by those who work.

While conspicuous individual success is pointed to by proponents of the conservative approach to inequality, examples of co-ordinated political activity and statistics on the lack of mobility of groups at the lower end of American society are pointed to by proponents of the socialist approach to inequality. Each of these political positions—conservative, liberal, and socialist—holds that different criteria are fundamental to the equality-inequality dimension. Socialism requires reordering the control over the means of production and redistribution of material goods according to criteria of need rather than inherited privilege. Liberalism requires the provision of accessibility to means of preparation for entry into fair competition for what society has to offer. Conservatism requires the retention of the existing distribution of resources, and it assumes that this distribution is justly ordered.

In the conservative article, Kristol maintains that equality cannot be clearly defined. No one can precisely determine a fair distribution of income or a just pattern of intergenerational social mobility. Human talents and disabilities are naturally distributed according to a bell-shaped curve, with a few people at the high and low ends and most lumped in the middle. The unequal distribution of income follows from the unequal distribution of talent. The just society is one in which inequalities are accepted as necessary for the common good. Moreover, the current attack on inequality does not really represent a genuine concern for the poor and underprivileged. It is an ideological weapon utilized by intellectuals to attack the business class. Intellectuals, jealous of the prerequisites of businessmen, merely use arguments in favor of equality to justify a redistribution of power to themselves.

In the socialist article, Walzer rejects the notion of a single bell-shaped curve according to which all talents and abilities are unequally distributed. He does not deny the existence of inequalities of talent. Instead of one curve, Walzer sees many. There are a variety of human talents and abilities. Some people have one kind of talent; other people have another kind of talent. Moreover, needs are also differentially distributed. For example, some people require considerable medical attention and others require relatively little. Each talent or need should be viewed within its own sphere. Money should not be allowed to be the principle of access. Unjust inequalities are created when people who are rich get more medical care than people who are sicker but poor. What is necessary to life itself (food, clothing, shelter, medical care) should be distributed according to need. Goods and services that are beyond what is necessary to life may be distributed in exchange for money.

In Walzer's theory each activity of life is allotted its own sphere and a distributive principle appropriate to the particular activity. He does not believe that the traditional socialist distribution principle of need is either necessary or appropriate as an ordering principle for every area of life. Walzer also lists instances where merit is the correct distributive principle. Under socialism, these alternative principles of distribution would suffice. However, under capitalism, where persistent inequities based on race and class exist, quotas are justified to redress the balance against those who have historically been excluded from desired occupations. The good society is one in which equality, in its different spheres, is combined with individual freedom of choice.

In the liberal article, Gans describes the rising demand for greater equality by minorities, wage earners, and the poor. Their complaints are justified as America has persistent patterns of economic and political inequality. In an earlier era these inequalities could be justified because they generated entrepreneurial energy and capital. At present, however, inequalities are a source of social instability and unrest. Feelings of individual inferiority and self-hate induced by inequalities result in crime and violence as well as political protest. It is necessary to reduce inequalities so that social conflicts may be moderated. When society is relatively equal, differences among citizens can be settled by fair compromise. Most approaches to reducing inequality call for collectivist solutions such as nationalizing industries. Although overall economic inequality is reduced, political inequality is increased since government officials gain increased power through control of the economy.

An American approach to reducing inequality would retain economic incentives to create wealth for the well-to-do and at the same time through tax and subsidy policies encourage the less well-to-do to maximize their earnings through their own efforts. The need for equality must be balanced against other competing goods such as liberty. America is rich enough so that the condition of the less well-to-do may be improved without taking too much away from the well-to-do. The affluent must be persuaded that it is in their interest to exchange some of their wealth for social peace by allowing more equality.

Notes

1. Kingsley Davis and Wilbert Moore, "Some Principles of Stratification," *American Sociological Review* 10 (1945). 242-249.

Conservative

Irving Kristol: About Equality

There would appear to be little doubt that the matter of equality has become, in these past two decades, a major political and ideological issue. The late Hugh Gaitskell proclaimed flatly that "socialism is about equality," and though this bold redefinition of the purpose of socialism must have caused Karl Marx to spin in his grave—he thought egalitarianism a vulgar, philistine notion and had only contemptuous things to say about it—nevertheless most socialist politicians now echo Mr. Gaitskell in a quite routine way. And not only socialist politicians: in the United States today, one might fairly conclude from the political debates now going on that capitalism, too, is "about equality," and will stand or fall with its success in satisfying the egalitarian impulse. To cap it all, a distinguished Harvard professor, John Rawls, recently published a serious, massive, and widely acclaimed work in political philosophy whose argument is that a social order is just and legitimate *only* to the degree that it is directed to the redress of inequality. To the best of my knowledge, no serious political philosopher ever offered such a proposition before. It is a proposition, after all, that peremptorily casts a pall of illegitimacy over the entire political history of the human race— that implicitly indicts Jerusalem and Athens and Rome and Elizabethan England, all of whom thought *in*equality was necessary to achieve a particular ideal of human excellence, both individual and collective. Yet most of the controversy about Professor Rawls's extraordinary thesis has revolved around the question of whether he has demonstrated it with sufficient analytical meticulousness. The thesis itself is not considered controversial.

Reprinted by permission of Irving Kristol from *Two Cheers for Capitalism* (New York; New American Library, 1979).

One would think, then, that with so much discussion "about equality," there would be little vagueness as to what equality itself is about—what one means by "equality." Yet this is not at all the case. I think I can best illustrate this point by recounting a couple of my editorial experiences at the journal, *The Public Interest*, with which I am associated.

It is clear that some Americans are profoundly and sincerely agitated by the existing distribution of income in this country, and these same Americans—they are mostly professors, of course—are constantly insisting that a more equal distribution of income is a matter of considerable urgency. Having myself no strong prior opinion as to the "proper" shape of an income-distribution curve in such a country as the United States, I have written to several of these professors asking them to compose an article that would describe a proper redistribution of American income. In other words, in the knowledge that they are discontented with our present income distribution, and taking them at their word that when they demand "more equality" they are not talking about an absolute leveling of all incomes, I invited them to give our readers a picture of what a "fair" distribution of income would be like.

I have never been able to get that article, and I have come to the conclusion that I never shall get it. In two cases, I was promised such an analysis, but it was never written. In the other cases, no one was able to find the time to devote to it. Despite all the talk "about equality," no one seems willing to commit himself to a precise definition from which statesmen and social critics can take their bearings.

As with economists, so with sociologists. Here, instead of income distribution, the controversial issue is social stratification, i.e., the "proper" degree of intergenerational social mobility. The majority of American sociologists seem persuaded that American democracy has an insufficient degree of such mobility, and it seemed reasonable to me that some of them—or at least one of them!—could specify what degree would be appropriate. None of them, I am sure, envisages a society that is utterly mobile, in which *all* the sons and daughters of the middle and upper classes end up in the very lowest social stratum, where they can live in anticipation of *their* sons and daughters rising again toward the top, and then of their grandsons and granddaughters moving downward once again! On the other hand, there is much evident dissatisfaction with what social mobility we do have. So why not find out what pattern of social mobility would be "fair" and "just" and "democratic"?

I regret to report that one will not find this out by consulting any issue of *The Public Interest*. I further regret to report that nowhere in our voluminous sociological literature will one find any such depiction of the ideally mobile society. Our liberal sociologists, like our liberal economists, are eloquent indeed in articulating their social discontents, but they are also bewilderingly modest in articulating their social goals.

Now, what is one to infer from this experience? One could, of course, simply dismiss the whole thing as but another instance of the intellectual irresponsibility of our intellectuals. That such irresponsibility exists seems clear enough, but *why* it exists is not clear at all. I do not believe that our intellectuals and scholars are genetically destined to be willfully or mischievously irresponsible. They are, I should say, no more perverse than the rest of mankind, and if they act perversely there must be a reason, even if they themselves cannot offer us a reason.

I, for one, am persuaded that though those people talk most earnestly about equality, it is not really equality that interests them. Indeed, it does not seem to me that equality per se is much of an issue for anyone. Rather, it is a surrogate for all sorts of other issues, some of them of the highest importance; these involve nothing less than our conception of what constitutes a just and legitimate society, a temporal order of things that somehow "makes sense" and seems "right."

A just and legitimate society, according to Aristotle, is one in which inequalities—of property, or station, or power—are generally perceived by the citizenry as necessary for the common good. I do not see that this definition has ever been improved on, though generations of political philosophers have found it unsatisfactory and have offered alternative definitions. In most cases, the source of this dissatisfaction has been what I would call the "liberal" character of the definition: it makes room for many different and even incompatible kinds of just and legitimate societies. In some of these societies, large inequalities are accepted as a necessary evil, whereas in others they are celebrated as the source of positive excellence. The question that this definition leaves open is the relation between a particular just and legitimate society and the "best" society. Aristotle, as we know, had his own view of the "best" society: he called it a "mixed regime," in which the monarchical, aristocratic, and democratic principles were all coherently intermingled. But he recognized that his own view of the "best" regime was of a primarily speculative nature—that is to say, a view always worth holding in mind but usually not relevant to the contingent cirucmstances (the "historical" circumstances, we should say) within which actual statesmen have to operate.

Later generations found it more difficult to preserve this kind of philosophic detachment from politics. The influence of Christianity, with its messianic promises, made the distinction between "the best" and "the legitimate" ever harder to preserve against those who insisted that *only* the best regime was legitimate. (This, incidentally, is an assumption that Professor Rawls makes as a matter of course.) The Church tried—as an existing and imperfect institution it had to try—to maintain this distinction, but it could only do so by appearing somewhat less Christian than it had promised to be. When the messianic impulse was secularized in early modernity, and science and reason and technology took over the promise of redemptive power—of transforming this dismal world into the wonderful place it "ought" to be—that same difficulty persisted. Like the Church, all the political regimes of modernity have had to preserve their legitimacy either by claiming an ideal character which in obvious truth they did not possess, or by making what were taken to be "damaging admissions" as to their inability to transform the real into the ideal.

The only corrective to this shadow of illegitimacy that has hovered threateningly over the politics of Western civilization for nearly two millennia now was the "common sense" of the majority of the population, which had an intimate and enduring relation to mundane realities that was relatively immune to speculative enthusiasm. This relative immunity was immensely strengthened by the widespread belief in an afterlife, a realm in which, indeed, whatever existed would be utterly perfect. I think it possible to suggest that the decline of the belief in personal immortality has been the most important *political* fact of the last hundred years; nothing else has so profoundly affected the way in which the masses of people experience their worldly condition. But even today, the masses of people tend to be more "reasonable," as I would put it, in their political judgments and political expectations than are our intellectuals. The trouble is that our society is breeding more and more "intellectuals" and fewer common men and women.

I use quotation marks around the term "intellectuals" because this category has, in recent decades, acquired a significantly new complexion. The enormous expansion in higher education, and the enormous increase in the college-educated, means that we now have a large class of people in our Western societies who, though lacking intellectual distinction (and frequently lacking even intellectual competence), nevertheless believe themselves to be intellectuals. A recent poll of American college teachers discovered that no fewer than 50 percent defined themselves as "intellectuals." That gives us a quarter of a million American intellectuals on our college faculties alone; if one adds all those in government and in the professions who would also lay claim to the title, the figure would easily cross the million mark! And if one also adds the relevant numbers of college students, one might pick up another million or so. We are, then, in a country like America today, talking about a mass of several millions of "intellectuals" who are looking at their society in a highly critical way and are quick to adopt an adversary posture toward it.

It is this class of people who are most eloquent in their denunciations of inequality, and who are making such a controversial issue of it. Why? Inequality of income is no greater today than it was twenty years ago, and is certainly less than it was fifty years ago. Inequality of status and opportunity have visibly declined since World War II, as a result of the expansion of free or nearly-free higher education. (The percentage of our leading business executives who come from modest socioeconomic backgrounds is much greater today than in 1910.) Though there has been a mushrooming of polemics against the inequalities of the American condition, most of this socioeconomic literature is shot through with disingenuousness, sophistry, and unscrupulous statistical maneuvering. As Professor Seymour Martin Lipset has demonstrated, by almost any socioeconomic indicator one would select, American society today is—as best we can determine—*more* equal than it was one hundred years ago. Yet, one hundred years ago most Americans were boasting of the historically unprecedented equality that was to be found in their nation, whereas today many seem convinced that inequality is at least a problem and at worst an intolerable scandal.

The explanation, I fear, is almost embarrassingly vulgar in its substance. A crucial clue was provided several years ago by Professor Lewis Feuer, who made a survey of those American members of this "new class" of the college-educated— engineers, scientists, teachers, social scientists, psychologists, etc.—who had visited the Soviet Union in the 1920s and 1930s, and had written admiringly of what they saw. In practically all cases, what they saw was power and status in the possession of their own kinds of people. The educators were enthusiastic about the "freedom" of educators in the USSR to run things as they saw fit. Ditto the engineers, the psychologists, and the rest. Their perceptions were illusory, of course, but this is less significant than the wishful thinking that so evidently lay behind the illusions. The same illusions, and the same wishful thinking, are now to be noticed among our academic tourists to Mao's China.

The simple truth is that the professional classes of our modern bureaucratized societies are engaged in a class struggle with the business community for status and power. Inevitably, this class struggle is conducted under the banner of "equality"—a banner also raised by the bourgeoisie in *its* revolutions. Professors are genuinely indignant at the expense accounts which business executives have and which they do not. They are, in contrast, utterly convinced that *their* privileges are "rights" that are indispensable to the proper workings of a good society. Most academics and professional people are even unaware that they are among the "upper" classes of our society. When one points this out to them, they refuse to believe it.[1]

The animus toward the business class on the part of members of our "new class" is expressed in large ideological terms. But what it comes down to is that our *nuovi uomini* are persuaded they can do a better job of running our society and feel entitled to have the opportunity. This is what *they* mean by "equality."

Having said this, however, one still has to explain the authentic moral passion that motivates our egalitarians of the "new class." They are not motivated by any pure power-lust; very few people are. They clearly dislike—to put it mildly—our liberal, bourgeois, commercial society, think it unfit to survive, and seek power to reconstruct it in some unspecified but radical way. To explain this, one has to turn to the intellectuals—the real ones—who are the philosophical source of their ideological discontent.

Any political community is based on a shared conception of the common good, and once this conception becomes ambiguous and unstable, then the justice of any social order is called into question. In a democratic civilization, this questioning will always take the form of an accusation of undue privilege. Its true meaning, however, is to be found behind the literal statements of the indictment.

It is interesting to note that, from the very beginnings of modern bourgeois civilization, the class of people we call intellectuals—poets, novelists, painters, men of letters—has never accepted the bourgeois notion of the common good. This notion defines the common good as consisting mainly of personal security under the law, personal liberty under the law, and a steadily increasing material prosperity for those who apply themselves to that end. It is, by the standards of previous civilizations, a "vulgar" conception of the common good: there is no high nobility of purpose, no selfless devotion to transcendental ends, no awe-inspiring heroism. It is, therefore, a conception of the common good that dispossesses the intellectual of his traditional prerogative, which was to celebrate high nobility of purpose, selfless devotion to transcendental ends, and awe-inspiring heroism. In its place, it offered the intellectuals the freedom to write or compose as they pleased and then to sell their wares in the marketplace as best they could. This "freedom" was interpreted by—one can even say experienced by—intellectuals as a base servitude to philistine powers. They did not accept it two hundred years ago; they do not accept it today.

The original contempt of intellectuals for bourgeois civilization was quite explicitly "elitist," as we should now say. It was the spiritual egalitarianism of bourgeois civilization that offended them, not any material inequalities. They

---

1. One of the reasons they are so incredulous is that they do not count as "income"—as they should—such benefits as tenure, long vacations, relatively short working hours, and all of their other prerogatives. When a prerogative is construed as a "right," it ceases to be seen as a privilege.

anticipated that ordinary men and women would be unhappy in bourgeois civilization precisely because it was a civilization of and for the "common man"—and it was their conviction that common men could only find true happiness when their lives were subordinated to and governed by uncommon ideals, as conceived and articulated by intellectuals. It was, and is, a highly presumptuous and self-serving argument to offer—though I am not so certain that it was or is altogether false. In any case, it was most evidently not an egalitarian argument. It only became so in our own century, when aristocratic traditions had grown so attenuated that the only permissible anti-bourgeois arguments had to be framed in "democratic" terms. The rise of socialist and communist ideologies made this transition a relatively easy one. A hundred years ago, when an intellectual became "alienated" and "radicalized," he was as likely to move "Right" as "Left." In our own day, his instinctive movement will almost certainly be to the "Left."

With the mass production of "intellectuals" in the course of the 20th century, traditional intellectual attitudes have come to permeate our college-educated upper-middle classes, and most especially the children of these classes. What has happened to the latter may be put with a simplicity that is still serviceably accurate: they have obtained enough of the comforts of bourgeois civilization, and have a secure enough grip upon them, to permit themselves the luxury of reflecting uneasily upon the inadequacies of their civilization. They then discover that a life that is without a sense of purpose creates an acute experience of anxiety, which in turn transforms the universe into a hostile, repressive place. The spiritual history of mankind is full of such existential moments, which are the seedbeds of gnostic and millenarian movements—movements that aim at both spiritual and material reformations. Radical egalitarianism is, in our day, exactly such a movement.

The demand for greater equality has less to do with any specific inequities of bourgeois society than with the fact that bourgeois society is seen as itself inequitable because it is based on a deficient conception of the common good. The recent history of Sweden is living proof of this proposition. The more egalitarian Sweden becomes—and it is already about as egalitarian as it is ever likely to be—the more *enragés* are its intellectuals, the more guilt-ridden and uncertain are its upper-middle classes, the more "alienated" are its college-educated youth. Though Swedish politicians and journalists cannot bring themselves to believe it, it should be obvious by now that there are *no* reforms that are going to placate the egalitarian impulse in Swedish society. Each reform only invigorates this impulse the more, because the impulse is not, in the end, about equality at all but about the quality of life in bourgeois society.

In Sweden, as elsewhere, it is only the common people who remain loyal to the bourgeois ethos. As well they might: it is an ethos devised for their satisfaction. Individual liberty and security—in the older, bourgeois senses of these terms—and increasing material prosperity are still goals that are dear to the hearts of the working classes of the West. They see nothing wrong with a better, bourgeois life: a life without uncommon pretensions, a life to be comfortably lived by common men. This explains two striking oddities of current politics: (1) The working classes have, of all classes, been the most resistant to the spirit of radicalism that has swept the upper levels of bourgeois society; and (2) once a government starts making concessions to this spirit—by announcing its dedication to egalitarian reforms—the working class is rendered insecure and fearful, and so becomes more militant in *its* demands. These demands may be put in terms of greater equality of income and privilege—but, of course, they also and always mean greater inequality vis-à-vis other sections of the working class and those who are outside the labor force.

Anyone who is familiar with the American working class knows—as Senator McGovern discovered—that they are far less consumed with egalitarian bitterness or envy than are college professors or affluent journalists. True, they do believe that in a society where so large a proportion of the national budget is devoted to the common defense, there ought to be some kind of "equality of sacrifice," and they are properly outraged when tax laws seem to offer wealthy people a means of tax avoidance not available to others. But they are even more outraged at the way the welfare state spends the large amounts of tax moneys it does collect. These moneys go in part to the nonworking population and in part to the middle-class professionals who attend to the needs of the nonworking population (teachers, social workers, lawyers, doctors, dieticians, civil servants of all description). The "tax rebellion" of recent years has been provoked mainly by the rapid growth of this welfare state, not by particular inequities in the tax laws —inequities, which, though real enough, would not, if abolished, have any significant impact on the workingman's tax burden. After all, the 20 billion dollars—a highly exaggerated figure, in my opinion—that Senator McGovern might "capture" by tax reforms would just about pay for his day-care center proposals, which the working class has not displayed much interest in.

Still, though ordinary people are not significantly impressed by the assertions and indignations of egalitarian rhetoric, they cannot help but be impressed by the fact that the ideological response to this accusatory rhetoric is so feeble. Somehow, bourgeois society seems incapable of explaining and justifying its inequalities and how they contribute to or are consistent with the common good. This, I would suggest, derives from the growing bureaucratization of the economic order, a process which makes bourgeois society ever more efficient economically, but also ever more defenseless before its ideological critics.

For any citizen to make a claim to an unequal share of income, power, or status, his contribution has to be—and has to be seen to be—a human and personal thing. In no country are the huge salaries earned by film stars or popular singers or professional athletes a source of envy or discontent. More than that: in most countries—and especially in the United States— the individual entrepreneur who builds up his own business and becomes a millionaire is rarely attacked on egalitarian grounds. In contrast, the top executives of our large corporations, most of whom are far less wealthy than Frank Sinatra or Bob Hope or Mick Jagger or Wilt Chamberlain, cannot drink a martini on the expense account without becoming the target of a "populist" politician. These faceless and nameless personages (who is the president of General Electric?) have no clear title to their privileges—and I should say the reason is precisely that they are nameless and faceless. One really has no way of knowing what they are doing "up there," and whether what they are doing is in the public interest or not.

It was not always so. In the 19th century, at the apogee of the bourgeois epoch, the perception of unequal contributions was quite vivid indeed. The success of a businessman was taken to be testimony to his personal talents and character— especially character, than which there is nothing more personal. This explains the popularity of biographies of successful entrepreneurs, full of anecodotes about the man and with surprisingly little information about his economic activities. In the 20th century, "entrepreneurial history," as written in our universities, becomes the history of the firm rather than the biography of a man. To a considerable extent, of course, this reflects the fact that most businessmen today are not "founding fathers" of a firm but temporary executives in a firm: the bureaucratization of modern society empties the category of the bourgeois of its human content. To the best of my knowledge, the only notable biography of a living businessman to have appeared in recent years was that of Alfred P. Sloan, who made his contribution to General Motors a good half century ago.

Nor is it only businessmen who are so affected. As the sociological cast of mind has gradually substituted itself for the older bourgeois moral-individualist cast of mind, military men and statesmen have suffered a fate similar to that of businessmen. Their biographies emphasize the degree to which they shared all our common human failings; their contributions to the common good, when admitted at all, are ascribed to larger historical forces in whose hands they were little more than puppets. They are all taken to be representative men, not exceptional men.

But when the unequal contributions of individuals are perceived as nothing but the differential functions of social or economic or political roles, then only those inequalities absolutely needed to perform these functions can be publicly justified. The burden of proof is heavy indeed, as each and every inequality must be scrutinized for its functional purport. True, that particular martini, drunk in that place, in that time, in that company, might contribute to the efficiency and growth of the firm and the economy. But would the contribution really have been less if the executive in question had been drinking water?[2]

So this, it appears to me, is what the controversy "about equality" is really about. We have an intelligentsia which so despises the ethos of bourgeois society, and which is so guilt-ridden at being implicated in the life of this society, that it is inclined to find even collective suicide preferable to the status quo. (How else can one explain the evident attraction which totalitarian regimes possess for so many of our writers and artists?) We have a "New Class" of self-designated "intellectuals" who share much of this basic attitude—but who, rather than committing suicide, pursue power in the name of equality. (The children of this "New Class," however, seem divided in their yearnings for suicide via drugs, and in their lust for power via "revolution.") And then we have the ordinary people, working-class and lower-middle-class, basically loyal to the bourgeois order but confused and apprehensive at the lack of clear meaning in this order—a lack derived from the increasing bureaucratization (and accompanying impersonalization) of political and economic life. All of these discontents tend to express themselves in terms of "equality"—which is in itself a quintessentially bourgeois ideal and slogan.

It is neither a pretty nor a hopeful picture. None of the factors contributing to this critical situation is going to go away; they are endemic to our 20th-century liberal-bourgeois society. Still, one of the least appreciated virtues of this society is its natural recuperative powers—its capacity to change, as we say, but also its

---

2. As Professor Peter Bauer has pointed out, the very term "distribution of income" casts a pall of suspicion over existing inequalities, implying as it does that incomes are not personally *earned* but somehow *received* as the end product of mysterious (and therefore possibly sinister) political-economic machinations.

capacity to preserve itself, to adapt and survive. The strength of these powers always astonishes us, as we anticipate (even proclaim) an imminent apocalypse that somehow never comes. And, paradoxically enough, this vitality almost surely has something to do with the fact that the bourgeois conception of equality, so vehemently denounced by the egalitarian, is "natural" in a way that other political ideas—egalitarian or anti-egalitarian—are not. Not necessarily in all respects superior, but more "natural." Let me explain.

The founding fathers of modern bourgeois society (John Locke, say, or Thomas Jefferson) all assumed that biological inequalities among men—inequalities in intelligence, talent, abilities of all kinds—were not extreme, and therefore did not justify a society of hereditary privilege (of "two races," as it were). This assumption we now know to be true, demonstrably true, as a matter of fact. Human talents and abilities, as measured, do tend to distribute themselves along a bell-shaped curve, with most people clustered around the middle, and with much smaller percentages at the lower and higher ends. That men are "created equal" is not a myth or a mere ideology—unless, of course, one interprets that phrase literally, which would be patently absurd and was never the bourgeois intention. Moreover, it is a demonstrable fact that in all modern, bourgeois societies, the distribution of income is also roughly along a bell-shaped curve, indicating that in such an "open" society the inequalities that do emerge are not inconsistent with the bourgeois notion of equality.

It is because of this "natural tyranny of the bell-shaped curve," in the conditions of a commercial society, that contemporary experiments in egalitarian community-building—the Israeli kibbutz, for instance—only work when they recruit a homogeneous slice of the citizenry, avoiding a cross-section of the entire population. It also explains why the aristocratic idea—of a distribution in which the righthand section of the bell curve is drastically shrunken—is so incongruent with the modern world, so that modern versions of superior government by a tiny elite (which is what the communist regimes are) are always fighting against the economic and social tendencies inherent in their own societies. Purely egalitarian communities are certainly feasible—but only if they are selective in their recruitment and are relatively indifferent to economic growth and change, which encourages differentiation. Aristocratic societies are feasible, too—most of human history consists of them—but only under conditions of relative economic lethargy, so that the distribution of power and wealth is insulated from change. But once you are committed to the vision of a predominantly commercial society, in which flux and change are "normal"—in which men and resources are expected to move to take advantage of new economic opportunities —then you find yourself tending toward the limited inequalities of a bourgeois kind.

This explains one of the most extraordinary (and little-noticed) features of 20th-century societies: how relatively invulnerable the distribution of income is to the efforts of politicians and ideologues to manipulate it. In all the Western nations—the United States, Sweden, the United Kingdom, France, Germany— despite the varieties of social and economic policies of their governments, the distribution of income is strikingly similar. Not identical; politics is not entirely impotent, and the particular shapre of the "bell" can be modified—but only with immense effort, and only slightly, so that to the naked eye of the visitor the effect is barely visible.[3] Moreover, available statistics suggest that the distribution of income in the communist regimes of Russia and Eastern Europe, despite both their egalitarian economic ideologies and aristocratic political structure, moves closer every year to the Western model, as these regimes seek the kind of economic growth that their "common men" unquestionably desire. And once the economic structure and social structure start assuming the shape of this bell-shaped curve, the political structure—the distribution of political power—follows along the same way, however slowly and reluctantly. The "Maoist" heresy within communism can best be understood as a heroic—but surely futile—rebellion against the gradual submission of communism to the constraints of the bell-shaped curve.

So bourgeois society—using this term in its larger sense, to include such "mixed economies" as prevail in Israel or Sweden or even Yugoslavia—is not nearly so fragile as its enemies think or its friends fear. Only a complete reversal of popular opinion toward the merits of material prosperity and economic growth would destroy it, and despite the fact that some of our citizens seem ready for such a reversal, that is unlikely to occur.

The concern and distress of our working- and lower-middle classes over the bureaucratization of modern life can, I think, be coped with. One can envisage reforms that would encourage their greater "participation" in the corporate structures that dominate our society; or one can envisage reforms that would whittle down the size and power of these structures, returning part way to a more traditional market economy; or one can envisage a peculiar—and, in pure principle, incoherent—combination of both. My own view is that this last alternative, an odd amalgam of the prevailing "Left" and "Right" viewpoints, is the most realistic and the most probable. And I see no reason why it should not work. It will not be the "best" of all possible societies. But the ordinary man, like Aristotle, is no utopian, and he will settle for a "merely satisfactory" set of social arrangements and is prepared to grant them a title of legitimacy.

The real trouble is not sociological or economic at all. It is that the "middling" nature of a bourgeois society falls short of corresponding adequately to the full range of man's spiritual nature, which makes more than middling demands upon the universe, and demands more than middling answers. This weakness of bourgeois society has been highlighted by its intellectual critics from the very beginning. And it is this weakness that generates continual dissatisfaction, especially among those for whom material problems are no longer so urgent. They may speak about "equality"; they may even be obsessed with statistics and pseudo-statistics about equality; but it is a religious vacuum—a lack of meaning in their own lives, and the absence of a sense of larger purpose in their society— that terrifies them and provokes them to "alienation" and unappeasable indignation. It is not too much to say that it is the death of God, not the emergence of any new social or economic trends, that haunts bourgeois society. And *this* problem is far beyond the competence of politics to cope with.

---

3. It must be kept in mind, of course, that retaining the shape of the curve is not inconsistent with *everyone* getting richer or poorer. The bell itself then moves toward a new axis.

Liberal

Herbert J. Gans: The New Egalitarianism

In a "nation of equals" many are considerably less equal than others and have grown impatient about not getting their share.

Although the fundamental idea of the Declaration of Independence is that "all men are created equal," Americans traditionally have been more interested in life, liberty, and the pursuit of happiness than in the pursuit of equality. In the last decade, however, their interests have begun to shift, and equality may be on its way to becoming as significant as liberty in the hierarchy of American goals.

The shift began approximately on the day in 1955 when Mrs. Rose Parks of Montgomery, Alabama, decided that she was no longer willing to sit in the rear of a bus. Much has been written about the ensuing political and social unrest, but few observers have emphasized that the revolts of the blacks, the young, and others have a common theme: the demand for greater equality by the less than equal. Blacks have agitated for racial equality through black power; students, in high schools as well as in colleges, have demanded more power on the campus; teen-agers have begun to claim the sexual freedom now available to young adults, and in less public ways they—and even younger children—have sought more equality within the family. And, of course, many women are now demanding equality with men, and homosexuals with heterosexuals.

Similar developments have been occurring in the economy and the polity. Wage workers have begun to demand guaranteed annual incomes and the other privileges that salaried workers enjoy. Public employees have struck for wage equity with workers in private industry. Assembly line workers have sought better working conditions and more control over the operation of the line. Enlisted men have called for reductions in the power of officers.

In politics the 1960s saw the emergence of the drive for community control—attempts by urban residents to obtain more power over their neighborhoods. Subsequently, community control broadened into a movement to reduce the power of bureaucracies at all levels of government and of professionals over their clients; for example, of doctors over patients, teachers over parents, and planners over home owners. Consumers have called for more control over what goods are to be produced and sold, environmentalists over how they are to be produced. Stockholders have demanded a greater role in the decisions taken by management.

Few of these demands have been explicitly phrased in terms of equality; most of those making the demands have spoken of autonomy and democracy. Many have actually asked for more liberty. Still, if all of these demands are put together, they mean more income for some and higher costs for others, more power for some and less for others. If the demands were heeded, the eventual outcome would be greater overall equality.

No one can accurately predict whether or not these demands will be heeded, but egalitarian ideas are cropping up with increased frequency among politicians and in the media. Senator Fred Harris's populist presidental campaign, which called for some income redistribution, was short-lived, but Senator George McGovern has proposed a comprehensive tax reform program along the same lines, and Governor George Wallace occasionally injects egalitarian notions into his campaign speeches. Widely read journalists, such as Tom Wicker, Jack Newfield, and *New Republic's* TRB, have talked and written about the need for equality. In March an article entitled "Equality" appeared in *Fortune*; it sought, rather gingerly, to prepare the business community for a more egalitarian future.

The current interest in equality cannot be explained away as the plaints of discontented minorities and newly radicalized public figures. It stems from the fact that America is, and always has been, a very unequal society. Take the distribution of income. The poorest fifth of the U.S. population receives only 4 per cent of the nation's annual income, and the next poorest fifth, only 11 per cent, while the richest fifth gets about 45 per cent, and the 5 per cent at the top, over 20 per cent. Inequality of assets is even greater: 1 per cent of the people control more than one-third of the country's wealth. Although many Americans now own some stocks, 2 per cent of all individual stockholders own about two-thirds of stocks held by individuals.

The same inequality exists in the business world. Of the almost two million corporations in America, one-tenth of 1 per cent controls 55 per cent of the total corporate assets; 1.1 per cent controls 82 per cent. At the other end of the spectrum, 94 per cent of the corporations own only 9 per cent of the total assets. Even the public economy is unequal, for the poor pay a larger share of their incomes for taxes than other groups; people earning less than $2,000 pay fully half of their incomes in direct and indirect taxes as compared with only 45 per cent paid by those earning $50,000 or more. Moderate income groups are not much better off; people earning $8,000-$10,000 a year pay only 4 percent less of their income than those making $25,000-$50,000.

Of course, the poor get something back from the government through welfare and other subsidies, but then so do the affluent, especially through indirect subsidies in the guise of tax policies, such as the oil-depletion allowance, crop supports, and tax exemptions granted to municipal-bond purchasers. Philip Stern, author of *The Great Treasury Raid* and himself a multimillionaire, recently described these subsidies as "a welfare program that reverses the usual pattern and gives huge welfare payments to the superrich but only pennies to the very poor." Stern estimated that the annual subsidies came to $720,000 per family for people with million-dollar incomes, $650 per family for the $10,000-$15,000 middle-income group, and $16 per family for the under-$3,000 poor.

Political inequality is also rampant. For example, since about 13 per cent of the population is poor in terms of the official poverty line, an egalitarian political system would require that almost fifty congressmen and thirteen senators be representatives of the poor. This is not the case, however, even though big business, big labor, and even less numerous sectors of the population have their unofficial representatives in both houses of Congress. While Supreme Court action has finally brought about the one-man, one-vote principle in electing these representatives, the seniority system maintains the traditional pattern of inequality, and so a handful of congressmen and senators, many from rural districts, still hold much of the real power on Capitol Hill. Affluent individuals and well-organized interest groups in effect have more than one vote per man because they have far greater access to their elected representatives than the ordinary citizen and because they can afford to hire lobbyists who watch out for their interests and even help to write legislation.

These patterns of inequality are not new; although America has sometimes been described as a nation of equals and as a classless society, these are simply myths. To be sure, America never had the well-defined classes or estates that existed in Europe, but from its beginning it has nevertheless been a nation of unequals. For example, in 1774, among the minority of Philadelphians affluent enough to pay taxes, 10 per cent owned fully 89 per cent of the taxable property. Over the last 200 years the degree of economic inequality has been reduced somewhat, but in the last sixty years—since reliable statistics on income distribution have become available—that distribution has changed little.

Although the ideal of a nation of equals has existed in American life from the beginning, it has, in fact, never been pursued very energetically in either the economy or the polity. Even the ideal that every boy could be President of the United States or chairman of the board of General Motors has rarely been achieved; most of our presidents have been rich, and studies of the origins of American businessmen show that in the nineteenth century, as now, the large majority have themselves been sons of businessmen.

Nevertheless, over the last 200 years most Americans seem to have put up quietly with the prevailing inequality. Today, however, the traditional patience with inequality has disappeared, and for three reasons.

First, many Americans are now beginning to realize that the frontier, by which I mean the opportunity to strike out on one's own and perhaps to strike it rich, is closing down. The literal frontier in the West was closed before the turn of the century, but until recently, other frontiers were still thought to be open. Rural people hoped that they could become independent by saving up for a farm; factory workers, by going into business, perhaps opening a gas station or small workshop; and middle-class people, by entering the independent professions.

Today these hopes have begun to disappear, for the family farm is economically obsolete, the small store cannot compete with the chain, and the independent professions now consist more and more of salaried employees. Of course, there are still exceptions, and every year a few well-publicized individuals strike it rich, but their small number only proves the rule. Most Americans now realize that they will spend their working lives as employees and that they can best improve their fortunes by making demands on their employers and, because the government's role in the economy is rapidly increasing, on their political representatives.

Second, as people have voiced more political demands, they have also become less patient with political inequality, particularly with their increasing powerlessness as bureaucracies and corporations continue to get bigger. Indeed, many of the demands for change that sprung up during the 1960s were fledgling attempts to fight powerlessness and to redress the political imbalance.

Third, the affluence of the post-World War II era has enabled many Americans to raise their incomes to a point where they are no longer preoccupied solely with making ends meet. As a result, new expectations have emerged, not only for a higher standard of living but also for improvements in the quality of life and for greater power to control one's destiny. And, more than ever before, people believe that the economy and the government should help them achieve their new expectations.

What people demand is not necessarily what they will get, as the lingering recession of the last few years and the continuation of the war in Vietnam have persuasively demonstrated. Still, the demands associated with the equality revolution will not recede, and if America is to have any chance of becoming a more stable society, it must also become a more egalitarian society.

Once upon a time inequality helped to make America great. The country was built out of the energy of restless entrepreneurs, the labor supplied by the unequal, and the capital generated from both. Today, however, inequality is a major source of social instability and unrest and is even a cause of the rising rates of crime, delinquency, and social pathology—alcoholism, drug addiction, and mental illness, for example. The conventional wisdom maintains that crime and pathology are caused largely by poverty, but during the 1960s poverty declined while crime and pathology increased. In these same years, however, inequality did not decrease; by some estimates, it actually grew worse.

One conventional measure of inequality is the number of people who earn less than half of a country's median family income. In the U.S. between 1960 and 1970, when this median rose from $5,620 to $9,870, the number earning half the median dropped only 1 per cent—from 20 to 19. One can also define inequality by measuring how far the poor are from the median income. In 1960 income at the poverty line, earned only by the richest of the poor, came to 50 per cent of the median; by 1970 it came to only 40 per cent. In other words, during the decade the poverty line rose far more slowly than the median income, and the inequality gap between the poor and the median earners actually widened by a full 20 per cent.

This gap is not just economic, however; it also produces social and emotional consequences. Inequality gives rise to feelings of inferiority, which in turn generate inadequacy and self-hate or anger. Feelings of inadequacy and self-hate, more than poverty, account for the high rates of pathology; anger results in crime, delinquency, senseless violence—and, of course, in political protest as well. But inequality also has less dramatic consequences. For example, because they cannot afford to dress their children properly, some poor mothers refuse to send them to school; shabby clothes may protect a youngster from the elements —a flour sack made into a suit or dress will do that—but shabby clothes also mark the child as unequal, and mothers want to protect their children from this label even at the cost of depriving them of schooling.

The social and emotional consequences of inequality are also felt by moderate-income people, especially the almost 40 per cent of Americans who earn above the poverty line but below the median income. For example, many young factory workers now realize, as their fathers could not afford to realize, that they hold unpleasant jobs without much chance of advancement or escape, and that much blue-collar work is inferior to white-collar jobs, which are now the norm in the American economy. In fact, the pathology and the protest normally associated with the poor is beginning to develop among factory workers as well. Hard drugs are now showing up in blue-collar neighborhoods, and strikes over working conditions, such as the recent one at the General Motors plant in Lordstown, Ohio, are increasing in number and intensity.

Indeed, if the most serious inequalities in American life are not corrected, people who feel themselves to be most unequal are likely to find new ways of getting even with America. New kinds of school, factory, and office disturbances, ghetto unrest, and dropping out of the system can be expected, and more crime in middle-class urban neighborhoods and suburbs is likely, for crime has always been a way by which at least some poor people can obtain a primitive kind of income redistribution when society pays no heed to their inequality.

Inequality does not harm only the unequal; it hurts the entire society. The last ten years have demonstrated the fragility of the American political fabric, but the social fabric is also weak. Old sources of stability have disappeared, as has much of the traditional American culture that once provided satisfactions even under inegalitarian conditions. The small towns and rural areas that gave people a sense of rootedness, which compensated them for their poverty, are being depleted by out-migration. In the cities the ethnic groups, which maintained the peasants' necessary resignation to European inequality and provided group cohesion and a close-knit family life as compensation, are now Americanized. (Although a revival of ethnic identity may be taking place currently, the old cultures are not being resuscitated, for the new ethnic identity is political and actually calls for more equality for ethnics.) Increasingly, Americans today are members of a single mainstream culture, partly urban, partly suburban, and distinguished primarily by differences in income and education. The main-stream culture pursues values long identified with the American way of life, mainly individual and familial comforts, security, and self-improvement, but it strives for ever higher levels of these, and with ever rising expectations that they will be achieved. As a result, mainstream culture rejects traditional rural, ethnic, and other values that call for modest expectations of comfort, security, and self-improvement and that thus accept the prevailing inequality.

The continued rise in expectations makes it likely that American will enter a period of greater economic and political conflict, for, when almost everyone has higher expectations, there must inevitably be conflict over how these expectations are to be met and just whose expectations are to be met first and foremost.

America has always endured conflict, of course; after all, economic competition is itself a form of conflict. But conflict can tear society apart unless it can be resolved constructively. This is possible only if the participants in the conflict have, and feel they have, a chance to get what they want or, when this is not feasible, to get about as much as everyone else—if, in other words, the conflict ends in a compromise that meets everyone's needs as fairly as possible. But if the participants in the conflict are unequal, those with power and wealth will almost always get what they want, whether from government or from the economy.

Conflicts can best be compromised fairly if the society is more egalitarian, if differences of self-interest that result from sharp inequality of income and power can be reduced. The more egalitarian a society, the greater the similarity of interests among its citizens, and the greater the likelihood that disagreements between them can be settled through fair compromise. Also, only in a more egalitarian society is it possible to develop policies that are truly in the public interest, for only in such a society do enough citizens share enough interests so that these policies can be considered to be truly public ones.

Consequently, the time has come to start thinking about a more egalitarian America and to develop a model of equality that combines the traditional emphasis on the pursuit of liberty with the newly emerging need to reduce inequality. As Daniel Patrick Moynihan put it in the famous "Moynihan Report" of 1965, Equality of Opportunity must be transformed into Equality of Results. Equality of Opportunity simply enables people with more income and better education to win out over the less fortunate, even when the competition itself is equitable. Equality of Results means that people begin the competition more equal in these resources; therefore, the outcome is likely to be more equitable. Equality of Results does not mean absolute equality, however, either of income or of any other resource. It does mean sufficient reductions in present inequities to erase any insurmountable handicaps in the competition.

Models or methods for achieving equality have generally been *collectivist*; they call for replacing private institutions with public agencies that will take over the allocation of resources, typically through a nationalization of industry. This approach assumes that all resources belong equally to all people and that public ownership will bring about equality. When all the people own everything, however, they really do not own anything, enabling the officials who govern in the name of the people to make themselves more than equal politically and to restrict others' political liberties. This seems to be an almost inevitable outcome of collectivist policies, at least in poor countries, even though these policies have also reduced overall economic inequality.

An American equality model must be *individualist*; it must achieve enough equality to allow the pursuit of liberty to continue but not restrict equal access to liberty for others. An individualistic model of equality begins with these assumptions: that people are not ready to stop competing for material or nonmaterial gain or self-improvement; that they will not, for the sake of equality, become altruists who repress their ego-needs for the public good; and that they are not ready to surrender control over their own lives to a government, however democratic, that doles out liberty and equality through collective ownership of all resources. Consequently, an individualist model would aim for greater economic equality, not by nationalizing industry but by distributing stock ownership to larger numbers of people, as Louis Kelso, among others, has suggested.

Similarly, the model would not provide the same public or private goods and services to everyone; rather, it would attempt to equalize income and then let people decide to spend that income on goods and services of their own choosing. Nor would everyone have the same income. Instead, the model would enable people to maximize their earnings through their own efforts; it would create more equality through tax and subsidy policies, as in Sweden and Great Britain, for example. Greater equalization of incomes after taxes should not significantly reduce incentive, for even now rich people continue trying to make more money although most of the additional earnings goes to the tax collectors.

The reconciling of equality and liberty is not simple, and only a great deal of public debate can determine how it ought to be done. It is not simply a matter of giving up a little liberty for a little equality. There are many kinds of equality — economic, social, political, and sexual, among others. Which kinds are most important, how much equality is needed, and which resources, powers, rights, and privileges need to be equalized and which need to be allocated on libertarian principles must be debated.

Nevertheless, some of the basic requirements of a more egalitarian society can be outlined. The American political-bureaucratic complex must be restructured so that it will attend to the demands of average citizens rather than of those best organized to apply maximal political pressure or the largest campaign contributions. The right combination of centralization and citizen control has to be found to make this complex both effective and democratic, responsive to majority rule as well as to the rights of minorities, at state and inferior levels as well as at the federal level. Some basic services, such as health, education, legal aid, and housing, should be available to everyone at a decent level of quality, so that, for example, the poor would not be confined to slums or public housing projects but could choose from the same kind of housing as everyone else. They would obtain rent subsidies to help pay for it.

The economy must also be democratized; corporations need to become more accountable to consumers and the general public, and they must be required to shoulder the social and other indirect costs of their activities. Stock ownership has to be dispersed, taxes must be made progressive, and subsidies should be used extensively for egalitarian purposes. Unemployment and underemployment have to be eliminated and the poverty line raised so that the gaps between those at the bottom, middle, and top are reduced and so that eventually no one will earn less than 75 per cent of the median income: $7500 by today's income figures. Whether a ceiling on top incomes is economically necessary remains to be seen, although it may well be socially desirable. Even now there is considerable uproar over millionaires who pay no taxes. Nevertheless, more income equality cannot be achieved solely by redistributing some of the great wealth of the superrich; redirecting the benefits of future economic growth to the now less than equal and imposing higher taxes on the corporations and the top fifth of the population would also be necessary. Still, greater income equality can be brought about without excessive soaking of the rich; S.M. Miller has estimated that if only 10 per cent of the after-tax incomes of families earning more than $15,000 were shifted to those earning less than $4,000, the income of persons earning less than $4,000 would increase by more than half.

America is today sufficiently affluent to afford more income equality without great sacrifice by anyone. The Gross National Product is currently so high that if it were divided equally among all Americans, a family of four would receive $19,000. Part of the GNP must be used for investment, of course, but if what economists call Total Personal Income were divided up, a family of four would still receive $15,600, fully half as much again as the current median family income.

A more egalitarian America is thus economically feasible, but it would not be politically achievable without considerable political struggle. The more than equal would fight any inroads on their privileges, but even the less than equal might at first be unenthusiastic, fearful that promises would not be kept and that, as has so often happened in the past, high-sounding policy proposals would continue to result in legislation benefiting the wealthy and powerful. The less than equal would soon rally to genuinely egalitarian legislation, but the affluent would still have to be persuaded that money and privilege alone cannot buy happiness in a conflict-ridden society and that the current American malaise, from which they suffer as much as others, will disappear only with greater equality. Indeed, I am convinced that what Daniel Bell has called the postindustrial society cannot be held together unless private and public resources are shared sufficiently to give every American a fair chance in the pursuit of liberty. That is why equality is likely to become an increasingly insistent item on the agenda of American politics.

Socialist

Michael Walzer: In Defense of Equality

At the very center of conservative thought lies this idea; that the present division of wealth and power corresponds to some deeper reality of human life. Conservatives don't want to say merely that the present division is what it ought to be, for that would invite a search for some distributive principle—as if it were possible to *make* a distribution. They want to say that whatever the division of wealth and power is, it naturally is, and that all efforts to change it, temporarily successful in proportion to their bloodiness, must be futile in the end. We are then invited, as in Irving Kristol's recent *Commentary* artile, to reflect upon the perversity of those who would make the attempt.[1] Like a certain sort of leftist thought, conservative argument seems quickly to shape itself around a rhetoric of motives rather than one of reasons. Kristol is especially adept at that rhetoric and strangely unconcerned about the reductionism it involves. He aims to expose egalitarianism as the ideology of envious and resentful intellectuals. No one else cares about it, he says, except the "new class" of college-educated, professional, most importantly, professorial men and women, who hate their bourgeois past (and present) and long for a world of their own making.

I suppose I should have felt, after reading Kristol's piece, that the decent drapery of my socialist convictions has been stripped away, that I was left naked and shivering, small-minded and self-concerned. Perhaps I did feel a little like that, for my first impulse was to respond in kind, exposing anti-egalitarianism as the ideology of those other intellectuals—"they are mostly professors, of course" —whose spiritual course was sketched some years ago by the editor of *Commentary*. But that would be at best a degrading business, and I doubt that my analysis would be any more accurate than Kristol's. It is better to ignore the motives of these "new men" and focus instead on what they say: that the inequalities we are all familiar with are inherent in our condition, are accepted by ordinary people (like themselves), and are criticized only by the perverse. I think all these assertions are false; I shall try to respond to them in a serious way.

Kristol doesn't argue that we can't possibly have greater equality or greater inequality than we presently have. Both communist and aristocratic societies are possible, he writes, under conditions of political repression or economic

Reprinted from *Dissent*, Vol. 20, No. 4, Fall, 1973.

underdevelopment and stagnation. But insofar as men are set free from the coerciveness of the state and from material necessity, they will distribute themselves in a more natural way, more or less as contemporary Americans have done. The American way is exemplary because it derives from or reflects the real inequalities of mankind. Men don't naturally fall into two classes (patricians and plebeians) as conservatives once thought; nor can they plausibly be grouped into a single class (citizens or comrades) as leftists still believe. Instead, "human talents and abilities...distribute themselves along a bell-shaped curve, with most people clustered around the middle, and with much smaller percentages at the lower and higher ends." The marvels of social science!—this distribution is a demonstrable fact. And it is another "demonstrable fact that in all modern bourgeois societies, the distribution of income is also along a bell-shaped curve...." The second bell echoes the first. Moreover, once this harmony is established, "the political structure—the distribution of political power—follows along the same way...." At this point, Kristol must add, "however slowly and reluctantly," since he believes that the Soviet economy is moving closer every year to its natural shape, and it is admittedly hard to find evidence that nature is winning out in the political realm. But in the United States, nature is triumphant: we are perfectly bell-shaped.

The first bell is obviously the crucial one. The defense of inequality reduces to these two propositions: that talent is distributed unequally and that talent will out. Clearly, we all want men and women to develop and express their talents, but whenever they are able to do that, Kristol suggests, the bell-shaped curve will appear or reappear, first in the economy, then in the political system. It is a neat argument but also a peculiar one, for there is no reason to think that "human talents and abilities" in fact distribute themselves along a *single* curve, although income necessarily does. Consider the range and variety of human capacities: intelligence, physical strength, agility and grace, artistic creativity, mechanical skill, leadership, endurance, memory, psychological insight, the capacity for hard work—even, moral strength, sensitivity, the ability to express compassion. Let's assume that with respect to all these, most people (but different people in each case) cluster around the middle of whatever scale we can construct, with smaller numbers at the lower and higher ends. Which of these curves is actually echoed by the income bell? Which, if any, ought to be?

There is another talent that we need to consider: the ability to make money, the green thumb of bourgeois society—a secondary talent, no doubt, combining many of the others in ways specified by the immediate environment, but probably also a talent which distributes, if we could graph it, along a bell-shaped curve. Even this curve would not correlate exactly with the income bell because of the intervention of luck, that eternal friend of the untalented, whose most important social expression is the inheritance of property. But the correlation would be close enough, and it might also be morally plausible and satisfying. People who are able to make money ought to make money, in the same way that people who are able to write books ought to write books. Every human talent should be developed and expressed.

The difficulty here is that making money is only rarely a form of self-expression, and the money we make is rarely enjoyed for its intrinsic qualities (at least, economists frown upon that sort of enjoyment). In a capitalist world, money is the universal medium of exchange; it enables the men and women who possess it to purchase virtually every other sort of social good; we collect it for its exchange value. Political power, celebrity, admiration, leisure, works of art, baseball teams, legal advice, sexual pleasure, travel, education, medical care, rare books, sailboats —all these (and much more) are up for sale. The list is as endless as human desire and social invention. Now isn't it odd, and morally implausible and unsatisfying, that all these things should be distributed to people with a talent for making money? And even odder and more unsatisfying that they should be distributed (as they are) to people who have money, whether or not they made it, whether or not they possess any talent at all?

Rich people, of course, always look talented—just as princesses always look beautiful—to the deferential observer. But it is the first task of social science, one would think, to look beyond these appearances. "The properties of money," Marx wrote, "are my own (the possessor's) properties and faculties. What I am and can do it, therefor, not at all determined by my individuality. I *am* ugly, but I can buy the most beautiful woman for myself. Consequently, I am not ugly, for the effect of ugliness, its power to repel, is annulled by money . . . . I am a detestable, dishonorable, unscrupulous, and stupid man, but money is honored and so also is its possessor."[2]

It would not be any better if we gave men money in direct proportion to their intelligence, their strength, or their moral rectitude. The resulting distributions would each, no doubt, reflect what Kristol calls "the tyranny of the bell-shaped curve," though it is worth noticing again that the populations in the lower, middle, and upper regions of each graph would be radically different. But whether it was the smart, the strong, or the righteous who enjoyed all the things that money can buy, the oddity would remain: why them? Why anybody? In fact, there is no single talent or combination of talents which plausibly entitles a man to every available social good—and there is no single talent or combination of talents that necessarily must win the available goods of a free society. Kristol's bell-shaped curve is tyrannical only in a purely formal sense. Any particular distribution may indeed be bell-shaped, but there are a large number of possible distributions. Nor need there be a single distribution of all social goods, for different goods might well be distributed differently. Nor again need all these distributions follow this or that talent curve, for in the sharing of some social goods, talent does not seem a relevant consideration at all.

Consider the case of medical care, surely it should not be distributed to individuals because they are wealthy, intelligent, or righteous, but only because they are sick. Now, over any given period of time, it may be true that some men and women won't require any medical treatment, a very large number will need some moderate degree of attention, and a few will have to have intensive care. If that is so, then we must hope for the appearance of another bell-shaped curve. Not just any bell will do. It must be the right one, echoing what might be called the susceptibility-to-sickness curve. But in America today, the distribution of medical care actually follows closely the lines of the income graph. It's not how a man feels, but how much money he has that determines how often he visits a doctor. Another demonstrable fact! Does it require envious intellectuals to see that something is wrong?

There are two possible ways of setting things right. We might distribute income in proportion to susceptibility-to-sickness, or we might make sure that medical care is not for sale at all, but is available to those who need it. The second of these is obviously the simpler. Indeed, it is a modest proposal and already has wide support, even among those ordinary men and women who are said to be indifferent to equality. And yet, the distribution of medical care solely for medical reasons would point the way toward an egalitarian society, for it would call the dominance of the income curve dramatically into question.

II

What egalitarianism requires is that many bells should ring. Different goods should be distributed to different people for different reasons. Equality is not a simple notion, and it cannot be satisfied by a single distributive scheme—not even, I hasten to add, by a scheme which emphasizes need. "From each according to his abilities, to each according to his needs" is a fine slogan with regard to medical care. Tax money collected from all of us in proportion to our resources (these will never correlate exactly with our abilities, but that problem I shall leave aside for now) must pay the doctors who care for those of us who are sick. Other people who deliver similar sorts of social goods should probably be paid in the same way—teachers and lawyers, for example. But Marx's slogan doesn't help at all with regard to the distribution of political power, honor and fame, leisure time, rare books, and sailboats. None of these things can be distributed to individuals in proportion to their needs, for they are not things that anyone (strictly speaking) needs. They can't be distributed in equal amounts or given to whoever wants them, for some of them are necessarily scarce, and some of them can't be possessed unless other people agree on the proper name of the possessor. There is no criteria, I think, that will fit them all. In the past they have indeed been distributed on a single principle: men and women have posssessed them or their historical equivalents because they were strong or well-born or wealthy. But this only suggests that a society in which any single distributive principle is dominant cannot be an egalitarian society. Equality requires a diversity of principles, which mirrors the diversity both of mankind and of social goods.

Whenever equality in this sense does not prevail, we have a kind of tyranny, for it is tyrannical of the well-born or the strong or the rich to gather to themselves social goods that have nothing to do with their personal qualities. This is an idea beautifully expressed in a passage from Pascal's *Pensées*, which I am going to quote at some length, since it is the source of my own argument.[3]

> The nature of tyranny is to desire power over the whole world and outside its own sphere.
>
> There are different companies—the strong, the handsome, the intelligent, the devout—and each man reigns in his own, not elsewhere. But sometimes they meet, and the strong and the handsome fight for mastery—foolishly, for their mastery is of different kinds. They misunderstand one another, and make the mistake of each aiming at universal dominion. Nothing can win this, not even strength, for it is powerless in the kingdom of the wise....
>
> *Tyranny.* The following statements, therefore, are false and tyrannical. "Because I am handsome, so I should command respect." "I am strong, therefore men should love me...." "I am...etc."

Tyranny is the wish to obtain by one means what can only be had by another. We owe different duties to different qualities: love is the proper response to charm, fear to strength, and belief to learning.

Marx makes a very similar argument in one of the early manuscripts; perhaps he had the *pensée* in mind.

Let us assume man to be man, and his relation to the world to be a human one. Then love can only be exchanged for love, trust for trust, etc. If you wish to enjoy art you must be an artistically cultivated person; if you wish to influence other people, you must be a person who really has a stimulating and encouraging effect upon others. . . . If you love without evoking love in return, i.e., if you are not able, by the manifestation of yourself as a loving person, to make yourself a beloved person, then your love is impotent and a misfortune.[4]

The doctrine suggested by these passages it not an easy one, and I can expound it only in a tentative way. It isn't that every man should get what he deserves—as in the old definition of justice—for desert is relevant only to some of the exchanges that Pascal and Marx have in mind. Charming men and women don't deserve to be loved: I may love this one or that one, but it can't be the case that I ought to do so. Similarly, learned men don't deserve to be believed: they are believed or not depending on the arguments they make. What Pascal and Marx are saying is that love and belief can't rightly be had in any other way—can't be purchased or coerced, for example. It is wrong to seek them in any way that is alien to their intrinsic character. In its extended form, their argument is that for all our personal and collective resources, there are distributive reasons that are somehow *right*, that are naturally part of our ideas about the things themselves. So nature is reestablished as a critical standard, and we are invited to wonder at the strangeness of the existing order.

This new standard is egalitarian, even though it obviously does not require an equal distribution of love and belief. The doctrine of right reasons suggests that we pay equal attention to the "different qualities," and to the "individuality" of every man and woman, that we find ways of sharing our resources that match the variety of their needs, interests, and capacities. The clues that we must follow lie in the conceptions we already have, in the things we already know about love and belief, and also about respect, obedience, education, medical care, legal aid, all of the necessities of life—for this is no esoteric doctrine, whatever difficulties it involves. Nor is it a panacea for human misfortune, as Marx's last sentence makes clear: it is only meant to suggest a humane form of social accommodation. There is little we can do, in the best of societies, for the man who isn't loved. But there may be ways to avoid the triumph of the man who doesn't love—who buys love or forces it—or at least of his parallels in the larger social and political world: the leaders, for example, who are obeyed because of their coercive might or their enormous wealth. Our goal should be an end to tyranny, a society in which no man is master outside his sphere. That is the only society of equals worth having.

But it isn't readily had, for there is no necessity implied by the doctrine of right reasons. Pascal is wrong to say that "strength is powerless in the kingdom of the wise"—or rather, he is talking of an ideal realm and not of the intellectual world as we know it. In fact, wise men (at any rate, smart men) have often in the past defended the tyranny of the strong, as they still defend the tyranny of the rich. Sometimes, of course, they do this because they are persuaded of the necessity or the utility of tyrannical rule; sometimes for other reasons. Kristol suggests that whenever intellectuals are not persuaded, they are secretly aspiring to a tyranny of their own: they too would like to rule outside their sphere. Again, that's certainly true of some of them, and we all have our own lists. But it's not necessarily true. Surely it is possible, though no doubt difficult, for an intellectual to pay proper respect to the different companies of men. I want to argue that in our society the only way to do that, or to begin to do it, is to worry about the tyranny of money.

III

Let's start with some things that money cannot buy. It can't buy the American League pennant: star players can be hired, but victories presumably are not up for sale. It can't buy the National Book Award: writers can be subsidized, but the judges presumably can't be bribed. Nor, it should be added, can the pennant or the award be won by being strong, charming, or ideologically correct—at least we all hope not. In these sorts of cases, the right reasons for winning are built into the very structure of the competition. I am inclined to think that they are similarly built into a large number of social practices and institutions. It's worth focusing again, for example, on the practice of medicine. From ancient times, doctors were required to take an oath to help the sick, not the powerful or the wealthy. That requirement reflects a common understanding about the very nature of medical care. Many professionals don't share that understanding, but the opinion of ordinary men and women, in this case at least, is profoundly egalitarian.

The same understanding is reflected in our legal system. A man accused of a crime is entitled to a fair trial simply by virtue of being an accused man; nothing else about him is a relevent consideration. That is why defendants who cannot afford a lawyer are provided with legal counsel by the state: otherwise justice would be up for sale. And that is why defense counsel can challenge particular jurors thought to be prejudiced: the fate of the accused must hang on his guilt or innocence, not on his political opinions, his social class, or his race. We want different defendants to be treated differently, but only for the right reasons.

The case is the same in the political system, whenever the state is a democracy. Each citizen is entitled to one vote simply because he is a citizen. Men and women who are ambitious to exercise greater power must collect votes, but they can't do that by purchasing them; we don't want votes to be traded in the marketplace, though virtually everything else is traded there, and so we have made it a criminal offense to offer bribes to voters. The only right way to collect votes is to campaign for them, that is, to be persuasive, stimulating, encouraging, and so on. Great inequalities in political power are acceptable only if they result from a political process of a certain kind, open to argument, closed to bribery and coercion. The freely given suport of one's fellow citizens is the appropriate criteria for exercising political power and, once again, it is not enough, or it shouldn't be, to be physically powerful, or well-born, or even ideologically correct.

It is often enough, however, to be rich. No one can doubt the mastery of the wealthy in the spheres of medicine, justice, and political power, even though these are not their own spheres. I don't want to say, their unchallenged mastery, for in democratic states we have at least made a start toward restricting the tyranny of money. But we have only made a start: think how different America would have to be before these three companies of men—the sick, the accused, the politically ambitious—could be treated in strict accordance with their individual qualities. It would be immediately necessary to have a national health service, national legal assistance, the strictest possible control over campaign contributions. Modest proposals, again, but they represent so many moves toward the realization of that old socialist slogan about the abolition of money. I have always been puzzled by the slogan, for socialists have never, to my knowledge, advocated a return to a barter economy. But it makes a great deal of sense if it is interpreted to mean *the abolition of the power of money outside its sphere*. What socialists want is a society in which wealth is no longer convertible into social goods with which it has no intrinsic connection.

But it is in the very nature of money to be convertible (that's all it is), and I find it hard to imagine the sorts of laws and law enforcement that would be necessary to prevent monied men and women from buying medical care and legal aid over and above whatever social minimum is provided for everyone. In the U.S. today, people can even buy police protection beyond what the state provides, though one would think that it is the primary purpose of the state to guarantee equal security to all its citizens, and it is by no means the rich, despite the temptations they offer, who stand in greatest need and protection. But this sort of thing could be prevented only by a very considerable restriction of individual liberty—of the freedom to offer services and to purchase them. The case is even harder with respect to politics itself. One can stop overt bribery, limit the size of campaign contributions, require publicity, and so on. But none of these things will be enough to prevent the wealthy from exercising power in all sorts of ways to which their fellow citizens have never consented. Indeed, the ability to hold or spend vast sums of money is itself a form of power, permitting what might be called preemptive strikes against the political system. And this, it seems to me, is the strongest possible argument for a radical redistribution of wealth. So long as money is convertible outside its sphere, it must be widely and more or less equally held so as to minimize its distorting effects upon legitimate distributive processes.

IV

What is the proper sphere of wealth? What sorts of things are rightly had in exchange for money? The obvious answer is also the right one: all those economic goods and services, beyond what is necessary to life itself, which men find useful or pleasing. There is nothing degraded about wanting these things; there is nothing unattractive, boring, debased, or philistine about a society organized to provide them for its members. Kristol insists that a snobbish dislike for the sheer productivity of bourgeois society is a feature of eqalitarian argument. I would have thought that a deep appreciation of that productivity has more often marked the work of socialist writers. The question is, how are the products to be distributed? Now, the right way to possess useful and pleasing things is by making them, or growing them, or somehow providing them for others. The medium of exchange is money, and this is the proper function of money and ideally, its only function.

There should be no way of acquiring rare books and sailboats except by working for them. But this is not to say that men deserve whatever money they can get for the goods and services they provide. In capitalist society, the actual exchange value of the work they do is largely a function of market conditions over which they exercise no control. It has little to do with the intrinsic value of the work or with the individual qualities of the worker. There is no reason for socialists to respect it, unless it turns out to be socially useful to do so. There are other values, however, which they must respect, for money isn't the only or necessarily the most important thing for which work can be exchanged. A lawyer is surely entitled to the respect he wins from his colleagues and to the gratitude and praise he wins from his clients. The work he has done may also constitute a good reason for making him director of the local legal aid society; it may even be a good reason for making him a judge. It isn't, on the face of it, a good reason for allowing him an enormous income. Nor is the willingness of his clients to pay his fees a sufficient reason, for most of them almost certainly think they should be paying less. The money they pay is different from the praise they give, in that the first is extrinsically determined, the second freely offered.

In a long and thoughtful discussion of egalitarianism in the *Public Interest*, Daniel Bell worries that socialists today are aiming at an "equality of results" instead of the "just meritocracy" (the career open to talents) that he believes was once the goal of leftist and even of revoluntary politics.[5] I confess that I am tempted by "equality of results" in the sphere of money, precisely because it is so hard to see how a man can merit the things that money can buy. On the other hand, it is easy to list cases where merit (of one sort or another) is clearly the right distributive criteria, and where socialism would not require the introduction of any other principle.

1. Six people speak at a meeting, advocating different policies, seeking to influence the decision of the assembled group.

2. Six doctors are known to aspire to a hospital directorship.

3. Six writers publish novels and anxiously await the reviews of the critics.

4. Six men seek the company and love of the same woman.

Now, we all know the right reasons for the sorts of decisions, choices, judgments that are in question here. I have never heard anyone seriously argue that the woman must let herself be shared, or the hospital establish a six-man directorate, or the critics distribute their praise evenly, or the people at the meeting adopt all six proposals. In all these cases, the personal qualities of the individuals involved (as these appear to the others) should carry the day.

But what sorts of personal qualities are relevant to owning a $20,000 sailboat? A love for sailing, perhaps, and a willingness to build the boat or to do an equivalent amount of work. In American today, it would take a steelworker about two years to earn that money (assuming that he didn't buy anything else during all that time) and it would take a corporation executive a month or two. How can that be right, when the executivie also has a rug on the floor, air-conditioning, a deferential secretary, and enormous personal power? He's being paid as he goes, while the steelworker is piling up a kind of moral merit (so we have always been taught) by deferring pleasure. Surely there is no meritocratic defense for this sort of difference. It would seem much better to pay the worker and the executive more or less the same weekly wage and let the sailboat be bought by the man who is willing to forgo other goods and services, that is, by the man who really wants it. Is this "equality of result"? In fact, the results will be different, if the men are, and it seems to me that they will be different for the right reasons.

Against this view, there is a conventional but also very strong argument that can be made on behalf of enterprise and inventiveness. If there is a popular defense of inequality, it is this one, but I don't think it can carry us very far toward the inequalities that Kristol wants to defend. Consider the case of the man who builds a better mousetrap, or opens a restaurant and sells delicious blintzes, or does a little teaching on the side. He has no air-conditioning, no secretary, no power; probably his reward has to be monetary. He has to have a chance, at least, to earn a little more money than his less enterprising neighbors. The market doesn't guarantee that he will in fact earn more, but it does make it possible, and until some other way can be found to do that, market relations are probably defensible under the doctrine of right reasons. Here in the world of the petty-bourgeoisie, it seems appropriate that people able to provide goods or services that are novel, timely, or particularly excellent should reap the rewards they presumably had in mind when they went to work. And which they were right to have in mind: no one would want to feed blintzes to strangers, day after day, merely to win their gratitude.

But one might well want to be a corporation executive, day after day, merely to make all those decisions. It is precisely the people who are paid or who pay themselves vast sums of money who reap all sorts of other rewards too. We need to sort out these different forms of payment. First of all, there are rewards, like the pleasure of exercising power, which are intrinsic to certain jobs. An executive must make decisions—that's what he is there for—and even decisions seriously affecting other people. It is right that he should do that, however, only if he has been persuasive, stimulating, encouraging, and so on, and won the support of a majority of those same people. That he owns the coproration or has been chosen by the owners isn't enough. Indeed, given the nature of corporate power in contemporary society, the following statement (to paraphrase Pascal) is false and tyrannical: because I am rich, so I should make decisions and command obedience. Even in corporations organized democratically, of course, the personal execise of power will persist. It is more likely to be seen, however, as it is normally seen in political life—as the chief attraction of executive positions. And this will cast a new light on the other rewards of leadership.

The second of these consists in all the side-effects of power: prestige, status, deference, and so on. Democracy tends to reduce these, or should tend that way when it is working well, without significantly reducing the attractions of decision-making. The same is true of the third form of reward, money itself, which is owed to work, but not necessarily to place and power. We pay political leaders much less than corporation executives, precisely because we understand so well the excitement and appeal of political office. Insofar as we recognize the political character of corporations, then, we can pay their executives less too. I doubt that there would be a lack of candidates even if we paid them no more than was paid to any other corporation employee. Perhaps there are reasons for paying them more—but not meritocratic reasons, for we give all the attention that is due to their merit when we make them our leaders.

We don't give all due attention to the restaurant owner, however, merely by eating his blintzes. Him we have to pay, and he can ask, I suppose, whatever the market will bear. That's fair enough, and no real threat to equality so long as he can't amass so much money that he becomes a threat to the integrity of the political system and so long as he does not exercise power, tyrannically, over other men and women. Within his proper sphere, he is as good a citizen as any other. His activities recall Dr. Johnson's remark: "There are few ways in which man can be more innocently employed than in getting money."

V

The most immediate occasion of the conservative attack on equality is the reappearance of the quota system—newly designed, or so it is said, to move us closer to egalitarianism rather than to maintain old patterns of religious and racial discrimination. Kristol does not discuss quotas, perhaps because they are not widely supported by professional people (or by professors): the disputes of the last several years do not fit the brazen simplicity of his argument. But almost everyone else talks about them, and Bell worries at some length, and rightly, about the challenge quotas represent to the "just meritocracy" he favors. Indeed, quotas in any form, new or old, establish "wrong reasons" as the basis of important social decisions, perhaps the most important social decisions: who shall be a doctor, who shall be a lawyer, and who shall be a bureaucrat. It is obvious that being black or a woman or having a Spanish surname (any more than being white, male, and Protestant) is no qualification for entering a university or a medical school or joining the civil service. In a sense, then, the critique of quotas consists almost entirely of a series of restatements and reiterations of the argument I have been urging in this essay. One only wishes that the critics would apply it more generally than they seem ready to do. There is more to be said, however, if they consistently refuse to do that.

The positions for which quotas are being urged are, in Amerian today, key entry points to the good life. They open the way, that is, to a file marked above all by a profusion of goods, material and moral: professions, conveniences, prestige, and deference. Many of these goods are not in any plausible sense appropriate rewards for the work that is being done. They are merely the rewards that upper classes throughout history have been able to seize and hold for their members. Quotas, as they are currently being used, are a way of redistributing these rewards by redistributing the social places to which they conventionally pertain. It is a bad way, because one really wants doctors and (even) civil servants to have certain sorts of qualifications. To the people on the receiving end of medical and bureaucratic services, race and class are a great deal less important than knowledge, competence, courtesy, and so on. I don't want to say that race and class are entirely unimportant: it would be wrong to underestimate the distortions introduced by an inegalitarian society into these sorts of human relations. But if the right reason for receiving medical care is being sick, then the right reason for giving medical care is being able to help the sick. And so medical schools should pay attention, first of all and almost exclusively, to the potential helpfulness of their applicants.

But they may be able to do that only if the usual connections between place and reward are decisely broken. Here is another example of the doctrine of right reasons. If men and women wanted to be doctors primarily because they wanted to be helpful, they would have no reason to object when judgments were made about their potential helpfulness. But so long as there are extrinsic reasons for wanting to be a doctor, there will be pressure to choose doctors (that is, to make medical school places available) for reasons that are similarly extrinsic. So long as the goods that medical schools distribute include more than certificates of competence, include, to be precise, certificates of earning power, quotas are not entirely implausible. I don't see that being black is a worse reason for owning a sailboat than being a doctor. They are equally bad reasons.

Quotas today are a means of lower-class aggrandizement, and they are likely to be resolutely opposed, opposed without guilt and worry, only by people who are entirely content with the class structure as it is and with the present distribution of goods and services. For those of us who are not content, anxiety can't be avoided. We know that quotas are wrong, but we also know that the present distribution of wealth makes no moral sense, that the dominance of the income curve plays havoc with legitimate distributive principles, and that quotas are a form of redress no more irrational than the world within which and because of which they are demanded. In an egalitarian society, however, quotas would be unnecessary and inexcusable.

VI

I have put forward a difficult argument in very brief form, in order to answer Kristol's even briefer argument—for he is chiefly concerned with the motives of those who advocate equality and not with the case they make or try to make. He is also concerned, he says, with the fact that equality has suddenly been discovered and is now for the first time being advocated as the *chief* virtue of social institutions: as if societies were not complex and values ambiguous. I don't know what discoverers and advocates he has in mind.[6] But it is worth stressing that equality as I have described it does not stand alone, but is closely related to the idea of liberty. The relation is complex, and I cannot say very much about it here. It is a future of the argument I have made, however, that the right reason for distributing love, belief, and, most important for my immediate purposes, political power is the freely given consent of lovers, believers, and citizens. In these sorts of cases, of course, we all have standards to urge upon our fellows: we say that so and so should not be believed unless he offers evidence or that so and so should not be elected to political office unless he commits himself to civil rights. But clearly credence and power are not and ought not to be distributed according to my standards or yours. What is necessary is that everyone else be able to say yes or no. Without liberty, then, there could be no rightful distribution at all. On the other hand, men are not free, not politically free at least, if *his* yes, because of his birth or place or fortune, counts seventeen times more heavily than *my* no. Here the case is exactly as socialists have always claimed it to be: liberty and equality are the two chief virtues of social institutions, and they stand best when they stand together.

Notes

1. "About Equality," *Commentary*, November 1972.

2. *Early Writings*, trans. T. B. Bottomore (London: Watts, 1963), p. 191.

3. I am also greatly indebted to Bernard Williams, in whose essay "'The Idea of Equality" (first published in Laslett and Runciman, *Philosophy, Politics and Society*, second series [Oxford: Blackwell, 1962]) a similar argument is worked out. The example of medical care, to which I recur, is suggested by him. The Pascal quote is from J. M. Cohen's translation of *The Pensées* (London and Baltimore: Penguin Classics, 1961), no. 244.

4. *Early Writings*, pp. 193-94.

5. "On Meritocracy and Equality," *Public Interest*, Fall 1972.

6. The only writer he mentions is John Rawls, whose *Theory of Justice* Kristol seems entirely to misunderstand. For Rawls explicitly accords priority to the "liberty principle" over those other maxims that point toward greater equality.

Part 4

WHO'S IN CHARGE?

Power—the ability to get people to do what you want even when it's not what they want to do—is the subject matter here. As implied by this definition, there are two kinds of power: (1) *coercion*, the application of force to accomplish desired ends, and (2) *authority*, the ability to get people to undertake an action because they believe its originator has the right to order its execution and they are thus obliged to accede.[1]

The question, Who's in charge? or, Who rules America? becomes controversial as soon as one treats skeptically the premise of the usual high school civics textbook that America is ruled by the people through their elected representatives. An alternate thesis is that the major decisions which shape our society are made by a small group of powerful men rather than by all the citizens through their participation in the democratic process.

According to the elite thesis in its various forms, one dominant group makes all the major decisions in our society. This group is a self-perpetuating one and holds within its grasp the predominant economic, military, and political power of our society. Although some of its component members seem to represent diverse groups, in reality they work together in a coordinated effort to maintain control. This thesis of a ruling elite is both contrary to the idea of what America is supposed to be and painful to entertain for it shows how powerless most of us are. The existence of a ruling elite as a definable class of people is in accordance with Marxist theory. Orthodox Marxists state that any capitalist society is basically ruled by its economic leaders and that politicians and the political process carry out decisions made elsewhere by those who control the economy.

Research conducted by C. William Domhoff describes the existence of an upper economic class based on its control of wealth, education at elite schools, and membership in elite clubs.[2] C. Wright Mills, though a proponent of a similar thesis, selected different sources of power: according to Mills's argument in *The Power Elite*,[3] the major decisions in American society are made by a very small number of individuals in three institutional areas of American society: the military, joint chiefs of staff; the polity, that is, the office of the presidency; and the economy, that is, heads of major corporations.

After the publication of this work of Mills, the question of power in American society, traditionally left to political scientists to debate, became a topic of sociological interest. Reviewers in sociological journals charged that Mills lacked specific evidence to back up his theory, and sociologist Arnold Rose authored a work specifically designed to refute Mills.[4] In *The Power Structure*, Rose argued that a multiplicity of groups in American society contest for power: businessmen, unions, political organizations, and voluntary associations. His thesis was that on a particular issue, one group—or several in concert—may exercise power, but no single group controls all the levers of power. Rather, every group which is a major source of power is also at times controlled through power exercised by others.

Pluralism is the name for the thesis which argues that different and competing groups share in deciding what happens in American society. On a particular issue, some groups may be allies, while on another issue they may be on the opposite side. No group wins everything it wants on all issues. A common agreement on the rules of the game maintains a stable balance between the different groups. The pluralist thesis holds that bargaining on issues takes place in the give and take among elected representatives who arrange compromises and trade votes in order to pass legislation.[5]

By contrast, the elite thesis holds that the electoral level of politics is a sham which is manipulated through use of the economic power and control over the media by an elite. According to this premise, important decisions are made privately by the elite, and a lesser level of relatively unimportant decision-making is left to elected officials in order to maintain a facade of popular government.

One clear difference between Mills and Rose is the type and magnitude of decision each had in mind when he referred to the exercise of power. Mills thought the great decisions were those which would make the difference between World War III and peace. On Rose's level of analysis, key decisions were the nomination of a presidential candidate or the passage of major legislation through Congress.

Pluralism is, of course, what the liberal sees. The elite thesis describes the socialist view. The conservative view is mixed: sometimes openly and sometimes tacitly, it maintains overtly the pluralist position, although at the same time it offers justifications for the existence of elites.

Notes

1. For a further theoretical discussion of power, see Hans, Gerth and C. Wright Mills, Trans., *From Max Weber* (New York: Oxford University Press, 1953).

2. C. William Domhoff, *Who Rules America* (Englewood Cliffs, N. J.: Prentice-Hall, 1967), and *The Higher Circles* (New York: Random House, 1970).

3. C. Wright Mills, *The Power Elite* (New York: Oxford University Press, 1956).

4. Arnold Rose, *The Power Structure* (New York: Oxford University Press, 1967).

5. Robert Dahl, *Who Governs?: Democracy and Power in an American City* (New Haven: Yale University Press, 1961).

Chapter 10

MASS MEDIA

The mass media became a social problem in the late 1960s when a public debate erupted over whether one political viewpoint was presented to the exclusion of others. Groups to the left and the right of the political spectrum charged that their views were excluded. The left has long felt that its access to the mass media was limited to third party candidates presented in off hours on radio and television under equal time provisions of the Federal Communications Act. However, this exclusion was a matter of concern only to people on the left as few others paid attention to their charges of media bias.

Media bias became a national issue when former Vice President Spiro Agnew charged in a 1969 speech that TV newscasters and commentators criticized the Nixon administration from a liberal perspective. He claimed that the media portrayed the administration unfairly in news casts. They distorted the president's speeches by offering post delivery analyses. Agnew warned the media to change its treatment of the administration or it would be subject to sanctions from the federal government. One television network immediately dropped its post-presidential speech comments and some observers thought that another network muted its comments. Several high level television network executives charged that Agnew's speech was an attempt to muzzle the media and take away its First Amendment rights. This countercharge was supported by editorials in major newspapers. The ensuing confrontation between the media and the Nixon administration, further exacerbated during

317

the Watergate events, insured that the question of media bias remained a national issue.

The three articles included in this section were written within the context of this controversy. In the conservative article, Phillips argues that mass media has replaced business as the dominant institution in American society. A shift in power has also taken place within the communications industry. Through the 1950s the conservative perspective of the owners of newspapers, magazines and broadcasting companies was reflected in the content of the media. Beginning in the 1960s the liberal and left perspectives of reporters and newscasters replaced the conservative opinions of the owners as the dominant ideologies of the media. What caused this media revolution? According to Phillips, the expansion of major newspapers and their news services and the growth of the major TV networks shifted power downwards from the owners to the level of the working press. Reporters and newscasters used this independence to focus attention on the social conflicts and social movements emerging in American society during the 1960s. The media encouraged the growth of dissent and became more powerful itself as a spokesman for liberal causes. According to Phillips the "mediacracy" represents a new concentration of power in American society that must be limited.

In the liberal article, Tuchman argues that there is a three-sided struggle, between media owners, media professionals, and the government for control over what is disseminated as news. Television broadcasters whose stations exist on the basis of a license from the government wage a constant battle to have themselves considered as owners with the same prerogatives as newspaper publishers. Although ownership gives publishers legal control of the press, editors and reporters have attained a degree of autonomy by successfully advancing the claim to professional rights. As professionals they believe that they should decide what is news.

Nevertheless, reporters and journalists utilize narrow criteria for conceptualizing events as news. Ultimately news professionals legitimate the status quo. Viewing news as a succession of discrete events they remove underlying socio-economic structures from consideration. Reporters believe that their standards of interpretation produce facts, but the result is typically a story that eschews broader implications and reflects a middle class perspective on the world.

These professionally determined criteria are occasionally overridden by so-called "must " stories. Ordered by owners, they have to be printed. Tuchman concludes that a division of power within the media produces a diversity of viewpoints, if only from the right to the middle of the political spectrum.

In the socialist article, Ehrlich argues that there is no real conflict between media, government and business. The media protects business interests and aids the government. Nevertheless, the media is attacked by business and government. How can this apparent contradiction be explained? Ehrlich argues that although the elites of business, government, and media share common values, their different occupational positions result in minor disputes, which are fought within a framework of common interests. Business, government, and media are interrelated and the media are corporate controlled. This control is reflected in news policies that limit the reporting of dissent and minimize the existence of social conflict.

How can these analyses be so different? One explanation is the level at which the issue of media control is addressed. Whereas Ehrlich views the upper level of corporate ownership as ultimately significant, Phillips focuses primarily on the lower level of newscaster and reporter and Tuchman takes a balanced view. They differ over whether ownership of the media gives the owner power to determine the content of the news. Ehrlich argues that the media are controlled by the same capitalist class that controls large corporations. He provides data on the interrelations between major communications corporations and other major corporations to document this thesis.

But do corporate interlocks at the upper levels of organizational structures necessarily explain the actions of employees at a lower level? Tuchman argues that news media professionals have achieved considerable autonomy to present the news according to their own professional standards. Yet these standards are narrowly conceived. They funnel events into rigid predetermined categories, which often neglect the broader implications of stories. Nevertheless, the criteria are chosen by the news professionals and are only occasionally suspended from above. Phillips agrees that news professionals have achieved autonomy but does not view these editorial criteria as merely technical. Most reporters and newscasters share a liberal to radical political orientation, which influences the content of their reporting. Phillips argues that reporters and newscasters are out-of-control of their more conservative corporate superiors, and he would like to see this situation rectified.

Liberals tend to believe that diversity of viewpoints exists in the media. They assume that the presentation of more than one viewpoint, even if they are merely two variations of a liberal perspective, is evidence of media fairness. Conservatives and socialists would only be satisfied of the existence of media diversity if their viewpoints were specifically and extensively presented. Each argues that the other's viewpoint is presented to the virtual exclusion of its own.

Conservative

Kevin P. Phillips: Mediacracy

Among the most important trends of the 1970s has been a spreading perception of the pivotal, well-nigh dominant, role the media have come to play in
American life. If the Industrial Revolution created a new elite and launched a
new, business domination of politics, the knowledge revolution raises the prospect of dominant *media* influence—of mediacracy instead of aristocracy or
democracy.

As of the mid-seventies, this possibility is just beginning to be taken seriously.
From various perspectives—political science, sociology, economics—theorists
are pinpointing the new centrality of the media. Author Joseph Epstein has even
argued that the media may play the same role in the post-industrial era that Wall
Street played in the earlier period: that of socioeconomic-elite-*cum*-bogeyman:

> The next national villain, if they have not already arrived in that role, figures to be
> the Media. . . . To break a politician, to make a celebrity, to turn an issue, these are not
> small things. Wall Street and Madison Avenue had money at their disposal, which gave
> them power; the Media have the attention of the public at their disposal, which gives
> them an equivalent if not greater power. . . . Should the country fall into a full depres-
> sion, who better to hold responsible than the party thought to hold the most power in
> the nation, and at the moment, that party is thought to be the media.[1]

While most Americans may not perceive the economic nature of the Post-
Industrial Revolution, they *have* perceived its impact. A survey taken in early
1974 by *U. S. News & World Report* found a cross section of national leaders
ranking television ahead of the White House as the country's number one power
center. In this respect, the past two decades have witnessed a vital quantum shift.
Economic data make this clear. The media have not simply become more powerful in the old context of things; *their growth has changed the old industrial-era
equation.*

By definition, the communications industry must serve as the linchpin of the
economy's new knowledge sector. But, through the nineteen fifties, while the
industrial era prevailed, the still relatively small and subservient communications industry had no particular ideological coloration of its own. Magazines,
broadcasting companies, newspapers, and advertising firms tended to be conservative, like the business community as a whole. This remains true in most
parts of the South, Midwest, and Rocky Mountains, where traditional economic
forms still dominate.

Then, as the communications industry ballooned during the late fifties and
early sixties, along with other knowledge-sector elements, it began to take on a
distinctly liberal ideology. The first media affected were those in the fashionable

Excerpted from Mediacracy: *American Parties and Politics in the Communications Age*, by
Kevin P. Phillips. Copyright © 1975 by Kevin P. Phillips. Reprinted by permission of
Doubleday and Co., Inc.
    1. Joseph Epstein, "The Media As Villain," *More*, September 1974, p. 24.

urban areas. Such media as *Time, Life, Newsweek*, the New York *Times*, the Washington *Post*, the Boston *Globe*, the Baltimore *Sun*, the Cowles publications, and the TV networks—many of them on the conservative side in the thirties—started becoming distinctly more liberal than the country as a whole. As the media revolution intensified, so did its ideological impact.

Here one must note that there is no real parallel outside the United States. Other countries have relatively small private-media sectors. Elsewhere, television is generally government controlled and not a massive private enterprise like CBS, NBC, and ABC. The concentration of private-media economic power in the United States—backstopped by other knowledge-sector enterprises, notably education—dwarfs that of any other nation. The United States is as far ahead of the rest of the world in the Post-Industrial Revolution as circa-1850 Britain was in the Industrial Revolution.

Most of the key U.S. media are owned by large communications conglomerates. Newspapers own broadcasting stations. Broadcasting companies own magazines and publishing houses. Since the communications business mushroomed in the sixties, it has begun creating its own culture—or, as Nixon-administration spokesmen argued, adversary culture. Even though most small-town and small-city newspapers remain conservative and Republican, the provincial print media have barely held their own since the fifties. With the rise of the knowledge industry, communications affluence and influence have tended to concentrate in the New York-Washington corridor (and in a few other areas such as Los Angeles and Chicago, where two important media baronies that were once conservative stalwarts—the Los Angeles *Times* and the Chicago *Tribune*—have become increasingly middle-of-the-road). It is this "New York-Washington media axis," with its "Ivy League elitist adversary culture," that triggered conservative animosity.

CHART 5
The Postwar Rise of the Communications Industry

	All figures in millions of dollars									
	1930	1935	1940	1945	1950	1955	1960	1965	1970	1973(Est)
Newspaper Receipts	1,073	668	846	1,792	2,375	2,926	4,136	5,156	6,967	8,310
Magazine Receipts	507	300	409	1,019	1,119	1,413	2,132	2,626	3,195	3,655
Radio Station Revenues	—	87	147	299	445	543	597	793	1,137	1,465
TV Station Revenues	—	—	—	0.3	106	745	1,269	1,965	2,808	3,700
Advertising Volume	2,607	1,690	2,088	2,874	5,710	9,194	11,932	15,255	19,600	25,765
Electronic Computer Sales	—	—	—	—	1	105	500	1,400	3,630	4,750

Source: Kevin R. Phillips.

Chart 5 shows the late-nineteen-fifties and early-nineteen-sixties coming of age of the communications industry. The rise of the New York-Washington media axis is less easy to chart, but here are some statistics. Since 1940, the New York *Times* has increased its circulation 30 per cent in its home city and 150 per cent beyond New York. The New York *Times* news service, purchased by only sixteen North American newspapers in 1956, is sold to about 250 today. The Washington *Post*/Los Angeles *Times* service, started in 1962 with twenty-one subscribers, now has over two hundred. In the years from 1940 to 1968, *Time*, *Newsweek*, and *U. S. News & World Report* increased their circulation by 585 per cent. Those are the big guns in the print media.

Television's growth is bigger still; just a few households had television in the years after World War II—few are without it today. Television has become a multibillion-dollar business, and the three New York-based television networks, via their news and documentary programs, have become the principal arbiters of American opinion. Survey after survey spotlights television as the most influential medium in the United States. One estimate has 90 per cent of U.S. national news coverage originating with UPI, AP, the New York *Times* Syndicate, Time Inc., the Washington *Post* (which owns *Newsweek*), and the television networks.[2]

Since the New York *Times*, the Washington *Post*, and three networks and major newsmagazines are all based in New York and Washington, as are most other opinion magazines (*Harper's Magazine*, *The New Republic*, etc.), most publishing houses, and many small broadcasting companies, the existence of a cultural-geographic "media axis" seems indisputable. Liberal opinions are virtually *de rigueur* within this milieu, and failure to advance them is professionally crippling. Daniel P. Moynihan errs in harping on elite Ivy League origins. Columnist Robert Novak best capsuled the dynamics this way, in April 1972: "The national media is a melting pot where the journalists, regardless of background, are welded into a homogenous ideological mold, joined to the liberal establishment and alienated from the masses of the country."[3]

This overwhelming left-liberal tilt has been strengthened by the interaction of the major media and the social upheavals of the sixties. Media expert Ben H. Bagdikian, in his book *The Information Machines*, noted that the communications revolution of the 1840s (Morse's telegraph, railroads, steam vessels, etc.) helped stir up Europe's revolutions of 1848, and he argues that "the spasms of change in American society in the mid-Nineteen Sixties are attributable in large part to new methods of communication."[4] Obviously, the media—television in particular—fueled the civil-rights revolution by spreading information, hope, and interracial examples across the South. Television also fanned youthful consciousness of poverty and the contradictions of U.S. society.

Besides spurring upheaval, the media were in turn strongly influenced by it. The fashionable media substantially interacted with other involved and growing segments of the knowledge industry: universities, think-tanks, foundations, social and welfare workers, urban planners, and so forth. The New York-Washington media axis became closely linked, in succession, to the liberal integration, anti-poverty, anti-hunger, anti-war, and ecology causes. Article followed article, in-depth studies abounded, and television documentaries—many later proven partially erroneous and distorted—stirred additional controversy. While the media in Chillicothe or Peoria might be spokesmen for local families, banks, or industries, the New York-and-Washington-based media were emerging as pre-eminent spokesmen for the causes of interest-group liberalism.

Until the Post-Industrial Revolution, the media—indeed the entire knowledge industry—did not represent a power concentration in their own right.

---

2. Louis Lapham, "The Temptation of a Sacred Cow," *Harper's Magazine*, August 1973, p. 46.

3. Patrick Buchanan, *The New Majority* (Philadelphia: 1973), p. 15.

4. Ben Bagdikian, *The Information Machines* (New York: Harper and Row, 1971), p. 3.

Instead, they reflected the politics of other U.S. subcultures. The 1956 edition of C. Wright Mills's book *The Power Elite* makes little mention of the media.[5] But, by the late sixties, the communications industry was the center of a new, knowledge economy six or eight times as rich as it had been in 1956, and capable of sustaining an affluent intelligentsia. Lionel Trilling, Irving Kristol, Daniel P. Moynihan, and others have described major elements of the new class as an "adversary culture" hostile to the prevailing middle-class values of work, patriotism, and traditional morality. Its power lies in the fact that it is not some starving assemblage of garret pamphleteers but an *affluentsia* with substantial control over the knowledge and information functions of an economy and society in which those functions are becoming dominant. This makes concentration of media power—and television power especially—a vital question. Patrick Buchanan, the Nixon-administration aide who most frequently expressed conservative antimedia philosophies, offered this analysis in his 1973 book *The New Majority*:

> The growth of network power, and its adversary posture towards the national government, is something beyond the tradition—something new in American life.
>
> The executives, anchormen and correspondents of the network news would have us believe that they are the direct heirs of John Peter Zenger and Elijah Lovejoy. That is not the case.
>
> These men are not victims of society or government in any sense of the word. They are ranking members of the privileged class, the most prestigious, powerful, wealthy and influential journalists in all history. The corporations in whose studios they labor are not struggling journals; they are communications cartels, media conglomerates holding positions within their industry comparable to that of Ford and General Motors.[6]

Coming years are likely to see the media increasingly at the center of U.S. political conflict: first, because of their ongoing increment of power; second, because of their espousal of adversary-culture views; third, because of the increasing articulation by young conservatives of anti-media politics; and fourth, because media influence is becoming so determinative of the fate of politicians and political ideas. The media are seen replacing party organizations and corporations in influence.

Meanwhile, the law is in flux. In 1973, the Florida Supreme Court acted upon the complaint of one spurned politician in handing down a decision that the Miami *Herald*, having attacked an office seeker, was obliged to give him space to reply. But the U. S. Supreme Court overturned the ruling. On the television front, new dispute has been focused on the Fairness Rule. Indeed, media theoretician Marshall McLuhan asserts that the Communications Revolution has turned politicians, bureaucrats, and experts into mere "servants" of the "new electronic citizenry who create and exchange information as a way of life."[7] In bygone eras, politicians were much less at the mercy of the media. Even if the press was solidly against a President or a governor, it was only one factor in opinion molding. As late as FDR's day, political opinion was largely a product of courthouses and clubhouses, rallies, torchlight parades, Tammany picnics, turkeys at Christmastime, jobs for the needy, and the rest of the "old politics." Per

---

5. C. Wright Mills, *The Power Elite* (New York: Oxford University Press, 1956).
6. Patrick Buchanan, op. cit., p. 18.
7. Marshall McLuhan, New York *Times*, July 29, 1973.

McLuhan, the Communications Revolution has changed this: politicians and political ideas are now largely merchandized via the media, and if the people are to have a full choice, the media cannot be allowed to decide who and what should be advanced or suppressed.

Media focus on the supposed guarantees of the First Amendment may be missing the overriding factor: the massive metamorphosis of socioeconomic power in the 180 years since the ratification of the Bill of Rights. Via the knowledge revolution, the weak, halfpenny press of the eighteenth century has become one of the most influential forces in the nation. John Peter Zenger's ideas were subject to the whims of the government; now many politicians argue that *they* are subject to the whims of the media.

Returning to the idea that the media represent an emerging new concentration of power akin to the railroads, trusts, and monopolies of the late-nineteenth century, a similar legal debate may also be beginning: how to square the rights of the public with the rights of the media. Bear in mind that, one hundred years ago, railroads, utilities, and trusts were *also* claiming the protection of the Bill of Rights. Then it was not the First Amendment at issue but the Fourteenth, under which a person's or a corporation's right to "due process" was deemed infringed by legislation applying unprecedented limitations on practices and rates. For years, the courts overextended the protections of the Bill of Rights, but, ultimately, the balance of public interest was perceived, and regulation triumphed. Thus, the Bill of Rights is hardly a static legal concept. If the Fourteenth Amendment could mean something different in 1938—in recognition of changing circumstances—from what it did in 1888, then perhaps the First Amendment may undergo a shifting interpretation of its own to reflect the new status of the communications industry. The media may be forced into the status of utilities regulated to provide access. Marshall McLuhan's speculation in this direction— that the idea of "a right to global 'coverage' has taken the place of the older right of each individual to express his opinion"—may very well prophesy a major post-industrial-society political battleground.[8]

---

8. Ibid.

Liberal

Gaye Tuchman: Whose Freedom of Speech? Whose Right to Know?

Since the eighteenth century the media have identified their activities with freedom of speech as provided for the in the First Amendment of the Bill of Rights. But some recent claims of the media to freedom of speech also blur the distinction between the public and private spheres. Additionally, the media have identified contemporary journalistic methods aiming for fairness with free speech.

Like the Constitution itself, the First Amendment is based on ideas prevalent during the Enlightenment. Drawing upon a rationalist notion of discourse and truth, the Enlightenment presupposed that when conflicting ideas and opinions compete freely with one another, the truth will emerge. This supposition builds two different and potentially antithetical rights into the First Amendment. The first, freedom of speech, provides that amendment with its popular name. The other and less frequently discussed provision is the right to know. According to the Enlightenment model of rational discourse, the public must be exposed to competing ideas if truth is to prevail. Unless the public can determine truth by assessing diverse opinions, it cannot wisely decide how it will be governed. To protect the public's right to know, the various branches of government must guarantee free speech.[1]

Ultimately, of course, freedom of speech and the right to know can interfere with governmental activities. Thomas Jefferson's views on the primacy of the First Amendment are particularly popular with the news media, for Jefferson insistently confirmed his faith in the Enlightenment model. In 1787 he wrote: "Were it left to me to decide whether we should have a government without newspapers or newspapers without a government, I should not hesitate to prefer the latter." In 1807, during his presidency, Jefferson reiterated his faith in the Enlightenment model despite the press' scurrilous attacks upon him. At least, his language continues to juxtapose "the press" and "truth." "It is a melancholy truth that suppression of the press could not more completely deprive the nation of its benefits, than is done by its abandoned prostitution to falsehood. Nothing can now be believed which is seen in a newspaper. Truth itself becomes suspicious by being put in that polluted vehicle." Finally, in 1823, he strongly reaffirmed, "The only security of all is in a free press." (All quotes are from Cater, 1959: 75.)

Several assumptions in this model are keys to understanding its applicability to contemporary conditions. First, in the eighteenth century the term "public" still connoted a general responsibility to the community and the community's

Reprinted with permission of Macmillan Publishing Co., Inc., from *Making News* by Gaye Tuchman. Copyright © 1978 by The Free Press, a Division of Macmillan Publishing Co., Inc.

1. An interesting contrast of French and American interpretations of these ideas is found in Habermas (1973).

assessment of its own interests. Second, those subscribing to the journals of opinion and, accordingly, those constituting the community and responsible for the assessment of truth were mostly the mercantile elite. Third, the rationalist model of determining truth was based upon the Enlightenment assumption that the methods of scientific discourse aimed at determining truth could be extended to social and political phenomena.

We have seen that the first two assumptions of the First Amendment were transformed during the nineteenth century. Economic self-interest and professionalism replaced public responsibility as pervasive motives for action. The penny press replaced the partisan press. These two changes enter into an assessment of the propriety of viewing science as a model for ascertaining social and political truth, for the model is heavily based upon the rationalists' own patterns of discourse through face-to-face social interaction. Gathering at salons in France, coffee shops in England, and clubs and taverns in New York, these men of ideas explored and debated philosophic issues concerning the conduct of inquiry and the laws of nature and of political systems.[2] For them, public discourse presupposed active personal interaction in which ideas were assessed and from which social organization proceeded. Agreeing to the identification of truth through informed and rational dialogue, the public could organize to implement social policy and bring about conceptually valid social change. Since "public" had a specific referent—the rationalists and the mercantile elite with whom the editors associated—public discourse as envisioned by the authors of the Bill of Rights was undermined by the introduction of the penny press. As noted, these journals were the first newspapers lacking face-to-face connections with their readers.

But even when one can locate a group that resembles a public in the eighteenth-century sense of that term, one finds that truth does not necessarily emerge from rational debate; nor is it necessarily cumulative. Consider the "community of discourse," to use Chaney's (1977) term, upon which the Enlightenment model is based: the community of science. The rationality of scientific argument (the assessment and revision of ideas accomplished through interactive exchange and empirical testing) supposedly establishes what is true of natural phenomena. And the eighteenth-century rationalists extended that tenet of natural science to social and political phenomena. Through what we now think of as their naive empiricism, eighteenth-century thinkers assumed a nonreflexive relationship between social thought and social phenomena. (Indeed, that assumption continued to hold sway in American social science well into the twentieth century.) Pointing out that contemporary philosophies insistently distinguish between social science and natural science, in part because of the role of reflexivity in social inquiry (Giddens, 1976;) puts a dent in the Enlightenment model.[3] An even more important criticism is implicit in histories and sociologies of natural science.

Recent work on patterns of scientific thought (Kuhn, 1962) and publication (Mullins et al., 1977) demonstrates that the state of a natural science depends not only on its topic but also on the structure of interaction among scientists. What is

2. I stress New York, since it has historically served as the center of American journalism, where most new developments have been introduced.
3. Reflexivity also plays an important role in the Heisenberg principle.

identified as scientific truth is embedded in a complex of professional arrangements, including networks of associations (described as invisible colleges by Crane, 1972) and norms about publication of ideas and findings. For an idea to be influential, it must gain access to leading professional journals, and that access is associated with specific career patterns (Reskin, 1977). Noting such patterns as the young gradually taking power from older scientists and then imposing their own theories, Kuhn argues that scientific "advances" are not cumulative. The discontinuity in the progression of dominant scientific paradigms, he claims, necessarily suggests that the truth does not evolve through a straightforward linear progression of the assessment of ideas. Rather, an era's truths emerge from the social organization of science and scientists during a specific historical period.

Of course, using twentieth century findings to debunk eighteenth-century ideas announces that in the long run, the Enlightenment model of the emergence of truth through conflict may well be true. Yet contemporary findings about the community of science remain pertinent because they alert us to the importance of *access* to the media in the determination of truth. Questions of access are embroiled in contemporary court cases involving the First Amendment. Those questions are particularly problematic because of legal distinctions between owning a newspaper and holding the license for an electronic medium.

Newspapers and the First Amendment: Because of the introduction of advertising, the pervasiveness of the wire services, the processes of centralization, concentration, and conglomeration of ownership, and the emergence of journalistic professionalism, newspapers no longer resemble the eighteenth-century press whose freedom Jefferson so strongly affirmed. Nonetheless, newspapers are identified as private property, and those who own newspapers have the right to publish what they will—within certain limitations pertaining to national security (see Porter, 1976). Newspapers are not legally required to grant access to their pages to anyone who wants it. And publishers are well within their rights to challenge the news professionals' claims to be the arbiters of what is newsworthy. That newsworkers claim the right to determine what is news and how it will be covered is an indication of their claim to professional expertise. But ultimately, for newspapers, "Freedom of the press is guaranteed only to those who own one," as A. J. Liebling so perceptively remarked. As Benét (1978) explains, although an owner may rarely interfere with news coverage, he or she has the last word on how an issue will be handled.

The Supreme Court affirmed the right of owners in a case involving the *Miami Herald*, a member of the Knight newspaper chain.[4] In 1972 a candidate for public office sued for access to the *Herald* in order to rebut its charges against him. Denying the right of access, one judge argued that the Constitution guaranteed a free press, not a fair press. Editors may edit according to their judgment. Newspaper owners may publish what they will. Yet the clear affirmation of the press' right to free speech contains problems.

First, as Barron (1973: 19) points out, government has interfered with the free press by passing the Newspaper Preservation Act of 1970. That legislation was

---

4. This account and the next few pages draw heavily on Friendly (1976), although his interpretation is quite different from mine.

designed to support economically faltering newspapers in order to increase the published viewpoints available to consumers. Barron argues, "If Congress has constitutional power to enact legislation to encourage diversity of viewpoints in the press, Congress . . . can enact legislation to give readers rights of access to the press." In other words, by interfering in the marketplace of publishing, the private sphere, Congress has blurred the distinction between private and public rights, and so opened the door to limiting the freedom of speech as the freedom of newspaper owners.

Second, the Newspaper Preservation Act assumes that newspapers compete only with one another. But most news consumers get their information from television and trust its credibility more than that of newspapers (Roper Organization, Inc., 1971). Newspapers have altered their format to maintain readership in the face of electronic competition. And, in any one area, there are inevitably more television stations than newspapers. For instance, in Miami in 1972, the *Herald*, with a circulation of 396,797, competed directly with a weak afternoon paper, the *Miami News* of the Cox chain, with which it shared printing facilities and advertising staff. Miami also had three UHF and six VHF television stations.[5] Does federal regulation of television interfere with competition between the two media? The question has not been raised in the courts, so far as I know. But it, too, points to the transformation of the meaning of open competition and the blurring of distinctions between the public and private spheres. And it raises the complex issue of the right to free speech in the electronic media.

Television and the First Amendment: Since 1928 the federal government has regulated access to the airwaves, for the number of frequencies available for broadcasting has been limited by the physical properties of the medium (until the advent of cable television), and the "airwaves belong to the people," as Herbert Hoover announced when he was Secretary of Commerce (quoted in Tuchman, 1974). The government directly regulates only television and radio stations, not the networks, since the networks are essentially suppliers of programs who rent time from their affiliates.[6] However, because each network owns five VHF stations, the Federal Communications Commission can influence the networks by pressuring their stations or by regulating affiliates who carry network programming. Legally, according to various communications acts, those who hold licenses for television and radio stations are not "owners." Although the buying and selling of stations are still only loosely regulated, the government recognizes the holders of the right to broadcast on a specific frequency as "licensees."[7] Legally, licensees hold a public trust; owners have private rights.

Needless to say, the broadcasting industry is displeased with the definition of broadcasting licenses as public trusts. License holders claim to be owners, and thus to have the same freedom of speech as those who own newspapers. When he was president of NBC News, Reuven Frank defended the broadcasters' rights to unfettered freedom of speech. He argued that government limitations suggest "that the First Amendment might become the first constitutional provision

---

5. One of the VHF stations also broadcast on UHF.

6. Exempt from direct regulation by the FCC, the networks are nonetheless the largest suppliers of national news.

7. The FCC must approve sales of licenses, but it does not get to choose the new owner from among those seeking to purchase the license from its present owner.

repealed by technological advance" [quoted in Friendly, 1976: 211]." For some lawyers, though, such as Barron (1971-72: 106), "It is one of the great public relation triumphs of the twentieth century over the eighteenth that broadcasters have managed to identify themselves so completely with the First Amendment."

Broadcasters willing to accept a definition of their licenses as franchises do so in the name of twentieth-century understanding of the role of the news media. They present themselves as defenders of the people against the excesses of government, and so as the purveyors of truth. Like Lippmann and his colleagues of the 1920s, these media owners take a proprietory attitude toward the public. In the 1920s:

> The educated middle class no longer heard in "public opinion" its own voice, the voice of reason. The professional classes now took public opinion to be irrational and therefore something to study, direct, manipulate and control. The professions developed a proprietory attitude toward "reason" and a paternalistic attitude toward the public [Schudson, 1978: 146].

Consider the defense of licenses as franchises offered by Charles H. Crutchfield, president of a broadcast group:

> At no time has the government even remotely interfered with us or applied any pressure . . . as far as trying to limit what we say . . . . If we in the media spent half the time defending the rights of our people against the excesses of the federal government that we do in protesting the real and imagined assaults upon our own "rights," not only the public, but we ourselves would be better served [quoted in Friendly, 1976: 211].

Not only does Crutchfield identify the media as the defenders of the people, but he also emphasizes that for all intents and purposes, his stations broadcast without government interference. Thus, he implies, the distinction between franchise and private ownership is moot.

For the government, though, the question of access is more than who will hold a license to operate a public medium. It also entails access to a station's airwaves, as set forth in the Fairness Doctrine. In its 1959 version, Section 315(a) of the Communications Act, the Fairness Doctrine states:

> Nothing in the [equal-time rule, a provision that all sides of an electoral issue must be presented] shall be construed as relieving broadcasters in the presentation of newscasts, news interviews, news documentaries and on-the-spot coverage of news events from the obligation imposed on them . . . to operate in the public interest and to afford reasonable opportunity for the discussion of conflicting views on issues of public importance [quoted in Friendly, 1976: 27].

A 1961 ruling of the Federal Communications Commission adds:

> A broadcast licensee has an affirmative obligation to broadcast programs devoted to discussion and consideration of public issues, and may engage in editorializing. However, the licensee also has an obligation to see that persons holding opposing viewpoints are afforded a reasonable opportunity for the presentation of their views. Where attacks of a highly personal nature have been made on local public officials, the licensee has an affirmative duty to take all appropriate steps to see to it that the persons attacked are afforded the fullest opportunity to respond [quoted in Friendly, 1976: 30].

At one time or another, the three commercial networks, the National Association of Broadcasters, the Radio-Television News Directors Association, assorted holders of radio and television licenses, Walter Cronkite, David Brinkley, and Harry Reasoner have all claimed that such regulations impinge on their freedom of speech. The networks and others who have licenses for stations base their objections on their self-definition as owners, not as holders of franchises. But they and the news professionals raise other arguments, too. Foremost among them is that government regulation interferes with their activities and so has a "chilling effect" upon them.[8] And, they claim, professional news practices guarantee a fair presentation, so regulation is unnecessary.

In testimony before the Senate Subcommittee on Constitutional Rights, Walter Cronkite argued that the fairness regulations constituted a chilling effect: "News and dissemination cannot be accomplished without fear of failure. . .and if the reporter or editor constantly must be looking over his shoulder for those who would have this product reflect their standard of right and wrong, of fairness and bias. . .[news dissemination] cannot be achieved [quoted in Friendly, 1976: 209]."

The Radio-Television News Directors Association took a similar tack in the Red Lion case, a Supreme Court case involving the application of the Fairness Doctrine to a fundamentalist radio station in Red Lion, Pennsylvania. That case is particularly interesting because the RTNDA sought to dissociate itself from the ultraconservative radio station, as did the National Association of Broadcasters and two television networks that also filed briefs before the court.[9] Rather than defend the right of extremist views to be heard, RTNDA argued that the Fairness Doctrine interfered with the work of its members as responsible professionals. In the words of a subsequent opinion, filed several years later by Justice Warren E. Burger about another case:

> For better or for worse, editing is what editors are for and editing is the selection and choice of material. That editors—newspaper or broadcast—do abuse this power is beyond doubt. . .but there [is] no accepted remedy other than a spirit of moderation and a sense of responsibility—and civility—on the part of those who exercise the guaranteed freedoms of expression [quoted in Friendly, 1976: 136].

By refusing to uphold the right of an extremist view to be heard without the rebuttal mandated by the Fairness Doctrine, the RTNDA, National Association of Broadcasters, the networks, and the court seem to be affirming the "scientific model" of journalism. They are asserting that the media are to establish and present "the true account" to the public, including the views of all responsible parties to a dispute. The public is not to choose between conflicting opinions, each presented by a different newspaper or news source, as was thought proper in the eighteenth century. Instead, the methods of contemporary journalism guarantee a fair presentation and capture "a spirit of moderation. . .a sense of responsibility. . .and civility."

---

8. That is, the possibility of being taken to court makes them overly cautious in expressing and disseminating potentially controversial ideas.

9. The RTNDA wanted the ruling to focus on its professional claims, and the claims of the radio station as those of a little guy being pushed around. It feared that network briefs would prompt a concern with the activities of major corporations and would thus contaminate the issue. The station lost the case. This account draws on Friendly (1976).

This view of news processing was not implied but explicitly invoked by NBC when the fairness of one of its documentaries was challenged before the FCC.[10] The documentary was "Pensions: The Broken Promise." Accuracy in Media, Incorporated, contended that NBC had presented a one-sided account that would leave viewers with the impression that all pension plans are inadequate. NBC replied that the program had included the appropriate disclaimers: The script pointed out that it was not possible to generalize from the flaws of some plans to make statements about all plans. It was true, NBC argued, that its staff had not balanced every criticism with a defense. But, acting in good faith, it had contacted each of the worst offenders mentioned in the program and invited them to appear before NBC's cameras. Through no fault of its own, the staff could not convince a representative to defend his or her company. NBC did obtain a general defense of pension plans through interviews with pension holders, employers, and industry spokespersons, including an executive of the National Association of Manufacturers. Finally, NBC cited Justice Burger's opinion that "editing is what editors are for." Taken together, NBC's arguments state that professional news practices ensure fairness and so guarantee the public's right to know.

In this formulation, the right to know is the right to know the facts established by NBC, not the right to know all possible opinions on the topic. For the practices cited by NBC, including offering time for rebuttal to the worst offenders, are core elements of the web of facticity. The notion that carefully assessed facts, including the fact that some people disagree, constitute freedom of speech is also contained in another of NBC's contentions. It claimed that its program was not controversial because it did not discuss specific legislative reforms. Rather, NBC felt, as David Brinkley wrote independently to the FCC: "To be found guilty of 'unfairness' for not expressing . . . the view that most people are not corrupt or that pensioners are not unhappy is to be judged by standards which simply have nothing to do with journalism [quoted in Friendly, 1976: 153]."

For NBC, then, fair speech is equated with free speech; governmental regulations interfering with newsworkers' professional activities inhibit free speech by interfering with newswork. That stations carrying NBC's documentaries are legally public franchises is irrelevant to this argument. NBC invoked professionalism, practices common to both ink and electronic journalism, not the rights of owners. Like news professionalism itself, the NBC argument blurs distinctions between what properly belongs to and in the public sphere and what belongs in the private sphere of life.

News professionalism claims independence of both ownership and management by claiming the right to judge what news is. As might be expected, the principle of professional dominance conflicts with the principle of control by owners and managers and can be a source of bitter dispute. Fred Friendly resigned from his position as head of CBS News when network officials refused to broadcast live the first Senate hearings on the Vietnam war (Friendly, 1967). Preferring to air profitable reruns of situation comedies, the network insisted that coverage on the evening news would suffice to tell the story; they rejected Friendly's news judgment. Similarly, according to the *New York Times* (1977: 15),

----

10. Again I draw on Friendly (1976), the best source on recent Fairness Doctrine cases. His interpretation stresses, though, that you can't tell the "good guys" from the "bad guys" when it comes to First Amendment rights.

the editors of two papers owned by the Pan-Ax newspaper chain were fired after they refused to run a story by Washington correspondent George Bernard, hired by the publisher, John P. McGoff. A former employee of the *National Enquirer*, which eschews the web of facticity, George Bernard wrote that President Carter condones promiscuity for his male staff and is grooming his wife for the vice-presidency. One complaint of the editors—that the correspondent's story took material out of context—is a professional affirmation of the web of facticity. Their refusal to run the disputed story is an affirmation of the claimed license (E.C. Hughes, 1964) of professionals: They should determine what is news.

It would, however, contradict available data to state that news professionals always fight to maintain their right to determine news. Both newspaper and television stations carry "must stories," items that the business office, advertising staff, or front office say "must be carried" to satisfy either advertisers or friends of well-placed executives in the news organization.[11] Newsworkers dislike this practice, found more commonly at newspapers than at television stations, but journalism textbooks adhere to organizational constraints. Thus Hohenberg (1962: 45) instructs students that the slug "must" can be used to label only such stories, since they "must" be run and are exempt from the competition for dissemination applied to other items uncovered by the news net. Using the "must" label to identify an optional story unearthed by the reporter would interfere with the editors' appropriate exercise of their own news judgment.

Additionally, television newsworkers follow organizational mandates by occasionally linking their news judgment to the preferences of advertisers. For instance, if a bank and an airline company take turns sponsoring the evening news, sponsorship may influence the ordering of stories about bank robberies and plane crashes. When there was a newsworthy bank robbery on the day the bank sponsored the NEWS program, a newsworker would call both advertisers and arrange for the airline to run its commercials that evening. A similar procedure would be followed when an air crash occurred when the airline was scheduled to be the sponsor. When there were items about both a bank robbery and an air crash, the "touchy" item would not be run next to the related commercial, even if news judgment suggested that as the appropriate placement in the ranking of the day's news.

Newsworkers' adherence to organizational realities in these cases does not invalidate their claim to professionalism. It suggests that professional practices are encouraged so long as they uphold the interests of news organizations (see Molotch and Lester, 1975). And, once again, it affirms that the same practices and associated problems crop up in both media. To be sure, newspapers carry more "musts" than newscasts. But newspapers generally carry more items than newscasts, and so their "musts" are less conspicuous. Technological differences provide marginal distinctions in professionalism between the two media. The dissimilar technologies do not mean that the relationship of newspaper professionals to owners is intrinsically different from the relationship of their TV counterparts to holders of television licenses.

In practice, the distinction between private ownership and public ownership is blurred. In both spheres new professionalism claims to hold sway. In both

---

11. Additionally, executives may recommend interviews with their friends when the friends are experts on a topic in the news. However, such recommendations are very rare. I learned of only one example of this during my observations at NEWS.

spheres professionalism connotes the web of facticity and places itself between newsmakers and the public. And the television news narrative is a visual enactment of the web of facticity. In both spheres those responsible for management and finances may either resist or accede to professional dominance (see Freidson, 1971) In sum, the distinction between the free speech of the press and that of the electronic medium is empirically invalid and hence theoretically problematic. Furthermore, as we have seen, professional practices found in both media limit the access of radical views to news consumers, and so limit everyone's use of the media as a political and social resource. Those practices limit the right to know.

References

Barron, Jerome. *Freedom of the Press for Whom* Bloomington: Indiana University Press, 1973.

Barron, Jerome. Testimony before Senate Subcommittee on Constitutional Rights. Washington, D.C.: U.S. Government Printing Office. 1971-72.

Benét, James. "Conclusion." pp. 266–271 in Tuchman, Daniels and Benét eds. *Hearth and Home: Images of Women in the Mass Media*. New York: Oxford University Press, 1978.

Cater, Douglas. *The Fourth Branch of Government*. Boston: Houghton Mifflin, 1959.

Chaney, David. "Communication and Community." *Working Papers in Sociology*, No. 12. University of Durham, Great Britain. 1977.

Crane, Diana. *Invisible Colleges*. Chicago: University of Chicago, 1972.

Giddens, Anthony. *New Rules of Sociological Method*. New York: Basic Books, 1976.

Friedson, Eliot. *Profession of Medicine*. New York: Dodd, Mead. 1971.

Friendly, Fred. *The Good Guys, the Bad Guys and the First Amendment*. New York: Random House. 1976.

Friendly, Fred. *Due to Circumstances Beyond Our Control*. New York, Random House, 1967.

Habermas, Jurgen. *Theory and Practice*. Boston: Beacon Press. 1973.

Hohenberg, John. *The Professional Journalist*. New York: Holt, Rhinehart & Winston, 1962.

Hughes, C. Everett. *Men and Their Work*. New York Free Press, 1964.

Kuhn, Thomas. *The Structure of Scientific Revolutions*. Chicago: University of Chicago Press, 1962.

Molotch, Harvey and Marilyn Lester. "Accidental News: The Great Oil Spill." *American Journal of Sociology*, 81 (1975), pp. 235–260. (1975).

Mullins, Nicholas C., Lowell Hargens, Pamela Hecht, and Edward Kock. "The Group Structure of Co-citation Structures: A Comparative Study." *American Sociological Review* 42:4 (1977), pp. 552–562.

New York Times. "Two Editors Dismissed in Articles Dispute: Michigan Paper, Refused Orders to Publish Reports Concerning Carter's Wife and Staff." June 26, 1977, p. 15.

Porter, William E. *Assault of the Media: The Nixon Years* Ann Arbor: University of Michigan Press, 1976.

Reskin, Barbara. "Scientific Productivity and the Reward Structure of Science." *American Sociological Review* (1977), 42:3 pp. 491–504.

The Roper Organization. "An Extended View of Public Attitudes Toward Television and Other Mass Media: 1959–71." Pamphlet. New York Television Information Office. 1971.

Schudson, Michael. *Discovering the News*. New York. Basic Books. 1978.

Tuchman, Gaye. *The TV Establishment: Programming for Power and Profit*. Englewood Cliffs, N.J.: Prentice-Hall, 1974.

Socialist

Howard J. Ehrlich: The Politics of News Media Control

The Basic Consensus

The relationship between the news media and the two major political forces in American society—government and business—only appears to be contradictory. In some situations, the connections seem to be conspiratorial; in others they may seem to be in conflict, but in fact they are not.

The media, on the one hand, protect business interests for their own economic well-being. The suppression of anti-business news is common. The media also "front" for the government by assuming its actions to be more legitimate than those who oppose it, and by generally ignoring its victims. These journalistic behaviors are buttressed by the social class identifications of reporters and by a professional ideology in which built-in arguments help rationalize what occurs. These range from the need for "objectivity" and "responsibility" to the necessity of maintaining continuing news sources. (The range of these arguments is narrow, and the arguments themselves are not very well developed.)

On the other hand, the media are bombarded with criticism from the agents of government and business. A large number of government officials see the media as a subversive force of sorts, particularly in times of political crises. And many newspapers are often charged with running materials that are "bad for business."

Two ideas to be developed below may help explain this apparently contradictory relationship. One describes the explicitly conservative role of the media in minimizing the *density of revolutionary symbols* that they will permit to be exposed to the general public. The other affirms the existence of this counter-revolutionary conspiracy by explaining the conflicts in terms of *pluralistic ignorance*.

American elites, whether they represent government, business, or the news media share basically the same set of values. They share remarkably common biographies, and as research on elites has demonstrated, a general satisfaction with their status, power, and the basic distribution of income and privilege in society. Their conspiracy is less one of secret plotting than it is an index of their position and common socialization. They act in the same manner, not because they agree to do so (although at times this occurs), but mainly because they share the same interests, the same facilities, the same objectives.

Their occupational positions, however, often lead them to perceive the interests of the other as antagonistic. And there are, of course, just enough genuine conflicts, although mainly of a superficial nature, that they and their publics come to believe that they do interact from positions of conflicting if not countervailing interests. For example, the disputes of government and business today are not over the legitimacy of unemployment in an affluent society, but rather

The Insurgent Sociologist, Vol. 4 (Summer 1974), pp. 31–43. Reprinted by permission.

concern how the unemployed are to be managed. It is not American capitalism that is questioned, but how its profits, risks, and pathologies are to be controlled. Similarly, when the news media battle with the government over the right to know, as in the case of the Pentagon papers, they aren't battling over the legitimacy of American investments in Southeast Asia.

These skirmishes, which derive from the idiosyncratic interests of each sector, create a smokescreen that baffles not only the public, but even the participants who come to believe that they are defending not a different set of selfish interests, but a fundamental set of selfless values. Thus, while they all behave to support the same set of values, they come to believe that they are operating from fundamentally different sets of value positions. They exist in a state of pluralistic ignorance, each sector unaware of their basic consensus.

Certainly, one of their consensual beliefs is the inherent goodness of the American system; and business, government, and the media are united in their opposition to the socialist and anarchist politics which characterize the current movements for protest and change in America. Here the media front for those interests they share with government and business. They simply do not print most challenges to the legitimacy of the system, nor do they doubt the existence of social justice in American society. The suppression of this kind of news by the media is a rational act. Theorists of revolution have only recently come to comprehend what social psychologists and practical politicians have known for years. In the language of a new theorist (government-certified and sponsored): the greater the density of symbols of revolution in the mass media, the greater the likelihood of revolutionary actions in the population. (See Ted Robert Gurr's, *Why Men Rebel*, Princeton University Press, 1970.) Some news is clearly not fit to print; and obviously newspapers of record need only record what is official, not what is anti-official.

The news media operate to continually underscore the legitimacy of business and government, to enhance their perpetuation in the name of order and stability, and to romanticize their agents with publicity and sometimes affectionate attention.

To get the news—which is usually defined as the actions of public officials and the business elite—the media compete for the time and cooperation of these men of power. Obviously, this is to be gained by placating, if not outright pleasing, news sources. Media managers have long taught their employees that a competitive advantage lies in pacifying their sources of news; and reporters who have been spurned by the elite are confined to the disadvantageous role of reporting what is already known or is public record by law.

The cooperative and friendly press becomes a trusting repository for the presentation of manipulated news leaks and trial balloons for new corporate or political ventures. Even more, the friendly press is rewarded with almost all the news it may have room to print in the form of press releases, speeches, and official documents.

The interrelationship of government, business, and the media has been built around the political-economic gains they realize cooperatively, and the values and ideals they share, even if they are unaware of their basic solidarity.

The Corporate Structure of Media Control

To better understand where we have been so far, we should examine the concentration and control of the news media. News is what the media say it is. The decision to report or not to report an item; where that item is placed in print or scheduled for broadcast; the length of time or space allocated; and the tone with which it is reported are some of the means by which the media regulate the news.

While 95 percent of homes in America have television sets, and while radios are everywhere, the newspaper remains the major source of national news—and probably local news as well. A study by Audits and Survey's, Inc. (*Editor and Publisher*, February 10, 1973) indicates that newspaper reading among persons 18 years old and older is twice as frequent as the viewing of the early evening network television newscasts. In fact, over a two-week period, 53 percent of the public do not see a single national newscast. In contrast, almost 90% of adults read at least one daily newspaper during the week, reading, on the average, 4.3 papers over a five-day span.

Broadcast news is often no different from the printed news. Radio and television spend considerably less time and money than newspapers to gather news. Most radio stations rely almost exclusively on wire service releases. Thus Associated Press which not only feeds news to 1,259 daily newspapers also sends to 62% of all radio and television stations in the country. If a station does not have the AP wire, then it probably subscribes to United Press International—or nothing. UPI, with approximately 3,900 domestic subscribers, feeds proportionately more newspapers than broadcast media. Some radio and television stations may have their own crews for local news, but they depend exclusively on the networks and wire services for national and international news. The result is that broadcast news offers almost no items that could not be found in the newspaper.

We turn now to the newspaper. There are about 1,748 daily newspapers in the country, but only 63 have competition. And, at least half of these 63 are strange competitors because they share facilities for printing, circulation or business. Only one city in the United States has more than two separately owned general circulation daily newspapers. What may be more critical is that almost three of every five daily papers is owned by a chain. Thus, the centralization of news control is even more extensive than the local monopoly that already exists through single ownership in 97% of American cities.

Monopolies, of course, charge monopoly prices. Grotta, reporting his dissertation study of 154 newspapers from 1950-1968, concludes: "If there are indeed significant economic efficiencies from larger scale operation in the industry, this study indicates that those benefits are not being passed on to the consumers; in fact, there is evidence that the concentration through merger and/or suspension may result in higher prices and lower quality" (*Journalism Quarterly*, 1971).

Monopolistic control has other consequences. One critical effect is that there is no pressure to even report the news. Sandman and associates (*Media*, Prentice-Hall, 1972) present a rough breakdown of the content of a typical daily newspaper:

60%	advertising
15%	wire service news (state, national, and international)
10%	syndicated features and columns
10%	sports, society, other specialized departments
5%	local hard news

There is actually less news in newspapers than even those figures indicate. Among that small set of news items that do appear, some of them are really not new, some of them are pre-packaged (usually commercial) press releases, and a good part of them are simply reports on local rituals (e.g., the garden club had its annual planting) or reports on the routine activities of symbolic leaders (e.g., the mayor visited the trolley museum). There is, in fact, substantial evidence to indicate that newspapers are unaware of most segments of community leadership and focus almost exclusively on the symbolic leaders (Ehrlich and Bauer, *American Sociological Review*, 1965).

The public cannot even rely on other news media as a means of escape from the concentration of control evident in newspapers. Newspapers own a major share of other news media, establishing a unique form of control. For example, in Columbus, Ohio, the major newspaper owns 49% of the stock of the second newspaper, which also shares its facilities. It also owns one of the major radio stations in the city and one of the network affiliated television stations. In Milwaukee, the Journal Company owns both daily newspapers and the leading television, and AM and FM stations. In Cheyenne, Wyoming, Frontier Broadcasting went one better by controlling all media (except one FM station) including the CATV system. (Although the Justice Department seemed bothered by this, the FCC had no objections.)*

Owning media facilities is profitable, but using the media as a corporate subsidiary makes it doubly profitable. As Nicholas Johnson, then an FCC Commissioner said:

> Media control by a conglomerate creates a situation in which the incentives are almost irresistable for the holding company to view the mass media subsidiary as only a part of its advertising and public relations...for its more...profitable industrial subsidiaries.

One confirming instance of Mr. Johnson's thesis occurred at the time when Congress was considering legislation to reverse a court order directing the DuPonts to sell their General Motors stock. In the state of Delaware, DuPont interests then controlled 88% of daily newspaper circulation—and their newspapers went into three of every four households in the state. Actually, the two major papers, the *Morning News* and the *Evening Journal* of Wilmington, Delaware were controlled by Christiana Securities. Christiana, a holding company, owned

---

* These examples are not unusual. In perhaps as many as 100 cities, newspapers control the only other local media (radio or TV). In 90 cities, the daily newspaper owns at least one local television station. In 230 cities, the newspaper publisher owns at least one radio station. In fact (according to a 1968 Justice Department study, single owners controlled at least two broadcast media in all of the "top 50 market areas"—the major metropolitan areas.

27% of the stock in DuPont. At the time of DuPont's attempts to maintain their G.M. holdings, Christiana ordered its papers not to print stories that would antagonize Senator Byrd, who was then chairman of the Senate Finance Committee.

The major news broadcasting networks are themselves conglomerates. There are many ways to depict their status, but the simplest is in the accompanying (and incomplete) Appendix.

This Appendix may astound people—a fact, itself, that points to the absence of the communication of significant social information. There are two other things that the table points out to us. First, we can see that the directors of the media are integrally enmeshed within the corporate and governmental structure of the entire society. Secondly, we can understand that *by their social positions* these moguls of the mass media have an inescapable investment in the status quo.

Two Case Studies

It is difficult to avoid a non-conspiratorial interpretation of the corporate structure of the news media. To remove ourselves from abstract interpretation, let us look at two case studies to see how directly and openly the media are controlled.

The first case study involved the treatment of a single event in the media of Baltimore and Washington. The event, the Children's March for Survival, took place on a Saturday afternoon, March 25, 1972, in Washington, D.C. The major aim of the march and rally was to express opposition to the Moynihan-Nixon Family Assistance Plan.

Now whenever an event occurs that protests the very structure of society, the news media respond in a stereotyped fashion. Most blot out the event. That is they either do not report what happened at all, or they minimize the happening by the nature of their coverage. When the events are too big or too public to be conveniently ignored or minimized, there are two alternative media strategies. If they are truly hostile, the press can cope with the event through editorials, columns, or follow-up features that play on the "unintended" consequences of the protest. If they are pushed to "journalistic neutrality," they describe the event—often in tedious detail. But what they invariably leave out is an analysis of the causes of the protest or the solutions proposed by the government or the political dissidents.

As you might expect, the Children's March was blotted out by the Baltimore media and distorted in the Washington press.

In Baltimore, the *News-American's* Sunday edition printed absolutely nothing about the march. On channel 11 (WBAL), the NBC affiliate owned by the *News-American's* parent corporation, the blackout was consistent.

The Baltimore *Sun*, in contrast to its Hearst competitor, acknowledged the march. It ran a picture. At the top and center of page two, the *Sun* ran an AP photograph displaying some so parading children in the foreground and the White House in the background. As the newspaper article goes, it was a nice photograph. But it bore the peculiar caption, "Marching for Welfare," and a two-sentence cut: "*A group paraded in front of the White House yesterday in a 'Children's March for Survival' to protest President Nixon's programs for welfare, child care, and hunger. The President was spending the weekend at Camp David.*" The group referred to by the *Sun* was estimated by Park Police to be 30,000 people in size. A very large "group" indeed.

The *Sun's* television outlet, channel 2 (WMAR, a CBS affiliate), like its competitor followed the news policy of its parent corporation. Channel 2 presented only two or three still photos and a brief acknowledgment of the march on its late news.

In Washington, the *Evening Star* began its extensive coverage on page one. Five reporters were credited with their story which covered almost a full page. And one of the reporters wrote a separate feature mainly about the children on the march. Relatively few of the relevant political details surfaced, and nowhere were the political, economic, or societal issues developed.

The *Washington Post* also gave the front page treatment and what amounted to probably more than a page of copy and photographs. Their lead story contained even fewer relevant details, and their two accompanying feature stories both dealt with unintended consequences of the event—one on the number of children who got lost and the other on a group of children whose bus didn't arrive.

The day before, the *Post* had editorialized against a vital tactic of the march organizers. They had persuaded the District school board—the only elected body in this Congressionally ruled city—to encourage kids to march, through use of parental permission slips and the provision of school buses. The *Post's* lengthy and angry March 24th editorial was headlined "Making Political Puppets Out of School Children." The gist of their editorial was that "the politicization of elementary school children who are a long way from being consenting adults" was wrong, and that "Washington's school administrators were wrong to have toyed with young minds about big issues."

That there is often nothing subtle about the treatment of social protest is illustrated by the second case study which I have called "The News Blackout in Iowa." From Iowa City where I lived and worked for six years, I compiled a lengthy report on the treatment of social and political protest by the news media in that state. For example, the *Des Moines Register,* a powerful statewide newspaper would not report a key demand of a two-day student boycott of classes at the University of Iowa in 1968. I remember writing a 7½ column inch reply to their coverage which they printed. However, one sentence was omitted from my letter, just as it had been omitted from the news reports to which I also objected. That item was "that since corporations were the prime beneficiaries of the university, they should be especially taxed to pay their fair share of the costs of higher education." That curious deletion was, of course, never explained by that major corporate enterprise, the *Register* (of Cowles Communication and Meredith Publishing, of *Family Circle* and *Venture,* of the *Minneapolis Star and Tribune,* of *Harper's Magazine,* of *The New York Times,* and of much more).

About a year later in Iowa City, some 500 protesters marched past the *Iowa City Press-Citizen* building as part of the November anti-war "moratorium" activities. The *Press-Citizen* apparently never saw the noon parade because it had assigned no reporter to it. No story ever appeared, even though the march and attending events were reported—although with varying accuracy—in other Iowa newspapers. Subsequently, LIFE Magazine reported in its December issue that October moratorium activities in Iowa City "were miserably attended, and in November they were scrapped entirely in deference to a last-minute cold snap." In reality, the October protest drew upwards of 5,000 persons while the November activities, although not as faithfully attended, were not called off and, in fact, resulted in some rather interesting confrontations between protesters and university officials and Selective Service authorities. LIFE's fictionalized account apparently stemmed from the total lack of coverage afforded the November protest by Iowa City's "newspaper of record"—the *Press-Citizen*.

LIFE magazine refused to retract their report which had been a part of series dealing with the presumed failure of the anti-war movement.

Racism and Sexism

Imprecise, distorted, inaccurate, or downright fabricated reporting characterizes the news media at every level of local and national organization—especially when it comes to dealing with Black/White relations.

When it comes to routine news, Black Americans are still invisible. When it comes to conflict, racial conflicts are under-reported and when mentioned, the violent or sensational aspects are overreported.

Consider two studies from different parts of the United States, one from Los Angeles, California and one dealing with the entire state of Iowa. In Los Angeles, David Sears and his associates studied the press coverage of Black Americans from 1893 up until the Watts riot of 1965. They found that during this time press coverage in the two major city newspapers had significantly declined relative to the percentage of Negroes in the city. Not even the civil rights movement of the 1950's resulted in any change. Ironically, the researchers said, and we quote: "Perhaps it is just as well that press coverage of Blacks was so rare for so many years, because the content of it was mostly degrading."

In Iowa, studies by journalists and social scientists indicate that for all the major newspapers in that state, as Black-White conflicts increased over the United States in the 1960's, Iowa newspapers actually cut down their coverage of race-related conflict. The *Des Moines Register*, for example, actually reduced their line coverage of civil disorders in the mid-1960's by almost 50%.

Media control and coordination across media outlets seems more explicit and deliberate in instances of social conflict. In whatever form, the media of communication remain a mass means for the transmission of group stereotypes and the continued subordination of Black Americans, among other minorities, by the cumulative misrepresentation of their social and economic conditions. That subordination, which has its major societal expression through economic exploitation, is clearly congruent with the interests of the large corporations that own and control the media.

The news media control women in two ways. First, by limiting the number of women journalists, and by keeping most of these in low-level or segregated positions. Second, by controlling the amount and kind of news presented about women.

Both methods of control serve to keep women in their so-called "traditional place." That place, of course, is the home—even at a time when 43% of all women have full-time jobs. What this narrow definition means in terms of news media control is, for example, the "woman's page"—that segregated section of the newspaper which is devoted largely to gossip columns, recipes, how to raise children, advice on furniture refinishing, and marriage announcements (although *not* divorce notices). On radio and television, there is often an equivalent—that is, special programming for women, although television does add a unique twist. Its obvious visual strength is used to focus on women as sex objects, as indicated by the overrepresentation of younger women, even in dramatic presentations that demand an older person, and the gross use of women in commercials for personal hygiene products. In fact, one study of prime time commercials indicated that women were *seven times* more likely than men to be shown in ads for personal hygiene products (Dominick and Rauch, *Journal of Broadcasting*, 1972). Television's second contribution is in its perpetuation of women in traditional roles from commercial through dramatic productions and in the news.

What news media control of women also means is that the news audience is treated to distorted coverage of women's activities. This distortion includes outright lies, half-truths, and the refusal to cover women who don't fit into the conventional mold. One example of a media-created lie which is accepted as truth is "bra-burning." Most Americans probably believe that the activists who protested the Miss America contest in 1968 burned their bras for some incomprehensible reason. And they believe it because the news media told them so.

In fact, the truth is much less sensational. What *really* happened was this: The women who demonstrated in Atlantic City decided to make several symbolic gestures of protest. Since women, far more than men, are defined by their physical appearance and clothing, they set up a so-called "freedom trashcan." And into it they threw several articles of old clothing—such as girdles, high-heeled shoes, and brassieres. They also discarded such non-clothing items as hair curlers and women's magazines. Somehow, the news media reported that a bunch of crazy man-hating women had burned their bras. In fact, none were burned.

When the news media deliberately present women as worthy only of contempt, they make it that much easier for sexism to flourish. A person who is the butt of jokes is a person who is oppressed economically, politically, and personally.

Public Broadcasting

I turn now to public broadcasting. Most people know that the commercial media are controlled by large corporations. But when we think of educational television or public radio, we think of non-commercial, educational radio and television under public control.

The Ford Foundation established and controlled educational television between 1951 and 1966. Ford funded it; Ford organized it; and thus Ford set the course of it. In effect, Ford and its operational arm, National Educational Television (NET), had direct and practically total control over educational television in America.

In 1967, the government stepped in. Congress passed the Public Broadcasting Act which provided for the establishment of a non-profit, private, non-political agency, the Corporation for Public Broadcasting. CPB's mandate was to develop public broadcasting while insuring that the medium would be protected from outside interference and control. However, educational radio and television are still controlled by private economic interests, and not by the public. First of all, Congress appropriated no money for the Corporation for Public Broadcasting until 1969—and then, it was terribly inadequate: only $27,000 per station. How have the so-called media survived? The Ford Foundation continues to provide the major portion of their funds. It does so through direct grants to stations, thereby avoiding undesirable publicity and maintaining the illusion of public control. Most of Ford's grants have been for programming—thus giving them control over what is actually put on the air. Xerox and Mobil Oil are the two other major corporate sponsors.

The Corporation for Public Broadcasting has a 15-member Board of Directors, appointed by the President. The Public Broadcasting Act specified that the directors be selected from fields such as education, cultural and civic affairs, and the arts, including radio and television. The Board is in fact controlled by representatives of private commercial media, and members of the political, economic, and military elite. Five of the fifteen board members have ties with commercial radio, television, film, and print. The military establishment is particularly well-represented by the former Chairman of the Corporation Frank Pace and Former Vice-chairman, and now chairman, James Killian. Pace was Secretary of the Army from 1950 to 1952, as well as chairman of the board and Chief Executive Officer of General Dynamics Corporation. In 1968, during his tenure as chairman, General Dynamics was the nation's largest defense contractor. Killian has served in a number of public and private positions, predominantly in the area of military policy and military production. For example, since 1959 he has been Chairman of the Board of Mitre Corporation, a leading producer of missiles and radar homing devices; he is a former chairman of the Institute for Defense Analysis; and was chairman of the President's Foreign Intelligence Advisory Board, an agency which oversees the operations of the CIA. Dr. Killian was also Chairman of the Corporation for Public Broadcasting's Special Projects Committee, whose purpose was "to concentrate especially on public broadcasting and civil disturbances."

Not much is known about the current president of CPB, Henry Loomis. Under Eisenhower, he was the director of the Voice of America, and, more recently served the U.S. Information Agency as its deputy director.

The CPB has only one representative of the arts, Irving Kristol, former editor of the CIA-funded *Encounter* magazine and now one of the founding editors of the academic, conservative magazine, *The Public Interest*.

The Corporation for Public Broadcasting does not represent the public; it is the servant of the politically and economically powerful. This institution, which supposedly was established to provide an alternative to media controlled by giant corporations, has been placed in those same hands.

Public television is no small matter. With 203 stations it is larger than ABC and only 16 stations smaller than the other networks. It has a potential audience of 75 million, and in 1972 an estimated 50 million persons watched at least two hours of public television during the survey week.

Most important is that public television has devoted 30% of "prime time" to public affairs programming. This compares to 2% on the three commercial networks.

In early January, 1973 the Board of CPB announced that it was taking charge of all national programming. The announcement which pretended to be in the interest of a free media, was actually a step towards the control of politically relevant programming. Their action was a response to the pressures brought to bear on them by the White House. The basis of Presidential pressure was two-fold. First, it was an attempt to force public TV to decrease the time allotted to news coverage and analysis as well as the cancellation of its public affairs programming. Second, it was an attempt to purge public TV of people and programming which was opposed to government policies. (These attempts were so blatant that on May 31, 1973, the American Civil Liberties Union and others filed suit against the CPB, the Public Broadcasting Service, and White House aides, Clay Whitehead and Patrick Buchanan. The defendants were charged with violating the Public Broadcasting Act and the First Amendment.)

Under the Public Broadcasting Act, the CPB served to receive and distribute the funds appropriated by Congress. The Act also authorized CPB to set up an interconnection network for distributing programs to local stations. The Public Broadcasting Service (PBS), which is controlled by the station managers themselves, served this network function. Since the most direct way to control porgramming is to control what can and can not be sent out over the network, CPB attempted to take over control of the network from the Public Broadcasting Service.

The full details of the political infighting (much as they are known) are not worth reporting. Some of the after-effects are. On April 17, 1973, Thomas Curtis, a conservative Republican appointed by Nixon and who had been elected to the CPB board chairmanship in September, 1972, submitted his resignation. Curtis, commenting only obliquely about the attempts of the Nixon administration to control the board's decisions, declared that he could no longer defend the integrity of the board.

The Public Broadcasting Service basically capitulated to the White House. This came about with the Ford Foundation's offer of eight million dollars to PBS and the President's acceptance of James Killian as new board chairman of CPB. The Corporation for Public Broadcasting can now fund—as the *New York Times* put it—"whatever programs it considers hygienic." PBS can now interconnect whatever privately funded programs it and its sponsors choose. The network schedule itself will be decided jointly by the White House controlled CPB and the Ford Foundation controlled PBS. Listener control, of course, remains irrelevant to public broadcasting.

Concluding Remarks

People are not free if the critical events of their society are systematically unreported or distorted. In American society where the news media are controlled, almost monopolized by persons of wealth, power and high political office, most persons are imprisoned in a network of myths and lies, in an environment where the media have become a mass means for pacification.

In all modern societies, freedom of the press belongs only to those who control the press or the transmitter. No really good solutions to the problems of media control seem apparent; certainly not within the sociological realities of any existing nation-state. The mass media of communication are, after all, instruments of the state. While it remains problematic whether a free and open media can be constructed anywhere, the rise (and repression) of alternative and underground media is inevitable. For the moment, perhaps all we can ask about the news media of any nation-state is whether or not its citizens would move against its ruling class if freedom of information actually existed.

Acknowledgments

Parts of this article were taken from Great Atlantic Radio Conspiracy program scripts, and I am strongly indebted to my co-conspirators for their several years of support and criticism. The case materials on Iowa and the section on consensus are based on an article I wrote with Fred Karnes. William V. D'Antonio, Carol Ehrlich, Janet Kohen, and Fred Pincus all provided detailed comments on an early draft which were extraordinarily helpful.

APPENDIX

Corporate Control of the Three Major Commercial Networks

ABC OWNS:

ABC TV networks (1968 affiliates)—and five television stations

Four ABC radio networks (1,254 affiliates)

Largest motion-picture distribution chain in the U.S. (American Broadcasting—Paramount theaters, over 434 theaters)

ABC records (Dunhill, Impulse, Bluesway, Westminister, Command, Probe)

ABC publishes three midwestern farm journals

Three tourist centers in Florida and California

ABC International has controlling interests in 16 foreign companies operating television stations and is associated with TV stations in a total of 26 foreign countries.

ABC Worldvision owns 64 foreign TV stations.

Composite Ownership (Controlled mainly by Morgan banking groups):

65% of voting shares to: State St. Bank & Trust Co., Bankers Trust Co., Bank of New York, Chase Manhattan, Chemical Bank, Irving Trust Co., First National Bank of Boston, First Jersey National Bank, City National Bank & Trust, National Shawmut, Bank of California, Merrill Lynch, First National City Bank, First National Bank of Denver, Mellon National Bank & Trust, Continental Bank, Bessemer Trust, Firestone Bank, Massachusetts Mutual Life Insurance, St. Paul Fire & Marine, Allendale Mutual Insurance Co.

Interlocks with Other Financial Institutions:

Marine Midland Corp., Lehman Bros., Mutual of New York, Mutual Benefit Life, East River Savings Bank, Bowery Savings Bank, Manufacturers Hanover Trust, National Bank of Detroit, Penn Mutual, Metropolitan Life.

Other Major Corporate Interlocks:

Allied Stores, Chrysler Corp., American Airlines, Boise Cascade, American Electric Power, St. Regis Paper, Western Pacific R. R., Albertsons, Hiram Walker, Adams Express, Squibb-Beech-Nut, Shearson-Hammill, N.Y. Telephone, GAF Corp., Belding Hemmingway Co., Bethlehem Steel, Diebold Computer, Amerad Hess Oil Corp., Erie-Lackawanna Railway, N.Y. Jets Football Club, Lily-Tulip Cup, Western Union Telegraph.

Institutional Interlocks:

Brigham Young U., Idaho State U., Stanford U., College of the Virgin Islands, College of Idaho, California Institute of Technology, Adelphi College, Carnegie Institute of Technology, George Washington U., Catholic U. of America, Aspen Institute, Center for the Advanced Study in the Behavioral Sciences, Catholic Charities, Inc., N.Y. Foundling Hospital, U.S. Chamber of Commerce, Committee for Economic Development.

NBC (a wholly owned subsidiary of RCA)

RCA is one of the 20 largest corporations in the world with 143 foreign markets. RCA has 64 manufacturing plants, produces 12,000 different products, and is a leading supplier of electronic equipment for military and police purposes.

RCA *owns (partial listing)*

NBC TV network (215 affiliates)

NBC radio network (250 affiliates) and five television, six AM and six FM stations

Random House Publishers (which includes Pantheon, Vintage, Alfred A. Knopf, Singer, and Modern Library);

RCA Victor records, Banquet Foods, Coronet Industries (carpets and furniture), Arnold Palmer Enterprises, Hertz Car & Truck Rentals, Cushman and Wakefield (reality).

Composite Ownership (control divided among Rockefeller, Morgan, and Manufacturers Hanover Trust Banking groups):

30% of the voting shares to: Chase Manhattan, Bankers Trust, Continental Illinois B & T, First National Bank of Chicago, Swiss Bank Corp., First National City Bank, State Street B & T, Irving Trust, Northwestern National Bank of Minnesota, First National Bank of Jersey City, Chemical Bank, Merrill, Lynch, Investment Co. of America, Investors Mutual & Investors Stock Fund, Massachusetts Investors Trust & Mass. Investors

Growth, Fidelity Capital Fund & Fidelity Trend Fund, Brown Bros. Harriman, Enterprise Fund, Bache & Co., Technology Fund, Founders Mutual Fund, Prudential Insurance, Lumbermans Mutual Casualty, Mutual Life Insurance, Hartford Insurance, Bankers Life.

Interlocks with Other Financial Institutions:

Girard Trust, Lehman Corp., St. Louis Union Trust, Stockyards National Bank, Peoples National Bank of Naples (Fla.), New England Mutual Life, First National Bank of Hamilton Sq. (N.J.), Penn Mutual Life Ins., First Pennsylvania B & T, Charter New York Corp., Metropolitan Life, Diebold Venture Fund.

Other Major Corporate Interlocks:

ITT, Macy's, Atlas Chemicals, Continental Can, Ralston Purina, Texas Gulf Sulphur, Hess Oil, W.R. Grace, Midland-Ross, American Home Products, Brinks, Clupack, John P. Maguire & Co., Cheesebrough-Ponds, ICI America, Seven-up Co., Meyer Blanke Co., Atlantic-Richfield, J.H. Foley Corp., Marconi Telegraph Cable Co., Trane Co., Systems, Science & Software, Inc., Archon Pure Products, Acme Cleveland Corp., Leesona Corp., Jewel Companies, May Department Stores, U.S. Plywood-Champion Papers, Inc., Hertz, Avon Products.

Institutional Interlocks:

Boy Scouts, Peace Corps, Whitney Museum of American Art, Franklin & Marshall College, Roper Public Opinion Research Center (Williams College), American Arbitration Assoc., American Red Cross, Lafayette College, Ithaca College, Harvard Business School, Pomfret School, Committee for Economic Development.

CBS OWNS

CBS TV network (247 affiliates)

CBS radio network (246 affiliates) and five television and fourteen radio stations

Viacom (CATV)

Columbia Records (the largest U.S. recording operation with 21 wholly or partially owned subsidiaries and 25 licensees doing business internationally in over 100 countries)

Fender Guitar & Amplifier Co., Buchia Synthesizer, Rogers Drums, Holt, Rinehart & Wilson, publishers, Dryden Press, W.B. Saunders (world's leading medical textbook publishers), Field and Stream Magazine, Creative Playthings, Franklin School of Science & Art, Memorex.

CBS also produces commercial films, educational films and audio cassettes, and newsfilms.

CBS Labs are involved in R & D for space and military programs and have produced, among other things, techniques of reconnaissance photography for police surveillance and a special mask for the protection of chemical-bacteriological weapons producers.

Composite Ownership (control shared by Morgan and Rockefeller banking groups)

47% of voting shares to: Chase Manhattan, Bankers Trust, Continental Illinois B & T, Bank of New York, Morgan Guaranty, Fidelity-Philadelphia Trust, State Street B & T, Bank of Delaware, Dreyfus Fund, Mass. Investors Trust, Mass. Investors Growth Stock, Fund Investors, Inc., Fidelity Management & Research, Investment Company of America, Arthur Judson, Inc., United States Trust Co., Hamilton Funds, Technology Fund, Tri-Continental Cap., Ives Fund, National Growth Fund, Prudential Insurance, Bankers Life, Connecticut General Life Insurance, John Hancock Mutual Life, Equitable Life Insurance, Teachers Insurance & Annuity.

Interlocks with Other Financial Institutions:

First National City Bank, Chemical Bank, Brown Bros. Harriman, New York Life, First Boston Corp., Manufacturers Hanover Trust, Royal Globel Insurance, Diebold Venture Fund, Oppenheimer Management Corp., Wm. A. M. Burden Co., W.E. Hutton & Co., Glen Ridge (N.J.) Savings & Loan, Federal Reserve Bank of Dallas, Federal Reserve Bank of New York.

Other Major Corporate Interlocks:

City Stores, Union Pacific R. R., Los Angeles & Salt Lake R. R., Oregon Short Line R. R., Oregon-Washington R. R. & Navigation Co., Atlantic-Richfield, Eastern Airlines, Pan American World Airways, Borden, American Electric Power, Fairchild Camera and Instrument, International Paper, Continental Oil, Brown and Root (second largest building contractor in the world, including Indochina), ITT, IBM, Delaware River Terminal & Warehouse Co., Atlantic Racing Assoc., Allied Chemical, Aerospace Corp., American Metal Climax, Inc., Lockheed Aircraft, Uris Building Corp., National Gypsum Co., National Wire Products, Safe-T-Ways Corp., Mine Publications, Inc., Smith, Kline & French Labs, Rockefeller Center, Data Dimensions, Inc., North American Aviation, Cummins Engineering Co., Aerospace Corp., Corning Glass, North American Rockwell Corp.

Institutional Interlocks:

Council on Foreign Relations, Museum of Modern Art, Lincoln Center, National Petroleum Council, Radio Free Europe (the CIA-funded propaganda agency), Resources for the Future, Inc., International Executive Service Corps., Columbia U., Greenpark Foundation, Rand Corp., N.Y. Rand Institute, U.S. Information Agency Advisory Commission, Center for Advanced Study in the Behavioral Sciences, The Business Council, Rockefeller Foundation, Washington U. (St. Louis), Carnegie Institution, Stanford Institute, American Red Cross, Albert Einstein Medical Center, American Institute of Aerospace and Astronautics, Institute for Defense Analysis, Smithsonian Institution, International Chamber of Commerce, Franklin D. Roosevelt Foundation, Boys Latin School (Md.), National Foundation for the Improvement of Education, U.S. State Department Advisory Commission on International Book & Library Programs, New Jersey Public Broadcasting Authority, Committee for Economic Development, American Petroleum Institute, Ballet Theatre Foundation, American Film Institute, Univ. of

Notre Dame, Carnegie Corp., California Institute of Technology, Univ. of Chicago, Lovelace Foundation, Anderson Foundation, Aspen Institute, National Merit Scholars Corp., Institute for International Education, Massachusetts Institute of Technology, Woodrow Wilson Foundation, Metropolitan Museum of Art, Population Council N.Y.C. Public Library, N.Y. Urban Coalition, J.H. Whitney Foundation.

Notes

A corporate interlock refers to the presence of *at least* one common member of the board of directors.

This table is based on a two-part article by Richard Pelton in *PL Magazine* February, 1970 and January, 1973) and draws heavily from The Network Project's Notebook Number Two, *Directory of the Networks* (New York, 1973). Additional materials by the author.

This table is reprinted from Howard J. Ehrlich, "The Politics of News Media Control," *Research Group One Report* Number 15.

Chapter 11

CORPORATIONS

Corporate power first became a major public issue around the turn of the century. Monopolies such as U.S. Steel and Standard Oil dominated their industries. They set prices, controlled production and kept wages low. Corporations suppressed the organization of unions. Many current proposals for reducing corporate power such as anti-trust laws and nationalization originated during this era.

In the early nineteenth century, the large corporation as we know it today did not exist. Most business was conducted by individuals or partners. Employees were limited to the number that one or two persons could supervise. Corporations originally involved a limited grant of state power to a group of persons for a specific purpose. For example, corporations were formed to build canals and roads. Once a corporate charter was granted, it was always subject to revision by the state to insure that a public purpose continued to be fulfilled.

Entrepreneurs, bankers, and lawyers collaborated during the nineteenth century to reorganize the corporation into an independent institution. The initial loss of public control over corporations occurred as a side effect of the Dartmouth College controversy. In 1819 the Supreme Court decided that the state of New Hampshire had no right to intervene to change the charter of Dartmouth College. This decision was construed to apply to business corporations also. Independence of the state, a major attribute of the present day corporation, was achieved.

The next step to the modern corporation was taken when the equal protection clause of the

Fourteenth Amendment to the Constitution was applied to corporations. The intent of this 1868 constitutional amendment was to guarantee former black slaves the right to full citizenship. The courts created a legal fiction: the corporation was to be treated as a person before the law. This decision freed individuals who acted for a corporation from personal liability for actions that they initiated on behalf of the corporation. Under the law the corporation was the actor.

The final step in creating conditions for the existence of the modern corporation was taken when legislators under corporate influence in states such as Delaware and New Jersey revised their incorporation laws to remove virtually all remaining restrictions on corporate actions. Now the modern corporation in its full panoply of rights and powers could be said to exist. This entity could: (1) hold assets beyond the life span of individual persons; (2) enable owners to divide the tasks of coordination among a large number of managers so that the work of thousands of persons could be organized and controlled; and (3) be free from direct government control of its operations and purposes.

Most conservatives believe that large corporations are the best means to produce abundant goods efficiently. They identify the growth of the modern corporation with the expansion of American power in the world. These conservatives believe that corporations serve the national interest. As President Eisenhower's Secretary of Defense and former head of General Motors, Charles Wilson, summed it up, "What's good for General Motors is good for the country."

Other conservatives, whose roots are in small and medium sized businesses, are not as sanguine about the large corporation. Large corporations become bureaucratized and rigidified as elaborate procedures have to be followed to make a decision. These conservatives feel that the sense of individual initiative and entrepreneurial spirit that made America great is being lost as large corporations displace small business. Yet they are wary of government intervention to redress this situation.

Most liberals also feel that corporations are the best way to run our economy. They are impressed with the variety of goods produced by American industry and by its sheer ability to produce and distribute massive quantities of products. However, many of these liberals are also concerned with the lack of competition in American industry. They are disturbed by reports of unsafe products and environmentally dangerous production processes. Although they accept the existence of the private corporation, they want government to act to eliminate its abuses. These liberals look to the various government agencies, such as the Federal Trade Commission and the Food and Drug Administration, to see that the public interest is served.

However, many liberals have become skeptical of the effectiveness of these agencies, finding that their policy-making apparatuses have become captured by the very corporations they were supposed to regulate. Some liberals argue that the regulatory agencies can be made to perform their original function by forbidding agency personnel from working for industry for long periods of time. Rules such as these, they feel, will insure a sufficient separation between regulator and regulated to enable the agency to function as an independent entity.

Some liberals and almost all socialists argue that concentrated economic power will always find a way to express itself no matter how many legal and administrative restrictions are placed on it. Liberals who take this position argue that large corporations must be broken up into smaller units to protect the public interest. To achieve this goal divestiture bills have been introduced in Congress. A major legislative and lobbying campaign was initiated in the mid-seventies to divide the major oil companies into separate production, refining, and distribution units, reducing their horizontal and vertical integration and thus their power over the industry and the consumer.

Socialists believe that large corporations are the basic social problem in American society. Corporations are the means by which economic resources are concentrated in the hands of a small upper class. This capitalist class translates the economic wealth produced by the corporations into political power through contributions to political candidates, lobbying, and public relations campaigns. Through these means control of economic resources by a small group is enforced by the state and legitimated by public opinion.

Most socialists believe that the solution to this private concentration of power is public ownership of the means of production. Corporations should be nationalized and run by the government for the people. To make this possible the people must first take control of the government from the capitalist class. Socialists expect that the relatively small rewards that workers receive in exchange for their work, in comparison to owners and managers, will lead to dissatisfaction with the corporate system. With this class consciousness workers could be organized to take over an existing political party or to form a new one to contest for political power using the electoral process. Other socialists argue that the most effective tactic is a general strike in which all workers withhold their labor until their demands are met. Still others feel that only a revolution can bring about the transition from capitalism to socialism.

Socialist anarchists are concerned that a change from private to govern-ment-run corporations may change little or nothing. A small group would be in control of decision making in either case. A more fundamental restructuring of economic organization is required. Decision making should be turned directly over to the workers who run the enterprise. Organizations should be reduced to the smallest possible size consistent with efficient production so that democratization of the workplace can be carried out. Both the alienation that results from loss of control over work process and over the results of one's labor must be eliminated if socialism is to be achieved.

In the conservative article, Crandall argues that corporate power, exercised through monopolies, is no longer a problem. Instead, the problem is the growth of the power of the federal government over corporations. During the 1970s the government expanded the areas in which it regulates the conduct of corporations to include health, safety, and environmental protection. These new regulations are costly, ineffective, and inefficient. They increase the cost of producing goods and reduce economic growth. Loss of economic growth is a major problem, since revenues produced through expansion of the economy is the best way to provide the means to deal with social problems.

Most regulations have been instituted at the behest of special interest groups, such as environmental organizations, rather than on behalf of the general public interest. If controls on corporate actions in the interest of protecting the environment are necessary, they should be undertaken through market type of incentives such as taxes. But it would be far better to leave matters now regulated by the government to the individual choice of the consumer. Consumers should be allowed to choose between exercising caution in using less safe products or reducing their standard of living by paying more for products with higher safety standards. Decisions should be made within the framework of the market instead of being taken over by government. If the present trend toward increased government regulation continues, the cost of producing goods will become so high that the economy will stagnate. Few taxpayers are aware that regulation costs so much. Excessive government regulation has not gained sufficient attention as a public issue.

In the liberal article, Nader, Green, and Seligman argue that excessive corporate power still exists. Corporations are run by a small, self-perpetuating oligarchy, which acts in its own interest rather than the public interest. The problem is that there is too little outside influence on corporate management. Corporate autarchy results in excessive financial benefits to corporate executives, inefficiency through lack of checks on management, and widespread illegal and corrupt activities.

Corporations have weakened controls over themselves by playing off one state against the other. Although formally under the aegis of state law, corporations have attained virtual autonomy. To redress this situation a broader regulatory authority is required. Nader, Green, and Seligman propose that the federal government undertake the chartering of corporations so that stricter standards can be set to make corporations obey the law and operate efficiently. Federal charters should include provisions for boards of directors to have greater oversight powers over corporate actions and to be more broadly representative of shareholders. Additional checks and balances on corporations could be introduced by allowing workers, consumers, communities, and other interested parties affected by corporate activities greater access to the courts to press their grievances against corporate actions. Dividing power among a variety of groups through a congressional act is the method to break up the concentration of power within the corporation. Inside the corporation, managers would compete with directors for power, and both would be further counterbalanced by interest groups acting through the legal system.

In the socialist article, Harrington argues that private corporate decision making impedes the operation of the economy and hurts the public interest. Private profit as a guideline to decision making does not result in public good. Corporations act against the public interest by producing wasteful and expensive products in the interest of maximizing profits. The automobile and oil industries have received billions of dollars of public subsidies. The development of these industries according to internally set corporate priorities has had antisocial results. The automobile oil economy isolates the poor and minorities, threatens the environment and causes urban crises. The actions of corporations in their own interest have similar negative consequences for other desired social goals such as full employment.

To achieve social goals government must determine economic priorities through a democratic process of decision making. Several structural changes in the American economy are required. Public works programs should be undertaken by the government both to provide useful social goods, such as housing, and to make useful employment available to all people. Railroads should be nationalized and rebuilt to save energy, protect the environment and provide jobs. A major oil company should be nationalized to develop energy resources on public lands.

A variety of financial institutions should be created that would make capital available to locally run cooperatives and community development corporations. The goal is to find ways to make investment decisions democratically by removing them from corporate control without centralizing them in the federal government. Harrington's proposals would not eliminate corporations. If instituted, they would result in a mixed economy in which private corporate decision making would be subordinated to public goals.

Conservative

Robert Crandall: Is Government Regulation Crippling Business?

Three-quarters of a century ago the great issue pitting business against government was monopoly power; after that it was unionism; today the provocation to battle is the issue of regulation. Nothing angers businessmen large and small more than federal intervention in matters of safety and environmental control. And nowhere is the state more intrusive and demanding in its relation to the private sphere. Their contest, waged in courtrooms, in the press, in the corridors of Washington, proceeds from the question: How much protection do workers, consumers, and the public need? But posing the question in that form has permitted regulators and interest groups to ride public sympathy to even more expensive, ill-considered forms of government control. The relevant question should be, how can regulation be designed so as to minimize expense and confusion, without sacrificing safety and health? The regulatory problem is one of method as much as scope.

Until as recently as a decade ago, the word regulation was applied almost exclusively to the government's attempt to control prices and licensing in such fields as transportation, electrical and gas utilities, communications, and oil and gas production. Today such agencies as the Civil Aeronautics Board, the Interstate Commerce Commission, and the Federal Communications Commission have this role.

But the 1970s have witnessed the growth of a new form of regulation that involves health, safety, and environmental protection. In less than 10 years Congress has created a federal bureaucracy employing 80,000 people, with the mission of protecting consumers or workers from harm. Among the more important of the new agencies, and their dates of creation, are:

> The Environmental Protection Agency (EPA), 1970
> The National Highway Traffic Safety Administration (NHTSA), 1970
> The Occupational Safety and Health Administration (OSHA), 1970
> The Consumer Product Safety Commission (CPSC), 1972
> The Office of Surface Mining Reclamation and Enforcement (in the Department of the Interior), 1977

At least another 15 lesser agencies or offices have also been created, and many existing organizations—such as the Federal Trade Commission—enjoy greater authority.

These groups act as agents for the public (including workers), which has no way of bargaining with business over product safety, pollution, or workplace hazards. We owe to these various organizations a substantial reduction in the quantity of noxious particulates and sulfur dioxide in the air, less muck in our waterways, and a sizable decrease in the number of fatal mining accidents, among other achievements.

Yet balanced against these notable successes is an even heavier load of failure. The promulgation of thousands of highly detailed standards has proved both confusing and costly. Automobile safety requirements have had no demonstrable effect on the highway death toll. The EPA's sulfur emissions standards will cost industry $1 billion more per year than more flexible, though equally safe, measures. A new program to make public transportation available to the handicapped costs more than providing them limousine service. OSHA's industrial-noise standards might run to $2 billion a year, neglecting much less expensive forms of worker protection.

There are two problems with this new "social" regulation, both of them locked in the design of the agencies themselves. First, it is impossible to calculate adequately either the costs or the benefits of the standards which these agencies impose. Had Congress used pollution taxes or insurance schemes to force or cajole companies to devise health and safety standards, the cost of the programs could have been easily computed. But the deliberate decision to have agencies mandate standards for business means that firms will simply add the costs of compliance into the price of products. The ultimate cost of a given standard is thus anybody's guess, a great boon to those seeking to disguise the true costs of regulation.

The second problem is the powerful influence that special-interest groups have been able to wield. These groups include public-interest organizations as well as unions and large firms. Again, because the agencies are so little accountable for their actions, they have proved an easy mark for highly organized lobbies.

The cost of social regulation has grown to vast proportions because society is billed for it indirectly. Here the contrast with the traditional rate-setting form of regulation is instructive. If the ICC were to suggest a 50 percent increase in railroad and trucking rates tomorrow, furious cries of collusion would fill the air. If a state commission were to grant a local electrical utility a 50 percent boost, consumers would storm the walls. If, however, EPA or OSHA were to announce that it was tightening all of its standards by 25 percent (which might increase compliance costs by 50 percent), the reaction would probably range from indifference to mild approval that businesses were being forced to stop polluting or endangering workers. The fact that costs and, therefore, prices would soon reflect this change would not be advertised by EPA or OSHA, understood by most citizens, or even believed by the ardent proponents of regulation.

EPA's standard for photochemical smog provides a noteworthy example of this heedless expenditure of society's resources. Congress has established a goal of reducing automobile emissions by 90 percent from their earlier, uncontrolled levels. Two of these pollutants, hydrocarbons and nitrogen oxides, are thought to create smog through a reaction with sunlight. A major component of this smog, ozone, has been thought to have harmful effects upon chronic respiratory diseases and breathing capacity. Unfortunately, there is little evidence of either effect at low levels of exposure. EPA has discovered that the only study linking ozone to respiratory disease is 22 years old, and has never been verified. No one even knows for sure how ozone exposure was measured in this study. But EPA, undaunted, is proposing to keep a very tight air standard for ozone—0.1 parts per million—at an annual cost of $14 to $19 billion per year. A looser standard, though reducing costs, would put congress in the embarrassing position of having to roll back automobile emissions standards. To avoid this outcome, EPA simply argues that there is *some* danger to health from allowing higher levels of ozone concentration, regardless of the evidence; few consumers will understand how much this will cost them, or how little it may help.

Since agencies generally do not have any interest in calculating the costs of their actions—indeed, they would prefer to avoid such embarrassments—it is not surprising that we do not know how much NHTSA, OSHA, or EPA is really costing us. The estimated cost of complying with EPA regulations in 1976 was $15 billion; if the agency enforced all of its standards the cost could reach at least $40 billion by the early 1980s. OSHA, which has not moved so fast nor so aggressively, may be costing us only $2 or $3 billion per year. Automobile safety regulation probably requires at least another $3 billion per year. Regulation of safety in coal mines has probably reduced labor productivity by about 50 percent. There is clear evidence that FDA regulation has reduced the rate of introduction of new therapeutic drugs. The total cost of all of these forms of regulation is thus immense, but we do not know with precision what the total burden is today or what it will be tomorrow.

The secondary effects of regulation increase the bill even further. Edward Denison of the Brookings Institution has estimated that productivity growth was reduced by nearly 20 percent in 1975 owing to increasing environmental control costs and health and safety regulations imposed upon private nonfarm business. But in 1975, Denison estimates, business spent only $9 billion on environmental control. This number will probably increase four- or fivefold by the mid 1980s if EPA implements the laws which it administers and enforces the resulting standards.

In short, we have considerable evidence that growing social regulation could eat into our ability to grow economically. Productivity growth has slowed to about 1 percent per year, a rate which will permit very little improvement in the average standard of living and even less ability to address other pressing social problems. There can be little doubt that regulation has contributed to this sharp deceleration in growth.

Regulation is supposed to protect the public; but the workings of the political process insure that general welfare will be overlooked in order to satisfy a few powerful groups. Public policy in a pluralistic, democratic society is rarely based, as it is generally supposed to be, upon providing the greatest good for the greatest number. Actually, policy-makers seek to mollify specific constituencies or "common interest" groups. These groups needn't be large; it is more important that they be well-organized and clamorous in their pursuit of self-interest. Truckers are no more numerous than members of many other groups, but their economic well-being is very much dependent upon monopolistic practices, while a consumer's welfare depends to a much lesser degree upon low shipping rates. So the ICC has largely regulated competition out of the trucking industry.

Another classic example of the extraordinary power of special-interest lobbying is EPA's decision on limiting sulfur emissions by electrical utilities. In 1977, EPA and the White House agreed on a proposal to require sulfur-removing equipment, called flue-gas scrubbers, on all new coal-fired utility plants. The idea had been vigorously advanced by the odd couple of midwestern coal-mining unions and environmentalists, in order to cope with the shift to cleaner western coal. The miners were concerned about the loss of jobs, since utilities, who consume large quantities of coal, would be loath to burn the dirtier midwestern variety if they were to be held responsible for the cleanliness of the air. So the miners argued for an amendment to the Clean Air Act that would focus on the installation of scrubbers—no matter what sort of coal is used—rather than on reaching a required level of purity in the atmosphere. According to EPA's own analysis, the cost of installing scrubbers is $1 billion more per annum than the option of giving utilities their choice of coal and technology to realize the same sulfur emissions rate. In fact, the final standard proposed by EPA administrator Douglas Costle is the most costly he could have chosen and may even generate more pollution than a slightly looser (partial scrubbing) standard. The final irony is that EPA's analyses show that employment in midwestern coal mines would not decline under any clean-air policy being contemplated.

Not all powerful interest groups have profit as their rallying cry. Environmentalists and other public-interest lobbies are best understood as ideologically united organizations seeking to tax the many for policies often desired by only a small, vocal minority. Groups such as the Environmental Defense Fund and the Natural Resources Defense Council lobby for goals that they believe to be in the interest of the general public, but they generally do not inform this larger constituency of the true costs or benefits of what they propose. On the other hand, the AFL-CIO is perfectly aware that worker safety can only be bought at the expense of consumers. In either case, it is important to keep the public from understanding how much this new regulation will cost. People must be led carefully into the brave new healthy world of the future, not knowing how many cars, television sets, or trips to Disney World they must sacrifice.

Despite the individual horror stories of misguided and inefficient regulation, the new social regulatory agencies will neither be disbanded nor sharply cut back in the foreseeable future. Nor should they be. But substantial reform is both possible and needed. In an article of this scope, it is possible only to summarize some of the more important suggestions for reform.

First, Congress must begin requiring regulators to measure both the costs they are forcing upon the economy and the benefits of their regulations. The Carter administration, concerned over slowing the pace of inflation, has already initiated this process by pressuring agency heads to soften some of their more expensive requirements. But a more permanent step in this direction would be the creation of a "regulatory budget"—an annual summation of all of the costs mandated by each agency. Agencies would be instructed not to exceed the budget total in any year, but would be free to determine how much to spend on each program in their domain. EPA could be given, for example, $40 billion per year to grow by a fixed percentage annually. It would then have to decide whether to spend $1 billion by requiring scrubbers for all electrical utilities, or by seeking reductions, in, say, water pollution. This proposal would have the additional advantage of provoking an annual debate in Congress on the size of EPA's or OSHA's budget. Such a debate would force proponents to measure the benefits of the various regulatory programs, something now totally lacking in the political process.

Second, Congress and the regulators should attempt to devise simple, market-like incentives for the promotion of environmental purity or human health and safety. A pollution tax or other form of market instrument confronts all polluters with the same "price" for polluting and assures that the cost of getting to a desired pollution level is minimized. As yet, the use of such alternatives as penalties and taxes has been rare, since they would make the cost of pollution or safety regulation more visible. Tax collections are public information; regulatory costs are not. The use of taxes would also make it more difficult for the politically powerful to lobby for favorable treatment, since the IRS is not likely to allow polluters to beg for favorable treatment. Finally, small firms would be penalized less than big firms since engineering standards usually require large fixed investments which can only be operated profitably at large outputs. To its credit, EPA is beginning to experiment with various forms of "pollution rights" in implementing the Clean Air Act.

Third, we should seriously question the tendency of regulators to limit our choices between product prices and safety. Not all of us want our standard of living reduced through substantially higher product prices in return for absolute safety. For instance, I would appreciate the opportunity to buy a fairly inexpensive lawnmower and to be careful in using it.

Finally, the strategy for reducing automobile emissions and hazards should be reexamined by Congress. Emissions standards for automobiles are set not by EPA, but by Congress, which has felt that it must eliminate any possibility of Detroit influence over an administrative agency. The result has been continual postponing of deadlines, inefficient automobile design, a needless collision with fuel-economy objectives, and higher vehicle costs to the consumer. It is painfully obvious that we can do better.

A few years ago, a colleague remarked to a conference on communications regulations that reform would not come easily in that area because there was no "crisis." We are not yet at a crisis point in regulation, but this partially owing to public ignorance. As long as most taxpayers do not realize that their $500 or so per year is often being wasted, they are not likely to raise regulation as an issue that competes with inflation, the Middle East, or abortion in forthcoming political campaigns. But when they finally discover that the new regulators have succeeded in reducing our economic growth to zero, and that we are rapidly becoming the next Great Britain, reform will become an urgent priority. One only hopes that the process can be improved before reaching such a state.

Liberal

Ralph Nader, Mark Green and Joel Seligman: The Myth of Corporate Democracy

It makes terrific sense on paper. The shareholders (electorate) choose directors (legislature) who in turn select the managers (executive branch) to administer the enterprise day to day. In theory, at least, corporations seem very much like "the little republics" 19th-century legislators imagined them to be.

That corporate democracy has been an illusion for nearly 100 years has not deterred businessmen and the New York Stock Exchange from annually proclaiming its viability. But the recent rash of corporate crime—over 100 companies have so far acknowledged illegal payoffs at home or abroad—raises important questions about who governs the largest corporations. Why has corporate law failed to keep corporations law-abiding? What is the scope of management power and what are the checks upon it?

In nearly every large American business corporation, one man variously titled the President, or the Chairman of the Board, or the Chief Executive Officer—or a small coterie of men have unquestioned operational control. In theory, this small group of managers is selected by the board of directors to run the corporation; in reality it is just the reverse. The chief executive or executive clique chooses the board, and, with its acquiescence, controls the corporation.

The legal basis for such a consolidation of power is the proxy election. Every year, the shareholders of each publicly held corporation are invited to attend a meeting where directors will be nominated and elected.

In political elections we can go a few steps down the street to vote. In corporate elections we have to go to someplace like Wilmington, Delaware. The result is that few stockholders attend these meetings. Sylvia Silver, a Reuters correspondent who covers over 100 Wilmington annual meetings each year, described representative 1974 meetings: "At Cities Service Company, the 77th largest industrial corporation with some 135,000 shareholders, 25 shareholders actually attended the meeting; El Paso Natural Gas, with 125,000 shareholders, had 50 shareholders; at Bristol Meyers, with 60,000 shareholders, 25 shareholders appeared. Even 'Campaign GM,' the most publicized shareholder challenge of

Reprinted from *The Washington Monthly*, July–August, 1976, by permission.

the past two decades, attracted no more than 3,000 of General Motors' 1,400,000 shareholders, or roughly two tenths of one per cent."

Since almost no one goes, the stockholders are represented only by their mailed in proxy votes. And company insiders have so totally dominated the proxy machinery that corporate elections have come to resemble the Soviet Union's "Communist ballot," on which only one slate of candidates appears. Of the 6,744 corporations required to file data with the Securities and Exchange Commission in 1973, incumbent management retained control in at least 6,734 companies, or 99.9 per cent. In the 500 largest industrial corporations—corporations which account for some 66 per cent of the sales of all industrial corporations in the United States—no incumbent management was even challenged in 1973.

The key to what British law Professor L. C. B. Gower calls "this solemn farce" is money—specifically, the cost of mounting a proxy challenge. Under current corporate law, the only real chance to nominate directors belongs to the incumbent management. With practically unlimited power to use corporate funds in the elections, the management simply overpowers opponents, who must prepare separate proxies and campaign literature at their own expense. Consider, for example, the techniques of the Northern States Power Co. in 1973. At that time Northern States Power voluntarily employed the "cumulative" voting system, which meant that only 7.2 per cent of outstanding shares was necessary to elect one director to Northern's 14-person board. Troubled by Northern's record on environmental and consumer issues, a broadly based coalition of public interest groups called the Citizens' Advocate for Public Utilitiy Responsibility nominated Alpha Snaby, a former Minnesota state legislator, for a seat on the board. These groups then successfully solicited the votes of over 14 percent of all shareholders, or more than twice the votes necessary to elect her to the board. Northern States then, in effect, bought the election back. By soliciting proxies a second and then a third time, the Power Company was able to persuade (or confuse) those who cast 71 per cent of Ms. Snaby's votes to change their minds.

Emphasizing the Positive

Larger, more experienced corporations are usually less heavy-handed. Typically, They will soften up the opposition with a series of "build-up" letters. In the 1971 'Campaign GM' contest, General Motors raised this strategy to a new plateau by encasing the Project on Corporate Responsibility's single 100-word proxy solicitation within a 21-page booklet specifically rebutting each of the Project's charges. The Project, of course, could never afford to respond to GM's pamphlet —postage alone for soliticing GM's 1.4 million shareholders would have exceeded $100,000. The cost of printing a document comparable to GM's 21-page booklet and mailing it out, accompanied by a proxy statement, a proxy card, and a stamped return envelope might have cost half a million dollars.

Nor is it likely that the Project or any other outside shareholder could have matched GM's ability to hire "professional" proxy solicitors, such as Georgeson and Company, which can deploy up to 100 solicitors throughout the country to contact shareholders personally, given them campaign speeches, and urge them to mail in their proxies.

Management's "army" in a proxy war also includes: attorneys, who can distract the opposition with costly litigation; accountants and statisticians, who will prepare the most self-serving financial analysis allowable; and public relations advisors, who will create advertisements for trade journals and the financial sections of major newspapers. Management can also exploit corporate personnel and resources on its own behalf. Clerical help and clerical facilities, including printing presses, photo-copying machines, and computer addressing machines, are invariably called into action.

Management's grip on company power is tightened by its authority to print and distribute annual, quarterly, and other reports to shareholders. Besides the formal proxy statement, these reports usually embody the only detailed information shareholders receive about their corporation. The reports, however, "may be in any form deemed suitable by the management" and are not subject to the same standards of truthfulness that the text of a proxy solicitation is subjected to. Consequently, though every word of an insurgent shareholder's communications with other shareholders may be challenged if it is arguably "false or misleading," most management reports are subject to no textual regulation whatever.

Unfortunately, management reports are frequently "false and misleading." They are often written in an upbeat public relations jargon which emphasizes "positive" aspects of the past business year while rationalizing or ignoring management mistakes, financial losses, corporate or executive criminal violations, or civil actions successfully prosecuted against the corporation. For example, although subsequent congressional testimony made clear that Lockheed would have gone bankrupt unless it received an emergency loan guarantee from the federal government, Lockheed's 1969 annual report managed to ignore the prominent debate in Congress over whether the federal government should "bail out" the firm. And just a few months before the comptroller declared the Franklin National Bank insolvent, the corporations' management reported to its shareholders that "in 1973 Franklin crossed an important threshold so that it is now in a position to move forward in establishing itself as a major worldwide financial institution and a leading money center banking operation." Nowhere in the report was any mention made of the foreign currency speculation or improvident real estate loans which four months later caused the bank's demise.

The aggregate costs to management of all these approaches to stockholders can easily exceed $1 million. In the past 25 years there have been no more than a dozen cases in which insurgents have been able to match management expenses in a major proxy fight. During the past decade, only in the MGM proxy context of 1967 were the insurgents able to match management's expenses in a costly struggle for control.

State corporation law has done nothing to offset this imbalance of corporate resources. No decision since 1907 in either Delaware or New York, the two leading chartering states, has denied management the power to expend corporate funds or use corporate personnel exactly as management chooses. Even such seemingly "unreasonable" expenditures as public relations counsel, "entertainments," chartered airlines, limousines, and the indirect cost to the corporation of using officers and employees on behalf of an incumbent director slate, have survived judicial scrutiny. By contrast, state courts have firmly established the rule that insurgents, unlike management, are not entitled to reimbursement of any campaign expenses as a matter of right. If this is the way it is chosen, it is no surprise that the board of directors has ceased to perform its statutory function of "managing the business and affairs of every corporation." Indeed, it is often hard to tell whether the boards of many corporations perform any independent function at all other than mirroring managers' desires. "Directors," William O. Douglas complained as early as 1934, "do not direct."

In a 1975 survey of 394 of the country's largest corporations, Korn/Ferry International (a New York executive recruitment firm) found that boards averaged only seven meetings per year. In most large corporations, the board meetings have withered, through neglect, into a ritualized one- to three-hour ceremony. Much of that time is consumed by a pro forma review of operations by the president or vice presidents and equally routine approvals of the capital appropriations that management wants.

The meetings are so infrequent, the inquiry so tame, that the boards cannot hope to "manage" their corporation. Professor Myles Mace of the Harvard Business School, in *Directors: Myth and Reality*, has summarized hundreds of interviews with corporate officers and directors and concluded that boards perform none of their legally implied roles. Because the chief executive effectively selects the new members of a board, it does not establish the basic policies of a firm, does not select the president or other chief executive officers, and does not serve as disciplinarian of the corporation. "In the years that I've spent on various boards," says Robert Townsend, businessman and former chairman of Avis, "I've never heard a single suggestion from a director (made as a director at a board meeting) that produced any result at all."

Directors do not even ask rough or knowing questions. "In many corporations," Professor Melvin Eisenberg found, "the executives go so far as to wholly deny the board—supposedly entrusted with supreme power over the corporation—access to certain categories of information." Yet it is considered "discourteous," a breach of "corporate manners," for directors to "challenge" the president or other corporate officers. This can be a very expensive form of decorum, as the Penn Central's shareholders painfully discovered. At the time of its collapse in June 1970, Penn Central was the largest railroad in the country and the sixth largest industrial corporation overall. Within a two-year period, shareholders, watch their shares plummet from 86½ to 1¾.

Inner-Directed

Why? "The board was definitely responsible for the trouble," says E. Clayton Gengras, one of the "outside" (non-management) members of the board. "They took their fees and they didn't do anything. Over a period of years, people just sat there. That poor man from the University of Pennsylvania (President Gaylord P. Harnwell), he never opened his mouth. They didn't know the factual picture and they didn't try to find out." As the Penn Central rushed towards its monumental crack-up, the board routinely approved every proposal forwarded by management. Although Penn Central was desperate for capital, the directors paid nearly $100 million in dividends. The board never saw a capital expenditures budget. It never understood the inaccuracies published in Penn Central's annual reports. Just six hours before the corporation filed its bankruptcy petition, the board routinely approved new contracts for eight corporate executives, apparently unaware even then of the dimensions of the Penn Central's crisis. "All of this," concluded the House Banking and Currency Committee, "raises the serious question as to whether giant corporations affecting the everyday lives of our population...should continue to be governed in the traditional fashion or whether a new system of corporate directorships should be devised."

Exceptions to this pattern become news events. In reporting on General Motors' 1971 annual shareholders' meeting, *The Wall Street Journal* noted that, "The meeting's dramatic highlight was an impassioned and unprecedented speech by the Rev. Leon Sullivan, GM's recently appointed Negro director, supporting the Episcopal Church's efforts to get the company out of South Africa. It was the first time that a GM director had ever spoken against management at an annual meeting."

How, then, can one reconcile the grand imperative, "The business and affairs of every corporation...shall be managed by...a board of directors," with the reality of this non-decision-making body? The fashionable response is that the board is a legal fiction. Management control has overwhelmed the rule of law.

This widely held view is only half right. Management has deposed the board of directors—but it has done so with the law's approval. No rule within modern corporation statutes prohibits management from nominating and serving as directors. And two provisions found in most state corporation laws further erode authority.

The first provision is exemplified by the corporation law in Delaware. The section provides that a director shall "be fully protected in relying in good faith upon...reports made to the corporation by any of its officers." The meaning of this provision is very simple. Directors have no "duty to know." Unless something occurs to make them suspicious that something is wrong, directors are not required to "put into effect a system of watchfulness." They need not anticipate problems or verify the accuracy of reports upon which they rely.

A second provision of the Delaware General Corporation Law accomplishes the same result by allowing the board to formally delegate responsibility for most corporate business to a committee dominated by inside directors. Our survey of the 200 largest industrial corporations indicates that the practice is very widespread. Of all the corporations which reported, two thirds had transferred directorial powers from the full board to an executive committee, at least half of whose members were insiders. (A smaller number of corporations accomplish a comparable result by delegating authority to an insider-dominated finance committee.)

Attorney John A. McMullen has described several examples:

"At IBM four directors, all top-level officers of the corporation, control the all-important executive and finance committees; in addition, three of them are members of the powerful Corporate Office. At GM, four of five men, all inside directors of the company, dominate the executive and finance committees of the board as well as the administration committee comprised of key officers and directors...du Pont's executive committee consists of the company's chairman of the board, president, and six senior vice presidents."

Yet, whether or not the board formally delegates authority to an executive committee, the managers who choose both board and committee *always* exercise control. Senior executives invariably call the shots, which is why corporate law today is a hopelessly inaccurate reflection of corporate realities. As Professor Bayless Manning, the former dean of Stanford Law School, put it, "We have nothing left but our great empty corporation statues—towering skyscrapers internally welded together and containing nothing but wind."

Self-Dealing

Autocratic corporate government is not a phenomenon of interest only to corporate law professors. It entails serious economic and social costs—in terms of self-dealing, inefficiency and illegality.

1. *Self-dealing*—Current Delaware law permits the chief executive of a corporation and other senior corporate executives to serve on the board of directors of compensation committee which:

   a. sets executive salaries;

   b. sells or purchases property from corporate executives;

   c. loans money—on a secured or unsecured basis; with or without interest —to corporate executives; and

   d. establishes pension plans, profit-sharing plans, stock bonuses, retirement, benefit, incentive, and compensation plans.

Not only does the Delaware law permit such self-dealing, but it also renders shareholders virtually powerless to call a halt. Any contract or transaction between the corporation and an interested executive is permissible as long as it is "fair." But, in Delaware, "fairness" is presumed by the law. As Professor Ernest Folk, the leading commentator on Delaware's General Corporation Law, explains: "Given Delaware's presumption of sound business judgment with respect to board decisions, the courts will try to determine whether the decision can be attributed to any rational business purpose, and if so, there will be no judicial preemption of the decision."

There are few practical limits to this doctrine. For example, if a corporate chief executive were so graceless as to embezzle $500,000 even in Delaware he would probably be required to return the money and perhaps to go to jail. Yet if that same executive simply raised his salary by $500,000 and could point to similar salary increases in his industry, Delaware court would probably call this "fair."

Inefficiency & Illegality

With no law to hold it back, excessive remuneration has become the norm. In 1974 the executive compensation (salary, bonus, deferred income, and directors' fees) of the highest paid executives at the 50 largest industrial corporations averaged about $400,000. This is roughly as much in one year as many of their employees earn in a lifetime, and two-and-one-half times the equivalent executive pay rate in 1963.

Often these salaries don't go down even when sales or profits do. According to Professor Wilbur Lewellen of Purdue, the mean salary for the top executive at 50 large manufacturing corporations increased steadily during every year of the recent recession, from $251,867 in 1970 to $287,759 in 1971, $323,802 in 1972, and $389,277 in 1973.

But salary, bonus, and deferred income are only the most obvious benefits. Equally important is ownership income. Nearly every large industrial corporation offers its top executives stock options. These options allow executives to buy shares of stock in their corporation at a fixed price at any time or at specified times —often with the help of company-secured, low-interest or interest-free loans— and subsequently sell them at the most advantageous moment. From the shareholders' point of view, the result is a classic case of "heads we lose, tails you win." Over time, executives are able to build up a substantial fortune in corporate stock without personal risk. The more they do so the more the value of other stockholders' shares is diluted.

In 1974 (after eliminating from consideration the seven chief executives whose stock holdings were either largely inherited or largely "founder's shares") the 43 highest-paid chief executives at the 50 largest industrial firms owned an average of $1,566,009 of the corporation's stock.

Pension and retirement benefits have also swollen. We found in a survey that 21 chief executives of the 50 largest corporations (the rest did not report dollar figures) looked forward to retirement benefits of $133,910 each year. Of course, executives also reap a whole range of other prequisites: life and medical insurance, free medical service, educational grants for their children, indemnification insurance, country club memberships, free legal or tax counseling, expense accounts, and other amenities. When all the stock bonuses, insurance policies, and benefit programs are taken into account, the executives' incomes rise by 50 to 75 per cent above the nominal average level of $400,000 to an average of $600,000 to $700,000 each year.

High levels of pay are not limited to the chief executive. At General Electric, the chairman of the board, Reginald Jones, received direct remuneration of $501,200 in 1974. Walker Dance, Jack Parker, and Herman Weiss, the next three highest-paid executives, each received $400,000. The next 107 highest were paid an average of $121,240 in salary alone, with none of the extra benefits taken into account.

2. *Inefficiency*—Business defenders enjoy ridiculing a Post Office or Department of Health, Education and Welfare as examples of big government inefficiency. But recent history has demonstrated that corporate autocracy itself is inefficient.

As corporate operations have grown more complex and technologies more sophisticated, checks upon senior management have all but disappeared. The result has often been irrational decisions, hurried decisions, decisions based upon inadequate factual analysis or executive self-favoritism. Surveying a decade that had seen the wreck of the Penn Central, cost overrun catastrophes at both Lockheed and Douglas Aircraft, the slow, resistible decline of A&P, and a host of conglomerate stock collapses, J. Irwin Miller, president of Cummings Engine, concluded, "I think we've just gone through a decade of rather surprisingly bad decisions by businessmen worldwide. Some of them so bad that nobody would have guessed it."

3. *Illegality*—There is also, of course, the wave of corporate illegality which now fills our business pages and even front pages. The prominent exposure of these crimes makes it unnecessary for us to recite them in detail. But it is important to understand how the existing system of corporate governmence

tolerates or encourages corrupt decisions. As Roderick Hills, chairman of the Securities and Exchange Commission, said, "The problem as we see it is the breakdown of corporate accountability."

We have repeatedly mentioned Delaware corporate law for the same reason that law school corporations courses inevitably revolve around that self-proclaimed "little home of big business." Because that state's corporate statutes, and its judicial interpretations of them, so favor management interests, one half of *Fortune's* top 500 industrials have chartered there. Worse, other states have followed Delaware's lead and weakened their corporate laws so as not to lose too much chartering business to this "corporate Reno."

Federal Chartering

In other areas—employment discrimination, unfair labor practices, pollution—Congress has understood how states would compete among themselves for plant sitings by offering high-pollution, low-wage environments, Hence, national minimum standards were essential. So too for the system of state chartering, espeically since it's so much easier to move a piece of paper to Delaware than relocate a plant in Alabama.

Federal chartering is a vehicle to bring the kind of democracy and probity to corporate governance that has been glaringly absent. Redesigning rights and obligations between shareholders, boards of directors, and executives can encourage giant companies to be both more efficient and law-abiding. To help accomplish this goal involves a full-time outside board of directors, selected by "cumulative voting" of beneficial owners in entirely company-funded elections. And the victims of corporate malfeasance—workers, consumers, local communities, shareholders, and small businessmen—should be accorded greater access to the court system to redress their complaints. These and other proposals are spelled out in detail in our report, *"Constitutionalizing" the Corporation: the Case for the Federal Chartering of Giant Corporations*. That study emphasizes that national standards for national corporations are essential to reverse the historic flow of power to an executive clique—and that corporate autocracy is not a necessary attribute of a productive economy.

Socialist

Michael Harrington: How to Reshape America's Economy

The following sumary of socialist ideas for reshaping the American economy is taken from testimony that Michael Harrington, chairman of the Democratic Socialist Organizing Committee, gave before the Joint Economic Committee of the U.S. Congress last November. Harrington began with a discussion of the Hawkins-Humphrey bill (the Equal Opportunity and Full Employment Act of 1975):

The basic presuppositions of the bill before us assert a fundamental—to my mind, erroneous—Keynesian principle: that the private corporate infrastructure of the American economy is sound, so that the role of government is to supplement and facilitate its decisions with regard to what investments should be made, what kinds of jobs should be created, and how the benefits of this process are to be distributed.

My rejection of this thesis is not the unique consequence of a socialist analysis, though it is shaped by such an analysis. In a just published book, *The New American Ideology*, Professor George C. Lodge of the Harvard Business School asserts similar criticisms of the Lockean assumptions about the American political economy, including our faith in a benign providence that somehow is thought to have created an economic universe in which private greeds interact to achieve a public good.

This faith is not merely a matter of conservative orthodoxy. In May 1967, for instance, Gardner Ackley, a leading spokesperson of the liberal point of view, said:

> If one were to examine all of the thousands of decisions made daily by the managers of the modern corporations, I think he would be struck by the relatively small number in which significant questions of conflict between public and private interest arise. In the vast majority of these decisions, businessmen need not explicitly consider the "public interest"; nor does government have reason for concern. What sources of material are cheapest, what product sells best, which production method is most efficient—these are questions to which answers that maximize private profit in most cases also maximize public welfare.

A similar, if unformulated, view underlies the Hawkins-Humphrey bill. Before turning to its specifics, some basic criticisms of this proposition are in order.

It is simply not true, certainly in terms of our recent experience, that answers that maximize private profit in most cases also maximize public welfare. Two related, and quite momentous, cases in point, the oil and auto industries, provide persuasive evidence on this count.

For more than a generation, the United States government has assumed that the welfare of the giant oil companies promotes the nation's interest. This was the rationale behind the special tax treatment devised for these companies in

Reprinted from *Dissent*, Spring, 1976 by permission.

1950—which was really a secret, undemocratic foreign aid program for reactionary Arab oil potentates, in which Washington had American corporations effectively operate as the tax collectors for foreign powers. (Senator Church's hearings on the multinationals documented this point brilliantly.) It was the theory behind the oil import quota system that kept Arab oil out of the United States when it was cheap and without political strings. It motivated percent depletion and the expensing of intangible costs; it was a subsidiary reason for the commitment of more than $70 billion for interstate highways dedicated to the glory of the private car and the destruction of mass transit. It was the explicit argument for effectively absolving the oil companies from the criminal provisions of the antitrust laws when the Department of Justice openly abandoned their enforcement in 1953-54. I could go on citing more examples, but the basic point now is plain: America paid tens of billions in direct and indirect public expenditures in order to support the private purposes of oil companies on the assumption that those purposes would benefit the public interest.

They did the opposite. These multinational corporations were given governmental incentives, not to develop our coal reserves, not to invest in new energy technologies, not to develop refinery capacity within the United States, and so on. After more than 40 years of federal support, the oil companies succeeded in creating a wasteful, environmentally destructive energy economy that is needlessly vulnerable to the OPEC cartel.

Similarly the automobile. Back in 1949, the United Auto Workers' union asked the car manufacturers to build a small, efficient vehicle. Detroit refused to do so for about a quarter of a century. It took advantage of the enormous, publicly financed infrastructure created for the care and feeding of the private car to build bigger and bigger, less and less efficient, more and more polluting automobiles. It imposed upon the American people the tremendous social costs of a corporate technology that maximized antipublic values. A few years back, the Ford Foundation reported one of the incredible ironies in all of this. Poor people, it found, got more mileage to the gallon than members of other social classes and this was the only area in which the poor had any advantage—and this because they drove older, and therefore somewhat more efficient, cars!

To generalize, it is an ideological, unscientific proposition to assert that the investment decisions of the private sector, even the ones made on a much more sophisticated profit calculus than those of the robber barons, promote the common good. The technology of the giant corporations has more "externalities" than "internalities"—i.e., its social cost regularly and massively exceeds its private costs and benefits.

This, in turn, means that government must have a much more systematic and conscious method for determining its priorities—democratically, on the basis of maximizing social values—and of effecting them in the economy. Earlier this year, the U.S. Railway Association told us that federal subsidies to transportation, from the early 19th century on to the present, totaled $450 billion, most of that money being spent during the last 50 years. Yet there was no plan for allocating these subsidies.

The result was that tens of billions were assigned to private corporations on the basis of an intraindustry competition held in the corridors of power. So the victory of truckers and private cars over the railroads was accomplished at the public expense and at an enormous dollar cost. It has, among other things, also helped to isolate the central city along with the poor and the minorities who live there, threatened the environment, promoted suburban sprawl, and so on. Indeed, to speak of the New York City crisis for a moment, a good deal of our problem derives from the fact that Washington spent so much money on cheap housing and publicly subsidized roads to help the middle class flee the City.

So private corporate priorities cannot empirically be assumed to be social in character, and government subsidy programs cannot go on in their present chaotic way, financing revolutions in the American way of life without any democratic discussion. And a similar point applies to present government full-employment policy.

The recession that began in 1969 was initiated by the White House. This is not a Watergate secret that had to be extracted from the President; it is a fact he himself confirmed at the time. We are going to strive for price stability by "cooling off" the economy, Mr. Nixon said. One of the reasons impelling him to act in this fashion was that sustained full employment is a threat to private corporations. For when there is a full employment, the labor market tightens up, unions become more combative, and wages tend to rise at the expense of profits. When the commanding heights of the economy are occupied by corporations that can administer prices, as is the case in America today, the result is inflation. So there was a corporate demand in 1969 to restore profitability and price stability by means of the classic remedies: deflation, or, to put it less technically, through the suffering of working people and the poor. This policy was too politically dangerous, as the 1970 elections demonstrated, and it was followed by a preelection heating of the economy in 1971-72, and a postelection slamming-on of the brakes in early 1973, a catastrophic decision from which the nation still suffers.

There are many instructive aspects to this history but only one of them is germane to the particular theme of this analysis: that corporations feel uncomfortable with full employment. If I can go back to, and contradict, Mr. Ackley's optimistic assumptions—in this rather basic case, what maximizes public welfare, i.e., full employment, does not maximize private profit. If the priorities of the latter prevail, as they have under the Nixon and Ford administrations, the former is impossible to achieve. We have a basic, structural conflict, not a providential harmony.

So on three counts—the antisocial tendencies of the corporate development of technology; the chaotic, antipublic character of a public subsidy system subordinated to corporate priorities; the contradiction between corporate profits and full employment—the Keynesian assumptions have been subverted. My policy conclusion is that government cannot relegate itself to an ancillary role, that it must intervene actively with regard to basic investment priorities, and to the best use of our human resources. This cannot be accomplished by "indicative" planning that leaves the fundamental corporate determinants in charge of the direction of the economy. It does not require totalitarian compulsion, which is economically inefficient as well as abhorrent on many other grounds. It demands a degree of democratic planning and socialization of the investment process, which means some structural changes in the American economy.

Let me now apply these general remarks to an analysis of a few important aspects of the Hawkins-Humphrey bill.

In Section 3 of the bill, the president is cast in a passive role. His analysis of the economy is assumed to accept private investment plans as a given and to tailor federal policy to that reality. I believe that we should provide for a much greater role for the public sector, as a source of jobs and as a means of planning production for social use (the specifics of how this might be done will be outlined in a moment).

A related point: Section 4 of the bill emphasizes local planning councils as the prime instrumentality for identifying needs that can be met in the course of providing useful employment to people. There are two limitations to this notion. First, the macro-economic planning of basic priorities in the economy is once more slighted—or rather left to the corporations. Second, experience with the planning councils under the Comprehensive Employment and Training Act of 1973 does not suggest that they have been as efficient or democratic as they should be. Let me stress one aspect of this last point. I think there should be as much local involvement, decision-making, and administration as is possible. We have overwhelming evidence with regard to the political and economic costs of a totally centralized economy. But the instruments of that local participation must be much more effective than CETA councils have been, and the possibility of serious local participation is conditioned by the success of federal efforts to get some kind of democratic control of the society's basic investment decisions.

Another and very important related point: Section 4 of the Act refers to the CETA councils creating "reservoirs" of useful, potential jobs. And Section 6 calls for the creation of a "standby" Job Corps. The unstated assumption of both of these proposals is that the private employment of labor is the most efficient and socially desirable, and that federally financed work is a matter of last resort, to be found in "reservoirs" on "standby." I disagree. I do not think that the best use of human talent in this society is inevitably to be found in the private profit-maximizing occupations. Do we want workers to build Nevada casinos or another generation of Florida condominiums in preference to applying their energies to erecting housing for working people and the poor?

I think there are occasions when government should be an employer of *first* resort. In specifying some job-generating activities that I think should be undertaken here and now, these criticisms can be seen in more explicit, counterposed detail.

I believe that the Congress should consider a number of projects, valuable and urgent in themselves, which could provide work for the unemployed and a means whereby society could assert a democratic social control over at least some of the investment decisions in the economy. While I see these things within the framework of my own democratic socialist analysis, all of them have been proposed by non- and even by antisocialists. I would be less than candid if I did not say that I hope that these ideas will become the first step toward a basic democratization of corporate power in American and the world. But liberals and reformers who disagree with my vision can share my immediate agenda.

First, we should nationalize the railroads in the United States. Current legislative proposasls do involve nationalization but only of the losses and decrepit property of a system that the government and greedy managements did so much to destroy. We should not have the public pay for the private cannibalization of the rail system. We should establish a national transportation plan that would determine, on the basis of social needs, how subsidies are allocated to the private sector and that would have a public sector of sufficient weight to influence the entire industry. The public railroad corporations should be designed according to the plan devised by the rail unions right after world War I: with a board of directors composed one-third of workers' representatives, one-third of public representatives, and one-third of representatives of the operating managers.

The nationalization and refurbishment of the American rail system would save energy, protect the environment and, as the UAW pointed out in its energy proposals, create an enormous number of socially useful jobs.

Second, we should nationalize one existing major oil company and provide it with privileged access to the development of energy resources on public property. In this regard, the proposals of President Ford and Senator Jackson, for socializing the developmental costs of new energy technologies while turning the benefits over to private corporations, should be rejected. It was Adam Smith who argued, rightly in this case, that risk-takers should be decision-makers and profit-takers. If the people take the risks in this area—and they are so large that the private sector refuse to take them—the people should make the decisions and reap the benefits. This is why the expansion of the public energy sector is so crucial.

Third, we should explore Congressman Reuss's proposals for the creation of a mechanism of national credit allocation. Along similar lines, we should consider the creation of a national bank—but not one that would simply get the risky leavings from the private banks.

Fourth, we should look toward the federal chartering of all major corporations, as Ralph Nader, George C. Lodge, and others have suggested. Those charters should require public and employee representation on the board of directors as a condition for doing business in interstate commerce.

Fifth, we should learn from the enormously effective experience of the Rural Electrification law. Washington provided subsidized credit to electrification co-ops and thus helped to facilitate one of the most important gains farm people have made in recent decades. That principle can and should be applied to consumer cooperatives, housing cooperatives, community development corporations, and the like. It is a perfect example of how the socialization of investment decisions need not be centralized in Washington.

Finally, an obvious question arises: How does one finance these things without incurring a ruinous inflation? There are a number of ways in which this can be done, two of them particularly relevant to my analysis.

It is, of course, necessary to resist increases in the Pentagon budget and to look for possible reductions in it. Any cutbacks requiring the closing of defense installations and the loss of jobs must, of course, be accompanied by an explicit plan for redeploying the people involved in work at least as remunerative as what is being abolished. But beyond that point, I think the time has come to consider a suggestion made sometime ago by John Kenneth Galbraith: we should nationalize all those major defense contractors whose prime, or only, client is the goverment. In those cases the private risk is a fiction and the private gain at the public expense a reality. This is one source of funds, along with other cuts in Pentagon waste.

The Treasury this year published a list of "tax expenditures" in the federal budget. They total around $94 billion, and we know from an analysis prepared for Senator Mondale that they discriminatorily reward the rich: e.g., the privileged character of capital-gains income, or the multibillion-dollar subsidy to the housing of the wealthy and the upper middle class contained in the perverse priorities of the deduction of interest on the mortgage. There are enormous savings to be made in these areas simply by following in fact the principle we now honor in the breech: that those best able to pay should bear their share of the tax burden.

Clearly, my proposals for government action are far from exhaustive. They are, rather, illustrative of an analysis and of a trend of possible action. We cannot assume, as the Hawkins-Humphrey bill does, that full employment can, or should, be achieved by making the government the subordinate of the private corporate economy. To achieve socially useful full employment, we must be prepared to take steps to democratically plan and control some of the major investment decisions in this country. In the particular cases in which I have urged action, In think the pragmatic liberal can agree with me in seeing its necessity. I therefore do not make these proposals in terms of some distant utopia: they are necessary to the creation of full employment in this decade and in the rest of this century.

Let me stress my conviction that we are at one of those moments in American history when sructural change is on the agenda. In the 1890s this country, and European capitalism, responded to the two-decade-long crisis of the laissez-faire economy by the creation of the modern corporation, the trusts, and the oligopolies. The problems of competition were ameliorated; the problems of monopoly were created. In the 1930s the United States, the last industrial democracy to build a welfare state, backed into a system of Keynesian planning. It assumed that all the government had to do was to establish a proper economic climate for the private economy by stimulating, or restraining, aggregate demand and investment. We demonstrated—by means of the war economy of 1940—45, and later by the Kennedy-Johnson tax cuts of the '60s—that we know how to put unused capacity back to work in this manner. But now we face the problems inherent in our old solutions: inflationary pressures; the manipulation of the business cycle for political purposes, as under President Nixon; the threat to private profit in a full-employment economy; and so on.

We surely are going to get structural change; the questions is what kind. The corporate rear guard fulminates about "socialism" while the corporate avant-garde propses new RFCs to socialize investment for private purposes. Under such conditions, I believe that full-employment policy is a focal point, and we must demand that it be implemented by a socialization of more and more investment on behalf of the people. We have been funding "socialism" for the rich, leaving free enterprise to the small shopkeepers, the workers, and the poor. We now must see to it that we do not continue that outrageous trend, buying full employment by further increasing the maldistribution of wealth and the corporate misuse of resources. We should, rather, achieve full employment by democratically investing in our social needs.

Chapter 12

ENERGY

In 1979, ordinary Americans waiting in gas lines and experts on television panels debated the cause and cure of the energy crisis. They asked: Is the crisis real? Does a shortage of oil actually exist or has scarcity been artificially created? In his 1977 speech in which he called for Americans to confront the energy problem with the moral equivalent of war, President Carter maintained that there was an actual shortage of oil. However, subsequent polls showed that most Americans disagreed with the President, believing that the oil shortage is contrived.

Over the past several decades estimates of oil reserves, presumed to be limited and decreasing, have continually been revised upward as new discoveries have been made. Nevertheless oil resources, created by the decay of fossils millions of years ago, are finite and eventually will run out. There is considerable disagreement as to just how long oil can continue to be a major source of energy. Whether it will last only a few or several decades is disputed, but it is generally agreed that sooner or later we will run out of oil.

Observers of the oil industry such as Robert Engler believe that, at present, there exists considerable oil resources both in the United States and abroad that remain untapped.[1] These resources include shale rock and tar sands from which oil can be extracted by known technologies. In the past the major oil companies have shown considerable

---

1. Robert Engler. Talk presented to City University of New York socialist discussion group, New York City, May, 1979.

reluctance to utilize these sources of oil, fearing that they would contribute to an oversupply of petroleum.

Until quite recently the energy problem was too much oil. Young adults can recall price wars between gas stations, offers of bonus trading stamps to get customers to buy gas from one company instead of another, and distribution of free glasses and trinkets to encourage motorists to fill up at a particular station. Advertisements touted the superior virtues of various fuel additives and the transmogrification of animal strength into engine power if you, "Put a tiger in your tank" by purchasing Esso gas. These artifacts of American culture disappeared in 1973.

The 1973 gas shortage had drastic effects on people's lives in most parts of this country. The car was necessary for getting to work, visiting family and friends, and carrying out everyday activities. The gas shortage separated suburb from city, and individuals from family, friends, and work. Everyone suddenly realized how dependent we were on fuel and how fragile our life support system had become.

The gas shortages of 1973 and 1979 showed that lack of fuel can create a crisis for most Americans. Inexpensive and easily available energy has been central to United States economic development and to a way of life that emphasizes personal mobility. Both of these assumptions have been called into question.

Shortages mean hours in gas lines, homes with inadequate heat in the winter, and the threat of factory closings due to lack of fuel. Rising fuel prices are a major source of inflation. Fuel price increases translate into higher costs of producing goods and growing food. They also lead to higher rents on apartments and raise the costs of maintaining a private home.

There is a continuing controversy as to whether the action of the OPEC countries to initiate massive price increases was taken independently or in coordination with the major international oil companies. In any event, OPEC price increases gave the oil companies the opportunity to add their own increases on to the original ones. The oil industry has been shown to operate as a private government comprised of the major companies since the 1920s. The major companies at that time agreed to divide the world market according to their existing market share and coordinate discovery, production, and distribution activities.[2] Based on this history of joint decision making it is a reasonable assumption that any major action of the oil companies, such as a change in pricing policies, is a result of consultation among themselves.

Much public attention since the shortages began has focused on the potential of alternate sources of energy to replace waning oil supplies. Since World War II U.S. government policy has been to concentrate on the development of nuclear energy to substitute for diminished oil supplies. The program to develop nuclear power plants to produce electricity was an outgrowth of the wartime Manhattan project, which developed the atomic bomb.[3] Since 1954 dozens of nuclear power plants have been put into

---

2. Robert Engler. *The Politics of Oil*. Chicago: University of Chicago Press, 1961.
3. Henry Etzkowitz, "Atoms for Peace," *WIN* Magazine, April 12, 1979.

operation throughout the country, and more are presently under construction. However, the rising costs of nuclear fuel coupled with the environmental, health, and safety hazards of nuclear power plants have called this policy into question.

The antinuclear movement emerged as a major political force in the late seventies. Nuclear power plant accidents, lawsuits, demonstrations, occupation of construction sites, and the inability of the nuclear industry or government to come up with a safe and secure method to dispose of nuclear wastes contributed to a slowing down in the growth of the nuclear industry. The question mark placed over nuclear energy has led to increased public interest in alternative sources of energy. The articles in this chapter discuss the development of solar energy. The prospects for solar energy provide a way of viewing conservative, liberal, and socialist solutions to the energy crisis irrespective of whether it is real or fake.

Conservatives view the existing structure of a few, huge, integrated energy corporations as the most efficient and productive way to develop our energy resources. Any change in the structure of the oil industry would result in additional costs and higher prices.

The oil companies view themselves as part of the free enterprise economy, taking risks with their capital to develop new sources of energy. The oil companies say that they have no control over the foreign governments that band together to raise prices. They maintain that they are doing the best they can in difficult circumstances to maintain the flow of oil to American industry and consumers. Shortages could be reduced if the federal government would eliminate price controls on oil. If domestic oil prices were allowed to rise, the prospect of increased profits would encourage increased investment in exploration for new sources of oil.

Conservative solutions to the energy crisis emphasize huge capital intensive projects, even in the area of solar energy. One such proposal is for giant space satellites to be sent aloft. Solar cells mounted on these satellites would produce electricity that would be beamed back to earth through microwaves. Solar energy that is developed this way would be compatible with corporate structures, for it would require a large scale technology, which only major corporations would have the resources to construct. Solar energy from space satellites would perpetuate corporate control of energy.

Liberals accept the oil companies as the vehicle for energy production and distribution. However, major oil companies such as Exxon, Mobil, and Texaco should be divided into smaller units to make them competitive with each other.

Most liberals feel that energy policy can be successfully modified through congressional action. Concerned citizens should mobilize lobbying groups to counter the power of the oil lobby. Legislation should be passed to provide government aid to help entrepreneurs undertake the development of alternative forms of energy as a strategy to break the control of oil companies over energy policy.

The socialist perspective takes two forms. Some socialists believe that the major oil companies should be nationalized and operated by the government. Other socialists, believing that corporate influence in politics is too strong to make such a policy feasible, argue that alternative forms of energy should be developed independently as a strategy to destabilize a major sector of corporate capital.

A number of confluences exist between proponents of the different perspectives creating an interesting potential for future political realignments to develop around this issue. Liberals and socialists agree that the existence of an oil energy industry dominated by a few major corporations is the basic problem. Some conservatives are also opposed to the major oil companies. These conservatives, primarily owners and operators of small or medium sized businesses, fear that large corporations will use their economic power to take them over or force them out-of-business. Many of these same individuals, also concerned about the growth of government bureaucracy, favor the development of solar energy both to reduce the power of the major oil companies and to make governmental environmental regulations unnecessary. Presumably if an energy source was nonpolluting by its very nature, there could be no argument for a government agency to regulate it.

Liberals also favor the development of solar energy both for environmental reasons and to create a balance of power to the major oil companies. Socialists view the development of solar energy as a means to eliminate energy scarcity and concentrated control of resources, two bases of a capitalist economy.

In the conservative article, the Mobil Oil Corporation states its view of the prospects for solar energy. Solar energy is one of several alternate sources of energy that have a role to play in the future. There are many technical difficulties to overcome before solar can become a practical source of energy, and the development process will take decades before solar energy can make a significant contribution. Mobil is interested in moving this development process forward. Through its solar energy subsidiary it is working on perfecting a process to produce solar electricity. Proponents of solar energy who believe that it can be developed quickly are simply mistaken. In the short term we will have to rely on oil and nuclear energy to fuel our economy. In the long term we can rely on the oil companies to develop alternate forms of energy.

In the liberal article, Welch argues that there is no real energy shortage, only a lack of will to make the necessary decisions to develop new sources of energy. Government energy policy is a mix of contradictions. Alternate policies that stalemate each other are simultaneously pursued. Despite this administrative paralysis the superior technical feasibility of solar electricity is inexorably emerging.

Although the executive branch of government is doing little to further the development of solar energy, Congress shows signs of taking effective action. Energy policy in the executive branch is heavily influenced by an elite group of scientists who are committed to the development of nuclear energy. In their reports and studies for the government, solar energy is played down, despite its decreasing costs, environment benefits, and the increasing costs and health and safety hazards of nuclear energy. If the Federal government dropped its support for nuclear energy, solar energy would be rapidly developed. The government's science advisory system should be overhauled to provide unbiased recommendations for policy makers. Despite the checks and balances exercised by special interests on government energy policy, a solar age is dawning.

In the socialist article, Etzkowitz suggests a strategy for the development of solar energy that combines political, social, and technological change. Corporations develop large scale and expensive energy technologies such as nuclear power to insure their control over the means of production. However, smaller scale, yet highly productive, technologies have recently been invented, but not put to wide use. If these new middle level technologies, such as solar cells for the production of electricity, were developed by socialist groups, the power that corporations exert over the economy through their control of technology could be broken. The campaign against nuclear energy by radicals and environmentalists will fail to overcome the argument that nuclear energy is necessary to maintain a modern economy until a viable alternative source of energy is developed. Mobilizing resources for alternative technological development is a means to contest the control of corporate capital over energy. Socialists should view technological development as a force to be shaped. The development of new means of production, rather than contesting for control of existing means of production, is proposed as a strategy to attain socialism.

Conservative

Mobil Oil Corporation: A Cloudy Day for Solar Energy

Just about everyone concerned with energy these days—ourselves included—has high hopes for the eventual contribution solar energy will make. But some self-styled experts sound as if they've been out in the sun too long.

Up in Vermont, for example, a candidate for nomination to the House of Representatives spent a lot of his stump time running against Mobil. His theme: Mobil, through its interest in Mobil Tyco Solar Energy Corporation, is doing promising research toward the development of low-cost, energy-efficient photo-voltaic cells. But because Mobil wants to wring out every cent of profit from its oil investments, runs his arguments, he's afraid Mobil will drag its heels on the photovoltaic project.

The trouble with this particular candidate was that he plowed old, familiar ground by airing a charge that has long been refuted. Where was he back last

April, when the U.S. Senate's Joint Economic Committee asked this question of Dr. A. I. Mlavsky, executive vice president of Mobil Tyco:

"Is there any truth to the allegation that major oil companies (like Shell and Mobil), who are funding solar energy R&D, may have an incentive to slow down the commercial development of solar energy in order to maintain profits from other competing energy sources?"

Here's how Dr. Mlavsky answered:

". . . Mobil has provided essential support in the program to develop our photovoltaic technology. Without Mobil's backing, this promising technology might have been abandoned by now.

"My involvement with Mobil Oil corporation dates back only 18 months when the joint venture, Mobil Tyco Solar Energy Corporation, was formed. My previous background was with Tyco Laboratories, Inc. Because my work during the 18 months has focused solely on managing the development of photovoltaics technology, it would be presumptuous of me to speak for Mobil.

"Nonetheless, as a citizen and a photovoltaics practitioner, I find it difficult to see how Mobil could have an incentive to slow the development of solar energy, for two pragmatic reasons:

"The first reason is timing. It will take 20 or perhaps 30 years before photovoltaics or any other solar technology can have a major impact on total energy supply. This will be at about the time when oil itself will become a scarce material.

"Moreover, electrical energy from photovoltaics cannot replace several critical uses of oil—namely, gasoline and petrochemicals.

"So, both on the basis of the time frame of photovoltaics development, and on the specific uses of crude oil and natural gas, I see solar energy and the oil business as complementary, not competitive. From my experience with Mobil, I think that oil companies have a positive incentive to accelerate the development of solar energy."

The facts, of course, seem never to get in the way when a politician scents an issue. Still, we're confident that common sense will prevail—and that solar energy will eventually shine through even the clouds of political opportunism.

Liberal

Bruce Welch: The Reality of Solar Power

It is no longer resources that limit decisions. It is the decision that makes the resources. That is the fundamental revolutionary change—perhaps the most revolutionary that mankind has ever known.

—U Thant

There is no shortage of energy, only a shortage of initiative for making energy accessible in usable form. We are still in a position to choose our future energy sources and, hence, to shape other important characteristics of society that depend upon them. The process of making that choice and the forces that shape it are of major public concern.

Fortunately, ours is a government of contradictions, of checks and balances, so complex that it can harbor, even nurture, the seeds of contradicition to administrative intent. Candidate Carter said there would be no more nuclear power except as a last resort. Yet the thrust of the Department of Energy's emerging program is to speed up the development of nuclear power while doing no more for solar energy—indeed, even less—than was done by the Ford adminstration.

Secretary of Energy James Schlesinger's attitude toward solar energy was succinctly expressed in a recent CBS television documentary. Asked to justify the accelerated development of nuclear fission, he called it a "last resort"; asked whether the energy crisis was not critical enough to justify an all-out effort to develop solar energy, he grinned indulgently: "The crisis is not yet *that* serious." In the same documentary, the President said that important contributions from solar energy are very far away.

Yet, like the truth that will out, superior technologies tend to come to the fore. Quietly, as inexorably as the sun rises, a solar electric age is being born. Acting against the major thrust of adminstrative policy and the inadequate advice of "prestigious" scientific committees, the Congress is paving the way.

In Congressional committee, the ERDA (Energy Research and Development Administration) Authorization Act for fiscal 1978 was amended to provide $13 million for the purchase of flat-plate solar cell arrays to generate electricity, and $6 million for research and development related to their automated production. Appropriation of these funds seems assured.

In addition, funds for the Department of Defense to buy solar cell systems, staggered over three years commencing in fiscal 1979, were included in both the House ($39 million) and the Senate ($98 million) versions of the National Energy Act. A conference committee on October 27 decided to provide $98 million for this purpose, of which $53 million will be for the purchase of silicon solar cell arrays and the remainder for supporting services and equipment. Congress expects that these purchases will save the Department of Defense $328 million net, in 1975 dollars, over a twenty-five year period and make solar cell systems competitive in conventional energy markets by 1983. The production of this equipment for the DoD is expected to lower the open market price of the arrays by 1983 to a point where large sustaining markets (e.g. residential power) will develop, possibly at prices as low as $750 per peak kilowatt. Additional purchases from other quarters may well cause even greater price reductions within this period of time.

While the cost of nuclear power has climbed over the past two decades at about twice the general rate of inflation, the cost of generating electricity from sunlight —even uncorrected for inflation—has sharply and consistently declined. In 1955, an assembly of solar cells capable of generating a kilowatt of electric power in full sunlight (a "peak" kilowatt) cost about $600,000. Today, such units can be bought in modest quantities for less than $10,000 per peak kilowatt. These remarkable savings have occurred despite the facts that solar manufacturing plants are not yet automated and that the total U.S. production, while steadily increasing, was only 330 to 350 kilowatts in 1976.

Moreover, a Federal Energy Administration report of July 1977 demonstrated that, if a purchase contract for 152 megawatts of flat-plate silicon solar cell arrays were staggered over three years, a first buy of 32 megawatts in 1978 to be followed by buys of 50 megawatts and 70 megawatts at one-year intervals, the last delivery to be made in fiscal 1983 (purchases customarily call for delivery dates in future years), the total cost of the 152-megawatt purchase would be $240 million, an average of $1,570 per kilowatt; and that the open market price could be driven as low as $500 per kilowatt in constant 1975 dollars for the last solar cells delivered in fiscal 1983. These projections are fully consistent with historical experience for other semi-conductor products. Moreover, they are based upon actual estimates obtained from three leading manufacturers. The FEA circulated these projections widely to industry and government in draft form before releasing its report, and they were judged to be attainable. A market impact analysis released by the BDM Corporation of McLean, Va. last October estimated that such a purchase might drive array prices as low as $440 per peak kilowatt by 1983.

The total cost of installing the 152 megawatts of flatplate solar cell arrays in the illustrative case, including the solar cell arrays, power conditioning equipment, support structures and storage batteries, would be about $450 million. If, for example, the Department of Defense were to make a purchase of that size, it could replace 20 percent of its gasoline-powered generators with solar cells at a net savings, in 1975 dollars, of $1.5 billion over twenty-five years from reduced operating, maintenance and fuel costs. These are conservative estimates, because purchase costs of gasoline generators and their fuel tanks, installation costs and the expense of training mechanics were not included.

The staggered purchase of the relatively modest quantity of 152 megawatts of peak solar cell electrical generating capacity would justify the capital investment to automate three to five companies in this fledgling industry, and the consequent reduction in the price of solar cells would open vast new markets and thereby drive prices even lower. The FEA has estimated that potential annual markets for public lighting and for driving small electrical motors and water pumps could alone reach 7,900 peak megawatts—an annual market which, incidentally, is about three times the current annual sales of nuclear generating capacity in the United States. Moreover, prices that would tap a 13,000-megawatt per annum market for the on-site solar generation of residential electricity may then be expected to come rapidly into range.

A contract just awarded for solar cells capable of delivering 362 peak kilowatts of electricity to meet all the power needs of Mississippi County Community College in Blytheville, Ark , was signed at a price of $3,026 per peak kilowatt of capacity, about half what informed observers had expected the contract to command. This development suggests that the FEA's estimates of the price-lowering effect of orders more than 420 times that large were greatly understated.

The installation cost, in comparable 1975 dollars, of some nuclear plants now under construction, and which will come on line in the early to mid-1980s, is about $1,000 per kilowatt of electrical generating capacity (later construction will probably cost more). But this figure does not include the first fuel loading of a plant, which will add 15 to 20 percent to capital costs. Nor does it include such extras as design for added resistance to earthquake, flood or aircraft impact, the purchase of more than 3 square miles of land, at a minimum, for siting; the cost of power lines and other distributing equipment, operating and maintenance expenses, security, decommissioning, waste storage and disposal; or the cost of government assistance, regulation, subsidy, insurance and emergency services. Moreover, large nuclear plants have been found to operate only about 50 percent of the time at their installed capacity rating, and up to 20 percent of the power that they do generate is lost internally and in transmission.

Solar cells, because of variations in sunlight, have an average capacity of only about 25 percent, and about 30 percent of the power generated is lost if cycled through storage batteries. Yet, solar cells installed on one's own roof to power direct current appliances at a cost of about $500 per peak kilowatt of generating capacity may seem an attractive alternative to nuclear power in some locations, even considering the appreciable added cost of a power storage system. More authorities anticipate that, in addition to economies from increased production, substantially lower costs will be brought about through technical advances now in sight. This means that within a decade electricity from solar cells could actually become much cheaper than nuclear power for consumers in many areas of the United States. The equation will be affected by the relative lifetime of solar arrays and nuclear plants, a comparison that cannot yet be made because of insufficient experience with either system. However, solar cells should last as long as their encapsulation maintains its integrity to protect them from weather. Compared to nuclear power plants, they are extremely simple devices. For the former, we lack even such important information as the pattern of aging-associated neutron bombardment embrittlement of metal in reactor pressure vessel walls. Claims that large nuclear power plants will have a forty-year life are wholly conjectural; indeed, it has not yet been determined that they can function safely and reliably for a single decade.

A solar electric age is coming no matter what the federal administration does. The government can merely speed or slow its coming. If we wish it to be so, solar cells for generating electricity can become cost-competitive with nuclear fission in widespread applications within little more than half the time that it takes to build a new nuclear power plant. The nation has the realistic option to meet much of its need for further expansion of electrical generating capacity with autonomous solar cell arrays powered by the sun.

For this to happen, large amounts of government money are not required. Indeed, considering the promise that the solar electric age offers for bringing needed diversity and competition into world energy markets, it is regrettable, in a way, that it is to be born of government funds. The absurdity is that government spending is required to offset the inhibitory effects of other government spending. (See Welch: "Nuclear Energy on the Dole," *The Nation*, February 26, 1977.)

Solar cell electricity would have come into widespread use spontaneously, and much sooner, had it not been for the false promise of economic competitiveness given nuclear fission by more than a quarter century of indulgent government support of the nuclear industry, support that continues and is even growing. Solar technologies would develop rapidly if the government would simply withdraw all support from the nuclear industry. The $450 million that the FEA estimated would be required to lower the price of solar cells to $500 per peak kilowatt or less, with a resulting savings of about $1.5 billion to the Department of Defense, is considerably less than one-third the amount provided in the fiscal 1978 budget for continued research, development and demonstration related to nuclear power.

Why, then, does the Carter administration press so obdurately for rapid expansion of nuclear power? Why does it so resist a major solar initiative? One reason is that nuclear interests have pervasive influence among the small "elite" corps of scientists who provide technical advice on such subjects at the top echelon of government. Solar energy interests have almost no voice at all. True, scientists are supposed to be totally objective, to seek persistently and weigh all relevant information. But, sadly, that ideal is not always achieved. All too often the authority and credibility of reports from major scientific study groups or committees, and hence the justification for using them to guide public policy, is assumed from the prestige of the study's sponsors and participants. This is commonly true even when the panel participants are obviously not qualified in, and have not carefully considered, all important areas of science that their advice appears to weigh. The study report, *Nuclear Power, Issues and Choices*, is a case in point.

Its prestigious backing with a $500,000 Ford Foundation grant administered by the Mitre Corporation and its stellar cast of panelists* would guarantee it high visibility under any conditions. The facts that it appeared while President Carter was formulating his energy program and that two members of the study group were given key positions in his new administration could only enhance its chance to influence national policy. A copy of the report was hand-delivered to the new President by his science adviser. On the day that the report was released, the study group was called to the White House to brief the President in person. In the ensuing months, the President's energy program and his acts and comments on energy issues have been in remarkable accord with the recommendations of the Ford-Mitre report. Bias and inadequacies in the structure and conduct of this study are therefore of major consequence and of public interest.

With regard to alternative energy sources, the report acknowledged that, "An assessment of the need for nuclear power should consider potential alternatives that might be economically competitive or might avoid specific serious problems associated with nuclear power and fossil fuels." However, it stated that the

---

* Spurgeon M. Keeney Jr., Chairman; Seymour Abrahamson, Kenneth J. Arrow, Harold Brown, Albert Carnesale, Abram Chayes, Hollis B. Chenery, Paul Doty, Philip J. Farley, Richard L. Garwin, Marvin L. Goldberger, Carl Kaysen, Hans H. Landsberg, Gordon J. MacDonald, Joseph S. Nye, Wolfgang K. H. Panofsky, Howard Raiffa, George W. Rathjens, John C. Sawhill, Thomas C. Schelling and Arthur Upton.

"goal" should be to have supplies of energy available at moderate cost when present resources are "gone"; that solar energy in general, and solar cells for generating electricity in particular, will be too expensive to compete with coal and nuclear power through the next three decades, that there is "little value in demonstrating clearly noncompetitive technology," and that it would be "inefficient and unnecessarily limiting" to try to make alternative energy sources available "prematurely."

While the panel's remarkable assurance about the appropriate timing for transition to alternative fuels may not be reflected in the President's thinking, there is every indication that its recommendations are reflected in the administrative policy of the new Department of Energy in ways that could cause the deployment of solar energy technologies to be drastically delayed. This is regrettable, because the panel's judgement that the solar technologies could not be competitive are unduly pessimistic and are not based upon a careful analysis of the relevant available information.

To focus upon but one crucial error: in summarily dismissing solar cells, the Ford-Mitre report said that "current collector costs are about $200,000 per kilowatt of peak electrical capacity." In fact, that price—which was not a misprint (I confirmed this with the author of that section of the report)—was almost twenty years out of date. Solar cells costs $200,000 per peak kilowatt in 1959; in September 1976, eight months before the Ford-Mitre report was released, ERDA purchased solar cell arrays for less than 8 percent of the price quoted by the Ford-Mitre study group—$15,500 per peak kilowatt in quantities as small as 130 kilowatts. The price had been $21,000 per peak kilowatt six months earlier, and $31,000 per peak kilowatt in March 1975, which was about the time the Ford-Mitre study group was assembled.

Superficiality, inaccuracy and lack of percipience were not confined to the panel's treatment of solar cells; they characterized their comments on other "solar" technologies as well. These deficiencies may be understood in terms of the relative vacuum in which the analysis of solar energy technologies evolved. The sections of the report on solar energy were the primary responsibility of an experimental physicist who for more than twenty years has had active professional interests in nuclear energy; he is currently involved in laser separation techniques for uranium enrichment. He has never been directly involved in any aspect of solar energy research or application, although, in 1975, he was chairman of a National Research Council committee formed to explore the optimal role and organizational characteristics of the then prospective Solar Energy Research Institute. And he is the only member of the Ford-Mitre study panel who had had prior professional experience in any way related to solar energy. The chairman of the panel lists his professional interest in *American Men and Women of Science* as "military and civilian applications of nuclear energy."

The Mitre Corporation, where the Ford-Mitre study was actually conducted, has been a major center of activity for quality research and systems analysis in solar energy technology for more than five years. Yet, the Ford-Mitre study group worked in total isolation from the solar energy experts who were under the same roof. I heard this first from a member of the Mitre solar energy group, and later confirmed it with the author of the solar energy section of the Ford-Mitre report. In our conversation, he justified not seeking and evaluating ideas and information from people in the solar energy field by classifying them collectively as "enthusiast nuts." (The accuracy of this label must be weighed against the historical facts that the price of nuclear power has consistently outstripped the enthusiastic projections of its advocates, whereas the cost of solar energy has consistently declined more rapidly than the relatively conservative predictions of professionals in that field.)

When a prestigious panel makes recommendations on an important public issue, it implies that those recommendations are based upon a thorough and balanced weighing of all relevant information. When that is not the case, and the deficiencies are not clearly stated, their recommendations comprise at best an irresponsible disservice to the scientific community, the government and the public at large.

For years after penicillin was developed it was so expensive that physicians took care to collect urine from the few favored patients who received it so that the penicillin could be recycled. Today, thanks to the economies of a large market and mass production, penicillin is available in every physician's office at an almost trivial price.

Similarly, solar cells will soon be cheap enough to generate electricity in widespread applications. It has been estimated that the basic electrical power requirements of a village of 250 people in Iran could be met by 20 peak kilowatts of solar cells. Such a need can reasonably be expected to be met for about $10,000 within little more than five years. Similar needs exist in innumerable villages throughout the world, and it will soon be possible for such needs to be profitably met.

The rate at which solar cells will actually spread throughout this and other industrialized countries will depend upon the development of adequate low-cost ways to store the electrical energy. It is in the administration's tepid encouragement of new storage technologies that its reluctance to promote solar energy really shows. The budget authority for fiscal 1978 provides only $48.4 million for all aspects of energy storage research, development and demonstration—less than 3 percent of the amount provided for nuclear fission. Almost four times as much is being spent by the federal government for research, development and demonstration related to the storage of commercial nuclear waste. Although hydrogen is a strong bet to be the major energy storage medium of the future, the fiscal 1978 budge provides only $6 million toward that goal. It is no exaggeration to say that the Department of Energy has not set up a crash program to find better ways to store electrical power. For nuclear power, storage of electrical energy is not particularly important; for distributed solar systems it is crucial.

The federal government should withdraw its multifarious supports from the nuclear power industry and remove remaining institutional obstacles to the rapid development of distributed solar energy systems. If this were done, electrical power production would gradually return to the private sector, the economy would be stimulated dramatically, and the nation would develop a safer, less wasteful and more resilient electric power base.

Finally, and viewing all areas of the nation's continued welfare, it is imperative that we evolve a more reliable science advisory system. To its credit, the Congress has shown that it knows that the recommendations of "prestigious" scientific committees cannot be taken as gospel. It is increasingly essential, for the shaping of national policy, to have scientific advice that can be relied upon to be comprehensive, competent and unbiased.

Socialist

Henry Etzkowitz: The Liberation of Technology

Technology is a double edged sword. At one and the same time it is a means of oppression and a means to realize a utopian vision.

Radicals usually scrutinize technology for its potential as a means of social control. Assembly lines, bugging devices and computers are among the technologies that are instruments of domination. The ill effects of assembly lines on the physical and mental health of workers have been extensively documented. The recent use of the Freedom of Information Act to obtain government documents has provided numerous instances of the use of electronic surveillance measures by the FBI and other police agencies against radical groups. Current proposals for the creation of a nationwide interconnected network of government computers that would exchange the information that different federal agencies collect about citizens have brought the spector of 1984 closer.

Technology also has a potential for liberation. Xerography, the offset press and videotape are examples of technologies that individuals and groups have used to further radical goals. Daniel Ellsberg's use of the xerox machine to reproduce the Pentagon Papers is the best publicized and most important example of the effect that easily accessible duplicating equipment has had on opening up secretive bureaucracies to public scrutiny. The development of efficient and relatively simple printing techniques such as the offset press has enabled radical publications to control their own presses. Stories about the refusal of printing firms to set type for radical manuscripts have become less common with the development of radical printing collectives. The availability of relatively inexpensive videotape equipment has made possible the organization of a radical software movement. Videotape collectives have demonstrated how the creation and dissemination of visual images for radical political and aesthetic goals may be undertaken.

The successful use of these technologies to carry out radical aims indicates that the potential of technology as a means of liberation should be further explored. Until quite recently the development of new technology has been associated with increasing centralization of power. New technologies such as atomic energy and computers have enabled economic and political elites to increase their control over the rest of us. However, in the past few years developments in technology have occurred that appear to lead in the opposite direction. The

Reprinted from *WIN* magazine, 503 Atlantic Avenue, Brooklyn, NY 11217. Subscriptions: $13 per year.

miniaturization of parts and the reduction in cost of transistors and other devices produced by the semi-conductor industry have made technologies that were formerly accessible only to those with considerable economic resources widely available to individuals and groups with modest means. The organization of radical news services has partly been based on the increased availability of motion picture and videotape equipment that occurred through these technological advances and consequent reductions in cost.

The very existence of technologies that can be used by large numbers of people makes it difficult for elites to monopolize the control of technical resources. I will suggest how some recent trends in the development of new technology may be consciously utilized to further radical goals. Control of technology influences who gets access to information and economic resources. The ability to direct and use technology is also a means to attain political power in an industrial society.

How can the process of creating new technology be used as a means to attain radical social change? The question of how to take control of the existing means of production then becomes one of how to bring into existence and thus control future means of production. To develop a theory of social change based on developing new technology it is necessary to determine the characteristics of an emerging technology that has the potential to supercede an existing mode of production.

Areas of technology must be identified in which two conditions hold:

1. A significant sector of corporate capitalism rests on the control of the technology in question; and

2. A feasible alternative technology exists that can be developed without enormous capital and scientific resources.

Once this analysis is completed a social movement must be created in which scientific and financial resources are mobilized to develop the technological alternative. If elements of a new mode of production can be initiated then the class power based on the existing mode of production will be eroded. This strategy necessitates the organization of sufficient economic and technical resources to establish a new mode of production and sufficient political power to protect this new mode of production from being coopted by existing economic and political power structures.

Middle Level Technology

Given the moderate level of resources that are likely to be available to insurgent groups, technologies that are chosen for development must be limited in scale yet technically superior. Large scale technologies require enormous capital investment to develop and an extensive bureaucracy to administer. Small scale technologies offer the advantage of low capital investment but seldom can provide the necessary productivity to replace existing large scale technologies.

Middle level technology is technically sophisticated but not capital intensive. It is larger in scale and use of resources than simple devices and may be constructed with existing knowledge and inexpensive and easily available materials such as solar collectors. Yet it is smaller in scale than complicated and expensive devices such as breeder reactors that require the development of massive new equipment with the expenditure of large amounts of funds. Nor does middle level technology imply archaic technology such as machetes or arcadian technology such as spinning wheels.

Middle level technology is the development of devices that are at the edge of the scientific and technological frontier. Relatively sophisticated equipment and knowledge are required, but not enormous funds or huge laboratories. Middle level technology must meet the requirements of environmental safety and high productivity necessary to sustain an industrial society. The photovoltaic solar cell is a prototypical middle level technology. Dave Elliot, a British writer on alternative technology, considers the thin film deposition process utilized in experiments on the mass production of solar cells to be not a particularly sophisticated technique, although hardly a backyard craft.

The Solar Cell

The solar cell produces electricity from sunlight. It can substitute for oil, coal and nuclear energy as a source of electric power. Solar cells have the potential to develop into a new mode of production because they derive electricity from a renewable source of energy—the sun. The only potential source of energy that can meet both environmental and productivity requirements is the sun. The sun provides an ever renewable form of energy, light as photons, that by its very nature does not deplete resources on the earth. Rather, sunlight provides additional resources to the earth by heating land and water and causing tides and winds. Available over most of the planet, most of the time, the sun offers a virtually limitless supply of energy. But only if effective ways are developed to use it can the sun provide pollution-free energy.

Solar cells are fundamentally different from energy technologies based on non-renewable supplies of oil, coal or uranium. Fully developed, solar cells could sharply reduce or even eliminate energy scarcity. At present solar cells are extremely costly to produce. Because of this, they are not considered practical alternatives to the existing means of producing electricity. The problem in their development is to find an inexpensive method to produce thin layers of silicon. Solar cell production is still virtually at the handicraft stage of manufacture. Skilled workers use diamond saws to hand cut crystalline cylinders into the thin plate which can be made into solar cells. Although sophisticated technical processes and machinery are used, the cells are essentially made by jewelers' techniques.

The solar cell, at present, is a machine for the production of electricity that is made by an archaic process. Modern industry is based on the production of machines by other machines. Standardized parts for many machines are produced by the machine tool industry on an automated basis. The machines for the production of oil drills, turbines and other technology of the fossil fuel industry are produced by this capital goods technology. With a capital goods sector the cost of producing solar cells could be significantly reduced.

Successful development of a method to mass produce solar cells will be the basis of a new energy industry. Control of solar cell production technology will enable existing energy corporations to retain complete control over a major segment of the economy or enable alternative groups to wrest some of this control away from these major corporations. As an anti-capitalist strategy the development of new technology has the advantage of offering a positive alternative to existing technologies with their environmental and other defects.

The development of new technology concentrates and expands the resources of the anti-capitalist movement. Rather than using up resources in struggles where the controllers of corporate capital have the greatest strength, i.e. within the existing industrial and political structures, the new technology strategy attacks corporate capital at its potentially weakest link—the technology it is dependent upon for its very existence. Every industry is always concerned that its technology and products may become outmoded. Corporations are aware that their control over an industry or market is ultimately dependent upon the control of the technology in their area of production. If another firm develops a technology or product that is superior to an existing one and the maker of the existing product cannot block or control the introduction of the new process or product its control over the industry will eventually be lost.

New Institutions and Radical Science

Alternate institutions have primarily been developed in the retail, media and service sectors. The production of information through alternative newspapers, magazines, and radio stations is one of the few areas in which radicals have attempted to organize institutions that utilize significant technologies. Most efforts have been directed toward creating alternative means of distribution. Food coops, free schools, and newspapers are now commonplace. Printshops, crafts and truck farms are among the alternative economic institutions in manufacturing and agriculture. With the exception of videotape in the media, most alternative economic institutions use standard or even archaic technologies. The research and development (R & D) sector of the economy has not been focused upon for the construction of alternative institutions.

Perhaps one reason for this lacunae is the relatively small number of radical scientists and engineers. Most radicals have tended to be educated in the social science and humanistic disciplines. They orient their work plans in alternatives to areas that they are already familiar with or that at least do not require an extensive technical background. The few radical scientists and engineers that do exist have largely organized themselves to do general radical political work or to critique dangerous developments in science and technology.

Radical scientists have used their professional skills in struggles against the development of harmful technologies. Their participation in the anti-nuclear and anti-bacteriological warfare campaigns has been a key factor in those successes. As scientists they provided legitimated information that was used to gain a wide hearing for the case against these technologies.

Radical science and engineering in the United States has seldom conceived of itself as a different way of doing science. The development of areas of research to achieve radical goals has seemed outside of the realm of possibility to groups who, with great financial difficulty, manage to publish magazines and hold conferences.

Perhaps another reason for the lack of interest of radical scientists and engineers in R&D has been that the very development of new technology appeared to lead inevitably to increased ruling class power. The only radical act possible seemed to be to renounce the laboratory for political organizing work.

An Alternative Research and Development Institution

I have been a participant for the past three years in an alternative research and development institution: Consumers Solar Electric Power Corporation (CSEP). CSEP was founded to develop solar energy technology as an alternative to the nuclear and petroleum industries. In both these areas R&D is heavily controlled by industry and government advisory councils are dominated by industry representatives. Research into alternate forms of energy is limited. Most of the available funds are distributed to large corporations that have little interest in the immediate development of a technology that would be competitive to their existing processes. University researchers and independent inventors comprise the other areas of R&D activity in this field.

The first step in the development of this alternate R&D institution was the collection and evaluation of information on alternate energy research that had thus far taken place. The purpose of the evaluation was to determine which area was closest to fruition, and had the potential to produce low cost environmentally safe energy. The other key factor was the amount of financial and technical resources that would be required to bring an area of research to the goal of economic viability, i.e. a working process that was cost-competitive with nuclear, coal and oil fuels.

The initial "Technology Assessment" phase of the development of this institution was completed by students and teachers on a part-time basis. Full time commitment occurred only after a particular technology was identified that had promise to realize the goals of the project. Initial full time commitment to the project came not from scientists and engineers but from a social scientist and students. The first phases of research were carried out by scientists on a part-time basis. However, their level of dissatisfaction with established institutions had not reached a sufficient level to enable them to make a full-time commitment to a financially unstable new institution. When their employers became aware of their consultation work for the alternative R&D institution they requested withdrawal of their efforts and received compliance. Some consulting relationships with employees of established R&D organizations were maintained but on a secret basis.

Our next effort was to obtain scientific personnel from the ranks of independent inventors who either work on their own funded by independent backers or occasionally in R&D labs when the goals of the labs and the inventors coincide. As the new institution established its own laboratory, it began to attract scientists with a commitment to its political goal of developing an alternative to the nuclear and petroleum industries.

The establishment of an alternative R&D institution rests only partly on recruiting the necessary scientific talent. An organizational support structure to provide supplies and equipment is necessary. The raising of sufficient financial resources to carry on these activities is also essential. An alternative R&D organization engaged in the development of a middle level technology requires the commitment of several hundred thousand dollars per year for operation. These funds have been raised both from financially well off individuals who are ideo-logically committed to the goals of the project as well as from persons who are interested in the project solely from motives of financial gain. Whatever their individual motivation, these persons' financial resources have typically been gained in the non-oligopolistic sectors of the economy. Psychotherapists, enter-tainers, and farmers are among the professions of persons who have supplied capital to the alternative R&D organization.

At this writing the alternative R&D organization has yet to achieve its goal of producing a cost competitive solar electricity process. Nevertheless, this project has demonstrated it is possible to organize alternative institutions in the R&D area. Scientific talent and financing were available once an organizational struc-ture with political goals was formed to mobilize these resources. The alternative R&D institution also demonstrated the possibility of building alternative institu-tions on a larger scale and in more expensive areas of the economy than usually thought possible. Most alternative economic institutions employ small amounts of capital and rarely undertake macroscopic goals such as the construction of a new solar electricity industry as an alternative to the oligopolistic corporations of the oil-energy industry.

Delegitimation

The institutionalization of a new mode of production must be accompanied by the delegitimation of the existing mode. According to Jurgen Habermas in *Legiti-mation Crisis*, delegitimation occurs as a virtually concommitant consequence of the economic and political crisis of capitalism. Individuals are shaken when institutions do not function smoothly. Institutional discontinuity results in dis-belief in the capitalist system. It is our contention that crisis offers only a poten-tial for delegitimation. To become an actuality, politically active individuals and groups must take advantage of the situation. Alternate analyses and social move-ments must be organized in order for people to understand the meaning of the crisis. A radical crisis analysis does not appear to most people without such active intervention. The anti-nuclear movement is one example of a potential crisis in capitalism being transformed into an actual instance of delegitimation. Although this process has not yet reached a final conclusion, sufficient disbelief in the nuclear industry has been created to make it a prime candidate for deinsti-tutionalization. No other sector of the capitalist economy seemed to have so much potential for growth twenty years ago and yet, at present, is in such a precarious situation.

Loss of belief by the public in corporate energy policy grew as the contradic-tions of nuclear power emerged. Reactor accidents, the inherent difficulties of insuring safe production of power from nuclear reactors, and the consequent dangers of radiation to the surrounding population led environmental and sci-ence activists to initiate a public campaign against the development of the nuclear industry. These campaigns were typically carried on by local and regional groups in areas where utilities proposed to build new reactors. Legal tactics, demonstrations, occupations, and public hearings were the forums through which wider attention was sought for the anti-nuclear argument. The publicity surrounding new accidents at reactor sites and the defection of scien-tists and engineers from within the nuclear industry lent additional momentum to the delegitimation process. The anti-nuclear movement has succeeded in gaining requirements that additional safeguards be built into new nuclear plants. The rising cost of uranium to fuel reactors is coupled with the unsolved problem of disposing of radioactive waste products. The escalating cost of constructing new atomic reactor power plants is rapidly making the nuclear industry uneconomical according to conventional capitalist criteria.

The last remaining theme in the argument for legitimation of nuclear energy is the contention that there is no viable alternative to nuclear energy as a source of power. The development of an environmentally safe source of electricity, such as solar cells, that can provide power of an equal or greater amount at an equal or lesser cost than nuclear reactors is the answer to this argument. The maintenance of this last contention of "no alternative" enables the proponents of nuclear power to stave off the collapse of the nuclear energy industry. The discrediting of this claim will enable opponents of nuclear energy to take the political initiative to move from delegitimation to deinstitutionalization.

The existence of the nuclear industry rests on the economic power of the large corporations that have invested in it, the entrenched bureacratic interests within the federal government that have developed in the atomic energy agencies and their successors and the myth of the potential beneficence of the atom that has been circulating since World War II. All of these three factors are necessary for the maintenance and growth of the nuclear industry. Government support is essential as the nuclear industry is inherently uneconomic. Without federal subsidies corporations would have little incentive to invest in nuclear power. Participation of the corporations is necessary as it would be politically impractical for such a large-scale non-military economic enterprise to be carried out by government. Public acquiescence is also essential. Without it, it would have to be conceded that the institutional forms of democratic government are meaningless. Opposition must be cooled out before it reaches massive proportions. If this cannot be done a program or tactic may have to be abandoned so that the system as a whole is not called into question.

The development of nuclear power and the suppression of solar technologies has been a key part of the energy program of the major oil corporations. In the past few years this policy has sustained a loss of public and legislative support. Proposals for divestiture of the major oil companies have gained increasing support. Interest in development of alternate energy technologies is becoming widespread. Corporate domination of US energy and technology policy is increasingly contested by environmental and consumer groups. Political pressure from these sources has made energy policy a national issue open to alternate analyses and policy proposals. The ideological hegemony of the major corporations is breaking down. The next step is to break their organizational control over energy policy and technology.

Alternative Technology

Most proponents of alternative technology view its development as a means of escape from industrial society. Some look to small-scale rural communities based on simple technologies to reduce dependence on technology and environmental degradation. Others have developed intermediate technologies that are appropriate for Third World countries. These technologies have usually not been seen as part of an anti-capitalist strategy.

Most observers accept the premise that to meet ecological criteria of industrialization, a lower standard of living than afforded by contemporary technologies will have to be accepted. Alternative technologies, it is assumed, are inherently less productive since they will consume less resources. The requirement that the populations of advanced industrial societies reduce their standard of living has been seen as a major obstacle to the introduction of alternative technology. However, if new technology that captures and uses renewable resources can be employed on a wide scale, this problem may be resolved. Technologies based on renewable sources of energy such as solar power have the potential to provide equal or greater productivity than technologies based on non-renewable fuels.

A major difficulty in instituting the widespread adoption of ecologically sound technology has been the fear that it would cost people jobs and lower their standard of living. Some proponents of alternative technology, who accept the necessity for a lower standard of living, argue that reduction in the use of resources can be achieved by reduction in consumption by elites. Others hold that a shift in public values will allow a general reduction in the standard of living to be accepted without social disruption or the need to redistribute existing resources from elite to non-elite sectors of the population. Yet few Americans show any great inclination to reduce their consumption. Proponents of the existing large scale technology use the fear that introduction of environmentally sound alternative technology will reduce the standard of living to legitimate the status quo. This argument can be met through the development of ecologically sound middle level technology that is as or more productive than ecologicaly unsound technology. When this is done, alternative technology will be viable.

As new technologies are developed according to ecological principles, a new society can be created that is not hostile to and destructive of nature. Technologies are at hand that minimize use of non-renewable resources and cause little interference with natural ecological cycles. Solar technologies to produce electricity and heat, hydroponics to produce food and agricultural use of sewage are among the technological alternatives to contemporary large scale industrial technology.

The Technology of Socialism

The direction in which technology is developed may be shaped by insurgent groups attempting to take power as well as by those currently in control of the economy. Different technologies will be developed by elites and insurgents in their efforts to maintain or overturn the class structure. As an emerging bourgeoisie used the development of industrial technology to overthrow a feudal landed aristocracy, a contemporary radical movement could develop new solar technologies to displace some of the ruling class power that is now based on control of fossil fuel and nuclear technologies. As the handmill represented the technology of feudalism, the steam engine, capitalism, the solar cell may well represent the technology of socialism.

Current attempts to realize the liberating potentialities of technology may yet fail for lack of sufficient resources or inability to overcome opposition. Nevertheless, attempts to realize alternative means of production can help to create the political and social conditions that will enable alternate technologies to be fully utilized. For each effort increases the number of people with the technical background and organizing skills to carry on the movement in the future. The development of middle level technology is neither an inevitable outgrowth of capitalism or a promise of socialism. The new solar technologies could well be captured and controlled by capitalist institutions. Yet the possibility of middle level solar technologies with their promise of abundance with environmental safety presents a critical juncture. If these technologies are developed by radicals they may be used to achieve qualitative social change. Depending upon the form of social relations in which solar energy is developed a step toward the achievement of socialism may be taken or capitalism perpetuated.

The corporate strategy of control of an industry rests on controlling its technology as well as its labor force. The liberation of technology through the research and development of new middle level technologies is one means of carrying on the struggle against corporate capital.

References

Consumers Solar Electric Power Corporation, P. O. Box 25856, West Los Angeles, CA 90025.

David Dickson, *The Politics of Alternative Technology*, New York: Universe Books, 1975.

Dave Elliot, "Lucas, Soft Technology for Hard Times," *Undercurrents*, March, 1974.

Peter Harper, "What's Left of Alternative Technology," *Undercurrents*, March, 1974.

Bernhard Stern, "The Frustration of Technology," *Science and Society*, 1937, No. 1.

Conclusion

IS AMERICA POSSIBLE?

To pose the question, Is America Possible? is to ask: is democracy feasible in the United States? Can we still realize the principles upon which the United States was founded? Can we attain the goals set forth in the Declaration of Independence and the Constitution given the enormous shift in social structures from the small scale social institutions of the eighteenth century to the large scale organizations of the twentieth century? Concentrated power is now the central issue and basic social problem in American society. Each specific issue and social problem is related to the larger question of who should make the decisions that affect our lives.

The premise of American political theory is that every citizen should have an equal voice in the political process. The institutions of the United States government were structured with the intention that no single group establish itself as a ruling elite. It was expected that the division of authority among different governmental institutions would balance one group against another and prevent the concentration of power. At present, this theory of American government often serves as an ideology to manage discontent with inequalities of power. Yet the original premise of political equality also serves as a standpoint from which to criticize persistent inequalities and as an ideal to be realized.

Political power has become concentrated and unequal as a result of economic and social inequalities. The principle of one person one vote has been reaffirmed in amendments to the Constitution and brought closer to actuality by the Voting Rights Act of 1964. Yet formal political equality accompanied by economic inequality is a contradiction because the individual or group with access to greater economic resources has a greater ability to translate political goals into actuality.

The Declaration of Independence contains an implicit demurrer if not a direct attack on inequality. Property is not listed along with rights to life, liberty, and the pursuit of happiness. By substituting happiness for property in the Lockean phrase "life liberty and property," Thomas Jefferson, author of the Declaration, stated a broader goal of human welfare for the people of the United States than making legitimate existing economic privilege. Jefferson's intellectual mentor, Francis Hutchinson, "held that property, depending on agreement (compact) for its delimitation, or division, *follows* on society rather than precedes it."[1] Private property, then, is not one of the inalienable rights associated with human existence. According to Hutchinson and Jefferson, wealth is fundamentally social, produced on the basis of cooperation among people. By calling for the pursuit of happiness instead of property, the Declaration stated a communal instead of an individualistic ideal. Jefferson, in using "happiness" in the eighteenth century sense, meant the doing of publicly useful acts that result in the improvement of conditions of life for all the people in a society.

The expectation of the founders of the United States that individual citizens would remain relatively equal was called into question by the economic concentration that occurred during and after the Civil War. National attitudes toward large scale manufacturing initially changed from negative to positive during the war of 1812 when the U.S. was partially cut off from receiving goods from Europe. Jefferson's fears that the growth of manufacturing would result in a concentration of political power were amply realized, first on the local and then on the national level, as the men who controlled the industrial means of production became the pre-eminent source of power in American society.

The Rise Of The Corporate Elite

In the United States during the 1870s and 1880s, the factory system caught up with demand and began to produce more goods than could be sold. The resulting drop in prices and profits led manufacturers to devise new means of organizing production and distribution. Initially, trade associations were formed representing manufacturers of each type of product. Members agreed to limit production and share the market between them. Since each company kept its operations secret, it was difficult to ensure that agreements were kept.

The second step taken by capitalists to contain the forces of production occurred when the largest companies in an industry bought stock in the smaller firms of their industry. As important stockholders they had access to information about the companies' rate of production and could determine whether agreements to limit production were adhered to. Finally, large companies increased their holdings of stock until they controlled the small companies. They operated the small companies as part of their own organization.

This process of amalgamation is exemplified in the conduct of the Dupont company. In the first stage,

> as production capacity caught up with demand after 1870, prices began to drop. The explosive industry's response to falling prices was precisely the same as that in the petroleum, whiskey, fertilizer, iron and steel, and other trades during the same period. The manufacturers joined together to form a federation, or association, to control price and production.[2]

In the second stage Dupont bought a minority interest in several explo- sives companies. The third stage was the acquisition of a major explosives company, Laflin & Rand. By acquiring Laflin & Rand, Dupont also acquired their stock in other companies. By combining both companies' stock in smaller companies a single entity controlled "close to 70% of the dynamite produced in the United States east of the Rockies."[3]

Eventually a new operating structure was devised to realize the potential of these acquisitions. "Costs of production and distribution could now be cut by reducing the number of administrative and sales offices and by concentrating production in large plants advantageously located in relation to markets and raw materials."[4] Techniques of hierarchical organization of human beings employed in the mass armies created after the French Revolution were subsequently intro- duced into the large scale factories created during the Industrial Revolution. Chains of command and the use of written rules were used to maintain order.

The new organization—the modern corporation—included a headquarters group to plan strategy for the entire organization. Separate groups, subordinate to the central planning office, conducted purchasing, sales, and financing for the organization. Factories were grouped into several operating divisions. Each divi- sion was responsible for the production of a particular type of product or a related group of products and reported to headquarters.

Production for a national market was made possible by the extension of rail- ways across the country.[5] National sales organizations were established. Previ- ously, most sales of products were made by companies to commission agents or wholesalers who in turn dealt with retailers. Large corporations, by creating their own sales organizations, eliminated many of these independent middle- men.[6] Located in cities across the country, these wholesalers served the tradi- tional urban marketing function of bringing together buyers and sellers. The incorporation of the middleman function into the bureaucratic structure of the corporation had few visible effects on cities in the late nineteenth and early twentieth century. Yet the loss of many middleman activities by the city and their consolidation into the corporation was a fundamental step that made possible the abandonment of cities by many major corporations in the mid-twentieth century.

Associated with the elimination of middlemen was the formulation of stan- dardized branded products that could be sold directly to the public. Through advertising, corporations formed direct links with the consumer. Simultane- ously, many corporations extended their operations to include the acquisition of raw materials and the production of components for their final products. By the end of the century, the individual factory was often merely one cog in an inte- grated system that controlled the production of goods from their inception to their consumption.

The problem for existing companies caused by the formation of new enterprises to produce goods in competition was largely resolved by making the scale of operation very large. It was difficult for a new company without access to a large source of capital to enter an industry. Integration of the production process, control over distribution, and national advertising made it possible for the large corporation to control the amount of goods produced and to set the prices at which they were sold either as price leaders or in direct collusion with the few other major members of their industry. Through these mechanisms the explosive forces of capitalism were contained and placed under control.

The Effects of Corporate Power

After major corporations consolidated their control over their respective industries during the late nineteenth century, they used their economic power to protect themselves from political attack. An antitrust movement consisting largely of middle-class reformers sought to break up the large corporations into smaller units and thus reduce their economic and political power.

Corporations met the external threat from the antitrust movement by gaining sufficient influence in national politics to ensure that antitrust laws passed by Congress were rarely applied by the attorney general and the new federal agencies such as the Federal Trade Commission set up to administer them. Corporate contributions to political campaigns, congressional lobbying, and the nomination and election of pro big business presidential candidates such as Harding and Hoover ensured that laws such as the Clayton Antitrust Act had little effect on major corporations. In addition, corporations developed tactics of legal delay to fight any antitrust actions that were initiated. Even those antitrust actions that were successful such as the 1912 breakup of the Standard Oil Company had little effect in reducing corporate concentration. The Standard Oil breakup resulted in five companies that divided the national market into regional segments and otherwise cooperated with each other despite the formal dissolution of the oil monopoly.

At the local level, control over large numbers of jobs allowed industrialists to become the pre-eminent source of power in their communities. This was especially apparent in the new industrial towns often based on a few companies or a single industry. In Muncie, Indiana, the Ball family, prominent local industrialists, along with other members of their class, dominated politics. They were able to suppress the formation of strong unions that would have provided an alternative source of political power.[7]

Corporate relocation decisions have turned thriving cities into depressed areas. Corporations have moved factories from the north and east to the south and west to avoid unions and hire employees at lower wages. New York City's loss of most of its garment industry to the south has been a major cause of the depopulation of working class neighborhoods in the south Bronx, eventually resulting in the deterioration and destruction of their housing. New Jersey's older industrial cities have suffered the loss of plants to other parts of the country and to Third World countries such as Taiwan, South Korea, and the Philippines, where multinational corporations protected by local political elites can pay low wages. Many workers lost their pensions while others were forced to retire early. Youths who expected to find employment in these factories have often been unable to find other jobs and have been forced to remain idle and dependent upon their parents. While relocation of plants are justified by corporations as necessary economic decisions, they have widespread effects on employees and citizens who have no voice in these decisions.

Major corporations influence the direction of technological innovation to increase their control over the means of production. They tend to develop those new technologies that are in accord with their corporate structure. For example, electric utilities prefer nuclear technology that is capital intensive and requires centralized control to solar technology that is decentralized and labor intensive. A larger capital investment increases a utilities rate base. Expensive new facilities provide justifications for rate increases and greater profits. Of course, decentralization of energy production to individual homes, apartment houses, or factories would eliminate much of the need for central generating facilities and thus for the utility itself.

Motor transportation, in displacing trolley cars and much of rail transport, has been shown to be an instance of manipulation rather than technological superiority of one form of transport over another. According to the Snell Report prepared for the U.S. Senate,[8] General Motors deliberately purchased and then put out of business trolley and interurban railway companies so that a larger market could be created for the buses that it manufactures. According to this same study, General Motors, through use of false data, persuaded railroads to replace steam engines with less efficient diesel locomotives that GM manufactured. Adoption of the diesel engines placed the railroads at a further disadvantage with truck transport and furthered their decline. Through stratagems such as these, General Motors and other corporations have been able to maintain control of the technology used for land transportation in the United States for almost fifty years.

In the oil industry the ability to control the flow of production enables the oil companies to create artificial shortages. By raising prices and restricting the availability of gasoline the oil companies disrupted peoples' lives in 1973–1974 and again in 1979. They also engineered a huge increase in profits. Shortages and increased profits enabled the major oil companies to further increase their control over the energy industry. Major oil companies also used their profits to gain control of corporations in other industries. Mobil took over Montgomery Ward Department Stores and Exxon Corporation moved to take control of the Reliance Electric Motor Company. Oil companies also purchased a variety of energy-related corporations in the coal, nuclear, and solar industries to further consolidate their power.

Corporations have concentrated wealth in the hands of a small segment of the population. In 1962 1% of all shareholders owned 72% of all corporate stock. "Based on census data, the top 5 percent of Americans hold 52% of net private wealth, and the bottom 60% hold only 7.5 percent. While the poorest fifth of the U.S. earned 3.7 percent of the nation's income, the top fifth earned 47.3 percent; the top one percent earned 10.5 percent of all income, or 51 times the per capita income earned by the poorest fifth."[9]

Control over the largest concentrated share of economic wealth in the United States translates easily into political power. Money gives a relatively few persons the ability to match groups that are much larger in number. Political action committees to provide campaign funds, direct participation by business leaders in electoral politics, along with public relations and lobbying campaigns are among the political techniques used by the corporate elite.

The extent of corporate power cannot be measured simply by examining the role of corporations in the economy or even by their ability to contribute heavily to political campaigns or engage in extensive public relations and lobbying campaigns. As we have seen, corporate power also involves the ability to: control the worklife of employees, increase the concentration of wealth, and disrupt the structure of everyday life. It includes the relocation of industries and jobs as well as the ability to shape the direction of technological innovation. This ability to generate power to affect many areas of life makes the corporate elite the single most powerful group in American society. The corporate elite comprises the oligopolistic corporations in each major industry. It may be viewed as both an institutional and a membership elite including both the corporations and their chief executive officers and major stockholders.

While the major corporations that were organized in the late nineteenth and early twentieth centuries have been able to constitute themselves as the greatest single source of power in the United States; this does not mean that corporate leaders are so powerful that they function as an executive committee arriving at decisions that are then automatically legitimated by the political system. The corporate elite was shaken by the depression of the 1930s. Some corporate leaders feared that revolution was imminent. But New Deal reforms of the economy, undertaken against the opposition of much of the corporate elite, rescued the capitalist system from destruction. Corporate production of war material during the Second World War, accompanied by full employment, enabled corporations to regain some of the legitimacy lost during the depression.

During the post war era a new corporate ideology was formulated to reassert corporate identity with the national interest. Advertising campaigns attempted to show that "better living" derived from Dupont's chemical research. Institutional advertisements in newspapers and on television identified the "free enterprise" system with traditional American values. In the social sciences a group of theorists developed the thesis that corporations were merely one group among many who had the ability to affect public policy.

The pluralists argued that farmers, doctors, lawyers, businessmen and other interest groups each had the ability to influence public policy on those few issues that were especially important to them. According to the pluralists, issues are typically decided by compromise among the different groups concerned. Politics is a shifting series of alliances between groups in which coalitions shift depending upon the issue at hand. While no single group is believed to be able to shape public policy on a wide variety of issues; each group is held to have the ability to block a policy that threatens its vital interests. According to David Riesman:

> The various business groups, large and small, the movie censoring groups, the farm groups and the labor and professional groups, the major ethnic groups and major regional groups, have in many instances succeeded in maneuvering themselves into a position in which they are able to neutralize those who might attack them.[10]

This defensive ability led Riesman to label them "veto groups".

Pluralist theorists have shown that the corporate elite is not omnipotent since other groups are often able to checkmate its moves in the political arena. However, pluralist theorists usually view as political only those decisions made in legislatures and other explicitly defined political institutions. Thus decisions made by corporations to relocate offices and plants or to replace one technology with another tend to be excluded from their definition of politics.

C. Wright Mills argued that the pluralist analysis of politics was inadequate as well. Mills held that pluralist theorists only dealt with the middle levels of decision making such as who was nominated for president or the passage of congressional acts.[11] Real power, for Mills, involved decisions that affected the future viability of the United States. Decisions on developing the hydrogen bomb or intervening in Vietnam were made by a power elite, operating according to a different structure and existing on a higher plane than the forces of pressure group politics.

The power elite derives from three sources: concentrated corporate power developed since the late nineteenth century, an increase in presidential power deriving from the depression era, and the development of the military as a major power center with the growth of the armed forces during World War II and in the post war years. Mills identified the increase in presidential power and the development of military power with the shift of decision making from domestic to foreign policy. Power elite policy decisions primarily concern decisions involving war and peace that arise from American-Soviet relations and other important issues of foreign policy. Power elite decision making affects domestic policy since it encourages an expanded military budget linked to important sectors of the corporate economy. These issues include decisions on developing new weapons systems costing billions of dollars. Such decisions influenced regional economic development and have, for example, played a major role in fueling the economy of the sun belt in the post-World War II era.

The Promise of Social Movements

Mills viewed individual citizens as divided among themselves into an atomized mass. He believed that they could no longer affect decisions at the upper levels of power. Mills's pessimistic view of Americans as powerless was challenged by the social movements of the 60s. The peace movement was able to combine civil disobedience, electoral politics, and effective use of the media to amass sufficient power to affect decision making at the level that Mills thought was beyond the reach of citizens. The peace movement brought about a major foreign policy change in forcing the executive branch of the government to move toward ending the Vietnam war.

The antiwar movement caused a division within the corporate elite as important sectors of corporate and financial wealth lent their support to the antiwar movement. However, this split was subsidiary to the major achievement of the peace movement; mobilizing a significant number of citizens to engage in political activity. The peace movement demonstrated that when a loosely organized movement of citizens can be motivated to engage in politics, the highest levels of power can be affected.

Those who wish to preserve the status quo tend to view political inactivity by most Americans as a virtue. The failure of many citizens to vote is taken as an indication of satisfaction with the way things are. However, most citizens are politically inactive, not because they are not dissatisfied, but because they feel powerless to effect change.

When a social movement invents a tactic that encourages citizens to directly confront problems, people have an incentive to become politically active. The contemporary feminist movement hit upon the use of small face-to-face groups in which women discuss their personal experiences with sexual inequality. Consciousness raising (CR) groups gave the feminist movement an organizing tool in which private problems could be seen in the context of broader issues. CR groups enabled the feminist movement to spread rapidly. They were easy to organize and simple to run. CR groups typically followed a list of topics that could be obtained by mail from a New York radical feminist collective. A woman who heard about the operation of a CR group from a participant could learn enough to invite her friends to form a group. CR groups could not, by themselves, eliminate sexual inequalities, but participation in consciousness raising groups reduced women's feeling of powerlessness. CR groups also provided emotional and social support for their members and encouraged women to participate in demonstrations and other political actions. CR groups connected women to the network of activities within the feminist movement and encouraged participants to initiate new political actions.

Social movements provide a way for citizens to join together, fight concentrated power, and sometimes win. The contemporary antinuclear movement, involving mass participation, was inspired by an act of civil disobedience by a Vermont commune farmer and political activist. He overturned an electric power transmission tower that was under construction for a nuclear power plant at Montague, Massachusetts. The Clamshell Alliance grew out of this act of civil disobedience. The alliance was organized on the basis of affinity groups, each consisting of a relatively small number of persons. These groups came together periodically to conduct demonstrations and occupations of the nuclear power plant construction site at Seabrook, New Hampshire. The activities of the Clamshell Alliance were spread by word of mouth and through radical periodicals such as *WIN* magazine.

In 1977, a Clamshell demonstration attracted several thousand people. The governor of the state of New Hampshire ordered the state police to arrest demonstrators who entered the construction site. The mass arrests attracted the attention of the national news media and the Clamshell model of antinuclear protest spread even more rapidly to other regions of the country undergoing nuclear power plant development. By 1979, several dozen antinuclear alliances with names such as SHAD and ABALONE were conducting protests against nuclear power. The various regional antinuclear alliances work to place local government restrictions on nuclear energy. In Charleston, South Carolina the City Council banned the transport of nuclear wastes through their town. These efforts represent a serious threat to the nuclear industry. As an opponent of the Charleston ordinance put it, "If enough communities that straddle interstates passed these ordinances, if enough east coast ports passed these ordinances, it would shut down the nuclear industry."[12]

Prior to the mass movements there was a period of gestation. Individuals and groups published articles analyzing the issues, organized lawsuits, lobbied, presented information at legislative hearings, and otherwise used established channels of political activity. But none of the movements gained momentum until a format was invented that dramatized the issue and encouraged mass participation. Demonstrations in Washington brought antiwar activists face to face with the government leaders who initiated the Vietnam war. Sit-ins at lunch counters dramatized the operation of segregation in everyday life. The contrast between the mild mannered, carefully dressed black college students and the unruly white crowds that taunted them further intensified the drama.

In each of the social movements a small number of activists devoted themselves full time to organizing activities. Occasionally, a few persons would gain prominence in the media as movement leaders but the movements were not solely dependent upon them for direction. Most leadership was exercised at the local level by a constantly shifting set of individuals. Government authorities who attempted to investigate the leadership of social movements had great difficulty in defining who was in charge. They assumed the existence of tightly controlled organizations. But the movements mainly operated through loose coordination between local centers of activity. When nationwide demonstrations were organized in Washington the leadership group typically acted as a national coordinating organization for the period of the particular action. For example, President Carter wanted to meet with the leaders of the antinuclear movement after the May, 1979 Washington demonstration. His advisers invited them to the White House but had difficulty organizing a meeting because the coordinating structure had almost entirely disbanded a few days after the demonstration. The civil rights, environmental, antiwar, and feminist movements all engendered national organizations. But these groups could never be said to encompass more than a small portion of the activities that occurred on behalf of these movements.

How have social movements affected national policy? The environmental movement during the 1970s succeeded in gaining federal laws requiring corporations to modify their activities to meet environmental standards. While corporations are presently attempting to eviscerate these restrictions using arguments of loss of employment and the need to develop sources of energy, the necessity of organizing this effort shows that the environmental movement had a significant effect on corporate policy. During the 1960s the civil rights movement achieved significant changes in employment practices. While the civil rights movement is certainly not anti-capitalist in its intention, nevertheless its actions resulted in federally ordered changes in corporate hiring policy that has been resisted by many companies as an unwarranted restriction on their freedom.

The corporate elite successfully resisted the formation of unions in most industries until the 1930s. The labor movement that did arise during the late nineteenth and early twentieth century largely eschewed participation in politics in order to gain a foothold in industry. This policy and balance of power shifted during the depression of the 1930s. The growth of large industrial unions and the formation of the Congress of Industrial Organizations (CIO) were aided by federal laws such as the Wagner Act that legitimated and protected union organizing efforts for the first time. While reforms of the New Deal ultimately enabled capitalism to survive in America and thus supported the status quo they also represented a modest shift in power from capital to labor. In succeeding years the major unions became an important force in the Democratic party by providing the party with a campaign apparatus through its local unions largely replacing the urban political machines that were in decline.[13]

The contemporary consumer movement dates from the publication of Ralph Nader's *Unsafe At Any Speed* in 1965. The book presented his study of safety defects in the Chevrolet Corvair. General Motors Corporation, fearful of the adverse publicity to its automobiles that might be generated by Nader's book, hired private detectives to investigate Nader to determine if he engaged in any activities that might be used to discredit him. The investigation failed to find anything in Nader's past that could be used against him so they hired women to create situations in which Nader could be compromised. Nader became aware of these activities and brought them to the attention of Senator Ribicoff of Connect-icut. The president of General Motors accepted responsibility for the actions of the detectives before a Senate hearing called by Ribicoff. The resulting national attention given to General Motors's campaign against Nader publicized Nader's analysis of the safety defects in the Corvair. Nader's analysis shifted the burden of safety from the actions of the driver to the construction of the automobile. Instead of the driver virtually automatically being held responsible for acci-dents, Nader showed that safety flaws (that the auto companies were often aware of) were responsible for many automobile accidents. The auto companies were often unwilling to correct these defects because the cost of making the necessary changes would reduce profits. Public exposure that the auto companies held the profit motive to be a higher value than human life, in a series of well publicized safety defects discovered in succeeding years, has negatively affected their credi-bility. These events also provided the political clout to create a federal agency to establish auto safety standards.

On the basis of his initial success, Nader organized a series of investigative efforts into the practices of other industries and government agencies. His tactic of amassing specific detailed information and presenting it to the public by showing the direct negative impact on public safety, health, and welfare gained greater acceptance for his findings than a more theoretical analysis of corporate activities would have achieved. The exposure of a series of instances of defective products, often produced by the same companies, demonstrates that this phe-nomena is not an accidental occurrence but is an inevitable result of the corpo-rate quest for profits rather than for serving the needs of consumers.

Nader's strategies and tactics, until quite recently, have remained within the confines of accepted pressure group behavior. He lobbies, provides information to senators, representatives, and the press to encourage the passage of legislation. His goals have been to regain the independence of regulatory agencies captured by industry and to re-establish them as an independent check on corporate activities. For the past several years he has also worked to establish a new regula-tory agency, the Consumer Protection Agency, that would directly represent consumer interests before the other regulatory agencies. Each year the passage of a bill to establish such an agency has been blocked by massive corporate lobby-ing. Nader's proposals for federal chartering of corporations have also been stymied. Their purpose is to regain some of the public control over corporations that was lost at the turn of the century when several states, influenced by corporations, competed with one another to offer more favorable terms for incorporation. As a result Nader appears to be reconsidering his approach to the problem of corporate power, both tactically and strategically. Nader's appearance as a major speaker at the May, 1979 Washington demonstration against nuclear power marked his acceptance of social movement tactics of political organizing. Nader's call for the "...displacement of the Republican and Democratic parties by new political alignments..." represents a realization that a new political force must be brought into existence to confront "...the matrix of corporate power."[15]

The coming radicalization of the consumer movement presents an opportunity to construct a new political alliance with other social movements opposed to corporate power and economic and social injustice. The growth of neighborhood movements to oppose bank redlining and disinvestment in older housing, citizens groups to oppose highway construction that destroys existing urban areas and promotes suburban spread, and a variety of other block, neighborhood, and citywide organizations constitute a potential grassroots base of support for such a political realignment. The civil rights, feminist, minority, and anti-nuclear movements also represent a potential base of support for a new political movement. Elements within the labor movement have also recently shown signs of interest in moving beyond conventional political activities. Douglas Fraser, President of the Autoworkers Union and organizer of the Progressive Alliance, and William Winipisinger, President of the Machinists Union, have both begun to explore alternatives to the traditional role of unions within the two party system. Winipisinger has appeared at union meetings and labor-community alliances to state his basic socialist program of four rights: "The right to a fair share of America's wealth and income. The right to participate in decisions governing public and private investment. The right to a job. And finally, the right to live a life of peace."[16]

The search for common ground between these various movements and the construction of a unifying ideology will be the first step toward the development of a national movement for equality and social justice in the 1980s. The indigenous American radical tradition provides a source of inspiration for this task. During the past two decades, radical historians such as Herbert Apthekar, Staughton Lynd and Eric Foner have attempted, through their writings, to revive this tradition and demonstrate its relevance to the contemporary American condition.

The Future of American Radicalism

Thomas Paine said that the fruits of the earth, the land, and its resources belong to all the people.[17] Everyone should share in the resources that derive from nature. No people should have the right to control nature and extract its benefits for their private use. Instead, the benefits of nature should be placed in the service of all the people. The Declaration of Independence does not make private property a national principle. Where it might have been included in the right to life, liberty and . . . the key phrase that follows is, of course, the pursuit of happiness, not property. Nor does pursuit mean a chase after happiness or a perpetual struggle to attain it. The pursuit of happiness is a "calling" to a state of personal fulfillment for all citizens.[18]

Conscience is another fundamental principle of radical American political theory. Every human being has the capacity to decide what is right and what is wrong. Once this decision is made each person has the moral responsibility to translate the moral knowledge into political action. Each person has the right and duty to challenge existing institutions if they do not meet human needs. The early nineteenth century abolitionist who refused to return escaped slaves to their owners, the 1960s southern black student who refused to obey local ordinances forbidding service at lunch counters reserved for whites, and a 1970s activist who toppled a nuclear power plant electricity transmission tower that was dangerous to health and life, all took a stand, starting from the first principle of their individual conscience.

These individual acts of conscience, rejecting the laws of their time on the grounds that they contravened moral principles, ignited social movements that made each of these individual acts concerning slavery, segregation, and nuclear energy into national issues. Each individual act of conscience inspired additional acts of conscience. Educational campaigns, organizing efforts, and political activities followed. In the formation of each movement an act of conscience made the fundamental issue clear. It excited potential supporters and moved them to action. The assumption of the theory of conscience is that other individuals share the same basic human nature and will be moved to undertake their own acts of conscience. Of course, not all individual acts of conscience precipitate mass political movements. Henry Thoreau's refusal to pay war taxes that he considered illegitimate did not inspire a mass tax refusal at the time. Yet his individual act and his essays kept the idea of civil disobedience alive and provided inspiration to Mahatma Gandhi and Martin Luther King, among others.

An act of civil disobedience against constituted authority is a right to revolution since accepted procedures, rules, or laws should not be followed if they do not meet the test of conscience. The right to revolution is also incorporated in the Constitution in the amendment process.[19] Amendments to the Constitution may deal with any issue and may even change the basic principles of the Constitution itself. Revolution is not necessarily defined as a change that takes place through violence. Rather, the criterion for whether a revolution has or has not occurred is the extent to which a fundamental and far reaching change has been instituted. The United States Constitution contains within it a potential for revolution since its amendment process provides a means for making fundamental changes. The amendment process is not subject to the checks and balances built into the legislative process. Bills calling for far reaching or even modest changes are typically whittled down by compromise before they become laws. Nor is the amendment process eroded by the restraints of the judicial system. Court decisions are subject to legal precedent, legislative modification, and executive unwillingness to carry out a judge's mandate. The nature of the amendment process, in setting forth a clear and simple principle that must be voted for or against offers an opportunity to pose choices on major issues in a way that opponents cannot subject to compromise. The abolitionist movement to end slavery used the amendment process to the Constitution to carry out its goals in the mid nineteenth century. The late nineteenth and early twentieth century feminist movement used the amendment process to gain women the right to vote. The contemporary feminist movement is presently using the amendment process to add an Equal Rights

Amendment to the Constitution. Socialists and other radicals who wish to eliminate economic inequality should also explore the amendment process as a means to attain this goal.

The radical heritage of the early years of the United States has largely been suppressed. A mythology was created to make it appear that the United States, from its inception, was a conservative or liberal nation or perhaps an amalgam of these two perspectives. As we have seen, the fundamental principles of the United States include radical proto-socialist elements as well. The success or failure of our collective efforts to put these principles into practice will determine whether America is possible.

Notes

1. Gary Wills, *Inventing America*. New York: Random House, 1978, p. 231.

2. Alfred Chandler, *Strategy and Structure: Chapters in the History of the Industrial Enterprise*. Cambridge: MIT Press, 1962.

3. Alfred Chandler and Stephen Salsbury, *Pierre S. Dupont and the Making of the Modern Corporation*. New York: Harper & Row, 1971, p. 56.

4. Ibid., p. 57.

5. Ibid., p. 75.

6. Alfred Chandler, ed., *The Railroads: The Nation's First Big Business*. New York: Harcourt, Brace & World, 1965.

7. Robert Lynd and Helen Merell Lynd, *Middletown in Transition*. New York: Harcourt, Brace and World, 1937.

8. Bradford C. Snell, *American Ground Transport: A Proposal for Restructuring the Automobile, Truck, Bus and Rail Industries*. Washington, D.C.: U.S. Government Printing Office, 1974.

9. Ralph Nader, Mark Green, and Joel Seligman. *Taming the Giant Corporation*. New York: W.W. Norton, 1976. pp. 29, 30.

10. David Riesman, *The Lonely Crowd*. New Haven: Yale University Press, 1950, p. 213.

11. C. Wright Mills, *The Power Elite*. New York: Oxford University Press, 1956.

12. *WIN* Magazine, July 26, 1979.

13. David Greenstone, *Labor In American Politics*. New York: Knopf, 1969.

14. Ralph Nader, *Unsafe At Any Speed*. New York: Grossman, 1965.

15. John Herbers, "New Party Hopes to Attract Old Parties Disillusioned." *New York Times*, August 12, 1979, p. 2 Section 4.

16. Joe Conason, "The Importance of Being Wimpy." *Village Voice*, June 25, 1979.

17. Eric Foner, *Tom Paine and Revolutionary America*. New York: Oxford, 1976.

18. Staughton Lynd, *Intellectual Origins of the American Revolution*. New York: Pantheon, 1968.

19. Herbert Apthekar, *Early Years of the Republic*. New York: International Publishers, 1976.

†